ON THE ROAD

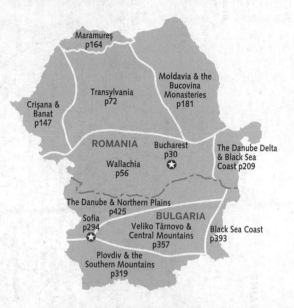

- Maramureş p164
- Transylvania p72
- Crişana & Banat p147
- Moldavia & the Bucovina Monasteries p181
- ROMANIA
- Bucharest p30
- Wallachia p56
- The Danube Delta & Black Sea Coast p209
- The Danube & Northern Plains p425
- BULGARIA
- Sofia p294
- Veliko Târnovo & Central Mountains p357
- Black Sea Coast p393
- Plovdiv & the Southern Mountains p319

SURVIVAL GUIDE

VITAL PRACTICAL INFORMATION TO HELP YOU HAVE A SMOOTH TRIP

THIS EDITION WRITTEN AND RESEARCHED BY

Mark Baker

Chris Deliso, Richard Waters, Richard Wat

Jun 2013

›Romania & Bulgaria

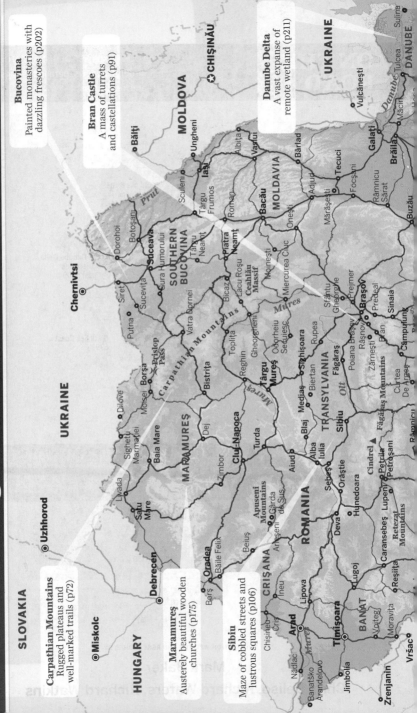

Bucovina
Painted monasteries with dazzling frescoes (p202)

Bran Castle
A mass of turrets and castellations (p91)

Danube Delta
A vast expanse of remote wetland (p211)

Carpathian Mountains
Rugged plateaus and well-marked trails (p72)

Maramureş
Austerely beautiful wooden churches (p175)

Sibiu
Maze of cobbled streets and lustrous squares (p106)

SLOVAKIA

HUNGARY

UKRAINE

MOLDOVA

ROMANIA

TRANSYLVANIA

SOUTHERN BUCOVINA

MOLDAVIA

MARAMUREŞ

CRIŞANA

BANAT

Carpathian Mountains

Făgăraş Mountains

Retezal Mountains

Apuseni Mountains

Ceahlău Massif

Miskolc

Uzhhorod

Debrecen

Chernivtsi

CHIŞINĂU

Bălţi

Ungheni

Iaşi

Sculeni

Târgu Frumos

Roman

Bacău

Oneşti

Mărăşeşti

Adjud

Focşani

Tecuci

Bârlad

Vaslui

Albita

Galaţi

Brăila

Buzău

Râmnicu Sărat

Macin

Tulcea

Sulina

DANUBE

Vulcăneşti

Suceava

Gura Humorului

Dorohoi

Botoşani

Siret

Sucevita

Putna

Vatra Dornei

Câmpulung

Târgu Neamţ

Piatra Neamţ

Bicaz

Lacu Roşu

Mercurea Ciuc

Gheorgheni

Toplita

Reghin

Bistriţa

Borşa

Prislop Pass

Moisei

Dilove

Sighetu Marmatiei

Baia Mare

Dej

Turda

Cluj-Napoca

Zimbor

Livada

Satu Mare

Beiuş

Argeşeni

Gârda de Sus

Oradea

Băile Felix

Bors

Chişineu Criş

Ineu

Lipova

Arad

Nădlac

Banatsko Arandelovo

Jimbolia

Zrenjanin

Vršac

Moravita

Vojteg

Timişoara

Lugoj

Reşiţa

Caransebeş

Deva

Hunedoara

Orăştie

Sebeş

Alba Iulia

Aiud

Blaj

Mediaş

Biertan

Sighişoara

Târgu Mureş

Odorheiu Secuiesc

Rupea

Făgăraş

Sibiu

Cindrel

Petrila Petroşani

Lupeni

Curtea De Argeş

Râmnicu

Sinaia

Predeal

Poiana Braşov

Braşov

Zărneşti

Bran

Râşnov

Sfântu Gheorghe

Prejmer

Câmpulung

Cernei

Pruț

Prut

Mureş

Mureş

Olt

Danube

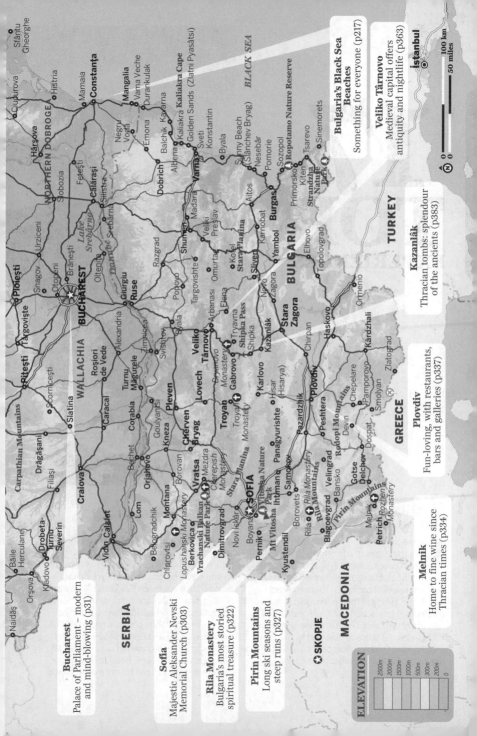

Bucharest
Palace of Parliament – modern and mind-blowing (p31)

Sofia
Majestic Aleksander Nevski Memorial Church (p303)

Rila Monastery
Bulgaria's most storied spiritual treasure (p322)

Pirin Mountains
Long ski seasons and steep runs (p327)

Melnik
Home to fine wine since Thracian times (p334)

Plovdiv
Fun-loving, with restaurants, bars and galleries (p337)

Kazanlâk
Thracian tombs: splendour of the ancients (p383)

Veliko Târnovo
Medieval capital offers antiquity and nightlife (p363)

Bulgaria's Black Sea Beaches
Something for everyone (p217)

ELEVATION

2500m
2000m
1500m
1000m
500m
300m
200m
0

0 100 km
0 50 miles

SERBIA

MACEDONIA

☆ SKOPJE

GREECE

TURKEY

Istanbul ◉

BULGARIA

WALLACHIA

NORTHERN DOBROGE

BLACK SEA

BUCHAREST

SOFIA

Carpathian Mountains

Stara Planina

Rodopi Mountains

Pirin Mountains

Rila Mountains

Vitosha Nature Park

Mt Vitosha

Vrachanski Balkan Nature Park

Lopushanski Monastery

Strandzha Nature Park

Ropotamo Nature Reserve

Danube

Lake Srebarna

Ploieşti
Târgovişte
Piteşti
Craiova
Drobeta-Turnu Severin
Orşova
Băile Herculane
Naidâş
Ciuperova
Sfântu Gheorghe
Histria
Constanţa
Mamaia
Năvodari
Năvodari
Mangalia
Varna Veche
Durankulak
Kavarna
Kaliakra Cape (Zlatni Pyasâtsi)
Golden Sands
Albena
Balchik
Dobrich
Varna
Sveti Konstantin
Byala
Nesebâr
Sunny Beach (Slânchev Bryag)
Pomorie
Burgas
Sozopol
Primorsko
Kiten
Tsarevo
Sinemorets
Ahtopol
Emona
Negru Vodâ
Silistra
Srebarna
Slobozia
Feteşti
Călăraşi
Giurgiu
Ruse
Svishtov
Zimnicea
Alexandria
Roşiori de Vede
Turnu Măgurele
Caracal
Slatina
Corneşti
Piteşti
Drăgăşani
Filiaşi
Vidin
Calafat
Belogradchik
Chiprovtsi
Berkovica
Montana
Vratsa
Mezdra
Cherepish Monastery
Botevgrad
Pleven
Cherven Bryag
Lovech
Troyan
Troyan Monastery
Gabrovo
Dryanovo Monastery
Veliko Târnovo
Arbanasi
Tryavna
Shipka Pass
Shipka
Kazanlâk
Stara Zagora
Chirpan
Haskovo
Kârdzhali
Zlatograd
Smolyan
Pamporovo
Chepelare
Devin
Dospat
Peshtera
Pazardzhik
Plovdiv
Hisar (Hisarya)
Karlovo
Koprivshtitsa
Panagyurishte
Samokov
Ihtiman
Pernik
Boyana
Kyustendil
Rila
Borovets
Blagoevgrad
Bansko
Velingrad
Gotse Delchev
Petrich
Melnik
Rozhen Monastery
Dimitrovgrad
Novi Iskâr
Lom
Bechet
Orjahovo
Goulyantsi
Kneza
Brovan
Razgrad
Popovo
Târgovishte
Shumen
Madara
Veliki Preslav
Omurtag
Kotel
Elena
Sliven
Yambol
Karnobat
Aitos
Nevo
Zagora
Topolovgrad
Elhovo
Ormenio
Zlatograd
Ornenio
Shagov
Otopeni
Brăneşti
Oltenita
Urziceni
Harşova
Cernavodă
Negru Vodă
Emona
Byala

17 TOP EXPERIENCES

Hiking in the Carpathians

1 Dense primeval forests that leap straight from the pages of a Brothers Grimm story, with bears, wolves, lynx and boar, rugged mountain plateaus, well-marked trails and a network of cabins en route to keep you warm. Hiking is the best way to absorb this vibrant landscape (p72) of forests and rolling pastureland. There are also some terrific guides out there to lead you to the best that Romania has to offer; be it bear watching, birdwatching, homestays or hikes.

Bulgaria's Black Sea Beaches

2 Whether you're looking for all-day tanning, all-night clubbing, or something a little more discrete and relaxing, you're sure to find some patch of sand to your liking along Bulgaria's Black Sea coast. Away from the big, brash package resorts, you'll come across charming seaside towns standing above smaller sandy coves, while the cities of Varna (p412) and Burgas (p395) both have lengthy, less-crowded urban beaches. If it's solitude you seek, head for the more remote beaches to the far north and south.

Rila Monastery

3 Set peacefully in a forested valley south of Sofia, Rila Monastery (p322) is Bulgaria's biggest and most storied spiritual treasure; a former centre of learning and culture that kept national spirits up during the Ottoman occupation. A Unesco World Heritage site since 1983, the monastery grew from a 10th-century hermit's hut, and has been rebuilt many times since. Its elaborate arches and precious frescoes and icons create a sublime and sumptuous atmosphere. Today's architectural incarnation of the monastery is considered a masterpiece of 19th-century Bulgarian Renaissance.

Painted Monasteries of Bucovina

4 Tucked in the Carpathian foothills, the Unesco-listed painted monasteries of Bucovina proudly show off Romania's unique, Latin-flavoured Orthodox tradition. The churches are at one with their natural surroundings and the dizzying kaleidoscope of colours and intricate details in the frescoes bring to life everything from biblical stories to the 15th-century siege of Constantinople. The monasteries are the genius of Moldavian Prince Stephen the Great (Ştefan cel Mare), who was later canonised for his works. Suceviţa Monastery (p206)

Wildlife in the Danube Delta

5 After flowing some 2800km across the European continent, the mighty Danube River passes through a vast expanse of remote wetland in eastern Romania – the delta – before finally emptying into the Black Sea. Under international environmental protection, the region (p211) has developed into a sanctuary for fish and fowl of all stripe and colour. Birders, in particular, will thrill to the prospect of glimpsing species such as the roller, white-tailed eagle, great white egret, mute and whooper swans, falcon, and even a bee-eater or two.

Veliko Târnovo

6 The unquestioned highlight of Bulgaria's central heartland, the grand old city of the tsars – Bulgaria's capital in medieval times – offers a mix of antiquity, boutique bliss and nightlife. This university town, set high above the ribboning Yantra River, is popular with visitors both local and foreign, who marvel at the oddly endearing 'Sound and Light Show' held nightly at the impressive Tsarevets Fortress (p364), a still-robust medieval citadel. It's also a great base for local hikes.

Bulgarian Wine Tasting

7 Bulgaria's winemaking tradition dates to ancient Thracian times, and fine wine has been enjoyed here by everyone from Roman writers and French crusaders to former British Prime Minister Winston Churchill, who used to order barrels of the local red from Melnik (p334) – a village in the southwest of the country that remains a great place for sampling wines. Distinct wine-growing regions exist from the Danube to the Black Sea to the Thracian Plain, and numerous wineries offer tastings that are usually complemented by meats, cheeses and memorable rustic views.

Aleksander Nevski Memorial Church, Sofia

8 Rising majestically over the rooftops of the Bulgarian capital, this beautiful Orthodox church (p303), dedicated to the memory of the 200,000 Russian soldiers who died in the Russo-Turkish War (1877–78), took 30 years to construct, and was completed in 1912. The shimmering golden domes are visible several streets away, while the vast, candlelit interior is decorated with Italian marble, alabaster and fading murals. Daily services are led by robed, white-bearded priests, accompanied by chanting choirs.

Bran Castle

9 Perched on a rocky bluff in Transylvania, in a mass of turrets and castellations, Bran Castle (p91) overlooks a desolate mountain pass swirling with mist and dense forest. Its spectral exterior is like a composite of every horror film you've ever seen, but don't expect to be scared. Inside, Bran is anything but spooky, with its white walls and geranium-filled courtyard. Legend has it Vlad the Impaler (the inspiration for Count Dracula) was briefly imprisoned here, and you can follow his footsteps through an 'Escheresque' maze of courtyards and hidden passages.

Skiing in the Pirin Mountains

10 High in the Pirin Mountains are Bulgaria's most famous ski areas: Bansko (p330) and Borovets (p325). With the highest pistes starting from 2500m, Bansko is known for its long, steep runs and extended ski seasons. It's also an international party scene, offering everything from refined restaurants and spa treatments to crowded bars and clubs. The slopes at Borovets, north beyond Mt Musala, also top 2500m. While the trails at this long-established favourite are less challenging, there is plenty of trickier, open terrain for thrill seekers.

Palace of Parliament, Bucharest

11 Depending on your point of view, this modern colossus (p31) is either a mind-blowing testament to the waste and folly of dictatorship or an awe-inspiring showcase of Romanian materials and craftsmanship, albeit applied to sinister ends. We think it's a bit of both, but whatever emotions the 'House of the People' happens to elicit, the sheer scale of Romania's entry into the 'World's Largest Buildings' competition – on par with the Taj Mahal or the Pentagon – must be seen to be believed

10

11

Wooden Churches of Maramureş

12 Rising from forested hillsides like dark needles, the exquisite wooden churches of Maramureş (p175), in northern Romania, are both austere and beautiful, with roofs of shingle, and weather-beaten Gothic-style steeples. Inside, you'll discover rich interiors painted with biblical frescoes, some of which date back to the 14th century. On Sundays villagers wear traditional dress for church, and attending a service is a special treat. Don't miss the eight Unesco-listed churches of Bârsana, Budeşti, Deseşti, Ieud, Plopiş, Poienile Izei, Rogoz and Surdeşti. Bârsana

The Perils of Plum Brandy

13 Big meals traditionally begin with a shot of Romanian moonshine, *ţuică*, but treat this innocent-looking liquid with a measure of respect. Home-brewed batches can weigh in at as much as 60% alcohol, and the wallop can be fast and furious. Classic *ţuică* is usually distilled from plums – purists say only plums – but we've seen other fruits, like apricots and pears, employed to this nefarious end. In smaller villages, you'll likely be offered some of grandpa's best, or look for it sold in plastic bottles at roadside rest stops by friendly old ladies with a glint in their eye. *Noroc!*

Thracian Tombs

14 Bulgarians are rightly proud of their Thracian heritage, and the ancient tribes who produced slave leader Spartacus and the semidivine, lyre-playing Orpheus were fantastically skilled artists and craftspeople. Today, the most obvious reminders of their culture are the elaborate tombs that have been unearthed across southern and central Bulgaria. The best of these is the amazing beehive tomb in Kazanlâk (p383), erected for a 4th-century-BC king, and adorned with remarkably well-preserved murals of chariot racing and feasting. It is now a Unesco World Heritage site.

Sibiu

15 Bursting with exhibitions and nightlife, tasteful Sibiu (p106) instantly dazzles with its maze of cobbled streets winding into lustrously coloured baroque squares. By day the tapping of guildsmen – for which this Romanian city is famous – still fills the streets; by night this old charmer is aglow with sidewalk cafes and authentic subterranean restaurants where you can tuck into your goulash by candlelight. Almost every month, Sibiu, a former European Capital of Culture, hosts some kind of special-interest event, be it a film, rock or folk fest.

Plovdiv

16 Arty, fun-loving Plovdiv (p337) makes a great alternative to Sofia. It's an eminently walkable and safe student city, loaded with great restaurants, bars and galleries, and boasting a dynamic cultural scene. The evocative Old Town features National Revival–era homes clinging to cobble-stoned lanes, museums and galleries, and a magnificent Roman amphitheatre; while the hip Kapana district is home to unpretentious indie cafes and bars. Plovdiv also makes a great base for forays into the Rodopi Mountains, famous for hiking and caving.

Stuffed Cabbage Leaves & Polenta

17 Romania's de facto, delicious national dish of stuffed cabbage (or sometimes grape) leaves, *sarmale cu mămăligă*, is traditionally served at weddings, Christmas dinners and big celebrations. It's also a staple on restaurant menus around the country. The leaves are typically filled with spiced pork, but occasionally veal or lamb is mixed in. *Mămăligă*, a thick porridge made from yellow corn (maize) flour, is a welcome sidekick to soak up the savoury juices. Our favourite bit is the dollop of sour cream usually dropped on top. *Pofta buna!*

Romania

Romania

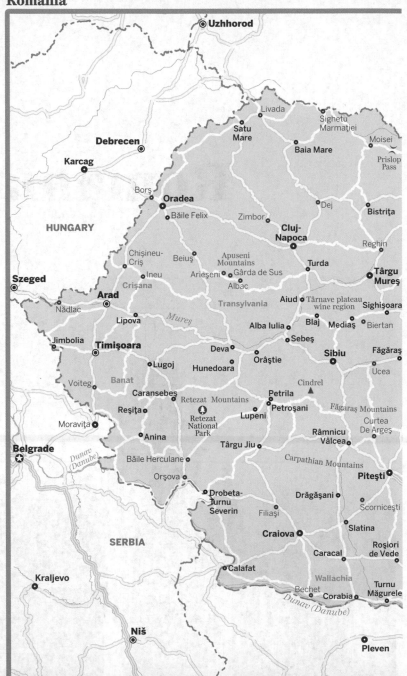

0
200 km
0
100 miles
Chernivtsi
Siret
Dorohoi
Putna
Suceviţa
Botoşani
Bălţi
Gura Humorului
Suceava
Carpathian Mountains
Cotnari wine region
MOLDOVA
Vatra Dornei
Târgu Neamţ
Târgu Frumos
Sculeni
Ungheni
Iaşi
Chişinău
Topliţa
Bicaz
Piatra Neamţ
Roman
Tiraspol
Gheorgheni
Albiţa
Ceahlău Massif
Moineşti
Bacău
Vaslui
Miercurea Ciuc
Odorheiu Secuiesc
Oneşti
Moldavia
Bârlad
Olt
Rupea
Adjud
Sfântu Gheorghe
Mărăşeşti
Tecuci
Codlea
Prejmer
Odobeşti wine region
Focşani
Prut
Zărneşti
Braşov
Galaţi
Râmnicu Sărat
Sinaia
Brăila
Câmpulung
Măcin
Tulcea
Sulina
Pucioasa
Câmpina
Buzău
Făurei
Bucegi Mountains
Horia
Sfântu Gheorghe
Târgovişte
Ploieşti
Ciucurova
Găeşti
Snagov
Urziceni
Hârşova
Ialomiţa
Otopeni
Slobozia
Histria
Bucharest
Brăneşti
Feteşti
Mamaia
Călăraşi
Constanţa
Olteniţa
Silistra
Alexandria
Giurgiu
Negru Vodă
Mangalia
Vama Veche
Zimnicea
BULGARIA

welcome to Romania

Natural Beauty

The Carpathian Mountains draw a wide arc through the centre of the country, leaving a swath of exposed rocky peaks surrounded by groves of pine and deciduous trees, and stretches of bright green meadow below. Hiking trails skirt the peaks, and a network of mountain huts provides somewhere to rest your head at night. Europe's second-longest river, the Danube, marks Romania's southern border before turning suddenly northward and emptying into the Black Sea. The Danube Delta is a vast and unique protected wetland, perfect for hiking, fishing, boating and birdwatching.

Castles & Medieval Villages

The land that gave us Dracula has no shortage of jaw-dropping castles pitched precariously on rocky hilltops. There's spooky Bran Castle of course, with its spurious connection to Bram Stoker's fictional count, but don't overlook beauties such as Hunedoara's 14th-century Corvin Castle or King Carol I's sumptuous 19th-century pile, Peleş Castle. North of Curtea de Argeş, you'll find the ruins of a fortress that really was the stomping ground of old Vlad Țepeș. In Maramureş you'll discover towns and villages that seemingly stepped out of the Middle Ages, complete with hay racks, horse carts and stately wooden churches.

Fortified churches and painted monasteries stand regally amid a pristine landscape. In the cities, former Saxon settlements such as Sibiu and Braşov ooze charm, while vibrant Bucharest is all energy.

(left) Moldoviţa Monastery (p204)
(below) Romanian man, Transylvania (p72)

Folk Culture

Romanian history is filled with tales of heroic princes battling fierce Ottoman warriors. That's all true, but it partly obscures the reality that much of Romania, for centuries, was a productive peasant culture. The hilly geography and lack of passable roads necessitated the emergence of literally hundreds of self-sufficient villages, where old-school crafts such as bread making, pottery, tanning and weaving were honed to an art. These days much of the country has moved on to more modern methods, but a fondness for that 'simpler' way of life persists. Folk museums, particularly open-air *skansens*, are a must. In smaller villages, many old folkways are still practised.

Friendly Faces

A country is only as good as its people, and you'll find Romanians in every region to be open, friendly, proud of their history and eager to share it with visitors. While tourism is growing, Romania is still considered something of an off-the-beaten-track destination for foreigners, and you'll get kudos from the locals just for showing up. While Romanians themselves decry what they see as the brashness, even rudeness, of their countrypeople in Bucharest, even there you'll discover plenty of friendly faces and impromptu drinking buddies if you make the effort.

need to know

Currency
» Romanian leu/lei (singular/plural)

Language
» Romanian

When to Go

Warm to hot summers, mild winters
Warm to hot summer, cold winters
Mild summers, cold winters
Cold climate

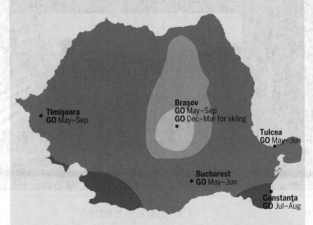

Timișoara
GO May–Sep

Brașov
GO May–Sep
GO Dec–Mar for skiing

Tulcea
GO May–Jun

Bucharest
GO May–Jun

Constanța
GO Jul–Aug

High Season
(Jun–Aug)

» Sunny weather from June through August, but temperatures can get oppressively hot.

» Locals head for the Black Sea; Mamaia is packed.

» Castles, museums, water parks and spas open and in high gear.

Shoulder
(Apr–May & Sep–Oct)

» Some museums, monasteries and attractions are closed or have shorter hours.

» Trees in full blossom by April; later in higher elevations.

» Birdwatching in the Danube Delta at its best in late May.

Low Season
(Nov–Mar)

» Ski season runs from mid-December to early March.

» Romantic cities such as Brașov and Sibiu look great in coats of snow.

» Museums and castles in smaller towns shut down or open only on weekends.

Your Daily Budget

Budget: Less than
130 lei

» Hostel dorm room or guesthouse: 50 lei per person

» Street food and self-catering: 30 lei

» Train/bus ticket: 30 lei

» Museum/sundries: 10 lei

Midrange:
130– 350 lei

» Double in a midrange hotel or pension: 100 lei per person

» Meals in good restaurants: 60 lei

» Train/bus tickets: 30 lei

» Museums/sundries: 30 lei

Top end: More than
350 lei

» Double in the best place in town: 180 lei per person

» Lunch and dinner at the best restaurants: 80 lei

Money

» ATMs widely available. Credit cards widely accepted in hotels and restaurants.

Visas

» Generally not required for stays of up to 90 days. Passport holders of EU member states can stay indefinitely.

Mobile Phones

» Local SIM cards can be used in European, Australian and some American phones. Other phones must be set to roaming.

Transport

» Mostly trains for long-distance travel; buses and minibuses (also called 'maxitaxis') within regions.

Websites

» **Bucharest Life** (www.bucharestlife .net) Casts a keen but critical eye on the capital.

» **Lonely Planet** (lonelyplanet.com) Go to the Thorn Tree to talk with travellers about Romania.

» **Romania National Tourism Office** (www .romaniatourism.com) Official tourism site.

» **Rural Tourism** (www .ruralturism.ro) Rural B&Bs across Romania.

» **Sapte Seri** (www .sapteseri.ro) What's-on listings.

Exchange Rates

Australia	A$1	3.66 lei
Canada	C$1	3.59 lei
Europe	€1	4.54 lei
Japan	¥100	4.52 lei
New Zealand	NZ$1	2.93 lei
UK	£1	5.70 lei
USA	US$1	3.53 lei

For current exchange rates see www.xe.com

Important Numbers

Call ☑112 for an ambulance or other emergency services in Romania.

Arriving in Romania

» **Henri Coandă International Airport (Bucharest; p264)**
Bus – 3.50 lei; express bus 783 to centre; 40 minutes
Taxi – 60–70 lei to centre; 30–40 minutes
Train – 8 lei to Gara de Nord; 30 minutes

» **Cluj Airport (p264)**
Bus – 2.50 lei; bus 8 to centre; 30 minutes
Taxi – 50 lei to centre; 25 minutes

» **Timişoara Airport (p264)**
Bus – 2.50 lei; express bus E4 to centre; 30 minutes
Taxi – 50 lei to centre; 25 minutes

Street Scams & Annoyances

Romania is a relatively safe country, but there are some common scams to be aware of. Watch out for rip-off taxi drivers, particularly at airport arrivals halls and train stations. Strangers who approach you speaking in English and offering rides or claiming to represent a hotel or hostel, are likely to be dodgy. Firmly decline any such approach.

We've outlined strategies for finding an honest ride outside of Bucharest's airport and main train station in the Bucharest chapter (p53). Trustworthy taxis will post their rates on the door, with honest drivers charging anything from 1.40 to 1.80 lei per km.

Stray dogs are an annoyance, but rarely pose a danger. Avoid the temptation to pet the dogs. The best strategy is to stay out of their way and they will stay out of yours.

if you like...

Folk Culture

Folk traditions are alive and kicking, especially in Romania's rural areas. There's tremendous variety across regions. The open-air museums are a treat, and every town or city has some type of ethnographic exhibition.

Maramureş Large parts of this remote rural area to the north of Transylvania still feel untouched by modern life (p164)

Ethnographic Museum An overlooked gem in Craiova, showing off regional bread making, pottery, painting and weaving skills (p66)

National Village Museum Romania's humbler origins are on display at the this well-done *skansen* (open-air museum), situated incongruously in the middle of Bucharest (p41)

ASTRA Museum of Traditional Folk Civilisation This museum in Sibiu holds some 300 reconstructed peasant huts and farmhouses in a lovely park setting (p108)

Ethnographic Museum Iaşi's most interesting museum resurrects rural life in 16 rooms that display everything from fishing and hunting to festive masks and woodworking (p200)

Castles & Fortresses

While the 'real Dracula's castle' may only have been a figment of Bram Stoker's imagination, there are dozens of worthy, even worthier, replacements. You'll find ruins on rocks as well as opulent restored residences of old royals.

Viscri The fortified church in this signature Saxon village dates from around 1100 (p103)

Bran Castle This mighty fortress got its start under the Teutonic Knights as guard over a strategic pass between Transylvania and Wallachia (p91)

Peleş Castle If your taste runs to more aristocratic piles, this former residence of King Carol I will not disappoint (p73)

Poienari Citadel Climb the 1480 steps to this hilltop fortress that really was the stomping ground of feared Wallachian prince Vlad Ţepeş, aka Dracula (p65)

Neamţ Citadel Târgu Neamţ's historic 14th-century citadel has a grand and tumultuous history as the site of battles with Hungarians, Turks and Poles (p194)

Medieval Towns & Villages

Medieval towns in Romania run the gamut from the historic cores of Sibiu and Braşov to the isolated, tiny hamlets of Transylvania and Maramureş.

Sighişoara Climb the cobblestones up to the town's ancient citadel and marvel at how little has changed in more than five centuries (p96)

Ieud One of at least a dozen historic Maramureş villages; this one has two wooden churches and many traditional wooden gates (p178)

Măgura The peaks of the Piatra Craiului mountains form a breathtaking backdrop to this tiny village (p94)

Biertan A biscuit-coloured church towers over a medieval marketplace amid tussocky hills and vineyards – stunning (p102)

Curtea de Argeş This former Wallachian capital boasts a Princely Court with an intact, frescoed 14th-century church (p64)

» Stained-glass window, Peleş Castle (p73)

Wilderness

Romania's geography is as varied as its history. Whether you're looking to scale a mountain, spend a day in a cave, or take a dip in the Black Sea, there's something for everyone.

Danube Delta The Danube ends its epic, transcontinental journey in a maze of pristine marshes and waterways (p211)

Apuseni Mountains Not the country's highest mountains, but arguably the best caves, including a rare cave still filled with ice-age ice (p142)

Iron Gates National Park The dramatic and perilously narrow gorge here that separates Romania from Serbia has bedevilled sailors since Roman times (p70)

Făgăraş Mountains Home to the country's tallest and most majestic mountains, with at least six peaks topping 2500m (p104)

Black Sea Barren stretches of sand and dune and some terrific wild camping await along the southern coastline near Vama Veche (p225)

Nightlife

Romanians love to party. Clubs can be dressy affairs, so pack some nightlife garb. University towns get manic on weekends. In summer, the party moves to the coast.

Bucharest's Old Town The tiny lanes that once surrounded the old Princely Court have been converted into an unbroken string of bars, pubs and clubs (p49)

Mamaia Romania's most popular Black Sea resort is ground zero for the country's best summer beach clubs (p223)

Timişoara You'd expect the home of the biggest university in the west of the country to hold epic parties and you'd be right (p149)

Cluj-Napoca Not to be outdone by Timişoara, this is another big-league college town with pubs and clubs on every corner (p133)

Vama Veche Locals contend you haven't really partied on the Black Sea until you've pulled a beachside all-nighter here over an August weekend (p225)

Architecture

Whether it's Greek or Roman ruins, medieval masterpieces or modern mega-projects, Romania has its share of historic buildings. The Black Sea coast is especially rich in antiquity.

Painted Monasteries of Bucovina Known for their massive fortifications and stunning frescoes, these treasures express the vitality of late-Byzantine religious fervour (p202)

Oradea This border city was home to some exuberant art-nouveau experimentation in the early 20th century – and that's an understatement (p155)

Transfăgărăşan Road A feat of genuine road-building chutzpah, this high-altitude highway winds its way around (and through) the country's tallest mountains (p105)

Palace of Parliament Former dictator Nicolae Ceauşescu's must-see alabaster albatross displays the country's material riches in grand (or grandiose) style (p31)

Ruins of Trajan's Bridge The brainchild of Roman Emperor Trajan and creation of Greek architect Apollodorus of Damascus, this epic bridge spanned the mighty Danube two millennia ago (p69)

month by month

Top Events

1 **Pageant of the Juni**, April

2 **Transylvania International Film Festival**, May

3 **Medieval Arts Festival**, July

4 **Peninsula Félsziget**, August

5 **George Enescu Music Festival**, September

January

Expect snow and ice everywhere during, statistically speaking, the country's coldest month. Avoid slushy Bucharest and head instead for the mountains, where ski resorts and winter sports are in full gear.

⭐ Winter Sports Festival

Held in Moldavia's Câmpulung Moldovenesc on the last Sunday of January. While sports are indeed the focus, they're mainly an excuse for revelry.

February

Ski resorts crowd up as school kids take their annual week long winter break. Elsewhere, the winter freeze is still going strong, and many museums and attractions in the countryside are closed or have only weekend hours.

⭐ Enchanted Water Springs

Târgu Jiu's annual folk-music festival is held over the third weekend of the month.

April

If you're partial to blossoming trees and blooming flowers, this is the most beautiful month of the year. Easter is the high point of the Orthodox calendar, and Easter fairs and painted-egg festivals abound.

⭐ St George Days Festival

Held in Sfântu Gheorghe (Transylvania) on the last weekend in April, this three-day festival honouring the church's patron saint is all about folk music, street food and nightly concerts.

⭐ Pageant of the Juni

Braşov's most colourful, biggest street festival begins in the first week after Easter, late in April or early May.

May

Temperatures warm a bit in May, but expect periods of rain. Romanians traditionally spend the Labour Day holiday (1 May) at the seashore, but it's still too cold to swim. Birdwatching starts in the Danube Delta.

⭐ Sibiu Jazz Festival

The second week in May brings headline jazz acts to Sibiu for the city's annual jazz festival. (p109)

⭐ Transylvania International Film Festival

The international film world decamps to Cluj-Napoca in late May and early June for the Transylvania International Film Festival (www.tiff.ro).

June

The formal arrival of summer brings reliably warm, even hot, days and lots of sunshine throughout the country. The Black Sea resorts get rolling and high-altitude zones are rich with wildflowers.

⭐ Craftsman's Fair

Bucharest's Village Museum is the venue for this annual celebration of pottery, woodworking and weaving in early June. (p44)

⭐ Dragaica

Held since the Middle Ages, this pagan pre-harvest celebration is held annually in Târgovişte in the last week of June.

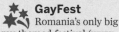

GayFest

Romania's only big gay-themed festival (www .gay-fest.ro). Six days of events are planned in late June and early July at venues around Bucharest.

July

The summer sun starts to boil. Bucharest and other large cities are often unbearable as temperatures can top 40°C. Locals hit the beaches on the Black Sea.

Medieval Arts Festival

This annual celebration of all things medieval is held in Sighişoara in mid-July and is arguably the country's best time-travel event.

Maramuzical Festival

Vadu Izei, together with the neighbouring villages of Botiza and Ieud, hosts this four-day international folk-music festival in the middle of July.

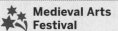

Nedeia Munţilor

Not far from Braşov, Fundata holds an annual 'mountain celebration' folk festival around 20 July. The location is appropriate; at 1360m, it's the highest village in Romania.

August

If you can take the heat, this is an ideal month to visit. Long days filled with sun bring crowds to the coast and the mountains. There's a mid-month holiday (15 August), so book hotels in advance.

International Folk Festival of the Danubian Countries

In odd-numbered years, the Danube Delta gateway city of Tulcea hosts visiting folk troupes from around Central and Eastern Europe.

Hora de la Prislop

A folk-music festival held on the second Sunday in August at the Prislop Pass in Maramureş celebrating the sheep returning from the mountains.

Sfântu Gheorghe Film Festival

Europe's most remote film festival (www.festival -anonimul.ro) takes places annually in late August at this Danube Delta outpost.

Peninsula Félsziget

Billed as 'Romania's biggest festival', this rock and indie fest (www.peninsula.ro) brings thousands to Târgu Mureş in late August.

September

Another great month to visit. The days are still warm and sunny, with plenty of daylight. The start of mushrooming season pushes city dwellers out into the woods in search of the perfect fungus.

International Theatre Festival for Children

Bucharest's Ion Creangă Theatre is the venue for this youth-oriented festival (www.fitc.ro) that brings troupes from around the world.

Pro Istoria Fest

This catch-all festival (www.proistoriafest.ro) held in early September brings various musical acts and medieval arts to Suceava.

George Enescu Music Festival

This highly acclaimed classical music festival (www. festivalenescu.ro) is held in odd-numbered years, with many performances at Bucharest's Athenaeum. (p44)

October

The cultural calendar is in full swing in cities and towns, with concerts and theatre performances. With all the spooky castles, there can't be a better place in the world to spend Halloween than Transylvania.

International Astra Film Festival

Sibiu's film festival (www. astrafilm.ro) focuses on the best regional documentaries. Held in mid to late October. (p110)

December

The month begins with a national holiday on the 1st and then descends into cold and darkness. By mid-month, the sun is all but gone by 4.30pm each day. Christmas brings welcome relief, with parties, festivals and markets.

Winter Festival

Sighetu Marmaţiei's undisputed annual highpoint comes just after Christmas, featuring food, music, masks and a colourful oxen parade.

itineraries

Whether you've got six days or 60, these itineraries provide the starting point for a trip of a lifetime. Want more inspiration? Head online to lonelyplanet.com/thorntree to chat with other travellers.

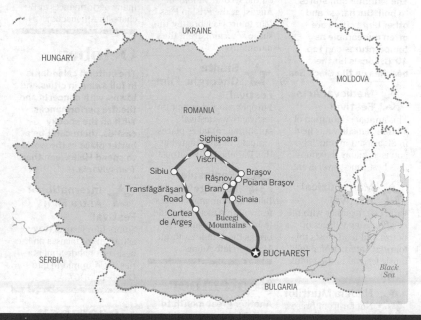

10 Days
Classic Romania

This classic route for travellers wanting a taste of Transylvania starts in the capital, **Bucharest**, where most flights arrive.

Hire a car at Bucharest or hop a train northward toward the mountains, stopping in **Sinaia** for a couple of nights and checking out **Peleş Castle**.

From there, take a cable car up into the **Bucegi Mountains** for hiking or biking. Drive or bus north for a couple of nights in **Braşov**, a lively hub with a cobbled centre.

Take day trips to the infamous 'Dracula's Castle' at **Bran** and another stunner at **Râşnov**, with the option of skiing and hiking at nearby **Poiana Braşov**.

If you have a car, spend a night in **Viscri** before continuing on for a night in **Sighişoara**, where the dramatic citadel offers B&Bs, espresso and Dracula's birthplace. From here, head southwest for a night or two in **Sibiu**.

If you have a car (and it's summer), drive south along the breathtaking **Transfăgărăşan Road**, which tackles the biggest of the Carpathians. South of the pass, stop at the 'real Dracula's castle' of **Poienari Citadel** outside **Curtea de Argeş** before returning to Bucharest.

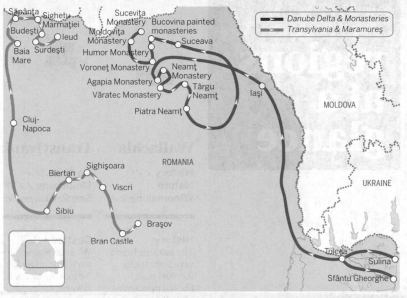

7-10 Days
Danube Delta & Monasteries

This tour starts in **Tulcea**, the gateway to the delta, though it could be done in reverse, beginning in **Suceava**. If you're arriving in Bucharest, take the bus or drive (3 to 4 hours) to Tulcea.

If you've only got a day or two for the delta, stay overnight in Tulcea and enter the delta via boating day trips. If you've got a few days or longer, skip Tulcea and grab a passenger ferry to deeper, more scenic destinations such as **Sulina** or **Sfântu Gheorghe**.

After getting your birdwatching and boating on, return to Tulcea and take the bus or drive north to **Iaşi**, Moldavia's largest city. Spend a day taking in the sights. Use Iaşi as a base to explore the **Agapia**, **Văratec** and **Neamţ** monasteries or head west and settle in at **Piatra Neamţ** or **Târgu Neamţ**.

From here, it's a short hop to **Suceava**, a good base for exploring the **Bucovina painted monasteries**. Highlights include the **Voroneţ**, **Humor**, **Moldoviţa** and **Suceviţa** monasteries. Accessing the monasteries is tricky without a car. If travelling by public transport, allow a couple of extra days.

10-14 Days
Transylvania & Maramureş

If you're coming to Romania to get a taste of small-town life, this tour is for you. **Braşov** makes a good base; if you're starting from **Bucharest**, take the train north on arrival. Spend at least a day or two in Braşov, and use it as a base for exploring **Bran Castle** and amazing fortified churches such as the one in **Viscri**.

From here, head north to the Unesco-protected town of **Sighişoara** and its historic citadel. Spend the night before heading south to the former Saxon stronghold of **Sibiu**. If you've got your own wheels, make a detour to take in another gorgeous village at **Biertan**. Sibiu is one of the liveliest cities in Romania, and well worth a couple of nights.

From here, you'll have to backtrack towards Sighişoara or head north through **Cluj-Napoca**. If you've got the time, this is another lively metropolis that merits at least a night.

From here push northward to **Baia Mare** or to **Sighetu Marmaţiei**, bases for further exploration of Maramureş. Don't miss the **Merry Cemetery** near Săpânţa. From Sighetu Marmaţiei, it's just a short hop to the pretty villages of **Budeşti**, **Surdeşti** and **Ieud**.

regions at a glance

Bucharest

Museums ✓✓✓
Entertainment ✓✓✓
Food ✓✓

Museums
Bucharest is home to the country's top museums of art, history and natural science, among many, many others. Lovers of folk art have both a quirky peasant museum and a grand, open-air collection dedicated to Romanian villages to choose from.

Entertainment
The capital has a thriving cultural calendar that runs from September through spring, and is especially strong on classical music. In addition, nightly throughout the year, you'll have your pick of jazz, rock, indie or blues at dozens of smaller music clubs. Many of these are concentrated in the Old Town.

Food
Bucharest is the food capital of Romania. Not only are the best Romanian restaurants here, but there's a thriving ethnic food scene as well, led by our new favourite 'local' nosh: Middle Eastern food.

p30

Wallachia

History ✓✓
Nature ✓
Winemaking ✓✓

History
The modern Romanian state traces its roots back to the old principality of Wallachia, once ruled over by the feared Vlad Ţepeş. The princely courts of Curtea de Argeş and Târgovişte tell this history.

Nature
The Danube River defines Wallachia's southern border. In the west, below Drobeta-Turnu Severin, the river winds its way through a series of dramatic narrow gorges – called the 'Iron Gates' – now protected as a natural park.

Winemaking
Home to some of the country's finest winemaking regions, including the Dealu Mare area north of Târgovişte, and a promising new region in the west, at Drăgăşani.

p56

Transylvania

Castles ✓✓✓
Mountains ✓✓✓
Scenic Villages ✓✓

Castles
Who can blame author Bram Stoker for looking to Transylvania for inspiration on spooky castles? Bran is a national treasure, but don't neglect Corvin Castle, at Hunedoara, or Râşnov, not far from Braşov.

Mountains
Transylvania's natural borders are defined by a string of 2500m peaks that cut through the country in a sweeping arc. We're partial to the Bucegi Mountains, accessible by cable car from Sinaia.

Scenic Villages
Isolated 17th-century villages, defined by a towering fortress church and ringed by majestic peaks, are par for the course in Transylvania. Don't miss Viscri; other musts include Biertan and Măgura.

p72

Crişana & Banat

Architecture ✓
Hiking ✓✓
Arts ✓✓

Architecture
Western cities such as Timişoara and Oradea were heavily influenced by architectural styles in Budapest and Vienna. Oradea, in particular, was drenched in glorious art-nouveau detail at the start of the 20th century.

Hiking
Often overlooked for higher peaks elsewhere, the Apuseni Mountains, southeast of Oradea, offer miles of rugged, isolated trails and dozens of caves that can be explored.

Arts
Timişoara takes its performing arts – theatre, opera, dance and classic music – seriously. For something less high-brow, the city's student complex is filled with bars and dance clubs that stay open till dawn.

p147

Maramureş

Village Life ✓✓✓
Folk Music ✓✓
Churches ✓✓✓

Village Life
The whole of Maramureş feels like one large open-air exhibition of peasant life as it was practised 100 years ago or more. Traditional crafts, including the making of strong plum brandy, still thrive.

Folk Music
Much Romanian folk music traces its roots to Maramureş, and traditional song and dance is on display throughout the year at festivals such as the Hora de la Prislop, held in August.

Churches
Simple, sombre wooden churches in villages such as Budeşti, Bârsana and Ieud are a testament to both the villagers' piety as well as their immense woodworking skills. Try to take in a service during your visit.

p164

Moldavia & the Bucovina Monasteries

Monasteries ✓✓✓
History ✓✓
Food ✓

Monasteries
Bucovina's painted monasteries, all from the 15th and 16th centuries, are considered masterpieces for the way they harmonise colour and architectural style with the surrounding countryside.

History
Moldavia was the scene of some of the greatest military triumphs against the Ottoman Turks in the 15th century, carried out by Moldavian prince Stephen the Great (Ştefan cel Mare).

Food
Moldavia is renowned for some of the best regional traditional cooking. They lay claim to *mămăligă* (cornmeal mush) here, but we're partial to *ciorbă Rădăuţi*, chicken soup with mashed garlic and vinegar, doused with sour cream.

p181

The Danube Delta & Black Sea Coast

Wildlife ✓✓✓
Beaches ✓
History ✓✓

Wildlife
The Danube Delta is an internationally protected wetland that stretches on as far as the eye can see. It's ideal for boating and hiking, fishing and birdwatching.

Beaches
Romania's coastline is dotted with beachfront from the Danube Delta to the Bulgarian border. We love the isolated, sandy beaches at Sulina and Sfântu Gheorghe in the delta and Vama Veche in the south.

History
The Black Sea coastline was settled by the ancient Greeks as far back as 700 BC, and then came the Romans. Museums in Tulcea, Histria and Constanţa are particularly rich in finds from antiquity.

p209

> **Every listing is recommended by our authors, and their favourite places are listed first**

> **Look out for these icons:**

 Our author's top recommendation

 A green or sustainable option

 No payment required

See the Index for a full list of destinations covered in this book.

On the Road

Bucharest

POP 2,100,000

Best Places to Eat

» Caru' cu Bere (p46)
» Malagamba (p46)
» Divan (p46)
» Lente & Cafea (p47)
» Sale e Pepe (p47)

Best Places to Stay

» Rembrandt Hotel (p44)
» Z Hotel (p44)
» The Doors (p45)
» Hotel Amzei (p45)
» Vila Arte (p45)

Why Go?

Romania's capital gets a bad rap, but in fact it's dynamic, energetic and more than a little bit funky. It's where still-unreconstructed communism meets unbridled capitalism; where the soporific forces of the EU meet the passions of the Balkans and Middle East. Many travellers give the city just a night or two before heading off to Transylvania, but we think that's not enough. Budget at least a few days to take in the good museums, stroll the parks and hang out at trendy cafes. While much of the centre is modern and garish, you will find some splendid 17th- and 18th-century Orthodox churches tucked away in quiet corners, and graceful art-nouveau villas. Communism changed the face of the city for good, and nowhere is this more evident than at the gargantuan Palace of Parliament, the craziest and arguably crassest tribute to dictatorial megalomania you'll ever see.

When to Go
Bucharest

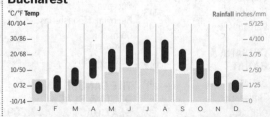

Apr & May City parks erupt into colour as trees blossom and flowers bloom.

Jul & Aug Avoid Bucharest in midsummer, when temps can be oppressively hot.

Sep & Oct Sunny and cooler, but still warm enough for terrace drinking and dining.

History

Lying on the Wallachian plains between the Carpathian foothills and the Danube River, Bucharest was settled by Geto-Dacians as early as 70 BC. By 1459 a princely residence and military citadel had been established under the chancellery of infamous Wallachian Prince Vlad Ţepeş. By the end of the 17th century, the city was the capital of Wallachia and ranked among southeastern Europe's wealthiest centres. It became the national capital in 1862, as it lay on a main trade route between east and west.

The early 20th century was Bucharest's golden age. Large neoclassical buildings sprang up, fashionable parks were laid out and landscaped on Parisian models and, by the end of the 1930s, the city was known throughout Europe as 'Little Paris' or 'the Paris of the East'.

Bombing by the Allies during WWII, coupled with a 1940 earthquake, destroyed much of Bucharest's prewar beauty. In 1977, a second major earthquake claimed 1391 lives and flattened countless buildings. Former dictator Nicolae Ceauşescu's massive redevelopment of the city in the 1980s, culminating in his grandiose Palace of the Parliament (sometimes still referred to as the 'House of the People'), drove a stake through the heart of Bucharest's elegant past.

The violent revolution of 1989 inflicted serious wounds, both physically and psychologically. Many buildings still bear bullet holes as testament to those chaotic days in 1989 when the anticommunist uprising resembled nothing so much as a civil war. Less than a year later, in June 1990, miners poured into the centre to support a government crackdown on protesting students in a shocking wave of violence that reopened scars that had barely had time to heal.

Although it's still haunted by its recent bloody past, more than two decades on, Bucharest is clearly recovering. The historic core, the Old Town, particularly the area around Str Lipscani, has received a long overdue revamp and there isn't a more enjoyable place in Romania to spend a night out.

◎ Sights

PALACE OF PARLIAMENT & AROUND

Palace of Parliament   HISTORIC BUILDING
(Palatul Parlamentului; ☑tour bookings 021-414 1426; www.cdep.ro; B-dul Naţiunile Unite; standard tour adult/child 25/13 lei; ☉10am-4pm; Mizvor) Facing B-dul Unirii is the impossible-to-miss Palace of Parliament, the world's second-largest building (after the Pentagon near Washington, DC) and Ceauşescu's most infamous creation. Built in 1984 (and still unfinished), the building has 12 storeys and 3100 rooms covering 330,000 sq metres – an estimated €3.3 billion project. Entry is by guided tour only. Bring your passport as they check IDs.

Several types of tours are available, including a 'standard' tour and a 'complete' tour. Both take around 45 to 60 minutes – the complete tour includes a view of the terrace and the basement. Don't expect a particularly accomplished (or polite) tour guide, but this is the only way to get a glimpse inside. Entry to the palace is from B-dul Naţiunile Unite on the building's northern side (to find it, face the front of the palace from B-dul Unirii and then walk around the building to the right). You don't normally have to book tours in advance, but we recommend giving them a call beforehand since the walk to the entrance is long indeed.

**National Museum of
Contemporary Art**   GALLERY
(Muzeul Naţionale Arta Contemporana; ☑021-318 9137; www.mnac.ro; Calea 13 Septembrie 1; adult 5 lei, student free; ☉10am-6pm Wed-Sun) The Palace of Parliament houses a superb art gallery that displays temporary, ever-changing exhibitions of eclectic installations and video art. There's also a top-floor, open-air cafe. The entry is from the southwestern side of the building (opposite from the Palace of Parliament tour entrance). Check the website in advance to make sure something is on during your visit to spare yourself a long walk.

PIAŢA UNIVERSITĂŢII

If Bucharest has a true centre, which we're not sure it does, it would be somewhere around here, midway between Piaţa Victoriei in the north and Piaţa Unirii in the south, with two major north–south arteries on each side: B-dul IC Brătianu to the east and Calea Victoriei to the west. Many university buildings are situated here (hence the name), plus government institutions, grand old buildings and lots of restaurants and bars. This was also the scene of the some of the fiercest fighting during the 1989 revolution and the subsequent miners' revolt in June 1990. Journalists observed both outbursts of violence from the relative security of the upper floors of the Hotel Inter-Continental. Scour the area and you'll still find bullet marks in some buildings.

Bucharest Highlights

1 Taking a stroll through former dictator Nicolae Ceauşescu's madhouse, the **Palace of Parliament** (p31)

2 Getting your photo snapped with Emperor Trajan holding a Dacian wolf at the **National History Museum** (p37)

3 Kicking back in Bucharest's surprisingly peaceful **Cişmigiu Garden** (p44)

4 Learning why you don't appreciate granny enough at the quirky but cool **Museum of the Romanian Peasant** (p41)

5 Going absolutely nuts in the **Old Town** (p46), Romania's biggest concentration of cafes, bars, pubs and clubs

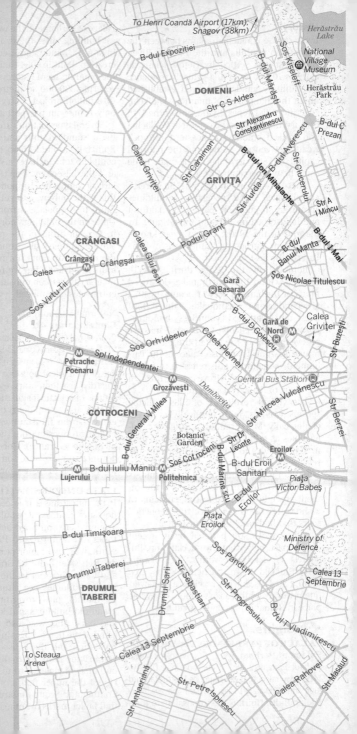

Central Bucharest

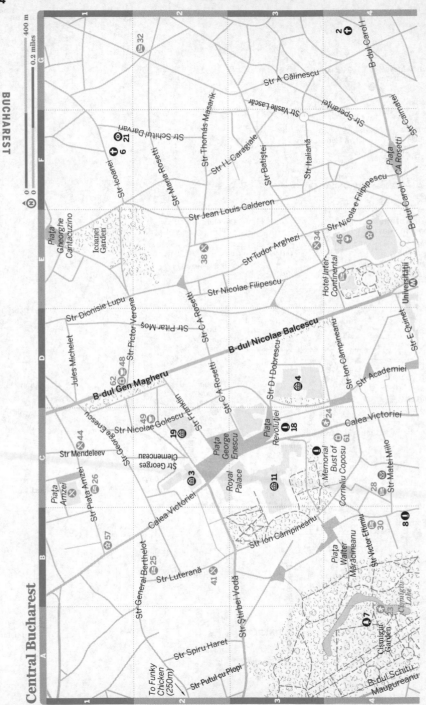

400 m
0.2 miles

Str A Călinescu

Str Vasile Lascăr

Str Speranței

Piața C.A. Rosetti

B-dul Carol I

Str Carmatei

2

Str Schitul Dârvari

Str Thomas Masarik

Str I L Caragiale

Str Batiștei

Str Italiană

6
21

Str Icoanei

Str Maria Rosetti

Piața Gheorghe Cantacuzino

Icoanei Garden

Str Jean Louis Calderon

Str Tudor Arghezi

Str Nicolae Filipescu

46
60
34

38

Hotel Inter-Continental

Str Nicolae Filipescu

Piața Universității

Str Dionisie Lupu

Str Pictor Verona

Str Pitar Moș

Str C A Rosetti

B-dul Nicolae Balcescu

Jules Michelet

48
62

B-dul Gen Magheru

Str D I Dobrescu

Str Ion Câmpineanu

Str Academiei

Str E Quinet

Str George Enescu

Str Nicolae Golescu

49

Str Franklin

19

4

24

Calea Victoriei

Str Mendeleev

44

Str Georges Clemenceau

Piața George Enescu

Piața Revoluției

18

Memorial Bust of Corneliu Coposu

61

Str Matei Millo

Piața Amzei

26

Str Piața Amzei

Royal Palace

3

11

28

Str General Berthelot

25

Calea Victoriei

30

Str Victor Eftimiu

8

57

Str Luterană

41

Str Știrbei Vodă

Str Ion Câmpineanu

Piața Walter Mărăcineanu

7

Cișmigiu Lake

Cișmigiu Garden

B-dul Schitu Măgureanu

To Funky Chicken (250m)

Str Spiru Haret

Str Putul cu Plopi

32

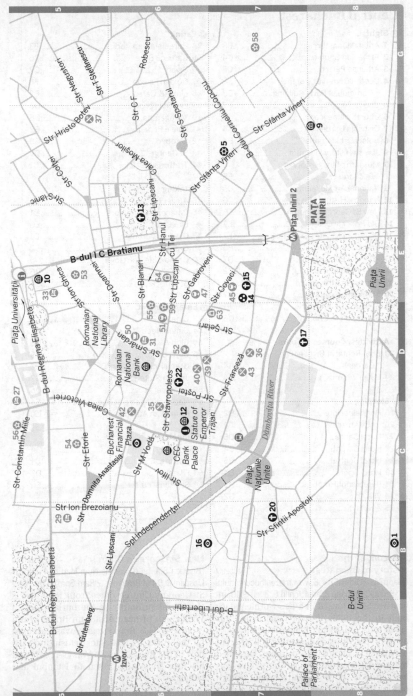

Central Bucharest

**Museum of the
History of Bucharest** MUSEUM
(Map p34; ☑ 021-3156858; www.muzeulbucurestiului
.ro; B-dul IC Brătianu 2; adult/child 6/3 lei; ☉10am-
6pm Wed-Sun) Housed in a neo-Gothic palace
built in the 1830s to host fancy balls, this
small museum, facing Piaţa Universităţii, is
a lovely spot with an interesting collection of
old artefacts, photos and costumes. Designed
by two Austrian architects, the palace was
built in 1832–34 for the Şuţu family, notorious for their high-society parties.

New St George's Church CHURCH
(Biserica Sfântul Gheorghe-Nou; Map p34; cnr Str
Lipscani & B-dul Brătianu; ☉8am-6pm) The New
St George's Church dates from 1699 and is
significant primarily as the burial place of
Wallachian prince Constantin Brâncoveanu
(r 1688–1714). Brâncoveanu was captured
by the Turks in 1714 after refusing to take
part in the Russo-Turkish War (1711). He and
his four sons were taken to Istanbul and
beheaded.

BUCHAREST IN...

One Day

Bucharest is a sprawling city, so if you've only got one day, get an early start and make your way over to the **Palace of Parliament** for a guided tour. Afterwards, stroll along **Calea Victoriei** and stop in at one of the big museums, such as the **National Art Museum**, and admire the **Rebirth Memorial** to the 1989 revolution. Afterwards sit for a beer at **Cişmigiu Garden** and spend the evening in the **Old Town (Lipscani)**.

Three Days

After day one, spend the second day in the leafy northern part of the capital, visiting **Herăstrău Park** and allowing time to see the open-air **National Village Museum** on its western bank. Walk along pretty Şos Kiseleff, stopping to admire the **Triumphal Arch** and possibly taking in another museum, the **Museum of the Romanian Peasant**. For your last day, consider a day trip to **Lake Snagov** to visit Dracula's, er, Vlad Ţepeş', final resting place.

OLD TOWN (LIPSCANI)

South of Piaţa Universităţii is a fascinating area that's both the heart of the city's historic core and the centrepiece of current efforts to transform Bucharest into a livable urban centre and tourist attraction. The Old Town, sometimes referred to as 'Lipscani' after one of the area's main streets, is home to Bucharest's Old Princely Court, dating back to the 15th century, when the city competed with former royal capitals, such as Curtea de Argeş and Târgovişte, to lead the Wallachian principality. Bucharest eventually won out, though the core of the Old Princely Court (Palatul Voievoda; Curtea Veche; Map p34; Str Franceză 21-23; ⊘10am-5pm) was allowed to fall into disrepair over the centuries. During our visit the court was undergoing a thorough renovation and temporarily closed to visitors. Even so, you could still peek through the fence to see a menacing statue of Vlad Ţepeş.

The area around the court thrived from roughly the 16th to the 19th centuries as a merchant quarter for artisans and traders, whose occupations are still reflected in street names such as Str Covaci (street of the blacksmiths) and Str Şelari (street for saddle-makers). During much of the 20th century, until as recently as a few years ago, the area had become a slum, a poor excuse for public housing for impoverished Roma.

These days, the saddle-makers are long gone and the Roma are quickly being pushed out to make way for arguably the liveliest, hippest, bawdiest and loudest quarter in the entire country.

Old Princely Court Church   CHURCH
(Biserica Curtea Veche; Map p34; Str Franceza; ⊘7am-8pm) The Old Princely Court Church, built from 1546 to 1559 during the reign of Mircea Ciobanul (Mircea the Shepherd), is Bucharest's oldest church. The faded 16th-century frescoes next to the altar are originals. The carved stone portal was added in 1715.

Stavropoleos Church   CHURCH
(Map p34; Str Stavropoleos; ⊘7am-8pm) The tiny and lovely Stavropoleos Church, which dates from 1724, perches a bit oddly just a block over from some of Bucharest's craziest Old Town carousing, but it's one church that will make a lasting impression, with its courtyard filled with tombstones and an ornate wooden interior. Romanian architect Ion Mincu designed the courtyard and restored this little gem in 1899.

National History Museum   MUSEUM
(Muzeul National de Istorie a Romaniei; Map p34; ☑021-315 8207; www.mnir.ro; Calea Victoriei 12; adult/student 8/2 lei; ⊘10am-6pm Wed-Sun) This is an excellent collection of maps, documents and artefacts on Romanian national history. It's particularly strong on the country's Roman ties, including a replica of the 2nd-century Trajan's Column. Our favourite piece, though, is not inside the museum at all, but rather on the steps outside: a controversial Statue of Emperor Trajan standing naked holding a Dacian wolf.

The statue was added in 2012 and has quickly become the most ridiculed (and photographed) monument in Bucharest. We wonder why?

Gară de Nord

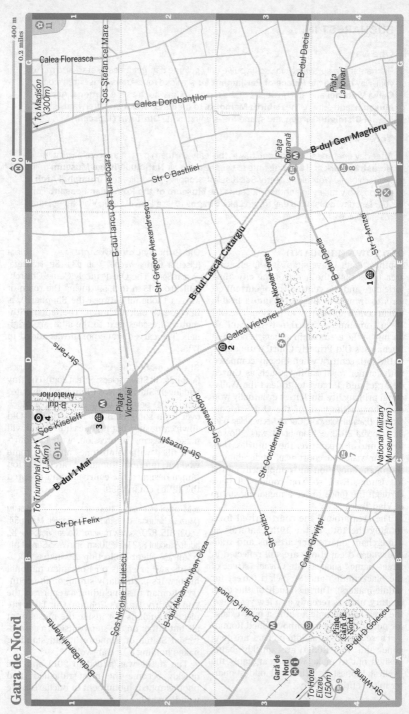

400 m
0.2 miles

Calea Floreasca

To Madison (300m)

Șos Ștefan cel Mare

Calea Dorobanților

B-dul Dacia

Piața Lahovari

Str C Bastiliei

Piața Romană

B-dul Gen Magheru

B-dul Iancu de Hunedoara

Str Grigore Alexandrescu

B-dul Lascăr Catargiu

Str Nicolae Iorga

B-dul Dacia

Str B Amzei

Calea Victoriei

Str Paris

Piața Victoriei

B-dul Aviatorilor

Șos Kiseleff

To Triumphal Arch (1.5km)

B-dul 1 Mai

Str Buzești

Str Sevastopol

Str Occidentului

National Military Museum (1km)

Str Dr I Felix

Șos Nicolae Titulescu

B-dul Alexandru Ioan Cuza

B-dul I G Duca

Str Polizu

Calea Griviței

B-dul Banul Manta

Piața Gară de Nord

B-dul D Golescu

Gară de Nord

To Hotel Elizeu (150m)

Str Witine

Gara de Nord

PIAŢA REVOLUŢIEI

To the north of Piaţa Universităţii, along Calea Victoriei, stands Piaţa Revoluţiei, a part of the city indelibly marked by the events surrounding the overthrow of the Ceauşescu regime in 1989. Ceauşescu's infamous final speech was given here, from the balcony of the former **Central Committee of the Communist Party building** (Map p34; www.mai.gov.ro; Piaţa Revolutiei 1; ⊙closed to the public), on 21 December 1989. Amid cries of 'Down with Ceauşescu!' he escaped (briefly) by helicopter from the roof. Meanwhile, the crowds were riddled with bullets, and many died. The building now houses the Interior Ministry.

On an island in front of the building on Calea Victoriei stands the **Rebirth Memorial** (Memorialul Renaşterii; Map p34; Calea Victoriei) – a white obelisk piercing a basketlike crown (a doughnut on a stick?). It was ridiculed when it was first erected in 2005, but the public has now grown accustomed to it, and it's one of the most photographed objects in Bucharest.

National Art Museum   MUSEUM
(Muzeul Naţional de Artă; Map p34; ✆021-313 3030; www.mnar.arts.ro; Calea Victoriei 49-53; admission 15 lei; ⊙11am-7pm Wed-Sun) Housed in the 19th-century Royal Palace, this massive, multipart museum – all signed in English – has three collections, including one on ancient and medieval Romanian art, modern Romanian painting and European art. The ancient collection is strong on icons and religious art, while the Romanian painting section has an excellent survey of 19th-century masters.

Save time for the Gallery of European Art, a 12,000-piece collection laid out by nationality. The Royal Palace itself is a treat. Built from 1812 to 1815 by Prince Dinicu Golescu, the palace became the official royal residence in 1834 during the reign of Prince Alexandru Ghica (r 1834–42). The current facade dates from the 1930s. Until 1989 it was the seat of the State Council and was called the Palace of the Republic.

Romanian Athenaeum   HISTORIC BUILDING
(Ateneul Român; Map p34; Str Benjamin Franklin; admission 7.50 lei) The exquisite Romanian Athenaeum is the majestic heart of Romania's classical music tradition. Scenes from Romanian history are featured on the interior fresco inside the Big Hall on the 1st floor; the dome is 41m high. A huge appeal dubbed 'Give a Penny for the Athenaeum' saved it from disaster after funds dried up in the late 19th century.

Inside, the peristyle is adorned with mosaics of five Romanian rulers, including Moldavian prince Vasile Lupu (r 1512–21), Wallachian Matei Basarab (r 1632–54) and King Carol I (r 1881–1914). It was built in 1888, and George Enescu made his debut here in 1898, followed five years later by the first performance of his masterpiece, 'Romanian Rhapsody'. Today it's home to the George Enescu Philharmonic Orchestra.

Athénée Palace   HISTORIC BUILDING
(Map p34; Str Episcopiei 1-3) Just to the north of the National Art Museum is the Athénée Palace, so evocatively captured in its postrevolutionary, prostitute-teeming state by Robert Kaplan in his book *Balkan Ghosts*. Designed to outdo Paris in 1918, the hotel later served as a hotbed for Romania's KGB, the Securitate. Now the Hilton organisation has thoroughly cleaned it up – and priced its rooms to the stratosphere.

PIAŢA UNIRII & AROUND

South of the Old Town, Piaţa Unirii stands at the centre of the new socialist city that Ceauşescu began building in earnest in the 1980s (knocking down much of old Bucharest in the process). The area's broad boulevard, B-dul Unirii, was originally intended as a kind of communist-era Champs-Élysées, with big apartment blocks on both sides housing the party elite. It was never finished, but the sheer scale conveys something of the intent. These days, Piaţa Unirii is a lively place with a huge roadway roundabout and a convenient metro station, and marks the southern border of the central city area. The main sights, ironically, are a handful of beautiful historic churches that miraculously survived the rebuilding and demolition project.

Patriarchal Cathedral CHURCH
(Catedrala Patriahală; Str Dealul Mitropoliei; ⊙7am-8pm) From the centre of Piaţa Unirii, look southwest to the Patriarchal Cathedral, the centre of Romanian Orthodox faith, built between 1656 and 1658. It triumphantly peeks over once-grand housing blocks on B-dul Unirii designed to 'hide' Bucharest's churches. One such fatality is the Antim Monastery, which dates from 1715. It's northwest, just one block before the boulevard ends.

St Apostles' Church CHURCH
(Biserica Sfinţii Apostoli; Map p34; Str Apostoli 33a; ⊙7am-8pm) Tiny St Apostles' Church, north of B-dul Unirii (west of the Piaţa Unirii), survived Ceauşescu's 1980s demolition project – to a degree. The church, built in 1636, was not moved, but the surrounding parkland was ripped up and replaced with blocks of flats. It's overgrown, with trees and near-abandoned buildings.

Antim Monastery MONASTERY
(Mânăstirea Antim; Map p34; Str Antim; ⊙7am-8pm) This beautiful walled complex was built in 1715 by the metropolitan bishop Antim Ivireanu. Today it's hidden by communist-era housing blocks.

Princess Bălaşa Church CHURCH
(Biserica Domniţa Bălaşa; Map p34; Str Sfintii Apostoli; ⊙7am-8pm) Another impressive church that survived the 1980s demolition is the candy-striped Princess Bălaşa Church. The church, just northwest of Piaţa Unirii, is named after Wallachian Prince Constantin Brâncoveanu's sixth daughter, who had a small wooden church built here in 1744 that was rebuilt over the years to the 19th-century structure that stands today.

Prince Mihai Monastery MONASTERY
(Mânăstirea Mihai Vodă; Map p34; Str Sapienţei) The former symbol of Bucharest, the 16th-century Prince Mihai Monastery was built from 1589 to 1591 under the orders of Mihai Viteazul (r 1593–1601). Ceauşescu moved it 279m east in 1985 to this patch of wasteland between apartment blocks.

PIAŢA VICTORIEI & AROUND
Piaţa Victoriei is an important traffic hub and square that marks the northern edge of the central city. The metro station is a good access point for walks north along Şos Kiseleff or south into the centre.

George Enescu Museum MUSEUM
(Muzeul George Enescu; Map p38; ☎021-318 1450; www.georgeenescu.ro; Calea Victoriei 141; adult/child 6/1.50 lei; ⊙10am-5pm Tue-Sun) A few blocks south of Piaţa Victoriei is this museum dedicated to national composer George Enescu (1881–1955). The real lure is the chance to peek inside the lovely building housing the museum: the turn-of-the-century art-nouveau Cantacuzino Palace.

Art Collection Museum MUSEUM
(Map p38; ☎021-212 9641; www.mnar.arts.ro; Calea Victoriei 111; ⊙10am-6pm Wed-Sun) This grab-bag of several dozen private collections is particularly strong on folk and religious art and Romanian painting from the 19th and early 20th centuries. It's now part of the National Art Museum.

ŞOSEAUA KISELEFF
Home to some of Bucharest's finest villas and a handful of its best museums, Şos Kiseleff (metro Piaţa Victoriei) stretches north from Piaţa Victoriei to Herăstrău Park. The major landmark in this neck of the woods is the Triumphal Arch (Arcul de Triumf; off Map p38; Piaţa Arcul de Triumf; ⊙occasionally open to the public), which stands halfway up Şos Kiseleff. The 27m arch, based on Paris' namesake monument, was built in 1935 to commemorate the reunification of Romania in 1918. Heavy traffic makes it difficult to get anywhere close to the arch, and the viewing platform is not always open to the public. The arch was scheduled for renovation in 2013.

TOP CHOICE **Grigore Antipa Natural History Museum** MUSEUM
(Muzeul de Istorie Naturală Grigore Antipa; Map p38; ☎021-312 8826; www.antipa.ro; Şos Kiseleff 1; adult/student/child 20/10/5 lei; ☀) One of the few attractions in Bucharest that are squarely aimed at kids, this natural history muse-

JEWISH BUCHAREST

Once a thriving part of Bucharest, the city's Jewish community occupied many of the old streets that surrounded today's Piaţa Unirii. While much of the area was razed in the 1980s to make way for Ceauşescu's redevelopment plans, here there are scattered reminders of this once-vital group.

The first stop would be the well-arranged **Jewish History Museum** (Muzeul de Istorie al Comunitaţilor Evreieşti din România; Map p34; ☑021-311 0870; Str Mămulari 3; admission free; ⊙9am-2pm Mon-Thu, 9am-1pm Fri & Sun), housed in the beautiful Tailor's synagogue. Exhibits highlight Jewish contributions to Romania, while the Holocaust room is dedicated to the around 200,000 Romanian Jews who were deported to camps in Transdniestr and Ukraine, and the well over 100,000 Jews from Transylvania who died at Auschwitz-Birkenau. The synagogue dates from 1850 and is one of three pre-WWII synagogues to survive. Bring your passport.

The **Choral Temple** (Map p34; ☑021-312 2196; Str Sf Vineri 9-11; ⊙closed for renovation), built in 1857, is the city's main working synagogue and is visually stunning inside. A memorial to the victims of the Holocaust, erected in 1991, fronts the temple. It was closed in 2012 for renovation and at the time of writing it was not clear when it would reopen.

South of the Piaţa Unirii area, the old **Sephardic Jewish Cemetery** (Cimitirul Evreiesc de rit Sefard; Calea Şerban Vodă; ⊙noon-6pm) lies opposite **Bellu Cemetery** (metro Eroii Revoluţiei). Two rows of graves dated 21 to 23 January 1941 mark the Iron Guard's pogrom against the Jewish community, during which at least 170 Jews were murdered. From the metro, walk 100m towards the modern City Hall; it's to the right.

North of Piaţa Unirii is the country's formal **memorial** (Map p34; Str Ion Brezoianu; ⊙24hr) to Romanian Jews and Roma who died in the Holocaust. The monument was unveiled in 2009 and was widely seen as the government's first step in acknowledging Romania's part in the destruction of European Jewry.

um has been thoroughly renovated and now features modern bells and whistles such as video displays, games and interactive exhibits. Much of it is signed in English.

Museum of the Romanian Peasant MUSEUM
(Muzeul Ţăranului Român; ☑021-317 9661; www.muzeultaranuluiroman.ro; Şos Kiseleff 3; adult/child 8/2 lei; ⊙10am-6pm Tue-Sun) One of the best museums in Bucharest is this collection of traditional peasant bric-a-brac, costumes, icons, artwork and partially restored houses and churches. There's not much English signage, but little cards in English posted at each room's entrance give a flavour of what's on offer. An 18th-century Transylvanian church is in the back lot, as is a gift shop.

Don't miss the jarring communism exhibition downstairs, which focuses on the Ceauşescu-era program of land collectivisation, which almost completely destroyed the traditional way of life.

National Village Museum OUTDOOR MUSEUM
(Muzeul Naţional al Satului; ☑021-317 9103; www.muzeul-satului.ro; Şos Kiseleff 28-30; adult/child 10/5 lei; ⊙9am-7pm Tue-Sun, to 5pm Mon; ▣) On the shores of Herăstrău Lake, this museum is a terrific open-air collection of several dozen homesteads, churches, mills and windmills relocated from rural Romania. Built in 1936 by royal decree, it is one of Europe's oldest open-air museums and a good choice for kids to boot.

National Museum of Geology
(Muzeul National de Geologie; Map p38; ☑021-212 8952; www.geology.ro; Şos Kiseleff 2; adult/child 8/4 lei; ⊙10am-6pm Tue-Sun) Another highly worthwhile museum, this one features Romania's varied geological formations, with enough English signage on hand to give you the general idea of what's on display. The impressive building dates from the early 20th century and was originally built to house the country's Royal Geological Society.

HERĂSTRĂU PARK & AROUND

A couple of blocks east of the Triumphal Arch in northern Bucharest, **Piaţa Charles de Gaulle** (metro Piaţa Aviatorilor) is in the heart of some of the city's most well-to-do areas.

'PAUPERS' GRAVES'

About 3km west of the Palace of Parliament, Ghencea Civil Cemetery (Cimitirul Civil Ghencea; Calea 13 Septembrie; ⊘8am-8pm) has two infamous inhabitants: Nicolae Ceauşescu and his wife, Elena. The pair were secretly buried here – and notably not at Bellu Cemetery, the city's most reputable resting place – on 30 December 1989, in hastily prepared graves. Both lie before the small chapel that faces the entry.

Nicolae lies in row I-35, to the left of the path. No tomb adorns his earth grave. There is only a simple stone inscription with name and dates of birth and death (26 January 1918 to 25 December 1989).

Elena is buried in a separate location, in row H-25, directly across the cemetery to the right (just behind a modern marble tomb). The markings are even simpler and there's no sign of flowers or candles. The decision to keep the couple apart in death was intentional. The body of their playboy son, Nicu, who died from cirrhosis of the liver in 1996, lies nearby.

Former Ceauşescu Residence
HISTORIC BUILDING

(B-dul Primăverii 50; ⊘closed to the public) Just east of Piaţa Charles de Gaulle is the former main residence of Nicolae and Elena Ceauşescu, also known as the Primăverii Palace. It's off-limits to everyone but state guests, but it is easy to look over the wall at the lush and leafy pad.

Zambaccian Museum
MUSEUM

(Muzeul Zambaccian; ☑021-230 1920; www.mnar .arts.ro; Str Muzeul Zambaccian 21a; adult/ student 7/3.50 lei; ⊘10am-6pm Sat-Wed) Tricky to find, the little Zambaccian Museum is in a restored villa between B-dul Aviatorilor and Calea Dorobanţilor (just north of Piaţa Dorobanţilor). The small collection boasts mostly Romanian paintings from the early 20th century, plus a Matisse, a Cezanne and a couple of Renoirs – all collected by the late Armenian businessman Krikor Zambaccian.

EAST BUCHAREST

The city's Old Town gets the fabled glory these days, but many of the cobbled blocks east of Piaţa Romană and Piaţa Universităţii are some of Bucharest's most evocative. This area has undergone a facelift in the past couple of years, and hidden among the crumbling buildings are some beautifully restored villas and spruced-up parks.

Church of the Icon
CHURCH

(Biserica Icoanei; Map p34; Str Icoanei 12; ⊘8am-8pm) This church was built by monk and former privy secretary Mihail Băbeanu from 1745 to 1750.

St Slujbă's Monastery
MONASTERY

(Mănăstirea Sfânta Slujbă; Map p34; Str Schitul Darvari 3; ⊘8am-6pm) Pretty St Slujbă's Monastery is surrounded by a lush walled garden.

Armenian Church
CHURCH

(Map p34; ☑021-313 9070; B-dul Carol I 43; ⊘9am-6pm Mon-Sat, 8am-1pm Sun) Along B-dul Carol I, east of Piaţa Universităţii, is the alabaster Armenian Church, which originally dates from 1781 (though this church was built in 1915).

Theodor Pallady Museum
MUSEUM

(Muzeul Theodor Pallady; ☑021-211 4979; Str Spătarului 22; adult/student 5/2.50 lei; ⊘10am-6pm Tue-Sun) The Theodor Pallady Museum is housed inside the exquisite early-18th-century Casa Melik, a former merchant's house. It contains the private art collection of the Raut family (part of the National Art Museum today).

WEST BUCHAREST

National Military Museum
MUSEUM

(Muzeul Militar Naţional; off Map p38; ☑021-319 5904; Str Mircea Vulcănescu 125-127; adult/student 5/2.5 lei; ⊘9am-5pm Tue-Sun) The National Military Museum doubles nicely as a Romanian history museum, with its chronological rundown of how the country defended itself. In the museum entrance, note the 1988 communist mural that celebrates the Palace of Parliament (a year before the revolution). In back is a hangar with early aviator Aurel Vlaicu's historic 1911 plane.

Cotroceni Palace
MUSEUM

(☑021-317 3107; www.muzeulcotroceni.ro; B-dul Geniului 1; adult/student incl guided tour 27/21 lei; ⊘9.30am-4.30pm Tue-Sun by appointment only) Cotroceni Palace dates from the late 19th century and is the official residence of the Romanian president. Many rooms are open to visitors, but call in advance to ensure a spot in the tour. The palace has an illustrious place in Romanian history, most notably as the home of Queen Marie, the English wife of Ferdinand I. Bring your passport.

SOUTHERN BUCHAREST

The area south of Piaţa Unirii is mostly devoid of traditional tourist sights but has some nice parks and important cemeteries.

Carol I Park
PARK

(⊗24hr) About 1km southwest of Piaţa Unirii, Carol I Park was inaugurated in 1906. The main sights here are an eternal flame burning for an unknown soldier and a 20m black-granite mausoleum. The mausoleum, topped with five arches made of red Swedish granite, was put up in memory of the 'Heroes for the Struggle for the People's and the Homeland's Liberty for Socialism'. Enter the park from the north at Piaţa Libertăţii or from the south along Calea Şerban Vodă.

Youth Park
PARK

(Parcul Tineretului) A couple of blocks east of Carol I Park along Calea Şerban Vodă (near metro Tineretului) is the bigger Youth Park, where various sporting events and open-air concerts take place in the Sports & Culture Palace. It's been thoroughly renovated and there's lots of space and playground equipment for younger children to run and play.

Martyr-Heroes of the December 1989 Revolution Cemetery
CEMETERY

(Cimitirul Eroii Martiri ai Revoluţei din Decembrie 1989; Calea Şerban Vodă; ⊗noon-sunset) Going west from the southern end of Carol I Park (near metro Eroii Revoluţiei), the road curves past this cemetery, where many of the 1000 victims of the 1989 revolution are buried.

Bellu Cemetery
CEMETERY

(Cimitirul Bellu; ☎021-636 3571; www.bellu.ro; Calea Şerban Vodă 249; ⊗8am-5pm) Bellu Cemetery is the city's most prestigious burial ground and houses the tombs of many notable Romanian writers. A map inside the gate points out locations. Many Romanians pay their respects to national poet Mihai Eminescu (1850–89) and comic playwright and humorist Ion Luca Caragiale (1852–1912), who are only separated by a bloke named Traian Savulescu; go to Figura 9 (to the right after you enter).

Activities

Bucharest is highly urbanised and the main activities include walking and sightseeing. In warm weather, you can hire row boats or pedal boats on lakes at several parks, including **Cişmigiu Garden** (Map p34; Cişmigiu Garden; 2-person pedal boat per hr 10 lei; ⊗9am-7pm May-Sep) and **Herăstrău Park** (Herăstrău Park; 2-person pedal boat per hr 10 lei; ⊗10am-7pm May-Sep). Thirty-minute pleasure cruises are offered on the lake at Herăstrău Park for 5 lei.

Bucharest is a dangerous city for cycling and we do not recommend it; nevertheless the bike-sharing scheme **I'Velo** (☎021-310 6397; www.ivelo.ro; Herăstrău Park; per hr 4 lei; ⊗9am-6pm May-Oct) offers bikes for hire at Herăstrău Park. The rental location is near the main entrance to the park, by the ExpoFlora zone. Phone or consult the website for location details.

Tours

Bucharest City Tour
DOUBLE-DECKER BUS

(www.bucharestcitytour.ratb.ro; per 24hr adult/child 25/10 lei; ⊗10am-8pm) The RATB offers

---

BUCHAREST FOR CHILDREN

Bucharest is not an extremely child-friendly destination, particularly if you're travelling with younger children. Distances between sights are vast and getting around involves a lot of legwork and tedious climbing up and down metro stairs.

Children of any age will appreciate the sheer vastness of the Palace of Parliament (p31) building. The most popular museums with younger visitors are likely to be the National Village Museum (p41) and the Natural History Museum (p40). The Geology Museum (p41) will appeal to older kids, especially those with a geek streak. Many kids will get a kick out of the plane hangar at the National Military Museum (p42), with parachute displays, a host of planes and all sorts of tanks outside.

The city's parks, particularly Cişmigiu Garden (p44), Herăstrău Park (p44) and Youth Park (p43), have set up play areas for kids and have lakes where you can rent paddle or row boats.

City Mall (p50) and Bucureşti Mall (p50) have supervised play areas for children.

BUCHAREST PARKS

Escape the heat or honks at some of Bucharest's urban oases. They tend to be best during the week, when fewer people are enjoying the outdoors. All have nice areas to sit in and drink beer or espresso, and many have swings or small rides for children.

Cişmigiu Garden (Grădina Cişmigiu; Map p34) Central and peaceful; open-air cafes look over the pond and plenty of benches (and flirters – it's known as 'lovers' park' locally).

Herăstrău Park (Parcul Herăstrău; ☉24hr) Lots of water and a 2-sq-km park.

Youth Park (p43) This large and renovated park has heaps of play areas, lakes and grassy fields.

a daily double-decker DIY tourist bus that's a convenient way of seeing the main sights as well as being an efficient alternative to buses and metros for moving around town. The bus runs every 15 minutes along the major north–south axis from Piaţa Unirii to the National Village Museum. Buy tickets on board at designated stops.

Cultural Travel & Tours   TRAVEL AGENCY
(☑021-336 3163; www.cttours.ro) Offers several half- and full-day city tours, including excursions to Snagov, from 140 to 200 lei per person. It also offers longer trips around the country.

TravelMaker   TRAVEL AGENCY
(Bucharest City Tour; ☑021-232 0331, 0735-525 710; www.bucharestcitytour.com) Full-service travel agency offering local city tours, as well as excursions around the country, including a popular trip to Bran Castle for around 300 lei per person.

★ Festivals & Events

Bucharest International Film Festival FILM
(www.b-est.ro; ☉Apr) Bucharest's only international film festival focuses on off-beat, arthouse fare from up-and-coming directors.

EuropaFest   MUSIC
(www.jmevents.ro; ☉May) Two weeks of jazz, blues and pop from the best European musicians, as well as performers from other continents, held at venues around the city.

Craftsman's Fair   FOLK CRAFTS
(Târgul Meşterilor Populari; ☉May & Jun) Local craft fair hosted by the National Village Museum with guest craftspeople from all over Romania.

**Bucharest Street
Music Festival**   PERFORMING ARTS
(D'ale Bucureştilor; ☉Jun) Weeklong carnival with street dancers, street theatre, folk danc-

ers and live bands performing in Bucharest's historic heart.

George Enescu Music Festival MUSIC
(www.festivalenescu.ro; ☉Sep in odd-numbered years) This prestigious classical music festival attracts some of the best orchestras and performers from around the world.

🛏 Sleeping

Hotels in Bucharest are typically aimed at businesspeople, and prices are higher here than in the rest of the country. Tips for getting discounts include booking in advance or using the hotel's website. Room rates can drop by as much as half in midsummer (July and August), which is widely considered low season. The situation with hostels continues to improve and Bucharest now has some of the best cheap lodging in the country.

CENTRAL BUCHAREST

TOP CHOICE Rembrandt Hotel $$
(Map p34; ☑021-313 9315; www.rembrandt.ro; Str Smârdan 11; s/d 'tourist class' Mon-Fri 330/371 lei, Sat & Sun 294/334 lei; ✴@🖥) It's hard to say enough good things about this place. Stylish beyond its three-star rating, this 16-room, Dutch-owned hotel faces the landmark National Bank in the historic centre. Rooms feature polished wooden floors, wall-size timber headboards, and DVD players. Book in advance, as the few tourist-class rooms go quickly.

Z Hotel   HOTEL $$
(Map p34; ☑031-140 0200; www.zhotels.ro; Str Ion Nisor 4; s/d 220/320 lei; P✴@🖥) This sleek, beautiful executive boutique is sandwiched nicely between Piaţa Universităţii and the Old Town. The rooms are stylish and upbeat, and the staff are warm and welcoming. There's a high-quality spa and fitness club on-site.

Hotel Capşa HOTEL $$$

(Map p34; ☑021-313 4038; www.capsa.ro; Calea Victoriei 36; s/d 400/500 lei; P☺❄@🛜) Behind the charming 1852 facade, this central hotel served as a bohemian hang-out through the 1930s. Rooms benefit from old practices – high ceilings – and newer touches including fleur-de-lys designs, dark-wood panelling and a fitness centre.

Hotel Amzei HOTEL $$$

(Map p34; ☑021-313 9400; www.hotelamzei.ro; Piaţa Amzei 8; s/d 450/550 lei; ☺❄🛜) This tastefully reconstructed villa just off Calea Victoriei has 22 rooms on four floors. The wrought-iron atrium in the lobby lends a refined feel. The rooms are in a more restrained contemporary style, but everything about the place says quality.

Berthelot Hotel HOTEL $$$

(Map p34; ☑031-425 5860; www.hotelberthelot.ro; Str Gen Berthelot 9; s/d 400/500 lei; ☺❄@🛜) This modern boutique hotel offers bright and clean rooms, with air-conditioning and LCD TVs. The location, just off the Calea Victoriei, is in the heart of the city's fashion and boutique quarter, and is excellent for shopping. The rack rates put this property between midrange and top end, but check the hotel website for discounts that practically put it in the budget category.

Midland Youth Hostel HOSTEL $

(Map p38; ☑021-314 5323; www.themidlandhostel.com; Str Biserica Amzei 22; dm 35-60 lei; ☺❄@🛜) This is a bright, cheerful, well-run hostel, with an excellent central location not far from Piaţa Romană. Accommodation is in six-, 10- or 14-bed dorms. There's a common kitchen and free breakfast.

Hotel Central HOTEL $$$

(Map p34; ☑021-315 5635; www.thhotels.ro/hotel-central; Str Ion Brezoianu 13; s/d 400/500 lei; ☺❄🛜) Very nice hotel that sits somewhere between top end and midrange for Bucharest. Half of the 61 rooms overlook busy B-dul Regina Elisabeta, so request something off the street if noise is an issue.

Hotel Carpaţi HOTEL $$

(Map p34; ☑021-315 0140; www.hotelcarpati bucuresti.ro; Str Matei Millo 16; s/d 160/220 lei; 🛜) This popular backpacker option in an old early-20th-century landmark hotel exudes a kind of communist-era charm; nevertheless, some of the 40 rooms have been renovated and offer good value. If you're on a strict budget, go for the even cheaper rooms that don't have en-suite bathrooms.

Hotel Opera HOTEL $$$

(Map p34; ☑021-312 4857; www.thhotels.ro/hotel-opera; Str Ion Brezoianu 37; s/d 300/340 lei; P☺❄🛜) Set on a back-street corner, this 33-room, faintly art-deco, music-themed hotel enjoys membership with Top Hotels Group, offering – among other things – Mercedes airport transfer. The rooms are small but nicely arranged.

GARA DE NORD & AROUND

Though the area around the Gara de Nord is not the most appealing, there are several decent accommodation options within an easy walk of the station.

Vila 11 GUESTHOUSE $

(Map p38; ☑0722-495 900; www.vila11.hostel.com; Str Institutul Medico Militar 11; s/d 60/100 lei; ☺❄@) Run by a welcoming expat family, this homey *pensiunea* is on a back street. Ask for a top-floor room, with pretty views and air-conditioning, but watch the narrow stairways.

Hotel Elizeu HOTEL $$

(off Map p38; ☑021-319 1734; www.hotelelizeu.ro; Str Elizeu 11-13; s/d 200/280 lei; ❄@🛜) This 54-room hotel within easy walking distance of the train station is comfortable and modern, with quiet rooms, minibar and decent buffet breakfast (included).

OUTSIDE THE CENTRE

Don't be put off that these choices aren't near the historic core of Bucharest. Many of the city's best options – including hostels – are just outside the centre.

TOP CHOICE The Doors HOSTEL $

(☑021-336 2127; www.doorshostel.com; Str Olimpului 13; dm 45-60 lei, d 150 lei) Our favourite hostel *du jour* in Bucharest is 15 minutes' walk southwest of Piaţa Unirii and all the better for it, with a quiet, residential location and a beautiful garden set up like a Moroccan tearoom. There are six- and eight-bed dorms, one quad and one private double. Friendly and welcoming staff.

Vila Arte BOUTIQUE HOTEL $$

(Map p34; ☑021-210 1035; www.vilaarte.ro; Str Vasile Lascăr 78; s/d 260/320 lei; ☺❄@🛜) A renovated villa transformed into a superb boutique hotel stuffed with original art that really pushes the envelope on design and colour. The services are top drawer and the

APARTMENTS

A short-term apartment rental makes sense if you're planning to stay longer than three days. Prices are generally cheaper than hotels, and you get a functioning kitchen and washing machine so you can regain control over your diet and dirty clothes at the same time. Note that you'll usually have to pay cash up front (sometimes in euros), so make sure you get a good look at the place before turning over your money. Most of the apartments are a little worn, but serviceable. Rarely will they actually look anywhere near as nice as they do in the online photos advertising them. The longer your stay, the more negotiating power you have over price.

RoCazare (☑0768-001 001; www.rocazare.ro) Decent selection of apartments in good, central locations, ranging from 200 to 400 lei per night.

Cert Accommodation (☑0720-772 772; www.cert-accommodation.ro) Has a good selection of apartments, with most being close to the centre. Insist in advance on a clean apartment, and double-check to make sure standard items such as toasters and coffeemakers are there and in working order. Prices range from 250 to 500 lei per night.

helpful reception makes every guest feel special. The 'Ottoman' room is done in an updated Turkish style, with deep-red spreads and fabrics, and oriental carpets.

Hotel Duke   HOTEL **$$$**
(Map p38; ☑021-317 4186; www.hotelduke.ro; B-dul Dacia 33; s/d 520/600 lei; P✪❄🐾🕸) At Piaţa Romana, the 38-room Duke is a pleasant business-style hotel with mint-and-caramel rooms, attentive staff, internet in the lobby, and a casual bar where suits chat.

Funky Chicken   HOSTEL **$**
(off Map p34; ☑021-312 1425; www.funkychic kenhostel.com; Str Gen Berthelot 63; dm 40-45 lei; ✪@) This hostel occupies a historic home on a shaded street, with four dorm rooms that sleep 24. No private rooms and no breakfast.

Pullman Bucharest World Trade Center   HOTEL **$$$**
(☑021-318 3000; www.pullmanhotels.com; Piaţa Montreal 10; s & d from 800 lei; ✪❄@🕸) Adjoining the World Trade Centre, this 12-floor high-rise has 203 classy rooms – geometric shapes, purple carpets in the hallways – with incredible views over the city, and four distinctive eating and drinking areas in the luxe lobby, plus a small fitness centre.

Hotel Helios   HOTEL **$$**
(Map p38; ☑021-310 7084; www.hotelhelios.ro; Str Iulia Haşdeu 16; s/d 150/220 lei; ❄@) This 15-room hotel is a good budget option and only a few blocks from the train station. It faces a quaint Orthodox church, and has stylish rooms and floor-to-ceiling wardrobes. Prices drop 20% Saturday and Sunday.

✖ Eating

Many of Bucharest's restaurants are concentrated in the Old Town, with the rest spread out all around the city. Self-caterers will want to head to the daily market on Piaţa Amzei, with a good selection of fresh fruit and veg.

OLD TOWN (LIPSCANI)

TOP CHOICE Caru' cu Bere   ROMANIAN **$$**
(Map p34; ☑021-313 7560; www.carucubere.ro; Str Stavropoleos 3-5; mains 15-40 lei; ⊗8am-midnight) Despite a decidedly tourist-leaning atmosphere, with peasant-girl hostesses and sporadic traditional song-and-dance numbers, Bucharest's oldest beer house continues to draw in a strong local crowd. The colourful belle-epoque interior and stained-glass windows dazzle, as does the classic Romanian food. Dinner reservations recommended.

Malagamba   ITALIAN **$$**
(Map p34; ☑021-313 3389; www.malagamba.ro; Str Sf Dumitru 2; mains 20-40 lei; 🕸🍴) Creative Italian cooking, with an inventive mix of pasta dishes and delicious salads. On weekends there are babysitters on hand and special kiddie shows, so that parents can take a break over diinner.

Divan   MIDDLE EASTERN **$$**
(Map p34; ☑021-312 3034; www.thedivan.ro; Str Franceză 46-48; mains 20-30 lei; ⊗10am-1am; 🕸) Deservedly popular Turkish and Middle Eastern place, where snagging a prized terrace table will take a mix of patience and good fortune. The waiter will first bring around a tantalising selection of starters, such as hummus and babaganoush. Select a few of these

and then settle back for the enormous platters of grilled meats and kebabs.

Sindbad
MIDDLE EASTERN **$$**

(Map p34; ☑021-317 7788; www.restaurantsind bad.ro; Str Lipscani 19; mains 20-30 lei; ☎) This small Lebanese restaurant may lack a little something in presentation, but it makes up for this with great food, belly-dancing and water pipes. In a word: authentic.

St George
HUNGARIAN **$$**

(Map p34; ☑021-317 1087; www.stgeorge.ro; Str Franceză 44; mains 20-45 lei; ☉11am-11pm; ☎) A festive and popular Hungarian restaurant on a lively strip in the Old Town. The cuisine on offer – stews and pork dishes – tends towards the heavy side, but you can wash it down with some very good wine. Dine on the terrace in nice weather.

Les Bourgeois
BISTRO **$$**

(Map p34; ☑021-310 6052; www.lesbourgeois.ro; Str Smârdan 20; mains 20-65 lei; ☉11am-midnight; ☎) French bistro–styled place with a mouthwatering range of salads as well as chicken, fish and beef dishes. We opted for the lamb chops and were not disappointed. Eat on the terrace along a bustling corner of the Old Town.

BEYOND THE OLD TOWN

Lente & Cafea
INTERNATIONAL **$$**

(Map p34; ☑021-310 7424; www.lente.ro; Str Gen Praporgescu 31; mains 20-35 lei; ☉11.30am-1am; ☎) Eclecticism is apparently the theme at this trendy, in-the-know restaurant. The menu is an assortment of tempting fish and chicken concoctions (many with curry, wild rice, mushrooms etc) interspersed with pages of musical lyrics and musical '10 Best' lists, such as, 'What are the best songs for a long road trip?'. Their choice: Muse 'Butterflies and Hurricanes'.

⌐TOP⌐
CHOICE Golden Falcon
MIDDLE EASTERN **$$**

(Map p34; ☑021-314 2825; www.goldenfalcon.ro; Str Hristo Botev 18-20; mains 35 lei; ☉noon-11pm) OK, we admit it, there's rarely more than a handful of diners at this upscale Turkish restaurant. Still, the yoghurt and hummus salads (10 lei per dish) are to die for, the flatbread is fresh from the oven and big as a hubcap, and the spicy lamb and beef kebabs are the best around.

Sale e Pepe
ITALIAN **$$**

(Map p34; ☑021-315 8989; www.saleepepe.ro; Str Luterană 3; pizzas 15-30 lei; ☉10am-midnight Mon-Fri, 3pm-midnight Sat & Sun) This tiny pizza and pasta place specialises in crunchy thin-crust pizzas – and for once in Romania, they don't undercook them. Pizza 'Pepperoni' comes topped with sliced red pepper and spicy sausage, and is served with hot sauce on the side on request. There's dining on two levels, with the more popular seating upstairs. It does breakfast, too.

Burebista Vanatoresc
ROMANIAN **$$$**

(Map p34; ☑021-211 8929; www.restaurantvanat oresc.ro; Str Batiştei 14; mains 40-60 lei; ☉noon-midnight) This is a touristy, traditional grill restaurant, where the staff don 19th-century peasantwear and everything feels kind of forced. On the other hand, the food is very good and the terrace is a relaxing spot for a beer and some grilled meats.

Trattoria Il Calcio
ITALIAN **$$**

(Map p34; ☑0722-134 299; www.trattoriailcalcio. ro; Str Mendeleev 14; mains 22-46 lei; ☉10am-midnight; ☎) This upscale local Italian chain is run by 'Romania's George Best' (football legend Gino Iorgulescu), complete with framed *Futbol* journals from the 1960s on the walls. The food's great, with hearty meals and good salads. It gets busy at lunchtime.

Karishma
INDIAN **$$**

(☑021-252 5157; www.karishma.ro; Str Iancu Capitanu 36; mains 20-36 lei; ☉8am-10.30pm; ☑) The best (and arguably the most authentic) Indian restaurant in the country. Excellent curries, spiced to order, along with the usual accoutrements of rice and bread. Good vegetarian selection.

⌐ Drinking

Drinking options can be roughly broken down into cafes and bars, though there's little distinction in practice. Most of the popular places these days are in the Old Town.

OLD TOWN (LIPSCANI)

⌐TOP⌐
CHOICE Atelier Mecanic
CAFE

(Map p34; ☑0726-767 611; Str Covaci 12; ☉11am-4am; ☎) The laid-back mood and the arty, mix-and-match junk-shop decor are a breath of fresh air compared with many other Old Town cafes and pubs that are lined with corporate tat and tie-ins. They serve great coffee here, as well as wines and an impressive range of single-malt scotches. DJs play tunes in the evening.

Old City   BAR
(Map p34; ☎0729-377 774; www.oldcity-lipscani.ro; Str Lipscani 45; ☺10am-5am; ⊛) This remains one of our favourite go-to bars in the Old City and most nights, especially weekends, bring big crowds and theme parties. There's a large, handsome bar area and a big garden out back.

St Patrick   PUB
(Map p34; ☎021-313 0336; www.stpatrick.ro; Str Smârdan 25; ⊛) This popular pub gets the authentic Irish bar look down with dark woods and green ceiling. Grab a table on busy Str Smârdan and settle back with a pint of Guinness or cider. They also do good renditions of standards including steak and kidney pie (24 lei) and Irish breakfast (24 lei).

Grand Cafe Van Gogh   CAFE
(Map p34; ☎031-107 6371; www.vangogh.ro; Str Smârdan 9; ☺8.30am-midnight Mon-Fri, 10am-midnight Sat & Sun; ⊛) This well-positioned and lively cafe stands at the entrance to the Old Town. Very good coffee and other drinks. They also prepare light meals including breakfasts (20 lei) and burgers as well as daily luncheon specials. The 1st floor is nonsmoking.

Fire Club   BAR
(Map p34; ☎021-312 7019; www.fire.ro; Str Gabroveni 12; ☺10am-5am; ⊛) A crowded, smoky, student-oriented bar and rock club that's much less flash and more relaxed than some of the other venues around the Old Town.

BEYOND THE OLD TOWN

TOP CHOICE Grădina Verona   CAFE
(Map p34; ☎031-425 1480; Str Pictor Verona 13-15; ☺9am-1am; ⊛) A garden oasis hidden behind the Cărturești bookshop, serving standard-issue but excellent espresso drinks and some of the wackiest iced-tea infusions ever concocted in Romania, such as peony flower, mango and lime (it's not bad). One drawback that we try to ignore on our visits: the service here is arguably the slowest and most inept in all of Bucharest.

Cafeneaua Actorilor   PUB
(Map p34; ☎0721-900 842; www.cafeneauaactorilor.ro; B-dul Nicolae Bălcescu 2; ☺9am-3am; ⊛) Located on the ground floor of the National Theatre (the entrance is just behind the Inter-Continental Hotel), this is an oasis of good drink and good pizza in the middle of the centre. Drink (and breathe) on the open-air terrace in summer; in winter, the action shifts to the labyrinthine (and admittedly claustrophobic) rooms inside.

Grand Cafe Galleron   CAFE
(Map p34; ☎021-313 4565; www.grandcafegalleron.ro; Str Nicolae Golescu 18a; sandwiches 20 lei; ☺9am-midnight; ⊛) A block east of Piața Revoluției, this stylish cafe has indoor nooks and outdoor seats for ice cream, sandwiches, drinks and all-day breakfast. A perfect spot for a quiet chat or to hang out over your laptop with a coffee and wi-fi.

☆ Entertainment

Bucharest has a lively night scene of concerts, theatre, and rock and jazz. Check the weekly guide Șapte Seri (p50) for entertainment listings. Another good source for what's on is the website www.iconcert.ro. To buy tickets online, visit the websites of the leading ticketing agencies: www.myticket.ro and www.eventim.ro

In addition to regular programs at popular night spots, Bucharest hosts a number of big-name concerts throughout the year, including performers such as Lady Gaga and the Red Hot Chilli Peppers in 2012 and Depeche Mode in 2013. Many mega-events take place at Piața Constituției in front of the Palace of Parliament (p31) or the 55,000-seat National Arena (Arena Națională; www.nab.ro; B-dul Basarabia 37-39), which opened in 2011.

Cinemas

Most films are shown in their original language. Check www.cinemagia.ro for film information.

Cinemateca Eforie   CINEMA
(Map p34; ☎021-313 0483; Str Eforie 2; tickets 12 lei) Plays an eclectic and often amusing mix of art-house, kitsch and Romanian films.

Cinema Pro   CINEMA
(Map p34; ☎031-824 1360; www.cinemapro.ro; Str Ion Ghica 3; tickets 10-16 lei) Shows first-run features from Romania and big films from around the world.

Hollywood Multiplex   CINEMA
(☎021-327 7020; www.hmultiplex.ro; Calea Vitan 55-59, București Mall; tickets 17-34 lei) Comfortable multiplex cinema with about a dozen screens, located in the Bucharest Mall.

Classical Music

Bucharest National Opera House   OPERA
(Opera Națională București; ☎021-314 6980, box office 021-313 1857; www.operanb.ro; B-dul Mihail

Kogălniceanu 70-72; tickets 6-65 lei; ☻box office 9am-1pm & 3-7pm) The city's premier venue for classical opera and ballet. Buy tickets online or at the venue box office.

Romanian Athenaeum　　CLASSICAL MUSIC
(Ateneul Roman; Map p34; ☑021-315 6875; www.fge.org.ro; Str Franklin 1-3; tickets 15-65 lei; ☻box office noon-7pm Tue-Fri, 4-7pm Sat, 10-11am Sun) The historic Athenaeum is home to the respected George Enescu Philharmonic and offers a wide array of classical music concerts from September to May as well as a number of one-off musical shows and spectacles throughout the year. Buy tickets at the venue box office.

Nightclubs & Live Music
Expect to pay a cover at the door of anywhere from 5 to 25 lei, which may or may not include a drink.

Control　　CLUB
(Map p34; ☑0733-927 861; www.control-club.ro; Str Constantin Mille 4; ☻6pm-4am; 🛜) This favourite among club-goers who like alternative, indie and garage sounds decamped to this new space not far from Calea Victoriei in 2012. Regulars were relieved to find the new digs to be nicer and airier and the old vibe was still intact. Hosts both live acts and DJs, depending on the night.

Green Hours 22 Jazz Club　　JAZZ
(Map p34; ☑0788-452 485; www.greenhours.ro; Calea Victoriei 120; ☻24hr) This old-school basement jazz club runs a lively program of jazz nights through the week and hosts an international jazz fest in June. Check the website for the schedule during your trip and try to book in advance if you see something you like.

La Muse　　CLUB
(Map p34; ☑0734-000 236; www.lamuse.ro; Str Lipscani 53; ☻9am-3am Sun-Wed, to 6am Thu-Sat) Just about anything goes at this popular Old Town dance club. Try to arrive early, around 11pm, since it can get crowded later. La Muse draws everyone from university students to young professionals in their 20s and 30s. Everyone looks great.

Club A　　CLUB
(Map p34; ☑021-316 1667; www.cluba.ro; Str Blănari 14; ☻9pm-5am Thu-Sun) Run by students, this club is a classic and beloved by all who go there. Indie pop-rock tunes play until very late Friday and Saturday nights.

Spectator Sports
Bucharest is home to several local football (soccer) clubs, but the two main ones are rivals Steaua București and Dinamo București. Both play in the country's top division, *Liga I*. The football season runs from the end of July through the following May, and catching a match during your visit is easy. With the exception of grudge matches between the two, games rarely sell out. Steaua plays its matches at **Steaua Arena** (☑021-410 2082, tickets 0752-121 159; www.steauafc.com; Str Ghencea 34-35; tickets 5-50 lei; ☻ticket office 10am-6pm Fri, 10am-5pm Sat), while Dinamo normally plays at **Dinamo Stadium** (Map p38; www.fcdinamo.ro; Șos Ștefan cel Mare 7-9), but also plays an increasing number of matches at the National Arena. Buy tickets for both teams in advance at their respective stadium box offices or at the ticket window before matches. Most international matches, including those involving the Romanian national team, are played at the National Arena.

Theatre
Bucharest's theatres offer a lively mix of comedy, farce, satire and straight contemporary plays in a variety of languages, though normally in Romanian. Tickets usually cost no more than 30 lei. Theatres close in July and August.

National Theatre of Bucharest　　THEATRE
(Teatrul Național București; Map p34; ☑box office 021-314 7171, theatre 021-313 9175; www.tnb.ro; B-dul Nicolae Bălcescu 2; ☻box office 10am-4pm

---

GAY & LESBIAN BUCHAREST

Bucharest has a large and active gay and lesbian population, though venues are not well publicised and change regularly from year to year. The best advice is to check the website of **Accept Romania** (☑021-252 5620; www.accept-romania.ro), a local rights group that promotes tolerance for gays and lesbians. The website has a good page of links to various clubs and happenings. The high point of the calendar is the annual six-day **Gay-Fest** (www.gay-fest.ro), held normally over the summer, with events, films and club nights around the city.

Mon, to 7pm Tue-Sun) The National Theatre is the country's most prestigious dramatic stage. The building is a 1970s-era big box, but the facilities inside are excellent. Most dramatic works are performed in Romanian. Check the website for the program during your visit. Buy tickets at the box office.

Jewish State Theatre
THEATRE

(Teatrul Evreiesc de Stat; Map p34; ✆theatre 021-323 4530, ticket reservation 0721-332 436; www .teatrul-evreiesc.ro; Str Iuliu Barasch 15; tickets 13-18 lei; ⊙box office 10am-noon Mon-Thu) Plays in Romanian and Yiddish.

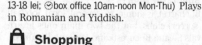

Shopping

What remains of Bucharest's fashion and boutique quarter (the global economic slump hit these places especially hard) is centred on **Calea Victoriei** (Map p34; Calea Victoriei), with off-shoots along Str Ion Câmpineanu and Str General Berthelot. The Old Town is populated mostly by clubs and bars, but here and there you can still find some interesting shops.

Anthony Frost
TOP CHOICE   BOOKS

(Map p34; ✆021-311 5136; www.anthonyfrost. ro; Calea Victoriei 45; ⊙10am-8pm Mon-Fri, to 7pm Sat, to 2pm Sun) Serious readers will want to make time for arguably the best English-language bookshop in Eastern Europe. Located in a small passage next to the Creţulescu Church, this shop has a carefully chosen selection of highbrow contemporary fiction and nonfiction, as well as books on art and architecture and a handful of Romanian authors in translation.

Museum of the Romanian Peasant Gift Shop
FOLK CRAFTS

(Map p38; www.muzeultaranuluiroman.ro; Şos Kiseleff 3; ⊙10am-6pm Tue-Sun) For beautifully made woven rugs, table runners, national Romanian costumes, ceramics and other local crafts, don't miss the excellent folk-art shop at the Museum of the Romanian Peasant; access to the shop is from the back of the museum.

Madison
PERFUMES & COSMETICS

(off Map p38; ✆021-231 6131; www.madisonper fumery.com; Calea Dorobanţilor 152; ⊙10am-9pm Mon-Fri, to 7pm Sat) Madison is an upscale perfume shop selling high-end personal-care products and made-on-request scents.

Str Hanul cu Tei
GIFTS

(Map p34; Str Hanul cu Tei, enter from Str Blănari 5 or Str Lipscani 63) The little courtyard Str Hanul cu Tei is a hidden passageway in the Old Town with a few art galleries and art supply and antique shops.

Filatelia
STAMPS & COINS

(Map p34; Str Covaci 2; ⊙10am-7pm Mon-Fri, to 4pm Sat) Filatelia is a tiny shop in the Old Town with an excellent selection of old Romanian stamps, coins and medals.

City Mall

(✆021-319 3522; www.city-mall.ro; Şos Olteniţei 2; ⊙10am-10pm Mon-Thu, to midnight Fri & Sat) Has children's activities and a movie theatre.

Bucureşti Mall

(✆021-327 6100; www.bucurestimall.com.ro; Calea Vitan 55-59; ⊙10am-10pm) This mall has a movie theatre.

Cărtureşti

(Map p34; ✆031-425 1480; www.carturesti.ro; Str Pictor Verona 13-15, cnr B-dul Nicolae Bălcescu; ⊙9am-9pm Mon-Sat, from 11am Sun) This bookshop, music store, tearoom and funky backyard garden is a must-visit. Amazing collection of design, art and architecture books, as well as carefully selected CDs and DVDs, including many classic Romanian films with English subtitles. Also sells Lonely Planet guidebooks.

Information

Emergency

Ambulance, Fire & Police (✆112) Some operators know a smattering of English.

Internet Access

Best Cafe (B-dul Mihail Kogălniceanu 19; per hr 5 lei; ⊙24hr; 🖥)

Media

International newspapers can usually be found at newsagents in major hotels.

Bucharest In Your Pocket (www.inyourpocket .com; 15 lei) Bi-monthly, comprehensive guide to Bucharest (there's a cover price, though you can find it free at big hotels), with opinionated and often very funny entertainment, hotel and restaurant listings.

Nine O'Clock (www.nineoclock.ro) English-language news daily; including some restaurant reviews and movie listings.

Şapte Seri (www.sapteseri.ro) Widespread, complimentary entertainment listing in Romanian only; the useful website is also in English. Find it at bars and clubs around town.

Medical Services

You'll find pharmacies all over the centre. **Sensi-Blu** (www.sensiblu.com) is a highly recommended chain with branches around town, including on **B-dul Nicolae Bălcescu** (www.sensiblu.com; B-dul Nicolae Bălcescu 7; ☺8am-10pm Mon-Fri, 9am-9pm Sat & Sun) and **Calea Victoriei** (www .sensiblu.com; Calea Victoriei 12A; ☺8am-10pm Mon-Fri, 9am-9pm Sat & Sun).

Emergency Clinic Hospital (☎021-9622, 021-599 2300; www.urgentafloreasca.ro; Calea Floreasca 8; ☺24hr) The first port of call in any serious emergency. Arguably the city's and country's best emergency hospital.

Medicover (☎021-9896, 021-310 1599; www .medicover.ro; Calea Plevnei 96; ☺8am-8.30pm Mon-Fri, to 2pm Sat) Good but expensive private clinic.

Pro-Dental Care (☎021-313 4781; www.pro dentalcare.ro; Str Hristo Botev 7; ☺10am-8pm Mon-Fri, to 4pm Sat) Offering dental care.

Money

You'll find hundreds of bank branches and ATMs in the centre. Most banks have a currency-exchange office and can provide cash advances against credit or debit cards. Always bring your passport, since you will likely have to show it. Most banks operate only on weekdays, though some may have limited Saturday morning hours.

Outside of normal banking hours, you can change money at private currency booths (*casa de schimb*). There is a row of these along B-dul Gen Gheorghe Magheru, running north of Piaţa Universităţii. We generally don't recommend using these, as the rates they offer tend to be the same as or lower than the banks', often with higher commission fees. If you do exchange money at a private booth, before you surrender your cash, tell the cashier exactly what you want to exchange and ask him or her to write down the amount you will receive in lei. You'll usually have to show a passport here as well.

For more on money matters, see p261

Post

Branch Post Office (www.posta-romana.ro; Str Gării de Nord 6-8; ☺7.30am-8pm Mon-Fri)
Central Post Office (☎021-315 9030; www .posta-romana.ro; Str Matei Millo 10; ☺7.30am-8pm Mon-Fri)

Tourist Information
Bucharest Tourist Information

Center (☎021-305 5500 ext 1003; http://en.seebucharest.ro; Piaţa Universităţii, in the underpass; ☺10am-6pm Mon-Fri, to 2pm Sat & Sun) This small, poorly stocked tourist office is the best the city can offer visitors. While there's not much information on hand, the English-speaking staff can field basic questions, make suggestions and help locate things on a map. Regular hours are posted on the door, though in practice the office is not always open when it should be.

Info Tourist Point (☎0371-155 063; www .infotourist.ro; Gara de Nord; ☺10am-6pm Mon-Fri) This small booth situated in the main terminal at the point where the rail tracks meet the station can help with basic information and hotel booking, though it falls far short of a true tourist information office. Though the booth claims to operate regular hours, in our experience it's often closed.

ℹ️ Getting There & Away
Air

All international and domestic flights use Henri Coandă International Airport (p264), often referred to in conversation by its previous name 'Otopeni'. Henri Coandă is 17km north of Bucharest on the road to Braşov. Arrivals and departures use separate terminals (arrivals is to the north). The airport is a modern facility, with restaurants, newsagents, currency exchange offices and ATMs. There are 24-hour information desks at both terminals.

The airport is the hub for the national carrier **Tarom** (☎call centre 021-204 6464, office 021-316 0220; www.tarom.ro; Spl Independenţei 17, City Centre; ☺8.30am-7.30pm Mon-Fri, 9am-1.30pm Sat). Tarom has a comprehensive network of internal flights to major Romanian cities as well to capitals and big cities around Europe and the Middle East. At the time of writing, there were no direct flights from Bucharest to North America or Southeast Asia. For a fuller discussion of flight options, including a list of major and budget carriers that service Bucharest, see p264.

Bus

DOMESTIC DESTINATIONS

It's possible to get just about anywhere in the country by bus from Bucharest, but figuring out where your bus or maxitaxi departs from can be tricky. Bucharest has several bus stations and they don't seem to follow any discernible logic. Even Bucharest residents have a hard time making sense of it.

The best bet is to consult the websites www .autogari.ro and www.cdy.ro. Both keep up-to-date timetables and are fairly easy to manage, though www.cdy.ro is only in Romanian. Be sure to follow up with a phone call just to make sure a particular bus is running on a particular day. Another option is to ask your hotel to help with arrangements or book through a travel agency.

Chief bus 'stations' – some are lots, or spaces by a curb – include the following:
Autogara Diego (☎021-311 1283; http://auto garadiego.ro; Spl Independenţiei 2K) Near the

intersection with Calea Victoriei. Destinations can include Iaşi, Piatra Neamţ and Suceava as well as several international destinations in Western Europe.

Autogara Filaret (☎021-335 3290, information 021-336 0692; www.acfilaret.ro; Piaţa Gării Filaret 1) Three kilometres south of Piaţa Universitaţii; take bus 7 and 232 from Piaţa Unirii. Regular services to Calafat, Giurgiu, Baia Mare, Iaşi and Suceava.

Autogara Militari (☎021-434 1084; B-dul Iuliu Maniu 141) Eight kilometres west of the centre; metro station Păcii. Destinations include Curtea de Argeş, Târgu Jiu and Timişoara.

CDI (☎0722-418 886, reservations 0723-187 789; www.cdy.ro; Str Ritmului 35) Located about 3km east of Piaţa Romana, and four blocks north of metro station Piaţa Iancului. Regular services to Braşov, Tulcea, Piteşti and Craiova, among other destinations.

INTERNATIONAL DESTINATIONS

Bucharest is the hub for long-haul coach services to Western Europe as well as parts of southeastern Europe and Turkey. Bus travel is comparable in price to train travel, but can be faster and require fewer connections. See p265 for a fuller discussion of destinations as well as companies offering services to and from Bucharest.

Car & Motorcycle

Driving in Bucharest is sheer lunacy and you won't want to do it for more than a few minutes before you stow the car and use the metro. If you're travelling around the country by car and just want to visit Bucharest for the day, it's more sensible to park at a metro station on the outskirts and take the metro into the city.

In theory, hourly parking rates apply in the centre, particularly off Piaţa Victoriei and Piaţa Universitaţii – look for the wardens in yellow-and-blue uniforms – or there's paid metered parking. In many places, though, you can just pull onto the sidewalk like everyone else. Petrol costs around 6 lei per litre.

Bucharest offers some of the country's cheapest car-hire rates. Major rental agencies can be found at the Henri Coandă International Airport arrivals hall. Most large companies also have an in-town branch.

The cheapest rates available are from **Autonom** (☎airport branch 021-232 4325, call centre 0721-442 226; www.autonom.com; Henri Coandă International Airport), offering a Dacia Logan for around 140 lei per day (including unlimited mileage and insurance, minimum two days); rates drop if you rent for more than a week. Rates for the major international car-hire companies tend to be higher, starting at about 220 lei per day, depending on the make and length of the rental.

Avis (☎021-204-1957; www.avis.ro; Henri Coandă International Airport; ☺8am-8pm)

Budget (☎021-204 1667; www.budgetro.ro; Henri Coandă International Airport; ☺8am-8pm)

Europcar (☎reservations 021-310 1797; www.europcar.ro; Henri Coandă International Airport; ☺8am-8pm)

Hertz (☎021-204 1278; www.hertz.com.ro; Henri Coandă International Airport; ☺8am-10pm)

Train

Gara de Nord (☎021-319 9539, reservations 021-9521/22; www.cfr.ro; Piaţa Gara de Nord 1) is the central station for most national and all international trains. The station is accessible by metro from the centre of the city.

Buy tickets at station ticket windows or in advance at **Agenţia de Voiaj CFR** (☎021-313 2642; www.cfr.ro; Str Domnita Anastasia 10-14; ☺7.30am-7.30pm Mon-Fri, 8am-noon Sat). A seat reservation is compulsory if you are travelling with an InterRail or Eurail pass. For international tickets, the private travel agency **Wasteels** (☎021-317 0370; www.wasteels.ro; Gara de Nord; ☺8am-7pm Mon-Fri, to 2pm Sat), located inside the train station, can help sort out complicated international connections.

Check the latest train schedules on either www.cfr.ro or the reliable German site www.bahn.de (when searching timetables, use German spellings for cities, ie 'Bukarest Nord' for Bucharest Gara de Nord).

Below are sample fares and destination times from Bucharest to major Romanian cities on faster IC (Inter-City) trains.

DESTINATION	FARE (LEI)	DURATION (HR)	DAILY IC DEPARTURES
Braşov	70	2½	frequent
Cluj-Napoca	90	7½	4
Constanţa	60	2-4	3
Craiova	40	2½	5
Iaşi	80	6	3
Sibiu	70	5	3
Sighişoara	80	4½	3
Suceava	80	8	3
Timişoara	100	8	2

Daily international services include two trains to Budapest's Keleti station (13 to 15 hours), one to Sofia (nine to 11 hours) and one to Belgrade (12 hours), Chişinău (13 hours) and Kiev (26 hours).

For more information on train transport, see p266.

Left Luggage (Gara de Nord; large/small bags 7/4 lei; ☺24hr) On the main level of the Gara de Nord in the long hallway near the information stand. It's on the right side as you're walking away from the tracks.

❶ Getting Around

To/From the Airport

BUS

To get to Henri Coandă International Airport from the centre, take bus 783, which leaves every 15 minutes between 5.37am and 11.23pm (every half-hour at weekends) from Piaţas Unirii and Piaţas Victorei and points in between. The Piaţa Unirii stop is on the south side.

Buy a ticket, valid for one round trip or two people one way, for 7 lei at any RATB bus-ticket booth near a bus stop. Once inside the bus remember to feed the ticket into the stamping machine. Henri Coandă International Airport is 45 to 60 minutes from the centre, depending on traffic. The bus stops outside the departures hall then continues to arrivals.

To get to the centre from Henri Coandă, catch bus 783 from the downstairs ramp outside the arrivals hall; you'll need to buy a ticket from the stand at the north end of the waiting platform (to the right as you exit).

TAXI

Taking a reputable taxi from the centre to Henri Coandă International Airport should cost no more than 70 lei. The company Fly Taxi monopolises airport transfers to the centre, though at 3.30 lei per kilometre, they're the most expensive. To find a cheaper cab, exit the airport at the arrivals area (push your way through the legions of touts), cross the street and then enter the parking lot. This is where the cheaper cabs line up. Look for prices on the door (about 1.40 to 1.80 lei per kilometre) or agree on a fixed price.

TRAIN

There's a regular shuttle train service (8 lei, 35 minutes) from Gara de Nord to Henri Coandă International Airport (Otopeni). The trains leave hourly at 10 minutes past the hour, starting at 8.10am and continuing until 7.10pm.

Public Transport

Bucharest's public transport system of metros, buses, trams and trolleybuses is operated by the transport authority **RATB** (Regia Autonomă de Transport Bucureşti; ☑info 021-9391; www .ratb.ro). The system runs daily from about 5am to approximately 11.30pm.

For buses, trams and trolleybuses, buy tickets at any RATB street kiosk, marked 'casa de bilete', located at major stops and public squares. Tickets for standard buses cost 1.30 lei per trip and are sold in two-ticket increments for 2.60 lei. Tickets for a small number of express buses, such as bus 783, which goes to the airport, cost

7 lei (good for two journeys). Punch your ticket on board or risk a 50 lei on-the-spot fine.

Metro stations are identified by a large letter 'M'. To use the metro, buy a magnetic-strip ticket available at ticketing machines inside station entrances (have small bills handy). Tickets valid for two journeys cost 4 lei. A 10-trip ticket costs 15 lei. The metro is a speedy way of moving up and down the central north–south corridor from Piaţa Victoriei to Piaţa Unirii, passing through the convenient stations of Piaţa Romană and Universitate. The metro is also useful for travelling from the Gara de Nord to the centre of town and back.

Taxi

Rogue drivers are still a problem, so watch for rip-offs. Always opt for a cab with a meter, and avoid the guys who line up outside the Gara de Nord as well as at Piaţa Unirii, the Inter-Continental Hotel and just outside the main arrivals hall at Henri Coandă International Airport.

Drivers are required to post their rates on both the passenger- and driver-side doors. The rate in an honest cab ranges from 1.40 lei to 1.80 lei per kilometre. Any fare significantly higher is a sign the taxi is a rip-off and should be avoided.

It's best to call one in advance – or have a restaurant or hotel call one for you. Reputable companies include **Cobalcescu** (☑021-9451; www.autocobalcescu.ro), **CrisTaxi** (☑021-9461; www.cristaxi.ro) and **Meridian** (☑021-9444; www.meridiantaxi.ro).

AROUND BUCHAREST

Snagov

POP 7040

Serpentine Snagov Lake, 40km north of Bucharest and running north–south, serves as the main weekend retreat for residents of the capital looking for a place to relax. The lake has a lovely rural setting, and there are plenty of opportunities for swimming, boating, fishing and sunbathing. Summer weekends can get crowded as nature-seeking hordes from Bucharest descend. Weekdays are more peaceful. In the past few years, Snagov has become a favourite haunt of Bucharest's newly moneyed classes, who buy plots of land and plunk down their very own McMansions. Indeed, the shoreline is ringed with new villas.

Snagov may have an even bigger claim to fame: a small island at the northern end of the lake holds a fine monastery that also happens to be the reputed final resting place

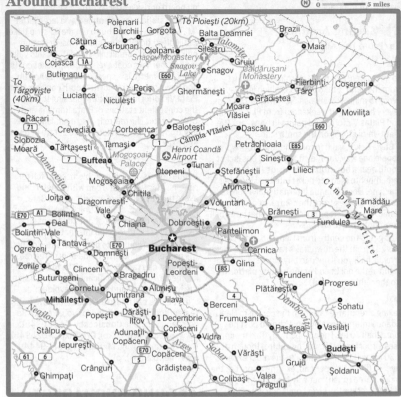

of none other than Vlad Ţepeş (aka 'Vlad the Impaler'), the legendarily brutal Wallachian prince who served as the inspiration for Bram Stoker's *Dracula*.

⊙ Sights

Snagov Monastery   MONASTERY
(Mănăstirea Snagov; ☎021-323 9905; www.snagov.ro; Snagov Island; adult/child 15/10 lei; ⊙9am-6pm) A tiny island at the northern end of Snagov Lake is home to Snagov Monastery (and Vlad Ţepeş), a small stone church dating from 15th century with a lovely interior.

There's been a church here since at least the 11th century, when Mircea cel Bătrân first built a wooden structure. The monastery was added in the late 14th century during the reign of King Dan I (r 1383–86), and in 1453 the wooden church was replaced by a stone edifice that later sank into the lake. The present church came after that.

Vlad Ţepeş' alleged grave is located inside the church, at the centre towards the back. The interior is small and the grave marker and portrait of Vlad are the main highlights. As with many aspects of the 'Dracula' story, there is some debate as to whether the body buried here actually belongs to Ţepeş. The bloodthirsty prince died in 1476 battling the Turks near Bucharest. His head was famously lopped off and carried back to Istanbul, where it was paraded on a stick. What happened to the rest of the body was never made clear.

Whether or not he's actually buried here, Vlad Ţepeş apparently had strong connections to Snagov. In 1456 he built fortifications around the monastery. He also built a bridge from the lake to the mainland, a bell tower, a new church, an escape tunnel and a prison and torture chamber. The remains of the prison (behind the present-day church) can still be seen.

Snagov Island is accessible by boat from Snagov village or various resorts along the shore. You can hire a rowboat from Complex Astoria (about 20 lei per hour) and row here yourself, or make a deal with one of the motorboat owners along the shore. Expect to pay around 100 lei for a ride out and back for up to four persons, allowing about 30 minutes on the island.

Snagov Palace   HISTORIC BUILDING
(☑021-320 8954; www.palatulsnagov.ro; Snagov; ⊙closed to the public) On Snagov Lake's western shore you'll see an impressive-looking villa, Snagov Palace. It was built by Prince Nicolae, brother of King Carol II, in neo-Renaissance style in the 1930s. During the Ceauşescu era, the palace was used for meetings of high-level government officials. Today, the building serves as a retreat for state guests.

🛏 Sleeping & Eating

Most people visit Snagov on a day trip, though there are a couple of pleasant overnight options.

Dolce Vita   HOTEL $$
(☑0723-580 780; www.dolcevitasnagov.ro; Snagov Parc; r 200 lei) This hotel and restaurant complex is located directly across the lake from Snagov village on the western shore, at the edge of a protected nature reserve. There are simple rooms here for rent and pretty lakeside-terrace dining (mains 20 to 30 lei). To get here, either drive or take a maxitaxi to Snagov village and phone for someone to fetch you in a motorboat.

Complex Astoria   BUNGALOWS $$
(☑0374-203 443, 0744-372 640; Sos Snagovului; r 160-190 lei; P ✱ ⓪) This 9-hectare wooded resort complex east of Snagov, on the lake's northern end, has three- and four-star villas as well as space to pitch a tent. On weekends, crowds from Bucharest descend and it can get packed; on weekdays it's quieter. There's a pool (20 lei), tennis courts and boats to hire as well places to eat.

To get to here by car drive through Snagov village for a further 3km northeast

to the complex (signposted 'Baza Turistică Snagov').

Hanul Vlasiei   ROMANIAN $$
(☑0749-114 778; www.hanulvlasieisnagov.ro; Str Hanul Vlasiei 1; mains 25-40 lei; ⊙11am-11pm) On the western side of the lake across from Snagov village, this upscale terrace restaurant is one of the nicest places to eat in the Snagov area. There's an indoor restaurant, too, that borders on the stuffy and is popular with wedding parties. The menu centres on grilled meets and traditional Romanian cooking.

El Capitan   BAR
(☑0756-385 638; Snagov Parc; ⊙2-9pm Mon-Thu, 11am-midnight Fri-Sun) Upscale terrace coffee and cocktail bar, just south of Dolce Vita on the western side of the lake across from Snagov village, attracts a glamorous boating crowd and their entourage. Relax on lakeside sofas and gaze out over lovely Snagov Lake.

ℹ Getting There & Away

Though it's only 40km north of Bucharest, it's not that easy to get to Snagov without your own wheels. The best bet is to catch a maxitaxi (6 lei) from stands at Piaţa Presei Libera in the north of Bucharest. The maxitaxi will drop you at the centre of Snagov village. The Complex Astoria, from where you can get a boat ride to Snagov Monastery, is a further 3km along the road to the northeast. To cross the lake from Snagov village, try to negotiate a private motorboat (around 10 lei per crossing) or call Dolce Vita, and they will send a boatman across the lake to get you (free ferry for customers).

To reach Snagov by car from Bucharest, follow the signs out of the city to the airport and then keep heading north along the E60 until you see the turn-off for Snagov, which lies 11km from the main road. To reach the western side of the lake, drive past the Snagov exit and turn off at Ciolpani, following the road marked 101N for a few kilometres as it meanders through the forest, getting bumpier and bumpier until it dumps you out around the Dolce Vita hotel complex. Figure on about 60 to 90 minutes from central Bucharest, depending on traffic.

Wallachia

Includes »

Best Places to Eat

» Epoca (p68)

» Belvedere (p61)

» Boccaccio (p59)

» Curtea Veche (p66)

» Garden Pub (p63)

Best Places to Stay

» Hotel Argeş (p62)

» Hotel Victoria (p62)

» Pensiunea Ruxi (p65)

» Hotel Corona (p70)

» Hotel Rexton (p67)

Why Go?

Wallachia (Ţara Românească), the region between the Carpathians and the Danube River, admittedly lacks the must-sees of Transylvania and Moldavia. Nevertheless, it's rich in early Romanian history, particularly at the historic seats of the Wallachian princes in Curtea de Argeş and Târgovişte. This was Wallachian prince Vlad Ţepeş' old stomping ground, and north of Curtea de Argeş stands the ruins of what many consider the real 'Dracula's castle'. Lovers of modern sculpture will want to see Constantin Brâncuşi's work on open-air display in Târgu Jiu, close to the region of his birth.

The Danube flows along the southern edge of Wallachia and is best seen west of Drobeta-Turnu Severin, where it breaks through the Carpathians at the legendary Iron Gates. Drobeta-Turnu Severin was once a thriving Roman colony, and you can still see the remains of Emperor Trajan's mighty bridge (AD 103) that once traversed the Danube.

When to Go

Ploieşti

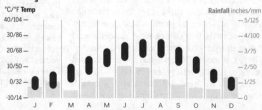

May Spring flowers cover the mountain highlands north of Curtea de Argeş.

Jun–Aug Warm summer afternoons for cruising the Danube near Iron Gates National Park.

Sep & Oct Regional cultural hubs like Craiova re-awaken after a long summer slumber.

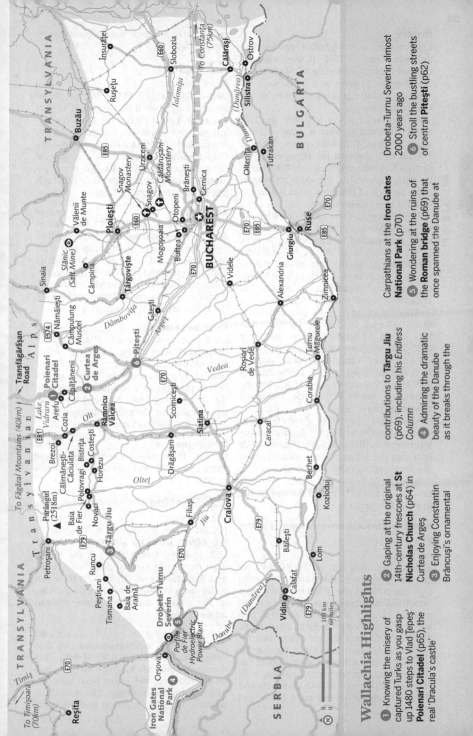

Wallachia Highlights

1 Knowing the misery of captured Turks as you gasp up 1480 steps to Vlad Ţepeş' **Poienari Citadel** (p65), the real 'Dracula's castle'

2 Gaping at the original 14th-century frescoes at **St Nicholas Church** (p64) in Curtea de Argeş

3 Enjoying Constantin Brâncuşi's ornamental contributions to **Târgu Jiu** (p69), including his *Endless Column*

4 Admiring the dramatic beauty of the Danube as it breaks through the Carpathians at the **Iron Gates National Park** (p70)

5 Wondering at the ruins of the **Roman bridge** (p69) that once spanned the Danube at Drobeta-Turnu Severin almost 2000 years ago

6 Stroll the bustling streets of central **Piteşti** (p62)

History

The principality of Wallachia was founded by Radu Negru in 1290. It was originally conceived as a vassal state of the Hungarian kingdom to serve as a buffer between Hungary and the growing influence of the Ottoman Turks.

As Hungarian power waned in the 13th and 14th centuries after a wave of Mongol invasions, Wallachian prince Basarab I (r 1310–52) defeated the Hungarian king Charles I in 1330 and declared Wallachia to be independent. The region is considered to be the first of the three main Romanian lands to gain independence.

The 14th century was a kind of golden age for the Wallachian princes, who established their first capital at Câmpulung Muscel, before moving on to Curtea de Argeş and Târgovişte. To this day, you can see the remains of the Princely Courts in both Curtea de Argeş and Târgovişte. Eventually, the Wallachian capital moved to Bucharest.

After the fall of Bulgaria to the Turks in 1396, Wallachia faced a new threat, and in 1415 Mircea cel Bătrân (Mircea the Old; r 1386–1418) was forced to acknowledge Turkish suzerainty. Other Wallachian princes, such as Vlad Ţepeş (r 1448, 1456–62, 1476) and Mihai Viteazul (r 1593–1601), became national heroes by defying the Turks and refusing to pay tribute.

Vlad Ţepeş' legendary disposition and gruesome tactics against the Turks served as inspiration for Bram Stoker's *Dracula*, four centuries on, although the author located the 'Prince of Darkness' in Transylvania.

In 1859 Wallachia was united with the province of Moldavia, paving the way for the modern Romanian state.

Ploieşti

POP 197,542

Ploieşti, the main city in the Prahova region, is the centre of Romania's oil production and ranks as one of the country's most important industrial cities. It's had an oil-refining industry since 1857 and this is a source of enormous pride for its inhabitants. That said, it's not a leading destination for visitors, and your main reason for coming is likely to be practical – the city sits at the centre of the country's rail network, with excellent connections to both Bucharest and Braşov. There are several good hotels and restaurants and some decent museums to pass the time.

Sights

Clock Museum
MUSEUM

(Muzeul Ceasului; ☑0244-542 861; Str Nicolae Simachei 1; admission 8 lei; ☺9am-5pm Tue-Sun) The city's unique Clock Museum has a collection of historic timepieces owned by several famous Romanians, including King Carol I, and an 18th-century rococo Austrian clock that belonged to Wallachian prince Alexandru Ioan Cuza. There's also a small collection of vintage gramophones.

Art Museum
MUSEUM

(Muzeul de Artă; ☑0244-522 264; www.artmuseum.ro; B-dul Independenţei 1; admission 8 lei; ☺9am-5pm Tue-Sun) The city's impressive art museum emerged from a renovation in 2012 looking fresher and with better lighting. The collection, housed in a grand Empire-style mansion, is strong on Romanian greats from the 19th and early 20th centuries.

Museum of Oil
MUSEUM

(Muzeul Naţional al Petrolului; ☑0244-597 585; Str Dr Bagdasar 8; admission 4 lei; ☺9am-5pm Tue-Sun) This modest museum highlights the important role of oil in the economic development of both the city and the country, especially in the 19th century when Romania was a petroleum pioneer. The technical nature of the displays will likely not appeal to all!

Synagogue
JEWISH

(☺closed to the public) Ploieşti's synagogue dates from 1901 and was lavishly restored in 2007.

🛏 Sleeping

Hotel Central
HOTEL $$

(☑0244-526 641; www.thr.ro; B-dul Republicii 1; s 220-360 lei, d 320-420 lei; ☀❄@☎) This beautifully restored landmark hotel sits in the dead centre of town. It offers both three- and four-star rooms, though there is not really much of a difference in quality. Some of the cheaper three-stars come without air-conditioning.

Hotel Prahova Plaza
HOTEL $$$

(☑0244-526 850; www.hotelprahova.ro; Str C-tin Dobrogeanu Gherea 11; r 504 lei; ☀❄☎) This communist-era hulk has been given a thorough makeover, and prices have been adjusted upward accordingly. The squawking parrot in the lobby is cute at first but starts

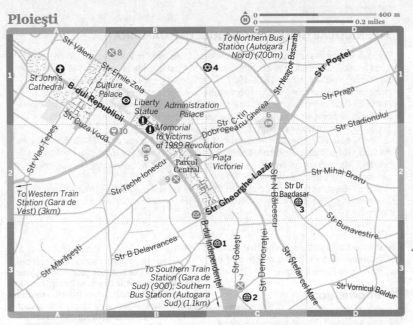

Ploieşti

◎ Sights
1	Art Museum	C3
2	Clock Museum	C3
3	Museum of Oil	C2
4	Synagogue	C1

🛏 Sleeping
5	Hotel Central	B2
6	Hotel Prahova Plaza	C1

🍴 Eating
7	Boccaccio	C3
8	Central Market	B1
9	Sport Pub Doroftei	B2

🍷 Drinking
10	Dublin Pub	B2

to get old very fast. The location couldn't be better, just a couple of minutes' walk from the central square.

Hotel Nord   HOTEL **$$**
(☎0244-516 774; www.nordhotelploiesti.com; Sos Vestului 31; s 130-200 lei; d 160-240 lei; P❄✿✳🛜) Nothing fancy here at this boxy business hotel 2km northwest of the centre, but the rooms are clean and good value. The Nord offers both two- and three-star rooms. There's

not much difference, except the latter have air-conditioning. Trolleybus 44 runs from the southern rail and bus stations to within 100m of the hotel.

✖ Eating & Drinking

Stock up on fruit, bread and cheese for the train journey at the monster-sized **central market** (B-dul Unirii; ⊘8am-6pm).

Boccaccio   ROMANIAN **$$$**
(☎0244-517 549; www.ristorante-boccaccio.ro; Str Goleşti 25; mains 25-50 lei; ⊘11am-11pm; 🛜) This is arguably the best dining experience in Ploieşti, with a large menu (English available) that's rich in well-prepared Romanian cuisine, plus a long list of grilled meats and fish. There's a classy dining room and an elegant summer terrace.

Sport Pub Doroftei   PUB **$$**
(☎0344-146 334; www.doroftei-pub.ro; Piaţa Victoriei 4; mains 20-30 lei; ⊘11am-1am; 🛜) Don't be deceived by the name, this 'sports' pub has great food and a fun 2nd-floor terrace that overlooks Piaţa Victoriei. After dinner, it does double duty as, well, a sports pub.

Dublin Pub   PUB
(☎0726-352 089; www.dublin-pub.ro; B-dul Republicii 19; ⊘11am-1am; 🛜) Popular spot to grab

WALLACHIA PLOIEŞTI

THE NICOLAE GRIGORESCU MUSEUM, CÂMPINA

If you've visited the art museums in Bucharest, Constanţa or Ploieşti, you've likely developed a taste for the talented and underrated (at least outside of Romania) 19th-century painter Nicolae Grigorescu (1838–1907). Best known locally for his starkly beautiful landscapes, his work ranges from portraiture to reportage (he was a war painter in the Romanian War of Independence). Grigorescu studied in Paris with Pierre Auguste Renoir and his later works were highly innovative, anticipating more modern styles, such as Impressionism, that were well in vogue by the end of his life.

The **Nicolae Grigorescu Museum** (Muzeul Nicolae Grigorescu; ☏0244-335 598; B-dul Carol I 166, Câmpina; adult/child 8/2 lei; ☺9am-5pm Tue-Sun) is a modest tribute to the painter's life, with collections on two floors in a traditional wooden village house where he lived during the last seven years of his life.

From Ploieşti's southern bus station there are several daily buses to Câmpina, 32km north of Ploieşti. There are also daily trains from Ploieşti's western station to Câmpina.

a beer or occasionally see some live music. The location is smack in the centre and an easy walk from Hotel Central.

ℹ Information

There's no tourist information office in Ploieşti. There are banks and ATMs all around the centre, with most on the main drag of B-dul Republicii and Piaţa Victoriei.

Agenţia de Voiaj CFR (☏0244-542 080; www.cfr.ro; B-dul Republicii 19; ☺8am-8pm Mon-Fri, 9am-1.30pm Sat) Sells domestic and international train tickets and seat reservations as well as domestic air tickets, and serves as an agent for some long-haul coach journeys.

Banca Transilvania (www.bancatransilvania.ro; B-dul Republicii 15) Convenient full-service bank and ATM, close to the centre.

Post Office (Piaţa Victoriei 10; ☺7am-1pm & 1.30-8pm Mon-Fri, 8am-1pm Sat) The central post office is located on Piaţa Victoriei, just south of Hotel Central following B-dul Republicii.

Sensi-Blu (Piaţa Victoriei; ☺8am-8pm Mon-Fri, 9am-7pm Sat, 9am-3pm Sun; ☎) Convenient pharmacy on the corner of Str Gheorghe Lazăr.

ℹ Getting There & Away

Bus

Ploieşti has several bus stations. The main station is the **southern bus station** (Autogara Sud; ☏0244-522 230; Str Depoului 9-11), which is adjacent to the southern train station. From here, you can catch buses to Bucharest (14 lei, one hour, several daily), Câmpina (6 lei, 30 minutes, eight daily) and Târgovişte (10 lei, 90 minutes, six daily). For other destinations, consult the website www.autogari.ro.

Train

The city has two main passenger train stations, so always ask which station your train departs from. Many domestic trains, including those to Bucovina and Moldavia, leave from the **southern station** (Gara de Sud; www.cfr.ro). This station also serves international destinations such as Moscow, Sofia and Chişinău. For trips to Transylvania and international destinations such as Budapest and Vienna, use the **western station** (Gara de Vest; www.cfr.ro). Bucharest trains arrive at and depart from either station, so consult the timetable.

Destinations for fast Inter-City trains include Bucharest (20 lei, 45 minutes, 15 daily), Braşov (30 lei, two hours, 10 daily) and Cluj-Napoca (100 lei, eight hours, two daily).

Târgovişte

POP 73,964

The small city of Târgovişte, 50km northwest of Bucharest, has played an outsized role in Romanian history. It served as the royal capital of Wallachia from 1418 until 1659, when the capital was moved to Bucharest. The ruins of the former royal court remain the town's leading attraction. During the 15th century, Vlad Ţepeş, of impaler fame, held princely court here. In more recent times, in 1989, the city made international headlines as the site where dictator Nicolae Ceauşescu and his wife, Elena, were executed. The choice of Târgovişte was coincidental. The Ceauşescus, fleeing arrest, were apprehended not far from here and brought to Târgovişte because the barracks were well fortified.

⊙ Sights

The town's main sights, including the Princely Court, are clustered along Calea Domnească, about 500m north of the centre and about 1.5km north of the train station. The **barracks** (contact@jandarmeriadambovita.ro; B-dul Carol I) where the Ceaușescus were executed on 25 December 1989 are closed to the public, but you can glimpse the premises from the road outside. The location is immediately to the right as you leave the train station along B-dul Carol I. It's strictly forbidden to take photographs. Visits are sometimes granted if requested in advance by email.

Closer to the centre, the city's 18th-century Orthodox **Cathedral** (Catedrala Metropolitana; ⊙8am-7pm) stands in the middle of the pretty Parcul Mitropoliei. At the park's western end is a **small chapel** (⊙closed to the public) and a statue to national hero **Mihai Viteazu**.

Princely Court   MUSEUM & RUIN
(Curtea Domnească; ☑0245-613 946; www.muzee-dambovitene.ro; Calea Domnească 181; adult/child 9/4.50 lei; ⊙9am-7pm Tue-Sun) The court was built in the 14th century for Mircea cel Bătrân (Mircea the Old) and remained a residence for Wallachia's princes, including Vlad Țepeș, until the reign of Constantin Brâncoveanu (r 1688–1714). Much of the court lies in ruin, though the 27m-high **Sunset Tower** (Turnul Chindiei) – the symbol of the city – has a museum exhibition.

Just north of the Sunset Tower is a lovely park for strolling. Each of the Wallachian princes gets his own bust here, but the biggest prize is reserved for Vlad Țepeș, who merits a big, suitably dramatic statue in the centre of the park – a great photo op.

Zoo   ZOO
(Grădina Zoologică; ☑0245-616 558; www.zootargoviste.ro; Zona Calea Domnească, Parc Chindia; adult/child 7/4 lei; ⊙9am-7pm Tue-Sun May-Sep, 10am-4pm Tue-Sun Oct-Apr; ⊞) Târgoviște's small zoo, in the park north of the Princely Court, is surprisingly comprehensive, with some large cats, a hippo, lots of chimps and a variety of other animals. The zoo shows obvious signs of wear and tear, but the animals appear adequately cared for. Kids will love how close you can come to the animals.

**Museum of Printing &
Old Romanian Books**   MUSEUM
(Muzeul Tiparului și al Cărții Românești Vechi; ☑0245-612 877; www.muzee-dambovitene.ro; Str Justiției 3-5; admission 4 lei; ⊙9am-5pm Tue-Sun)

Housed in a 17th-century palace built by Constantin Brâncoveanu for his daughter Safta, the museum is filled with original books from the beginning of Romania's printing age and manuscripts by 17th- and 18th-century Romanian writers.

Târgu Church   CHURCH
(Biserica Târgului; Str Ion Rădulescu; ⊙8am-6pm) Near the restaurants on Str Alexandru Ioan Cuza is the beautiful, partially frescoed Târgu Church. The 1654 church was painted during the 17th and 18th centuries, but destroyed during an earthquake in 1940. Extensive renovations followed in 1941 and the 1970s and were still ongoing at the time of research. The church is especially pretty when lit up at night.

🛏 Sleeping

TOP CHOICE Hotel Dâmbovița   HOTEL $$
(☑0245-213 370; www.hoteldambovita.ro; B-dul Libertății 1; s/d 130/170 lei; ℗🌼@🐾) If you're going to spend the night in Târgoviște, make it here, the nicest place in town. While the modern high-rise building doesn't look encouraging from the outside, the rooms are clean and quiet; some have balconies with views overlooking the park. Our favourite design touches are the funky yellow leather chairs in the lobby.

Pensiunea Chindia   PENSION $
(☑0345-566 900; www.cazaretargoviste.ro; Calea Domenască 200; s/d/tr 70/80/100 lei; ℗🐾🐾) Good-value pension located directly across the street from the entrance to the Princely Court.

✗ Eating & Drinking

Most of the best restaurants and bars are located in the historic centre, along Str Alexandru Ioan Cuza.

Belvedere   ROMANIAN $$$
(☑0723-493 641; Str Alexandru Ioan Cuza 22a; mains 25-40 lei; ⊙11am-midnight; 🐾) Grab an upper-level terrace table overlooking the pedestrian street and enjoy excellent Romanian and international dishes. We opted for Pui Bucovinean, a delicious chicken stew with sour cream. The wine list is the best in town, but service can be slow.

Don Quijote   ROMANIAN $$
(☑0720-209 686; Str Dr Marinoiu 9; mains 25 lei; ⊙9am-midnight; 🐾) This popular place has a small outside terrace and stone fireplace.

Bistro Alexo PIZZA $$

(☎0732-125 396; Calea Domenească 179; pizza 16-20 lei; ☺9am-11pm) The inviting garden terrace is a welcome spot for coffee or pizza. The salads are enormous; one is enough for the whole table. They also serve good espresso. It's just near the entrance to the Princely Court.

❶ Information

There is no tourist information office. The good people at Hotel Dâmboviţa (p61) stock city maps, which they are happy to hand out.

Arena Internet (B-dul Independenţiei 2-4; per hr 2.50 lei; ☺7am-10pm; 🛜)

Banca Comercială Română (BCR; B-dul Independenţiei 6; ☺9am-5pm Mon-Fri) Full service bank with a row of ATMs in the centre.

Central Post Office (Str Dr Marinoiu; ☺7.30am-8pm Mon-Fri, 8am-1pm Sat)

Farmacia Davilla (B-dul Mircea cel Bătrân; ☺7.30am-7.30pm Mon-Fri, 8am-1pm Sat & Sun) Convenient pharmacy across from the BCR building.

❶ Getting There & Away

Bus

Târgovişte has several bus stations. The main **bus station** (Autogara; www.autogari.ro; Str Gării) is located 2km south of the city centre and about 200m northwest of the train station. Buses to Bucharest (10 lei, five daily) depart from here. At the time of writing, buses to Ploieşti (10 lei, one hour, several daily) leave from a small stop on Str Gimnaziului 2, just off of Calea Domnească and about 1km south of the Princely Court. Buses to Braşov (15 lei, three hours, five daily) leave from a stop at B-dul Eroilor 38, about 1km north of the Princely Court. For other destinations, consult www.autogari.ro.

Train

Târgovişte's sleepy **train station** (Gara Târgovişte; www.cfr.ro; Piaţa Gării) is 2km south of the city centre, at the end of B-dul Regele Carol I. There are regular departures throughout the day to Bucharest Nord (10 lei, two hours, four daily), though some trains use Bucharest's smaller Basarab station. For other destinations, you're better off taking the bus.

Piteşti

POP 148,264

Piteşti is a pleasant, medium-sized city with a pretty, pedestrianised centre lined with cafes, bars and a handful of decent hotels. If you're planning an overnight stay in this neck of the

woods it's a strong candidate – not so much for the sights (they are strictly second-tier), but for the energy and lively atmosphere.

◉ Sights

The city's pride and joy is an enormous stretch of green that runs west of the centre called **Trivale Park**. North of the centre, you'll find a seemingly forgotten **memorial to the victims of communism** (Str Negru Vodă 32) that stands where the city's notorious prison was once located.

County History Museum MUSEUM

(Muzeul Judeţean de Istorie; ☎0248-212 561; www .muzeul-judetean-arges.ro; Str Armand Călinescu 44; adult/child 5/2 lei; ☺9am-5pm Wed-Sun) This sprawling museum has extensive collections on archaeology, history, natural sciences and folk art.

Art Museum MUSEUM

('Rudolf Schweitzer Cumpăna' Art Gallery; ☎0248-212 561; www.muzeul-judetean-arges.ro; B-dul Republicii 33; adult/child 5/2 lei; ☺9am-5pm Wed-Sun) This central museum showcases the best of modern and contemporary Romanian art, including works from Nicolae Grigorescu, Nicolae Tonitza and other luminaries of the late 19th and early 20th centuries.

Princely Church CHURCH

(Biserica Domnească; Str Victoriei; ☺8am-6pm) The unusual St George's Church (Biserica Sfântul Gheorghe), more commonly known as the Princely Church, was built by Prince Constantin Şerban and his wife Princess Bălasa between 1654 and 1658.

🛌 Sleeping

TOP CHOICE **Hotel Argeş** HOTEL $$

(☎0248-223 399; www.hotelarges.ro; Piaţa Muntenia 3; s/d 180/220 lei; 🅿 ❄ @ 🛜) On our shortlist for the best three-star hotel in the country. Ultra-clean rooms with high-thread-count linens, thick-weave carpets, sparkling baths and a warm reception add up to easily the best deal in the city. The location is dead centre. The only negative is a lacklustre breakfast, but there are plenty of cafes nearby.

Hotel Victoria HOTEL $$

(☎0248-220 777; www.victoriahotel.ro; Str Egalităţii 21; s 200-250 lei, d 225-280 lei; 🅿 ❄ @ 🛜 🐾) The Victoria, with both three- and four-star rooms, offers excellent value, especially the three-star rooms, which have the same quality linens, flat-screen TVs and updated baths

PITEŞTI PRISON & THE SECRET POLICE

In the years immediately following WWII, governments around the world experimented to various degrees with mind control, hoping to use (and in some cases abuse) breakthroughs in psychology and behavioural sciences for their own ends.

In Romania, this research took a particularly nefarious turn at Piteşti prison, where the former communist regime implemented a brainwashing scheme to 're-educate' political enemies. The program, which ran from 1949 to 1952, was initiated by one of the prisoners, Eugen Ţurcanu, acting on the orders of the secret police, the Securitate. The idea was to subject inmates to intolerable levels of abuse in order to break down their identities and make them more amenable to the communist system.

The program had three stages: in the first stage, prisoners were subjected to demeaning acts like scrubbing floors with rags between their teeth or having to lick toilets clean. Religious prisoners were humiliated through acts such as being baptised with buckets of urine.

Next, the prisoners were forced to betray fellow inmates who'd shown them any kindness or sympathy and then to renounce their own families. The point was to sever existing bonds of love or loyalty.

In the final stage, the prisoners were forced to prove their successful re-education by inflicting the same acts of mental and physical abuse on new prisoners. Failure to follow through meant having to spend weeks in a tiny isolation cell.

The program was eventually discredited by the communists themselves, and in 1954 Ţurcanu and 21 other prisoners were tried and sentenced to death for murdering and abusing prisoners. The Securitate at the time denied any knowledge of the program.

These days, the prison is long gone, replaced by a (now-crumbling) public housing estate. The only reminder is a memorial to the victims of communism that stands on the prison's former grounds.

as the more expensive rooms, but without the Jacuzzi and bidet. There's a beautiful spa and indoor pool, plenty of free parking and the best buffet breakfast in town.

Hotel Carmen HOTEL **$**
(☎0248-222 699; www.hotel-carmen.ro; B-dul Republicii 84; s 82-142 lei, d 94-154 lei; ❉ 🎧) This small, friendly place with contemporary decor offers two- and three-star accommodation. The two-star rooms are fine and also come with niceties like TVs and air-conditioning; the chief difference between two and three stars is size.

✖ Eating & Drinking

TOP CHOICE Garden Pub ROMANIAN **$$**
(☎0733-956 280; www.gardenpub.ro; Str Victoriei 16; mains 20-40 lei; ❤9am-1am; 🎧) This deservedly popular restaurant and pub draws everyone from visiting businessmen to students on their lunch break for excellent soups, salads and grilled meats and fish. There's a streetside terrace out front, more outdoor seating on the roof, and a handsome dark-wood interior for chilly evenings. Book in advance.

Tartine & Moi FRENCH **$$**
(☎0734-127 940; http://tartineetmoi.blogspot.ro; Str Egalităţii 29; mains 20-30 lei; ❤8am-6pm Mon-Wed, 8am-midnight Thu & Fri, 6pm-midnight Sat) This charming hole-in-the-wall off a busy street near the centre calls itself a bistro, but the feeling is more like being in someone's kitchen. Daily lunch offerings vary from traditional French to Italian, Swiss and even Indian, but it's all good. The desserts are a speciality.

Asia Flavour Company ASIAN **$$**
(Asian Food Concept; ☎0721-846 474; Str Plevnei 10; mains 20-30 lei; ❤noon-11pm; 🎧) This Asian restaurant is a pleasant surprise. Decent Thai and Vietnamese dishes are on hand, as well as passable sushi, though the *maki* sushi looks like something you might make at home. Ingredients including fresh ginger, wasabi and lemongrass hit the spot after endless renditions of grilled pork.

Guinness Pub PUB
(☎0722-375 621; www.guinnesspub.ro; Str Victoriei 30; mains 15-25 lei; ❤8.30am-midnight; 🎧) Sadly, there's no Guinness on tap, though this is still a fun and rowdy drinking option most nights. If you're hungry, there's a full menu of Romanian dishes and grilled meats.

Aysha Café CAFE, CLUB
(Str Armand Călinescu 36; ☺10.30am-1am Mon-Fri, 1pm-2am Sat & Sun; ☎) This popular cafe, club and water-pipe den is proof that Piteşti is not just about old geezers pining for the good old days – it draws a youngish crowd of late teens and 20s. Weekend belly-dancing nights can get crowded.

❶ Information

There's no tourist information office, though some hotels stock a small multilingual book *Turism in Argeş* (20 lei) that has a serviceable map of the city in the front sleeve.

Agenţia de Voiaj CFR (☎0788-036 229, domestic train information 021-9521; www.cfr .ro; Str Victoriei; ☺7am-8pm Mon-Fri) Sells domestic and international train tickets as well as seat reservations and couchettes. They also sell tickets for some domestic flights and long-haul coach journeys. Just around the corner from Hotel Argeş.

BRD (☎0248-218 306; Str Victoriei 7; ☺9am-5pm Mon-Fri) Full service bank and 24-hour ATM.

Central Post Office (Str Victoriei; ☺9am-7pm Mon-Fri, to noon Sat) The main post office is unmarked and there's no street address. To find it, walk south on Str Victoriei beyond the Princely Church. On the right side you'll see a large building with a row of florists in front. Ask one of the flower-sellers, who will point to an obscure staircase. The post office is up one flight.

Piteşti Net Cafe (Str Armand Călinescu 24; per hr 4 lei; ☺8am-midnight) Central internet cafe aimed more at teens and gamers.

Sensi-blu (Str Victoriei; ☺8am-10pm Mon-Fri, 9am-9pm Sat, 9am-2pm Sun) Conveniently located central pharmacy.

❶ Getting There & Away

Bus

Piteşti has several bus stations. Most buses, including bus and maxitaxi services to Bucharest (24 lei, two hours), leave from the **main bus station** (Autogara; Str Tudor Vladimirescu 86), about 300m south of the centre (200m north of the train station). Minibuses to Curtea de Argeş (5 lei, 45 minutes) and several other points north often leave from the northern suburb of Bascov, about 5km north of the centre. For other destinations, consult the website www.autogari.ro.

Train

The main train station is the **southern station** (Piteşti Sud; ☎0248-627 908, domestic train information 021-9521; www.cfr.ro; B-dul Republicii; ☺10am-5pm Mon-Fri). Services include

Bucharest (34 lei, five daily) and Craiova (43 lei, three daily).

Curtea de Argeş

POP 26,133

Curtea de Argeş has a humble, likeable charm, enriched by the captivating treasures left over from town's role as a Wallachian capital in the 14th century. St Nicholas Church in the former Princely Court is a must-see and considered to be one of the oldest monuments preserved in its original form in the country. The town's storied cathedral, sculpted from white stone, is unique for the important royal tombs it hides and its chocolate-box architecture. In addition, the town is a gateway to the Făgăraş Mountains and just a short bus ride away from the 'real' Dracula's castle.

◉ Sights

The main sights are located north of the town centre along a long stretch of B-dul Basarabilor. The Princely Court is at the southern end of B-dul Basarabilor, while the monastery complex is 2km to the north.

TOP CHOICE Princely Court CHURCH, RUIN
(☎0248-721 446; Str Negru Vodă 2; adult/child 5/2 lei; ☺9am-6pm) Curtea de Argeş was an early capital of Wallachia, and these ruins from the 14th century mark the spot where the court once stood. The main sight is St Nicholas Church, which dates from the time of Basarab I (1310–52). Many of the frescoes are originals. The tomb of early ruler Vladislav I Vlaicu (d 1377) stands in the main room. Vlaicu's tomb was first discovered and exhumed in the 1920s. He was found buried wearing an enormous gold buckle (not on display).

The wall paintings, painstakingly restored in the early 20th century, merit closer inspection. In the main room to the right, just below the upper window, look for a rare painting of a pregnant Mary dating from 1370.

Curtea de Argeş Cathedral & Monastery MONASTERY
(Mănăstirea Curtea de Argeş; ☎0248-721 735; B-dul Basarabilor 1; adult/child 2/1 lei; ☺8am-8pm) The cathedral and monastery complex here is considered one of the country's most important ecclesiastical sights. The church was originally built by Neagoe Basarab (r 1512–21), with marble and tiles brought in from

Constantinople. The current edifice dates from 1875, when French architect André Lecomte du Nouy was retained to save the complex, which was in near ruins.

The white marble tombstones of King Carol I (1839–1914) and his wife Elizabeth (1853–1916) lie on the right in the church's entrance hall. On the left of the entrance are the tombstones of King Ferdinand I (1865–1927) and British-born Queen Marie (1875–1938). Neagoe Basarab and his wife are also buried here.

🛏 Sleeping

TOP CHOICE Pensiunea Ruxi   PENSION $
(☎0727-827 675; www.pensiunea-ruxi.ro; Str Negru Vodă 104; r 80 lei; 🅿😊🛜) While the rooms are new and comfortable, the real treat is the homely atmosphere; the family will go to heart-breaking lengths to make sure you're taken care of. The only partial drawback is the town-centre location, about 1km from the Princely Court and 2km from the monastery complex. Walk or take a local minibus. Breakfast costs 15 lei.

Pensiunea Casa Domneasca   PENSION $$
(☎0248-721 008; www.casa-domneasca.ro; Str Plopiș 3; s 170-220 lei, d 190-240 lei; 🅿😊❄🛜❄) Beautiful four-star *pensiunea* (B&B) with an elegant reception area and rooms that look like a spread in *Town & Country* magazine. The standard rates include breakfast; the higher rates include use of the sauna and pool. To find it, make a right at the statue of Besarab I near the Princely Court and follow the street uphill about 100m.

Hotel Posada   HOTEL $$
(☎0248-721 451; www.posada.ro; B-dul Basarabilor 27-29; s/d 130/180 lei; 🅿❄🛜) Nicely remodelled three-star hotel with a quiet location at the far northern end of B-dul Basarabilor

WALLACHIA CURTEA DE ARGEȘ

THE 'REAL' DRACULA'S CASTLE

Many castles across Romania claim a connection (dubious or otherwise) to the notorious former Wallachian prince Vlad Țepeș (1431–76), aka 'Vlad the Impaler' or, better yet, 'Dracula'. But few claims are as legit and well documented as this evocative pile of rocks standing atop a mighty crag just 30km north of Curtea de Argeș, near the village of Căpățânenii.

The **Poienari Citadel** (Cetatea Poienari; Poienari; adult/child 5/2 lei; ☉9am-6pm Jun-Aug, 9am-5pm May & Oct; 🅿) was once a powerful fortress guarding the entry to a strategic pass linking Wallachia with Transylvania. The castle's vantage point was recognised as early as the 13th century, when Wallachian leaders first built a tower to guard the pass. Two centuries later Vlad Țepeș enlarged the castle, using it as both a fortress and a prison. Legend has it most of the work was carried out by captured Turks.

These days there's not much of the castle left to see, but it's still worth the short trip north from Curtea de Argeș to take in the spectacular setting and to make the invigorating climb (1480 steps) to the top. The entrance to the citadel lies just at the start of the towering Transfăgărășan Road (p105), so it's an especially easy stopover if you're planning on crossing the mountains here.

If you've got a few days, the area around the citadel is lovely. About 4km south of the citadel, the village of **Arefu** retains a special untouched-by-time charm. It's allegedly inhabited by descendants of the minions who served Vlad Țepeș, a point of pride the villagers still boast about to this day. About 1km north of the fortress lies the massive artificial **Lake Vidraru**, which was dammed in the 1960s to feed a hydroelectric power plant.

The surrounding villages are teeming with pensions and homes displaying *cazare* (accommodation) signs. In Căpățânenii, 1km south of Poienari, **Pensiunea Dracula** (☎0745-473 381; www.pensiuneadracula.ro; Căpățânenii 190; r 100 lei; 🅿🛜) is a clean and well-run pension, whose owners really get into the Dracula theme. Another good choice is **Pensiunea La Cetate** (☎0744-424 845; www.pensiunealacetate.ro; Poienari; r 110 lei; 🅿❄🛜), just 100m from the steps leading to Dracula's Castle. There's a great terrace here for lunch or dinner.

The best way to get here from Curtea de Argeș is by maxitaxi (5 lei, 40 minutes), signposted to Arefu. They leave regularly from the main bus station. Be sure to tell the driver where you are going. You'll alight in Căpățânenii village – the citadel is a 1km hike north.

by the monastery complex. Try to get a front room to watch the sunset over the mountains.

🍴 Eating

Curtea Veche ROMANIAN $$
(☎0348-108 114; www.curteavechekm0.ro; B-dul Basarabilor 121; mains 15-30 lei; ⊗9am-11pm) Handsomely restored villa with a big rambling porch and a lower level terrace with comfy pillow seating for lounging. The menu is textbook traditional Romanian; *tochitura argeseana* is a stewy mix of pork, peppers, onions and an egg, all poured over polenta. Does pretty good pizza too.

Crama Basarabilor ROMANIAN $$
(☎0744-653 750; B-dul Basarabilor 106; mains 10-32 lei; ⊗11.30am-11pm; 🔊) Nice summer camp–inspired terrace, but sit inside to enjoy the full menu of classic Romanian fare, with a few 'international' dishes for variety, including an 'English Breakfast'. Just 20m from the Princely Court.

ℹ Information

There is no formal tourist information office, though the private travel agency **Turism Posada** (☎0248-721 451; www.posada.ro; B-dul Basarabilor 27-29; ⊗9am-5pm Mon-Fri) in the Hotel Posada may be able to answer some basic questions.

Catena (www.catena.ro; B-dul Basarabilor 117-119; ⊗9am-8pm Mon-Fri, 8am-3pm Sat, 8am-2pm Sun) Convenient pharmacy, 100m north of the Princely Court.

Post Office (B-dul Basarabilor 17-19; ⊗7am-8pm Mon-Fri) Near the Hotel Posada.

Raiffeisen Bank (B-dul Basarabilor 31; ⊗8.30am-6.30pm Mon-Fri) One of several ATMs on B-dul Basarabilor. This one is next to the Hotel Posada, 100m south of the monastery complex.

ℹ Getting There & Away

The main bus station is near the town centre, on a side street about 200m west of Pensiunea Ruxi. Cities served include Bucharest (30 lei, two to three hours, four daily) and Braşov (30 lei, three hours, one daily). Frequent maxitaxis to Arefu (4 lei, 40 minutes) also leave from the main bus station. Other maxitaxis go to and from Piteşti (to the northern suburb of Bascov) from an unofficial maxitaxi stop in front of the Princely Court entrance.

Rail services have been greatly curtailed and trains are not recommended.

Craiova
POP 243,765

The university town of Craiova, founded on the site of the ancient Dacian and Roman stronghold of Pelendava, is a regional commercial centre and transport hub. All long-haul trains between Timişoara and Bucharest stop here, so it makes a convenient point to break a long journey. The modern city, frankly, is not much to look at; though the historic centre, bordered on one end by Romania's prettiest county prefecture buildings, is great for a relaxing stroll. On summer evenings, the town converges on the centre to see a 'singing fountain' display, during which the water jets rise and fall to the sounds of Mozart and Strauss.

◉ Sights

Craiova has a handful of interesting museums, including a very good art museum and one of the best regional folk museums in the country. There are also several churches worth seeking out.

Madonna Dudu Church CHURCH
(Str Madona Dudu 13; admission free; ⊗8am-7pm) Displayed inside the church is the Madona Dudu icon, said to perform miracles for those who pray in front of it.

TOP CHOICE Art Museum MUSEUM
(Muzeul de Artă; ☎0251-412 342; www.muzeul deartacraiova.ro; Calea Unirii 15) Craiova's Art Museum was closed for renovation during our research but was scheduled to reopen in late 2013. The highlight is a small but important collection of sculptures by Brâncuşi, including *The Kiss, The Thigh* and *Miss Pogany*. The museum is located in the amazing early-20th-century Dinu Mihail Palace, which was home to Polish president-in-exile Ignacy Mościcki in 1939.

TOP CHOICE Ethnographic Museum MUSEUM
(Muzeul Olteniei Secţia de Etnografie; ☎0351-444 030; www.muzeulolteniei.ro; Str Matei Basarab 16; adult/child 4/2 lei; ⊗9am-5pm Tue-Sun) This is a highly informative, well-organised exhibition of folk traditions in the Oltenia region surrounding Craiova. The exhibition begins downstairs with bread making and progresses through pottery, tanning, clothing, weaving and folk art. There's little Eng-

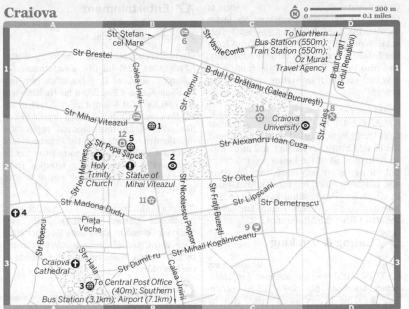

Craiova

Craiova

◎ Sights
1 Art Museum		B2
2 County Prefecture		B2
3 Ethnographic Museum		A3
4 Madonna Dudu Church		A2
5 Natural Science Museum		B2

🛏 Sleeping
6 Casa David		B1
7 Hotel Triconf		B1

🍴 Eating
8 Dolce Vita		D1

🍷 Drinking
9 Pub's Pub		C3

🎭 Entertainment
10 Marin Sorescu National Theatre		C1
11 Oltenia Philharmonic		B2

🛍 Shopping
12 Folk Arts Shop		B2

lish signage, but the director speaks English and can show you around. The setting is the historic Casa Băniei, dating from the 17th century. Recommended.

Natural Science Museum MUSEUM
(☏0251-411 906; www.muzeulolteniei.ro; Str Popa Şapcă 8; adult/child 4/2 lei; ◎9am-5pm Tue-Sun) Small collection on two floors dedicated to the natural sciences. The highlights are fossils on the ground floor that include some massive mammoth tusks. On the upper level are stuffed animals representing the various fauna in the country's regions and climate zones. Very little signage in English limits the appeal.

🛏 Sleeping

Sleep options are limited to a few midrange and top-end hotels that cater mostly to businesspeople.

Hotel Rexton HOTEL $$$
(☏0351-462 451; www.hotelrexton.ro; B-dul Carol I no 49; s/d 330/380 lei; P🐕❄@🛜) The city's nicest hotel is this four-star option that opened its doors in late 2012. The classical motifs are a bit over the top, but the rooms themselves are more sleekly furnished, with flat-screen TVs, big comfy beds and quality carpets. It's a 10-minute walk south on B-dul Carol I from the train and bus stations. Minimal parking out front (reserve in advance).

Casa David
HOTEL $$

(☑0251-410 205; www.casadavid.ro; Str Ştefan cel Mare 18a; s/d 250/270 lei; ⓅⒶ✳🕾) This small four-star *pensiune* is a step up from the hotels in terms of comfort and quality, and also price. The location is good, midway between the train station and the town centre.

Hotel Triconf
HOTEL $$

(☑0251-412 321; hoteleuropacraiova@yahoo.com; Calea Unirii 10a; s/d 150/180 lei; ✳🕾) Formerly the Hotel Europa, it's smaller and more intimate than most of the hotels around town, but the rooms are only so-so; they are clean and relatively quiet, but thoroughly lacking in character. The location is excellent, five minutes from the central square and across the street from the Museum of Art.

Eating & Drinking

TOP CHOICE Epoca
STEAKHOUSE $$$

(☑0732-707 002; www.epocarestaurant.ro; Str Alexandru Macedonski 51; mains 40-115 lei; ⊘noon-1am; 🕾) This luxury steakhouse, run by head chef Jakob Hausmann, is a must for lovers of high-quality imported beef. The menu is almost exclusively grilled steaks and chops, with the speciality being cuts from Argentina and the US, served on hot plates that allow you to cook it perfectly to your liking.

Dolce Vita
ITALIAN $$

(☑0251-466 604; Str Arieş; mains 20-30 lei; ⊘8am-midnight; 🕾) Relaxed, casual setting ideal for an evening meal. The menu is good-quality Italian with a pleasing range of homemade pasta dishes. These include a very passable pesto and delicious ravioli served with butter and sage. Book ahead on weekends.

Temple Bar
PUB

(☑0251-592 733; www.thetemplebar.ro; Str Brazda lui Novac 77b-77d) Proper, upscale Irish pub located 2km north of the centre (take a taxi since it's hard to find) and not a drop of true Irish food, but nevertheless one of the most popular and enjoyable spots in town for drinks or a bite to eat; there's a large menu of grilled meats, pastas and salads. The main draw is the lively atmosphere.

Pub's Pub
PUB

(www.pubspub.ro; Str Fraţii Buzeşti 4; ⊘6pm-2am) Popular, high-octane watering hole with weekend parties and occasional live music.

☆ Entertainment

A complete list of what's on can be found at www.craiova.ro/evenimente.

Marin Sorescu National Theatre
THEATRE

(☑box office 0251-413 677; www.tncms.ro; Str Alexandru Ioan Cuza 11; ⊘box office 9am-4pm Mon, 9am-4pm & 4.30-6.30pm Tue-Fri, 10am-1pm & 4.30-6.30pm Sat & Sun) Under director Silviu Purcărete, Craiova's main drama venue has enjoyed an international reputation for theatre excellence. Peformances are normally in Romanian, though the venue occasionally hosts visiting troupes from other countries. Buy tickets at the theatre box office.

Oltenia Philharmonic
CLASSICAL MUSIC

(Filarmonica Oltenia; ☑0351-414 697; www .filarmonica-oltenia.ro; Calea Unirii 16; ⊘box office 11am-7pm) Classical concerts are performed by the Oltenia Philharmonic. Buy tickets at the box office.

🛍 Shopping

Folk Arts Shop
ARTS & CRAFTS

(Magazin de Artă Tradiţională; Natural Science Museum, Str Popa Şapcă 8; ⊘9am-1.30pm 2.30-5pm Mon-Fri) This small shop inside the Natural Science Museum sells traditional textiles, ceramics and clothing.

❶ Information

There's no tourist information office and local travel agencies are more intent on getting Romanians out than helping visitors find their way around town.

Agenţia de Voiaj CFR (☑0351-100 110; www .cfr.ro; Complex Unirea; ⊘8am-8pm Mon-Fri) Sells domestic and international train tickets, as well as seat reservations and couchettes. Can help sort out international connections.

BRD (☑0251-412 282; Str Mihai Viteazul 2; ⊘ 9am-5.30pm Mon-Fri, 10am-2pm Sat) Centrally located bank and ATM.

Central Post Office (www.posta-romana. ro; Calea Unirii 54; ⊘7am-8pm Mon-Fri, 8am-1pm Sat)

Sensi-blu (Complex Unirea; ⊘8am-10pm Mon-Fri, 9am-7pm Sat, 9am-3pm Sun) Modern pharmacy with a central location.

❶ Getting There & Away

Air

Craiova Airport (Aeroportul Craiova; ☑251-416 860; www.aeroportcraiova.ro; Calea Bucureşti 325) is situated 8km east of the centre along the main highway (E70) to Bucharest. The budget

CONSTANTIN BRÂNCUŞI 'IN SITU' IN TÂRGU JIU

The blue-collar coal-mining town of Târgu Jiu is an unlikely setting for the archly minimalist, modern sculpture of internationally acclaimed Romanian master Constantin Brâncuşi (1876–1957). Commissioned as a war memorial in 1935, the four pieces the sculptor created in 1938 along the main street, Calea Eroilor (Avenue of Heroes), constitute arguably the high point of Brâncuşi's career, and certainly merit a detour for fans of modern art.

A logical place to begin a Brâncuşi tour is at the entrance to the town's Central Park, at the western end of Calea Eroilor. The first piece, the small but moving *Gate of the Kiss* (Poarta Sărutului), is in the shape of an arch meant to commemorate Romania's unification after WWI.

Continue along the park's central mall to the *Alley of Chairs* (Aleea Scaunelor). The dwarf-sized stone stools are in groups of three on either side of the avenue. The alley leads to a third sculpture, the riverside *Table of Silence* (Masa Tăcerii). Each of the 12 stools around the circular stone table represents a month of the year.

As public sculpture, these three relatively small works seem almost insignificant, but Brâncuşi is celebrated as a master of proportion, simplicity and symbolism.

The *Endless Column*, one of his best-known and most-celebrated works, sits at the eastern end of Calea Eroilor (20 minutes on foot from the other pieces). The 29.35m-tall structure, threaded with 15 steel beads, is meant to symbolise the synthesis of heaven and physical reality.

The communist leadership, unsurprisingly, didn't get and didn't like what it considered to be Brâncuşi's decadent style, and there was even talk in the 1950s of demolishing the pieces. In the end, the sculptures survived. It was a lucky break. Today, works by Brâncuşi fetch as much as €30 million each at auction, and the statues here are given a 24-hour armed guard.

Târgu Jiu itself is a relatively depressed industrial city. There are ample places to eat and stay the night, but it's not a place you'll want to linger. There's a regular train service to and from Bucharest (36 lei, five hours, three daily) via Craiova.

Buses and maxitaxis connect the city to Timişoara (40 lei, three daily) and Drobeta-Turnu Severin (two daily), among other places.

carrier **Carpatair** (☑0251-435 566; www.carpa tair.com; Craiova Airport; ☺6am-6pm) is part of Craiova's network of flights, servicing destinations across Europe, but flights usually require a change of planes in Timişoara.

Bus

The **main bus station** (Autogara; ☑0251-411 187; B-dul Carol I 1), about 50m to the left as you exit the train station, appears at first glance like utter anarchy, but is actually well organised. Regular maxitaxis leave from here to Bucharest (around 40 lei, hourly). There are also regular bus services to Timişoara (40 lei) and Drobeta-Turnu Severin (20 lei), among other cities.

Train

All fast trains between Bucharest and Timişoara stop at Craiova's **train station** (www.cfr.ro; B-dul Carol I). Services include trains to Bucharest (50 lei, three hours, 12 daily), Timişoara (50 lei, five hours, seven daily), Drobeta-Turnu Severin (33 lei, two hours) and Târgu Jiu (33 lei, two hours).

Drobeta-Turnu Severin

POP 86,475

Drobeta-Turnu Severin – usually shortened to 'Severin' in conversation – is on the bank of the Danube (Dunărea) River bordering Serbia. Though the modern city was laid out in the 19th century, the town has a rich history stretching back nearly 2000 years, when it was a Roman colony and had a population of some 40,000. It's best known as the base of Roman emperor Trajan's colossal bridge across the Danube. You can still see ruins of the bridge as well as a Roman fortress built to defend it.

◉ Sights

Iron Gates Museum   MUSEUM
(Muzeul Porţilor de Fier; Str Independenţei 2) While the museum houses an ethnographic and natural-sciences section, as well as an aquarium displaying Danubian species, the

highlight is a scale model of the Roman bridge constructed across the Danube in AD 103 by Greek architect Apollodorus of Damascus on the orders of Emperor Trajan (r AD 98–117). The museum was closed at the time of research but is due to reopen in 2013.

The bridge stood just below the site of the present museum, and the ruins *(ruinele podului lui Traian)* of two of its pillars can still be seen towering beside the Danube. In its day it was a tremendous feat of engineering and was more than 1100m in length and 15m wide. Nearby, you'll see scattered pieces of rock and debris that were once part of a Roman colony along the banks of the river.

Water Tower　　　　　HISTORIC BUILDING
(Castelul de Apă; cnr Str Crisan & Str Dr Saidac; admission free; ⊘9am-9pm) Severin's most strik-ing building is this massive water tower, dating from 1910. It was one of the first buildings in the country to use iron in its construction. These days you can walk the 159 steps to the top for amazing views out over the Danube (or take the lift).

🛏 Sleeping

There are a number of roadside *pensiunes,* motels and restaurants on the main E70 highway, signposted as Str Tudor Vladimirescu, about 2km north of the town centre.

TOP CHOICE **Hotel Corona**　　　　HOTEL $$
(☎0743-128 658; www.hotelcorona.ro; Str Tudor Vladimirescu 106a; s/d 150/180 lei; ⓟ🐾🌸@🛜) This clean, smart and well-run hotel occupies a nondescript strip of shops along Hwy

---

WORTH A TRIP

ORŞOVA & THE IRON GATES NATIONAL PARK

South and west of Drobeta-Turnu Severin, just below the town of Orşova, the Danube River begins a series of twists and turns between towering rocks that have bedevilled sailors from time immemorial.

The area is protected by the 1150-sq-km **Iron Gates National Park** (Parcul Natural Porţile de Fier). A similar protected area, the Djerdap National Park, sits across the river in Serbia. Highlights of the park include miles of rugged, unspoiled riverbanks and a massive stone carving of the former Dacian leader, Decebal (r AD 87–106). You'll also see scattered reminders of ancient settlements that were submerged in the 1960s during construction of the Porţile de Fier Hydroelectric Power Plant, 10km west of Drobeta-Turnu Severin. One of the most famous of these settlements was the island of Ada Kaleh, a Turkish enclave that had survived into the 20th century but was totally destroyed during construction of the dam.

There are two ways to access the park. If you have your own wheels, local Hwy 57 hugs the river for a distance of more than 100km from Orşova to Moldova Nouă. It's one of Romania's most dazzling road trips and cuts straight through the heart of the national park. To find it, follow Hwy E70 from Drobeta-Turnu Severin west in the direction of Timişoara. As you approach Orşova, cross a bridge and bear left on the road sign-posted 'Orşova Centru'. From here, follow the signs to Hwy 57 'Moldova Nouă'.

You can also take a **boat excursion** (Plimbări cu barca; ☎0722-169 837, English information 0725-083 352; www.pedunarelacazaneorsova.ro; Orşova Port; per boat of 6 passengers 300 lei; ⊘9am-5pm May-Oct) from Orşova. Several private operators line Orşova Port near the centre from May to October. They typically offer guided boat tours (two to three hours) through the most picturesque regions of the river.

Technology geeks might also want to take a tour of the **Porţile de Fier Hydroelectric Power Plant** (Hidrocentrala Porţile de Fier I; Hwy E70; adult/child 4/2 lei; ⊘9am-4pm Tue-Sun). This controversial project was a Romanian–Yugoslav joint venture, conceived in 1960 and completed 12 years later. There's a small museum on-site that takes you inside and provides a good idea of the scale of the plant. Guided tours (in Romanian only) go down five levels to the turbines. The museum is located along Hwy E70, 10km west of Drobeta-Turnu Severin.

There's a regular minibus service to Orşova from Drobeta-Turnu Severin as well as at least one train per day, though the Orşova train station is a good 2km hike to the centre of town.

E70, but it's set back from the highway so noise is not an issue. The rooms are bright and furnished in contemporary style. The reception is friendly and the restaurant, while lacking atmosphere, serves very good food. It's about 2km northeast of the centre of town.

Hotel Continental HOTEL $$

(☑0372-528 828, reservations 0372-121 721; www .continentalhotels.ro; B-dul Carol I 2; s/d 225/250 lei; P😊❄@🛜) This battered high-rise from the 1970s has seen better days, but the location is about as good as it gets, on a ridge above the river and within walking distance to the sights. Ask to see several rooms as they're in varying states of repair. The river-view rooms tend to be the nicest. Friendly English-speaking staff.

🍴 Eating & Drinking

There's a lively **food market** (Piața Mircea; cnr Str Numa Pompiliu & Str Dr Saidac; ⊘6am-9pm Mon-Fri, 7am-3pm Sat & Sun) just east of the town centre where you can buy fresh fruit and vegetables, breads and cheeses.

TOP CHOICE Trattoria Il Calcio ITALIAN $$

(☑0753-118 070; www.trattoriailcalcio.ro; B-dul Tudor Vladimirescu 143; mains 20-30 lei; ⊘11am-midnight; 🛜) This is the local branch of a Romanian chain of Italian restaurants, but don't let that deter you. The food and service are excellent. The baked lasagne, served with a side of fresh-baked pizza bread, might just be the best meal in Severin. It's in the new part of town, along the E70 highway in the direction of Craiova, about 2km from the centre of the old town.

16,50 BAR

(☑0252-310 478; www.1650.ro; Str Traian 50; ⊘11am-2am) About as cool as it gets in sleepy Severin. There's decent pizza and other nosh on hand, as well as a garden terrace furnished with wrought-iron sofas and chairs covered in big white pillows. Around sunset this place morphs into a full-fledged club-lounge.

ℹ Information

There is no central tourist information office, though there are large city maps posted at intervals around town, particulary along B-dul Carol I.

Agenția de Voiaj CFR (☑0252-313 117; www .cfr.ro; Str Decebal 43; ⊘8am-8pm Mon-Fri) Sells domestic and international train tickets as well as tickets for some international bus lines.

BRD (☑0252-316 074; B-dul Carol I 55, cnr Str Rahovei; ⊘9am-5pm Mon-Fri) One of several banks and ATMs scattered around town; close to Hotel Continental.

Eccofarm Nou Farmacie (cnr Str Numa Pompiliu & Str Dr Saidac; ⊘8am-9pm Mon-Fri, 8am-2pm Sat & Sun) One of at least a dozen pharmacies located around town. This one is conveniently situated within the food market complex.

Genex (Str Tudor Vladimirescu 81a; per hr 2 lei; ⊘1pm-midnight Mon-Fri, 2pm-midnight Sat & Sun) This down-at-heel internet cafe in a humble building on Hwy E70 is about the best option in town.

Post Office (Str Decebal 41; ⊘7am-8pm Mon-Fri, 8am-1pm Sat)

ℹ Getting There & Away

Bus

Drobeta-Turnu Severin, as with many Romanian towns and cities, has more than one bus and minibus station. Many long-haul buses and minibuses merely service designated stops along Hwy E70. To be sure, inquire at your hotel or consult the website www.autogari.ro. Buses and minibuses service the entire region, with frequent departures for Orşova (5 lei, 30 minutes) and Timişoara (35 lei, five hours), among other cities.

Train

The **train station** (Gara; www.cfr.ro; B-dul Dunărea) is located along the Danube River on the extreme western edge of the port, about 2km from the centre of town. On arrival, hike up the steps and turn right on B-dul Carol I to reach the centre or take a taxi (around 8 lei). The city has good train connections to both Bucharest (about 60 lei, five hours, five daily) and Timişoara (40 lei, four hours, four daily). Bucharest-bound trains stop in Craiova (25 lei, three hours). There's one daily train to Orşova (5 lei, 25 minutes).

WALLACHIA DROBETA-TURNU SEVERIN

Transylvania

Includes »

Why Go?

Transylvania conjures a vivid landscape of mountains, castles, fortified churches and superstitious old crones. The Carpathian Mountains are truly spectacular and outdoor enthusiasts can choose from caving in the Apuseni range, rock climbing at Piatra Craiului National Park, biking atop the flat Bucegi plateau, or hiking the Făgăraş. The skiing scene, particularly in the Bucegi Mountains, is a great draw, while well-beaten paths up to Bran and Peleş Castles are also worth the crowds.

A melange of architecture and chic sidewalk cafes punctuate the towns of Braşov, Sighişoara and Sibiu, while the vibrant student town Cluj-Napoca has the country's most vigorous nightlife. Many of southern Transylvania's Saxon villages are dotted with fortified churches that date back half a millennium. An hour north, in Székely Land, ethnic Hungarian communities are the majority. Throughout you're likely to spot many Roma villagers – look out for black cowboy hats and rich red dresses.

Best Places to Eat

- » Bella Muzica (p88)
- » Crama Veche (p144)
- » Crama Sibiu Vechi (p111)
- » Camino (p137)

Best Places to Stay

- » Casa Wagner (p87)
- » Am Ring (p110)
- » Casa Au Cerb (p99)

When to Go

Braşov

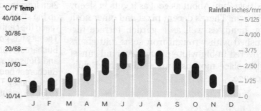

Jun–Sep Summer is a glorious time for hiking and seeing the medieval cities in full swing.

May A pleasant month, with the mountains rich in wildflowers and the weather cool.

Dec–Mar Plenty of snow for skiing, with plummeting temperatures.

History

For 1000 years, until WWI, Transylvania was associated with Hungary. In the 10th century a Magyar (Hungarian) tribe, the Székelys, settled in what they called Erdély ('beyond the forest' – the literal meaning of Transylvania). In the 12th century Saxon merchants arrived to help defend the eastern frontiers of Hungary. The seven towns they founded – Bistriţa (Bistritz), Braşov (Kronstadt), Cluj-Napoca (Klausenburg), Mediaş (Mediasch), Sebeş (Mühlbach), Sibiu (Hermannstadt) and Sighişoara (Schässburg) – gave Transylvania its German name, Siebenbürgen.

Medieval Transylvania was autonomously ruled by a prince accountable to the Hungarian crown, while the indigenous Romanians were serfs. After the 1526 Turkish defeat of Hungary the region became semi-independent, recognising Turkish suzerainty. In 1683 Turkish power was broken and Transylvania came under Habsburg rule four years later. The Catholic Habsburg governors sought to control the territory by favouring first the Protestant Hungarians and Saxons and then the Orthodox Romanians. In 1848, when the Hungarians launched a revolution against the Habsburgs, Romania sided with the Austrians. After 1867 Transylvania was fully absorbed into Hungary. In 1918 Romanians gathered at Alba Iulia to demand Transylvania's union with Romania.

This unification has never been fully accepted by Hungary, and from 1940 to 1944 it set about re-annexing much of the region. After the war, Romanian communists moved to quash Hungarian nationalist sentiments. Currently, however, feelings of resentment have subsided somewhat and Romania's relations with its western neighbour are pacific. Still, one feels an extant mistrust between the communities, and the Hungarians publish maps of the region with only Hungarian place names (even street names), as if they were not located in Romania.

PRAHOVA VALLEY

Wallachia funnels into Transylvania in this narrow valley at the foot of the fir-clad Bucegi Mountains. Sinaia, a king's summer retreat a century ago, is the finest town, but the real draw is up, way up, with hiking and biking trails along the flat plateau atop the mountains, and ski trails that carve down the mountainsides. If you're looking for just a taste, it's possible to do a day trip from Braşov

and take a cable-car ride up and take a short hike. But it's easier if you stay a night or two.

Sinaia

POP 11,470

Nestled in a slender fir-clad valley, this pretty town teems with hikers in summer and skiers in winter. Backed by the imposing crags of the Bucegi Mountains, it's a dramatic place for a day's hike or, using the network of cabanas open to walkers, several days.

The town itself is a melange of crayon-coloured wooden houses contrasted with the 'wedding-cake' style of its grander 19th-century buildings. Once home to Romania's first king, Carol 1, who created a summer retreat here, Peleş Palace is a dream of hidden passages, fairy-tale turrets, vertiginous galleries and classical statues; it's so beguilingly imaginative, it could raise a swoon from the most hardened cynic.

Sinaia is named after Mount Sinai, and you'll notice there's a cross on the mountain above the town; a bi-product of a nobleman's visit to Israel in 1965. Following his return he founded a monastery with a lustrously gilded interior up the hill.

Sinaia is administratively part of Wallachia but is most easily reached from Transylvania.

◉ Sights

Peleş Castle　　　　　　　　　　CASTLE
(www.visit.peles.ro; tours adult/child 20/5 lei, optional tour adult/child 70/7 lei, photos 3 lei; ⊙9am-5pm Tue-Sun; 🚻) A 20-minute walk uphill of the town centre, this one has to be the most magical of all the castles you'll marvel at in Transylvania. Fairy-tale turrets rise above green meadows, and grand reception halls fashioned in Moorish, Florentine and French styles collectively overwhelm.

Endless wood-carved ceilings and gilded pieces induce cross-eyed swoons, and even if you're bent on chasing creepy Dracula-type castles, it's hard not to get a thrill visiting this one. The first European castle to have central heating, electricity and vacuuming(!), Peleş was intended to be the summer residence of Romania's longest-serving monarch, King Carol I. Construction on the 3500-sq m-edifice, built in a predominantly German-Renaissance style, began in 1875. Some 39 years, more than 400 weary craftsmen and thousands of labourers later, it was completed, just months before the king died in

Transylvania Highlights

1 Wandering the cobbled alleyways and fairy-tale squares of medieval towns **Braşov** (p82), **Sibiu** (p106) and **Sighişoara** (p96)

2 Exploring the **Bucegi Mountains** (p79), where novices can bike or hike the plateau; or pressing on to the rugged **Apuseni Mountains** (p142)

3 Wandering bucolic valleys to discover **Saxon villages** and their **fortified churches** (p101) such as those in Viscri and Biertan

4 Squeezing yourself into a **bear hide** and watching the brown bear's picnic unfold around you with **Carpathian Nature Tours** (p86)

5 Hanging out with shepherds in agrotourism guesthouses such as those in **Sibiel** (p114) or the Hungarian **Huedin Microregion** (p141)

6 Head to **Poiana Braşov** (p92) to experience the 'Cold Mountain' location used in the Hollywood film, and for some great skiing too

7 Get your pulse racing in the spooky **Tihuta (Borgo) Pass** (p143), immortalised in Bram Stoker's *Dracula*

8 One of the creepiest looking castles in the country is **Bran Castle** (p91) a half-hour's journey from Braşov

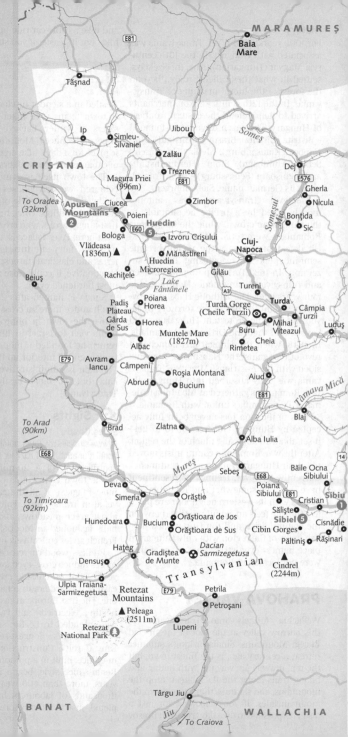

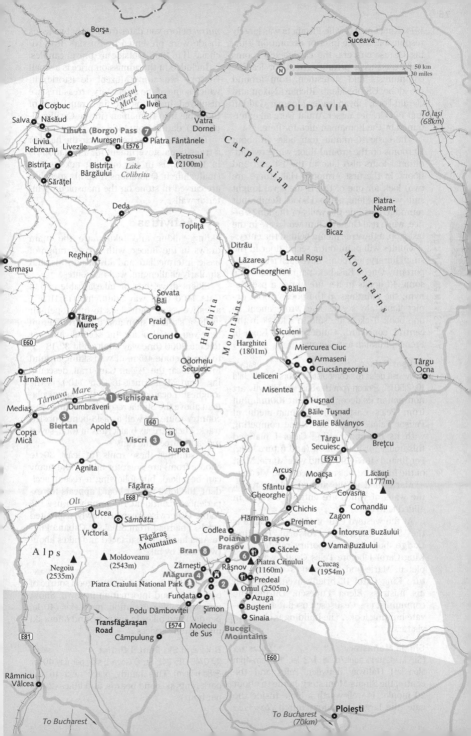

1914. King Carol I's wife Elisabeta was largely responsible for the interior decoration. During Ceauşescu's era, the castle's 160 rooms were used as a private retreat for leading communists and statesmen from around the globe. US presidents Richard Nixon and Gerald Ford, Libyan leader Moamar Gaddafi and PLO leader Yasser Arafat were all entertained by the Romanian dictator here.

The basic 40-minute tour takes in about 10 rooms on the ground floor, while two additional tours also take in the 1st and 2nd floors. In the first Armoury Hall (there are two) look for one of the 11 medieval knight suits with the long pointed boots. Rembrandt reproductions line the walls of the king's office, while real Gustav Klimt works are in the last stop, a theatre/cinema behind the entry.

Guides will point out a secret door in the small library; all rooms have such a door apparently. Queen Elisabeta painted and wrote some 43 books in her life under a pseudonym; the paintings in the poetry room depict 'fairy-tale' scenes she wrote about in one book. Tickets are sold in a kiosk in the central courtyard. Guides speak English, French, Russian and German.

Pelişor Palace   PALACE
(www.visit.peles.ro; compulsory tours adult/child 10/2.50 lei; ☺noon-7pm Thu-Sun; ♿) Heavily art nouveau in its decor, and about 100m uphill from Peleş Castle, the German-medieval Pelişor Palace has a hard time competing with its neighbour. King Carol I planned this house for his nephew (and future king) Ferdinand (1865–1927) and wife Marie. Most of the furniture was imported from Vienna.

Marie died in the arched golden room, the walls of which are entirely covered in gilded leaves.

At the western end of the Peleş estate is the Swiss-châlet-style **Foişorul Hunting Lodge**, built as a temporary residence by King Carol I before Peleş Castle was completed. Marie and Ferdinand's son, the future King Carol II, briefly lived here with his mistress Elena Lupescu. During the communist era, Ceauşescu used it as his private hunting lodge. The building is closed to visitors.

Sinaia Monastery   MONASTERY
(Str Mănăstirii; adult/child 4/2 lei; ☺10am-4pm Mon-Sat) Halfway between Peleş and the centre, the Sinaia Monastery, home to about 20 monks, is well worth a look. Inside the gate, the large Orthodox church (*biserica mare*) before you dates from 1846; two icons inside were presented by Russia's Tsar Nicholas II in 1903. Outside are prayer candles.

Included in the admission price is a small **History Museum** (Muzeul de Istorie) in which some of the monastery's treasures are displayed, including the first translation of the Bible into Romanian (in the Cyrillic alphabet), dating from 1668.

The **tomb of Tache Ionescu**, the head of a transitional government for a few months in 1921–22, is in the building next to the small church. Quotations from his speeches are carved in stone on the mausoleum's interior walls.

🏃 Activities

Skiing, hiking and biking are the main draws in the Bucegi with a good range of basic, intermediate and advanced runs, and similarly challenging walking routes.

Skiers drive, bus or take a cable car to Cota 1400 (one way adult/child 18/11 lei), a festive scene with sleds to hire, open-air grills, a ski-hire shop and a chairlift. From here you can also take the second cable car to Cota 2000 (one way adult/child 32/18 lei) to access some 40km of wild skiing around Mt Furnica; the 2½km Carp trail, descending from Mt Furnica to Cota 1400, is the toughest. Located on top of the Bucegi plateau above the Sinaia resort is an 8km cross-country route, as well as a 13-bend bobsled track. There are six black runs in total, seven red, and three blue runs.

In summer these trails (at least 30 to choose from) are great for hikers, and many can be biked, but following a recent accident, the local tourist board appeals for experienced, confident riders only to use the trails. Otherwise keep to newly asphalted roads. The road from Sinaia to Cabana Piatra Arsa has been resurfaced and takes about two hours by bike.

Snow   SKIING
(Str Cuza Vodă 2a; ☺9am-6pm) A good source of equipment and information in town, Snow, near the cable-car station, hires skis (40 lei per day) and bikes in summer, and offers ski instruction services.

Bike and Ski Rental Outlet   SKIING
(☎0745-015 241; Str O Goga 1; skis per day 40 lei; ☺8am-7pm) This handy place next to the park rents skis and boards, and bikes (20 lei per hour).

🛏 Sleeping

Hotel Caraiman   HOTEL $$
(📞0244-311 542; palace@rdslink.ro; B-dul Carol I nr 4; s/d/ste 145/200/240 lei; 🅿😊📶) Built in 1880, this austere yet welcoming multi-gabled hotel has bags of atmosphere: its stained-glass windows, chandeliers, sweeping stairways and wood panelling hint at the affluent elite who used to patronise it. Fragrant rooms enjoy thick carpets, decent fittings, en suite and cable TV. Ask for one facing the park for the restful babble of the nearby fountain.

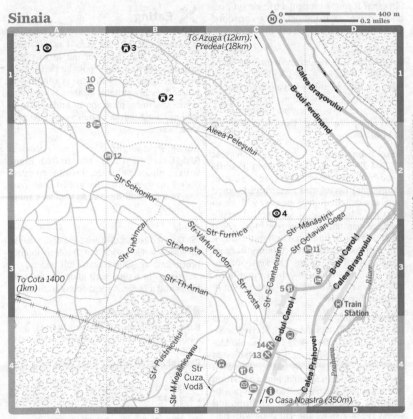

Sinaia

TRANSYLVANIA SINAIA

Sinaia

Hotel Palace
HOTEL $$

(☎0244-312 051/2; www.palace-sinaia.ro; Str O Goga 4; s/d 145-200 lei; 🅿😊🛜) A 'wedding-cake' style 19th-century beauty, this chandelier-dripping hotel has fine rooms finished in dark wood and lilac walls. You might want to opt for one with a balcony and view of the park. Remember The Overlook Hotel in *The Shining*? If you've brought a tricycle get pedalling down its hauntingly long corridors! Discounts available if you call in advance.

Anda Hotel
HOTEL $$

(☎0244-306 020; www.hotelanda.ro; B-dul Carol I 30; s 175 lei, d 300 lei; 🅿😊🛜) Anda is immaculate, if a little bland, with balcony-wrapped rooms with cable TV and modern en suites, and an attractive restaurant dishing up risotto and pasta dishes. Discounts available in low season.

Hotel Economat
HOTEL $$

(☎0244-311 151; www.apps.ro; Aleea Peleşului 2; s/d/tr 90/150/180 lei; 🌞🅿) Like a slice of Hansel and Gretel, this gingerbread-roofed hotel is a delight. Rooms are cosy with clean en suites. Staff, however, surrounded by pilgrimage paraphernalia in reception, could do with a lick of humour. Head to the excellent Vanatoresc, its sister restaurant across the courtyard and up the hill. Festooned in bear furs and stag antlers, this former hunter's lodge is a fun place to take your complimentary breakfast

Marami Hotel
HOTEL $$

(☎0244-315 560; www.marami.ro; Str Furnica 52; s/d/ste 160/180/200 lei; 😊🛜) Ten-year-old Marami is clean, modern and well positioned for visiting nearby Peleş Castle. There's a gym, a Jacuzzi and a sauna, plus an inviting restaurant for breakfast. Rooms are peach-coloured with pine-accented furniture and forest views. Ask for the 4th floor with balconies facing the mountains.

Hotel Cota 1400
HOTEL $

(☎0244-314 990; www.hotel-cota1400.ro; s/d 140/160 lei; 🅿🛜) Next to the Cota 1400 cable-car station, this hotel is paint-thirsty on the outside, but with mountain views this dramatic, who's complaining? There's a terrace bar to drink up the panorama, a drab restaurant, a sauna, a games room and myriad rooms with fresh en suites, TVs, and space. If you're bear-inclined, Yogis tend to visit the hotel car park after midnight.

Casa Noastra
HOTEL $

(☎0244 314 556; www.casanoastra.sinaia.ro; B-dul Carol 1; s/d/tr 70/100/120 lei; 🅿🛜) Five hundred metres south of the roundabout in the centre of town, this four-floor traditional-style hotel has clean rooms with sparkling en suites and fine views of the mountains. Outside of August there are decent discounts.

Eating

Irish House
INTERNATIONAL $$

(www.irishhouse.ro; B-dul Carol I nr 80; mains 15-25 lei; 🍴) Eat inside or out at this busy central watering hole, popular with families and après-skiers. Service is a little slow, but coffees are suitably frothy and there's a menu spanning pizza, pasta and salads, as well as Romanian fare such as smoked pork with beans.

Bucegi Restaurant
ROMANIAN $$

(B-dul Carol I; mains 20 lei) Next to Irish House with an alpine ambience, this alfresco eatery dishes up specialities like grilled bear, venison, omelettes and pizza, as well as a range of salads.

Snow
ROMANIAN $$

(Str Cuza Vodă; mains 15-40 lei) Next door you can hire skis, while inside the Tyrolean interior broths bubble, soup warms chilly skiers, and waitresses in alpine garb glide around with plaits and a smile. A meat-accented menu.

Information

Banca Transilvania (B-dul Carol I 14) Has a 24-hour ATM; foreign-exchange service is next door.

Central Post Office (Str Cuza Vodă; ⏰9am-7pm Mon-Fri, 9am-12pm Sat)

Salvamont (☎0244-313 131; Primărie, B-dul Carol I) This 24-hour mountain-rescue service is located at the Cota 2000 chairlift station.

SensiBlu Pharmacy (B-dul Carol I 8, Hotel Sinaia; ⏰8am-10pm Mon-Fri, 9am-9pm Sat, 9am-2pm Sun) SensiBlu stocks a wide range of toiletries.

Sinaia Tourism Information Centre (☎0244-315 656; www.info-sinaia.ro; B-dul Carol I 47; ⏰8.30am-4.30pm Mon-Fri) Run by the ever-helpful Paul, this dinky office packs a powerful punch, with free local maps, basic skiing and hiking maps, brochures, ideas for local activities and info on upcoming classical concerts.

Tea Tour Travel Agency (☎0244 310 745; B-dul Carol 1; ⏰9am-5pm Mon-Sat) Run by Vasi, TT books forward travel tickets and organises trekking with a reliable guide in the

Bucegi Mountains. One day for two people costs 100 lei.

❶ Getting There & Away

Sinaia is on the Bucharest–Braşov rail line – 126km from the former and 45km from the latter – so jumping on a train to Bucharest (38 lei, 1½ hours) or Braşov (13 lei, one hour) is a cinch.

The train station is downhill and a couple of blocks north from the centre of town. From the station climb up the stairway across the street to busy B-dul Carol I, which leads left past hotels, banks, travel agencies and the cable car.

Buses and maxitaxis run every 45 minutes between roughly 6am and 10pm from the train station to Azuga (4 lei) and Buşteni (3 lei, 10 minutes); some go all the way to Bucharest (25 lei, 1½ hours) or Braşov (16 lei, one hour). Rates are cheaper than the train; pay the driver when you board or seek out the bored guy wandering by the taxis with a laminated ID.

Bucegi Mountains

These sandstone and limestone mountains rising 2505m are hugely popular with Romanians (and a healthy population of bears). While some trails are poorly marked, there is a decent selection of cabanas and shelters should you lose your way, go trekking for a few days, or the weather turns inclement. Winter is severe, avalanches close wild-skiing options during the thaw and summer thunderstorms are common.

An added bonus is the hiker-friendly plateau above the horseshoe-shaped range, that stands between Bran and Sinaia. The best walking map is Dimap's fold-out *Five Mountains from the Carpathian's Bend* (34 lei; www.dimap.hu) covering the Piatra Craiului, Bucegi, Postăvarul, Piatra Mare and Ciucaş ranges, plus a Braşov city map. A visit to the Tourist Information Centre in

Bucegi Mountains

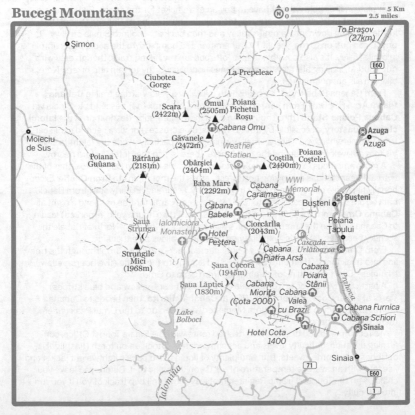

Sinaia is essential before setting off on ambitious hikes.

🛏 Sleeping

Camping in Bucegi is only allowed in clearly signed areas and is, in fact, not altogether recommended due to the likelihood of bear encounters. Cabanas provide blankets. It's sometimes hard to reserve a spot in cabanas, but they'll always make space.

FROM BUŞTENI

Cabana Omu CABIN $

(☎0744-567 290, 0244-320 677; www.cabana-omu.ro; per person 40 lei) This is a simple electricity-free refuge with beds but no running wa-

---

HIKING & BIKING

The two most common starting points are from the cable-car stations at Cota 2000 (from Sinaia) or from Cabana Babele (in neighbouring Buşteni).

From Buşteni take the cable car up to **Cabana Babele** (2206m). From Babele a trail leads to the giant WWI memorial cross at 2284m (one hour; it's marked with red crosses). From here a path (red crosses) leads to the top of Caraiman Peak (2384m). On the peak the path becomes wider, turning into a trail that continues towards Omu Peak across Bucegi Plateau. It gets close to the Coştila Peak (2490m) on top of which is a rocket-like TV transmitter. Nearby is a weather station that has accommodation.

Alternatively, a trail (three to four hours, blue crosses) leads from **Cabana Caraiman** (2025m), where you can pick up the trail to the WWI cross (30 to 45 minutes, red circles).

Cabana Babele is the best starting point for biking around the Bucegi – you can take your bike on the cable car, but have to buy an extra ticket for the space. Bike trails are generally not marked. Well-beaten routes include one starting at Cabana Cuibul Dorului, descending down into Ialomiţa Valley and then back around into Sinaia on Hwy 71, or you can puff up to the Coştila TV transmitter and bomb down the access road into Ialomiţa Valley. It's also possible to bike 'off-road' on the hiking trails, though only with due caution, staying alert for the sometimes non-bikeworthy terrain and hikers. Note, biking trails are not marked.

From Cabana Babele you can hike south following a yellow-stripe trail to **Cabana Piatra Arsă** (1950m). From here you can pick up a blue trail that descends to Sinaia via **Cabana Poiana Stânii** (three hours). An even more interesting destination is the **Ialomiciora Monastery**, accessible by trail (1½ hours, blue crosses) or via a second cable car from Babele, where you'll find a small hermitage built partially inside the Ialomiţa cave. Visitors are welcome to spend the night there; there is also the Hotel Peştera nearby.

A more ambitious expedition involves taking the cable car from Buşteni to either of the two cable-car stations and hiking northwest across the mountains to **Bran Castle**. Exceptionally fit people can do this in one strenuous day, assuming an early start from Babele, but you are strongly encouraged to take two days and camp for free or spend a night at **Cabana Omu**. From the TV transmitter there is a trail (two hours, yellow-marked) leading to Cabana Omu on the summit (Bucegi's highest point, at 2505m). North of Babele the scenery becomes dramatic, with dizzying drops into valleys on either side.

From Omu to Bran Castle is tough but spectacular – a 2000m drop through the tree line into thick forest, then onto a logging road leading to the castle (five hours, yellow triangles). Don't even think of climbing up from Bran to Omu.

A particularly nice route from Sinaia (seven to 10 hours, yellow and blue stripes) starts at either Cota 1400 or Cota 2000 at **Cabana Mioriţa**, then heads to Cabana Piatra Arsă, down to the Ialomiciora Monastery and then up to the Omul Peak (where there's also a cabana).

We recommend you discuss your desired route with the Sinaia Tourist Office, confirming duration, difficulty levels and accommodation. Stock up on torch (flashlight) batteries, take some sweets, fruit and plenty of liquids, and pack a lightweight jacket and fleece – with an average temperature of −3°C you'll be glad of it. Before you leave your châlet, sign the Tourists' Traffic Register, that way they can keep track of you if you run into difficulty.

ter. The nearby weather station has heat and electricity.

Cabana Babele CABIN $
(☎0744-567 290, 0244-315 304; www.babele.ro; per person 50 lei; ⊙year-round) Perched high at 2206m, this simple hikers' refuge dates from 1937. Doubles have private bathroom. There's a restaurant on the premises.

Cabana Caraiman CABIN $
(⊙May-Sep) Cabana Caraiman sits on an outcrop with vertiginous, breathtaking views of the valley below. Cosy and basic this makes for a memorable night's stay.

FROM SINAIA

Cabana Valea cu Brazi CABIN $
(☎0732-249 844; bed 25 lei) This is a so-so cabana at 1510m, a 10-minute walk up from Cota 1400.

Cabana Schiori CABIN $
(☎0244-313 655; Str Drumul Cotei 7; d from 100 lei) Walkable from Sinaia's centre, this is pretty fancy for a cabana, with a swank restaurant on-site too and 27 beds.

Getting There & Away

Roads wind up from Hwy 71 south of the mountains all the way to Cabana Babele – although much of the road as far as Piatra Arsa Cabana has been resurfaced, for the rest of the journey an ordinary car may struggle. The easiest way into the Bucegi from Sinaia is up two cable-car rides: one from the centre to the Cota 1400 station, then another up to Cota 2000 station. In the centre, the 30-person cable-car leaves half-hourly with two station points marked by elevation. Finally, buses outside Snow, just below the station, also go up to Cota 1400 (5 lei) when full; a taxi from the train station to Cota 1400 is a matter of negotiation, though expect to pay about 40 lei for the whole cab or 14 lei per person.

Predeal

POP 6740

Distinguished by its sci-fi-style train station, and ghostly wooden villas in varying states of decay on the hill opposite, Predeal's natural assets are a little more impressive: the surrounding forests are home to boar, wolves, foxes and deer. The town offers the first opportunity you'll hit heading south of Braşov. At 1033m, this resort is higher than Poiana Braşov or Sinaia, but the runs aren't as long and it misses the most popular access

HIKING TIMES

These are average times. People with higher or lower levels of fitness should adjust accordingly.

» **Babele to Bran** nine hours
» **Babele to Cota 2000** seven hours
» **Babele to Omu** two or three hours
» **Cota 2000 to Omu** four or five hours
» **Cota 2000 to Bran** 14 to 16 hours
» **Omu to Bran** eight hours

points into the Bucegi Mountains. Just south of town is the official border of Transylvania.

Activities

There are 13 hiking trails in the area. The loop from near Fulg de Nea up the mountain to the southern end of Str Poliştoaca takes about two hours. Trails north of town are open for cycling too.

Clăbucet Zona de Agrement SKIING
(☎0268-456 541) Clăbucet Zona de Agrement manages the eight-run mountain with two chairlifts and several drag lifts. Single-ride tickets for adult/child cost 18/10 lei. An all-day pass costs 118/80 lei. You can hire skis and snowboards near the base of the mountain.

Fulg de Nea SKIING
(Snow Flake; ☎0268-456 089; Str Telefericului 1) A good hub for winter and summer activity, Fulg de Nea, close to the ski lift, is Predeal's central ski school, and also offers ice skating, sleigh riding and hiking, plus biking and tennis in summer. Equipment rental is available for all diversions. It also runs a villa.

Sleeping & Eating

The tourist information centre can find you *cazare* (accommodation) to stay in for as little as 75 lei. The road to the lift is increasingly crowded with new three- and four-star places. Most hotels have a restaurant of sorts, and there are plenty of fast-food options along Str Mihai Săulescu. Some plush hotels are in the Trei Brazi district, a 20-minute walk northwest.

Fulg de Nea HOTEL $
(☎0268-456 089; Str Telefericului 1; per person 50 lei; P ☎) This pleasant 40-room, no-frills

accommodation has grotto-effect walls, and an inviting restaurant strung with skiing paraphernalia, that serves up decent steak and soup (mains 15 lei). The basic rooms are fine for flopping after the slopes. Right next to the button lift.

Vila Şoimulm GUESTHOUSE $
(☎0744-665 553, 0268-455 217; vilasoimul@yahoo.com; Str Şoimului 4; r 60 lei; P☎) With its faux log-cabin exterior and excellent self-catering area, this 18-room guesthouse is a winner. Fresh white walls, even fresher linen and modern en suites. About 60m up a zigzag street from the train station (behind the white church).

❶ Information

The **Tourist Information Centre** (☎0268-455 330; www.predeal.ro; ⊙8am-4pm Mon - Fri, 9am-2pm Sat & Sun) in a modern building in front of the train station offer info on *pensiunes*, as well as maps and info on hikes and bike rides.

Across B-dul Mihai Sălescu, the blue-and-white **Banca Comercială Romǎnǎ** (⊙8.30am-5pm Mon-Fri, to 12.30pm Sat) has a 24-hour ATM. In case of emergency, call **Salvamont** (☎0-SALVAMONT, 0726-686 696).

❶ Getting There & Away

The train station and bus/maxitaxi stop are right on the main street, B-dul Mihai Sălescu, which goes north to Braşov and south to Sinaia and Bucharest. The lifts are a 10-minute walk southeast.

The **Agenţia de Voiaj CFR** (☎0788-036 232) and the train-station ticket office share the same space.

Predeal is on the main Cluj–Napoca–Braşov–Bucharest line and you'll never wait long for a train heading to Braşov (14 lei, 40 minutes) or Bucharest (38 lei, two hours). Outside, buses or maxitaxis show up about every half-hour in the train-station parking lot where you can get to Braşov (6 lei, 30 minutes), Sinaia (5 lei, 30 minutes) or Bucharest (34 lei, two hours).

BRAŞOV

POP 274,400

Legend has it the Pied Piper reemerged from Hamelin in Braşov, and indeed there's something whimsically enchanting about it, with its fairy-tale turrets and cobbled streets. Dramatically overlooked by Mt Tâmpa, with trees sporting a russet-gold coat (and cocky Hollywood-style sign), this is a remarkably relaxed city.

Wander its maze of streets, stopping for caffeine injections at bohemian cafes between losing yourself in a beguiling coalescence of Austro-Hungarian gingerbread roofs, baroque gods, medieval spires and Soviet flat-tops. The city's centrepiece square is Piaţa Sfatului, a people-watcher's mecca. There are myriad things to see here, great restaurants and oodles of accommodation.

Many use Braşov as a base for skiing in nearby Poiana Braşov, trekking in the Piatra Craiului National Park, castle-watching at Bran and hairy drives on the Transfăgărăşan Road.

History

Established on an ancient Dacian site in the 13th century by Teutonic knights, Braşov became a German mercantile colony named Kronstadt (Brassó in Hungarian). The Saxons built ornate churches and townhouses, protected by a massive wall that still remains. The Romanians lived at Schei, just outside the walls, to the southwest.

One of the first public oppositions to the Ceauşescu government flared up here in 1987. Thousands of disgruntled workers took to the streets demanding basic foodstuffs. Ceauşescu called in the troops and three people were killed in the scuffle.

◉ Sights

Braşov is an outdoor type of place, best seen on DIY rambles around its medieval core.

The Town

Black Church CHURCH
(Biserica Neagră; adult/child 6/3 lei; ⊙10am-5pm Tue-Sat, to noon Sun, closed Mon) Braşov's main landmark, the Black Church is the largest Gothic church between Vienna and Istanbul, and still used by German Lutherans today. Built between 1383 and 1480, it was named for its appearance after a fire in 1689. The original statues from the exterior of the apse are now inside.

Worshippers drop coins through the wooden grates in the floor and hope for the best. The church's 4000-pipe organ, built by Buchholz of Berlin in 1839, is believed to be the only Buchholz preserved in its original form. Since 1891, organ recitals have been held in the church during July and August, at 6pm Tuesday, Thursday and Saturday (5 lei).

Note the scrape marks outside the church; some locals swear it's from soldiers' sharpened swords from centuries past. Also the original construction was intended to have a far larger bell tower (funds ran out); see how small it is in comparison to the mammoth base.

Piaţa Sfatului   SQUARE
This wide square, chock with cafes, was once the heart of medieval Braşov. In the centre stands the 1420 **council house** (Casa Sfatului), topped by a **Trumpeter's Tower** in which town councillors, known as centurions, would meet. These days at midday, traditionally costumed musicians appear from the top of the tower like figures in a Swiss clock, and trumpet songs. Apparently the tower is haunted; not surprising given that it was the site of countless tortures. Piaţa Sfatului was supposedly the scene of the last witch burning in Europe.

Braşov Historical Museum   MUSEUM
(☎0268-472 350; adult/student 7/1.50 lei) The old city hall today houses the two-floor, by-the-numbers Braşov Historical Museum, in which the history of the Saxon guilds is recounted (in limited English).

Hirscher House   GALLERY
Opposite the historical museum is the Renaissance Hirscher House (built 1539–45), also known as the 'Merchants House'. It was thoughtfully built by Apollonia Hirscher, the widow of Braşov mayor Lucas Hirscher, so that merchants could do business without getting rained on. Today it shelters a gallery.

Mureşenilor House
Memorial Museum   MUSEUM
(Muzeul Memorial Casa Mureşenilor; ☎0268-477 864; adult/student 4/1.50 lei, Sat & Sun free; ☉9am-5pm Tue-Fri, 10am-5pm Sat & Sun) On Piaţa Sfatului's western side stands the charming Mureşenilor House Memorial Museum, which honours the family of Jacob Mureşan, the first editor of the Romanian-language *Gazeta Transylvania*, a political newspaper published in the 19th century. No English is spoken.

EAST OF THE CENTRE
Mt Tâmpa   MOUNTAIN
Towering above town from the east is Mt Tâmpa, where Braşov's original defensive fortress was built. Vlad Ţepeş attacked it in 1458, finally dismantling it two years later and – out of habit – impaling some 40 merchants atop the peak. These days it's an easy trip up.

Many visitors go via the Tâmpa cable car offering stunning views from the top of Mt Tâmpa in a communist-era dining room. There's access to hiking trails up here. Walk south to reach the Hollywood-style Braşov sign, with a viewing platform.

You can also hike to the top in an hour following zigzag trails from the cable-car station (red triangles) or from the northeastern edge of the wall.

NORTH OF THE CENTRE
Running north of Piaţa Sfatului, the pedestrianised Str Republicii provides respite from the traffic that detracts from the charm of the rest of the Old Town. At the promenade's northern end is the wooden-cross **Memorial to Victims of the 1989 Revolution**. Across B-dul 15 de Noiembrie is the **Heroes' Cemetery**, a memorial slab listing 69 local victims.

A block west of the memorial, the **Art Museum** (☎0268-477 286; B-dul Eroilor 21; adult/child 3.50/1 lei; ☉10am-6pm Tue-Sun) and the **Ethnographic Museum** (☎0268-476 243; www.etnobrasov.ro; adult/child 5/1.50 lei; ☉9am-5pm Tue-Sun) adjoin each other. The former has a mishmash of Romanian paintings and decorative arts. The latter has laminated handouts (in English, German and French) explaining exhibits; ask for a demo of the early-20th-century eight-ribbon loom.

FREE **Citadel**   HISTORIC BUILDING
(Cetate; ☉11am-midnight) In 1524 a new wooden citadel was built in Braşov, on top of Citadel Hill just north, though the stone wall ruins you now see are from the 16th and 17th centuries. Today it houses a couple of beer patios.

FROM BRAŞOV WITH LOVE

Between 1950 and 1960, when Romania still considered itself Moscow's buddy, Braşov was named 'Oraşul Stalin', with the Russian dictator's name emblazoned into the side of Mt Tâmpa thanks to artistic deforestation. At the time the name was sadly apt, as ruthless forced industrialisation yanked thousands of rural workers from the countryside and plunked them down on the city in an attempt to crank the totalitarian motor of industry.

Braşov

To Agenţia de Voiaj CFR (300m);
Autogara 1 (3.2km);
Train Station (3.2km);
Autogara 2 (3.7km)

0   400 m
0   0.2 miles

5

32

To Opera
Braşov (1km)

To Kismet Dao
Villa (140m)

Piaţa
Teatrului

Str Mihai Eminescu

Str Nicolae Iorga

Str Lungă

Heroes'
Cemetery

Municipal
Council

Parcul
Central

B-dul 15 Noiembrie

District
Council
8

Str Gherea

1

B-dul Eroilor

Str Sadoveanu

Str Politechnicii

27

Şirul Livezii

33

18

Str Republicii

19

29

30

Str Sfântu Ioan

Str Postăvarului

Str Nicolae Bălcescu

Calea Poienii

Str Mureşenilor

Str Michael Weiss

35
34
28

Str Castelului

Str Piaţa
Enescu

36

16

24

Str Julius
Romer

17

Piaţa Sfatului

9 **4** **7**

Warthe
Hill

15

13

23

26

Str Dupa Ziduri

Str G Dinicu

MOUNT
TÂMPA

Str Hirscher

22

Str Stejerişului

37

2

Str Porta Schei

Str Cerbului

31

Str
Storii

To Poiana
Braşov (12km)

Str George Bariţiu

3

Str Paul
Richter

14

Str Traian Demetrescu

Str Cibinului

Str Castelului

10

Str Gheorghe Dima

Str Beethoven

Str G Coşbuc

Stadium

Aleea T Brediceanu

12

Aleea Tiberiu Brediceanu

Aleea Saguna

Str Gheorghe Băiulescu

Str Trotuş

Nisipului de Sus

Str Brâncoveanu

Str Prundului

Str L Arbore

Str Lacea

Military
Cemetery

Str Petöfi

Str După Inişte

20

Str Retezat

25

6

Piaţa
Unirii

11

Str Curcanilor

Str Piatra
Mare

21

Str Vasile Saftu

Str Democratiei

To Gabriel
Hostel (220m)

Braşov

TRANSYLVANIA BRAŞOV

AROUND THE WALL

Old Braşov is surrounded by a 12m-high and 3km-long 15th-century wall, built to defend the city from Turkish attacks. Seven bastions were also raised around the city at the most exposed points, each one defended by a guild whose members, pending danger, tolled their bastion bell.

The most popular viewing area is along the western section, which runs along a stream and pedestrianised Str Dupa Ziduri north to B-dul Eroilor. A good access point is 200m south of the Black Church. Above on the hillside are two towers – the **Black Tower** (Turnul Neagru) and **White Tower** (Turnul Alba); both are rather white actually – offering nice views, particularly when the setting sun casts a golden hue on Braşov.

On the wall's southeast corner, past the **Schei Gate** (Poatra Schei; 1825), is the 16th-century **Weavers' Bastion** (Bastionul Ţesătorilor; Str Castelui). Visit the **Weavers'**

Bastion Museum (Muzeul Bastionul Ţesătorilor; ✆0268-472 368; adult/child 4/1.50 lei; ✆10am-5.30pm Tue-Sun), housed in Braşov's only 15th-century building. The simple exhibits – in German and Romanian only – include an impressive fudge-coloured cityscape model of Braşov in the 17th century, made in 1896 by a German teacher in town.

SCHEI DISTRICT

In Saxon Braşov, Romanians were not allowed to enter the walled city but were banished to the Schei quarter in the southwest. Entry to this quarter from the walled city was marked by the Schei Gate. Passing through it, the sober rows of Teutonic houses change to the small, simpler houses of the Romanian settlement.

St Nicholas' Cathedral CHURCH
(St Nicolae din Scheii; ✆6am-9pm) St Nicholas' Cathedral, first built in wood in 1392, replaced by a Gothic stone church in 1495, and

later embellished in Byzantine style. Inside are murals of Romania's last king and queen, covered by plaster to protect them from communist leaders and uncovered in 2004.

First Romanian School Museum   MUSEUM
(Prima Scoala Romaneasca; adult/student 5/3 lei; ⊙Tues-Sun, 9am-5pm) This building packs a staggering amount of antique books, including the first Russian bible and 15th-century school books that admonish against theft in no uncertain terms: 'He who will steal this book shall be cursed!'.

🏃 Activities

Hikes are everywhere – from atop Mt Tâmpa in town, Poiana Brașov, Zărnești or into the Bucegi Mountains. Pick up maps from Himalaya or talk with a travel agent specialising in hikes. You can also ski on day trips to Poiana Brașov, Predeal and Sinaia.

TOP CHOICE Carpathian
Nature Tours   ADVENTURE TOUR
(☏0745-512 096; www.cntours.eu; Villa Hermani, Măgura Village, Piatra Craiului National Park) Based in the mountainside village of Măgura in Piatra Craiului National Park, this conservation-minded tour operator delivers immersive wildlife experiences, as well as trekking and cultural trips.

Roving România   GUIDED TOUR
(☏0744-212 065; www.roving-romania.co.uk) Tailored tours far from the madding crowd in the comfort of a Land Rover, and an expert on all things Romanian. Colin works with photographers, birdwatchers and history buffs, and has great contacts with local people giving you an authentic taste of rural life. Trips last a minimum of two days.

Dan Marin   GUIDED TOUR
(☏0744-319 708; www.transylvanian.ro) Run by an award-winning local Romanian, this tour company specialises in wildlife, and historical and cultural treks. Dan knows the forests well and is an expert tracker. For a group of four, a one-day hike costs €70.

DiscoveRomania   GUIDED TOUR
(☏0268-472 718; www.discoveromania.ro; Str Paul Richter 1; ⊙10am-3pm Mon-Fri) Encounters with Roma communities, visits with local craftsmen, birdwatching trips in the Danube Delta, wolf-tracking adventures in the Carpathians – all trips run by this environmentally sensitive company are designed to immerse you in Romanian culture.

Swimming Pool   SWIMMING POOL
(Str Aleaa Tiberiu 5; adult/child 12/5 lei; ⊙10am-8.30pm) A decent 25m pool for lane swimming, with a sun deck outside for the summer months.

★★ Festivals & Events

Brașov especially fizzes during the **Days of Brașov** festival, the first week after Easter (late April/early May), finishing with the fantastic **Juni Pageant**.

Brașov also hosts other events including the **International Chamber Music Festival**, which is usually held the first week in September in various venues around town, with a final concert at Bran Castle. Since 1968, the **Golden Stag Festival** (Cerbul de Aur; www.cerbuldeaur.ro), held in late September, has put pop music on the stage – folks such as James Brown, Joe Cocker and Kylie Minogue have performed – however, it was cancelled in 2011 and 2012.

TEDDY BEARS' PICNIC

Thanks to its megalomaniac dictator (under Ceaușescu none but he was allowed to hunt), 60% of Europe's brown bears are today found in Romania (an estimated 6000).

The chances of you seeing one of these sizeable Yogis are high if you're trekking or going to a bear hide (where you're more or less guaranteed a sighting; try Carpathian Nature Tours). A cousin of the grizzly, Romanian bears are smaller but have the same powerful hump of muscle on their back, and they can also move at 30 mph.

Hikers have been mauled and even killed by bears in recent years, usually as a result of surprising them, so here's a few tips. Try to pitch your tent in an open spot so they can see you, keeping your food at least 4m high in the branches of a tree. Also, any used sanitary material or trash should be kept in a ziplock bag. Should you find yourself in the presence of a mother and cub, stand still to signify you're not afraid, and make yourself bigger by waving your arms. Similarly, when walking through dense forest, talk loudly to announce your presence; the last thing a bear wants is to engage with you.

Etnovember is an imaginative festival, held in November since 1998, that highlights traditions of Romanians and many ethnic minorities. Watch out too for **Oktoberfest**; organised by the Saxon element of the city, it follows the Bavarian tradition of rivers of alcohol, tents and music.

🛏 Sleeping

TOP CHOICE **Casa Wagner** HOTEL $$
(📞0268-411 253; www.casa-wagner.com; Piaţa Sfatului; s/d incl breakfast 269/315 lei; @🤶) This former 15th-century German bank is now a boutique hotel with 24 well-appointed rooms. Right in the heart of the city, its exposed-brick walls, tasteful furnishings, modern en suites, welcoming breakfast area and pleasant management make this an excellent choice.

Bella Muzica HOTEL $$
(📞0268-477 956; www.bellamuzica.ro; Piaţa Sfatului 19; s/d 220/270 lei; 🤶) Within its wine-coloured corridors are 34 dark-wood and exposed-brick rooms. Very comfy beds, fans, en suites, friendly staff and cable TV all help make it a firm choice for aesthetes – and we haven't even mentioned its dead central location or fabulous restaurant yet.

Rolling Stone Hostel HOSTEL $
(📞0740-518 681, 0268-513 965; www.rollingstone .ro; Str Piatra Mare 2a; dm 38 lei, r from 115 lei; 😊@🤶) Run by helpful sisters with unlimited reserves of energy, super friendly Stone attracts a cosmo stew of travellers. Dorms are a little crowded, but for the smaller one downstairs. The private double room (without bathroom) has elegant couches and armoire. You'll be given a map and bags of info on arrival. Personal lockers, organised tours and basic breakfast. Laundry is 15 lei.

Casa Rozelor BOUTIQUE HOTEL $$$
(📞0268-475 212; www.casarozelor.ro; Str Michael Weiss 20; s/d incl breakfast 315/380 lei; @🤶) This hidden courtyard oasis has five beautiful apartments, some with split-level floors adjoined by spiral staircases. Each is defiantly individual but all fuse contemporary chic with traditional Saxon; think antique furniture and modern art on brick walls. Glorious!

Hotel Coroana HOTEL $$
(📞0268-477 448; www.aro-palace.ro/hotel-brasov -coroana; Str Republicii 62; s/d/tr 161/221/230 lei; 🤶) With its wide-screen views of Republic St, this fine art-nouveau and baroque beauty is plusher than its sister hotel right next door (The Postăvarul). Traditonal rooms are spacious, have cable TV, and fresh-looking en suites. Check out the stunning stained-glass windows in the stairwell.

Gabriel Hostel HOSTEL $
(📞0744-844 223; www.brasovtrips.com; Str Vasile Saftu 41a; dm/d/tr 40/80/120 lei; 😊@🤶) Spotless Gabriel has peaceful accommodation in uncrowded dorms. There's also an outside area for barbeques and a welcoming kitchen/self-catering area, plus individual lockers. Eponymous owner Gabriel offers myriad day trips (plus the odd shot of home-made plum brandy) and is a qualified guide. Take bus 51 from the train station to the last stop; the door is just across the street.

Pensiunea Curtea Braşoveană HOTEL $$
(📞0268-472 336; www.curteabrasoveana.ro; Str Băilor 16; r €60; ❄@🤶) This plush courtyard hotel in a 100-year-old house has eight lovely rooms with minibar, air-con, cable TV and all the mod cons. Some rooms have wood ceilings. Sauna, friendly management and free breakfast buffet top it off nicely.

Hotel Aro Palace HOTEL $$$
(📞0268-478 800; www.aro-palace.ro; B-dul Eroilor 27; s/d new 450/550 lei, old 300/350 lei; ❄❄🤶) Lounge music wafts across Aro's marbled lobby, dotted with Corbusier-style chairs, and over to its art-deco bar. As well as a swimming pool this comfy hotel has internationally accented rooms with great views, balconies and en suites. For cheaper rooms ask to stay in the old wing.

Hotel Postăvarul HOTEL $
(📞0268-477 448; Str Republicii 62; s/d/tr 80/138/166 lei; 🤶) This early-20th-century hotel with suitably creaky stairs, communal washrooms, endless corridors and tiny rooms with sloping ceilings, bureaus and basins, is like something out of an existentialist novel.

Kismet Dao Villa HOSTEL
(📞0268-514 296; www.kismetdao.com; Str Neagoe Basarab 8; dm 45 lei, d with shared bathroom 135 lei; 😊@🤶) There's a pleasant vibe here: maybe it's those colourful murals and friendly staff. Dorms are fresh with crayon-coloured walls, parquet flooring and individual lockers. Some are cosier than others, particularly 'Snorer's Den'. The private rooms are

winners with blue walls, TV, fan and reading lights. There's also a communal computer and film lounge.

Eating

The city has bags of choice from sugary eats at bakeries on Str George Barițiu, to shadowy boho restaurants and high-class steakhouses. Piața Sfatului is great for cafes and breakfast while Str Republicii is more suited to people-watching cafes.

TOP CHOICE Bistro de l'Arte BISTRO $$
(www.bistrodelarte.ro; Str Piața Enescu 11; mains 12-28 lei; 🕾) Tucked down a cobbled street straight out of a folk tale, this chichi joint has decidedly boho genes with walls dotted with local artists' work, and sculptures. Gazpacho soup, shrimps and tomato gratin, snails... or just a croque monsieur. Perfect for nursing a cappucino and working on your laptop.

Bella Musica ROMANIAN, MEXICAN $$
(Str George Barițiu 2; mains 20-30 lei; 🕾) In a vaulted grotto-like cellar aflicker with candlelight, Musica offers intimate dining. Its menu spans Mexican fare such as tasty fajitas, *ciorba* (soup), pasta, foie gras, salads and schnitzel steak. Try the goulash beef stew with dumplings.

Sergiana ROMANIAN $$
(Str Mureșenilor 28; mains 30 lei; ⊙10am-11pm) Authentically Saxon, this subterranean carnivore's heaven has two sections: the white room for 'pure' nonsmokers, and the exposed brick vaults for *fumeurs*. Choose from a menu of venison, stag, boar, pork ribs, sirloin steak, and Transylvanian sour soup with smoked gammon and tarragon (11.50 lei). A hunter's dream.

Keller Steak House STEAKHOUSE $$$
(www.kellersteakhouse.ro; Str Hirscher 2; mains: 85 lei; 🖮) One of Brașov's premier steakhouses, here you can eat inside its ochre interior or tackle your sirloin outside on the terrace. Steak and roquefort cheese, salad and boar... one thing is for certain: you won't leave here with an empty stomach.

Restaurant Gustari ROMANIAN $$
(Piața Sfatului 14; mains 15-25 lei) Settle into an umbrella-shaded wicker seat and ponder a menu of soups, salads, ice creams or a wide choice of spirits and coffees. The breakfast is great, as is the view of the midday trumpeters in the Trumpeter's Tower

Casa Româneasca ROMANIAN $$
(Piața Unirii; mains 15-30 lei) Piping out aromas of pork crackling in onion, meatball soup, chicken liver and bacon and *sarmalute cu mamaliguta* (boiled beef rolled with vegetables, spices and cabbage), this redolent restaurant can be smelled from down the street.

Baritiu 16 'Organic' JUICE BAR $
(Str George Barițiu 16; ⊙8.30am-8pm; 🍃) This bijou hole-in-the-wall cafe is the vitamin shot you need to give your feet sightseeing wings. Banish those carb-heavy meat dishes with a carrot and orange juice, or a healthy sandwich.

Spar SUPERMARKET $
(Str Nicolae Bălcescu; ⊙24hr) This fully stocked supermarket is in the basement of the Star department store.

Drinking

Deane's Irish Pub & Grill PUB
(Str Republicii 19) As if transplanted from Donegal, this subterranean Irish pub, with its early-20th-century cloudy mirrored bar, shadowy booths and old-world soundtracks, is a haven for the Guinness-thirsty. Live music some nights.

Festival 39 BAR
(Str Republicii 62; ⊙10am-1am) This romantic watering hole is an art-deco dream of stained-glass ceilings, wrought-iron finery, candlebra and leather banquettes, and has a bar long enough to keep an army of barflies content. Sheer elan.

☆ Entertainment

Vintage Pub BAR, CLUB
(www.thevintagepub.ro/brasov; Str Livada Postei 1) A spit from the centre, Vintage is the city's premier haunt for the young and beautiful. DJs interchange with live sets and, groan... karaoke.

Gheorghe Dima State Philharmonic LIVE MUSIC
(Str Hirscher 10) Performing mainly between September and May, this orchestra has a fine reputation.

Opera Brașov OPERA
(🕿0268-415 990; Bisericii Române 51) Stages mainly classics. Tickets for all performances can be purchased at the venues.

Sică Alexandrescu Drama Theatre THEATRE
(☎0268-412 969; Piaţa Teatrului 1) Come here
for plays, recitals and opera year-round.

Puppet Theatre THEATRE
(Teatrul de Păpuşi Arlechino; ☎0268-475 243; Str
Hirscher 10; tickets from 5 lei) This place stages
creative shows for kids on Sundays.

Alliance Française CULTURAL BUILDING
(☎0268-412 179; www.afbv.home.ro; B-dul Eroilor
33; ☺9am-5pm Mon, Wed & Fri, 1-8pm Tue &
Thu) Courses in French, poetry recitals and
French films screened occassionally.

🛍 Shopping

To avoid the predictable oeuvre of Dracula
mugs and spooky T-shirts, try the shop at
the Ethnographic Museum for handicraft
mementos.

Himalaya OUTDOOR EQUIPMENT
(www.himalaya.ro; Str Rebublicii 23; ☺10am-7pm
Mon-Fri, to 2pm Sat) Sells ski and hiking boots,
walking maps, fleeces, sleeping bags, tents
and rock-climbing gear.

Sport Virus OUTDOOR EQUIPMENT
(☎0268-418 115; www.sportvirus.ro; Str George
Bariţiu 24; ☺10am-7pm) Jackets, walking
shoes, tents, rock-climbing gear and backpacks. And don't be fooled by the sign that
reads 'Jack Wolfskin', this is Sport Virus.

Okian Bookstore BOOKSHOP
(Str Mureşenilor 1; ☺10am-6pm Mon-Fri) Up the
stairs on the 1st floor, this bookshop has a
generous selection of English-language novels at very agreeable prices; classics sucha as
Dracula, Moby Dick, and plenty of Poe and
Hardy.

Librăria George Coşbuc BOOKSHOP
(Str Republicii 29; ☺9am-7pm Mon-Fri, 10am-4pm
Sat) Nonfiction books only, but plenty of use-
ful hiking maps.

ℹ Information

EMERGENCY Salvamont (☎0725-826 668;
Str Varga 23) Emergency rescue service for the
mountains.
INTERNET ACCESS Red Net Internet (Str
George Bariţiu 8; per hr 2.50 lei; ☺7.30am-10pm)
Internet Cafe (Str Michael Weiss 11; ☺24hr)
LEFT LUGGAGE Train Station (per day small/
big bag 5/7 lei; ☺24hr) The left-luggage office
is in the underpass that leads out to the tracks.
MEDICAL SERVICES County Hospital
(☎0268-333 666; Calea Bucureşti 25-27;
☺24hr) Northeast of the centre.

ℹ
MAPS & PUBLICATIONS

The information centre hands out a
useful, free *Sam's City Guide* with
maps of Braşov and Poiana Braşov.
Braşov In Your Pocket (6 lei) is a
quarterly miniguide and has plenty of
worthy foodie and accommodation
tips. It's available at the tourist office
and some hotel lobbies.
The free, biweekly Romanian magazine *Zile şi Nopţi* (Days and Nights;
www.zilesin opti.ro) is found in bars and
cafes and has entertainment listings.
Check www.brasovtravelguide.ro or
www.brasov.ro for basic info.

Sensiblu (☎0268-411 248; Str Republicii 15;
☺9am-6pm Mon-Fri, 8am-3pm Sat) Well-
stocked pharmacy.
MONEY You'll find numerous ATMs and banks
on Str Republicii and B-dul Eroilor.
Raiffeisen Bank (Piaţa Sfatului) Charges 5%
commission for changing travellers cheques.
POST & TELEPHONE Central Post Office
(Str Iorga Nicolae 1) Opposite the Heroes'
Cemetery.
**TOURIST INFORMATION Tourist Informa-
tion Centre** (☎0268-419 078; www.brasovcity
.ro; Piaţa Sfatului 30) Easily spotted in the gold
city-council building in the centre of the square;
the English-language-speaking staff offer free
maps and brochures and track down hotel
vacancies and train and bus times. The centre
shares space with the history museum.
TRAVEL AGENCIES Active Travel (☎0268-
477 112; www.activetravel.ro; Str Republicii
50; ☺10am-6pm Mon-Fri, 10am-1pm Sat)
Leads trekking/hiking, mountain-biking and
cultural tours. It also rents bikes (three/24
hours 28/46 lei); €50 deposit required.

ℹ Getting There & Away
Bus

Maxitaxis and microbuses are the best way
to reach places near Braşov, including Bran,
Râşnov, Sinaia, Hârman and Sfântu Gheorghe.
Otherwise it's generally better to go by train as
the bus situation is ever-changing.
The most accessible station is **Bus Station 1**
(Autogara 1; ☎0268-427 267), next to the train
station, for maxitaxis and long-distance buses.
From 6am to 7.30pm maxitaxis leave every
half-hour for Bucharest (30 lei, 2½ hours),
stopping in Buşteni and Sinaia. About four or
five maxitaxis leave for Sibiu (35 lei, 2½ hours),

stopping in Făgăraş town. Nine or 10 go daily to Sighişoara (30 lei) en route to Târgu Mureş (40 lei, four to five hours). A handful of buses go to Bistriţa (33 lei, seven to eight hours), Constanţa (55 lei) and Iaşi (35 lei). Buses also head to Hărman (3 lei, 20 minutes).

A few daily buses to Sfântu Gheorghe (6 lei, 45 minutes) leave from a parking lot on the opposite side of the train station from Autogara 1. Look for the tiny blue sign 'Braşov-Sfantu Gheorghe'.

Nearly hourly buses go to Prejmer (4 lei, 30 minutes), which confusingly stop at the intersection 100m to the right (west) of the train station as you face away from the entrance. Catch it across the street from Restaurant Făget.

Bus 51 reaches the centre from the train station (prepurchase your ticket). From the centre, hail a bus at the corner of Str Nicolae Bălcescu and Str Gherea.

Bus Station 2 (Autogara 2; ☎0268-426 332; Str Avram Iancu 114), 1km northwest of the train station, sends half-hourly buses marked 'Moieciu-Bran' to Râşnov (3 lei, 25 minutes) and Bran (6 lei, 40 minutes) from roughly 6.30am to 11.30pm, Take bus 12 to/from the centre (it stops at the roundabout just north of the station). A dozen daily buses go to Zărneşti (6 lei, one hour)

The main bus stop in town is the 'Livada Poştei' at the western end of B-dul Eroilor in front of the County Library (Biblioteca Judeţeană). From here bus 20 goes half-hourly to Poiana Braşov (4 lei, 20 minutes). Buy your ticket from the kiosk opposite the Student Culture House before boarding.

All European routes are handled by **Eurolines** (TUI Travel; ☎0268-475 219; www.eurolines.ro; Piaţa Sfatului 18; ☺9am-8pm Mon-Fri, to 4pm Sat), which sells tickets for buses to Germany, Italy, Hungary and other European destinations.

Train

The train station is 2km northeast of the town centre, past grey block-housing neighbourhoods. Advance tickets are sold at the **Agenţia de Voiaj CFR office** (☎0268-477 015; Str 15 de Noiembre 43; ☺8am-7.30pm Mon-Fri).

Sample direct train services include the following (prices are for 2nd-class seats on rapid trains):

DESTINATION	PRICE (LEI)	DURATION (HOURS)	FREQUENCY (DAILY)
Bucharest	44	2½	10
Cluj-Napoca	73	6	5
Iaşi	83	8½	1
Sf Gheorghe	11	½	15
Sibiu	40	2¾	6
Sighişoara	35	2½	14

International train services include three daily trains to Budapest (seat/sleeper 155/200 lei, 14 hours), two to Vienna (250/320 lei, 18 hours) and also one daily train to Prague (479/559 lei, 21 hours) and Istanbul (129/164 lei, 19 hours).

❶ Getting Around

Bus 51 runs from the train station and Autogara 1 through the centre, stopping at Piaţa Unirii south of the centre. From Autogara 2, take bus 12 from the 'Stadion Tineretului' stop on nearby Str Stadionului (just north of the bus station).

Autonom (☎0268-415 250; www.autonom .com) usually has the best car-hire prices (Daewoo Matiz from 120 lei per day, with significant discounts for long-term rentals) and will deliver a car to you anywhere inside Braşov free of charge. **Budget** (☎0269-474 564) has an office inside the Hotel Aro Palace that's sometimes staffed. **Transilvania Travel** (☎0268-477 623; www.transilvaniatravel.com; Str Republicii 62; ☺10am-6pm Mon-Fri, to 2pm Sat) also hires cars (Dacia Logan starting at 128 lei per day).

The taxi stand outside the train station has a good reputation. A couple of reputable companies include **Martax** (☎0268-313 040) and **Tod** (☎0268-321 111).

AROUND BRAŞOV

This region of castles, Saxon churches and ski lifts provides a colourful alternative to Braşov's own attractions – making it easy to stay in the area for a week or more. The most popular trip – usually done as a day trip from Braşov – is to see the 'Dracula castle' at Bran.

Bran

POP 5177

On a rocky bluff rising from wolf-prowled forests perches a gaunt castle, its mass of turrets a sinister refrain...right? Sort of, but Bran Castle, despite its tenuous link to Vlad Ţepeş, is anything but gloomy. Inside it's positively sunny, with a geranium-festooned courtyard, bright white rooms, hidden stairways and a palpable effort on the part of its blue-blooded owner to distance the place from any mention of garlic.

Guarded from the east by the Bucegi Mountains and from the west by the Piatra Craiului massif, its setting is indisputably stunning. If you've a determined taste for the Gothic you'll find the castle is best seen from a distance, its grey facade often shrouded in mist. Creep a little closer and

Bran town itself is a carnivalesque gauntlet of stalls hawking vampiric T-shirts, and myriad day trippers who take away from the atmosphere. There's even a 'haunted castle' funhouse next to the entrance, complete with staff dressed as werewolves and vamps who chase you around. Embrace the tack!

The entrance to Bran Castle, signposted 'Muzeul Bran', is on the left as you enter the town. By far the bulk of visitors see Bran as a half-day trip, along with a stop at Râşnov Castle. Daring hiking trails down from the Bucegi wind up here too.

◉ Sights

Bran Castle
CASTLE

(☎0268-237 700; www.bran-castle.com; adult/student 25/5 lei, camera & video 20 lei; ⊙9am-7pm Tue-Sun, noon-7pm Mon May-Sep, 9am-5pm Tue-Sun Oct-Apr) Facing the flatlands and backed by mountains, the 60m-tall Bran Castle is spectacular. If you can manage to avoid bottlenecks from tour groups that appear in waves, you may enjoy the largely renovated interiors and claustrophobic nooks and crannies.

Built by Saxons from Braşov in 1382 to defend the Bran pass against Turks, the castle may have housed Vlad Ţepeş for a few nights on his flight from the Turks in 1462, following their attack on the Poienari fortress in the Argeş Valley. From 1920 Queen Marie lived in the castle, and it served as a summer royal residence until the forced abdication of King Michael in 1947. It became a museum in 1957. Much of the original furniture imported from Western Europe by Queen Marie is still inside the castle. A fountain in the courtyard conceals a labyrinth of secret underground passages. Your ticket for the castle includes entrance to the open-air village museum, with a dozen traditional buildings at the foot of the castle.

Opposite the former customs house are some remains of the old defensive wall, which divided Transylvania from Wallachia (best viewed from the soldiers' watchtower in the castle). On the southern side of the wall is an endearingly petite stone chapel, built in 1940 in memory of Queen Marie. The church, now boarded up, is a copy of a church in the queen's palace grounds in Balchik, Bulgaria (formerly southern Dobrogea). A memorial tomb where the queen's heart lies has been carved in the mountain, on the north side of the wall.

In 2006, after 60 years in communist/government hands, Bran Castle's keys were handed back to Dominic Habsburg, a New York–based architect and Queen Marie's grandson. The castle was initially put on the market in 2007 (a US$135 million final sale price was predicted), but in 2009 the family decided not to sell it, ensuring the castle would remain open as a museum.

Vama Bran Museum
MUSEUM

(adult/student 8/2 lei) The Vama Bran Museum, down the hill behind Bran Castle, has original items found in the castle – plates, furniture and various sundries – displayed in nine rooms.

✹ Festivals & Events

Sâmbra Oilor
FESTIVAL

The three-day Sâmbra Oilor, held in late September/early October, is a huge pastoral festival celebrated to welcome the sheep home from the hills.

🛏 Sleeping & Eating

Bran's coven of villas and *pensiunes* grows every year.

Hanul Bran
HOTEL $

(☎0268-236 556; www.hanulbran.ro; Str Principala 384; s/d 100/120 lei) Probably the plushest dead central option ('scuse the pun), this ochre-coloured hotel with a bubbly adjoining restaurant enjoys a dramatic view of the castle. Large genial rooms with comfy beds, TV and en suites.

Guesthouse
PENSION $

(☎0744-306 062; Str Principala; r 120-140 lei, tr 150 lei) With terrific views of Bran Castle, this guesthouse sits almost opposite Hanul Bran and is clean and family-friendly with a kids' adventure playground and communal lounge and dining room.

Popasul Reginei
PENSION $

(☎0268-236 834; www.popasulreginei.ro; Str Aurel Stoian 398; r 120 lei; 🐕) Just across the park and down the street from Bran Castle, this 16-room place has an attractive restaurant serving traditional fare (though waiters are a bit gruff). Tasteful rooms with white walls, en suites, TVs and flower-filled verandahs.

❶ Getting There & Away

Bran is an easy DIY day trip from Braşov. Buses marked 'Bran-Moieciu' (6 lei, one hour) depart every half-hour from Brașov's Bus Station 2 (Autogara 2). Return buses to Brașov leave Bran every half-hour from roughly 7am to 6pm in winter, and 7am to 10pm in summer. All buses to Brașov stop each way at Râșnov.

From Bran there are about a dozen buses daily to Zărnești (5 lei, 40 minutes), and a few to Pitești originating from Brașov.

AROUND BRAN

Be sure to stop at the roadside for fresh cheese and honey as you meander through green hills studded with farms and hayricks. Some 4km southeast of Bran, on a road that starts paved but quickly deteriorates to moonscape, is the village of Şimon, with shoulder-to-shoulder villas and hiking trails leading into the Bucegi Mountains. Mama Cozonacilor (☑0745-151 424; www.branturism. ro; r 80 lei; 🛜) is a pleasant 25-room complex backed by a steep hill; staff arrange activities such as hikes, biking, horse rides and paintball. Breakfast is 25 lei.

Moieciu de Jos, 4km southwest of Bran on the road to Câmpulung, is known for its cheese with a pine aroma. It celebrates a summer festival at the end of June. From Moieciu de Jos, a dirt track leads northwest to Peștera, named after the village's 160m-long cave said to be full of bats. From Peștera, it's an easy 6km ride or hike north through Măgura to Zărnești.

Continuing south along the upper course of the Moieciu River, you reach Moieciu de Sus, a long, cinematically perfect valley of low hills and rocky peaks, specked with clumps of fir trees and shepherd shacks. This meandering village is gorgeous Hobbit Shire material – if three-quarters of the Shire were guesthouses, that is. The endless line of *pensiunes* charge 100 to 140 lei for double rooms, without breakfast. Hiking trails into the Bucegi Mountains are marked from here.

Staggering views of the mountains unfold along the road signposted to Câmpulung, offering a breathtaking panorama of rolling green hills and farmhouses teetering on ridgetops at 1290m before reaching the minuscule Fundata, 25km south of Bran, where you can cross-country ski or cycle. On the last Sunday of August this village holds the fascinating Mountain Festival (Nedeia Munților), bringing together local artisans.

Continuing south along the same road, you come to Podu Dâmboviței, home to the Peștera Dâmbovicioarei. This 870m-deep cave is not particularly noteworthy but the drive to it is. Sheer rock faces line either side of the road, as do villagers, who frequently stand on the roadside selling homemade cheese (*cașcaval de casă*), sausages, smoked and dried meats, plus fresh milk.

Poiana Brașov

She might not be as starry as Verbier (though Jude Law and Nicole Kidman have left a sequinned trail), but with her winter coat on Poiana Brașov (1030m) is a very pretty ski resort and well serviced by a plethora of hotels and chalets. While advanced skiers will head for Sinaia, intermediates and beginners will appreciate gentle runs to practise their carve. Just 12km from Brașov, it's an easy day trip. Come summer, Poiana Brașov is also popular with hikers, thanks to its year-round cable car taking you right into the panorama of mountains and forests.

The recently built St Ivan Butezatorul church (Str Valea Dragă) in the centre is finished in Maramureș style – made entirely of wood, with a tall spire.

🏃 Activities

Skiing

Poiana Brașov has 12 runs – including two blacks (each about 2km long) – that are accessed by two cable-car lifts run by ANA (☑0268-262 413), with a chairlift and five drag lifts higher up. The main cable car, a 15-minute walk up the road southwest from the bus stop (past the St Ivan Butezatorul church), operates all year. Another is next to Hotel Sport. Ski rental starts at 40 lei per day, an all-day chairlift pass is about 250 lei and a five-trip pass is 120 lei.

The ski season runs from December to March, sometimes later. Check out www .poiana-brasov.ro for ski conditions.

ANA holds group and private lessons (it's about 110 lei per hour for two people) in English, French and German; check with its office situated at Hotel Sport. An alternative, Club Rossignol (☑0721-200 470; ⊙9am-5.30pm), across from the main lift, also hires skis or snowboards for 40 lei per day.

Hiking

The Postăvaru Massif nestles between the Cheii Valley, Timișului Valley and Poiana Brașov, and has dozens of trails of varying levels of difficulty to choose from.

From Poiana Brașov you can hike to Cristianul Mare (1802m, three hours, marked with red crosses), the massif's highest peak (or just take the cable car up). From the top the trail (marked with yellow bar) leads to another (marked with red triangles), that leads east down to the road that links Timişu de Jos (on the Sinaia–Braşov rail line) with Timişu de Sus (2½ hours). Turn left for Jos, right for Sus.

You can also hike directly down to Timişu de Jos from Cabana Cristianul Mare in three to four hours. The trail is marked from the cabana with blue stripes, then blue crosses. Instead of following the blue-cross trail where the path diverges, you can continue following the blue-stripe trail, which eventually takes you over the top of Mt Tâmpa to Braşov. This trail (1½ hours) follows the old Braşov road.

From Poiana Braşov you can also easily hike to Râşnov (two to three hours, yellow crosses, then left on the road to the trail marked with blue stripes) or tackle the more strenuous hike to Predeal (five to seven hours, yellow stripes).

🛏 Sleeping

Prices here are for high season (between December and mid-March); prices at all but lower-end places fall by 25% or more at other times.

Vila Zorile CHALET $$
(📞0268-262 286; www.vila-zorile.ro; Str Poiana Ruia 6; s/d/f incl breakfast 178/198/285 lei; 🅿🛜) Jude Law and Nicole Kidman stayed at this very cosy chalet – with denim blue rooms with minibar, pine furniture, armoire and cable TV – while filming *Cold Mountain*. Charming management.

TOP CHOICE Hotel Sport HOTEL $$$
(📞0268-407 330; www.anahotels.ro; s/d incl breakfast from €160/190; 🅿❄🛜) Renovated in 2011, new-look Sport packs a punch with 'Corbusier'-style leather couches, retro lights, granite walls and contemporary rooms with chocolate brown carpets, cool en suites and decked verandahs. You can even have a one-hour massage (€75).

Hotel Alpin HOTEL
(📞0268-262 343; www.hotelalpin.ro; s/d/apt 500/522/770 lei; 🅿❄🛜) This chandeliered giant is kitschy but comfortable, with a wide range of facilities including massage, bike rental, poool and sauna. Rooms are finished to an international standard, if a little bland.

Poiana Ursului CHALET
(📞0268-262 216; www.poianaursului.ro; s/d incl breakfast €65/75; 🛜) Ten minutes' walk from the ski lift, this hotel has 38 decent-sized rooms with comfy beds, green walls, minimal decor and the odd stained carpet.

Pensiune Cassandra PENSION
(📞0268-262 281; s/d 100/120 lei) Take the left turn at Restaurant Ambiance on the main road and follow a potholed track to its end. Cassandra's a little smoky and has comfy rooms with gaudy quilts and fresh en suites.

ℹ Information

There is no tourist information office in Poiana Braşov; check websites such as www.poiana-brasov.ro or www.poiana.info.ro (in Romanian). The local **Salvamont** (📞0725-826 688; Cabana Cristianul Mare) will come to the rescue any time of the day or in case of emergency.

ℹ Getting There & Away

From Braşov, bus 20 (3.50 lei, 20 minutes, every 30 minutes) runs from the Livada Poştei bus stop, opposite the County Library at the western end of B-dul Eroilor, to Poiana Braşov.

Râşnov

Eighteen kilometres south of Braşov, the hilltop ruins of 13th-century **Râşnov fortress** (Cetatea Râşnov; admission 10 lei; ⏰9am-8pm May-Oct, to 6pm Nov-Apr), built by Teutonic Knights as protection against Tartar and Turkish invasion, feel considerably less touristy than Bran's. Visitors can wander the grounds, where there's a church, a jail and nice views of the mountains. A small museum includes gruesome prints of torture, while there's also a 17th-century, 146m-deep well built by Turkish prisoners, who were promised freedom once it was completed (it took them 17 years!). The **Info Turist Centre** (📞0740-510 665; guteanu_25gabriel@yahoo.com; Str Republicii 13; ⏰8am-3pm Mon-Fri) is 50m from the main square.

Buses bound for Bran come within 200m of the centre of Râşnov; a few 'Râşnov' buses go through it – finishing at the edge of town.

Zărneşti

POP 26,370

There's a bit of tumbleweed blowing through low-slung, rustic Zărneşti, for not much happens save for trekkers alighting from Braşov, bound for stunning Piatra Craiului National Park. Nicole Kidman had to hang around here for the filming of *Cold Mountain* but you don't have to – instead push on up those forested hills to the pretty village of Măgura in the heart of Piatra Craiului. Buses stop at a roundabout, near the post office and about 100m past the city hall and centre along Str Metropolit Ion Meţianu. The train station is about 1km east of (before) the city hall.

Sleeping

Cabana Gura Raului   GUESTHOUSE $
(☎0722-592 375; per person 30 lei) Well positioned at the foot of the Craiului National Park (making it perfect for an early morning hike), the 17 rooms, all with shared bathrooms, in this large creaky edifice are boxy but adequate. Breakfast is an extra 10 lei.

❶ Information

BCR (Str Metropolit Ion Meţianu 8; ⊙8.30am-5pm Mon-Fri, to 12.30pm Sat) Has a 24-hour ATM.

Piatra Craiului National Park Office
(☎0268-223 165; www.pcrai.ro; Str Topliţei 150; ⊙8am-4pm Mon-Thu, to 2.30pm Fri) In a building shaped like a mountain range about 2km towards the mountains, west from the centre – follow the 'Plaiu Foii' sign at the bus-stop roundabout, then go left at the fork. It has excellent maps and guides available (from 82 lei per day).

Salvamont (☎0722-553 121; Str Metropolit Ion Meţianu 17; ⊙8am-5pm) The closed information centre (a pink building 50m east of the city hall) now houses this scraggly local rescue team which can help point your way (in English).

❶ Getting There & Away

There are 14 buses leaving weekdays to Autogara 2 in Braşov (6 lei, one hour), and about half that at weekends. About five or six daily buses head to Bran (4 lei, 40 minutes). If you're headed up to stay in Măgura village you'll need to organise a lift from up there or thumb a ride.

Măgura

Deep in Piatra Craiului National Park, this is an alpine idyll of rolling meadows, shepherd dogs, and pastel cottages piping smoke into the mountainous sky; all of them backed by the massive Mt Craiului (meaning 'big rock'). It's also a handy place from which to launch yourself into a number of hiking trails that begin from here. Villa Hermani, run by the Carpathian Nature Tours, is the best place to stay. Ask about going on a bear-watching trip, and for directions to the bat cave of Peştera, 1km away. Over a period of a year in this area, 50 shepherd dogs were taken by wolves.

❶ Getting There and Away

Măgura is 15 km from Bran and 20 minutes' drive from Zărneşti. From Braşov head past Râsnov towards Zărneşti, where you enter Piatra Craiului National Park along a knobbly road; 1km on head left across a small bridge then keep going uphill for about 3km. You'll need wheels to get here. Alternatively, if you're coming to stay with Carpathian Nature Tours it can pick you up from the train station at Zărneşti (35 lei). Trains leave regularly from Braşov for Zărneşti, while you can catch buses from Bus Station 2 (Autogara 2).

WORTH A TRIP

BEAR WATCHING

Your spine tingles with anticipation as you sit silently watching the forest clearing through the window of the hide, ravens circling overhead providing a suitably Gothic prelude. Hidden in logs are entrails and tasty biscuits to catch the bears' olfactory attention (they can smell them up to 1km away). It can take a while but the first arrival of the Carpathian brown bear is unforgettable as it shuffles into view; suspiciously eyeing you through the window on its hind legs. Usually it's mums and cubs who linger; the males – and remember these are cousins of the grizzly so they're big – only come as it gets dark.

This wildlife trip is organised by Carpathian Nature Tours (www.cntours.eu; Măgura village; s/d incl breakfast & dinner €40/80), which takes you by Land Rover from Măgura (an hour's drive) to the Stramba valley, home to shepherds' flocks and meadows rolling into forest. There are two packs of wolves here and over 60 bears. Highly recommended, it costs €40 to visit the bear hide. Book well ahead.

Piatra Craiului National Park

Climbers, hikers and lovers swoon about Piatra Craiului and its twin-peaked Piatra Mică ('Stone of the Prince'), marked by a large stone cross, and La Om (2238m), which offers climbers one of Romania's greatest challenges. The 25km-long range covers 148-sq-km from Zărneşti down to Podu Dâmboviţei and rises from the ground in near-vertical limestone towers.

The national park office has maps for sale, including Dimap's 1:70,000 *Piatra Craiului* (10 lei) and *Postăvarul* (15 lei).

In May/June and September, Piatra Craiului receives heavy rainfall. Summer storms are possible and in winter much of the mountain cannot be accessed. Avalanches are common.

HIKING

Day-hike loops from Zărneşti are an option. For one that takes four to six hours, follow blue-stripe markers south of town, past Cabana Gura Râului; the trail then veers northwest to **Cabana Curmătura** (☎0744-706 941; shared/ private room 30/70 lei), where you can follow yellow vertical-stripe markers back to Zărneşti. An alternative return splinters east on the blue-dot trail up **Piatra Mică** (a 1816m peak).

Several trails meet up behind Cabana Curmătura, from where you can follow a blue-stripe trail in a looping direction west and north to Colţul Chiliilor Monastery peak (1125m, two hours). The blue-stripe trail back to the northwestern edge of Zărneşti from here is relatively flat (about two hours).

More-experienced hikers eye the tougher stuff, back on the western side of the range. You should have a guide who knows the area (ask at the park office or in Braşov). From northwestern Zărneşti, a road marked with red-stripe signs goes 11km to 849m **Cabana Plaiu Foii** (☎0726-380 323; r 120 lei). It's best to hike as the road's pretty rough. From the cabana, a very difficult trail (red stripes, four hours) goes up limestone cliffs to **La Lanturi** (or 'to the chains', as you'll need to use the permanent cables to navigate some of the narrow canyon walls). Nearby is the vigorous climb up to the highest peak in the park, **La Om** (2237m).

ℹ Getting There & Away

By far the best access point to the park is from Zărneşti. If you're hiking from Bran, the quickest route is along the gravel road to Predulut, through the village of Tohaniţa.

North of Braşov

After the dramatic mountain approach to Braşov from Bucharest, the flatland settings for the Unesco-protected Saxon citadels of Hărman, Prejmer and Vama Buzăului lack a little punch. That said, if you have wheels, they're worth a visit.

HĂRMAN & PREJMER

Quiet Hărman, 12km north of Braşov and 7km from Prejmer, is a dusty Saxon village with a 16th-century peasant **citadel** at its centre. Inside the thick walls is a 52m weathered **clock tower** and a 15th-century **church** (admission by donation; ☉9am-noon & 1-5pm Tue-Sun summer, 10am-4pm winter). Hit the bell near the *'Bitte Läuten'* sign on the door to the left of the main door if the gate's locked. The colourful houses facing the main square are typical of the Saxon era, with large rounded doors and few windows.

Several kilometres off the main highway north from Braşov, Saxon Prejmer (Tartlau) was first settled in 1240, with a picturesque 15th-century **citadel** (adult/child 8/4 lei) surrounding the 13th-century Gothic evangelical **church** in its centre (near where the microbuses stop). The fortress was the most powerful peasant fortress in Transylvania, its 272 small cells lining the inner citadel wall intended to house the local population during Turkish sieges. The building's 4.5m-thick outer defensive walls are the thickest of all the remaining Saxon churches.

Frequent microbuses and maxitaxis from Braşov's Autogara 1 stop in Hărman (3 lei, 20 minutes), while it's fairly easy to visit Prejmer (4 lei, 20 minutes) on the same trip, heading there first from a stop near Autogara 1, then taking a Braşov-bound bus and exiting at the Hărman stop on the way back (it's a 20-minute walk from the highway to the church on the lone entry road).

SAXON LAND

No trip to Transylvania is complete without a ramble through the valleys and medieval villages and fortified churches in the area that Saxons colonised from the 12th century. The area lies north of the Carpathians, between Transylvania's 'big three': Braşov, Sighişoara and Sibiu.

TRANSYLVANIA PIATRA CRAIULUI NATIONAL PARK

Saxon Land

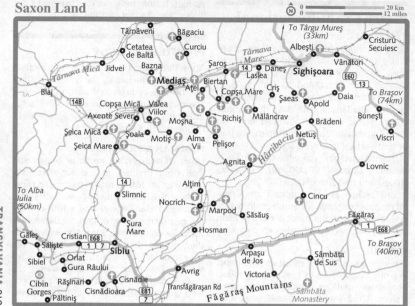

To Târgu Mureş (33km)

To Braşov (74km)

To Alba Iulia (50km)

To Braşov (40km)

Sighişoara

POP 26,370

So pretty it should be arrested; from the moment you enter its fortified walls, wending your way along cobblestones to its centrepiece square, Sighişoara burns itself into your memory. It's like stepping into a kid's fairy tale, the narrow streets aglow with lustrously coloured 16th-century houses, their gingerbread roofs tumbling down to pretty cafes. Horror fans won't be disappointed either, for this Unesco-protected citadel, the best preserved of its kind in Europe, was the birthplace of one of history's great monsters – Vlad Ţepeş (The Impaler).

The area was settled by the Romans, and it wasn't until the 12th century that immigrant Saxons established a thriving trading town here and the citadel you see today. It was later extended and enlarged in the 14th century. Grab a caffeine burst outside Ţepeş' house (opposite the fantastical church with the onion-dome spire); visit the sights of the citadel then wind yourself up for the climb to the church on the hill. Many use Sighişoara as a base from which to explore the enchanting Saxon villages of Viscri and Biertan. Cartographia publishes the highly detailed Sighişoara fold-out map, covering the city and environs.

⊙ Sights

Most of Sighişoara's sights are conveniently clustered in the compact old town – the magical medieval **Citadel** perched on a hillock and fortified with a 14th-century wall (to which 14 towers and five artillery bastions were later added). Today the citadel, which is on the Unesco World Heritage list, retains just nine of its original towers (named for the guilds in charge of their upkeep) and two of its bastions.

If you're here late July, the weeklong **Medieval Festival of the Arts** is a blast of colour, alcohol and Saxon merriment.

Clock Tower   TOWER

(Turnul cu Ceas; Piaţa Muzeului) With its stunning peacock-coloured roof tiles, the Clock Tower dates from 1280 and once housed the town council. Formerly the main entrance to the fortified city, the tower is 64m tall, with 2.35m-thick walls. Inside, the 1648 clock is a pageant of slowly revolving 80cm-high wooden figurines, each representing a character from the Greek-Roman pantheon: Peace bears an olive branch, Justice has a set of scales and Law wields a sword. The executioner is also present and the drum-player strikes the hour. Above stand seven figures, each representing a day of the week.

Under the clock tower on the right (if heading out of the old town) is the small, dark Torture Room Museum, with a very feeble compendium of exhibits. Give it a miss.

Church on the Hill   CHURCH
(Biserica din Deal; Bergkirche; ⊘mid-Apr–Oct) Reached by the 172 steps of the covered stairway *(scara acoperită)*, this 17th-century, 429m-high Lutheran church is the town's highest point. Facing its entry – behind the church when approaching from the steps – is an atmospheric, overgrown German cemetery.

Goldsmiths' Tower   TOWER
Around the citadel walls are the remnants of 14 towers erected by the guilds in the 14th to 16th centuries to protect the town from Turkish raids. The Goldsmiths' Tower defended the southwestern corner, one of the most sensitive points of the city of Sighişoara.

Roman Catholic Church   TOWER
(Str Bastionul) St Joseph Roman Catholic Church was built in 1894, after the demolition of the Franciscan convent. It is situated in the northeast of Sighişoara citadel, near the enclosure wall.

Tailors' Tower   TOWER
(Turnul Cizmarilor; Str Bastionul) Dating from the 14th century, the Taylor's Tower marks the second entrance into the citadel. The tower was destroyed by a fire in 1676, and rebuilt three years later.

History Museum   MUSEUM
(Piaţa Muzeului 1; adult/child 10/2.50 lei; ⊘9am-5.30pm Tue-Fri, 10am-5.30pm Sat & Sun) Inside the Clock Tower, the History Museum has small rooms that wind up to the 7th-floor lookout above the clock. On the 1st floor, don't miss the small exhibition on local hero

COMBO TICKET
You can visit the History Museum, the Medieval Arms collection and the Torture Room Museum for a combined ticket price of 17 lei (about the same price as the student discounts for all three).

PRINCE CHARLES: TREE HUGGER

Not content with attempting to save Borneo's rainforests, Prince Charles is also campaigning to save Transylvania's forests and Saxon architecture in villages such as Viscri and Biertan. Rapid economic growth in Romania has placed the Carpathian Mountains under threat from logging, and the prince, only too aware of how England's forests shrank to nothing during industrialisation, is keen to make his voice heard. A voice that ancestrally is connected to Vlad The Impaler. He was heard to say: 'The genealogy shows I am descended from Vlad the Impaler, so I do have a bit of a stake in the country'. The royal bought a five-bedroom 150-year-old house in the village of Zalanpatak, while his first house was purchased in Viscri in 2006.

---

and physicist Hermann Oberth; there are some English translations (as well as the sketch of Oberth's 'space suit'). A couple of floors up you can see the clock's famed figures, as well as the clanking innards of the clock behind them.

Collection of Medieval Arms   MUSEUM
(adult/student 6/1.50 lei; ⊘9am-5.30pm Tue-Fri, 10am-5.30pm Sat & Sun) This small collection of armoury has four rooms devoted to medieval helmets, shields, crossbows, maces (aka 'whips for fight') and cannonballs. Somehow an illustration of Napoleon made the cut too.

Church of the Dominican Monastery   CHURCH
(Biserica Mănăstirii) This 15th-century Gothic church, which was closed for renovation at research time, became the Saxons' main Lutheran church in 1556. Classical, folk and baroque concerts have been held here in the past. Hidden away behind it is a **statue of Vlad Ţepeş**, showing the legend with a bewildered look and his trademark circa-1981 porno moustache.

Continuing west towards Piaţa Cetăţii, you come to the site where Vlad Ţepeş was born in 1431 and reputedly lived until the age of four. The pretty, all-renovated **Casa Dracula** (Piaţa Cetăţii) is now a restaurant.

Sighişoara

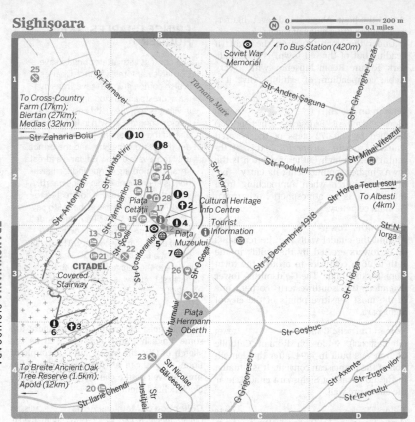

0   200 m
0   0.1 miles

Breite Ancient Oak Tree Reserve   FOREST

(☏0265-506 024; www.breite.ro) Escape the
crowds and visit the enchanting Breite Ancient Oak Tree Reserve, 2km out of town.
Its 133 hectares boast 800-year-old oaks,
with circumferences of 400cm to 600cm.
Ask at the Cultural Heritage Info Centre for
directions.

🏃 Activities

Cross-Country Farm   HORSE RIDING

(☏0372-772 890; www.cross-country.ro; horse riding per hr 70 lei) Cross-Country Farm, 17km
west of town, offers horse rides past traditional villages. There are wagons for beginners, and guides speak English.

🚲 Tours

Rent bikes in summer at Gia Hostel, Pensiune Cristina & Pavel and Bed & Breakfast
Kula.

Wanderlust Tour   CULTURAL TOUR

(☏0728-216 212, 0721-254 195; www.wanderlust
-tour.ro; Cultural Heritage Information Centre) Run
by Peter Suciu, Wanderlust offers day trips
to the Saxon villages, and cycling tours. You
can also experience rustic life by meeting
traditional charcoal burners and cheese
makers.

Eye Tours   CULTURAL TOUR

(☏0752-328 149, 0788-314 009; www.eye-tours
.com; day trips per person 80-100 lei) Offering
hiking excursions to Saxon churches, meeting shepherds and nature walks to the nearby Tarnava Mare.

Café International &
Family Centre   CULTURAL TOUR

(☏0265-777 844; Piaţa Cetăţii 8; adult/child 20/10
lei; ⏰8am-8pm Mon-Sat Jun-Sep, 1-7pm Mon-Sat
Oct-May) Walking tours of the town at 10am,
11.30am, 3pm and 4.30pm.

Sighişoara

TRANSYLVANIA SIGHIŞOARA

🛏 Sleeping

CITADEL

TOP CHOICE **Bed & Breakfast Kula**   PENSION $
(⌕0265-777 907; Str Tâmplarilor 40; r/apt per person 65/150 lei; ☀) Spilling with antique furniture, wood floors and rugs, this pension in a 400-year-old house feels like you're staying at a friend's; which you are by the time you've sat chatting with the owners in the pretty garden, as they ply you with homemade wine.

Casa Wagner   HOTEL $$
(⌕0265-506 014; www.casa-wagner.com; Piaţa Cetăţii 7; s/d/ste €39/49/69; ℗☀🖵) This appealing 16th-century hotel has 32 rooms spread across three buildings. Think peach walls, candlebra, dark-wood furniture and tasteful rugs. The rooms in the eaves are smaller but wood floored, cosy and very romantic for writing those Harker-esque diary entries. The ground-floor restaurant often has live music in the evenings.

Casa Au Cerb   HOTEL $$
(Stag House; ⌕0265-774 625; www.casaucerb.ro; Str Şcolii 1; s/d/tr €55/60/75; ☀🖵) Ten peaceful rooms in a higgledy-piggledy maze of corridors. Expect stunning views of the

square far below – especially from number 4 – wrought-iron beds, parquet floors, cable TV, and walls adorned with tasteful watercolours. Serene.

Casa Saseasca   HOTEL $
(⌕0265-772 400; www.casasaseasca.com; Piaţa Cetăţii 12; s/d 130/150 lei; 🖵) Delightful accommodation with authentic decor – traditionally painted Saxon furniture – and widescreen views of the nearby square, as well as en suites and cable TV. There's also an inviting courtyard out back and a terraced restaurant out front.

Casa Legenda   GUESTHOUSE $$
(Str Bastionului; r 170 lei; 🖵) Five pleasant, peaceful rooms with traditionally carved bedsteads, local art on mint-green walls and bijou en suites. There's a cool breakfast area downstairs (and we're not talking the Fonz); also a flowery courtyard and snug lounge.

Hotel Sighişoara   HOTEL $$
(⌕0265-771 000; www.sighisoarahotels.ro; Str Şcolii 4-6; s/d/apt 227/250/290 lei; ☀❄🖵) With its 16th-century facade, stained-glass windows and darkly cavernous lobby, you half expect to be greeted by a Count. Rooms are large and mustard-coloured with capacious

beds, flat-screens, arched ceilings and immaculate bathrooms. Rooms on the 3rd and 4th floors have air-con.

Pensiune Cristina & Pavel   PENSION $

(📞0744-159 667, 0744-119 211; www.pensiuneafaur .ro; Str Cojocarilor 1; dm/s/d 45/80/125 lei; P) The floors are so clean at this four-room, one-dorm guesthouse, you could eat your lunch off them. En-suite rooms are spearmint white, plus there's an idyllic garden bursting with flowers. The dining/self-catering area is welcoming, and should you need it, there's a laundry service.

It also rents bikes (45 lei per day) and arranges day trips to Biertan and other Saxon villages. Peaceful.

Burg Hostel   HOSTEL $

(📞0265-778 489; www.burghostel.ro; Str Bastionului 4-6; dm 40 lei, s/d without bathroom 70/90 lei, with bathroom 80/95 lei; 🛜) Basic Burg is ubiquitously wood-walled with a number of cosy rooms – the triples have the most space. Single rooms are adequate. There's a bar downstairs, plus a pleasant courtyard to read in.

OUTSIDE THE CITADEL

Gia Hostel   HOSTEL $

(📞0722-490 003; www.hotelgia.ro; Str Libertăţii 41; dm/d incl breakfast 39/99 lei; @🛜) Just 15 minutes downhill of the citadel, this hostel has two eight-berth and one four-berth dorms. All of them are clean and breezy. There's a vine-canopied terrace, a library and a TV basement with bags of DVDs. Check out the Dracula mural. There's also a free computer.

Nathan's Villa   HOSTEL $

(📞0265-772 546; www.nathansvilla.com; Str Libertăţii 8; dm 50 lei; @🛜) Cramped dorms, but thoughtfully placed linen screens on bunks allow for a little more privacy. The purple dorm is cosy: check out the retro boiler. Another plus is a sofa and a TV in dorms. Two minute's walk towards the train station from Gia Hostel.

Hotel-Restaurant Claudiu   HOTEL $

(📞0265-779 882; www.hotel-claudiu.com; Str Iiarie Chendi 28; s/d 135/165 lei; P🛜) Twelve fragrant rooms with white walls, dark furniture, laminate floors, flat-screens and bijou en suites. The management are friendly too. Check out the miniaturised Harley in the reception. Random?

✕ Eating & Drinking

Café International & Family Centre   CAFE $

(Piaţa Cetăţii 8; mains 13 lei; ⊙8.30am-7.30pm Mon-Sat Jun-Sep, 9am-6pm Mon-Sat Oct-May; 🛜🎵) This delightful family-run cafe dishes up delicious pies, cookies, quiche and cakes. Inside it's a Gustavian-meets-rustic-chic interior, while outside chairs and tables spill onto the cobbles come summer. Friendly staff wear traditional Saxon garb. Oh, and the blackberry muffins: they'll turn your day around.

Casa Dracula   ROMANIAN $$

(Str Cositorarilor 5; mains 28 lei; 🪑) Despite the ghoulish Dracula bust mounted to the wall, the house where Vlad was born could have been dealt a worse blow than this atmospheric, wood-panelled restaurant. The menu scuttles from tomato soup to salmon fillet – all with Dracula-related references. With a little embellishing from you, your kids will love it.

Cositorarului Casa   RESTAURANT $

(Str Cositorarilor 9; mains: 15-25 lei; ⊙9am-10pm) Refresh yourself with beautiful views of the old town and homemade lemonade. It also rustles up toasted sandwiches and breakfast. Inside is cosy, outside there's a small terrace.

Jo Pizzerie   PIZZERIA $

(Piaţa Hermann Oberth; mains 10-33 lei; ⊙10am-midnight) This lively pizzeria has a large terrace with views of the street below and over 20 different kinds of pizza.

Globus   SUPERMARKET $

(Str Ilarie Chendi 4; ⊙24hr) Globus is a small but well-stocked grocery store.

Market   MARKET

(Str Târnavei) The daily market has a good selection of fruits, vegetables and cheese.

Korona   BAR

(Str Turnului 1; ⊙8pm-4am) Enjoying a refurb when we visited, with its suitably Gothic interior of exposed brick walls and candlebra; you may just get bitten by this subterranean haunt. Just below the clock tower.

★ Entertainment

Occasional classical concerts are held in the city's churches; look for posted adverts.

Aristocrat   CLUB

(www.club.club-aristocrat.ro; ⊙10pm-late) In a converted theatre space, this is an Ibizacalibre place, with copious lounge space and balconies. Friday is retro night.

Shopping

TOP CHOICE House On The Rock ARTS & CRAFTS (www.thespoonman.ro; Piaţa Cetăţii 8; ⊙Mon-Sat 10am-8pm) In an old catacomb below Café International (p100) this may be the best place in Transylvania to buy a culturally meaningful souvenir. The work of six artists ranging from intricately carved wooden spoons to painted-glass icons, peasant-style clay statues, naive-style rustic stools and painted eggs will keep you busy.

Information

Many of the facilities you'll want are found along a short stretch of Str 1 Decembrie 1918.

LEFT LUGGAGE The **train station** (left luggage per day 5 lei; ⊙24hr) can hold your bags.

MEDICAL SERVICES Farmacia Genţiana (Piaţa Hermann Oberth 45; ⊙8am-8pm) Farmacia Genţiana stocks toiletries.

MONEY There are numerous ATMs and banks lining Sighişoara's main street, Str 1 Decembrie 1918.

BRD (Str 1 Decembrie 1918, 20; ⊙9am-6pm Mon-Fri) Has a 24-hour ATM.

Banca Transilvania (btwn Piaţa Cetăţii & Muzeulul) Just an ATM and along with Hotel Sighişoara's ATM, the only bank option in the citadel.

POST & TELEPHONE Post Office (☑0265-774 854; Str O Goga 12; ⊙7.30am-7.30pm Mon-Fri) Recently relocated.

TRAVEL AGENCIES Hotels and guesthouses can negotiate with honest taxi drivers for a return trip to Biertan for around 100 lei.

Cultural Heritage Info Centre (☑0788-115 511; www.dordeduca.ro; Piaţa Muzeului; ⊙10am-6pm Tue-Sun) Rents out bikes (5 lei per hour) and offers guided tours of Sighişoara and the fortified churches as well as DVDs on the same subject. It also has maps of the city and region.

Tourist Information (☑0265-770 415; Str O Goga; ⊙10am-4pm Mon-Fri, 9am-1pm Sat) This useful English-speaking resource can book beds and check bus and train times and has maps of the city.

Getting There & Away

About a dozen trains connect Sighişoara with Braşov (21 lei, two hours), nine of which (none of the slow ones) go on to Bucharest (65 lei, 4½ hours). Five daily trains go to Cluj-Napoca (59 lei, 3½ hours).

You'll need to change trains in Mediaş to reach Sibiu (16 lei, 2½ hours), but the four daily trains are timed for easy transfers. Three daily trains go to Budapest (145 lei, nine hours), and the night train has a sleeper (from 200 lei).

Buy tickets at the **train station** (☑0265-771 886).

Next to the train station on Str Libertăţii, the **bus station** (☑0265-771 260) sends buses of various sizes and colours to Bistriţa (33 lei, three hours, three daily), Făgăraş (19 lei, three hours, one daily) and Sibiu (20 lei, 2½ hours, four daily). Maxitaxis pass by every couple of hours for Târgu Mureş (12 lei, 1½ hours). There are regular services to Daneş (3 lei). Buses to Sibiu stop at Mediaş. Buses to Braşov (38 lei, 2½ hours) stop at the bus station a couple of times per day and require a **reservation** (☑0265-250 702).

Getting Around

Taxis greet incoming trains; it should be about 10 lei to reach the citadel. If driving into the citadel with a private car, there's a 15 lei access charge.

Gia Hostel (p100) hires cars from about 90 lei per day. **Mokai Rent a Car** (☑0744-605 816, 0265-777 113; www.rentacarsighisoara.com) charges about 90 lei per day for a Fiat Panda.

Fortified Saxon Churches

One of Romania's highlights is here in the belly of Saxon Land (aka the Târnave plateau), stretching more or less 120km between Hwy 1 (between Braşov and Sibiu) to the south, and Hwy 13 (Braşov to Sighişoara) and Hwy 14 (Sighişoara to Sibiu) to the north. The rolling hills are filled with fortified Saxon churches in towns that can easily feel lost in centuries past; especially when you see a horse and cart rattle past laden with milk churns, or a shepherd ushering his flock across your path. Bus service is practically nonexistent; visitors come by hire car, taxi, bike or tour bus. If you get stares as you pull in past a row of octogenarians in trad garb, they're just wondering who the folks are with a car!

A couple of highlights get nearly all the visits, notably Biertan and Viscri. Much of the restoration in the area has been carried out by the Mihai Eminescu Trust, of which Prince Charles is a major driving force, along with author William Blacker (*Along the Enchanted Way*).

It's best to explore when churches are open, failing which you may have to track down the caretaker to get entry (which is

TRANSYLVANIA FORTIFIED SAXON CHURCHES

often possible). Bring your own food or eat in Biertan.

History

In 1123 Hungarian King Geza II invited Saxons – mainly from the Franken region in western Germany – to settle here. In the 15th and 16th centuries, following the increased threat of Turkish attacks on their towns, the settlements were strengthened with bulky city walls and fortified churches. Defensive towers in the churches served as observation posts. Town entrances were guarded with a portcullis that could be quickly lowered.

After the 1990 revolution there was an exodus of Saxons back to Germany, leaving pretty villages ghostly and untended. Many were swiftly inhabited by the Roma.

BIERTAN
POP 2550

Your first glimpse of Biertan's medieval church is unforgettable: towering over the square below, clustered with vividly painted houses and backed by vineyards and tussocky meadows, this feels like a place that time forgot. There's a couple of places to stay, a decent restaurant and a market in the square that sells handicrafts.

◉ Sights

Biertan's fantastical 15th-century **church** (adult/child 8/4 lei; ☉10am-7pm Apr-Oct) was the seat of the Lutheran bishop from 1572 to 1867 and was listed as a Unesco World Heritage site in 1993. Its Viennese-style altar (1483–1550) has 28 panels and its three rings of walls stand up to 12m tall. This is the only fortified church in the region that holds regular services (once a month).

Near the altar in the church is the sacristy that once held treasure behind its formidable door with an even more formidable lock: it has 19 locks in one, and is such a marvel of engineering, it won first prize at the Paris World Expo in 1900. Inside the grounds are many buildings of interest, including a small bastion, which is famous in local lore: couples wanting a divorce were supposedly locked in here for two weeks as a last attempt to resolve differences. There was only one bed and one set of cutlery. The method has been so successful that only one couple decided to go through with divorce in 400 years!

If you're lucky enough to time your visit in mid-August you'll be here for the **Lună Plină (Full Moon) Horror Film Festival** (www.lunaplinaferstival.ro). Biertan also hosts a **Saxon Festival** in mid-September.

🛏 Sleeping

There are a dozen guesthouses around town, not all are signed.

TOP CHOICE **Casa Dornröschen** PENSION $
(☎0269-244 165; www.biertan.net; Str George Cosbul 25; s/d €20/39; ☉Apr-Oct ♿@⊚) Walk down the alley past the church entrance, and on past a pastel-green cottage to this ex-kindergarten. Sun-dappled rooms with tasteful bathrooms and a great dining area. Breakfast includes homemade cheese and jam. Secluded and restful, it's set within the citadel walls.

Pensiunea Thomas APARTMENT $$
(☎0269-806 699; Str 1 Decembrie 1; s/d incl breakfast €34/42) Central Thomas boasts two well-kitted-out apartments based around a small courtyard. Huge bathrooms, refined decor, fresh linen, plus wi-fi and cable TV. Ask the manager about cycle hire, archery and riding activities.

Pensiunea Unglerus PENSION $
(☎0269-806 699; www.biertan.ro; Str Aurel Vlaicu 10; s/d €18/34; ⊚) Mixing the rustic – the backyard gives onto a tumbledown shepherd hut – with the modern – a fresh interior of contemporary furnishings, and biscuit-yellow walls hung with watercolors – this is a nice place to stop. Call ahead.

🍴 Eating

Unglerus Medieval Restaurant ROMANIAN $$
(Str 1 Decembrie, 1; mains 16-24 lei; ☉10am-10pm; ⊚) With its high-backed chairs, wood-raftered ceilings, ornately carved bannisters and oil paintings of knights and maidens, this is an atmospheric place for lunch. Omelettes, breaded pork, tartar steak and pan-fried trout. Next to the church entrance.

❶ Getting There & Away

Four daily buses connect Biertan with Mediaş (11 lei, 40 minutes). You should be able to hire a taxi from Sighişoara for about 80 to 100 lei for the day.

AROUND BIERTAN

Five kilometres south of Biertan is the small village of **Richiş**, likewise dominated by a fantastic stone church. From Biertan you can also head east for 3km along a dirt track to **Copşa Mare** (Grosskopisch), a quaint town in a tight valley. The church there dates from the early 14th century.

A rough dirt road leads northwest from Biertan to Aţel (Heteldorf), but it's far easier to reach by looping back via the main highway. In 1959 the northern tower was levelled to uncover a secret tunnel leading to a neighbouring farmstead.

Back toward Sighişoara, 13km down an unpaved road south of Laslea, is the isolated village of Mălâncrav (Malmkrog), boasting the highest proportion of Saxons of any village in the region. The village church, in addition to possessing vast frescoes that are among the finest in Transylvania (some dating from 1375 to 1405), has an altarpiece (1520) said to be the best-preserved of its kind still occupying its original location.

The 15th-century Hungarian **Apafi Manor House** (2 0723-150 819, 0745-924 558; cvranceanu@mihaieminescutrust.org; per person 245 lei), painstakingly restored to its 18th-century layout, reopened in 2007. Built by the Hungarian princely family of Apafi, the manor is one of only a handful of manor houses ever built in a (Hungarian-governed) Saxon village. Renovation work on this highly atmospheric living museum (and guesthouse) was executed using traditional methods.

Cazare in some of the local houses (built using traditional tools and building methods) can be reserved using the same contact information (per person without breakfast 122 lei). Adjacent is an 80-hectare orchard and organic apple juice factory that can be visited.

SAXON CHURCHES AROUND MEDIAŞ
With its grim factories and power plants, Mediaş town may be an ugly vision of industry – but for its medieval centre – yet around it are some magnificent Saxon churches you should definitely not miss.

Bazna (Baassen in German), a small village first settled in 1302, is northwest of Mediaş (head north towards Tărnăveni for 10km then west for another 5km). Its late-Gothic St Nicholas' Church was built at the start of the 16th century on the ruins of a 14th-century original. Its highlight is the three pre-Reformation bells (1404) in the church tower.

Back on the Tărnăveni road, go another 5km north, then take the road to 'Delenii' for 6km to reach **Băgaciu** (Bogeschdorf in German). The pre-Reformation, late-Gothic altar in its church, restored in Vienna in 1896, is considered to be the best-preserved Saxon church altar.

About 10km south from Mediaş is **Moşna** (Meschen in German), with a 15th-century church built in late-Gothic style and an eight-storey bell tower.

About 5km southeast of Copşa Mică is **Valea Viilor** (Wurmloch in German). The village, dating from 1263, has a quaint fortified church, which was raised at the end of the 15th century and is surrounded by 1.5m-thick walls. The building is on Unesco's list of World Heritage sites.

Axente Sever, literally a minute south of Copşa Mică on the road to Sibiu, has a 14th-century church (fortified in the 15th century) with a testing bell-tower-climb requiring progress on all fours at times.

Şeica Mică (Kleinschelken in German) is 3km west of a turn-off 11km south of Copşa Mică on the road to Sibiu. The village was engulfed by fire several times during the 16th century, but remarkably its local church, built in 1414, survived. Its beautiful baptismal font is late Gothic (1447) in style and cast from iron.

VISCRI
POP 450

Nestled in buttery-soft hills, Viscri is as rustic as it gets; powder-blue shuttered houses with old ladies knitting socks on doorsteps, livestock wandering the streets past Roma children with grubby, nut-brown faces. The village is also one of the best-preserved Saxon villages in Romania, despite the fact only a handful (16) of Saxons now remain.

Up from town is a **fortified church** that Saxon colonists wrested from its Székely builders in 1185, recognised as a Unesco World Heritage site and supported by the **Mihai Eminescu Trust Foundation** (www.mihaieminescutrust.org). This vital organisation not only preserves Viscri's medieval houses, it also enlists the participation of the village's dominant Roma population in the cottage industry. Attached to the church is a dark tower, with a creaking stairway leading to the top. There's also a two-level **museum** (adult/student 4/2 lei) within the bastions.

A blacksmith shop is next to the bar at Str Principăla 36.

The **Tourist Information Centre** (2 0742-077 506, 0788-719 405; Str Bisericii 46) is in a yellow house just a few metres from the church gate. It can also accommodate groups of up to 18 people (per person without breakfast 35 lei). It has dial-up internet access in the office and a self-catering kitchen in the cool

GREAT READS: WILLIAM BLACKER'S 'ALONG THE ENCHANTED WAY' (2010)

Described by the *Sunday Times* as 'A lyrical description of an almost vanished way of life', *Along the Enchanted Way* tells of the author's abiding love for and immersion into rustic Romanian life. In his own words he was 'entranced by the Eastern Europe of wooden peasant cottages on the edge of forests inhabited by wolves and bears, of snow and sledges and sheepskin coats, and of country people in embroidered smocks and headscarves'. His story follows his life scything meadows next to peasants, wolf-troubled shepherds, and falling in love with a beautiful Roma girl.

Blacker, grandson of the first man to fly over Mt Everest, lived initially in Maramureş with an old couple who worked off the land, before he moved to Saxon country. It's largely thanks to Blacker's campaigning that the outside world knows of the existence of the 200-odd Transylvanian Saxon villages with their fortified churches dating back to the 14th and 16th centuries. In 1996 he wrote a pamphlet on the threat to their preservation that received the attention of Prince Charles. The two became friends after Blacker took the prince to a traditional Transylvanian wedding. He now lives in Tuscany and Yorkshire.

cellar. You will need your own transport to get here.

🛏 Sleeping

Staying in Viscri is special. Arrange a room in a traditional Saxon home by calling Carolina Fernolend (📞0740 145-397), who speaks English and can arrange accommodation for about €25 per night, including breakfast and dinner. Ask for one of the very few traditional rooms, with a 200-year-old 'Saxon bed', which is an oversized cabinet with a pullout mattress! Carolina can help arrange hikes, and popular three-hour horse-and-cart trips (50 lei per cart) that include stops at a new brick kiln, a picnic and a demonstration of charcoal making (10 lei extra). About half of the places have pit toilets – this is real-deal Saxon living. Call well ahead.

🏠 Viscri 125   GUESTHOUSE $$

(📞0741-411 490; www.viscri125.ro; main street; s/d/tr €60/100/120; 🅿🛜) Six upscale wood-beamed, rustic-style rooms in a renovated house and barn, backing onto meadows. Owner Mihai is friendly and organises traditional cooking classes for kids using fruit picked in the nearby forest. There's also wine-tasting for adults and cycling trips to the surrounding area.

🛍 Shopping

Cafe Artizanat   CAFE

(Str 9; ⏱10am-8pm) Close to the church, this cafe has a terrace next to a barn selling a range of felt slippers (33 lei) and 'hobbit'-style hats (60 lei). Each pair of socks is knit-ted by a different villager enrolled in the cottage industry. Sit outside in your new hat and enjoy a homemade slice of cake and glass of local wine.

Făgăraş Mountains

Looking over bucolic Saxon Land, the forbidding Făgăraş Mountains look like something from *Lord of the Rings*. The Transfăgărăşan Road – a real Transylvania highlight for those hiring wheels – sometimes opens only in early June, after the last of the snows melt from the road, closing by early October. Access points from the north – Făgăraş and Victoria – are situated outside the mountains and lack any sort of mountain-air quaintness.

FĂGĂRAŞ

Făgăraş (fuh-guh-*rash*) town is 25km east of the start of the Transfăgărăşan Road, but has more services than any access point north of the mountain range. Dead-centre Piaţa Republicii, where you'll find a bank, is one block northwest of the maxitaxi stop on B-dul Unirii. The train station and bus station are 1km north of the maxitaxi stop. The only attraction in Făgăraş is a real-live, moat-surrounded castle, a block north of the roundabout, which houses the **Valeriu Literat Făgăraş Museum** (📞0268-211 862; adult/student 5/2 lei; ⏱8am-6pm Tue-Fri, to 4pm Sat & Sun). The collection spans the town's history, and the highlight is the 20th-century sculpture of local artist Virgil Fulicea. The castle was originally built in the 13th century, but what you see dates from the mid-17th century.

SÂMBĂTA

At the foot of the mountains (20km via highway from Victoria, or 10km by a somewhat rough, but paved back road), the Sâmbăta complex is home to one of Romania's wealthiest monasteries and a key access point for Făgăraş hikes. Ceauşescu liked it enough to build a villa here on the monastery grounds.

Popular with Romanians, the lavish 1696 Sâmbăta Monastery (⏩0268-241 237; admission free; ☺8am-6pm) is also known as Brâncoveanu Monastery after its original founder, Wallachian prince Constantin Brâncoveanu (r 1688–1714). Forty monks live here. Sâmbăta's ruins were restored between 1926 and 1936.

THE TRANSFĂGĂRĂŞAN ROAD

The Transfăgărăşan Road (the 7C), Romania's highest asphalted road and voted by TV's *Top Gear* as the world's best road, provides an unforgettable experience behind the wheel. Boldly charging up and down one of Romania's highest mountains, this two-lane road sometimes has the narrowest of shoulders separating it from the edge of a cliff. Driving its length is an adventure in itself, with breathtaking scenery around every one of the dozens of twists and turns.

Ceauşescu's most celebrated project was built in the 1970s over the course of 4½ short years – 6 million kg of dynamite was used to blast out 3.8 million cu metres of rock, and 38 overworked soldiers died in accidents during its hasty construction – before it opened on 20 September 1974. While the scheme fitted well within the dictator's overall megalomania, he also had more practical reasons for building it. Though other routes east and west of here cut an easier north–south route, he thought it wise to secure the Carpathian crossing at the traditional border between Wallachia and Transylvania, just in case the Soviets invaded (as they had Czechoslovakia in 1968).

How to tackle it: Running from Piteşti via Curtea de Argeş in the south to Hwy 1 in the north (118km in all), the Transfăgărăşan Road is most commonly accessed from the northern end, where a 35km drive will take you up to the haunting glacial Lake Bâlea (2034m).

Starting from Hwy 1 in the north, the drive gets interesting at Km12, when the road begins a series of jagged turns through lush forest. As you keep climbing, the trees start to thin, their veil replaced by unfolding views of sheer rock face. By Km20, your ears are popping. At Km22, you arrive at the *cascadă* (waterfalls). The 360-degree views here are stunning: walls of mountains surround the area, and the distant waterfalls' slash of white appears like a lightning bolt in a grey sky. There are souvenir stands, a restaurant and the Cabana Bâlea Cascada as well as a cable car that whisks you up to Lake Bâlea. Alternatively, follow the scenic blue-cross trail (2½ hours). The remaining 13km up to Lake Bâlea is a maze of razor-sharp zigzags hanging over precipices framing breathtaking views.

The crowning glory: The climax is Lake Bâlea, hovering like a mirror among the rocks, sometimes totally enshrouded by clouds that come billowing over the peak above it. Cabana Bâlea is here, boasting a good restaurant and decent rooms. In winter an Ice Hotel is constructed, with walls, corridors, pillars, beds, and sculptures built entirely out of ice. Bathroom facilities are inside Cabana Bâlea. To get here during snows, you'll have to park at Cabana Bâlea Cascada and take the cable car the rest of the way. And remember, temperatures here can be near zero, even if it's boiling at the foot of the mountain, so wrap up.

No public transport follows this route, which is closed from October to May (roughly). After an 887m-long tunnel through rock under the Palţinu ridge, the road descends the less impressive south side along the Argeş Valley. After re-entering forest, just when you think the fun is over, the road suddenly hugs the shores of the picturesque Lake Vidraru and crosses a 165m-high arched dam (1968). Beyond the lake, just off the road, is the Poienari Citadel (p65), the real Dracula's castle (where Vlad Ţepeş ruled).

Făgăraş Mountains

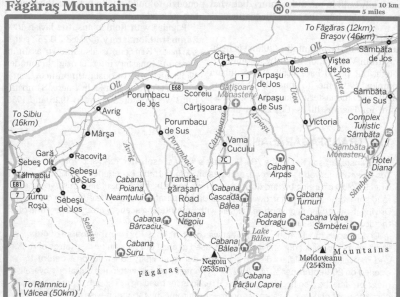

To Făgăras (12km); Braşov (46km)

Olt · Sâmbăta de Jos

Cârţa · Vistea de Jos · Ucea

Arpaşu de Jos · 1

Porumbacu de Jos · Scoreiu · Cârţişoara Monastery · Arpaşu de Sus · Sâmbăta de Sus

To Sibiu (16km) · Avrig · Cârţişoara

Porumbacu de Sus · Victoria · Complex Turistic Sâmbăta

Mârşa · Vama Cucului · Sâmbăta Monastery · Hotel Diana

Gară Sebeş Olt · Racoviţa · 7C

Tălmaciu · Sebeşu de Sus · Cabana Poiana Neamţului · Transfăgărăşan Road · Cabana Arpas

Turnu Roşu · Sebeşu de Jos · Cabana Cascadă Bâlea · Cabana Turnuri

Cabana Bârcaciu · Cabana Negoiu · Cabana Podragu · Cabana Valea Sâmbetei

Cabana Suru · Lake Bâlea · Cabana Bâlea

Negoiu (2535m) · Moldoveanu (2543m) · Mountains

To Râmnicu Vâlcea (50km) · Făgăraş · Cabana Pârâul Caprei

Its fame today is derived from its workshops of glass icons, run by the monastery's monks, residents since the early 1990s. There is a **glass icon museum** (⏱11am-4.45pm Mon, Wed, & Fri, 9am-4.45pm Tue, Thu & Sat, 8.30am-4.45pm Sun May-Oct), with lovely examples of 18th-century glass icons and other relics.

🛏 Sleeping

There are several signed *pensiunes* with rooms for around 90 lei without breakfast.

Complex Turistic Sâmbăta GUESTHOUSE $
(☎0740-920 138; 2-bed hut 40 lei; ⏱May-Sep) Just south of the monastery entrance, this plain collection of a dozen huts – with open-air bar-restaurant – is a popular start and stop point for Făgăraş hikers.

Academia Sâmbăta GUESTHOUSE $
(☎0730-556 342; d 80 lei; 🛈) The monastery's basic rooms are in an adjoining complex. Breakfast is 10 lei, and dinner costs 15 lei. Monday and Friday are vegie-only days.

❶ Getting There & Away

The complex isn't convenient to train or bus stations. Sâmbăta is 9km south of Sâmbăta de Sus village, where roads go west to Victoria, or north to Sâmbăta de Jos village on Hwy 1 and on to Făgăraş (26km northeast of Sâmbăta de Sus).

Sibiu

POP 154,458

Instantly charming with a maze of cobbled streets and baroque squares undulating downhill, Romania's cultural gem has a magic all of its own. Franz List and Johan Strauss were drawn here in the 19th century, and in 2007 the city was voted European Capital of Culture. In fact, the country's first hospital, school, library and pharmacy were all established here, so there must be a spirit of enterprise in the air.

Most months have myriad things going on, from festivals (more festivals here than any other city in Romania), exhibitions, theatre and opera, as well as plenty of cafes to people-watch in the city's three main squares. Sibiu has a bohemian yet stately ambience, which is perhaps what makes it so appealing; its back streets of wilting pea-green houses with their distinctive eyelid windows (imagine a benign 'Amityville Horror' House), watching a cast of artists, visiting guildsmen and buskers bustle below them, just as they did back in the 18th century when the city really blossomed.

History

Founded on the site of the former Roman village of Cibinium, during the peak of

Saxon influence, Sibiu had some 19 guilds (each representing a different craft) within the sturdy city walls protected by 39 towers and four bastions. Under the Habsburgs from 1703 to 1791 and again from 1849 to 1867, Sibiu served as the seat of the Austrian governors of Transylvania. Much remains from this colourful history. In 2000 Johannis Klaus of the German Democratic Forum was elected mayor and has remained hugely popular ever since, placing the city once again under German leadership.

◎ Sights

AROUND PIAŢA MARE
At the centre of the old walled city, the expansive Piaţa Mare is a good start for exploring Sibiu. Climb to the top of the former **Council Tower** (Turnul Sfatului; admission 2 lei; ◷10am-8pm), which links Piaţa Mare with its smaller sister square, Piaţa Mică.

Brukenthal Museum ART GALLERY
(www.brukenthalmuseum.ro; Piaţa Mare 5; adult/student 20/5 lei) The Brukenthal Museum is the oldest and likely finest art gallery in Romania. Founded in 1817, the museum is in the baroque palace (1785) of Baron Samuel Brukenthal (1721–1803), former Austrian governor, and hosts excellent collections of 16th- and 17th-century paintings.

Banca Agricola LANDMARK
(Piaţa Mare 2) Banca Agricola is Piaţa Mare's most impressive building; it now houses the town hall and tourist information centre.

History Museum HISTORY MUSEUM
(Str Mitropoliei 2; adult/child 20/5 lei) The History Museum displays Palaeolithic Age tools, ceramics, bronze, jewellery and life-sized home scenes, costumes and furniture. Other sections hold guild exhibits, an armoury, Roman artefacts and a treasury.

Biserica Evanghelică CHURCH
(Evangelical Church; Pieţa Huet; church tower adult/child 3/2 lei) The Gothic Biserica Evanghelică, built from 1300 to 1520, is partially scaffolded due to renovation but you can still climb the church tower; ask for entry at Casa Luxemburg. Its 1772 organ features a staggering 6002 pipes (the largest in southeast Europe). In summer, organ concerts (5 lei) are held every Wednesday (6pm) and Sunday (10pm). The tomb of Mihnea Vodă cel Rău (Prince Mihnea the Bad), son of Vlad Ţepeş, is in a closed-off section behind the organ (ask for entry). This prince was murdered in front of the church in 1510.

Pharmaceutical Museum MUSEUM
(adult/child 10/2.5 lei) Housed in the Piaţa Mică pharmacy (opened in 1600), the Pharmaceutical Museum is a three-room collection packed with pills and powders, old microscopes and scary medical instruments. Some exhibits highlight Samuel Hahnemann, a founder of homeopathy in the 1770s (Romania was one of Europe's first countries to legitimise the use of giving small doses of a disease in order to fight the disease itself).

Franz Binder Museum of World Ethnology MUSEUM
(☏0269-218 195; Piaţa Mică 11; adult/child 5/1.50 lei; ◷10am-6pm Tue-Sun) Named for a 19th-century collector from Sibiu, the great Franz Binder Museum of World Ethnology has an unexpectedly rich collection of North and Central African pieces (including a 2000-year-old mummy).

St Ursuline Church CHURCH
Heading northeast from Piaţa Mică, you come to the St Ursuline Church, founded by Dominican monks in the 15th century.

LOWER TOWN
To reach the lower town from Piaţa Mică, you can walk along the road that goes under the **Iron Bridge** (1859). The bridge's nickname is Liar's Bridge, after the tricky merchants who met here to trade and the young lovers who declared their 'undying' love on it. If you tell a lie upon it, it's supposed to creak.

CITY WALLS
South of Piaţa Mare, Str Cetăţii lines a section of the old city walls, constructed during the 16th century. As in Braşov, different guilds protected each of the 39 towers. Walk north up Str Cetăţii past a couple – the **Potters Tower** (Turnul Olarilor) and **Carpenters Tower** (Turnul Dulgherilor) – to reach the **Natural History Museum** (☏0269-213 156; Str Cetăţii 1; adult/child 30/3.25 lei; ◷10am-6pm Wed-Sun), which has an average collection of stuffed animals that dates from 1849, and frequent temporary exhibitions.

Further north, the street curls around the **Haller Bastion**. When Sibiu was hit by the plague, holes were drilled through the walls to enable corpses to be evacuated more

Sibiu

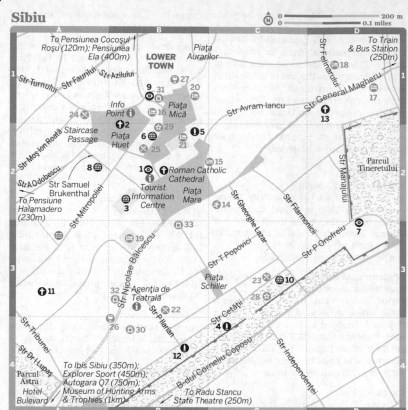

quickly from the city. The bastion was consequently dubbed the 'gate of corpses'.

OUTSIDE THE CENTRE

Railway Museum
MUSEUM

(Muzeul Locomotivei cu Abur; Str Dorobanţilor 22; admission negotiable; ⊙approximately 7am-3pm Mon-Fri) The so-called Railway Museum is an open-air collection of a couple of dozen old trains right off the tracks. South of the train station; it's across the tracks, 300m south.

Museum of Hunting Arms & Trophies
MUSEUM

(Muzeul de Arme şi Trofee de Vânătoare; ☎0369-101 784; Str Şcoala de Înot 4; adult/student 10/2.50 lei; ⊙10am-6pm Tue-Sun) A 15-minute walk southwest of the centre, this museum has a collection of muskets and stuffed heads. At the southern end of this street is the **Sub Arini Park** filled with tree-lined avenues, a tennis court and a swimming pool (open from May to September). There is also a **Municipal Stadium**, where Sibiu's football team plays.

Astra Museum of Traditional Folk Civilisation
MUSEUM

(Muzeul Civilizaţiei Populare Tradiţionale Astra; Calea Răşinarilor 14; adult/child 15/3.50 lei; ⊙museum 10am-6pm Tue-Sun, gift shop 9am-5pm Tue-Sun) Five kilometres from the centre, this sprawling open-air museum has a dazzling 120 traditional dwellings, mills and churches brought from around the country and set among two small lakes and a tiny zoological garden. Many are signed in English, with maps showing where the structures came from. There's also a nice gift shop and restaurant with creekside bench seats. Trolleybus 1 from the train station goes there (get off at the last stop and keep walking for under 1km, or take the hourly Răşinari tram for a couple of stops). Taxi here from the centre is about 12 lei.

Sibiu

Activities

Explorer Sport   ADVENTURE
(📞0269-216 641; Calea Dumbrăvii 14; ⊙9am-8pm Mon-Fri, 10am-2pm Sat) Explorer Sport rents bikes (about 23 lei a day), as well as skis in winter. It also sells packs and boots, and repairs bikes.

TOURS

Carpathian Travel Center   CULTURAL TOURS
(📞0740-843 678; www.carpathian-travel-center.com; Piaţa Mare 12; ⊙10am-6pm Mon-Fri, 11am-4pm Sat May-Oct) Offering city tours as well as hiking and cycling trips in the surrounding countryside.

Festivals & Events

Sibiu Jazz Festival   LIVE MUSIC
(www.sibiujazz.ro; ⊙May) In 2005 Sibiu resurrected its weeklong jazz festival, which died, along with its first founder, in the early 1990s.

Mayfest   LIVE MUSIC
(⊙1 May) Sibiu's remaining 5500 German-speaking Saxons flock to Dumbrava Forest for pagan frolicking and beer bingeing.

International Theatre Festival   THEATRE
(www.sibfest.ro; ⊙May/Jun) This festival is the most prominent annual performing arts event in Romania and draws as many as 60,000 people per day at 60 venues, with 70 countries involved.

Transylvania Tattoo Expo   FESTIVAL
(www.tattooexpo.ro; ⊙early Jun) Got a taste for the weird and wonderful? Then this communion of Romania's greatest flesh artists is the festival for you.

**Transylvania International
Film Festival**   CINEMA
(TIFF; www.tiff.ro; ⊙Jul) Taking place across the city over a week, and hosting 50 international films in competition, this is the most important film festival in Romania.

**International Country &
Folk Music Festival**   LIVE MUSIC
(⊙Jul) This lively festival features a vivid range of country and folk music from across Romania.

National Festival of Folk Traditions   FESTIVAL
(⊙early Aug) Displays of craft traditions at the Museum of Traditional Folk Civilisation, which holds many summer events.

Artmania Rock Festival
LIVE MUSIC

(www.artmania.ro; ☉Aug) Concerts, exhibitions, workshops, musical acts and events dedicated to the fine arts in this festival.

International Opera Music Festival
LIVE MUSIC

(www.filarmonicasibiu.ro; ☉late Sep) Welcoming a host of international acts, this popular festival is staged in September.

International Astra Film Festival
CINEMA

(www.astrafilm.ro; ☉mid-Oct) Going for 20 years now this important film festival is dedicated to East European and Romanian documentary filmmakers.

🛏 Sleeping

Oodles of quality hostels and boutique hotels in choice locations. Book well ahead during festivals or at the weekends, when everywhere seems to be full. **Antrec** (☎0744-542 365; www.antrec.ro) arranges rooms in *pensiune*-style accommodation in the countryside from 80 lei per person per night (excluding breakfast).

TOP CHOICE Felinarul Hostel
HOSTEL $

(☎0269-235 260; www.felinarulhostelsibiu.ro; Str Felinarul 8; dm/r 55/140 lei; ❄@🛜) More boutique than hostel, this labour of love is a wood-accented, courtyard oasis with one eight-berth and two six-berth dorms.

There are also two homely private rooms with en suites, a book exchange, wine-coloured cafe, antique-style kitchen, posh coffees from the bar and wi-fi. Prepare to stay a while. Oh, and the management are great too – when we passed the owner was trying to fix a visitor's Vespa for him. Book well in advance.

Am Ring
HOTEL $$

(☎0269-206 499; www.amringhotel.ro; Piaţa Mare 14; s/d/tr 250/290/420 lei; ❄🛜) This 26-roomed centrally placed diva is lavish with marbled busts of Hadrian and Achilles, and at every turn antique furniture, velvet curtains and wood-raftered ceilings. There's a nice bar too. Rooms have Gustavian period furniture, thick carpets and huge beds. The pièce de résistance has to be Room 103 for its imposing view of the square, four-poster and moody green walls.

Hotel Împăratul Romanilor
HOTEL $$$

(☎0269-216 500; Str Nicolae Bălcescu 2-4; s/d/tr €50/60/110; ❄🛜🏊) Within this 18th-century grand pile's powder-green exterior is an old-world landscape dripping in glass chandeliers, monogrammed carpets, huge beds and gilt paint furniture. Could do with a refurb in places but a stay here will be an atmospheric one.

Villa Astoria
HOTEL $$

(☎0369-446 917; www.villastoria.com; Piaţa Mică 31; d/q €59/125; 🛜) Four-person rooms and two doubles in a 14th-century building. Rooms are lovely with split levels, wood rafters, terrific views and regal furnishings. It's dead central too.

Casa Romana
GUESTHOUSE $

(☎0740-612 270; Str General Magheru 40; s/d 120/140 lei; 🅿🛜) Down the hill a few minutes' from Piaţa Mare, this pleasant guesthouse has great-value rooms with flat-screens, fridges, en suites, sofas and wi-fi. Staff are very friendly and there's a cosy restaurant and bar downstairs. Rooms are cheaper during the week.

Old Town Hostel
HOSTEL $

(☎0728-184 959, 0269-216 445; www.hostel sibiu.ro; Piaţa Mică 26; dm/d 55/180 lei; 🛜) In a 450-year-old building with three dorms and two private rooms (one with en suite), Old Town has sublime square views. It also has decidedly plush touches including parquet floors, fresh white walls, choice artwork, TV in dorms and considerably spaced beds (the antithesis of battery-hen mentality). It's a nice vibe too, from the communal kitchen to the lounge.

Ibis Sibiu
HOTEL $$

(☎0269-218 100; Calea Dumbravii 2-4; r 224 lei; 🅿❄❊🛜) It might not scream 'Transylvanian' but this slick high-riser complete with restaurant, cafe-bar and modern rooms (not to mention the incredible views) may prove to be an oasis if your first choices are full during festivals or at weekends. Surgically clean en suites with powerful showers, fluffy cloudlike beds and cable TV. Wi-fi in rooms and oodles of parking.

Pensiunea Cocoşul Roşu
PENSION $

(☎0369-427 482; www.cocosulrosu.ro; Str Ocnei 19; s/d 100/120 lei; 🛜) Down a cobbled, wilting alley this friendly *pensiune* has six pleasant rooms with some tasty touches such as blood-red chairs and a smattering of art, as well as a shaded patio for breakfast (15 lei extra). They forgot to spend much time on the en suites, sadly.

Casa Luxemburg
HOTEL $$

(☑0269-216 854; www.kultours.ro; Piața Mică 16; s/d/tr from 260/290/350 lei; ⊜🛜) Super rooms with parquet flooring, minimal but tasteful furnishings, and well-chosen artwork. There are flat-screens, armoires, bureaus and fresh-looking en suites. Overlooking the Evangelical Church and Piața Mică.

Pensiunea Ela
PENSION $

(☑0269-215 197; www.ela-hotels.ro; Str Nouă 43; s/d/tr 100/120/160 lei; 🛜) Down a quiet street in the Lower Town, so you might have to knock on the door a few times to get an answer. Within its flowery courtyard there are eight basic rooms with a rustic signature. Owner Ella is a welcoming host and there's a nice garden and chalet to read in.

Happy Day Pension
PENSION $$

(☑0269-234 985; www.pensiuneahappyday.ro; Str Lungă 2; s/d 150/170 lei; 🛜) These custard-yellow digs are set in a cheerless square 10 minutes' walk into the ugly side of town. It gets better inside though with a bizarre quasi Venetian cafe, and very appealing white en suite rooms with oxblood carpets and darkwood furniture.

Pensiune Halamadero
PENSION $

(☑0269-212 509; Str Măsarilor 10; s/d/tr without bathroom 60/80/100 lei) Basic digs with five triples in a house with a pleasant beer garden/cafe outside. Blue-walled rooms with fans and reading lights – some with en suite – and, unusual for Romanian guesthouses... a bath!

✖ Eating

TOP CHOICE Crama Sibiu Vechi
ROMANIAN $$

(Str P Ilarian; mains 25 lei) Hidden in an old wine cellar with its staff dressed in trad garb, this is the most rustically evocative restaurant in Sibiu. It's certainly the most authentic place to explore Romanian fare such as cheese croquettes, minced meatballs and peasant's stew with polenta. Dimly lit, brick walled... welcome to a local well-kept secret.

Pardon Café & Bistro
INTERNATIONAL, ITALIAN $$

(Str Cetatii 14; mains 20 lei; ⊘9am-10pm) Opposite the Philharmonic, this bijou treasure has walls stacked with old gramophones, clocks and antique telephones. Eat in the cosy interior or on the atelier enjoying a range of pasta, steak, soup or salad. The breakfasts are tasty too.

Zorba Greek Restaurant
GREEK $$

(Piața Mică 8; mains 25 lei; ⊘11am-2am) Next to the Franz Binder Museum, Zorba dishes up Aegean-fresh fare: colossal Greek salads, souvlaki, calamari, pizza and pasta.

Pasaj
BISTRO $

(www.lapasaj.ro; Str Turnului 3A; mains 12-20 lei; ⊘8.30am-10pm; 🛜✏) At the foot of the passage of stairs this is a perfect spot to catch a quiet frothy coffee and tuck into a menu of salads, pasta and pizza. Eat inside the low-lit interior or alfresco on wrought-iron tables and chairs.

🍷 Drinking

Piața Mică is the coffee-drinking HQ for Sibiu.

Imperium Club
BAR

(Str Nicolae Bălcescu 24; ⊘9am-dawn) Cosy barfly joint with vampish vaulted ceilings, dimly lit booths for canoodling, great cocktails – try the mojito – and live jazz some nights.

Bohemian Flow
BAR

(www.bohemianflow.ro; Piața Mică 26; ⊘Mon-Sun 4pm-5am) Lively backstreet cellar club beneath Old Town Hostel, piping out reggae and good vibes for a young crowd.

Music Club
BAR

(Piața Mică 23; ⊘8am-5am; 🛜) Playing an Escher-esque trick on you – descend two flights of stairs and just as you think you're entering the second dungeon, you emerge onto an outdoor terrace. Order cocktails (12 lei to 15 lei) using buttons on the tables. There's live music every Thursday, and other random nights.

☆ Entertainment

Studionul Astra
CINEMA

(Piața Huet 12; ⊘9am-5pm) On a rainy day head to Astra's attic and pore over thousands of documentaries before choosing one to watch in its screening room (small donation appreciated). This place also hosts the annual International Astra Film Festival in October.

Philharmonic
LIVE MUSIC

(www.filarmonicasibiu.ro; Str Cetății 3-5; adult/child 10/7 lei) Founded in 1949, this has played a key role in maintaining Sibiu's prestige as a main cultural centre of Transylvania.

Radu Stancu State Theatre THEATRE
(B-dul Spitelor 2-4; tickets 20 lei) Plays here are usually in Romanian, with occasional productions in German on Wednesday. It hosts the International Theatre Festival in May/June.

Shopping

Franz Binder
Museum Gift Shop HANDICRAFTS
(Piaţa Mică 11; ⊙9am-5pm Tue-Sun) This shop stocks lots of traditional pieces, which make good souvenirs.

Antik VINTAGE
(Str Nicolae Bălcescu 23; ⊙10am-5pm Mon-Fri, to 2pm Sat) Follow the cobbled alley through the courtyard to this Aladdin's cave of old books, oil paintings, traditionally painted crockery, medals, ornamental jewellery and soporifically ticking wall clocks. Perfect for a non-fang-related souvenir.

Hereus Art Bazaar HANDICRAFT
(http://hereus.blogspot.com; Piaţa Mică 18; ⊙Mon-Sat 11am-7pm) Delightful bijou craft and jewellery shop hawking necklaces, glass pendants, traditional ceramics, boho woolly hats and pashminas.

Librăria Humanitas BOOKSHOP
(Str Nicolae Bălcescu 16; ⊙10am-9pm Mon-Sat, 11am-5pm Sun) Lots of maps and English titles.

Librăria Schiller BOOKSHOP
(Piaţa Mare 7; ⊙8am-3pm Mon-Fri) Good source for maps and has a small collection of English-language classic novels.

ⓘ Information

The free biweekly *Şapte Seri* is a helpful Romanian listings booklet. You can pick it up in tourist offices and restaurants, or view it translated online at www.sapteseri.ro

Agenţia de Teatrală (Str Nicolae Bălcescu 17; ⊙11am-6pm Mon-Fri, to 3pm Sat) sells tickets for major events.

Emergency
Salvamont (☑0269-216 477, 0745-140 144) Provides 24-hour emergency rescue service for hikers and skiers in trouble.

Left Luggage
Train Station (per day 5 lei; ⊙24hr) In the 'ticket shed' across from the station.

Medical Services
Farmasib (Str Nicolae Bălcescu 53; ⊙7am-11pm Mon-Fri, 8am-11pm Sat & Sun) Farmasib sells a range of toiletries and over-the-counter medicine.

Hospital (☑0269-215 050; B-dul Corneliu Coposu 2-4)

Nippur-Pharm (Str Nicolae Bălcescu 5; ⊙9am-7pm Mon-Fri, 9.30am-2pm Sat) Nippur-Pharm sells a range of toiletries and medicine.

Money
ATMs are located all over the centre as well as in most hotels.

Banca Comercială Romană (Str Nicolae Bălcescu 11) Gives cash advances.

Post
Central Post Office (Str Mitropoliei 14; ⊙7am-8pm Mon-Fri, 8am-1pm Sat)

Tourist Information
Info Point (☑0269-244 442; www.kultours.ro; Piaţa Huet 1; ⊙9am-10pm) Info on local attractions, surrounding areas, booking bus tickets, car rental and bike hire (per day 35 lei). It also sells some decent souvenirs – books, bags and T-shirts. You'll find the tour company and booking agent Kultours here too.

Tourist Information Centre (☑0269-208 913; www.sibiu.ro; Piaţa Mare 2; ⊙9am-5pm Mon-Fri, to 1pm Sat & Sun) Based at the City Hall; staff here are fantastically helpful at guiding you to make the best of the city and cultural events, finding accommodation, and booking train and bus tickets. They also give away an excellent city map.

Travel Agencies
Casa Luxemburg (☑0269-216 854; www.kultours.ro; Piaţa Mică 16) Travel agent offering loads of city tours (9 to 14 lei) and day trips (50 to 90 lei); has a useful free map of the centre too.

ⓘ Getting There & Away

Air
Austrian Airlines (www.austrian.com) Flies between Vienna and Sibiu.

Blue Air (www.blueair-web.com) Flies variously to Stuttgart, London, Paris, Rome and Milan as well as others. The Agenţia de Voiaj CFR office sells tickets.

Tarom (☑0269-211 157; www.tarom.ro; Str Nicolae Bălcescu 10; ⊙9am-12.30pm & 1.30-7pm Mon-Fri, 9am-1pm Sat) Has daily flights to London, Bucharest, Barcelona, Munich, Vienna and many other destinations.

Bus
The **bus station** (Piaţa 1 Decembrie 1918) is opposite the train station. From this station and from Autogara Q7, bus and maxitaxi services travel to:

Alba Iulia (20 lei, one hour, 10 daily)

Braşov (25 lei, 2½ hours, three daily)
Bucharest (40 lei, 4½ hours, six daily)
Cluj-Napoca (30 lei, 3½ hours, 16 daily)
Deva (25 lei, two hours, three daily)
Timişoara (51 lei, six hours, three daily)
Târgu Mureş (20 lei, three house, five daily)

Maxitaxis to Cisnădie (6 lei) leave every half-hour from platform 9. Another microbus heads west a few times daily, stopping in Sălişte (8 lei), 4km from Sibiel, and ending in Jina (11 lei). Some village-bound buses also stop outside Hotel Parc. Three or four daily buses to Râşinari and Păltiniş (9 lei, 1¼ hours) leave from in front of the train station.

Eurolines sells tickets to many European destinations.

Several international buses leave from the lot next to Hotel Parc, 2km southwest of the centre.

Train

Sibiu lies at an awkward rail junction; often you'll need to change trains. There are seven daily direct trains to Braşov (35.60 lei, 2½ hours), three daily trains to Bucharest (67 lei, five hours) and Timişoara (67 lei, five hours), and one early-morning run to Arad (55 lei, five hours). To get to/from Sighişoara (13 lei) or Cluj-Napoca (55 lei), you'll have to change at Copşa Mică or Mediaş (about nine or 10 trains daily). For Alba Iulia (25 lei, 2½ hours), there are two direct, otherwise change at Vinţu de Jos.

For villages Rasinari and Paltinis it's necessary to catch a local bus from the train station (9 lei).

The **Agenţia de Voiaj CFR office** (📞 0269-212 085; Str Nicolae Bălcescu 6; 🕖7am-8pm Mon-Fri) sells advance tickets and serves as agents for Blue Air and Eurolines.

❶ Getting Around

Trolleybus 1 connects the train station with the centre, but it's only a 450m walk along Str General Magheru. Trolleybus 8 runs between the airport and the train station.

There's a taxi stand at the west end of Str Nicolae Bălcescu. To call a taxi dial 0269-953.

Car Rental

Autonom (📞 0269-235 538; www.autonom .com; Str Nicolae Bălcescu 1; 🕘9am-6pm Mon-Fri) Typically has the best rates, from €35 per day for a Fiat Panda, but if you're hiring for a week or more they're amenable to negotiating a heavy discount. Also has an office at Sibiu Airport.

Around Sibiu

Many visitors fail to capitalise on Sibiu's great nearby attractions – quiet villages and hiking trails past glacial lakes. It's possible

FUNERAL RITES IN TRANSYLVANIA

Some Romanians believe that for each person there is a star and a tree. When the person dies so too does the star. The passing of a person is sometimes marked by a fir tree which is placed at the head of their grave. The women of the village sing a special song about the tree and its obligation to dry and perish beside its human counterpart.

During a funeral and following wake, the body is never left alone but is very much part of the celebration as those gathered tell stories about the deceased right next to their coffin. In Transylvania a person's death is announced by the sound of alphorns blown in the garden of the dead at dawn, noon, evening, and on the way to the cemetery.

to hike across the Cindrel Mountains on a day trip, or rent a bike and go on trails from Păltiniş.

About 16km north of Sibiu towards the heart of Saxon Land, in the town of **Slim-nic**, is a great hilltop 15th-century fortified church that's fun to ramble around.

CISNĂDIE & RĂŞINARI

Cisnădie is worth a stop for its fortified 15th-century **Saxon church** (adult/chid 5/3 lei); especially if you make the vertiginous climb up the bell tower for its sweeping views of the town's roof-scape. A **museum of communism** is found on the 1st floor of the citadel walls; with English translations, identity cards and faded photos, it presents a stark reminder of communism's freedom-cloying reign.

Almost in the skirts of the Cindrel Mountains and 12km south of Sibiu, Răşinari is peppered with faded facades and has a little Ethnographic Museum (west of the centre, follow the brown sign, then take the first left). Hourly tram 1 connects Răşinari with the southern part of Sibiu (3 lei). Take bus 1 from the train station to reach the tram.

PĂLTINIŞ

Twenty kilometres southwest of Răşinari is the stunning low-key ski/summer resort of Păltiniş. There are five ski runs – green, blue and red – to suit most levels of skier, and come summer, the landscape of forested mountains has breathtaking hiking trails through it. The cable car costs 8 lei.

The **tourist information centre** (✆0269-574 035; centre Păltiniş; ☉8am-7pm), by Casa Turiştilor, has information on resorts, hiking trails and maps, and sells drinks and snacks. Bistro sits opposite and is a nice place to sit outside with a sandwich (15 lei) and drink up the mountain views. Accommodation-wise, **Hotel Cindrel** (✆0269-574 056; www.hotelcindrel.ro; main road into Păltiniş; s/d incl breakfast 170/220 lei), back up the hill, is a safe bet, and 100-room **Casa Turiştilor** (✆0269-574 035; s/d 2-star 125/155 lei, 3-star 200/250 lei) is ready for its grand opening after a €3.6m revamp, and promises sauna, pool and jacuzzi.

Halfway back towards Răşinari, **Curmătura Ştezii** (✆0269-557 310; www.curmaturastezii.ro; Km17; r/cabin 80/60 lei) is a happy little lodge with heaps of pelts and an appealing streamside location. There are trails nearby and a good restaurant. Breakfast is 15 lei.

MĂRGINIMEA SIBIULUI

The villages in the so-called Mărginimea Sibiului ('borders of Sibiu') represent the heart of traditional rural (ie Romanian) Transylvania. Scattered throughout the region west of Sibiu, they have preserved an old way of life: here you see not only the ubiquitous horse and plough, but also artisans engaged in woodwork, carving and weaving. Painting icons on glass and colouring eggs are pastimes here as much as vigorous text messaging is in Bucharest, and the local cuisine includes a tasty shepherd's polenta (with loads of fresh cream and milk).

It's great to ramble around by bike – get a map to take quiet backroads from Sibiu, as the Sibiu–Alba Iulia highway is unpleasantly flooded with traffic.

Look up www.ruraltourism.ro for details (and photos) of many guesthouses in the area.

Local trains from Sibiu to Sebeş stop at Cristian (15 minutes), Sibiel (3 lei, 35 minutes), Sălişte (3.20 lei, 45 minutes) and Miercurea Sibiului (5.50 lei, 1¼ hours).

SIBIEL & AROUND

If you only visit one Saxon village in this area ensure it's this one. Rural Sibiel reminds of Little Red Riding Hood country, with the village almost swallowed by the neighbouring forest, and in recent winters packs of wolves have been spotted. Bears too are regular visitors to Sibiel's orchards, stocking up on fruit.

Wander past rubicund-faced pensioners to its milk-white, late-18th-century church and gasp at its frescoed ceiling of gilded angels and icons. Then head to **Zosim Oancea Icons Museum** (✆0269-553 818; adult/student 5/3 lei, photos 10 lei; ☉8am-1.30pm & 2-8pm), one of Romania's largest icon collections, with some 700 icons collected by a priest who spent 17 years in prison during the commu-

CINDREL MOUNTAINS

These lovely mountains, topped with Mt Cindrel (2244m) and Mt Frumoasa (2170m), shelter two large glacial lakes, with well-marked trails cutting across. Visitors could start from Păltiniş and make their way overland to Mărginimea Sibiului as a day hike.

From Păltiniş, some trails are perfect for mountain biking too. You can pick up trail maps from the Păltiniş reception centre. There's a 4km trail to Şanta, where there's a refuge for campers to spend the night. The most popular route (3.5km, red circles) descends to the Cibin Gorges (Cheile Cibinului). From here the trail goes northeast, past Cibin River to Cabana Fântânele. The next day, continue in the same direction to Sibiel village (three to 3½ hours, blue crosses). Alternatively, follow another blue-cross trail to the neighbouring village of Fântânele. From Sibiel you can also take a 2½-hour walk to Cetatea Sibielului – it starts from the stream at the western end of the village.

Heading back south from Cabana Fântânele, a trail (red crosses and blue circles) cuts down a valley to Şaua Şerbănei, where you pick a separate trail leading to the Cânaia refuge (7½ to eight hours for the whole trip, blue circles).

More adventurous alpinists should follow the trail from **Cabana Păltiniş** (✆0730-651 699, 0724-313 908; r per person with shared/private bathroom 80/100 lei) south, past the Cânaia refuge (5½ to 6½ hours, red stripes) to the summit of Mt Cindrel. Heading northwards, red stripes also indicate the way to Răşinari village (six to seven hours), with its Cabana Mai.

nist reign for his religious deeds (if it's shut seek out curator Valerica).

Hiking trails line the hills to the east – follow the river upstream.

To reach Sibiel from Sibiu, catch the Transmixt bus (10 lei). From Sibiel, head 6km north to Săliște, another quaint village rich in local folklore. In Galeş, 2km west of Săliște, is a small **ethnographic and art museum**. It is at the southern end of the village, across the bridge opposite a salami factory. A dirt track leads from Galeş to Poiana Sibiului, famed for its fantastic coloured eggs, which are decorated with bright, geometric motifs.

📇 Sleeping

TOP CHOICE **Mioritica** GUESTHOUSE **$**
(📞0740-175 287, 0269-552 640; coldeasv@yahoo .com; s/d/tr 80/100/120 lei; 🅿@🛜) Rustic paradise and traveller's oasis, Mioritica sits in a bee-humming garden with a stream passing at its feet. Amid the vivid flowers are a shrine, intimate nooks for reading and even a small communist museum set up by the likeable owner, Sorin Coldea. The chalet-style buildings are enticing, housing a cosy breakfast room and nine rooms wrapped in verandahs to take in the forest views. Tours to the nearby mountains – where you may see bears – cost €25 per person. It's located towards the hills; follow the stream from the village centre on a rough road signed 'Pensiunea Sibiel' for about 700m.

🔒 Shopping

Artisans Shop HANDICRAFTS
(opposite the church; ⊙9am-8pm) The Artisans Shop is a little hut on the main street and has a tempting collection of hand-crafted bracelets, woollen rosettes, painted eggs, and ceramics.

SZÉKELY LAND

Technically it's wrong to call this central patch of Transylvania on the eastern realms of the Carpathians 'Hungarian Transylvania', but going around much of Székely Land (Ţara Secuilor in Romanian, Székelyföld in Hungarian) it can feel that way. It's so near to Saxon towns Braşov and Sighişoara, yet the spirit of many towns – such as Odorheiu Secuiesc (Székelyudvarhely in Hungarian) and Miercurea Ciuc (Csíkszereda in Hungarian), where ethnic Hungarians comprise the majority, or the even-split of Târgu Mureş

(Marosvásárhely in Hungarian) – feels almost foreign.

The area is home to many Székelys, ethnic Hungarians who live and communicate almost exclusively in their Hungarian dialect. A level of tension still exists between Romanians and Hungarians, who battled each other during WWI and WWII, and mention of Székely Land or ethnic Hungarians not learning the Romanian language in some parts of Romania will bring out verbal editorials; as does any notion of Romania's treatment of the Hungarians in the 20th century. In Târgu Mureş' main Orthodox church you can see a peasant Jesus dressed in Romanian costume being tortured by nobility in Hungarian costumes. Statues of Romulus and Remus stress Romania's Latin roots, purposefully placed during communist times to undermine the Hungarians' claim. Things haven't entirely settled, as one Hungarian-Romanian noted: 'I tell my son he's Romanian, as am I, but when a Transylvanian person hears my accent, I'm immediately treated as something less than a full-blooded Romanian.'

History

The origins of the Székely (see-kay) people are disputed. Debates rage as to whether they are descendants of the Huns, who arrived in Transylvania in the 5th century and adopted the Hungarian language, or whether they are Magyars who accompanied Attila the Hun on his campaigns in the Carpathian basin and later settled there. Three 'nations' were recognised in medieval Transylvania: the Székelys, the Saxons and the Romanian nobles.

During the 18th century the Székelys suffered at the hands of the Habsburgs, who attempted to convert this devout Protestant ethnic group to Catholicism. Thousands of young Székely men were conscripted into the Austrian army. Local resistance throughout Székely Land led to the massacre of Madéfalva in 1764, after which thousands of Székelys fled across the border into Romanian Moldavia.

Following the union of Transylvania with Romania in 1918, some 200,000 Hungarians – a quarter of whom were Székelys – fled to Hungary. Today, many Hungarian tourists flock to the area, especially to the 'capitals' of Odorheiu Secuiesc and Miercurea Ciuc, to experience pastoral customs already lost in their motherland.

Sfântu Gheorghe

POP 54,312

Blinker your vision against the dehumanising Lego-style apartment blocks, heading straight to the park fringed by attractive Habsburg-era buildings, and Sfântu Gheorghe (32km north of Braşov) merits a visit. In a 2011 census 77% of the city's inhabitants classed themselves as ethnic Hungarian.

Settled in the early 14th century and one of the oldest towns in Transylvania, it developed as a cultural centre for the Székelys from the 15th century onwards, when it became a free town. It was left devastated by Turkish attacks between 1658 and 1671, and a plague in 1717. Today its museum is the region's best place to investigate Székely culture.

There are a number of banks in town including the **Banca Comercială Română** (Str Jozef Bem; ⊘8.30am-6pm Mon-Fri, to 12.30pm Sat), as well as **Tourist Information Bureau** (☏0267-316 474; www.sepsiszentgyorgy.ro; Str 1 Decembrie 1918 2; ⊘7.30am-3.30pm Mon-Wed, to 5pm Thu, to 2pm Fri).

◉ Sights

About 200m south of Central Park, the **Székely National Museum** (Székely Nemzeti Múzeum; ☏0267-312 442; Str Kós Károly; adult/child 6/3 lei; ⊘10am-6pm Tue-Fri, 10am-4pm Sat & Sun) is housed in a building which is itself a masterpiece, designed by leading Hungarian architect Kós Károly between 1911 and 1912 (he designed many of the buildings around Central Park too). Three floors of exhibits include a Hungarian flag from the 1848 revolution, 17th-century knight suits, a stuffed boar and lots of Székely crafts and costumes.

North of the centre, following Str Kossuth Lajos and crossing a bridge over the Debren River, you'll come to the **Fortificată Reformată church**, in whose cemetery you can also see some lovely examples of traditional Székely wooden crosses and graveposts.

SLEEPING & EATING

A decent place to sleep is **Pensiunea Ferdinand Panzio** (☏0740-180 502; www.ferdinandpension.ro; Str Decembrie 1918 number 10; s/d 150/170 lei; P🐾), while **Tribel** (cnr Str 1 Decembrie 1918 & Piaţa Libertăţii; mains from 14 lei; ⊘7am-10pm Mon-Fri, 9am-10pm Sat & Sun; 🐾), near the park, is good for lunch, and **Szentgyörgy Pince** (St George Cellar; St Gábor Áron 14; mains 12-24 lei; ⊘9am-midnight), near the library, great for dinner.

ℹ Getting There & Away

The bus station is 50m north of the train station. Microbuses and maxitaxis go along Str 1 Decembrie 1918 (stops are marked); some finish at a stand north of the market. Frequent services go to Miercurea Ciuc (20 lei), Piatra Neamţ (30 lei) and Târgu Neamţ.

Buy advance train tickets at the **Agenţia de Voiaj CFR** (☏0267-311 680; Str Petrofi Sandor, opposite the Sugas building; ⊘8am-3pm Mon-Fri). While the train station is being renovated there's a blue portacabin next door selling tickets. From Sfântu Gheorghe three trains daily go to Covasna (4 lei, one hour) and 16 go to Braşov (5 lei, 30 to 45 minutes), with eight stopping in Hărman (4.50 lei, 30 minutes).

Spa Towns

COVASNA

The curative powers of mineral waters in the area around Sfântu Gheorghe – such as the 'Fairy Queen Valley' (Valea Zânelor) in Covasna (Kovászna in Hungarian), 28km east – draw a steady crew of older visitors seeking cures for what ails them. Up towards the hills in Covasna, **Hotel Montana** (☏0267-340 290; Str Toth 23; r from 68 lei) feels like stepping into a faded *National Geographic* article from 1979, with lots of old-timers in robes awaiting treatments.

BĂILE TUŞNAD

About 40km north of Sfântu Gheorghe (en route to Miercurea Ciuc) is the more peaceful Băile Tuşnad, in the volcano-made Harghita Mountains, featuring pools and springs in a lush valley. An **InfoTur stand** (☏0266-335 114; ⊘10am-10pm) has listings of 15 *pensiunes* in town (ranging from 90 to 180 lei for a double room); the nearby **Centrul de Informare Eco-Turistica** (☏0723-357 650; ⊘9am-2pm Mon, Wed & Fri), 100m north of the bus station, offers accommodation information too. Across the street is a **pool** (⊘Jun-Sep).

It's possible to hike 40 minutes up the path behind the train tracks to clifftop **Stânca Soimilor** for a valley view.

About 24km southeast, St Anne's Lake is a pretty spot with boats and picnic grounds (no accommodation). An annual pilgrimage is held there on 26 July. One hotel is **Sara Pension** (☏0266-335 110; r 100 lei), with pleasant rooms, a pool and sauna and plenty of activities including kayaking. There's a lakeside restaurant, **Lacul Ciucaş** (📞0266-335 555; mains 14-25 lei), down from the main road.

Buses between Miercurea Ciuc and Sfântu Gheorghe stop here.

Miercurea Ciuc

POP 42,032

Doing a competent impression of being nondescript, Miercurea Ciuc is not as bland as its Soviet-style housing blocks imply. Push on to the old centre, particularly pedestrianised Str Petöfi Sándor, and you'll find a languid gauntlet of restaurants spilling onto the cobbles and a lively cafe-society feel. Celebrated for its nationally loved Ciuc (pronounced 'chook') beer, or the town's hockey fascination, Miercurea Ciuc (Csíkszereda in Hungarian) is a friendly if rather dishevelled place where the population is over 80% ethnic Hungarian. If you're heading to Bicaz Gorges or Lacu Roşu in Moldavia, it's a worthwhile stop-off.

Founded during the reign of Hungarian King Ladislaus I (r 1077–95) around a castle that the king built for himself, Miercurea Ciuc quickly developed into a prosperous commercial centre and the hub of Székely Land cultural activities. Traditional Székely villages such as Leliceni (4km southeast), Misentea and Ciucsângeorgiu (another 2km and 4km south) and Armaseni (2km north of the latter along a dirt track) lie within easy reach of Miercurea Ciuc.

◉ Sights

Franciscan Monastery   CHURCH

Two kilometres south of the centre in the Şumuleu district (Csíksomlyó in Hungarian) is a fine Franciscan monastery, built in 1442 by Iancu de Hunedoara (János Hunyadi), governor of Hungary from 1446 to 1452, to commemorate his great victory against the Turks at Marosszentimre.

The monastery today is the site of the city's main tourist draw, the Pentecostal Pilgrimage. About 300,000 Székelys flock here on Whitsunday (late May/early June) to celebrate their brotherhood.

CITY CENTRE

Miercurea Ciuc's centrepiece, and the proud source of the Ciuc beer logo, is its **Mikó Castle**, which today houses the impressive **Székely Museum of Csík** (Csíki Székely Múzeum; 📞0266-311 727; adult/student 5/2.50 lei; ⏱9am-5pm Tue-Sun). Built from 1623 to 1630,

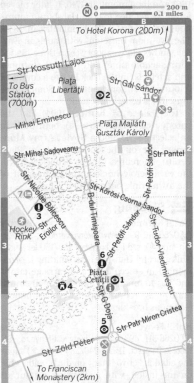

Miercurea Ciuc

the castle was burnt down by Tartars in 1661 and then rebuilt in 1716. It later played a role as defence for the Habsburg empire, housing the first Székely infantry in 1849. The five-room museum, with labels in English, shows old weaponry (eg a three-bladed spring-action knife) and regional costumes and artefacts. In the back lot are a couple of relocated traditional buildings. Some of the museum is being renovated.

The **Palace of Justice** (1904) and the baroque **city hall** (1884–98), both built in an eclectic style, and a **Soviet Army Monument** are on the opposite side of Piaţa Cetăţii. Miercurea Ciuc is a hockey town: there's a heroic **hockey statue** in front of the town's rink, next to Hotel Fenyő.

🛏 Sleeping

Hotel Korona
HOTEL $

(☎0266-310 993; www.korona.panzio.ro; Str Márton Áron 40; s/d incl breakfast 120/150 lei; P�) This graceful Habsburg-era building is ornamented in stucco casts and carriage lamps and has 15 functional rooms with en suites; annoyingly, room doors have glass panels. Generous breakfast.

Hotel Fenyő
HOTEL $$

(☎0266-311 493/5; www.hunguest-fenyo.ro; Str Nicolae Bălcescu 11; s/d 240/284 lei; ��) Near the citadel, Fenyő is ugly on the outside, chic on the inside, with an inviting restaurant and bar. Rooms are decent with bath-tubs, marbled en suites and cable TV, but feel overpriced. Ask for one with a view of the mountains. Great breakfast buffet.

Pension Nefelejcs
PENSION $

(☎0758 808 943; Str Toplita 75; s/d 70/90 lei) Located 1.2km from the centre, these motel-style digs have fresh rooms with rugs, TVs, en suites and reading lamps. Somewhat bland but at least there's a cafe that sells coffees and beers.

🍴 Eating & Drinking

The eating/drinking strip for Miercurea Ciuc is the pedestrianised Str Petöfi Sándor, comprised almost entirely of cafes, bars and pizza joints.

La Jupânul
ROMANIAN $

(Str Zöld Péter 1; mains 6-12 lei; ⊗9am-11pm) Popular with lively eaters and drinkers, this traditional restaurant has bench seats and locally recommended food (pork schnitzels, chicken breast etc).

San Gennaro
ITALIAN $

(Str Petöfi Sándor 15; pasta & pizza 10-15 lei; ⊗9am-midnight) The best place on the strip with tasty salads and delicious thin-crust pizza. There's a decked terrace or you can eat inside.

Café Bar Cuba
BAR

(Str Gál Sándor 6; ⊗8am-4am) This wood-fronted, jazz-piping joint is chichi inside with a hint of Havanesque glamour; or is it just the pics of Ché and Fidel on the walls puffing away at foot-long Cubans. Good coffees and devilish mojitos.

Hockey Klub
BAR

(Str Petöfi Sándor; mains 10-20 lei, beer 3 lei; ⊗9am-midnight) Popular with the local ice-hockey team, this rather old-fashioned bar has sport on the big TV at the end of the room, and low-lit booths for earnest conversations.

ℹ Information

Banca Comercială Română (Kereskedelmi Bank; ☎0266-271 766; cnr Str Kossuth Lajos & Str George Coşbuc; ⊗8.30am-6pm Mon-Fri, to 12.30pm Sat)

Left Luggage (Left Luggage; per 24hr 4 lei; ⊗24hr)

Post Office (Str Kossuth Lajos 3; ⊗7am-8pm Mon-Fri, 8.30am-1pm Sat)

Tourist Information Centre (☎0266-317 007; www.szereda.ro; Piaţa Cetăţii 1, Room 120; ⊗8am-4pm Mon-Fri) A well-hidden information office on the 1st floor of city hall, and probably as a result, rarely visited. Staff hand out a free town guide/map (in Hungarian and Romanian) and can help with area info.

ℹ Getting There & Away

The **Agenţia de Voiaj CFR** (☎0266-311 924; Str Kossuth Lajos 12, 1st fl; ⊗7.30am-6pm Mon-Fri) sells advance tickets. From Miercurea Ciuc there are more than 10 trains to Braşov (28.70 lei, two to 2½ hours) via Sfântu Gheorghe (22.70 lei, 1½ hours); three continue to Bucharest (65 lei, five hours). There are also 11 daily trains to Gheorgheni (18 lei, one hour), and two daily trains to Budapest (300 lei, 20 hours) and Iaşi (85 lei, seven hours).

The **bus station** (☎0266-324 334; Str Braşovului 1) is 50m north of the train station. A couple of daily buses go to Braşov (20 lei, two hours), six to Gheorgheni (10 lei, 1¼ hours), plus six to Sfântu Gheorghe (15 lei), nine to Odorheiu Secuiesc (12 lei), and three to Budapest (110 lei).

Gheorgheni

POP 19,705

Surrounded by stunning scenery on one of Romania's prettiest drives (the 13A and 13B, via Sovata), with the mountains surging over golden plains dotted with flocks of sheep, Gheorgheni is at best an overnight stop. Most of its limited life, including guesthouses, banks and restaurants, gravitates around the triangular park of Piaţa Libertăţii.

👁 Sights

The **Tarisznyás Márton County Museum** (Vàrosi Tarisznyás Márton Muzeum; ☑0266-365 229; Str Rácóczi 1; adult/student 6/3 lei; ⊙9am-5pm Tue-Sun), 400m east of Piaţa Libertăţii, is in an 18th-century Armenian trade house and it's well worth a visit to see the intricately carved wooden fence posts, craftworkers' tools, and other artefacts of Magyar and Székely culture. It backs onto an **Armenian Church**, which dates from the 17th century, when many Armenians lived in town.

Just 6km north of Gheorgheni on the road to Topliţa is the tiny village of Lăzarea (Gyergyószárhegy in Hungarian). Dating from 1235, the predominantly Hungarian village is dominated by its 16th-century **castle** (adult/child 13/10 lei; ⊙9am-5pm Tue-Sat), on the rim of green forested hills. It was to Lăzarea Castle that Gábor Bethlen, later to become prince of Transylvania (r 1613–29), came seeking solace following the death of his son in 1590. There's a small museum and views of the area and the neighbouring monastery from the bastions.

🛏 Sleeping & Eating

Lázár Panzió HOTEL $
(☑0730-118 703, 0266-364 446; www.lazarpanzio.ro; Str Fürdö 3; s/d 78/98 lei; 🅿🛜) Just 30m west of Piaţa Libertăţii, these 15 citrus-yellow rooms have plenty of space, cable TV, reading lights and fresh en suites. There's also a restaurant downstairs and cafe-bar (try the gypsy steak). Central and great value.

Rubin Hotel HOTEL $
(☑0266-365 554; www.rubinhotel.ro; Str Gábor Áron 1; s/d incl breakfast 100/120 lei; 🛜) Rubin has high ceilings and 18 colourful rooms in an early-19th-century building. There's internet in the reception, a welcoming restaurant and you can even get a massage here (30 lei per half-hour) after using its gym.

Astoria HOTEL $
(☑0266-362 333; www.astoria-hotel.ro; Str Două Poduri 2; s/d 80/100 lei; 🛜) Two hundred metres down a crumbling one-way street from the church on Str Márton Áron, Astoria boasts contemporary rooms with slick en suites, fresh white linen and cream walls. Ask for a double room in the turret for the best views. There's also a swanky restaurant (⊙10am to late) with a wood-fire oven.

Cafeteria Marzipán CAFE $
(Piaţa Libertăţii 15; mains 5-10 lei; ⊙8am-10pm) Secreted in a courtyard next to Rubin Hotel, this is a pleasant spot for an alfresco cappuccino and slice of cake or pastry.

ℹ Information

Associata Turistica (☑0744-420 626; www.visitgheorgeni.ro; Piaţa Libertăţii 27; ⊙8am-4pm Mon-Fri) Opened in 2012, this excellent tourist office has info on local things to do including Lăzarea's castle, Lacu Roşu, and the Bicaz Gorge, 26km east. Free walking maps too, as well as accommodation and trekking advice.

ℹ Getting There & Away

The **bus station** (☑0266-364 722) and **train station** (☑0266-364 587) are 1.5km west of the centre via Str Gării. There are two daily buses to Braşov (25 lei, 2½ hours); one to Târgu Mureş (25 lei, four hours), continuing to Cluj-Napoca (30 lei); one to Lacu Roşu (15 lei, one hour); and one to Odorheiu Secuiesc (5 lei, 2¼ hours). Trains going to Braşov (43 lei) and Baia Mare (70 lei), Bistriţa (38 lei) and Bucharest North (70 lei) stop here. There is no public transport to the stations, so many people lug their bags out there by foot. Ask Associata Turistica about getting a cab.

Odorheiu Secuiesc

POP 36,320

Of all Székely Land, nowhere is more 'Hungarian' than Odorheiu Secuiesc (or as locals prefer, Székelyudvarhely), with about 95% of the population being ethnic Hungarian. Surrounded by small hills, dominated by its centrepiece square and church and sprinkled with gelateries and cafes, Odorheiu Secuiesc is a low-key place to stretch your legs. Some weekends there's a market selling crafts on Str Kossuth Lajos.

Settled on an ancient Roman military camp, Odorheiu Secuiesc developed as a small craft town between the 11th and 13th centuries. The Craftmen's Market, held in the citadel in mid-July, carries on the town's tradition of craft guilds set up by King Matthias Corvinus in 1485. Politics is often a part of conversation, and you're more likely to hear about the tensions between Romanian and ethnic Hungarian politicians here than elsewhere in Székely Land.

The train and bus stations, reached via Str Bethlen Gábor, are a 10-minute walk north of the centre; the bus station is 100m southwest of the train station (west of the tracks). Streets (and everything else, actually) get two names here – Hungarian and Romanian.

⊙ Sights

Visiting Odorheiu Secuiesc can occupy an afternoon, or you can take up Herr Travel (p120) on one of its interesting walking tours.

Walk east past the impressive **city hall** (1895–96) to the 18th-century baroque **Hungarian Reformed Church** (Református Templom).

Behind the Hungarian Reformed Church is Piaţa Márton Áron. Just below the steps leading to the town's first **Roman Catholic church** (Római Katolikus Plébániatemplom; built 1787–91) is a statue of the square's namesake bishop, who received a life sentence for promoting Hungarian rights during the communist era. At the head of the park is a **WWI & WWII Monument**.

Franciscan Monastery & Church   CHURCH
(Szent Ferencrendi Templom és Kolostor; Piaţa Primeriei 15; ⊙10am-6pm Tue-Sun) At the western end of the main square, Piaţa Primeriei, stands the Franciscan Monastery & Church, built from 1712 to 1779.

Citadel   CHURCH
Odorheiu Secuiesc's medieval citadel (*vár*), built between 1492 and 1516, is almost fully intact today, and houses an agricultural college. Visitors can freely stroll about its inner walls.

Haáz Rezső Museum   MUSEUM
(www.hrmuzeum.ro; Str Kossuth Lajos 29; adult 5 lei; ⊙9am-4pm Tue-Fri, 9am-1pm Sat & Sun) South of the main square, this excellent museum hosts travelling exhibitions and had a compelling study of Leonardo Da Vinci's war machines when we passed.

Chapel of Jesus   CHURCH
(Jézus Kápolna; Str Bethlen Gábor) The town's best church lies 2km south of the centre on Str Bethlen Gábor. The small fortified Chapel of Jesus is one of the oldest architectural monuments in Transylvania, built during the 13th century. It's usually locked, but you can ask for entry at house No 143 on the main road next door.

☞ Tours

Herr Travel   CULTURAL TOUR
(☏0722-201 997; www.guide2romania.ro) An ambitious agency arranging hiking, biking, caving, food, culture and adventure tours around the region.

🛏 Sleeping

Herr Travel can arrange a room in university housing (pricey at 70 lei per person including meals).

Korona Panzió   HOTEL $
(☏0266-310 993; www.koronapanzio.ro; Piaţa Primeriei 12/2; s/d 91/140 lei; @🖧) Pine-accented rooms at this decent motel-style accommodation. Better still is its flowery courtyard garden and restaurant – try the traditional dishes such as chicken polenta, tripe soup and goulash. Free internet and, weirdly, free solarium!

Hotel Târnava-Kükülő   HOTEL $$
(☏0266-213 963; www.kukullo.ro; Piaţa Primeriei 16; s/d 215/290 lei; ☻@🖧) Boxy rooms with a few sticks of furniture, bureau, armoire, cable TV and small en suites. There's a sauna, a plunge pool, and massage on request (half-hour costs 25 lei).

Pensiune Petofi   GUESTHOUSE $
(☏0756-093 926; www.petofipanzio.ro; Str Petőfi Sándor 2; s/d 91/140 lei; 🅿🌂🖧) This popular central hotel has a decent restaurant serving Hungarian fare. Rooms are a little dark with tangerine-colored quilts, quality darkwood furniture and bijou en suites. Cable TV and air-con.

✗ Eating & Drinking

There are some fast-food joints along Str Bethlen Gábor north of Piaţa Márton Áron.

Pizza 21   ITALIAN $
(Str Crişan; pizzas 11-16 lei; ⊙10am-midnight) A couple of blocks north of the centre, this cosy pizzeria with Gustavian-green furniture and facade has tasty thin-crust pizza, calzone and pasta, as well as a few Thai dishes.

Gondüző   ROMANIAN $$
(Str Sântimbru; mains18 lei; ⊙10am-midnight) This upscale restaurant with flashy decor has tasty fare including soup, pork cutlets,

fried trout and roasted chicken breast with stewed fruit and rice. A few vegie dishes.

G Café/G Pub CAFE
(Str Sântimbru; ◷7.30am-11pm Mon-Fri, 9am-midnight Sat & Sun; ☎) Could this be Transylvania's coolest boho bar? Grab a coffee, sink into a faded leather armchair and let your eye wander across antique photos, candlebra, Edvard Munch–style paintings and walls plastered in old newspapers. Add to this a soundtrack of lounge music and the earnest chatter of intellectuals and you feel as if you've been airlifted from 1930s Paris.

ℹ Information

There are ATMs and banks along Str Kossuth Lajos.

Korona Panzió (Piaţa Primeriei 12/2; per hr 3 lei; ◷10am-11pm; ☎) Hotel with internet access.

Post Office (Str Bethen Gábor 56; ◷7.30am-7.30pm Mon-Fri, 8am-1pm Sat)

Tourinfo (☎0266-217 427; www.tourinfo.ro; Piaţa Márton Áron 6; ◷8am-8pm Mon-Fri) An organised place with maps, brochures and multilingual staff.

ℹ Getting There & Away

Transport into Odorheiu is limited. From the **bus station** (☎0266-218 495; Str Târgului 10), 100m southwest of the train station, there's one daily bus to Sovata (11 lei, one hour), one to Miercurea Ciuc (13 lei, one hour), eight to Târgu Mureş (20 lei, two hours) and a few to Budapest (100 lei, 12 hours). A few Hungary-bound buses are run by **Csavargó** (☎0266-249 253) and **Scorpion Trans** (☎0266-218 495); both have ticket windows at the bus station.

Only five daily trains clank out towards Sighişoara (1½ hours, 6 lei) – at research time they left at 6am, 2.30pm and 10.20pm.

Odorheiu Secuiesc to Târgu Mureş

CORUND

Twenty-five kilometres north of Odorheiu Secuiesc, this small village is basically a one-street gauntlet of stalls hugging the road. Expect to buy authentic embroidered chemises, woolly socks, waistcoats and felt hats, as well as animal-skin rugs and green, brown and cobalt-blue pottery.

Buses to Sovata go through here from Odorheiu Secuiesc.

PRAID

Eight kilometres north of Corund on the road to Sovata, Praid is home to a **salt mine** (☎0266-240 200; www.salinapraid.ro; Str Állomás 44; adult/child 20/12 lei; ◷8am-2pm Mon-Sat, 10am-1pm Sun summer, 8am-12.45pm Mon-Sat & 10am-12.45pm Sun winter), a bizarre underground world with a church, sculpture, swing sets, slides, a cafe selling soda and beer, and internet access(!). Locals come for extended underground treatments for bronchitis and other respiratory illnesses at the base, 120m below the surface. A bus leads down dark tunnels – it's almost apocalyptic.

There's a saltwater outdoor pool a couple of hundred metres west of the entrance to the salt mine.

SOVATA

Forty kilometres north of Odorheiu Secuiesc and 60km east of Târgu Mureş (but somewhere between St Moritz and Blackpool), with its green saltwater lakes surrounded by lush vegetation and forests, Sovata has a touristy feel. The most popular spot is **Lacu Ursu** (Bear Lake; ◷mid-Jun–Sep), enjoying a steady temperature of between 30°C and 40°C. People have been coming here for the lakes' restorative properties – said to cure infertility – since the 19th century, and with its faded summer villas lining the road, the place has the air of a lost snapshot from a Chekhov play.

Sovata Tourist Information Centre (☎0265-577 421; www.sovatatravel.ro; ◷9am-9pm Jun-Aug, to 5pm Tue-Sat Sep-May), 3km northeast of the crossroads and 750m from Lacu Ursu, helps find homes, hotels and *pensiunes*. It rents bikes for 20 lei per day. Profits support a local orphanage. There are also a couple of ATMs in the main town of Sovata itself.

A few minutes walk from Lacu Ursu, **Villa Sara** (☎0265-570 159; www.vilasara.ro; Str Trandafirilor 86; r 170 lei; ℗☎) is a cosy place to stay. Opposite the blackened church.

Five minibuses daily connect Sovata with Odorheiu Secuiesc (11 lei, one hour).

Târgu Mureş

POP 140, 674

Lively Târgu Mureş, with its nearly even Hungarian and Romanian populations, as well as a sizeable Roma population, offers a different slice of Transylvania past and present. Buildings in its centre sport a more colourful, even flamboyant, Habsburg spirit, with tiled rooftops of government buildings jutting over heroic statues and floral paint jobs.

Târgu Mureş (Marosvásárhely in Hungarian, Neumarkt in German) was first documented as 'Novum Forum Sicolorum' in 1322. It developed as a leading garrison town and later as an important cultural and academic centre. In 1658 it was attacked by Turks, who captured 3000 inhabitants and transported them back to Istanbul as slave labour.

During the Ceauşescu regime, Târgu Mureş was a 'closed city', with all ethnic groups other than Romanians forbidden to settle here, in an effort to dilute the Hungarian community.

Târgu Mureş

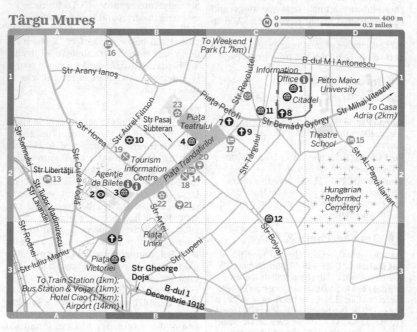

Târgu Mureş

◉ Sights
1 City Museum C1
2 County Council Building A2
3 Culture Palace B2
4 Ethnographic Museum B2
5 Greco-Catholic Cathedral B3
6 Memorial to Victims of the 1989
   Revolution B3
7 Orthodox Cathedral C1
8 Reform Church C1
9 Roman Catholic Church C2
10 Synagogue B2
11 Teleki House C1
12 Teleki Library/Bolyai Museum C2

🛏 Sleeping
13 Atlantic A2
14 Hotel Concordia B2

15 Pensiune Ana Maria D2
16 Pensiunea Tempo B1
17 Premier Hotel C2

✕ Eating
18 Dona Restaurant B2
19 Emma Vendéglő B2
   Hotel Concordia .... (see 14)
   Laci Csarda .... (see 16)

☕ Drinking
20 Old City Pub B2
21 Teresa Scara B2

✪ Entertainment
22 Cinema Arta B2
23 National Theatre B1
   State Philharmonic .... (see 3)

In 1990 Târgu Mureş was the scene of bloody clashes between Hungarian students, demonstrating for a Hungarian-language faculty in their university, and Romanians who raided the local Hungarian political party offices. The Romanian mob attempted to gouge out the eyes of playwright András Sütő, who remained blind in one eye until his death in 2006. According to Human Rights Watch World Report for 1990, the violence was stirred up by rumours that armed Romanian peasants were being bussed in from outlying villages to fortify Romanian protesters.

Today Hungarian seems to be undergoing a renaissance in Târgu Mureş, with many local songs in Hungarian only or in both languages. Carnival comes on the last weekend in June, when the city hosts its **Târgu Mureş Days. Felsziget Festival** (www.felsziget.ro) is a big five-day rock/DJ festival at the end of July.

To make the 15-minute walk into town from the train station, walk 1km straight up to Piaţas Victoriei, Unirii and Trandafirilor, the main thoroughfare where most hotels and travel agencies are. From the bus station, turn right along Str Gheorghe Doja and follow the street north 1.75km to Piaţa Trandafirilor.

The tourist information office offers free maps of the city.

Sights

PIAŢA TRANDAFIRILOR & AROUND
The effervescent central Piaţa Trandafirilor is filled with statues, open-air cafes, restaurants, a cinema and theatre. At the northeastern end of Piaţa Trandafirilor are two very different churches.

Culture Palace MUSEUM
(Palatul Culturii; ☑0265-267 629; cnr Piaţa Trandafirilor & Str Enescu; adult/student 10/4 lei; ☻9am-6pm Tue-Sun) Built 1911–13, this secessionist-style building is unlike anything you'll find around Transylvania. Inside its glittering, tiled, steepled roofs are ornate hallways, colourful walls, giant mirrors imported from Venice, and an often-used concert hall (with a dramatic 4463-pipe organ), not to mention several worthwhile museums (all included in the entry price).

The most enchanting is the Hall of Mirrors (Sala Oglinzi), with 12 stained-glass windows lining a 45m hallway; each depicts a Székely fairy tale – check out the creepy devil ravishing the country maiden. The

Art Museum (1st floor) houses many large late-19th-century and early-20th-century paintings; the Archaeological Museum (2nd floor) explains Dacian pieces found in the region (English signage).

County Council Building CULTURAL BUILDING
Next door to the Culture Palace is the County Council Building, with a tiled roof and bright-green spires. Its 60m watchtower *may* open for visitors, but presently the only glimpse of the building's interior you can get is the grand, colourful entry with hand-painted ceilings and stained glass facing the grand staircase upstairs.

Memorial to Victims of the 1989 Revolution MUSEUM
On Piaţa Unirii, just past the Romanian Orthodox Greco-Catholic Cathedral, is a memorial made of five connected wooden crosses in tribute to the eight locals killed here.

Teleki Library/Bolyai Museum MUSEUM
(www.telekiteka.ro; Str Bolyai 17; admission by donation; ☻10am-6pm Tue-Fri, to 1pm Sat & Sun) The Teleki Library (under renovation at the time of writing) contains some 230,000 (and counting) rare books. The adjoining Bolyai Museum (if locked, ask the front desk to open it) is dedicated to Târgu Mureş' sons Farkas and János Bolyai, 19th-century mathematicians whose advances superseded Newtonian theories, shaping space science as we know it. If that's boring to you, scalps and skull parts are also displayed.

Orthodox Cathedral CHURCH
The dominating Orthodox Cathedral (1925–34) was designed to impress, with gold icons (as well as a politically charged mural of a 'Romanian peasant' Jesus being whipped by nobles in Hungarian costumes inside; look to the left and right after entering).

Roman Catholic Church CHURCH
(Biserica Sfântul Jonos) Across the street from the Orthodox Cathedral is this airier, baroque-style church, which dates from 1728.

Ethnographic Museum MUSEUM
(☑0265-250 169; Piaţa Trandafirilor 11; adult/student 4/2 lei; ☻9am-4pm Tue-Fri, to 2pm Sat, to 1pm Sun) On the square's western side, just past adjoining Piaţa Teatrul, is the simple Ethnographic Museum, housed in the baroque Toldalagi Palace (1762). The collection of traditional fabrics, pots, looms and tools is

dryly explained in English. It was closed for renovation when we passed.

Synagogue JEWISH
(Str Aurel Filmon 21) A block west of the Ethnographic Museum is an ornate and well-preserved synagogue from 1900. Before WWII, 5500 Jews lived in Târgu Mureş; now only about 100 live here.

THE CITADEL & AROUND
A block northeast of Piaţa Trandafirilor, the huge citadel dates from 1492 and is best seen from outside. On its southern end, and accessed separately from the rest, is the Reform Church (1491), with the nicest grounds. Gates lead into the main area from either side, but it's easiest from the north-eastern side. There are a couple of theatres as well as an army recruitment centre inside.

City Museum MUSEUM
(adult/student 4/1 lei; ⊙9am-4pm Tue-Fri, 10am-2pm Sat & Sun) The citadel's most appealing attraction, in the 1492 gate tower on the western wall, is a small museum, with pottery fragments and old decrees.

Teleki House HISTORIC BUILDING
Towards Piaţa Trandafirilor, on Piaţa Bernády György, is the yellow-painted, baroque Teleki House (built 1797–1803). Joseph Teleki served as governor of Transylvania between 1842 and 1848.

Weekend Park SWIMMING POOL
(cnr Str Luntraşilor & Aleea Carpaţi; adult/child 5/2 lei; ⊙8am-midnight, closed Mon) In high summer when the mercury tops 40°C, this complex, 2.5km north of the centre, is a welcome oasis. There's a couple of giant pools, a few kids' pools, plus a beach volleyball area. Take Str Revoluţiei north, then go left on Str Luntraşilor. It's poorly sign-posted.

🛏 Sleeping
Târgu Mureş can often be full come weekends, and budget accommodation seems to wither no sooner than it has set up. If desperate, pick up a *Zile şi Nopţi* weekly, which includes accommodation listings. Contact Antrec (☎0744-707 799; mures@antrec.ro) for help finding *pensiunes* in the region.

TOP CHOICE Hotel Concordia BOUTIQUE HOTEL $$
(☎0265-260 602; Piaţa Trandafirilor 45; s/d €56/64; P✦🕸🛜🏊) By far the glitziest and most contemporary option in town; with its

retro-nodding aesthetics and minimal boho edge, it's as if a slice of London's Soho has been transplanted here. Rooms have zebra-patterned chairs, claret-red carpets and there's a glass-roofed pool, massage and a Jacuzzi.

Pensiunea Tempo PENSION $
(☎0265-213 552; Str Morii 27; s/d incl breakfast 120/160 lei) Festooned in baskets of flowers, this motel-style courtyard accommodation is very comfy. En-suite rooms include flat-screens, desks, swallow-you-up beds and a welcoming restaurant next door.

Premier Hotel HOTEL $$
(☎0365-430 951; www.hotelpremierms.ro; Piaţa Trandafirilor 54; s/d 150/170 lei; 🛜) Beneath the archway marked 'Pensiunea History' walk a few yards into the tunnel, then hang a right for this 1st-floor boutique hotel. With its ochre walls, large rooms, designer furniture, flat-screens and cable TV, Premier lives up to its name.

Pensiune Ana Maria PENSION $
(☎0265-264 401; Str AL Papui Ilarian 17; s/d incl breakfast 90/120 lei; P✦@🛜) This family-run hotel boasts traditional Austro-Hungarian furnishings, and some rooms even have wooden awnings over the blue beds. Rooms also have TVs and large en suites. Breakfasts here are so generous you may want to pay extra!

Atlantic HOTEL $$
(☎0265-268 381; www.atlantichotel.ro; Str Libertăţii 15; r 180 lei; P✦🕸🛜) This flamingo-pink hotel is smart and mercifully cool with a homely restaurant and garden. Rooms have flat-screens, large beds and accompanying rubber plants. Check out the compendium of animal pelts on the 1st floor.

Hotel Tineret HOTEL $
(☎0265-217 441; Str Nicolae Grigorescu 17-19; s/d 90/120 lei; P🛜) Around 1.5km from the centre, Tineret is unimaginative but smart. With a nice terrace to drink on and clean rooms with en suites and all the trimmings such as cable TV and minibar, it's a decent option. There's even a barber!

Hotel Ciao HOTEL $
(☎0265-250 250; Str Gheorghe Doja 143; s/d 119/139 lei; 🕸@🛜) Right next to the Autogara, rooms here are fresh and large with mustard brown walls, cable TV, and clean en suites. Perfect if you have an early bus departure. It's 1.5km outside the centre.

✖ Eating

Dona Restaurant
ROMANIAN $

(Piaţa Trandafirilor 36-38; mains 15 lei; ⊘24hr) Dona is a very tasteful, shall we say 'alpine-chic', 24-hour eatery. The menu dishes up crêpes, omelettes, grilled gypsy's nape of pork, pizza and pasta. There's a hole-in-the-wall bakery too, and an outside terrace to people watch.

Emma Vendéglő
ROMANIAN $$

(Str Horea 6; mains 11-25 lei; ⊘11am-11pm) This low-key Hungarian restaurant-bar brings in the locals for its borschts and four-course dinners. Best is the chicken with cucumber sauce and polenta.

Hotel Concordia
INTERNATIONAL $$

(☑0265-260 602; Piaţa Trandafirilor 45; 20 lei; ⊘closed Sun) With a bright, modern interior of wood floors and retro orange glass lamp-shades, this place is buzzing with trendy urbanites. A delicious menu of contemporary and traditional dishes – try the chicken liver and onion (10 lei) – as well as Chinese cuisine, pizza and salads.

Laci Csarda
ROMANIAN $$

(Str Morii 27; mains 15-25 lei; ⊘10am-12am) Attached to the Pensiunea Tempo, this terraced and indoor restaurant has a Hungarian-accented menu, with a lavish selection of cold plates, soups, goulash, pies, steaks and salads.

� Drinking

Old City Pub
BAR

This cosy wood-panelled and exposed-brick subterranean haunt draws a stew of students and moneyed urbanites. The decor is faintly Sherlock Holmes; the food's good too, with salads, spring rolls, nachos and bruschetta (mains 8 lei). Just off the square through an archway.

Teresa Scara
BAR

(Piaţa Trandafirilor; ⊘10am-10pm) This simple beer garden with slatted wooden tables, umbrella shades and a lively soundtrack packs in the locals come afternoon. With three tiers of seating, there's a pleasant summery vibe here.

☆ Entertainment

The lovely Culture Palace (p123) houses the **Agenţie de Bilete** (☑0265-212 522; ⊘10am-1pm & 5-7pm Mon-Fri, 10am-1pm Sat & Sun), which sells tickets for a wide variety of shows, including opera and the **State Philharmonic** (☑0265-261 420; tickets 20 lei) concerts (held Thursday nights).

National Theatre
THEATRE

(www.orizont.net/teatru; Piaţa Teatrului 1; tickets cost 20 lei) Events at this venue (with very 1978 decor) are in Hungarian and Romanian.

Cinema Arta
CINEMA

(Piaţa Trandafirilor; tickets 10 lei) Next to McDonald's, this cinema plays Hollywood films in their original language.

ℹ️ Information

There's left luggage at the bus station and train station (per day 7 lei, depending on size). ATMs are easy to find in the centre, including at **Banca Carpaţi** (cnr Piaţa Trandafirilor & Str Mihai Viteazul; ⊘8.30am-5pm Mon-Fri).

Information Office (☑0265-250 337; ⊘8am-3pm or 4pm Mon-Fri) There's a small information office near the citadel's northern gate; English-speaking staff can tell you if a concert or special exhibition is going on in the citadel.

Post Office (☑0265-213 386; Str Revoluţei 1; ⊘7.30am-7.30pm Mon-Fri, 8am-1pm Sat)

Tourism Information Centre (☑0365-404 934; www.cjmures.ro/turism; cnr Piaţa Trandafirilor & Str Enescu; ⊘8am-8pm Tue-Thu, to 4pm Mon & Sat) Occupying the enviable corner spot at the Culture Palace, this superbly run centre offers free maps and information on the region, as well as advice on accommodation and transport.

Transair (☑0265-266 592; www.transair.ro; Piaţa Trandafirilor 3¾, 2nd fl; ⊘9am-5pm Mon-Fri, 10am-2pm Sat) This busy travel agency can arrange trips to Roma villages to hear live music, car rental and a wealth of adventure trips around the area. There's no sign on the sidewalk. The office is upstairs through the first door to the right in the central courtyard.

ℹ️ Getting There & Away

Târgu Mureş Airport (p264) is 14km southwest of town (on the road to Cluj-Napoca). Catch a bus from outside the theatre (buses leave here two hours before every major flight). **Wizz Air** (www.wizzair.com) has regular flights to/from Budapest, and **Tarom** (☑0265-250 170; www .tarom.ro; Piaţa Trandafirilor 6-8; ⊘9am-5pm Mon-Fri, to noon Sat) flies several times per week to Bucharest.

The **bus station** (☑0265-237 774; Str Gheorghe Doja) sends daily bus and maxitaxi services, including hourly maxitaxis to Sighişoara (11 lei, 1½ hours), continuing on to Braşov (35 lei, four hours) and Bucharest (58 lei, seven hours). There are also five daily buses to Bistriţa (14 lei,

2½ hours), three to Budapest (90 lei), five to Cluj-Napoca (25 lei, 2½ hours), two to Sibiu (15 lei, three hours), and frequent services to Sovata (10 lei, 1¼ hours).

The **Agenţia de Voiaj CFR** (☑0265-236 284; Train Station; ⊘24hr) sells advance tickets. From Târgu Mureş there are two daily trains to Bucharest (85 lei, 8½ hours) and Sibiu (27 lei, 5½ hours), and one each to Budapest (160 lei, 7½ hours), Cluj-Napoca (38 lei, 2¼ hours), Iaşi (20 lei, 6½ hours) and Timişoara (70 lei, 6½ hours).

❶ Getting Around

Central Târgu Mureş is small enough to cover by foot. Bus 18 (1.5 lei) goes from the stop at Piaţa Teatrul and Piaţa Trandafirilor to the bus station; bus 5 goes to the train station. A taxi to or from the airport is about 30 lei.

Autonom (☑0265-250 424; www.autonom .ro; Piaţa Trandafirilor) Rents a variety of cars, including the Fiat Panda (from 175 lei per day); hire it for longer and the price drops sharply.

TUI Travel/Eurolines (☑0265-306 126; Str Călăraşilor 38; ⊘9am-8pm Mon-Fri, 10am-2pm Sat) Rents Dacia Logans from 158 lei per day.

SOUTHWEST TRANSYLVANIA

The patch of Transylvania between the Retezat Mountains and Apuseni Mountains, west of the Cluj-Napoca-Sibiu highway, is home to Dacian ruins, mountaintop citadels and one of Eastern Europe's greatest 'Dracula-style' castles (in Hunedoara).

The history is undeniable. The pre-Roman Dacia kingdom lived in full force in the area until Romans conquered the capital Sarmizegetusa in AD 106. The union of Transylvania with Romania occurred in Alba Iulia. Twice. It happened in 1599 and again after WWI.

Those willing to drive on back roads – such as the lovely hilly drive from Deva to Abrud – will get a break from often-industrial, highly trafficked roads.

Alba Iulia

POP 65,748

Alba Iulia is a good stop-off if you're heading between Cluj-Napoca and Sibiu. While the modern part of town does its best to put you off with a handful of hotels and banks back-dropped by an ugly concrete sprawl, the amazingly intact citadel is magical. Wander its rarefied collection of churches and mon-uments early morning to avoid the crowds, and come evening you may be lucky enough to hear the dulcet voice of a priest wafting from the Roman Catholic cathedral.

The nation announced the union of Transylvania with Romania here in 1599 and 1918, which were hugely important to Romanians. Alba Iulia was known by the Dacians as Apulum, serving both as the capital of Upper Dacia and, later, during Roman times, as the largest centre in the Dacian province of the Roman empire. From 1542 to 1690 Alba Iulia was the capital of the principality of Transylvania. Romania's national day (1 December) is a time of major celebrations in Alba Iulia.

◉ Sights

Alba Carolina Citadel   CASTLE
The imposing Alba Carolina Citadel, richly carved with sculptures and reliefs in a baroque style, is the dominant sight of the city of Alba Iulia, and worth stopping to see for a couple of hours. It was originally constructed in the 13th century, although the fortress you see today was built between 1714 and 1738.

Str Mihai Viteazul runs up from the lower town to the **first gate** of the fortress, adorned with sculptures inspired by Greek mythology. From here, a stone road leads to the **third gate** of the fortress, dominated by an **equestrian statue of Carol VI of Austria**. Above the gate is **Horea's death cell** (Celula lui Horea), where the leader of the great 1784 peasant uprising awaited his unpleasant end.

Just before you enter the third gate, a footpath leads 500m south to an out-of-sight **Orthodox church** (Biserica Memorială Sfânta Treime). The wooden church, brought to Alba Iulia in 1990 from Maramureş, stands on the site of a former Metropolitan cathedral built by Mihai Viteazul in 1597 and destroyed by the Habsburgs in 1713.

Inside the gates, about 200m west in a park, is the Soviet-style 22.5m Costozza monument, which commemorates the soldiers and officers of the 50th infantry regiment of Alba Iulia, who were killed while fighting in the Habsburg army against Italy in the battle of Costozza in 1866.

Just west is the Unification Hall (Sala Unirii; 1900), built as a military casino. In this hall the act of unification between Romania and Transylvania was signed during the Great Assembly of 1 December 1918.

Facing the hall from the south is a large **equestrian statue of Mihai Viteazul** (Michael the Brave), ruler of Romania from 1593 to 1601. On 1 November 1599 he visited Alba Iulia to celebrate the unification of Wallachia, Moldavia and Transylvania, a union that crumbled after his assassination in 1601. Behind the statue is the Princely Court, former residence of the princes of Transylvania, which was built in several stages from the 16th century onwards.

Immediately west is the 18th-century **Roman Catholic Cathedral**, built on the site of a Romanesque church destroyed during the Tartar invasion of 1241. Many famous Transylvanian princes are buried here.

Inside the former Babylon building (1851) is the impressive **Unification Museum** (Muzeul Unirii; ☎0258-813 300; adult/child 10/5 lei; ☉10am-7pm Tue-Sun summer, to 5pm Tue-Sun winter), one of Romania's most interesting museums. Many Roman sculptures, votives and pillars found in the area are subtitled in English. Don't miss the section devoted to the peasant revolutionaries Closca, Crișan and Horea. The highlight is a replica of the wheel used to crush Closca and Horea to death in 1785 (Crișan killed himself in prison before he could be tortured to death).

Near the western entrance of the citadel, the highly impressive **Orthodox Cathedral** (originally known as the 'Church of the Coronation') was built in 1921–22 and is designed in the shape of a Greek circumscribed cross, and surrounded by a wall of decorative colonnades enclosing its peaceful gardens within. A 58m-tall bell tower marks the main entrance to the complex.

There are English and French information panels placed throughout the citadel, making it easy to delve into its history without a guide.

🛏 Sleeping

TOP CHOICE Hotel Medieval   HOTEL $$$
(☎0374-079 990; www.hotel-medieval.ro; r 320-685 lei incl breakfast; ☺🖥) Housed in former 18th-century barracks within the citadel this new five-star belle retains much of its grandeur with antique furniture, costumed staff, grandfather clocks, marble floors and ornamental gardens. Rooms are divine with carved beds, wood ceilings, and enormous clawed baths. Don't miss the hotel's three restaurants.

Villa Precosia   HOTEL $$
(☎0258-814 033; www.precosia.ro; Str Lucian Blaga 10; s/d incl breakfast 185/280 lei; 🖥) This sumptuously columned hotel is a shot in the arm to Alba Iulia's sleeping scene, and has seven nice en-suite rooms with an international feel to them. There's also a sunny cafe and an inviting Italian restaurant.

Hotel Parc   HOTEL $$
(☎0258-816 642; www.hotelparc.ro; Str Primăverii 4; s/d 240/300 lei; 🅿❄🖥🏊) Looking like a 1970s cruise ship on the outside, this swish hotel has art-deco aspirations with a gold lift and spangly lobby. Rooms are sunny with mustard walls, thick carpets, minibar, cable TV and air-con.

Flamingo   PENSION $
(☎0258-816 354; Str Mihai Viteazul 6; r with shared/private bathroom 70/120 lei) Basic digs in

---

DISAPPEARING MOUNTAIN

Eighty kilometres from Alba Iulia or Deva, the **Roșia Montană** ('Red Mountain') has mines dating from Dacian times, 2000 years ago – indeed some of the gold mined here wound up in Rome. In recent years Canadian mining company Gabriel Resources launched a plan to create the continent's largest opencast cyanide goldmine here, a 16-year project that would reportedly extract 200 tonnes of gold and silver. Meanwhile, Unesco has been lobbying to preserve the mountain – and its 7km of historic Roman mines, resident bats, 91 species of birds, lynx and wolves – as a protected heritage site. The Romanian government has yet to decide the mountain's fate.

Also opposed to Gabriel Resources' plans is Alburnus Maior, an NGO based in the village of Roșia Montană. Forty families opposed to leaving farms they have occupied since the 16th century (and that Gabriel Resources is now attempting to purchase), form the backbone of the organisation, which organises Fun Fest – a coalescence of documentary-makers, musicians, artists and guest speakers, taking place in Roșia Montană in the middle of May. All proceeds from the festival go towards saving the mountain. Visit: www.rosiamontana.org to learn more.

Alba Iulia

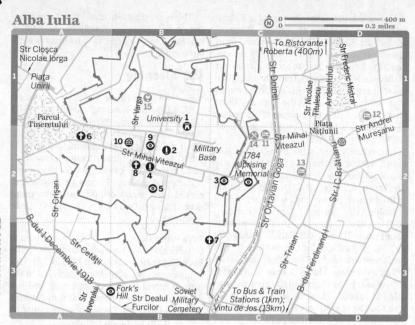

a guesthouse close to the eastern gate of the citadel. Rooms with shared bathroom are up a creaky spiral staircase with off-putting glass panel doors, but bearable if you're looking to save a few lei.

Eating & Drinking

TOP CHOICE Pub 13   STEAKHOUSE $$
(3rd Gate, Citadel; mains 20 lei; ⊗noon-2am) Built into the wall of the citadel, this ambiently lit cavern of a restaurant is hung with armour and candlebra, and has a menu bursting with steak, salad and pizza. Try the maize porridge served with cheese and sour cream (16 lei).

Ristorante Roberta   PIZZERIA $
(Str Tudor Vladimirescu 4; pizza & pasta 17 lei; ⊗9am-midnight) This Italian pizzeria has check cloth tables and stucco Corinthian columns, and dishes up very good pizza and pasta. Shame about the location on a busy road in the new town.

Pas   BAR
(Str Varga 4; ⊗8am-midnight; ☎) A bubble of bohemian flair hidden among the stately lines of the citadel, this bijou bar pipes Coltrane jazz onto its terrace from its bikers' lair interior.

Information

Albena Tours (☎0258-812 140; office@albena tours.ro; Str Fredric Mistral 2; ⊗9am-5pm Mon-Fri, to 1pm Sat) Central travel agent, more focused on travel from Romania, but can help with regional tours.

Banca Comercială Română (B-dul Regele Carol I 35; ⊗8.30am-6pm Mon-Fri, to 12.30pm Sat) Gives cash advances.

Left Luggage (train station; per day 6 lei; ⊗24hr)

Post Office (B-dul Brătianu 1; ⊗7am-8pm Mon-Fri)

Getting There & Away

Direct bus and maxitaxi services from Alba Iulia's **bus station** (☎0258-812 967) include five daily to Bucharest (51 lei), 13 to Cluj-Napoca (20 lei, two hours), four to Deva (17 lei, 1½ hours), 12 to Sibiu (15 lei, 1½ hours), three to Târgu Jiu (36 lei), three to Târgu Mureş (32 lei, 2¼ hours) and two to Timişoara (40 lei). Local buses 3 and 4 run from the stations to the citadel and centre.

The **Agenţia de Voiaj CFR** (☎0258-816 678; Calea Moţilor 1; ⊗8am-4pm Mon-Fri) sells advance tickets as well as acting as agent for **Blue Air** (www.smartflying.ro). There are three daily trains to Bucharest (106 lei, 6½ to nine hours), Cluj-Napoca (38 lei, 2½ hours), Deva (9 lei, two hours), Timişoara (58 lei, five hours) and

Alba Iulia

Sibiu (12 lei, 2½ hours). There are also a couple of daily trains to Prague (515 lei, 16 hours) and Vienna (261 lei, 12 hours).

Deva

POP 66,571

Deva is crowned by its 13th-century citadel and Hollywood-style sign. Apart from grabbing a cappuccino and pizza down the pedestrianised B-dul 1 Decembrie, or popping into a handful of museums, Deva does little to warrant an extended stay. That said, if you're on a castle hunt headed for Corvin Castle, stopping in Deva is *definitely* preferable to staying in Hunedoara's industrial sprawl.

◎ Sights

Rising some 270m from town on a rocky hilltop, the **citadel** (admission free) bestrides the town. A **funicular** (☑0254-220 288; return 10 lei; ⊙9am-9pm) saves visitors from the steep climb (which leads up behind Parcul Cetăţii at the west end of B-dul 1 Decembrie). At the top there are plenty of stone walls to ponder and 360-degree views of the surrounding hills.

Work started on the stone fortress in 1250. Legend says the wife of the mason was bur-

ied alive in the walls to ensure its safekeeping. In 1453 Iancu de Hunedoara expanded the fort, just in time to imprison Unitarian activist Dávid Ferenc (1510–79), who died here. In 1784, during the peasant uprising led by Horea, Crişan and Cloşca, the fortress served as a refuge for terrified nobles fearful of being killed by militant peasants. In 1849 Hungarian nationalists attacked Austrian generals held up in the fort. The four-week siege ended with the mighty explosion of the castle's gunpowder deposits, which left the castle in ruins.

Down by the park, at the foot of the hill, is the **County Museum** (Muzeul Judeţean Hunedoara-Deva; ☑0254-216 750; adult/student 4/1.50 lei; ⊙10am-6pm), housed in the 17th-century Magna Curia Palace. Expect an exhibition on local flora and fauna – including huge stuffed bisons – geology and a mix of classics thrown in for good measure.

⊨ Sleeping

Budget options are limited.

TOP CHOICE Pensiunea Sub Cetate   PENSION $
(☑0254-212 535; www.subcetate.ro; B-dul 1 Decembrie 37b; s/d 100/120 lei; ❋⊛) In the leafy end of town, this well-kept *pensiune* has a garden vivid with flowers. Its 10 en-suite rooms are capacious and clean. There's also a sun-dappled breakfast room. Best are the two front carpeted rooms with balconies.

Hotel Sarmis   HOTEL $$
(☑0254-214 731; www.unita-turism.ro; Str Mareşal Averescu 7; s/d 130/175 lei; P❋⊛) Recently renovated, this sickly, pastel-green and white Aztec-style colossus has 18-rooms decked in dark wood and biscuit-coloured bedspreads, with reading lamps and en suites. Not much character here but reasonable value.

✕ Eating

Pizzeria Veneţia   PIZZERIA $
(B-dul Iuliu Maniu; pizza 8-16 lei; ⊙9am-11pm) This modern indoor/alfresco restaurant covers all the doughy bases from Margherita to La Reine.

Restaurant Castelo   INTERNATIONAL $
(cnr B-dul 1 Decembrie & Str Avram Iancu; mains 15 lei; ⊙9am-midnight; ✐) Near the foot of the hill this shady terraced joint has a steak-heavy menu, as well as pizza, salad and spare ribs Romanian-style. If it gets hot outside, keep cool in its wine-dark interior.

Deva

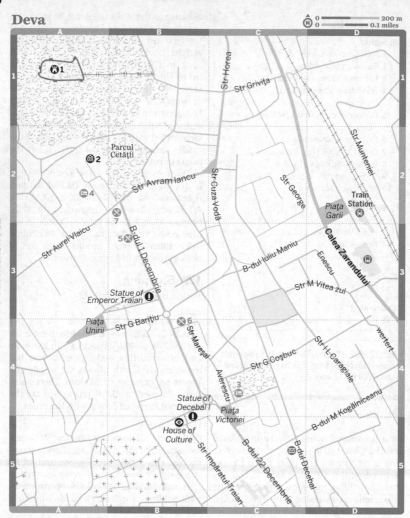

Arta   ICE CREAM **$**
(☺8am-10pm Mon-Fri, 10am-11pm Sat & Sun) Attractive alfresco gelaterie specialising in sugary treats. Grab a pew on the decked terrace and get your people-watching goggles on, between sipping fresh juices (7 lei) and ice cream.

ℹ Information

Internet Club (B-dul Iuliu Maniu; per hr 2.50 lei; ☺24hr) Follow the sign behind the building.

Post Office (B-dul Decebal; ☺8am-8pm Mon-Fri, to 2pm Sat)

Raiffeisen Bank (B-dul Iuliu Maniu; ☺9am-6pm Mon-Fri) At the train station.

Romtelecom (cnr B-dul 1 Decebrie & B-dul Iuliu Maniu; ☺9am-5pm) Has free wi-fi.

ℹ Getting There & Away

The train and bus stations are five minutes' walk north of the centre at Piaţa Garii. It's easy enough to pop into town for a quick citadel lookaround and then get back on the road. The 'information' desk by the train station tracks keeps bags if you ask, with no set price.

Deva

Bus

The bus station spills across the parking lot in front of the train station. Frequent buses and microbuses go to Orăştie (8 lei, 30 minutes) and Hunedoara (6 lei, 25 minutes). Other services include hourly runs to Petroşiani (15 lei), four daily to Timişoara (30 lei) and three weekly to Sibiu (25 lei). Private maxitaxis to Cluj-Napoca (36 lei, five daily) and Târgu Mureş (40 lei, two daily) leave from an alternate 'station' directly in front of the train station.

Minibus 6 also does a circuit of Deva, running when full and costing 2 lei per journey.

Train

Deva has many train links. Daily service includes a few direct trains to Bucharest (85 lei, 6½ to 7½ hours), three to Cluj-Napoca (51 lei, 3¼ hours), three with changes to Sibiu (35 lei, 3½ to 4½ hours) and a couple to Timişoara (47 lei, 3¼ hours), plus at least three daily trains to Budapest (200 lei, 6½ hours). Buy advance tickets at **Agenţia de Voiaj CFR** (☎0265-218 887; B-dul 1 Decembrie, Block A; ☺7am-8pm Mon-Fri)

Hunedoara

POP 71, 207

One of Romania's most communist-looking cities, Hunedoara's skeletal steel mills surround one of Eastern Europe's loveliest medieval endeavours, Corvin Castle. It's a surreal time-travel experience – one second you're in the midst of commie-drab architecture, the next in the Gothic turrets of the 14th century. But visit the castle as a day trip rather than staying overnight.

The adjacent bus and train stations are a few hundred metres from Hotel Rusca; take Str Avram Iancu 200m for a couple of long blocks east, then head right (south) on L-shaped B-dul Dacia to where it bends back towards the west.

◎ Sights

Corvin Castle CASTLE
(Castelul Corvinestilor; ☎0254-711 423; www.corvincastle.com; adult/student 10/5 lei; ☺9am-6pm Tue-Sun, 9am-3pm Mon) This creepy Gothic castle, with its drawbridge over a rushing river, leaps from all your favourite horror films but seems incongruously close to the industrialised, scarified buildings around it. And while it might lack crags and forests swirling round it, on the frightometer it beats Bran Castle with its eyes shut.

Play 'shoot the cabbage' (five arrows for 10 lei) with a bow and arrow, wander through the church-high vaulted darkness of the largely unrestored downstairs chambers and past a hunter's gallery of lynx, wolf, boar and bear pelts. In the upstairs banquet hall you can live out your inner Monty Python *Holy Grail* fantasy dressed as a maiden or knight in its fancy-dress wardrobe (5 lei for half an hour).

The fantastical monument stands as a symbol of Hungarian rule. The fairy-tale castle walls, believed to be built on old Roman fortifications, were hewn out of 30m of solid rock by Turkish prisoners. Eventually Jules Verne included the castle in his *Around the World in 80 Days* itinerary in 1873. The castle was fully restored in 2009.

From the bus or train station, the castle is about 1.5km southwest, but it's easier to take the bus to the old centre (2 lei) then walk the short distance from there.

❶ Getting There & Away

The **bus station** (B-dul Republicii 3) sends maxitaxis every 20 minutes to Deva (6 lei, 30 to 40 minutes). Daily buses, except Sundays, go to Timişoara (25 lei, 3½ hours). There's a night bus to Bucharest (70 lei) Monday, Wednesday and Friday.

The adjoining **train station** (☎0254-719 238; B-dul Republicii 3) sees little action. About eight daily trains connect Hunedoara with Simeria (4 lei); from there you can reach Braşov, Sibiu or Arad.

Retezat Mountains

Part of the Southern Carpathians, most of the stunning territory is covered by the **Retezat National Park** (☎0372-742 024; www.retezat.ro), Romania's oldest (established in 1935) reserve. Covering 381 sq km (including some 80 glacial lakes), the area is considered a Unesco Biosphere Reserve. Carnivores large and small (especially the cute marmot)

TRANSYLVANIA HUNEDOARA

Retezat Mountains

roam the region, as do black deer and chamois. The region provides unforgettable hiking experiences among its valleys, peaks, rivers and gorges. The **Retezat Tourist Information Point** (☎0723 392 210; www.turismretezat .ro; Str Horea 5) is in Haţeg.

🏃 Activities

Hiking is excellent here. The two main bases are Cabana Gura Zlata and Cabana Pietrele.

From Cabana Gura Zlata, which is reached by paved road south of Ulpia Traiana-Sarmizegetusa, there are oodles of well-marked hikes. Another 12km south of the cabin is **Lacu Gura Apei**, a glacial lake you can stick your feet in (it's cold).

Cabana Gura Zlata (☎0744-648 599; www .gurazlata.ro; s/d €25/30) has expensive rooms in a two-storey villa, with campsites 200m north (in a patch of woods across the river). Many cabanas and *pensiunes* are appearing in the area. One is **Pensiunea Iris** (☎0746-022 447, 0354-409 169; www.geraico.ro; r 90 lei), a modern lodge with small rooms, decent beds and a bar-restaurant on-site.

Another good base is south of Nucşoara. Hikers can catch a local train from Simeria (36km), Petroşani (44km) or Târgu Jiu (94km) to Ohaba de Sub Piatra, then follow the trail south, through Nucşoara and

onward for about two hours (blue stripes) to **Pensuinea Codrin** (☎0742-793 620; www .codrin.ro; r with shared bathroom 80 lei, dm 25 lei), which has simple rooms that are nonetheless heavenly after a long day of hiking, and breakfast for 15 lei. A minibus that theoretically meets every train at Ohaba de Sub Piatra makes this journey as well, but you should call to confirm (☎0722-667 511). Basic comfort can be found at the cabins around the remains of **Cabana Pietrele** (☎0722-715 595; huts from 30 lei), about 3½ hours from Nucşoara; the main cabana in the complex burned down in 2007. Both Codrin and Pietrele can be reached by standard car.

At the edge of Nucşoara there is an impressive **tourist information centre** (☎0254-779 969; www.retezat.ro; ⊗8am-4.30pm Mon-Thu, to 2pm Fri), doubling as the Retezat Park headquarters, with good maps for 15 lei. You can sleep in its cabins (per person 40 lei).

A popular hike is up **Mt Retezat** (2482m), a *very* full day trip from Cabana Gura Zlata or Pensiunea Codrin. Another popular hike is the six-hour hike up **Mt Peleaga** (2509m) from Pensiunea Codrin.

Other access points to the mountains are to the northeast and east of the mountains. From Ohaba de Sub Patria (9km from the park), take a local train to Pui train station, from where you can hike 5km south along a paved road to Hobiţa. From Hobiţa a trail leads to Cabana Baleia (4½ hours, blue triangles).

A starting point from the east is Petroşani. Daily buses run to Câmpu lui Neag, 28km west of Petroşani. There is a cabana in Câmpu lui Neag. From here a 3½- to four-hour trail leads to Cabana Buta in the southeastern Retezat.

NORTHERN TRANSYLVANIA

Stretching north towards Maramureş, Transylvania's treats don't stop. Cluj-Napoca is a pulsing student town chock with cafes and culture, and is a popular gateway to the caves and hikes of the Apuseni Mountains just southwest. Further north, the Bârgău Valley served as the perfect setting for Bram Stoker's *Dracula*.

During WWII, northern Transylvania fell under pro-Nazi Hungarian rule. Under the Diktat of Vienna of 30 August 1940, the Axis powers, Germany and Italy, forced Romania to cede 43,493 sq km and a population of 2.6 million to Hungary. During the four years of occupation, thousands of Romanians were imprisoned and tortured while entire villages were massacred. Northern Transylvania was not recovered until 25 October 1944 when, following the liberation of Satu Mare, the territory fell back into Romanian hands.

Cluj-Napoca

POP 294,800

It may not be flanked by epic mountains or be as instantly arresting as Braşov or Sibiu, but Cluj is big on charm and in no time you'll be infected by it. Film capital of Romania, the city is bursting with students and cineastes; in fact its Transylvania International Film Festival (www.tiff.ro), held each year in the last week of May, attracts plenty of international talent, while the Transilvania Jazz Festival (www.transilvaniajazzfestival.ro), held in October, is another cultural highlight.

Romania's largest student population make this city their home, and with its boulevards, baroque architecture, bohemian cafe society, and back streets animated with bon viveurs and subterranean bars, you can see why. It's also a great base for renting a car, has several good travel agencies, and serves as a common shooting-off point for the Apuseni Mountains and further-flung Maramureş.

Thanks to one-way streets complicating Central Cluj, your best bet is to park up and see the city by foot. The train station is 1km north of the town centre, where many of the sites and hotels are within walking distance of one another. Head to the excellent tourist office for a map of the city.

History

Cluj-Napoca attained municipal status in AD 124, during the reign of Emperor Hadrian; later, Emperor Marcus Aurelius elevated it to a colony between AD 161 and 180. From 1791 to 1848 and after the union with Hungary in 1867, Cluj-Napoca served as the capital of Transylvania.

⊙ Sights

PIAŢA UNIRII

St Michael's Church CHURCH

The vast 14th-century St Michael's Church dominates Piaţa Unirii. The neo-Gothic tower (1859) topping the Gothic hall church creates a great landmark, and the church is considered to be one of the finest examples of Gothic architecture in Romania. Daily services are in Hungarian and Romanian, and evening organ concerts are often held.

Statue of Matthias Corvinus STATUE

Flanking St Michael's Church to the south is the bulky 1902 equestrian statue of Matthias Corvinus, the famous Hungarian king and son of Iancu de Hunedoara.

National Art Museum ART GALLERY

(Piaţa Unirii 30; adult/student 5/3 lei; ⊙10am-5pm Wed-Sun) On the eastern side of Piaţa Unirii is the National Art Museum, housed inside the baroque Banffy Palace (1791). The couple of dozen rooms are filled with paintings and artefacts, including a 16th-century church altar and many 20th-century paintings. The inner courtyard (free entry) sometimes stages outdoor shows, as do the ground-floor halls.

Pharmaceutical Museum MUSEUM

(Str Regele Ferdinand I; adult/child 5.20/3.10 lei; ⊙10am-4pm Mon-Wed & Fri, noon-6pm Thu) Tours are led by a hilarious pharmacist in a white lab coat, who points like a game-show model towards (seemingly ho-hum) glass cases of ground mummy dust, medieval alchemist symbols and painted 18th-century aphrodisiac bottles.

Ethnographic Museum of Transylvania   MUSEUM

(Muzeul Etnografic al Transilvaniei; www.muzeul-etnografic.ro; Str Memorandumului 21; adult/student 6/3 lei; ⊙9am-4pm Tue-Sat) Freshly renovated, the Ethnographic Museum of Transylvania has two floors of well-presented displays featuring tools, weapons, hand crafts, toys and household items with detailed descriptions in English. It also runs the open-air **Ethnographic Museum** (adult 6 lei, child free; ⊙9am-5pm Tue-Sun, closed Apr), with 14 traditional buildings; take bus 26, 27 and 28 to Hoia forest from the train station or bus 30 from the centre.

NORTH OF CENTRE

Around Piaţa Muzeului, a couple of blocks north of Piaţa Unirii, this charming neigh-bourhood is pleasant to explore on foot, letting you dip into courtyards for a peek at local life and seeing remnants of archaeological digs that have been going on here since 1991 in the southern and northeastern sections of the square.

Franciscan Church   CHURCH

(Biserica Franciscanilor) On the eastern side of Piaţa Muzeului is a beautifully decorated 15th-century Franciscan church, one of the city's oldest structures. Services are held in Hungarian.

National History Museum of Transylvania   MUSEUM

(Str Constantin Daicoviciu 1; adult/child 6/3 lei) The National History Museum of Transylvania, which dates from 1859, was still closed at research time, with no set reopening date.

In these halls you will eventually again see a mummy from Egypt, lots of Roman

Central Cluj-Napoca

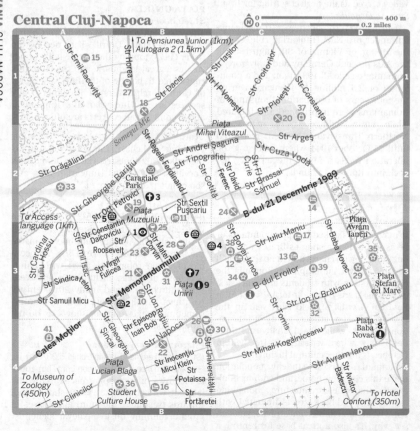

pieces, ghoulish remains of three humans from the area's first tombs (they were probably Indo-Europeans, as Dacians cremated corpses), and a map that tries to make sense of migration in the area.

Birthplace of Matthias Corvinus
HISTORICAL SITE

(Str Matei Corvin 6) A block south of the National History Museum is the politically charged birthplace of Matthias Corvinus, a 15th-century Hungarian king.

STUDENT GHETTO
The student ghetto, southwest of the centre, is full of open-air bars, internet cafes, fast-food shops – and students.

Museum of Zoology
MUSEUM

(Str Clinicilor 5-7; adult/student 3/1.5 lei; ⊙9am-3pm Mon-Fri, 10am-2pm Sat & Sun) This surprisingly rewarding museum is home to hundreds of jarred and stuffed specimens

Alexandru Borza Botanic Gardens
GARDEN

(Str Republicii 42; adult/student 5/3 lei) Through the campus housing, head past fast-food joints up Str Bogdan P Haşdeu to Str Pasteur to reach these fragrant 1930 gardens.

Hungarian Cemetery
CEMETERY

(Házsongárdi Temető) Just east of here, most easily reached from Str Avram Iancu down the hill, is an immense, highly memorable Hungarian cemetary.

🏃 Activities
Cluj-Napoca is a popular centre for caving and mountain-biking enthusiasts, with the Apuseni Mountains to the southwest offering a wealth of caves and trails.

Clubul de Cicloturism Napoca
CYCLING

(📞0744-576 836; office@ccn.ro) Clubul de Cicloturism Napoca is a group of outdoors-lovers who can help with all your two-wheeler questions.

TRANSYLVANIA CLUJ-NAPOCA

Central Cluj-Napoca

TOP CHOICE Green Mountain Holidays · HIKING

(📞0744-637 227; www.greenmountainholidays.ro) This terrific ecotourism organisation is recommended for an environmentally friendly, activity-filled week. Check its website for caving, hiking and biking tours in the Apuseni Mountains; with guides, transport, meals and accommodation, as well as self-guided trips.

🎓 Courses

Access language · LANGUAGE

(📞0264-420 476; www.access.ro; Str Ţebei 21, 3rd fl; ⏰10am-6pm Mon & Thu, 2-8pm Tue & Wed, 2-6pm Fri) Offers Romanian-language courses.

Tours

Pan Travel · TOURS

(📞0264-420 516; www.pantravel.ro; Str Grozavescu 13; ⏰9am-5pm Mon-Fri) Books accommodation, car rentals, self-drive tours and multi-day tours to the Apuseni Mountains (€200 including accommodation and guide), Saxon villages or around Maramureş with English- or French-speaking guides (€110 per person per day). Make advance contact online or by telephone. Bus 30 goes from near Piaţa Unirii to reach it.

Transylvania Ecological Club · ECOTOUR

(Clubul Ecologic Transilvania; 📞0264-431 626; www.greenagenda.org) One of Romania's most active grassroots environmental groups, operating since the mid-1990s, focusing on promoting ecotravel in the Huedin region and Apuseni Mountains. It can provide trail maps and find guides.

🎉 Festivals & Events

Cluj's biggest event is the **Transylvania International Film Festival** (www.tiff.ro), held in the last week of May. This rapidly expanding 10-day festival draws myriad visitors to see over 200 films from 50-odd countries. There is also a **Septemberfest**, a **Folk Crafts Fair** in May, the **Transilvania Jazz Festival** (www.transilvaniajazzfestival.ro) in October, and the nationwide **Festivinum Wine Festival** all May.

🛏️ Sleeping

The Cluj representative for **Antrec** (📞0264-406 363; cluj@antrec.ro) can help find a *pensiune* in the region.

TOP CHOICE Retro Hostel · HOSTEL $

(📞0264-450 452; www.retro.ro; Str Potaissa 13; dm/s/d/tr incl breakfast from 49/90/135 lei; ✉@🖥️) Well organised, central and with helpful staff, Retro has clean dorms and decent double rooms (all with TVs and shared bathrooms). There's also a pleasant cafe downstairs. The private rooms face the narrow road in which sit two noisy bars, so bring earplugs. Retro rents a car for €35 per day, and lends out its bikes for free. It also offers a great choice of guided tours to Maramureş, Scarisoara Ice Cave, Turda Salt Mine and hiking in the Apuseni Mountains.

TOP CHOICE Fullton · HOTEL $$

(📞0264-597 898; www.fullton.ro; Str Sextil Puşcariu 10; s 170-210 lei, d 196-236 lei; ✉❄️🖥️) This boutique hotel with a pea-green facade has a great location in the old town and a couple of places to park. Rooms are fragrant and fresh and have individual colour schemes (some, such as room 101, have four-poster beds) bureaus and en suites. There's also a welcoming patio bar.

Piccola Italia · PENSION $

(📞0264-536 110; www.piccolaitalia.ro; Str Racoviţă 20; s/d/tr 115/130/150 lei; P🖥️) Immediately left after you pass north over the river, Piccolo is a short haul uphill on a quiet road. It has nine clean, whitewashed rooms with reading lights, TVs and en suites. Add to this a garden dripping in vines, hearty breakfast and friendly management and it's a winner.

Hotel Agape · HOTEL $$

(📞0264-406 523; www.hotelagape.ro; Str Iuliu Maniu 6; s/d 200/225 lei; ❄️🖥️) With 60 rooms spread around a courtyard over three floors, Agape is well placed in the heart of the city. Some of its rooms feel a little lost in the '70s; that said, shop around for a corner double (such as room 302) and it's a different story: sunny, spacious and with great views. There are a number of excellent restaurants here too.

Hotel Confort · HOTEL $$

(📞0264-598 410; www.hotelconfort.ro; Calea Turzii 48; s/d 180/240 lei; ✉❄️🖥️) A steep 15-minute walk out of town, this cool modern hotel has 40-rooms with wireless connection, en suites, cable TV, minibar and fresh peach walls. Insist on taking one out back, away from the road.

Transylvania Hostel
HOSTEL $$

(☎0264-443 266; www.transylvaniahostel.com; Str Iuliu Maniu 26; dm 50 lei, d 150 lei; ☻@☎) Huddled around a leafy courtyard this mercifully cool hostel has spacious dorms, private lockers and a lounge with comfy sofas that you may find hard to prize yourself off. There's also a games room and communal PC and flat-screen with plenty of DVDs. Super-friendly management.

City Center Hostel
HOSTEL $

(☎0264-594 454; www.citycenterhostel.com; Str Ion Raţiu 2; dm/d incl breakfast 50/80 lei; ✳@☎) Just off busy Str Memorandumului this welcoming hostel, which has recently changed hands, has a new cafe run by a very respected chef, two generously spaced dorms with private lockers and one private double room. Smaller than Retro Hostel and still getting its act together, it should become a favourite by the time you visit.

Hotel Meteor
HOTEL $$

(☎0264-591 060; www.hotelmeteor.ro; B-dul Eroilor 29; s/d 138/177 lei; ✳☎) Close to the busy road this midranger has OK rooms with white walls, chocolate quilts, flat-screens and forgettable furniture. Ask for one out back, though.

Hotel Victoria
HOTEL $$

(☎0264-597 963; www.hotel-victoria.ro; B-dul 21 Decembrie 1989, 54-56; s/d 170/230 lei; P☻☎) This hotel aspires toward modern chic in its lobby; however, rooms are faded and edging toward spartan. But they're clean, with bouncy beds, en suites and TVs. Some rooms have mini step-out balconies.

Pensiunea Junior
PENSION $

(☎0264-432 028; www.pensiune-junior.ro; Str Câii Ferate 12; s/d 100/130 lei; P☎) About 300m from the train station and perfect for early departures. Its lobby glows with pastel nudes and '70s chairs; while upstairs, rooms have custard walls, TV, en suites and fresh linen.

Camping Făget
CAMPGROUND $

(☎0264-596 227; campsites per person 10 lei, 2-person huts 71 lei; ☎) This hilltop collection of OK cabanas and tent spots in the trees is 7km south of the centre. Take bus 35 from Piaţa Mihai Viteazul south down Calea Turzii to the end of the line. From here it is a marked 2km hike.

✖ Eating

Earthy bistros, sidewalk cafes, hole-in-the-wall gyros joints and upscale dark-wood dens of high cuisine, Cluj has it all.

TOP CHOICE Camino
CAFE $

(Piaa Muzeului 4; mains 15 lei; ☽9am-midnight; ☎) With jazz piping through its peeling arched interior decked in candlebra and threadbare rugs, this boho restaurant is perfect for solo book-reading jaunts or romantic dinner alfresco. Its homemade pasta is delicious, the salads and tapas full of zing. Breakfasts too.

Magyar Vendeglo
HUNGARIAN $$

(Str Iuliu Maniu 6; mains 25 lei) Based at the Hotel Agape, rustically painted wooden walls and finely carved furniture complement a menu spanning goulash, schnitzel, steak and, curiously, 'brain with egg'! Not sure whose brain.

Restaurant Matei Corvin
ROMANIAN $$

(Str Matei Corvin 3; mains 16-42 lei) With its Romanesque arched ceilings and walls strung with oils, this old trusty delivers with a flavoursome menu of broths, soup, pork roulade and tortillas. Authentic.

Napoca 15
ITALIAN $$

(Str Napoca 15; mains 15-20 lei) Delightful courtyard restaurant with giant fans keeping you cool as you tuck into an Italian menu of pasta, pizza or sugary pancakes. And with a decent wine list and pleasant tunes, it makes for a romantic spot.

Bricks
BRAZZERIE $$

(mains 25 lei; ✳☎) Bricks has risen from the ashes of a men's drinking den, as a chichi urban bistro. Rattan chairs shaded by an arbour look out across the river, while the menu excels with plenty of grilled dishes, vegie numbers, oriental cuisine and salads.

Memo 10
DELI $

(Str Memorandumului 10; mains 8 lei; ☽11am-6pm Mon-Fri; ✳) This smart, fresh buffet restaurant is a handy fast-food joint and has lasagne, slightly limp salads, cutlets and grilled chicken (which are much better). It's also very cool during summer. A three-course lunch costs 12 lei.

Self-Catering

For fresh produce, stroll through the **central market**, behind the **Complex Commercial Mihai Viteazul** shopping centre on

Piaţa Mihai Viteazul. The **Sora supermarket & shopping mall** (Str 21 Decembrie 1989, 5; ⊗24hr) is also useful for stocking up.

Drinking

Cluj Napoca's bars perpetuate Romania's vampiric, night-loving stereotype. Action pulses from darkness till dawn in dozens of cavernous underground cellars and tomb-like bars.

Klausenberg Café   CAFE
(www.klausenburgcafe.ro; Str Universităţii 1; ⊗9am-midnight; 🖶) This swanky bar, glittering with crystal, pulls you into its tasteful petals.

Stuf   CAFE
(Piaţa Unirii 19; ⊗24hr) Smoky and divey, the shadows are occasionally glowing with trippy murals, the remaining walls clad in bamboo.

Casa Tauffer Jazz Café   BAR, LIVE MUSIC
(Strada Vasile Goldiş 2; ⊗24hr) With its oxblood walls ornamented with Rat Pack prints and antique trumpets, and Armstrong and Gillespie jumping on the speakers, this smoky joint is a slice of New Orleans. There are piano evenings and exhibitions too.

Music Bar   BAR
(Str Horea 5; ⊗10am-4am Mon-Fri, 6pm-5am Sat & Sun) This cavernous, subterranean bar has enough space and darkness to keep a busload of vampires happy; good indie noise on the speakers and a lively crowd of bon viveurs.

☆ Entertainment

Janis Club   CLUB
(www.janis.ro; B-dul Eroilor 5; ⊗9pm-6am Thu, Fri & Sat) This sweaty cave magnetises locals like a fluorescent Venus fly trap with guest DJs, theme nights, karaoke and a backbone soundtrack of Pink Floyd, Joplin and The Doors.

Diesel   CLUB
(Piaţa Unirii 17; ⊗6pm-dawn) Its outside terrace might look innocent enough, but descend the stairway into the Sadean darkness and a dungeonlike interior awaits, complete with low-lit grotto bar, candlebra and a whole world of possibilities.

Cinema Arta   CINEMA
(Str Universităţii 3) This cinema plays Hollywood films in English. Closed for a refurb when we visited, but soon expected to open.

Hungarian State Theatre & Opera   THEATRE
(Str Emil Isac 26-28) This company, close to the river, stages Hungarian-language plays and operas. Tickets are sold in advance at the box office inside the theatre.

National Theatre Lucian Blaga   THEATRE
(Piaţa Ştefan cel Mare 2-4; tickets from 20 lei) National Theatre Lucian Blaga was designed by the Viennese architects Fellner and Hellmer; performances are well attended. The **Opera** (☑0264-595 363; National Theatre Lucian Blaga) is in the same building. Tickets for both can be bought from the **Agenţia de Teatrală** (☑0264-595 363; Piaţa Ştefan cel Mare 14; ⊗11am-5pm Tue-Fri) starting at 6.50 lei and 15 lei respectively.

State Philharmonic   LIVE MUSIC
(Filarmonica de Stat) The State had moved into the Student Culture House at research time. The improvised box office is just inside the front doors, on the right. Check with the Tourist Information Office to see where they are playing.

French Cultural Centre   CULTURAL BUILDING
(Centre Culturel Français; ☑0264-597 595; www.ccfc.ro; Str Ion Brătianu 22; ⊗library 2-7pm Mon, 10am-7pm Tue-Fri, to 1pm Sat Sep-Jul) Well-stocked library; hosts art, music and film events.

🛍 Shopping

The Ethnographic Museum has a gift shop chock with finely embroidered shirts, beaded jewellery and handicrafts.

King Art   HANDICRAFTS
(B-dul Eroilor 14; ⊗9am-5pm Mon-Fri) This pedestrian-only street sells a host of home-made candy, honey, painted icons and cheeses.

Sport Virus   BOOKS
(Str Calea Moţilor 22; ⊗10am-7pm Mon-Fri, to 2pm Sat) Outdoors shop with maps, rock-climbing gear, tents and sleeping bags, and hiking boots.

Gaudeamus   BOOKSHOP
(Str Iuliu Maniu 3; ⊗10am-7pm Mon-Fri, 11am-2pm Sat) Some maps, lots of art books and plenty of highbrow English novels.

Librăria Humanitas   BOOKSHOP
(Str Universităţii 4; ⊗10am-7pm Mon-Fri, to 6pm Sat) Stacks of English and American novels.

❶ Information

Zile și Nopți (www.zilesinopti.ro) and *24-Fun* are biweekly entertainment listings (in Romanian). Check www.visitcluj.ro for general information.

Internet Access

Most cafes have free wi-fi. The tourist office also has free internet, and if you're staying at Retro Hostel there's a communal computer you can use.

Left Luggage
Train Station (per 24hr 5 lei)

Medical Services
Clematis (Piața Unirii 11; ☺8am-10pm) A well-stocked and central pharmacy.

Money
The city is full of ATMs, and banks that exchange currency, including **Banca Comercială Română** (Str Gheorghe Barițiu 10-12), which also gives cash advances.

Post & Telephone
Central Post Office (Str Regele Ferdinand 33; ☺7am-8pm Mon-Fri, 8am-1pm Sat) The central post office, along with the telephone centre, faces Caragiale Park.

Telephone Centre (☺9am-6pm Mon-Fri, to 1pm Sat) In the building attached to the back of the post office, facing Caragiale Park. Fax services, free wi-fi and an internet-connected PC for public use.

Tourist Information
Tourist Information Office (☎0264-452 244; www.visitcluj.ro; B-dul Eroilor 6-8; ☺8.30am-8pm Mon-Fri, 10am-6pm Sat) Run by proactive Marius, this super-friendly office has bags of information on trekking, train and bus times, eating, accommodation as well as cultural sights and events.

Travel Agencies
Retro Hostel (p136) organises enjoyable, good-value trips.

❶ Getting There & Away

Air
Lufthansa (www.lufthansa.com) Sends two daily flights to Munich.

Wizz Air (www.wizzair.com) Budget carrier flies to London, Paris, Rome, Venice, Madrid, Barcelona and more.

Bus
Daily bus services from **Autogara 2** (Autogara Beta; ☎0264-455 249) include two daily buses travelling to Brașov (50 lei), three to Bucharest (60 lei), five to Budapest (75 lei), one to Chișinau (18 lei) and eight to Sibiu (28 lei, three

hours). There's also a handful of buses that travel to Bistrița (13 lei) and Baia Mare (25 lei). The bus station is 350m northwest of the train station (take the overpass). Note: there is no Autogara 1.

From a parking lot on Piața Mihai Viteazul, two companies run seven daily buses to Turda (7 lei) till about 8.30pm.

From Piața Unirii microbuses go via Oradea to Budapest's Ferihegy 2 Airport (75 lei, six or seven hours).

Note: it's quicker to get to Sibiu by bus, and Brașov by train from Cluj.

Train

The **Agenția de Voiaj CFR** (☎0264-432 001; Piața Mihai Viteazul 20; ☺8am-8pm Mon-Fri, 9am-1.30pm Sat) sells domestic and international train tickets in advance. Sample fares for *accelerat* trains:

DESTINATION	PRICE (LEI)	DURATION (HR)	FREQUENCY (DAILY)
Bistrița	15	2-3	3
Brașov	67	5	8
Bucharest	82	9	5
Budapest	140	5	2
Huedin	13	¾-1¼	23
Iași	82	9½	5
Oradea	39	2¼-4	2 every hr
Sibiu	48	5	2 (change at Vintu De Jos)
Sighișoara	55	3½	5
Suceava	67	7	5
Târgu Mureș	35	2¼	1
Timișoara	67	7	8
Zalău	20	4½	1 (not direct)

The smaller Gara Mică, 100m east of the central train station, is for short-distance trains only.

❶ Getting Around

To/From the Airport
Bus 8 runs goes to the airport every 10 minutes from 5.30am to 10.30pm on weekdays and every 30 minutes until 10pm on weekends, leaving from Piața Mihai Viteazul.

Car
Cluj has some of the best car-rental rates in the country. **Autonom** (☎0264-590 588; www.autonom.com; Str Victor Babeș 10) has excellent rates (Dacia Logan from 160 lei per day) and will deliver a car to you anywhere in the city, free of charge. It has a desk at Cluj Airport.

Taxi

Diesel Taxi (☏0264-946, 0264-953) is a well-regarded, meter-using local company. A ride from the train station to the centre is about 10 lei.

Tram, Trolleybus & Bus

Trolleybus 9 runs from the train station into town. Bus 27 takes you within a 10-minute walk of the open-air Ethnographic Museum northwest of the centre in Horea forest. At research time a two-ride ticket for either cost 3.5 lei.

Turda

POP 57,381

Since its main square was semi-pedestrianised back in 2010, Turda is more inviting. With its lustrously coloured Hapsburg facades and two ace cards – the epic Turda Gorge and eerily awesome Salt Mine – you may find yourself happily staying overnight here. Alternatively, visit from Cluj, a mere 27km away.

Turda was an important salt-mining town from the 13th century until 1932, when the main mine shut down. A quarter of the town's residents are Hungarian. Turda's central street, Str Republicii, is home to several banks, the post office and a taxi stand at its north end (at Piaţa Republicii, near where the roads go around the 15th-century Catholic church).

◎ Sights

Salt Mine   MINE

(www.salinaturda.eu; Str Salinelor 54; adult/child 15/8 lei; ☺9am-3.30pm daily summer, 9am-1.30pm Mon-Fri, 9am-3.30pm Sat & Sun winter; P☺) Like a Bond villain's hideout, these creepy caverns seem an apt place for hatching world domination; the most popular is Rolf Mine, some 40m-deep (13 storeys high).

To get to it pass through the crashed UFO-style entrance, then, feeling like an extra in an X-Box game, shuffle down a space-age stairway past a serenely lit shrine (where each morning a priest said prayers for those unfortunate miners about to be lowered by rope and basket into the chilly abyss). Your first glance from the slippery gallery into Rolf Mine is highly vertiginous, peering down at...well, a billiards table, table tennis area, carousel and bowling alley, far, far below. Oh, and Gollumesque boats that paddle around an island in a spectral green pond...all in all, very weird. Fortunately for you these days, there's a lift, or you can take the stairs.

The mine is about 1km north from the centre, towards Cluj; a sign points 200m off the road. If you're driving from Cluj, veer left at the first fork in the village (a sign points to '*centru*'). By the time you read this a zoo should be operating – at surface level – in the same complex.

🛏 Sleeping & Eating

Hunter Prince Castle   HOTEL $$

(Dracula Hotel; ☏0264-316 850; www.huntercastle.ro; Str Sulutiu 4-6; s/d 204/247 lei; P☀☺) This imposingly turreted, whitewashed castle of a hotel is enticing, with a courtyard dripping with plants and a cosy restaurant. Inside it gets amusingly Gothic, with traditional furniture, antlers, rugs and random wood statues. Highly camp, and if you have kids with you they'll love it.

Alegria Pizzeria   PIZZERIA $

(Piaţa Republicii; mains 15 lei; ☺8am-midnight) This is a good stop for a coffee, pizza or

---

WORTH A TRIP

TURDA GORGE

Turda Gorge (Cheile Turzii) is a short but stunning break in the mountains 7km or 8km west (as the stork flies). You can hike the bottom of the gorge's length in an hour. To get there, take a bus to the centre of Cheia; they leave right from the taxi stand in front of the church in Turda (3.50 lei). From there it's an easy 5km hike to the gorge (follow the '*cheile turzii*' signs). If you have wheels, you can drive down this road to the gorge, though this is not recommended in bad weather unless you have a powerful 4WD. Our Daewoo Matiz, at prudently low speed, did just fine when the road was dry.

Camping is possible in the area. There's a small bar at the cabana with drinks, but little to no food, so bring the essentials.

salad; eat inside its Europop-blasted interior or, even better still, outside on the Piața on its terrace.

ℹ️ Information

Tourist Information Centre (☏0364-108 229; www.turismturda.ro; Piața Republicii 45; ⊘9am-5pm Mon-Sat) You can get a Turda map and advice on hikes and local attractions, as well as info on forward travel.

ℹ️ Getting There & Away

Maxitaxis leave frequently from the centre for Cluj-Napoca's Piața Mihai Viteazul (7 lei, 40 minutes) until 8.30pm or so. Dacos buses leave from the 'Transit Stop' in front of Leonardo department store. The bus station (Autogara Sens Vest), in Piața Romană, 10 minutes' walk south of the tourist office, has buses heading for Alba Iulia (15 to 14 lei, frequent), Sibiu (27 lei) and Bucharest (65 lei, four daily, eight hours). Buses to Abrud (20 lei, three daily) and Campeni (15 lei, nine daily) in the Arieș Valley, hubs for the Apuseni Mountains to the south, are less frequent.

Huedin Microregion (Kalotaszeg)

Just off the Cluj-Oradea highway, like a more-accessible Maramureș, this bucolic paradise near the Apuseni Mountains includes 40 (chiefly) Hungarian villages bundled under the names 'Huedin Microregion' or Kalotaszeg. With a car there's much to explore, as men in Austrian-style hats and women in headscarves on horse carts return your waves as you bounce and weave towards superb mountain hikes and waterfalls.

The Kalotaszeg is much beloved by Hungarian folklorists as a stronghold of pastoral Transylvanian Magyar culture. In Budapest's Ethnography Museum, there is a huge, seven-room exhibit devoted entirely to Kalotaszeg. Centuries-old traditions persist here: staying at a home can open up makeshift tours of horseshoe-makers' workshops, shepherd huts and wooden churches, plus from May to October you can see how sheep-milk cheese is made.

You can plan trips with Davincze Tours in Sâncraiu or Green Mountain Holidays.

Restaurants are not to be found in much of the area; plan on eating at Huedin or at your guesthouse.

ALONG THE HIGHWAY

The area's namesake, Huedin (Bánffy-hunyad in Hungarian), 52km west of Cluj-Napoca, is an unengaging highway town that nevertheless can fill your mobile (cell) phone with credits, tummy with food and wallet with lei. You're better off heading to Sâncraiu or Mănăstireni for accommodation, though Hotel Montana, set on a very busy road is OK. Large rooms have TV, en suites and sleigh beds.

Seven kilometres east of Huedin, Izvoru Crișului is known as Körösfő to Hungarians, or just as 'souvenir village' to everyone else, as the roadside is lined with stalls selling traditional handicrafts.

Twelve kilometres west of Huedin is the village of Bologa. The ruins of a 13th-century **medieval fortress** tower above it. Equally interesting is the old **watermill** *(moară de apă)*, still in use today. The entrance to the mill is 3km from the main road (E60) on the left in the centre of the village.

Ciucea village, 22km west of Huedin, is principally a place of pilgrimage for Romanians and Hungarians alike, having been home to Romanian poet and politician Octavian Goga (1881–1939) and to Hungary's most controversial 20th-century poet, Endre Ady (1877–1919). One of Ady's houses is now a small **museum** (adult/student 4/2 lei; ⊘9am-5pm Tue-Sun). A nearby, petite 16th-century **wooden church** was moved here from near Cluj to preserve it.

In villages around Ciucea, on the first Sunday in May, are irresistible **Measurement of the Milk Festivals** (Masurisul Laptelui), when shepherds bring in their flocks and milk them for a contest; there's also a lot of eating, dancing and merriment. Buses go from Huedin to villages such as Magura Priei, 10km north of Ciucea, for the festival.

NEAR HUEDIN

These places are quickly accessed in a two-hour break on long drives, or serve as stepping stones to the Apuseni. Six kilometres south of Huedin, Sâncraiu is set at the base of sweeping hills, with a few dozen homes turned into guesthouses. Many are signed, though not all. Stop by **Davincze Tours** (☏0745-637 352, 0264-257 580; www.davincze .ro; No 291); run by Istvan, this travel agency (across from the Reformed church) can organise guides for you on the Padis Plateau ((270 lei per day). And while there are a staggering 40 *pensiunes* in this pretty village, the rooms at Davincze Tours are very homely with traditionally painted beds and wardrobes. Rooms are 34 lei per person, 85 lei including breakfast and dinner. They speak English.

Mănăstireni (Magyargyerömonostor in Hungarian), 16km southeast of Huedin via Căluta or 21km via Izvoru Crişului, is a quaint village noted for its 13th-century church – you can see the old steeple with bullet holes from Turk guns. During the 1848 revolution, 200 Hungarians died at the battle of Mănăstireni. They were buried in a mass grave, which today rests beneath lake waters at Lake Beliş – at low water levels, you can see the church top coming up for air.

TOWARDS THE MOUNTAINS

Toward the village of Rachiţele the landscape rolls through pastureland, the forest thickening as you pass farmsteads and locals sharpening scythes at roadside. The last base with guesthouses before the Apuseni Mountains is Rachiţele. Seven kilometres east of the village, reached by a patchy dirt road, is Rachiţele Falls. It's also on this road you'll find some welcoming *pensiunes*, including Cabana Susman (0788-938-696; No 167; r per person from 80 lei). Two kilometres short of the falls, these pretty wood lodgings are nestled in the hillside and have eight rooms with forest views.

A nice approach to the Apuseni is the 50km ride southwest from the main-highway town Gilău (16km west of Cluj) to Beliş. It's possible to find accommodation in towns such as Ruseşti, Mărişel and Lake Beliş.

ℹ️ Getting There & Around

Buses or trains go to Huedin. Huedin has taxis that can drop you off in villages, while another option is hitchhiking.

Apuseni Mountains (North)

Southwest of Cluj-Napoca, the popular Apuseni are dotted with caves and forested trails, with a world of subterranean rivers and a 3500-year-old underground glacier. Travellers head for the central Padiş Plateau – reached from the north or south – to camp or bunk at a cabana and make a week's worth of day trips from there.

PADIŞ PLATEAU

Rugged Padiş Plateau is an unspoilt wilderness of karst-laced meadows fringed by forests teeming with lynx and wolf. Imagine dense Hansel and Gretel–style forests – you may even see a crone, with bent Roma pensioners hobbling across the plateau – and you're getting close.

From Cabana Padiş, a popular circuit leads southwest along the polluted Ponorului River to the fantastic Cetăţile Ponorului or 'fortress cave' (Cetatea Ponorului; 2½ hours one way, blue circles), so called because of its sheer 70m entrance, like the portal to some mystical underworld. While much of this walk is on road, the last part is down an uneven path winding through forest. As the path veers sharply downhill you'll have to pick your way across boulders and sprawling tree roots and, for the final 200m descent, you'll need the aid of a ladder and cables to get you to the great mouth of the cave (those prone to vertigo should stop before this point).

The cave itself, with a main gallery 2km long, and one of the country's largest underground rivers – fraught with whirlpools and sinkholes – requires good boots, a helmet and a torch to make much of the damp underground chamber. See Dimap's *Padis Plateau* map for greater detail on the route once inside. The river sinks its way through the chamber's numerous holes, some as deep as 150m.

Another trail, marked first by red stripes then by red circles, leads from the cabana north for three or four hours to a meadow at Poiana Vărăşoaia. From here, red circles bear east two hours to the Rădesei Citadel (Cetăţile Rădesei), another underground chamber that has impressive rock formations (as well as tent sites). The route then circles Someşul Cald, a river in a deep gorge, before heading back south to the cabana. If you continue to follow the red stripes north through the Stâna de Vale ski resort you'll arrive at Cârligatele Peak (1694m).

🛏️ Sleeping

There are a couple of camping places including Padiş Plateau itself, and Glavoi, 8km south, where you can camp by a stream in the lee of a wooded valley. There is a seasonal cafe and toilet there.

TOP CHOICE Cabana Cetațile Ponorului CHALET $
(📞0732-625 928; www.padis.ro; s/d 30/50 lei)
Around 1.7km downhill from Glavoi, past the
turn-off for the fortress cave, this delightful
guesthouse delivers with fresh rooms, rustic
furniture, spanking clean linen, and modern
en suites. There's also a pleasant restaurant
and terrace bar.

Cabana Bradet GUESTHOUSE $
(📞0743-048 266, 0788-335 051; main street, Padiș
Plateau; cabanas 70 lei, r with/without bathroom
150/70) Slap bang on top of the plateau,
with serene views, Bradet has 10 comfy
rooms (some with bathrooms), a bar and a
cafe. And for those inclined to the elements,
outside there are barrel-shaped hobbit-style
cabanas (sleeps two small adults). It even
sells chocolate!

ℹ️ Information

Check www.padis.ro for details on the plateau.
One regional map is Dimap's *Zona Padiș din
Muntii Bihor*, which can provide more detail.

It's worth considering going with a guide.
Based in Oradea, **Apuseni Experience** (📞0756-
194 321, 0259-472 434; www.apuseniexperience
.ro) leads full weeklong hiking, cultural, caving and underground rafting trips. Other good
guides work with **Green Mountain Holidays**
(📞0744-637 227; www.greenmountainholidays.
ro) or Pan Travel (p136) in Cluj.

Getting to the Plateau

The best access road to Padiș is south of Huedin
from Rachițele. It's 21km from Rachițele to
Ponor and a further 10km to Padiș. Currently
the road around Ponor is in bad shape and you
should ensure you bring a spare tyre. Another
option is slower going: from Pietroasa in the
west (it's 16km to Boga then 6km to Padiș).

With the road under construction at the time
of research, journey time should be scythed by
the time you read this – it may soon take as little
as a few hours to Padiș Plateau from Cluj.

By bus head from Cluj-Napoca to Huedin and
hitch or catch a minibus to Rachițele. From here
it's another hike or hitch.

These roads can be hiked, as can trails from
Gârda de Sus (five to six hours, blue stripes) or
the lesser-used trail from Stâna de Vale in the
northwest (six to seven hours, red stripes).

Cluj-Napoca to Bistrița

Don't think this road, passing many industrial towns and with trucks racing past you,
is going to be a lovely leisurely experience.

Still, there are a few places worth stopping
at if you're headed north towards Bistrița,
Maramureș or Southern Bucovina.

BONȚIDA

Thirty kilometres northeast of Cluj and 3km
east of the highway, this village's crowning
jewel is **Banffy Castle** (www.heritagetraining
-banffycastle.org; admission 3 lei; ◷9am-8pm),
once home to the country's most impressive
gallery of statuary (back in the 18th century). Its buildings are being painstakingly restored and warrant a quick wander. There's
a cafe tucked in the corner of the grounds,
and to spot some of those titan, god and
hero statues, peer in the little annexe as you
enter through the archway.

Bistrița

POP 82,300

A must for any Dracula diehard, Bistrița
(Bistritz in German) was the town Jonathan
Harker visited on the eve of St George's day,
before passing onward for the nightmare
awaiting him at the Borgo Pass. For those
less fang-inclined the town may not be quite
as exciting. Dominated by its magnificent
14th-century church, from which radiate
pretty cobbled streets, it makes for a pleasant wander, stopping at a cafe or treating
yourself to a read of that blood-soaked novel
you keep hearing so much about. It's also a
worthy overnight base before setting out for
the nearby charms of idyllic Lake Colibița
and rugged Tihuța (Borgo) Pass.

First chronicled in 1264, Bistrița was one
of the seven towns founded by the Saxons,
whose presence still lives on in the old
town's quaint 15th- and 16th-century merchants' houses (only a few hundred Saxons
still call Bistrița home). Witch trials were
also common events here during medieval
times.

In August, the city hosts the **International Folk, Dance and Traditions Festival**
(Nunata Zamfirei). A good map of the town
can be acquired at the Tourist Information
Office (p145). A local 200-page colour guide,
Bistrița Năsăd Travel Guide, has some useful information on county sights in English.

⊙ Sights

What remains of the city's 13th-century walls
lies south of the town along the northwest
side of the municipal park. In 1530 Wallachian prince Petru Rareș (r 1541–46) besieged Bistrița, forcing its Saxon inhabitants

TRANSYLVANIA CLUJ-NAPOCA TO BISTRIȚA

to finally surrender. The Coopers' Tower remains at the east of the park.

Evangelical Church
CHURCH

(Biserica Evanghelică) At a staggering 76.5m, Bistrița's 14th-century, Gothic-style church dominates Piața Centrală. And though it's closed for restoration, you can still travel up the elevator in the tower for amazing views (8 lei).

Șugălete
HISTORICAL BUILDING

Facing the church on the north side of Piața Centrală is the fine Șugălete row of terraced buildings, which in medieval times was bustling with trading activities. The Galeriile de Arta (☎0745-454 032; Piața Centrală 24; ◷10am-6pm) is worth a peek, with regularly changing exhibitions.

Orthodox Church
CHURCH

Down the pedestrian B-dul Rebreanu, which is lined with cafes and restaurants, is an Orthodox church (1270–80), the centrepiece of Piața Unirii.

County Museum
MUSEUM

(Muzeul Judetean; B-dul General Grigore Bălan 19; adult/student 5/3 lei; ◷10am-7pm Tue-Sun) The open courtyard of the half-closed County Museum has a wooden church in its central garden. The museum's collection of minerals and stuffed animals is hardly worth a look though.

🏃 Activities

Codrișor Swimming Pool
SWIMMING

(adult/student 5/2 lei; ◷8am-8pm) To cool off there's the Codrișor swimming pool, an outdoor pool on the south side of the river.

🛏 Sleeping

Hotel Codrișor
HOTEL $

(☎0263-233 814; www.hotelcodrisor.ro; Str Codrișor 28; s 105-130 lei, d 140-170 lei; 🅰) A few minutes' walk out of town, pass over the bridge near Crama Veche Restaurant to reach this decent-value hotel. Conveniently, it's also right next to the public swimming pool. Classed as 'standard' or 'high comfort', rooms are clean with kitsch navy quilts, flat-screens, bureaus and en suites. High-comfort rooms are huge and, yes, pretty comfortable too.

Hotel Bistrița
HOTEL $$

(☎0730-660 837, 0263-231 154; www.hotel-bistrita .ro; s/d 130/175 lei; 🅿🅰) Guarded by a phalanx of conifers, this imposing hotel has 34 swish rooms, a plush 1980s feel and friendly staff. Rooms are darkly wooded and down-lit, with clean en suites, cable TV, safe deposit boxes and, in some cases, balconies.

Hotel Select
HOTEL $

(☎0262-233 814; s/d 90/110 lei) Right next to Hotel Codrișor, Select is 'commie-drab' on the outside, but much more fluffy within. Indeed, a smart restaurant and well-kept rooms fit for a lawyer en route to see a Count beckon. Dark-wood furniture, crisp linen, boutique-style wallpaper, TV and minibar.

Coroana de Aur
HOTEL

(☎0263-232 470; www.hotel-coroana-de-aur.ro; Piața Petru Rareș 4; s/d/apt 160/220/460 lei; 🅿🅰) It couldn't be less like the inn (of the same name) that Harker stayed at if it tried. This is a shambling, unatmospheric hotel with 1970s-style rooms, most of which are equipped with wi-fi, cable TV and non-Gothic trimmings such as air-con.

🍴 Eating

🔺TOP CHOICE Crama Veche
ROMANIAN $$

(Str Albert Berger 10; mains 20 lei; ◷noon-midnight; 🅰) Tucked behind the Cultural Centre, this authentic Transylvanian restaurant has stone floors, wood-carved tables and chairs, and beguiling black-and-white photos of peasants on the walls. The rustic menu lives up to the interior with shepherd's polenta, knuckle of pork, grilled boar, and Saxon dishes including schnitzel. Outside there's a welcoming terrace.

Restaurant Central
ROMANIAN $

(B-dul L Rebreanu 30; mains 15 lei; ◷9am-midnight) Restaurant Central is situated in an atmospheric medieval townhouse and excels with its dark interior of ancient arches strung with fairy lights, and a hearty traditional Romanian menu.

Coroana de Aur Restaurant
ROMANIAN $$

(Piața Petru Rareș 4; mains 25 lei; ◷10am-11pm) Inside the Coroana de Aur hotel, this restaurant is plastered with cheesy vampiric prints with quotes from the book, plus a couple of crimson cloaks hanging dejectedly on a coat stand. Get your teeth into its carnivorous menu with dishes such as venison with mushrooms, liver and onion, pork and polenta, and turkey in a...bacon cloak!

Carrefour Supermarket SUPERMARKET
(Str Garii; ☺8am-10pm Mon-Sat, 9am-7pm Sun) This big supermarket is across from the bus station.

Drinking

Café Rossmarket CAFE
(Piața Unirii 1; ☺8am-10pm) This bijou cafe has floral wallpaper and makes for a pleasant juice or caffeine stop.

Old House Pub BAR
(Piața Petru Rareș; ☺6pm-2am) Inside this old plum-coloured building next to the Coroana de Aur hotel is an interior boasting fin de siècle style, with wrought-iron chairs and belle-époque murals.

Any Time Bar BAR
(Str Piața Centrala 1; ☺6pm-3am) This exposed-brick haunt offers lively tunes and vampish late nights in its cellar.

ⓘ Information

Banca Comercială Română (Piața Petru Rareș; ☺8.30am-6pm Mon-Fri, to 12.30pm Sat) Cashes travellers cheques and has an ATM.

Raiffeisen Bank (Piața Unirii 1; ☺9am-6.30pm Mon-Fri)

Tourist Information Office (☎0263-235 377; www.primariabistrita.ro; Piața Centrala 13) This excellent tourist office comes equipped with brochures, maps, local info and stakes for Van Helsing–types (joking).

ⓘ Getting There & Away
Bus
The **bus station** (☎0263-233 655) sends four daily buses to Brașov (57 lei, seven to eight hours), three to Cluj (22 lei, 2½ to three hours) and Oradea (47 lei), two to Satu Mare (47 lei), three to Sibiu (53 lei, six hours), five to Suceava (39 lei) and nine to Târgu Mureș (23 lei, 2½ hours). There are as many microbuses to Brașov, Oradea and Sibiu, and more to Cluj; call ☎0263-213 621 or ☎0744-693 676 for more information.

Train
The **train station** (☎0263-223 572) sends one daily train to Bucharest (85 lei, 10 hours), four daily trains to Cluj (16 lei, three to four hours) and one to Vatra Dornei (16 lei, five hours). It's easier to reach Lunca Ilvei from Cluj. To reach Suceava (57 lei, eight hours) you must change trains in Beclan Someș. You can also buy tickets at the **Agenția de Voiaj CFR** (☎0263-213 938; Piața Petru Rareș; ☺9am-4pm Mon-Fri), which is also an agent for Blue Air.

Bârgău Valley

Bârgău Valley's **Tihuța Pass** is one of the most photogenic passes in the country: cast your eye over its forbidding pine forests and rocky crags and you can imagine a weary Harker rattling up here in the mysterious black coach towards the castle, for the Borgo Pass of the novel is today's Tihuța Pass. Your final destination (via Mureșeni) will be the little hamlet of **Piatra Fântânele**, (47km from Bistrița), at the head of the Tihuța Pass (1200m), home to the ever tacky but hugely fun Hotel Castle Dracula. But don't rush here without savouring first the woody charms of Lake Colibița and little Lunca Il-vei, west of the pass.

⊙ Sights

⬛TOP CHOICE Hotel Castle Dracula HOTEL
(☎0266-264 020, 0266-264 010; www.hotelcasteldracula.ro; s/d/apt 175/220/350 lei; ℗⚗) Positioned roughly on the promontory where the Count's castle would have stood, Hotel Castle Dracula is lazily Gothic from the outside, but more interesting within (particularly in reception, where a stuffed hawk, wolf, raven and ferret watch you signing in). Corridors are lined with cranberry-coloured carpets and dragon motifs, while rooms are rustically stylish, with bureaus for writing fraught diaries, and old-fashioned furniture. The apartments are more vampy with wine-dark walls, candlebra and dinner tables for impromptu séances. Meanwhile, the hotel's Fear Room is a creaky-stepped, ghosthouse-style crypt, with murals retelling the story of Dracula. We won't tell you the denouement but in the '90s someone had a heart attack (clue: since when did Dracula wear sneakers?). The restaurant is earthy with dishes such as pork suckling and mutton on the bone, and an outside terrace perfect for summer breakfasts. On a stormy night when the Pass is whipped by rain, wind rattles the casements and the odd wolf howls across the valley, the hotel can be genuinely creepy.

Outside in the car park there's a faded map detailing four colour-coded walks in the area as well as a sculpture of author Bram Stoker in a glass coffin. Immediately after is a gathering of stalls hawking snow globes, vampire mugs, masks, hats and garden gnomes! There's also tennis and a small ski lift next door.

A couple of daily buses between Bistriţa and Vatra Dornei pass by here.

LAKE COLIBIŢA

Protected by towering crags and dense forests, this glittering lake is a hidden treasure. With few developments it has an off-the-beaten-track feel and makes for a perfect sojourn to catch a kayak, a few rays or take a swim. You'll find it 15km southeast of the village of Prundu Bârgăului, some 20 or so kilometres from Bistriţa.

🛌 Sleeping

Fisherman's Hotel   HOTEL $
(☑0722-500 422; www.fishermans.ro; Colibiţa 46; r 150 lei; P🖵🌐🌐🖾) Enjoying a regal position on the lake, Fisherman's rooms are tasteful with murals, thick carpets, flat-screens and en suites, and there's an excellent restaurant with elevated views. You can fish from the jetty with the hotel's rods, hire its pedlo (25 lei per person) or take their three-person boat out for a putter (25 lei). There's also a kids' pool.

Pensiunea Ariniş   PENSION $
(☑0740-407 954; www.lacolibita.ro; d 100 lei) Rioting in flowers, timbered Ariniş sits atop a grassy knoll. There's a pretty terrace to enjoy breakfast and soak up the view of the green lake below, or try the freshly caught grilled trout for lunch (20 lei). Rooms are fresh wood-floored affairs with en suite, TV and wi-fi. The hotel also has a jetty and can rent you kayaks (10 lei).

Crişana & Banat

Best Places to Eat

» Casa Bunicii (p153)

» Graf (p157)

» Rosecas (p157)

» Nora (p153)

» Intermezzo (p153)

Best Places to Stay

» Hotel Elite (p157)

» Hotel Savoy (p153)

» Hostel Costel (p153)

» Pensiunea Belanco (p161)

» Casa Noastră (p160)

Why Go?

Western Romania, with its geographic and cultural ties to neighbouring Hungary and Serbia, and historical links to the Austro-Hungarian Empire, enjoys an ethnic diversity that much of the rest of the country lacks. Timişoara, the regional hub, has a nationwide reputation as a beautiful and lively metropolis, and for a series of 'firsts'. It was the world's first city to adopt electric street lights (in 1884) and, more importantly, the first city to rise up against dictator Nicolae Ceauşescu in 1989. Outside the metropolitan areas of Timişoara, Oradea and Arad, the remote and pristine Apuseni Mountains are littered with dozens of amazing caves that cry out for exploration and kilometres and kilometres of isolated hiking trails.

When to Go

Timişoara

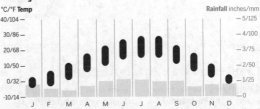

Apr & May
Budding tree blossoms make a striking backdrop to a city break to Timişoara or Oradea.

Jun–Aug Summer brings warm days filled with sunshine and perfect for hiking the Apuseni Mountains.

Sep & Oct Timişoara's cultural scene awakens with theatre, opera and classical music.

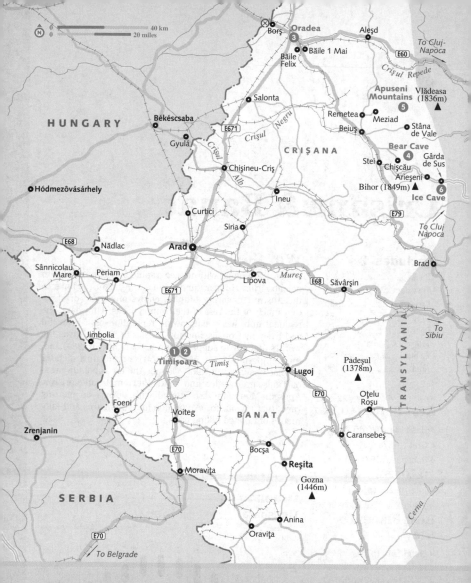

Crişana & Banat Highlights

1 Getting a riveting history lesson at the **Permanent Exhibition of the 1989 Revolution** (p149) in Timişoara

2 Indulging in a lazy day in **Timişoara** (p149), starting at the outdoor pool, then an evening at the opera, and finally a nightcap on Piaţa Victoriei or Piaţa Unirii

3 Taking in the stunning but crumbling art nouveau grandeur of **Oradea** (p155)

4 Looking at the ancient stalactites and stalagmites in the magnificent **Bear Cave** (p159)

5 Hiking around or simply gazing at the western **Apuseni Mountains** (p159)

6 Glimpsing ice from the Ice Age at the appropriately named **Ice Cave** (p159)

History

The western Romanian regions of Crişana and Banat have traditionally played the role of stepping stone between east and west. The area was first settled in the 6th century BC, and by AD 106 had become part of the Roman province of Dacia. The two regions fell under Hungarian rule around the end of the 9th century and remained part of the Hungarian kingdom until the Ottoman conquest of Crişana and Banat in 1552.

The Turks ruled these parts for around 150 years, finally losing control of Crişana and Banat to the Austrian Habsburgs in 1716 after the Turks were defeated in battle by Habsburg prince Eugene of Savoy. Two years later, the regions formally became part of the Habsburg Empire, ruled from Vienna.

Austria lost no time in shoring up the regions against any possible return of the Turks, building state-of-the-art military fortresses in Arad, Oradea and Timişoara – that remain standing to this day. As a way of furthering their claims to the Banat, the Austrians opened the area to settlement, and today you still come across small scattered communities of ethnic Czechs, Croats, Slovaks and others, living much as they did 100 years ago.

The anti-Habsburg bourgeois uprisings of 1848 were felt keenly in these parts. Independence-seeking Hungarians fought to make the areas part of a newly formed Hungary, against armed resistance from the Austrians and, in some cases, bands of Romanian fighters. The Austrians eventually prevailed, but ultimately ceded the territories to Hungary when Austria and Hungary agreed to form a dual monarchy in 1867 (the 'Ausgleich' as it was called).

Crişana and Banat largely thrived in the half century between the *Ausgleich* and WWI. The amazing art nouveau and Secession architecture of the major cities is evidence of this prosperity. Following WWI, Hungary lost large chunks of its former territory, including what are now the Romanian regions of Crişana and Banat, which were awarded to newly independent Romania.

BANAT

Timişoara

POP 303,700

Romania's third- or fourth-largest city (depending on the source) is also one of the country's most attractive urban areas, built around a series of beautiful public squares and lavish parks and gardens. It's known as Primul Oraş Liber (First Free Town), for it was here that anti-Ceauşescu protests first exceeded the Securitate's capacity for violent suppression in 1989, eventually sending Ceauşescu and his wife to their demise. With western Romania's nicest hotels and restaurants, it makes a perfect base for exploring the Banat region.

⊙ Sights

PIAŢA UNIRII & AROUND

Piaţa Unirii is Timişoara's most picturesque square, featuring the imposing sight of the Catholic and Serbian churches facing each other. A couple of blocks to the east, following Str Palanca, is the Cetate (Fortress), a classic 18th-century Austrian fortress that's been remodelled into a complex of shops and cafes.

Roman Catholic Cathedral CHURCH
(Catedrală Episcopală Romano-Catolică; ☑0256-430 671; Piaţa Unirii 12; ☉8am-6pm) The city's fine baroque cathedral was built in the mid-18th century, after the Austro-Hungarian Empire had finally secured the area from Turkish influence. The main altar painting was carried out by Michael Angelo Unterberger, who was the director of the Fine Arts Academy in Vienna at the time the cathedral was built.

Serbian Orthodox Church CHURCH
(Biserica Ortodoxă Sârbă; Str Ungureanu 12) Fronting Piaţa Unirii, the Serbian Orthodox Church was built at approximately the same time as its Catholic counterpart across the square. Local Banat artist Constantin Daniel painted the interior.

Art Museum MUSEUM
(Muzeul de Artă; ☑0256-491 592; www.muzeul deartatm.ro; Old Prefecture Palace, Piaţa Unirii 1; admission 5 lei; ☉10am-6pm Tue-Sun) The museum displays a representative sample of paintings and visual arts over the centuries as well as regular, high-quality temporary exhibitions. It's housed in the baroque Old Prefecture Palace (Palatul Vechii Prefecturi), built in 1754, which is worth a look inside for the graceful interiors alone.

Permanent Exhibition of the 1989 Revolution MUSEUM
TOP CHOICE
(☑0256-294 936; www.memorialulrevolutiei.ro; Str Popa Sapcă 3-5; admission by donation; ☉8am-4pm Mon-Fri, 9am-1pm Sat) This work in progress is an ideal venue to brush up on the December 1989 anticommunist revolution that began

Central Timişoara

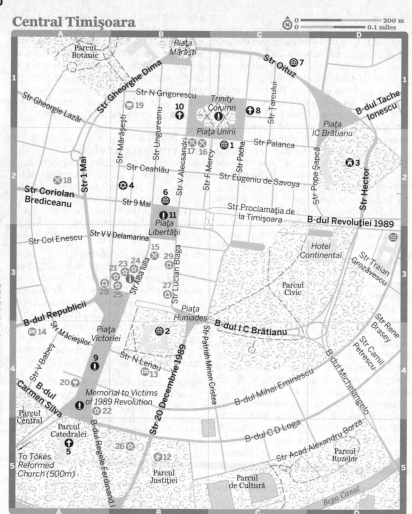

in Timişoara. Displays include documentation, posters and photography from those fateful days, capped by a graphic 20-minute video (not suitable for young children) with English subtitles. Enter from Str Oituz.

Great Synagogue
JEWISH

(Str Mărăşeşti 6) Built in 1865, the synagogue acts as an important keynote in Jewish history – Jews in the Austro-Hungarian Empire were emancipated in 1864, when permission was given to build the synagogue. It was closed at the time of research

for a multiyear renovation, but the fine exterior is worth taking in.

PIAŢA LIBERTĂŢII & AROUND

Sandwiched between Piaţa Unirii and Piaţa Victoriei is a shady square that lies at the heart of the city, Piaţa Libertăţii. There are few traditional sights here, but several interesting old buildings and monuments.

Fronting the square, the **Old Town Hall** (Piaţa Libertăţii 1; ⊘ closed to the public) was built in 1734 on the site of 17th-century Turkish baths. It was here that the leader of the 1514 peasant revolt, Gheorghe Doja, was tortured

Central Timişoara

before being executed. Doja's peasant army, after an initial victory, was quickly quashed, captured and killed.

The **statue of St John of Nepomuk and the Virgin Mary** was made in 1756 in Vienna and brought to Romania in memory of plague victims. The story of hapless St John of Nepomuk, who was said to have been flung off Charles Bridge in Prague to his death on the orders of the king for failing to reveal the confessions of the queen, can be seen etched around the monument's base.

PIAŢA VICTORIEI & AROUND

Begging to be photographed with your widest lens is Piaţa Victoriei, a beautifully green pedestrian mall dotted with central fountains and lined with shops and cafes. The square's northern end is marked by the 18th-century National Theatre & Opera House (p154). It was here that thousands of demonstrators gathered on 16 December 1989. A memorial on the front of the opera house reads: 'So you, who pass by this building, will dedicate a thought for free Romania'. Toward the centre, there's a **statue of Romulus and Remus**.

Metropolitan Cathedral   CHURCH
(Catedrala Ortodoxă; www.timisoara.org/catedrala; B-dul Regele Ferdinand I; ◷10am-6pm) The Orthodox cathedral was built between 1936 and 1946. It's unique for its Byzantine-influenced architecture, which recalls the style of the Bucovina monasteries.

Banat History Museum   MUSEUM
(Muzeul Banatului; Piaţa Huniades 1) Housed in the historic Huniades Palace, the museum was closed at the time of research for renovations expected to last until 2015. The exterior of the palace, though, is still worth a look. The origins of the building date to the 14th century and to Hungarian king Charles Robert, Prince of Anjou.

SOUTH OF THE CENTRE

The **Bega Canal** sneaks around the city south of Piaţa Victoriei. While the riverside is still scruffy in spots, the parks that line the canal on both sides are pleasant places to stroll.

Tőkés Reformed Church   CHURCH
(Biserica Reformată Tőkés; Str Timotei Cipariu 1) The 1989 revolution began at the Tőkés Reformed Church, where Father Lászlo Tőkés spoke out against Ceauşescu. You can

DON'T MESS WITH TIMIŞOARA

Even at the height of his power, Nicolae Ceauşescu never liked Romania's western-most metropolis. The dictator's visits to the city were few and brief, and required sur-reptitious, dread-fuelled travel and sleeping arrangements to allay his assassination concerns. So when the Romanian secret service, the Securitate, overplayed its hand in the already truculent city by trying to deport popular Hungarian pastor and outspo-ken Ceauşescu critic László Tőkés, the dictator should have sensed disaster looming; however, like most megalomaniacs, he didn't grasp the full scale of his folly until he was being shoved in front of a firing squad, looking genuinely stunned, a little more than a week later on Christmas Day 1989.

What started on 15 December 1989 as a human chain of Tőkés' parishioners protect-ing him from arrest mushroomed into a full-scale anticommunist revolt on 20 Decem-ber. Overconfident Ceauşescu actually left Romania during this time for a visit to Iran, leaving his wife Elena to cope with the escalating protests.

When Ceauşescu returned to Romania a few days later, the situation was critical. Facto-ry workers brought in by party officials to crush the demonstrations spontaneously joined the protesters in Piaţa Operei (today's Piaţa Victoriei), chanting antigovernment slogans and singing an old Romanian anthem ('Wake up, Romanians!') banned since the com-munists took power in 1947. The crowd, now over 100,000 strong, overpowered and then commandeered some of the tanks that had previously fired on demonstrators. Protests later ensued in Bucharest and around the country and Ceauşescu's fate was sealed.

Learn more about the revolution and see video footage of the events at the excellent Permanent Exhibition of the 1989 Revolution (p149).

sometimes peek in at the church, but the small apartment is private property.

NORTH OF THE CENTRE

Banat Village Museum   MUSEUM
(Muzeul Satului Banăţean; ☑0256-225 588; www.muzeulsatuluibanatean.ro; Str Avram Imbroane 1; admission 4.50 lei; ☉10am-6pm Tue-Sat, noon-8pm Sun) The open-air display was created in 1917 and exhibits more than 30 traditional peas-ant houses dating from the 19th century. Take tram 1 (black number) from the north-ern train station.

🏃 Activities

Rent **pedal boats** (per hr 15 lei; ☉May-Sep) to splash around the Bega Canal from below the Podul Mitropolit Şaguna bridge on the southern side of the canal. You can **hire bikes** from **i'velo** (www.ivelo.ro; Parcul Justitiei; per hr 5 lei; ☉11am-9.30pm Mon-Fri, 10am-10.30pm Sat & Sun Apr-Aug, to 7.30pm Sep & Oct), just east of the State Philharmonic Theatre.

☞ Tours

Several companies and individuals offer guided tours of the city and the Banat re-gion. Recommended guides include **Tymes Tours** (☑0256-203 015; www.tymestours.ro), **Al-exandra Irimia** (☑0742-112 174; http://alexandra irimia.com) and **Claudiu Preda** (☑0745-519 934; www.claudiupreda.eu). Prices vary accord-ing to the guide, but rates typically start at around 125 lei per two-hour tour for groups of up to five people.

🎭 Festivals

The city has an active cultural calendar throughout the year, with high points com-ing in spring and autumn. The tourist infor-mation centre (p155) website has a complete list.

**European Festival of
Performing Arts**   PERFORMING ARTS
(FEST-FDR; ☑0256-499 908; www.tntimisoara.com; ☉May) Annual nine-day festival that highlights the best of Romanian drama and theatre.

Timishort Film Festival   FILM
(www.timishort.ro; ☉May) Annual international film festival features the best in short films and draws visitors from around the world.

Plai   WORLD MUSIC
(www.plai.ro; ☉Sep) This annual, very popu-lar festival of ethnic and world music takes places on the grounds of the Banat Village Museum.

Sleeping

TOP CHOICE **Hotel Savoy** HOTEL $$$
(☎0256-249 900; www.hotelsavoytimisoara.ro; Splaiul Tudor Vladimirescu 2; s/d 270/325 lei; P⊖❄📶) Stylish refurbished villa from the 1930s, with a keen eye for art deco detail. The rooms are swank, with soft tones and white carpets. It's a short walk to the centre or to the banks of the Bega Canal.

Hostel Costel HOSTEL $
(☎0726-240 223; www.hostel-costel.ro; Str Petru Sfetca 1; dm 40-45 lei, d 135 lei; ⊖@📶) Run by affable staff, this charming 1920s art nouveau villa is arguably the city's only real youth hostel. The vibe is relaxed and congenial. There are three dorm rooms and one private double. There are lots of little rooms to relax in and a big garden out back. The hostel is a bit hard to find for the first time. It's about 1km east of the centre, across the Bega Canal near the Decebal Bridge; take tram 1.

Pension Casa Leone PENSION $
(☎0256-292 621; www.casaleone.ro; B-dul Eroilor 67; s/d/tr 125/150/200 lei; P⊖❄📶) This lovely seven-room pension offers exceptional service and individually decorated rooms. To find it, take tram 8 from the train station, alight at Deliblata station and walk one block northeast to B-dul Eroilor (or call ahead to arrange transport).

Hotel La Residenza HOTEL $$$
(☎0256-401 080; www.laresidenza.ro; Str Independenţei 14; s/d 400/480 lei; P⊖❄@📶) Charming converted villa recalls an English manor, with a cosy reading room and library off the lobby and a well-tended garden in the back. A first choice for visiting celebrities and *the* place to stay if price is no object. Located about 1km south of the city centre.

Hotel Central HOTEL $$
(☎0256-490 091; www.hotel-central.ro; Str N Lenau 6; s/d 160/180 lei; P❄📶) It's not exactly the Taj Mahal, but this communist-era hotel has had a decent facelift, leaving the rooms clean, modern and comfortable. You can't beat the price for the location, and there's ample guarded parking out front (per day 10 lei) if you're travelling by car.

Hotel Cina Banatul HOTEL $
(☎0256-490 130; www.hotelcina.ro; B-dul Republicii 7; s/d 120/140 lei; P❄📶) One of the best-value places in the centre, though not quite as appealing as the Central; this hotel has clean, ultramodern rooms and a good restaurant.

Eating

There are plenty of lovely terrace cafes lining Piaţa Unirii and Piaţa Victoriei that serve a mix of drinks and food. *The* spot for cheap eats, kebabs and pizza joints is the **student complex** (Complexul Studentesc), south of the centre across the Bega Canal. This area is home to many university buildings and dorms as well as street-food outlets, cheap cafes and restaurants that cater mostly to students.

TOP CHOICE **Casa Bunicii** ROMANIAN $$
(☎0356-100 870; www.casa-bunicii.ro; Str Virgil Onitiu 3; mains 18-30 lei; 👪) The names translates to 'Granny's House' and indeed this casual, family-friendly restaurant specialises in home cooking and regional specialities from the Banat. The duck soup and grilled chicken breast served in sour cherry sauce come recommended.

Nora ROMANIAN $$
(☎0256-218 204; www.restaurantnora.ro; B-dul Damboviţa 40, cnr Str Transilvania; mains 15-30 lei; ⊙noon-midnight) Reservations are a must to nab a spot on the terrace at this popular, casual Romanian restaurant with a reputation for grilled meats. About 2km out of the centre to the southwest but worth the taxi fare (about 10 lei)

Intermezzo ITALIAN $$
(☎0256-432 429; www.restaurant-intermezzo.ro; Piaţa Unirii 3; mains 22-36 lei, pizza 18-24 lei; ⊙noon-midnight) This place has great pizzas and even better pastas. Dine on the terrace on Piaţa Unirii or in the cellar restaurant.

Casa cu Flori ROMANIAN $$
(☎0256-435 080; www.casacuflori.ro; Str Alba Iulia 1; mains 18-28 lei; ❄) One of the best-known restaurants in the city and for good reason. Excellent high-end Romanian cooking with refined service at moderate prices. In nice weather, climb three flights to the flower-lined rooftop terrace.

Eclipse SANDWICHES $$
(☎0730-072 550; Piaţa Unirii 2; salads & sandwiches 17-21 lei; ⊙8am-midnight Mon-Fri, 9am-midnight Sat & Sun; 📶) The menu promises freshly made salads and sandwiches from organic ingredients, but we like the smoothies, fresh juices and full breakfast menu – perfect if your hostel or pension doesn't serve

breakfast. There's a pretty terrace to enjoy it all while looking out onto the square.

Open-Air Market
MARKET

(Str Coriolan Brediceanu; ⊘generally Mon-Sat 8am-6pm) Timişoara has a colourful central market two blocks west of Piaţa Libertăţii where you can buy produce, meats, cheeses and bread for train provisions or picnic lunches.

🍷 Drinking

In summer, Piaţa Unirii and Piaţa Victoriei are lined with cafes.

Opera
CAFE

(Piaţa Victoriei 6; ⊘8am-11pm; 🛜) One of over a dozen similar cafes on this large square, all serving a mix of hot and cold beverages and usually some variation of salads and sandwiches. We like this place for the pleasant staff, the ice-cream cart on site and occasional live music in the evenings.

Scârţ loc lejer
CAFE

(☏0751-892 340; Str Zoe 1; ⊘10am-11pm Mon-Fri, 11am-11pm Sat, 2-11pm Sun; 🛜) This is an old villa that's been retro-fitted into a funky coffeehouse with albums pinned to the wall and chill tunes on the turntable. There are several cosy rooms in which to read, talk and relax, but our favourite is the lush garden out back, with shady nooks and even hammocks to stretch out in. Located about 1km south of the city centre near Casa Bunicii.

Aethernativ
CAFE

(☏0724-012 324; Str Mărăşeşti 14; ⊘10am-1am Mon-Fri, noon-1am Sat, 5pm-1am Sun; 🛜) This informal art club, cafe and bar occupies a courtyard of a run-down building two blocks west of Piaţa Unirii and has eclectic furnishings and an alternative, student vibe. There are no signs to let you know you're here; simply find the address, push open the door and walk up a flight of stairs.

☆ Entertainment

Theatre & Classical Music

National Theatre & Opera House
THEATRE, OPERA

(Teatrul Naţional şi Opera Română; ☏opera 0256-201 286, theatre 0256-201 117; www.tntimisoara.com; Str Mărăşeşti 2) The National Theatre & Opera House features both dramatic works and classical opera, and is highly regarded. Buy tickets (from around 40 lei) in the nearby **Agenţia Teatrală** (☏0256-201 286; www.ort.ro; Str Mărăşeşti 2; ⊘10am-1pm & 5-7pm

Tue-Sun), but note that most of the dramatic works will be in Romanian.

State Philharmonic Theatre
CLASSICAL MUSIC

(Filharmonica de Stat Banatul; ☏0256-492 521; www.filarmonicabanatul.ro; B-dul CD Loga 2; ⊘box office 2-7pm Wed, 9am-1pm Thu & Fri) Classical concerts are held most evenings here. Tickets (from 40 lei) can be bought at the box office inside the theatre and one hour before performances.

German State Theatre
THEATRE

(Teatrul German de Stat; ☏0256-201 291; www.teatrulgerman.ro; Str Mărăşeşti 2) Close to the National Theatre is the German State Theatre, with regular performances in German. Buy tickets at its **box office** (☏0256-435 743; www.teatrulgerman.ro; Str Alba Iulia 2; ⊘10am-3pm & 5pm-7pm Tue-Fri, 10am-3pm Sat).

Clubs

The city's club scene changes with the season. For a decent listing of hotspots, pick up a free copy of *Şapte Seri* (Seven Evenings) at the tourist information centre.

Club 30
CLUB

(☏0256-247 878; www.club30.ro; Piaţa Victoriei 7; admission 10 lei; ⊘6pm-3am) This club has been a staple on the dance scene for years and shows no signs of slowing down, particularly on retro '80s and '90s dance nights. There's live music on some evenings.

Happy
CLUB

(☏0725-225 292; www.happytimisoara.ro; Cantina 4c, student complex; ⊘from 10pm) Fun club in the student complex (p153). You'll have to ask around within the complex to find it. Parties, DJs and the whole bit. Starts late.

Cinemas

Cinema Timiş
CINEMA

(☏0256-491 290; Piaţa Victoriei 7; tickets 6-8 lei) Centrally located cinema screens a mix of Hollywood blockbusters and popular European films. Movies are normally screened in their original language.

🛍 Shopping

Banat Souvenir
GIFTS, SOUVENIRS

(☏0721-481 130; Str Lucian Blaga 10; ⊘10am-7pm Mon-Fri, 11am-3pm Sat) The best place in town to buy souvenir glassware and T-shirts, plus old postcards, textiles and traditional shirts.

Librăria Humanitas
BOOKS

(☏0256-431 414; www.evive.ro; Str Lucian Blaga 2; ⊘9am-7pm Mon-Fri) Sells some English-language books about Romania as well as a good selection of maps.

Galerie Calina
GALLERY

(www.calina.ro; Str Mărăşeşti 1-3; ☺10am-6pm Mon-Fri, 11am-3pm Sat) High-end contemporary art gallery showcases the work of younger artists from Romania and abroad.

ℹ Information

Agenţia de Voiaj CFR (☎0256-491 889; www.cfr.ro; cnr Str Măcieşilor & Str V Babeş; ☺7am-8pm Mon-Fri) Sells domestic and international train tickets and seat reservations as well as domestic air tickets and serves as an agent for coach journeys with Eurolines and Atlassib.

Central post office (☎0256-491 999; B-dul Revoluţiei 1989 2; ☺8am-7pm Mon-Fri, to noon Sat)

Online Centers (B-dul Mihai Eminescu 5; per hr 5.40 lei; ☺24hr; ⑦) Internet cafe.

Sensi Blu Pharmacy (www.sensiblu.com; Piaţa Victoriei 7; ☺8am-8pm Mon-Fri, 9am-8pm Sat & Sun) One of at least half a dozen similar, modern pharmacies on or around Piaţa Victoriei.

Timişoara County Hospital (Spitalul Clinic Judeţean de Urgenţă Timişoara; ☎0356-433 111; www.hosptm.ro; B-dul Iosif Bulbuca 10) Modern hospital, located 2km south of the centre, with high-quality medical care and 24-hour emergency service.

Tourist information centre (Info Centru Turistic; ☎0256-437 973; www.timisoara-info.ro; Str Alba Iulia 2) This great tourism office can assist with accommodation and trains, and provide maps and Banat regional info.

Unicredit Tiriac Bank (www.unicredit-tiriac.ro; Piaţa Victoriei 2; ☺9am-4pm Mon-Fri)

ℹ Getting There & Away

Air

Timişoara Airport (p264) is 12km northeast of the centre. Timişoara has excellent air connections to nearly every big city in the country and destinations around Europe thanks to budget carriers **Carpatair** (☎0256-300 970; www.carpatair.ro; ☺7am-7pm Mon-Sat) and **WizzAir** (☎calls €0.60 per min 0903-760 160; www.wizzair.com). Express bus E4 connects the airport and the city centre (20 minutes).

Bus

Timişoara lacks a centralised bus station for its extensive domestic services. Buses and minibuses are privately operated and depart from several points around the city, depending on the company. Consult the website www.autogari.ro for departure points. Sample fares include Arad (15 lei), Cluj-Napoca (65 lei) and Sibiu (45 lei).

International buses leave from the **east bus station** (www.autogari.ro). The main international operators include **Atlassib** (☎0256-226 486; www.atlassib.ro; Calea Dorobantilor 59) and **Eurolines** (☎0256-288 132; www.eurolines.ro; Str M Kogălniceanu 20). Belgrade-based **Gea Tours** (www.geatours.rs) offers a daily minibus service between Timişoara and Belgrade (one way/return 125/200 lei). Book over the website.

Train

Trains depart from the **northern train station** (Gara Timişoara-Nord; www.cfr.ro; Str Gării 2), though it's actually 'west' of the centre. Daily express trains include Bucharest (200 lei, nine hours, two daily), Cluj-Napoca (127 lei, six hours, two daily) and Arad (20 lei, one hour, five daily). There's one daily train to Belgrade (70 lei, three hours), which leaves at 5.40am.

CRIŞANA

Oradea

POP 176,231

Fans of art nouveau and Viennese Secession architecture dating from the late 19th and early 20th centuries will want to make a special stopover in Oradea. While many of the once-elegant buildings here have been allowed to fall into disrepair, visitors with a sharp architectural eye will see Secession's signature lyric design elements and inlaid jewelwork on buildings up and down the main pedestrian walkway, Calea Republicii, and across the Crişul Repede river at the Black Eagle Arcade.

◉ Sights

The best way to see the city is to stroll along Calea Republicii, lined on both sides with architectural gems. Don't miss the **Moskovits Palace** (Palatul Moskovits; Str Republicii 13), a Secession-style masterwork from 1905.

Roman Catholic Cathedral
CHURCH

(Sirul Canonicilor; ☺9am-6pm) This cathedral, 2km north of the centre, was built between 1752 and 1780 and is the largest baroque church in Romania. Organ concerts are occasionally held here. The adjacent **Bishop's Palace** (☺closed to the public), from 1770, boasts 100 fresco-adorned rooms and 365 windows. **Canon's Corridor** (Sirul Canonicilor; Str Sirul Canonicilor), just east of the cathedral, forms a series of 57 arches built between 1750 and 1875, part of the original Baroque

Oradea

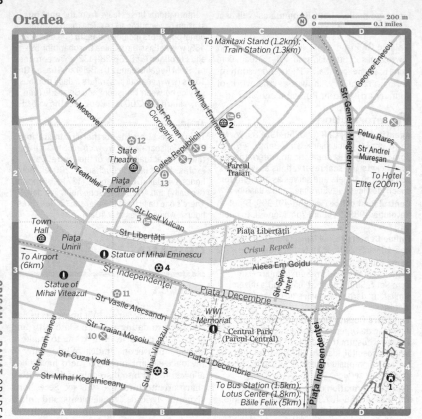

To Maxitaxi Stand (1.2km); Train Station (1.3km)

To Hotel Elite (200m)

To Airport (6km)

To Bus Station (1.5km); Lotus Center (1.8km); Băile Felix (5km)

design as laid out by the Austrian master architect FA Hillebrandt.

Orthodox Synagogue

JEWISH

(www.oradeajc.com; Str Mihai Viteazul 4; ⊙closed to the public) Oradea's Orthodox synagogue dates from 1890, and before WWII was the main house of worship for around a third of the city's residents. It survived the war intact, but was badly neglected afterward and is now undergoing a thorough multi-year renovation. Though it was closed during our visit due to the renovation work on the synagogue, you can contact the **Jewish Community Centre** (☎0359-191 021; www.fcer.jewishfed.ro; Str Mihai Viteazul 4) to take a look inside.

Just behind and to the left of the Orthodox synagogue is a small Holocaust Memorial (closed during our visit) to remember the around 30,000 Oradea Jews who perished. Most of the victims were executed at the German Nazi extermination camp at

Auschwitz-Birkenau in Poland following a series of transports in May–June 1944, after being forced to live in a cramped, sealed ghetto. The ghetto was located in the area surrounding the synagogue and remains depressed to this day.

Zion Temple Synagogue

JEWISH

(Neolog Synagogue; www.oradeajc.com; Str Independenței 22; ⊙closed to the public) Of the reform arm of Judaism and dating from 1878, this synagogue with its graceful dome is one of the most striking elements of the Oradea skyline. The synagogue was undergoing renovation to transform it into an exhibition centre during our visit and it was not clear when it would reopen to the public.

Cetatea Oradea

FORTRESS

(Piața Independenței; ⊙closed for renovation) Oradea's fortress dates from the 15th and 16th centuries and played a key role in

Oradea

conflicts between the Turks, Austrians and Hungarians over the years. The fortress is shaped like a pentagon, with five towers and thick defensive walls. At the time of writing it was closed for long-term renovation, but you can still stroll around the outside.

🛏 Sleeping

TOP CHOICE Hotel Elite HOTEL $$
(☎0259-414 924; www.hotelelite.ro; Str IC Bratianu 26; s/d 250/280 lei; P◉🤖🛜🏊) This beautiful and well-maintained hotel is fully worth the splurge, especially if you're travelling during the hot summer and have kids in tow. The rooms are spotless and well-maintained, but the major drawcard is a gorgeous heated (and child-friendly) pool straight out of a Hollywood mansion. Swim into the night and dine on the terrace.

Scorilo Hotel HOTEL $$
(☎0259-470 910; www.hotelscorilo.ro; Str Parcul Petőfi 16; s/d/apt 180/220/300 lei; P❄🛜) It's nearly impossible to book a room at this clean and way-too-popular family-run hotel. The location, 10 minutes' walk from the train station, is convenient if you're coming by train. The rooms are small but tidy; some have balconies over the garden. The outdoor restaurant is the most festive place in town for an evening meal.

Hotel Qiu HOTEL $$
(☎0733-666 555; www.qiu.ro; Calea Republicii 15; r 220 lei; ❄🛜) This modern hotel boasts an excellent location, right on Calea Republicii in the centre of town. There's no reception; instead book over the hotel website or by phone. The building is an art nouveau palace in need of renovation, but the rooms themselves have been given a stylish update and are clean, quiet and comfortable.

Hotel Atlantic HOTEL $$
(☎0259-426 911; www.hotelatlantic.ro; Str Iosif Vulcan 9; s/d 180/190 lei; ◉❄🛜) A renovated art nouveau villa that sports enormous rooms equipped with beds the size of trampolines and their own full-sized bars (BYO drinks). Unfortunately, the slightly over-exuberant contemporary style doesn't exactly fit the character of the building. Still, standards are high and the big rooms are good value for money.

🍴 Eating

Calea Republicii is a stroller's paradise, lined with cheerful eateries and cafes. Most of Oradea's terrace cafes and restaurants double as bars in the evening.

TOP CHOICE Graf INTERNATIONAL $$$
(☎0259-421 421; www.restaurantgraf.ro; Str Barbu Stefanescu Delavrancea 3; mains 30-70 lei; ⏰11am-11pm; 🛜) Graf is arguably Oradea's nicest restaurant and a perfect splurge option. The menu features wood-grilled steaks, fish and pork; the caramelized duck leg served on our visit was one of our best meals in Romania. Desserts feature cheesecake and homemade ice cream, and the wine list is top notch.

Rosecas ROMANIAN $$
(☎0745-265 673; www.rosecas.ro; Str Traian Moşoiu 17; mains 16-25 lei; 🛜) This informal everyman place serves excellent home-cooked Romanian and Hungarian fare, like chicken paprikash and duck, as well as delicious salads and homemade chicken soup. In summer, sit on the small terrace squeezed in between two buildings.

Lactobar CAFE $
(www.lactobarretrobistro.ro; Calea Republicii 11; mains 8-15 lei; ⏰8am-11pm; 🛜👶) Even if you're not hungry, stop by this charming, very kid-friendly 'retro bistro' on the main street. The colourful decor of period-piece found

CRIŞANA & BANAT ORADEA

objects is remarkable, topped off with an orange, ultra-cool Dacia automobile. The menu is less amazing, mostly burgers and sandwiches, but people come for the fun – not the food.

Cyrano ROMANIAN $$
(☑0740-163 943; Calea Republicii 7; mains 14-30 lei; ☺8.30am-midnight Mon-Fri, 9.30am-midnight Sat, 11am-midnight Sun; ☎) Popular hang-out ideal for people-watching from the coveted terrace tables. Though the menu teems with Romanian favourites, the incredible beef and veggie stew in a bread bowl (*ciorbă de vițet cu tarhon in chiflă*) is all the food you need.

☆ Entertainment

Tickets for performances at the **State Philharmonic** (Filarmonica de Stat; ☑box office 0259-430.853; www.oradeaphilharmony.com; Str Moscovei 5; tickets 15-25 lei; ☺box office 11am-5pm), with its traditional program of classical music, can be purchased in advance from the theatre box office or one hour before showtime. Kids will enjoy the shows at Oradea's **Arcadia Puppet Theatre** (Teatrul de Stat pentru Copii si Tineret Arcadia; ☑0259-433 398; www.teatrularcadia.ro; Str Vasile Alecsandri 8; adult/child 5/4 lei; ☺box office 10am-2pm Mon-Fri).

Shopping

Lotus Mall (☑0259-436 022; www.lotus-center.ro; Str Nufărului 30; ☺10am-10pm), 2km southeast of the centre, has a modern cinema, bowling alley, supermarket and a number of boutiques. **Humanitas** (☑0259-472 955; www.librariilehumanitas.ro; Calea Republicii 5; ☺10am-7pm Mon-Sat, 10am-5pm Sun) is a small but helpful bookstore, with a tiny collection of titles in English.

❶ Information

Oradea lacks a tourist information office but the bookshop Humanitas sells a handy map of the city.
24-hour Pharmacy (☑0259-18 242; Str Libertății 4)
Alpha Bank (☑0259-457 834; Piața Unirii 24; ☺9am-4pm Mon-Fri)
Internet Café (☑0359-454 566; Str George Enescu 24; per hr 3 lei; ☺8.30am-midnight Mon-Fri, noon-midnight Sat & Sun; ☎)
Post office (☑0259-435 040; Str Roman Ciorogariu 12; ☺8am-8pm Mon-Fri, to 2pm Sat)

❶ Getting There & Away

Bus

A small **bus station** (autogara; ☑0259-418 998; Str Râzboieni 81) is situated 2km south of the centre. From here you can catch frequent maxitaxis and regular buses to Băile Felix (4 lei, 10 minutes), Ștei (for access to Bear Cave; 13 lei, two hours) and Arieșeni (24 lei, three hours).

There's a small **maxitaxi** stand north of the train station for services to cities north of Oradea, such as Baia Mare (38 lei, three hours).

Train

Oradea's **train station** (☑0259-414 970; www.cfr.ro; Calea Republicii 114) is 2km north of the centre. Daily fast trains from Oradea include Budapest (150 lei, five hours, one daily), a slow overnight to Bucharest (about 105 lei, 12 hours), Cluj-Napoca (43 lei, three hours, six daily), Brașov (60 lei, nine hours, two daily) and Timișoara (47 lei, three hours, five daily).

Băile Felix

Băile Felix, 5km southeast of Oradea, is a summer oasis, with huge open-air kid-friendly swimming pools, with the water warmed by thermal springs. It's close enough to Oradea for an easy day trip, and the pools provide welcome relief if you get caught in a midsummer heatwave.

◉ Sights & Activities

Strand Felix SWIMMING POOL
(www.bailefelix.net; adult/child 25/12 lei; ☺8am-7pm Mon, 8am-8pm Tue-Sun May-Oct) The largest and most popular of the resort's two main public pools, located just beyond the Strand Apollo, near the Stația Băile Felix bus stop. The Felix has water slides and attracts families and kids.

Strand Apollo SWIMMING POOL
(www.bailefelix.net; adult/child 25/12 lei; ☺8am-7pm Mon, 8am-8pm Tue-Sun May-Oct) The smaller and quieter of the two main pools at the resort. The entrance is just opposite the Stația Băile Felix bus stop.

⌂ Sleeping & Eating

There are plenty of private rooms on offer, so if the places here are booked, simply look for signs saying *cazare* (rooms) or *pensiunea*.

Termal Hotel HOTEL $$$
(☑0359-437 398; www.hotel-termal.ro; half board s/d 240/340 lei, full board s/d 270/400 lei; ❂❂✱❂✸) This institutional-looking

modern building houses a comfortable spa resort. The rooms reek of cleanliness, with firm beds and balconies (request a forest view).

Pensiunea Veronica PENSION $$
(☎0259-318 481; www.casaveronica.ro; Str Primaverii 9a; d/tr/apt 150/180/250 lei; P⊖❄☜) This well-maintained mustard-yellow chalet was fully renovated in 2010 and is near the entrance to the pools and convenient for families.

Restaurant Union ROMANIAN $$
(☎0259-317 005; www.pensiuneaunion.ro; Băile Felix 106a; mains 15-25 lei; ⏲8am-midnight) Feast on a full menu with Romanian and Italian food, including a delicious bean soup with smoked ham.

Getting There & Away

Maxitaxis run either every 15 minutes or when full between Oradea bus station and Băile Felix (4 to 5 lei). Many maxitaxis and buses headed south for Ştei and the Apuseni Mountains stop at Băile Felix bus stop.

CAVING IN THE APUSENI NATURE RESERVE

The Apuseni Nature Reserve is prime caving territory. The area to the southeast of Oradea is filled with literally hundreds of caves, of which several dozen are open to the public. For serious spelunking, the best source of information is the **Apuseni Nature Reserve Visitors Centre** (Bear Cave Branch; ☎0259-329 339; www.parcapuseni.ro; Sudrigiu; ⏲8am-4.30pm Mon-Thu, 8am-2.30pm Fri), with headquarters on the approach to Bear Cave near the village of Chişcău or the branch (p160) near Arieşeni in the Apuseni Mountains.

Travelling from Oradea along Hwy E79 (local Hwy 76), the first major cave is **Meziad Cave** (Peştera Meziad; 4km from Meziad village; adult/child 15/10 lei; ⏲9am-1pm & 2-5pm, closed Thu morning), 24km northeast of the town of Beiuş. The cave features an enormous opening and is split into three levels, with some fairly treacherous climbs. Wear sturdy shoes and bring a torch (flashlight), as there's no electric light in the cave.

Meziad Cave is not easy to reach with public transport. From Beiuş, take a local minibus to the village of Meziad and hike the final 4km. By car from Beiuş, follow signs to the cave for 11km. At the village of Remetea, bear right at the Cămin Cultural building and continue for 9km to Meziad village. Pass through the village and eventually bear left across a small stone bridge to a gravel road, which brings you to the ticket office.

Bear Cave (Peştera Urşilor; ☎0742-115 303; Chişcău; adult/child 15/10 lei; ⏲10am-5pm), about 82km from Oradea, is one of Romania's finest and worth a special trip. The cave was discovered by quarry workers 40 years ago. It's named after skeletons of the extinct cave bear (*Ursus spelaeus*) found inside. The magnificent galleries extend over 1km on two levels. Guided tours allow you to spend an hour inside.

Without private transport, the region around the cave is tricky to navigate. Infrequent buses run between Beiuş, Chişcău and Ştei. From Oradea by car, head south through Beiuş, follow Hwy E79 a further 8km along the Crişul Negru River, then turn left at the turn-off for Pietroasa and Chişcău; continue for 8km. For an overnight option, **Pensiunea Laura** (☎0741-358 092; Chişcău, near the entrance to Bear Cave; r 90 lei; P☜) is a wooden chalet with eight rooms and a charming restaurant. **Transilvania Tours** (☎0259-318 491; www.transilvaniatour.ro) offers guided excursions from Băile Felix.

The most famous cave in the Apuseni Nature Reserve is the chillingly named **Ice Cave** (Peştera Gheţarul de la Scărişoara; ☎0742-010 347; accessible from Gârda de Sus; admission 7 lei; ⏲tours 9am, 10.20am, 11.40am, 12.20pm, 3.40pm, 5pm, 6pm, Sun to 5pm only May-Sep). The cave was first documented in 1863 by Austrian geographer Arnold Schmidt. Believed to be one of only 10 of its kind in Europe, the cave is filled with 7500 cu metres of ice dating back to the Ice Age, when the Apuseni Mountains were covered in glaciers.

Tours of 10 to 50 people depart throughout the day. The tour lasts 20 minutes and involves a steep descent to the opening, a quick peek inside, and then back up again. The cave can be reached on foot from Gârda de Sus (9km, two hours). You can drive to the cave via a paved but treacherously narrow road (18km, one hour) that leaves from the centre of Gârda de Sus.

Arieşeni & Gârda de Sus

Arieşeni and Gârda de Sus (often noted on signs as Gîrda de Sus) are wonderfully picturesque alpine villages that straddle both the Arieş River and scenic national Hwy 75 along a narrow valley in the Apuseni Mountains. Both are filled with guesthouses and make for an ideal stopover to relax and hike in the adjacent Apuseni Nature Reserve.

🏃 Activities

Most visitors come here just to relax and take in the mountain air or to hike or cave in the adjacent Apuseni Nature Reserve, a remote expanse of mountains in the 1600m to 1800m range that fans out to the north. Hiking trails leave from the villages of Vârtop, Arieşeni and Gârda de Sus. Pick up a hiking map from the visitors centre or buy the 1:150,000 *Apuseni Mountains* map, available from pensions or at most convenience stores. The website www.padis.ro is an excellent source of information in English.

🛏 Sleeping & Eating

There is no shortage of pensions, hotels and private rooms to let along Hwy 75. Look for *cazare* signs in the windows. Additionally, houses with the green sign reading '*Reţea Turistica*' means the owner has rooms for tourists (which are generally around 60 to 80 lei).

TOP CHOICE Casa Noastră PENSION $
(☎0258-779 122; www.pensiunea-casa-noastra.ro; Arieşeni; s/d 100/140 lei; ☺❋❈) This family-owned guesthouse is arguably the area's most handsome *pensiune,* with snug timber-lined rooms, a handsome garden along a babbling brook, and a lovely terrace perfect for an evening meal of grilled meats and a bottle of wine. It's 1km west of the centre of Arieşeni on Hwy 75.

Four Seasons HOTEL $$
(☎0729-989 515; www.4seasons.ro; Vârtop 30; d/apt 200/250 lei; ☺❋❈) Located along Hwy 75 in the village of Vârtop, 6km west of Arieşeni, this enormous chalet enjoys a commanding view over the valley. Most rooms have balconies. Request a view over the front of the house.

Mama Uţa CABINS, CAMPGROUND $
(☎0258-778 008; Gârda de Sus 97; campsite/cabin 15/100 lei; ❈) This popular summer spot, situated just on the western side of Gârda de Sus, has 14 wooden cabins. You can also pitch a tent, but it gets crowded in summer. The restaurant is one of the best around, so come for a meal even if you're not staying here.

Cabana Cetatile Ponorului HUT $
(☎0740-007 814, 0732-625 928; www.padis.ro; dm 40-50 lei; ☺) This well-equipped mountain hut offers 65 beds in dorm rooms of two, four and six beds. The more expensive beds have their own baths. Breakfast costs 12 lei. The hut is about three to four hours on foot from Vârtop along a red-marked trail, but is also accessible from many trails in the Padiş region.

ℹ Information

A branch of the **Apuseni Nature Reserve Visitors Centre** (☎main office 0259-329 339; www.parcapuseni.ro; ☺8am-4.30 Mon-Thu, 8am-2.30pm Fri) is located on Hwy 75 between Arieşeni and Gârda de Sus, about 1km west of Gârda de Sus. The office lacks English-language materials, but the helpful staff can advise on caving, camping and hiking opportunities. There's a handy **ATM** (Arieşeni 19) and **post office** (Arieşeni 19; ☺8am-4pm) in Arieşeni village.

ℹ Getting There & Away

Arieşeni and Gârda de Sus straddle Romanian Hwy 75, and there are decent bus and maxitaxi connections to Ştei, Beiuş, Oradea and Arad. The main bus station is located at the centre of Arieşeni village.

Arad

POP 160,000

The border town of Arad, around 50km from the Hungarian line, lies astride the main road and has rail connections in and out of the country. There are not many traditional sights here, but the city is a convenient stopover on your first or last night in the country. Fans of late-19th- and early-20th-century Viennese-influenced architectural styles like neoclassical and Secession will enjoy a stroll up the city's long tree-lined central boulevard.

◉ Sights & Activities

Town Hall HISTORIC BUILDING
(www.primariaarad.ro; B-dul Revoluţiei 75; ☺closed to the public) The U-shaped, neoclassical town hall is Arad's most impressive building. The clock atop the 1876 building was purchased in Switzerland in 1878.

Archaeology & History Museum   MUSEUM
(Muzeul de Arheologie si Istorie; ☑0257-281 847; Piaţa George Enescu 1; admission 2 lei; ☺9am-6pm Tue-Sun) Arad's modest history museum is a good primer for anyone interested in the city's complex origins, including 150 years of Ottoman occupation until 1699. After that the city served as a military bastion of the Habsburgs and, briefly, in 1849, as a centre of the Hungarian uprising, before being awarded to newly independent Romania after WWI.

Synagogue   JEWISH
(Str Dobra 10, entrance Str Cozia 12; ☺closed to the public) Arad's synagogue lies south and west of Piaţa Avram Iancu. It was built between 1827 and 1834 in Moorish style. It was closed to visitors at the time of research, but is worth a look anyway to see the last remnant of a once-vibrant community of around 10,000 Jews that lived in Arad pre-WWII.

Cetatea Arad   FORTRESS
(Citadel; ☺closed to the public) Arad's star-shaped fortress was built on orders of the Habsburg empress Maria Theresa between 1763 and 1783. It stands on the site of an old fortress built in 1551 by the Turks. Today it houses a military base.

Reconciliation Park   MONUMENT
(Parcul Reconcilieri) This monument park, three blocks west of Piaţa Avram Iancu, holds two amazing statues. In the centre, the Statue of Liberty was erected in 1890 to honour 13 Hungarian generals executed after the 1849 Hungarian uprising. Nearby, an even more impressive Arch of Triumph was built in 2004 to remember Romanian fighters killed in the same insurrection.

Neptun Water Park   SWIMMING POOL
(Strandul Neptun; general admission adult/child 5/3.50 lei, pool admission 10/6 lei; ☺9am-10pm May-Sep) The grounds of this sprawling water park are in various states of repair, but the pools themselves are clean and well maintained. There's a large popular thermal pool and a couple of smaller pools for children.

🛏 Sleeping

There are no youth hostels and few budget options in Arad. Enquire about booking a room in a private home (room 60 to 80 lei) through Info Tour Arad (p163).

⦿ᴛᴏᴘ Pensiunea Belanco   BOUTIQUE HOTEL $$
(☑0257-349 010; www.belanco.ro; Str Cocorilor 36; s/d 150/180 lei; P☺❀📶) This small family-run hotel opened for business in 2012, offering meticulously designed, well-proportioned singles and doubles, with air-conditioning and balconies. There's a lovely garden terrace for breakfast at the back of the house. The only downside is location, in an industrial neighbourhood 3km northwest of the centre. Take a taxi (10 to 15 lei) from the train station.

Hotel Continental Forum   HOTEL $$$
(☑reservations 0372-121 721; www.continental hotels.ro; B-dul Revoluţiei 79-81; s/d 350/400 lei; P☺❀@📶) Arad's upmarket choice has international standards of accommodation and service, and frequently discounts room rates during slow periods. In-room internet costs extra. The buffet breakfast is the best in town.

Hotel Arad   HOTEL $
(☑0257-280 894; www.hotel-arad.com; B-dul Decebal 9; s/d 125/145 lei; P☺❀📶) Old-fashioned but still in good shape, with huge rooms and an excellent central location about two minutes' walk from B-dul Revoluţiei.

✗ Eating

Transilvania Restaurant   ROMANIAN $$
(Sori Bar; ☑0257-281 478; Str N Bălcescu 2; mains 15-25 lei, lunch specials 15-18 lei) The square-side terrace is an excellent choice for lunch, offering good-value daily specials of traditional Romanian meals. In the evening it does double duty as a popular drinking spot.

Perla Mureşului   ROMANIAN $$
(☑0257-228 827; Str Malulul Mureşului; mains 15-25 lei; ☺11am-11pm) This popular riverside terrace is an excellent choice on a warm evening in summer, with a cool breeze blowing in (if you are lucky) and pretty glimpses of the river below. The food, traditional Romanian, is above average (but short of gourmet), though that doesn't diminish the festive feel.

Open Air Market   MARKET $
(Piaţa Catedralei; ☺6am-8pm Mon-Fri, 6am-2pm Sat, 6am-1pm Sun) Sprawling open-air food market has dozens of stalls offering fresh fruit and vegetables, breads, meats and cheeses. At the western end of Str Meţanu.

Arad

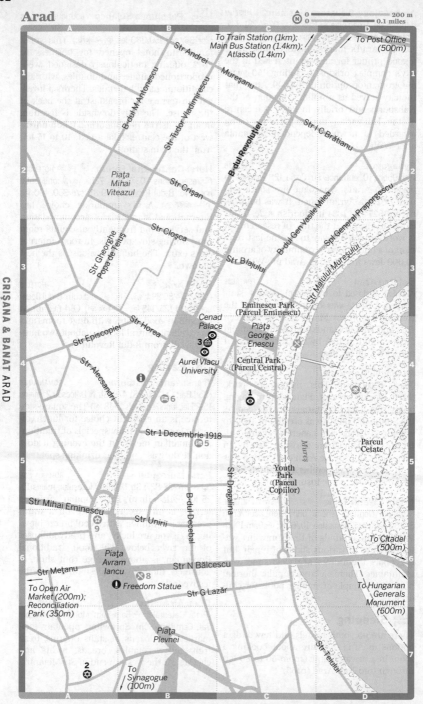

N 0 — 200 m
0 — 0.1 miles

To Train Station (1km);
Main Bus Station (1.4km);
Atlassib (1.4km)

To Post Office
(500m)

Str Andrei

Mureşanu

B-dul M Antonescu

Str Tudor Vladimirescu

Str I C Brătianu

B-dul Revoluţiei

Piaţa
Mihai
Viteazul

Str Crişan

Str Închisorii

Str Gen Vasile Milea

Spl General Praporgescu

Str Gheorghe Popa de Teiuş

Str Closca

Str Blajului

Str Malului Mureşului

Str Episcopiei

Str Horea

Eminescu Park
(Parcul Eminescu)

Cenad
Palace

Piaţa
George
Enescu

3

Central Park
(Parcul Central)

Aurel Vlacu
University

Str Alecsandri

1

4

6

Parcul
Cetate

Str 1 Decembrie 1918

5

Mureş

Str Draşalina

Youth
Park
(Parcul
Copiilor)

Str Mihai Eminescu

B-dul Decebal

9

Str Unirii

To Citadel
(500m)

Piaţa
Avram
Iancu

Str N Bălcescu

8

Str Meţanu

Freedom Statue

Str G Lazăr

To Open Air
Market (200m);
Reconciliation
Park (350m)

To Hungarian
Generals
Monument
(500m)

Piaţa
Plevnei

Str Tetului

2

To
Synagogue
(100m)

Arad

⊚ **Sights**

Archaeology & History Museum..(see 1)
1 Palace of Culture C4
2 Synagogue..A7
3 Town Hall B4

⊕ **Activities, Courses & Tours**
4 Neptun Water Park............................ D4

⊜ **Sleeping**
5 Hotel Arad..B5
6 Hotel Continental Forum B4

⊗ **Eating**
7 Perla Mureşului C4
8 Transilvania Restaurant B6

⊕ **Entertainment**
9 Ioan Slavici Theatre............................A6
Philharmonic Orchestra..............(see 1)

☆ Entertainment

Consult the helpful staff at Info Tour Arad to check on cultural happenings. The **Philharmonic Orchestra** (Filarmonica de Stat Arad; ☑box office 0257-281 554; www.filarmonicaarad.ro; Piaţa George Enescu 1; tickets from 15 lei), based in the **Palace of Culture**, holds classical music concerts. Tickets are sold at the venue box office two hours before performances begin. Arad's **Ioan Slavici Theatre** (Teatrul Ioan Slavici; ☑0257-280 016; www.teatrulclasic.ro; B-dul Revoluţiei 103; tickets 20-30 lei; ⊙box office 10am-2pm & 5-7pm Mon-Fri, 10am-noon & 5-7pm Sat-Sun) is nationally celebrated, though performances are in Romanian. The theatre also hosts concerts and musical performances.

ℹ Information

Agenţia de Voiaj CFR (☑0257-280 977; www.cfr.ro; Str Meţanu 16; ⊙8am-8pm Mon-Fri, 9am-1pm Sat) Sells domestic and international train tickets.

Banca UniCredit Ţiriac (Piaţa Avram Iancu 11; ⊙9am-3.30pm Mon-Fri, to 12.30pm Sat)

Eurocomputer (B-dul Decebal 20; per hr 3.50 lei; ☎) Internet cafe.

Info Tour Arad (☑0257-270 277; turism@primariaarad.ro; B-dul Revoluţiei 84-86; ⊙9am-6pm Mon-Fri, to 2pm Sat) Helpful staff provide brochures and free maps and give accommodation recommendations.

Post office (Str Caius Iacob 4; ⊙7am-7pm Mon-Fri)

ℹ Getting There & Away

Bus

Arad **bus station** (Calea 6 Vânători 2) is west of the train station. It's the hub for **Atlassib** (☑0257-270 562; www.atlassib.ro), the main international coach operator. Daily domestic destinations include Timişoara (about 15 lei), Bucharest (about 70 lei) and Oradea.

Car & Motorcycle

The border crossing into Hungary is 52km west of Arad in Nădlac. This is a major road crossing from Romania into Hungary, so expect to wait at the border.

Train

Arad train station (☑0257-230 633; Piaţa Gării 8-9) is a major railway junction. Daily fast services include several to Budapest (about 100 lei, four hours), with onward connections to Western Europe, Bucharest (105 to 140 lei, 10 hours, three daily), Timişoara (20 lei, one hour, five daily) and Cluj-Napoca (60 lei, four hours, three daily).

Maramureş

Includes »

Best Places to Eat

» Millennium (p168)

» Restaurant Tineretului (p173)

» Hotel Perla Maramuresului (p180)

Best Places to Stay

» Hotel Gabriela (p179)

» The Village Hostel (p176)

» Victoria Berbecaru (p178)

» Casa Iurca (p173)

Why Go?

Widely regarded as Romania's most traditional region, scattered with gothically steepled wooden churches and villagers' homes fronted by ornately carved gates, Maramureş feels as if you are climbing into a horse-drawn time machine and heading back 100 years. Smaller in scale and softer in contour than neighboring Transylvania, Maramureş' tapestry of pastureland, peopled by colourfully garbed crone-faced peasants, jumps straight from a Brothers Grimm story. Welcome to the heart of folkloric, medieval Romania where the last peasant culture in Europe continues to thrive. But don't wait forever to visit: even here the 21st century is making inroads.

Medieval Maramureş exists in the Mara and Izei Valleys. Eight of its churches, in the villages of Bârsana, Budeşti, Deseşti, Ieud, Plopiş, Poienile Izei, Rogoz and Surdeşti, are on Unesco's list of World Heritage Sites.

When to Go
Baia Mare

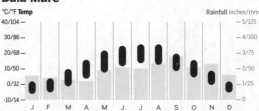

May–Sep Warm temperatures, meadows vivid with wildflowers and excellent trekking weather.

Dec–Mar The best time for skiers to head to Romania's snowy slopes.

Jun–Aug Summer months are the perfect time to hit the beach and cycle in the Carpathians.

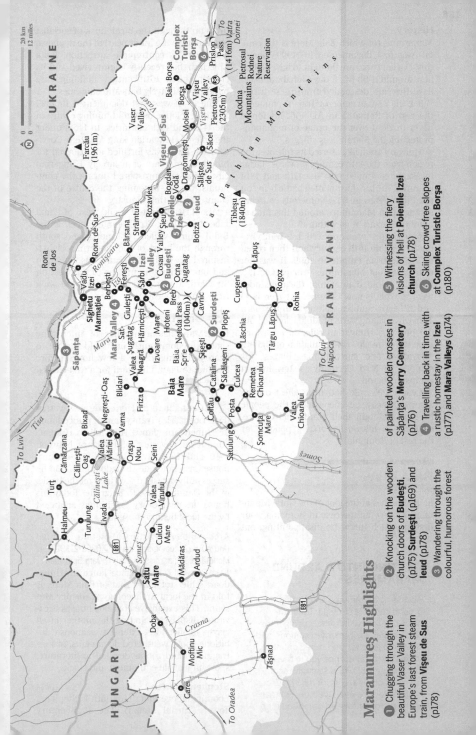

Maramureş Highlights

1 Chugging through the beautiful Vaser Valley in Europe's last forest steam train, from **Vişeu de Sus** (p178)

2 Knocking on the wooden church doors of **Budeşti** (p175) **Surdeşti** (p178) and **Ieud** (p169)

3 Wandering through the colourful, humorous forest of painted wooden crosses in Săpânţa's **Merry Cemetery** (p176)

4 Travelling back in time with a rustic homestay in the **Izei** (p177) and **Mara Valleys** (p174)

5 Witnessing the fiery visions of hell at **Poienile Izei church** (p178)

6 Skiing crowd-free slopes at **Complex Turistic Borşa** (p180)

History

Maramureş (of which Baia Mare is the capital) was first documented in 1199. Prior to this, Dacian tribes are thought to have settled here around 1000 BC; today's inhabitants believe they are descended from these tribes. When the Roman emperor Trajan conquered the rest of Romania in AD 106, his forces never made it over the range of mountains protecting the Maramureş villages.

Hungary gradually exerted its rule over the region from the 13th century onwards. Tartar invasions continued into the 17th and 18th centuries, the last documented battle being on the Prislop Pass in 1717. Numerous churches sprang up in Maramureş around this time to mark the Tartars' final withdrawal.

Maramureş was annexed by Transylvania in the mid-16th century and then ceded to the Austrian empire in 1699. It was not until 1918 that Maramureş – or part of it – formally rejoined Romania; the remainder went to what is now Ukraine. Between 1940 and 1944 Maramureş – along with northern Transylvania and parts of Moldavia – fell under pro-Nazi Hungarian rule, during which time the entire Jewish population of Sighetu Marmaţiei and surrounding villages was shipped to Nazi Germany's extermination camps in Poland.

Ceauşescu's rule had little effect on the area; curiously, he encouraged the people here to maintain their traditional culture, contrary to his *Systematizire* policies for the rest of Romania.

Baia Mare

POP 144,780

Baia Mare lies at the foot of the Gutâi Mountains. As is often the case in Romania, your first approach might be disappointing, but press on through the bleak husk of socialist tenements to the inner pearl of the medieval old town. Its centrepiece attraction, Piaţa Libertăţii, has recently been revived and its cheerily hued 16th-century buildings are bursting with lively bars and chic cafes.

The town was first documented in 1329 and it developed as a gold-mining center in the 14th and 15th centuries. In 1469, under the rule of Hungarian king Matthias Corvinus, the town was fortified and thrived for hundreds of years as a largely Hungarian city. Baia Mare prospered during the communist period, becoming the centre of the country's smelting industry.

About 10 minutes' walk west of Piaţa Libertăţii, along Str Gheorge Şincai, is the B-dul Unirii, which runs north and south through the heart of the modern, socialist-inspired city of the 1970s and '80s. The train and bus stations lie further to the west on Str Gării, and are about a 15-minute walk from Piaţa Libertăţii.

◎ Sights

Baia Mare has a number of interesting sights (predominantly in its old centre) to keep you amused for a few hours before heading to Piaţa Libertăţii for a well-earned coffee break.

FREE **Casa Iancu de Hunedoara**　MUSEUM
(Piaţa Libertăţii 18) Transylvanian prince Iancu de Hunedoara (János Hunyadi in Hungarian), royal governor of Hungary between 1446 and 1453, lived in the 15th-century house Casa Iancu de Hunedoara. In 1456 he successfully thrashed the Turks on the banks of the Danube, close to Belgrade. Today, his house has temporary exhibitions arranged by the local history museum.

Archaeology & History Museum　MUSEUM
(Muzeul de Arheologie şi Istorie; ☎0262-211 927; Str Monetăriei 1-3; admission 5 lei; ⊙9am-5pm Tue-Fri, 10am-2pm Sat & Sun) Prince Iancu de Hunedoara's life story, and that of Baia Mare, is told in the local Archaeology & History Museum. This expansive complex houses excavation displays, including the mother of all clay-pot collections, extensive weapons exhibitions, tools, weathered documents, bronze fragments and rooms devoted to literature, sport, industrial equipment and clocks.

Stephen's Tower　TOWER
Looming above Piaţa Libertăţii is Stephen's Tower (Turnul Ştefan). The 15th-century

---

GETTING INTO & AROUND MARAMUREŞ

Accessing Maramureş and getting around can be a struggle. Train entry often requires visitor-challenging transfers in small, lazily marked stations, and the same goes for the limited options for getting around once you're there. For DIY touring, car hire is strongly recommended, preferably from Baia Mare or Cluj. Make sure you have a decent map of the region or take an organised tour.

Gothic-style tower was originally topped with a bell, which was replaced by a mechanical clock in 1628. There's a noticeboard beside the tower with some descriptive information about the tragic fate of the adjoining church, which survived several fires and was eventually pulled down by the municipal authorities.

Baia Mare

◎ Sights

1 Archaeology & History Museum	D2
2 Art Museum	D3
3 Butchers' Tower	D3
4 Casa Iancu de Hunedoara	D2
5 Central Market	D3
6 Dealul Florilor Stadium	C1
7 Ethnographic Museum	C1
8 Mineralogical Museum	B4
9 Romanian Soldiers Monument	C2
10 Stephen's Tower	D2
11 Village Museum	C1

⊜ Sleeping

12 Euro Hotel/Best Western	A4
13 Hotel Carpaţi	C2
14 Hotel Mara	B4
15 Hotel Rivulus	C3
16 Pensiunea Floare De Colti	D2

⊗ Eating

17 Barbarossa	D2
18 Budapesta	A2
19 Café Lumiere	D2
20 Millennium	D2
21 Rustic	B4

✿ Entertainment

Agenţia Teatrală	(see 22)
22 Teatrul Municipal	D3

MARAMUREŞ BAIA MARE

Art Museum
MUSEUM

(Muzeul de Artă; ☑0262-213 964; Str 1 Mai 8; admission 7 lei; ⊙9am-4:30pm Tue-Sun) The Art Museum has 250 exhibits tracking local artists from 1896 to the present.

Central Market
MARKET

(cnr Str 22 Decembrie & Str Vasile Alecsandri) The central market is surrounded by the only remaining part of the 15th-century city walls and is beneath the **Butchers' Tower**, now fully restored, where famous brigand Grigore Pintea Viteazul was shot in 1703.

Dealul Florilor Stadium
STADIUM

(Stadionul Dealul Florilor) North across the footbridge over the Săsar River, the stadium is home to the Baia Mare football club.

Romanian Soldiers Monument
MONUMENT

(Monumentul Ostaşilor Români) The WWI Romanian Soldiers Monument is in the park to the west of Dealul Florilor Stadium. Open-air masses are often held next to the monument on Sunday.

Ethnographic Museum
MUSEUM

(Muzeul Etnografic; admission 5 lei; ⊙Tue-Sun 10am-4pm) Northwest of Dealul Florilor Stadium is the Ethnographic Museum, in which all the traditional trades of the Maramureş region are represented.

Village Museum
MUSEUM

(Muzeul Satului; adult/child 5/2 lei; ⊙8am-4pm Tue-Fri, from 10am Sat & Sun) The Village Museum displays traditional wooden houses and churches, for which the region is famed.

Mineralogical Museum
MUSEUM

(Muzeul de Mineralogie; B-dul Traian 8; admission 7 lei; ⊙9am-4:30pm Tue-Sun) This museum houses an interesting collection of rare minerals and gems from the Baia Mare region, but is suited more to enthusiasts than the general public.

🛏 Sleeping

Turn to the Tourist Information Centre for help with arranging private homestays.

Pensiunea Floare De Colti
PENSION $

(☑0262-250 216; Str Vasile Lucaciu 48; s/d 100/130 lei; P🅿❄🔊) Newish and very clean, this hotel is also close to the centre. Rooms are sizeable, with fresh en suites and cable TV. Breakfast is included and there's also parking.

Euro Hotel/Best Western
HOTEL $$

(☑0262-222 405; www.eurohotel-bm.ro; B-dul Bucureşti 23; s/d 175/210 lei; ⊖❄🔊) With a litany of shiny attributes including wi-fi, pool, sauna, fitness centre, bar, restaurant and bowling, this is good value. That said, it's on the main road, so ask for one of its modern rooms at the back.

Hotel Mara
HOTEL $$

(☑0262-226 660; www.hotelmara.ro; B-dul Unirii 11; s/d 170/210 lei; ⊖❄🔊) Despite the geometrical confusion of its ugly exterior, Mara has a graceful lobby with studded leather chairs, and a pleasant, low-lit bar. En-suite rooms are tight but pleasantly finished in old-world furniture. You can also get a massage here (35 lei, one hour).

Hotel Rivulus
HOTEL $$

(☑0262-216 302; www.hotelrivulus.ro; Str Culturii 3; s/d 170/210 lei; ⊖❄) Overlooking Piaţa Revoluţiei, Rivulus has a swank lobby and rooms to match with plush furniture, cable TV, air-con and choice oils on the walls.

Hotel Carpaţi
HOTEL $$

(☑0262-214 812; www.hotelcarpati.ro; Str Minerva 16; s/d 170/280 lei; ⊖❄🔊) With its shimmering lobby ablaze with mirrors, Carpaţi reminds us of 1970s Vegas. Rooms here are fresh and welcoming, dominated by flat-screen TVs and retro-kitsch furniture, and have air-con and en suites.

✖ Eating & Drinking

Piaţa Libertăţii is humming with lively cafes and alfresco restaurants.

Millennium
ROMANIAN $$

(Piaţa Libertăţii 5; mains 15-30 lei; ⊙10am-11pm) Boasting a prime people-watching spot on the square and an encyclopaedic menu of snacks, salads, ice cream and pizza, this place is a magnet for the town's youth.

Barbarossa
INTERNATIONAL $

(Piaţa Libertăţii; mains 15 lei; ❄🔊) Named after the infamous pirate, this nautically themed restaurant has an atmospheric interior hung with antique lanterns, and a terraced area of wrought-iron tables and chairs pumped with iced air. On offer are chicken, steak, pasta and salads.

Rustic
ROMANIAN $$

(B-dul Unirii 14a; mains 20 lei; ⊙11am-11pm) On an unnamed street behind the Olympic swimming pool, this carnivores' favourite has a bubbly terrace and a traditional interior. Rustic is all about pork fillets, steaks and cold plates of salami. Authentic.

Café Lumiere CAFE $
(Piaţa Libertăţii; ❀❆) Lumiere has a sense of Ibiza-chic with a terraced area with decked floors and billowing linen ceiling. Great coffee to wake you up to a menu of goulash, soup, bruschetta, pasta and salad.

Budapesta HUNGARIAN $$$
(Str Victoriei 94; mains 35-45 lei; ☺8am-10pm) Excellent Hungarian cooking in a refined setting. You'll have to look hard to find it; it's on the second level of a shopping complex at the far western end of Str Victoriei. Goose liver with crispy onion, lamb cutlet with rosemary jus, and many more dishes.

☆ Entertainment

Teatrul Municipal THEATRE
(Str Crişan 4) Plays are performed in Romanian. You can buy tickets in advance at the **Agenţia Teatrală** (☺10am-noon & 4-6pm Tue-Sun) in the lobby.

Cinema City CINEMA
(www.cinemacity.ro; Gold Plaza Baia Mare, Str Victorei 73; tickets 15 lei) Mall-style cinema with all the latest Hollywood blockbusters.

❶ Information

There are numerous banks and ATMs scattered around town.

Banca Transilvania (B-dul Unirii 5; ☺9am-6pm Mon-Fri, 9.30am-12.30pm Sat)

Bancpost (B-dul Traian 1B; ☺9am-5pm Mon-Fri)

Central Post Office (B-dul Traian 1B; ☺7am-8pm Mon-Fri, 8am-1pm Sat) There's another branch on B-dul Burcureşti.

Mara Holidays (☎0262-226 656; office@hotelmara.ro; B-dul Unirii 11; ☺9am-5pm Mon-Fri) Tourist agency inside Hotel Mara. Can help arrange car hire and international travel.

Sensi-blu (B-dul Traian 2; ☺8am-8pm Mon-Fri, to 4pm Sat & Sun) Pharmacy.

Tourist Information Centre Maramureş (☎0262-206 113; www.visitmaramures.ro; Str Gheorghe Şincai 46; ☺9am-4pm Mon-Thu, to 2pm Fri) This jewel of a tourist resource is hidden in a communist-era building with a verdigris roof. Helpful English-speaking Rada can recommend homestays, suggest itineraries and trekking guides, and sort out transport options.

❶ Getting There & Away

Air

The **airport** (☎0262-293 444) is 9km west of the centre at Tăuţi Măgherăuş. A taxi to the centre should cost about 40 lei.

Tarom (☎0262-221 624; B-dul Bucureşti 5; ☺9am-6pm Mon-Fri, to noon Sat) operates daily flights between Baia Mare and Bucharest (one way about 590 lei).

Bus

Infrequent services run from the **bus station** (☎0262-221 777; Str Gării 2) to outlying villages. There are daily buses to Satu Mare (12 lei, one to two hours), Cluj-Napoca (around 25 lei, three to four hours), and Sighetu Marmaţiei via Baia Sprie (14 lei, two hours).

Maxitaxis, departing from the bus station, run daily (except Sunday) to Satu Mare (15 lei) and to Bistriţa (about 25 lei). **Fulop Impex SRL** (☎0745-600 796; www.efitravel.ro/services.php) operates an overnight bus service to Budapest (90 lei, 10 hours).

Train

Advance tickets are sold at **Agenţia de Voiaj CFR** (☎0262-219 113; Str Victoriei 5-7). From Baia Mare **train station** (☎0262-220 950; Str Gării 4) there are around four daily trains to Satu Mare (7 lei, two hours); two to Bucharest via Braşov (about 104 lei, 13 hours); two to Cluj-Napoca (24 lei, three hours) and one to Timişoara (76 lei, six hours). At the time of research there were no direct trains to Budapest, but you can catch an early train (departing 4.30am, arriving 8.30am) to the Hungarian city of Debrecen, from where there are frequent departures to Budapest (about 55 lei, nine hours).

Around Baia Mare

SURDEŞTI & AROUND

Approaching Surdeşti from Baia Sprie, you pass through **Şişeşti** village, home to the Vasile Lucaciu Memorial Museum. Vasile Lucaciu (1835–1919), appointed parish priest in 1885, built a church for the village that was supposedly modelled on St Peter's in Rome.

The towering church (72m) at **Surdeşti** is one of the most magnificent in the Maramureş region and listed as a Unesco monument. It's well worth the hike for its wall and ceiling paintings. The church, signposted 'Monument' from the centre of the village, was built in 1724 as a centre of worship for the Greco-Catholic faithful. Two kilometres south in **Plopiş** is another fine Unesco-protected church with a towering steeple. Ask for the key at the house nearby. A further 14km south is the town of Lăschia. Its church dates from 1861 and has a bulbous steeple.

BAIA MARE TO IZVOARE

North of Baia Mare a small road twists and turns through the remote villages of Firiza, Blidari and Valea Neagră, culminating 20km north of Baia Mare at Izvoare, where there are natural springs.

Viewing churches is not on the agenda here; come to wallow in the mountainous countryside dotted with delightful wooden cottages and ramshackle farms. The most popular hiking destination in the area is Igniş Peak (1307m), also frequented by paragliders.

This route is not served by public transport. A hiking trail (five to six hours, marked with red triangles) leads from Baia Mare to Izvoare; it starts about 3km north of Baia Mare along the Baia Mare–Izvoare road.

Ţara Chioarului

The Ţara Chioarului region in the southwestern part of Maramureş takes in the area immediately south of Baia Mare. The numerous villages, most of which boast traditional wooden churches, form a convenient loop that is ideal for a two-hour drive by private transport.

◉ Sights & Activities

Follow the main road south from Baia Mare towards Cluj-Napoca for 14km to Satulung. Three kilometres south of Satulung, take the unmarked turn-off on the left, opposite Cabana Stejarul, to Finteuşu Mare and continue for 5km until you reach the village of Posta. A small wooden church dating from 1675 sits at the top of the hill.

Nine kilometres south of Şomcuţa Mare lies Valea Chioarului, the southernmost village in Ţara Chioarului. Its delightful tall church stands next to the bus stop in the centre of the village. Beside the church is a bust of Hungarian hero Mihai Viteazul (1994).

From Şomcuţa Mare, a minor road winds its way to Remetea Chioarului, 12km northeast. Its tiny church, dating from 1800, is the highlight of Ţara Chioarului. It stands majestically beside the village's extraordinarily ugly, seven-spired modern church (1996).

Săcălăşeni, 7km further north, has a small church built in 1442, but sadly a modern church dominates the village.

Sighetu Marmaţiei

POP 44,200

Sleepy 'Sighet' (its shortened nickname) has a few sights for a morning's browsing, a pretty square edged by a church, and the Ukrainian border crossing just a few minutes away; but your real reason for being in Maramureş is its rural charm, so you needn't linger long. For centuries Sighet formed a cultural and geographic border between Slav-dominated territories to the north and Hungary and Romania to the south. Its name is derived from the Thracian and Dacian word *seget* (fortress).

Sighetu Marmaţiei, first documented in 1334, was also an important Jewish settlement until spring 1944, when most of the Jews were transported to Auschwitz-Birkenau. After WWII the communist government established one of the country's most notorious prisons here, for dissidents, intellectuals and anyone else who could

---

FESTIVITIES & CULTURE

Outside of carefree, *horincă*-swilling wintertime, the most noteworthy celebration in Maramureş is the Hora de la Prislop folk-music festival, held annually on the second Sunday in August.

Additionally there is Tânjaua de pe Mara, a celebration of peasant work held in May in the villages of Hărniceşti, Hoteni and Sat-Şugatag. Revellers, young and old, are 'watered' in the river for purification, before retiring to a feast and party. Tourists are welcome. Other notable festivals include Sanzienele (St John's Day/Midsummer Day), in the third week of June, which revolves around rejoicing in the regenerative power of nature, and St Maria's Pilgrimage in Moisei on 15 August.

The Winter Festival (27 December) is the undisputed high point of the year, featuring food, music, masks, a parade of colourful peasant costumes and oxen carrying baked cakes between their horns!

Sighetu Marmaţiei

Sighetu Marmaţiei

challenge the regime. It's now one of the city's most important tourist sights.

Nearly all the hotels, shops and restaurants are located on or near the central Piaţa Libertăţii or avenues that lead off it. The train and bus stations are adjacent and situated north of the city centre (about 10 minutes away on foot). To buy a city map (5 lei), try the bookshop **Luceafărul** (Piaţa Libertăţii 10; ⊗9am-6pm Mon-Fri).

◎ Sights

On Piaţa Libertăţii stands the **Hungarian Reformed church**, built during the 15th century. Close by is the 16th-century **Roman Catholic church**.

Synagogue   JEWISH
(Str Bessarabia 10) Sighet's only remaining synagogue is found near Piaţa Libertăţii. You can look around for free, but it's customary to leave a donation (10 lei). Before

SUPERSTITION IN ROMANIA

Jonathan Harker noted in *Dracula*: '... every known superstition in the world is gathered into the horse-shoe of the Carpathians, as if it were the centre of some sort of imaginative whirlpool'.

Few peoples cherish their old-world folk tales as do Romanians, with a colourful panoply of witches, giants, ghosts, heroes, fairies and Nosferatu to keep them awake at night. Given that much of Romania is rural and remote, it's not surprising that some of these superstitions and tales survive to this day. As much as 20% of people in Maramureş still believe in witchcraft.

Some traditions are innocuous, like a tree strung with pots and pans in the front garden, advertising that there's a daughter in the household who's free to marry. However, in certain remote areas there are more disturbing beliefs. Garlic and crosses are still wielded, and bodies are exhumed and a stake driven through their hearts to stop them haunting, as in the case of the village of Marotinul-de-Sus (west of Bucharest) back in 2004. During the total eclipse of 1999, while urbanites were partying, others in Romania were lighting bonfires and ringing churchbells across the countryside to ward off vampires, werewolves and evil spirits (all of which are associated with the lunar phenomenon).

WWII the Jewish community was estimated at 50,000 – more than half of Sighet's pre-war population. Sadly, today the local Jewish community numbers around 200.

Most of the Jews perished at Auschwitz-Birkenau after being shipped there in 1944, when Hungary (which ruled over the area at the time) agreed to surrender its Jews to Nazi Germany. Some 38,000 eventually perished and the majority of the survivors chose to emigrate.

Jewish Community Centre   JEWISH
(☎0262-311 652; Str Bessarabia 8; ⏰10am-4pm Tue-Sun) Next door is the Jewish Community Centre, where you can also arrange to visit the town's **Jewish Cemetery** (Str Szilagyi Istvan), a couple of blocks south of the centre (follow Str Izei then turn right into Str Szilagyi Istvan and look for a long stone wall).

Elie Wiesel's House   HISTORIC BUILDING
The Jewish writer and 1986 Nobel Peace Prize–winner Elie Wiesel was born in (and later deported from) Sighet. His house, on the corner of Str Dragoş Vodă and Str Tudor Vladimirescu, is open to visitors. Along Str Gheorghe Doja there is a **monument** (Str Mureşan) to the victims of the Holocaust.

Maramureş Museum   MUSEUM
(Piaţa Libertăţii 15; adult/student 4/2 lei; ⏰10am-6pm Tue-Sun) The Maramureş Museum displays colourful folk costumes, rugs and carnival masks.

Village Museum   MUSEUM
(Muzeul Satului; ☎0262-314 229; Str Dobăieş 40; adult/child/photo 4/2/4 lei) Allow two to three hours to wander through the incredible constructions at the open-air Village Museum, southeast of Sighet's centre. Children love the wooden dwellings, cobbled pathways and 'mini villages'. You can even stay overnight in tiny wooden cabins (20 lei) or pitch a tent (5 lei per person).

🏃 Activities

Teofil Ivanciuc   TOUR
(☎0745-944 555; www.amizadil.com) Teofil Ivanciuc is a local author who works as a fixer with outfits such as National Geographic, and can take you to the mountains to explore remote villages (one-day tours €35 per person). Homestays can also be arranged in his traditional wooden house (single/double €20/30 including breakfast).

🛌 Sleeping

For homestays check out www.ruraltourism.ro or www.pensiuni.info.ro.

TOP CHOICE Cobwobs Hostel   PENSION $
(☎0745-635 673; www.cobwobs.com; Str 22 Decembrie 1989 nr; dm/d without bathroom 40/100 lei; ❄@🖥) Friendly Cobwobs sits down a grassy lane in a pleasant house whose garden is so crowded with apple and plum trees, rioting flowers and talkative chickens that you may forget you're in town. Owner Lia is charm itself and a great source

of local info (handy given there's no tourist office any more).

Doubles and family rooms are homely and large, with shared showers and bathrooms. There are also two dorms. Outside are tables to read at and bikes for rent.

TOP CHOICE Casa Iurca HOTEL **$$**

(☎0262-318 882; www.casaiurca.ro; Str Dragoş Vodă 14; r 150 lei, annexe s 92 lei, d 185-218 lei; ⊛✳🖭) Rooms are elegant and cool in this fine wood-accented villa. Expect tasteful furniture, flat-screen TVs, tiled floors, leather chairs and spotless linen for your money. There's also in-room wi-fi, fridge, cable TV and fan. Hands-down the best digs in town.

Hotel Marmaţia HOTEL **$$**

(☎0372-721 210; www.hotelmarmatia.ro; Str Mihai Eminescu 97; s/d 170/250 lei; ⊛✳@🖭) This appealing wood-clad building, finished in plum-coloured shutters and sitting at the foot of a nearby mountain, is welcoming and cosy, with international-style rooms (with cable TV on the flat-screen, and minibar), a posh lobby and an excellent restaurant, and all exuding a sense of peace. You can even take a dip in the nearby river if it gets too hot.

Motel Buţi HOTEL **$**

(☎0262-311 035; www.hotelbuti.ro; Str Ştefan cel Mare 6; s/d/tr 100/120/180 lei; ⊛✳@🖭) Admittedly, rooms may be a bit on the small side, but considering the hotel's cleanliness, and the rooms' flat-screens, decent furniture and crisp linen, this is very good value. There's a bar downstairs.

✕ Eating & Drinking

TOP CHOICE Restaurant Tineretului ROMANIAN **$**

(Str Ioan Mihaly de Apşa; mains 10 lei; ⊙7am-9pm) This rustically accented restaurant is hung with cowbells and lanterns and makes for a magical departure from the rest of Sighet's offerings. It's also lovely and cool in high summer. Gyros, cold meat platters, breakfast and grilled nape of pork.

Casa Iurca ROMANIAN **$$**

(Str Dragoş Vodă 14; mains 20-35 lei; ⊙9am-11pm; 🖭) In a leafy courtyard, carved tables huddle around a centrepiece wood-fired grill. With Pavarotti in the air, and flowers to admire, this is a wonderful place to eat. Dishes include seared pork, skewered lamb and Maramureş stew with polenta (28 lei).

Casa Veche ROMANIAN **$$**

(Str Iuliu Maniu 27; mains 14-30 lei; ⊙8am-11pm) Probably the busiest joint in town, Casa has a bubbly terrace come evening, and an elegant, high-ceilinged interior besmirched by pumping Euro-pop and (sorry!) a stratosphere of smoke. Succulent steaks, salads and huge pizza.

Market MARKET **$**

(Piaţa Agroalimentara) The town market is a good spot to pick up picnic provisions, with a large selection of fruit and vegetables as well as big loaves of bread and excellent, fresh-baked *covrigi* (0.50 lei).

Moak BAR

(Central Caffe; Piaţa Libertăţii 23; ⊙8am-10pm; 🖭) Local haunt with strong coffee, free wi-fi and a few sugary snacks to keep your stomach from rumbling. It's facing the square.

SIGHET PRISON: A SUFFERING NATION

In May 1947, the communist regime slaughtered, imprisoned and tortured thousands of Romanians who could or might oppose the new leadership. While many leading prewar figures were sent to hard-labour camps, the regime's most feared intellectual opponents were held in Sighet's maximum-security prison. Between 1948 and 1952 about 180 members of Romania's academic and government elite were imprisoned here and some 51 died.

The prison, housed in the old courthouse, was closed in 1974. In the early '90s it reopened as the **Memorial to the Victims of Communism and to the Resistance** (☎0262-319 424; www.memorialsighet.ro; Str Corneliu Coposu 4; admission 6 lei; ⊙9.30am-6.30pm Mon-Sun, to 4pm winter). Photographs and objects with short descriptions are displayed in the torture chambers and cells on two levels. There's also a small bookstore and gift shop. The heart-rending bronze statues in the courtyard, shielding themselves and covering their mouths in horror, are dedicated to those who died.

Immediately outside is a little kiosk selling doughy pretzels (get them early morning).

❶ Information

ATM (Piaţa Libertăţii 8) Outside Hotel Tisa.

Banca Română (Calea Ioan Mihaly de Apşa 24; ☺9am-5pm Mon-Fri) ATM, and cash transfer and exchange facilities.

Post & Telephone Office (Str Ioan Mihaly de Apşa 39) Opposite the Maramureş Museum.

❶ Getting There & Away

Bus

The **bus station** (Str Gării; ☺closed Sun) is opposite the train station. There are several local buses departing daily (except Sunday) to Baia Mare (12 lei, 65km) and Satu Mare (20 lei, 122km), and regular services to Borşa (10 lei), Budeşti (7 lei), Călineşti (7 lei) and Vişeu de Sus (10 lei), as well as Bârsana, Botiza, Ieud and Mara (all around 6 lei). From Borşa, there are daily maxitaxi services to Moldavia: Vatra Dornei (departing at 11am, 20 lei) and Iaşi (departing at 1pm, about 40 lei).

For Budapest buy bus tickets from **Hotel Coroana** (☏0362-103 244; hotelcoroana@ yahoo.com; Piaţa Libertăţii 8), where the bus leaves at 7pm (100 lei).

Atlassib (☏0262-519 365; Bogdan Vodă 5; ☺9am-5pm Mon-Fri, to 3pm Sat) Books bus trips to major Romanian destinations.

Eurolines (☏0729-618 009; Bogdan Vodă 5; ☺9am-5pm Mon-Fri, 10am-1pm Sat) Just off Piaţa Libertăţii. Offers Europe-wide long-distance coach service.

> ### ❶ BORDER CROSSING: TO UKRAINE
>
> There's a small car/foot bridge from Sighet to Ukraine about 2km outside the centre, making an excursion into Ukraine a snap. EU and US citizens need only fill out some forms and show a passport; nationals from other countries may need to secure a visa beforehand. Formalities on the Romanian side are fast and hassle-free: go straight to the front of the queue with your passport. To find the crossing point, from the centre of Sighet follow Str Titelescu north about 2km. The border is open 24 hours. The Ukrainian town on the other side is called Slatina and has a number of hotels.

Train

Advance tickets are sold at the **Agenţia de Voiaj CFR** (☏0262-312 666; Piaţa Libertăţii 25; ☺7am-8pm Mon-Fri). There's one daily fast train to Timişoara (93 lei, 12 hours), Bucharest (90 lei, 12 hours), Cluj-Napoca (60 lei, six hours) and Braşov (77 lei, eight hours). A sleeper train here costs 121 lei.

Mara Valley

The Mara Valley (Valea Marei), with its beautiful rolling hills, is the heart of Maramureş. Villages here are famed for their spectacular churches and carved gateways. Private rooms and homestays are fairly plentiful; the website www.pensiuni.info. ro has a good selection of *pensiunes* (pensions) in this valley.

GIULEŞTI & AROUND

Heading south from Sighetu Marmaţiei, you reach the tiny village of Berbeşti, famed for the 300-year-old *troiţă* (crucifix), a large Renaissance-style cross carved with solar emblems, which stands by the roadside at the village's northern end. Traditionally, travellers prayed by the cross to ensure a safe journey.

Continuing south you'll find Giuleşti, the main village in the Mara Valley, notable for its crumbling wooden cottages with 'pot trees' in their front yards, on which a colourful array of pots and pans are hung to dry. It was here in 1918 that the revolutionary Ilie Lazăr summoned delegates from all over Maramureş prior to their signing of Transylvania's union agreement with Romania. Ilie Lazăr's house is preserved and open to tourists as a memorial museum. During the communist crackdown in the early 1950s, Ilie Lazăr was arrested and imprisoned at Sighet prison.

The village of Deseşti is a few kilometres southwest of Giuleşti on the road to Baia Mare. Its tiny Orthodox church, built in 1770, was struck by lightning in 1925, destroying much of the outer walls and the steeple. Its interior paintings, by Radu Munteanu, date from 1780 and feature Sodom and Gomorrah.

Close to the church is an oak tree, hundreds of years old and measuring about 4.5m in diameter. It has been preserved as a monument to the extensive oak forest that once covered the area before people felled the trees to build their homes.

Mara, just a couple of kilometres south of Deseşti, is known for its elaborate wooden

WOODEN MARAMUREŞ: CHURCHES & GATEWAYS

Dating back to the 14th century when Orthodox Romanians were forbidden by their Hungarian rulers to build churches in stone, the carpenters of Maramureş used wood to express their people's spirituality. Of the eight Unesco-listed churches you can see today, all were built in the 18th and 19th centuries after the Tartar invasions finished in 1717. These churches' weatherbeaten exteriors have taken on an eerie, blackened hue, their gothic spires rising austerely to narrow pinpricks. However, inside you'll find them vibrant and cosy, with packed congregations of fervently religious villagers, and walls painted in naïve biblical frescoes and representations of rural traditonal life. These Orthodox churches are divided into the ante-nave, nave and altar, with towers rising up to 50m above.

Traditionally, homes of the Mara, Cosău and Izei Valleys used oak, while in Bârsana pine was used, and this is still the case. Roofs are tall and steep, many finished in shingle tiles that look like fish scales, while the oldest are covered in thatch.

Immense carved wooden gates fronting homes are common now, often used to illustrate the social status and wealth of the inhabitants, yet originally they were built only by royal landowners to guard against evil. The gates were the symbolic barrier between the safe interior and the unknown outside world, and people placed money, incense and holy water under them for further protection against dark forces. Gate carvings include the Tree of Life, the snake (guardian against evil), birds (symbols of the human soul) and a face (to protect from spirits).

---

porch fences. These porches are a unique architectural feature of the Maramureş region. In more recent times, the spiritual importance of these outside porches has been overridden by the social status attached to them.

SAT-ŞUGATAG & AROUND

Seven kilometres south of Giuleşti is Sat-Şugatag, home to a church dating from 1642. The church is famed for its fine, ornately carved wooden gate. Sat-Şugatag was first documented in 1360 as the property of Dragoş of Giuleşti, a voivode and probably Moldavia's first ruler.

Mănăstirea is 1km east of Sat-Şugatag. The church here was built by monks in 1633. By 1787 just one monk and four servants remained, and during the reign of Austro-Hungarian Emperor Joseph II the monastery was closed. The original monks' cells are on the northern side of the church.

Seven kilometres south of Mănăstirea is Hărniceşti, home to a marvellous Orthodox church dating from 1770. A footpath, signposted 'Spre Monument', leads from the village's primary school to the hillside church.

Nine kilometres southeast of the village of Ocna Şugatag is Hoteni, known for its Tânjaua de pe Mara folk festival held from 1 May to 14 May to celebrate the first ploughing.

EASTERN MARA VALLEY & COSĂU VALLEY

Heading south from Sighetu, bear left at Fereşti along the road leading to some of Maramureş' least accessible villages. From Baia Mare, you can approach this area through Cavnic, across the Neteda Pass.

Corneşti, the first village along this stretch, has a small 18th-century church with interior paintings by Hodor Toador. Călineşti, 7km further south, has two churches, known as Susani (sus meaning 'up') and Josani (jos meaning 'low'). The Susani church (1683) is on the left side of the road as you enter the village from the north. The Josani church, built 20 years earlier, is more spectacular.

From Călineşti a road leads to Sârbi, inhabited since 1402. Its two churches are built from oak. The Susani church dates from 1667, the Josani church from 1665. A traditional 'natural laundrette', ingeniously constructed by villagers to utilise the hydropower from the stream, is still used to wash clothes and blankets here.

If ever there was a place that conjoured bucolic Eden, Budeşti is it: men sport straw, nipple-shaped hats, women are garbed in floral headscarves, and all is backdropped by intricately carved wooden entrances to cosy cottages stacked with firewood. There are a couple of shops scattered about and a pension. The village also has one of the most beautiful churches in Maramureş. **Josani church**, built in 1643, features four small turrets surrounding the main steeple. The church's most prized piece is the 18th-century painting of the Last Judgment. If the church is locked, there's a phone number on the entrance door.

Budeşti is reachable from Sighet by bus or maxitaxi (or dedicated hitching). Pack a lunch as food here is scarce.

Sleeping

Babou Camping & Hostel
HOSTEL, CAMPING $

(0262-374 717; www.baboumaramures.com; Breb; tents/campervans 16/20 lei; dm incl breakfast 58 lei; Apr-Oct; P) Babou's sits in glorious hammock-strung meadowland with views of Ukraine. There's a pine-accented hostel with a four-berth dorm, a kitchen and a communal area, or a huge garden to pitch in. Extremely new, clean and efficiently run by Dutch people. Call to arrange a pick-up.

BREB

En route to Budesti from Ocna Sugatag, rustic Breb is an isolated village replete with ancient wooden houses and a 16th-century wooden church. A famous woodcarver (Patru Pop) lives here, and this tiny traditonal village is also home to the culturally immersive Somewhere Different tour company. For a price, owner Duncan can pick you up from Sighet. But there are also four buses running from Baia Mare and regular minibuses from Sighet.

Sleeping

The best accommodation in the area is in Breb.

TOP CHOICE Village Hostel
GUESTHOUSE $$

(0725-141 545; www.somewheredifferent.com; Breb; cottages per night 280 lei) Run by a charm-ing English couple – who also run the culturally immersive Somewhere Different tours – the hostel has five traditionally styled cottages with wood-beamed rooms, log burners, immaculate kitchens and bedrooms carpeted with sheepskin rugs. You're also given a mobile phone on arrival with useful contact numbers.

Dinner can be arranged at local houses, and your cottages are fully prepped for self-catering, with milk delivered daily along with cheese and freshly baked bread. Rustic chic gets no better.

SĂPÂNŢA

Săpânţa village, 12km northwest of Sighetu Marmaţiei and just 4km south of Ukraine, exudes pastoral charm with vividly hued rugs hanging over walls, hayrick-dotted cornfields as far as the eye can see, and horses and carts trundling at a snail's pace. The main draw of the village, however, is its unique **Merry Cemetery** (admission & camera each 4 lei): the church graveyard famous for the colourfully painted wooden crosses that adorn its tombstones. The crosses attract busloads of visitors who marvel at the gentle humour that created them and, curiously, villagers seem unfazed by the daily circus. Outside the church, a gauntlet of souvenir stalls hawk embroidered tablecloths, Russian dolls and some of the finest examples of woven rugs in the country.

Five hundred metres down a gravel road, a new **wooden church** claiming to be the tallest wooden structure in Europe (75m) has been built with a nontraditional stone base. Ask the resident nun to open the basement chapel.

Two buses per day go to Săpânţa (morning and afternoon, weekdays only) from Sighetu Marmaţiei, but with no return bus. The wooden church is signposted off the

MARAMUREŞ MARA VALLEY

MERRY CEMETERY

Săpânţa's Merry Cemetery was the creation of Ioan Stan Pătraş, a simple wood sculptor who, in 1935, started carving crosses to mark graves in the old church cemetery. He painted each cross in blue – the traditional colour of hope and freedom – and on top of each he inscribed a witty epitaph to the deceased. Every cross tells a different story, and the painted pictures and inscriptions illustrate a wealth of traditional occupations: shepherds tend their sheep, mothers cook for their families, barbers cut hair and weavers bend over looms.

Pătraş carved and painted his own cross, complete with a portrait of himself. Pătraş' grave is directly opposite the main entrance to the old church. Since Pătraş' death in 1977 his apprentice Dumitru Pop, as well as a number of other craftsmen, work in Pătraş' former house and studio, now a fascinating little **museum** (admission 3 lei). It's a short detour 300m to the right of the cemetery entrance.

main Sighet–Negreşti–Oaş road, though it's easier to just look up and follow the steeple.

🛏 Sleeping & Eating

Camping Poieni   CAMPING $
(☑0740-593 380; www.camping-poieni.ro; campsites/cabins 8/50 lei; 🛜) Located 3km out of town (heading south towards the mountains), Poieni is idyllically positioned by a stream, and has tiny wood cabanas and a restaurant in the main house. Guests can use the clay oven too. Shared showers and WC.

Pensiunea Ileana   PENSION $
(☑0745-491 756, 0262-372 137; sapantaileana@yahoo.com; d 80 lei) With its traditional rooms nestled round a courtyard, and its garden stacked with freshly sheared wool, Ileana is old-school Maramureş. Ileana, the eponymous host, is lovely and has her own weaving workshop she can show you. The pension is opposite the cemetery.

Izei Valley
POP 3000

The Izei Valley (Valea Izei) follows the Iza River eastward from Sighetu Marmaţiei to Moisei. A tight-knit procession of quintessential Maramureş peasant villages nestle in the valley, all featuring the region's famed elaborately carved wooden gates and tall wooden churches.

The region is best explored by car, heading south out of Sighet along the main highway (DN18) towards Baia Mare and then bearing left in Vadu Izei (6km south of Sighet) along a quieter road in the direction of Bârsana.

VADU IZEI

Vadu Izei is at the confluence of the Iza and Mara Rivers, 6km south of Sighetu Marmaţiei. Its museum is in the oldest house in the village (1750).

Ioan Borlean (☑0728-316 425, 0742-749 608) functions as a quasi-official source of tourist information. Give him a call if you need help.

🛏 Sleeping

TOP CHOICE Casa Muntean   PENSION $
(☑0766-755 267; www.casamuntean.ro; Str Dumbrava 505; s/d without bathroom 40/80 lei; ☺@🛜) Colourful rooms enlivened by richly coloured rugs, wooden ceilings and wall hangings, as well as cable TV. Owner Florin can

SLEEPING IN THE IZEI VALLEY

Botiza is particularly rich in homestays. Alternatively, www.ruraltourism.ro and www.pensiuni.info.ro list an array of *cazare* (accommodation) available along the Izei Valley. Note: if you're driving, phone ahead to get precise directions; if you're planning to arrive by bus or train in Sighet, ask the owner to pick you up at the station.

take you on a guided tour (60 lei) to local wooden churches or to the Merry Cemetery.

They also hire bikes (20 lei) and can organise a four-hour horse-and-cart trip (100 lei). The owners will pick you up at Sighet station.

Pensiunea Teodora Teleptean   PENSION $$
(☑0742-492 240; Str Dumbrava 503; r 120 lei; 🅿) Ten rooms in a pretty wood-carved building. Rooms are spacious and fragrant with antique armoires, wood-raftered ceilings, TVs and en suites.

BÂRSANA

From Vadu Izei continue for 12km through Onceşti to the village of Bârsana (formerly Bîrsana), dating from 1326. In 1720 it built its first church, the interior paintings of which were created by local artists Hodor Toador and Ion Plohod.

◉ Sights

Bârsana Monastery   MONASTERY
(Mănăstirea Bârsana) The famous Orthodox Bârsana Monastery is a popular pilgrimage spot in Maramureş, but the church you see today was built in the 1990s. The 11am service is a magical experience among the rolling hills and wildflowers, and every 30 June the monastery celebrates the 12 Apostles. Check out the beautiful church, shrine, museum and shop. Eleven nuns presently reside here.

Barsana Art Museum   MUSEUM
(Main St; ☺9am-8pm) Not a museum but a garden workshop, this place is operated by an artisan whittling wooden carvings, from life-size bears to miniature archways.

🛏 Sleeping

Mihai Paşca   PENSION $
(☑0262-331 165; Bârsana 377; r 70 lei) Situated 2km outside of Bârsana on the road to

Călineşti is this large wooden house offering cosy rooms with driftwood furniture, TV, clean linen, en suites and bright, fresh walls.

BOTIZA

Continue south to Şieu, then take the turn-off right for the sleepy village of Botiza, one of the prettiest in all of Maramureş and site of the some of the region's best homestays. Botiza's old church, built in 1694, is overshadowed by the giant new church, constructed in 1974 to serve devout Orthodox families.

The 9am Sunday service is the major event of the week in Botiza. The *entire* village flocks to the church to partake in the religious activities, which continue well into the afternoon.

🛏 Sleeping

George Iurca　　　　　　　　PENSION $
(☏0722-942 140, 0262-334 110; botizavr@sintec .ro; Botiza 742; r per person 90 lei; @☎) George is a friendly guide with a licence to conduct tours throughout Romania. He rents out clean, comfortable rooms as well as mountain bikes (25 lei per day) and vehicles with a driver-guide (300 lei per day for a group). You'll find his house four doors down from Botiza's new church.

Victoria Berbecaru　　　　　PENSION $
(☏0262-334 107; r incl breakfast 80 lei) Four spick-and-span rooms are available at this pension, run by the warm, French-speaking Victoria. Better still are her rooms in the 19th-century wooden house just opposite, where you can stay in simple, cosy cells that give the feeling of a ship's cabin. Downstairs there's a shop selling Victoria's beautifully woven rugs.

POIENILE IZEI

From Botiza a road leads west to Poienile Izei, home of a church with the most dramatic frescoes of hell you are ever likely to encounter. The early-17th-century church's frescoes eerily depict infernal visions of torments inflicted by the devil on sinners. Visit on a stormy day and it'll scare the pants off you. To visit, ask for the key at the priest's house, a large wooden place in the centre of the village, with an ornately carved terrace.

At **La Domniţa** (☏0262-334 383; house 135, Poienile Izie 138; r per person 40 lei) the friendly owner speaks French and does some excellent home cooking.

Four kilometres further north along a gravel track is the village of Glod, the birthplace of popular Maramureş folk-singing duo, the Petreuş Brothers.

IEUD

Packed with traditional houses and pensioners in traditional garb, this fervently Orthodox village (6km off the road south from Şieu) has as its main draw its 17th-century wooden church. Under its rooftop was found the 'Ieud Codex', a document that is considered to be the oldest writing in the Romanian language (1391–92; today the codex is kept in the archives of the Romanian Academy in Bucharest).

Ieud's other church (Biserica de Lemn din Şes), today Greco-Catholic in denomination, was built in 1717. The church, at the southern end of the village, is unique to the region as it has no porch. It houses one of the largest collections of icons on glass found in Maramureş. Cross the bridge to the modest **Ethnographic Museum** (adult/child 5/3 lei; ☺ 8am-12pm & 1-8pm Mon-Sun) to see an elderly woman spinning thread on a wheel like Rumplestiltskin.

🛏 Sleeping

Liviu Ilea　　　　　　　　　PENSION $
(☏0747-940 260; Ieud 333; r per person incl breakfast & dinner 90 lei; ℗☎) This wooden house (found at the base of a hill at the end of a lane) is signed 1km out of town, and has simple rooms with a nice family. The owner can arrange to pick you up in Baia Mare or Sighet for 1.25 lei per kilometre.

Vasile Chindris　　　　　　PENSION $
(☏0743-811 077, 0262-336 197; Ieud 201; r per person 90 lei; ℗) Rooms (with shared bathroom) are clean and homely in these central digs. The husband-and-wife team can drive you around. Meals cost 28 lei.

Vişeu & Vaser Valleys

Wooded mountains rise to dizzying heights around the picturesque Vişeu Valley (Valea Vişeu), which tracks the Vişeu River on its journey south. Regular buses and maxitaxis link the valley to Sighet, making it more accessible for travellers without private transport.

VIŞEU DE SUS

Essentially a one-street affair dotted with a few banks, cafes and restaurants, the town's narrow lanes radiate towards the **Vaser Valley railway station** (☏0262-353 381; Str Cerbului 5). If you're headed into the rural wilds of Maramureş this is a good stop to fuel up on gasoline and lei, and there are a couple of solid hotels.

STEAMED UP!

Operated by CFF Vişeu de Sus (p180), and variously known as the 'Vaser Valley Railway' or 'Carpathian Forest Steam Train', this former logging train travels a network of some 60km of narrow 12-gauge track, and is probably the last forestry railway still powered by steam working in Europe today. Started in 1932 as an alternative to transporting logs by river, the track winds through soaring forested crags that a traveller might otherwise have trouble reaching. It's a life-affirming experience as you sniff the woodsmoke, hear the train whistle blaring, and see smoke whorling from the gleaming black funnel.

The journey proper starts at 9am, but you'll need to secure a ticket by arriving at the train station at 8.30am (the train only seats 180). Thanks to damage to the track caused by flooding in 2008, the journey ends at Paltin, where you'll alight by the river for an hour's lunch. There are benches in a meadow, and grilled hot dogs and drinks are served for a fee. From Paltin the intrepid can trek higher into the mountains, or it's possible to camp near the warden's lodge (at Paltin) if you seek his permission (arrange with the CFF Vişeu de Sus office to catch a return train the following day).

This is a 'Hogwarts' train extraordinaire, loved by kids and adults alike, the mountain scenery up to the remote Valea Vaser (Vaser Valley) among the most stunning in Europe. Keep your eyes peeled along the way to see bears drinking at the river. The magic ends at 3pm as you return to the station. It has a pleasant cafe – so you can warm up with a coffee – and a small Jewish museum. The railway runs from spring to autumn.

To get to the station from the town of Vişeu de Sus, follow signs to: 'Moca Nita', turning left opposite Hotel Brad on the corner of Str 22 Decembrie and Str Iuliu Maniu, and continuing along Str Carpaţi for 2km. There's plenty of free parking at the train station, or you can walk from the centre (about 10 to 15 minutes). Remember to bring an extra layer to combat the chilly air, and if you plan to do some hiking at the top, bring food and water and wear sturdy boots. CFF sells a good hiking map of the Vaser Valley trails (12 lei).

First chronicled in 1363, for centuries Vişeu de Sus was an important logging area, and ethnically diverse, boasting communities of Jews and Germans. Though many Germans emigrated after WWII and particularly after 1989, there are still a handful of German speakers. The town's Jews largely perished in the Holocaust.

Most travellers come here for the chance to ride a steam-powered locomotive high into the hills, along a narrow-gauge track originally built for transporting logs. It's a grand day out and combines the thrill of a good ride with a chance to springboard on to a hike into the upper reaches of the Vaser Valley.

🛏 Sleeping

The area immediately surrounding the train station is filled with private *pensiunes* offering rooms for around 80 to 90 lei, often including breakfast. The owners may prepare an additional meal for you for around 20 lei per person.

Pensiunea Stancuta PENSION $
(☎0745-096 481, 0262-355 521; Str Alexandru Ioan Cuza 56; r 70 lei) Handy for catching the early-morning train, Stancuta is 1km past the train station from the centre of town. The rooms are clean and welcoming, with fine views of the nearby mountains. There's a large garden and a wood terrace to read on.

Hotel Brad HOTEL $
(☎0262-352 999; cnr Str 22 Decembrie & Stre Iuliu Maniu; s/d incl breakfast 70/105 lei; P 🖥) The Brad is somewhat sorry for itself on the outside, but things are sunnier within, with cream rooms, firm beds, bureaus, TVs and pine furniture. It's pretty good value given the price.

TOP CHOICE **Hotel Gabriela** HOTEL $
(☎0262-354 380; www.hotel-gabriela.ro; s/d 100/120 lei; P 🖥❄🖥) Located 2km east of town, Gabriela is reliable, offering clean, modern rooms with verandahs, cable TV, en suites and hearty breakfasts. The sister restaurant next door bubbles with life and makes pretty good pizza.

🍴 Eating

Moak CAFE $
(Str 22 Decembrie; mains 15 lei; ⏰7am-10pm; 🖥) Bijou-sized Moak is a welcome slice of chic, with leather couches and funky wallpaper.

It serves up toasted paninis, wraps, burgers and pasta.

Pizzeria Andra

PIZZERIA $

(Str 22 Decembrie; mains 15 lei; ⊙7am-midnight) Euro-pop on the tube and whorls of cigarette smoke hanging in its arches, Andra is a local favourite, with a huge menu of pizza, pasta, schnitzel and bruschetta to choose from.

Café Maya

CAFE $

(Str 22 Decembrie 12) With its vaguely Parisian, lemon interior, this is a good stop for cappuccinos and, come night-time, mojitos and daiquiris.

❶ Information

Alll your needs are taken care of by the tirelessly helpful staff at **CFF Vişeu de Sus** (☏0744-686 716, 0262-353 381; www.cffviseu.com; Str Cerbului 5; adult/child 45/29 lei; ⊙8am-6pm Mon-Sun), the agency that operates the narrow-gauge railway out of the steam-train station. They can assist you with walking maps and eating and accommodation advice, and can help organise a guide.

BORŞA

Buzzing little Borşa has a real ace up its sleeve: its proximity to the **Complex Turistic Borşa** 10km east, a ski resort set amid insanely pretty countryside with dark green forests, sun-dappled streams and mid-size mountains. As well as having some decent intermediate and beginner slopes, it's the main entry point for walkers keen to experience the **Rodna Mountains**, part of which forms the Pietrosul Rodnei Nature Reservation (5900 hectares). In winter the resort boasts the largest natural ski run in Europe.

Hiking information is scarce, but there are clearly marked trails leading from the top of the ski lift. Trails include a two-hour hike (in good weather) to the Prislop Pass and a pleasant one-hour hike signposted 'Cascada Cailor', which leads to the 100m high 'Horse' waterfalls. If you want to stretch your legs before starting on the trails, there's a path leading up underneath the **ski lift** (Str Brădet 10; one way/return 10/20 lei; ⊙7am-6pm).

In Borşa town, the **Hotel Perla Maramuresului** (☏0741-418 946, 0262-342 539; Str Victoriei 27; r 70 lei) has a delightful wooden facade and an old-world feel. Its restaurant serves up dishes like grilled veal (12 lei), and the dining room is festooned with plates and violins. Warped, creaky stairs lead to basic but cosy rooms with woollen blankets, wooden floors and plain en suites. Right outside is where buses and maxitaxis from Sighet drop you, and where maxitaxis to Vatra Dornei and Iaşi depart. At the Complex Turistic ski resort, **Pensiunea Vila Focus** (☏0262-344 038; r 100 lei), near the chairlift, is a timber and stone affair with a tempting restaurant and immaculate rooms. Try for digs facing the mountain.

Buses run between Borşa proper and the Complex Turistic all day. There are several daily buses to Sighet, stopping in most towns along the way. There are also daily maxitaxi services to Moldavia: Vatra Dornei (departing at 7am, about 25 lei) and Iaşi (departing at 1pm, about 45 lei), passing Gura Humorului.

Prislop Pass

From Complex Turistic Borşa, a tight, winding road climbs for 10km to the remote Prislop Pass. Hikers can trek north into the Maramureş Mountains or head south into the Rodna Mountains and onward to Moldavia. Red triangles, then blue stripes lead to the peak of the Gargalau Saddle (1925m, two hours). Then either continue east (red stripes) to the Rotunda Pass, then southeast to Vatra Dornei, or west to the highest part of the massif and on to La Cruce (four to five hours). From here the weather station on the summit of Mt Pietrosul (2305m, blue stripes) is only 90 minutes away, which among the mind-bending views allows for a good long gaze into Ukraine without the hassle of border checks. At this point, it's a direct hustle back down to Borşa (two to three hours).

Cabanas are scarce in this area; come prepared to camp out. Do not attempt to stray too far from these trails without a good map and compass.

Moldavia & the Bucovina Monasteries

Best Places to Eat

» La Castel (p189)
» Latino (p201)
» Hotel Lacu Roşu (p198)
» Buena Vista (p189)
» La Rustica (p189)

Best Places to Stay

» Hotel Unirea (p187)
» Hotel Sonnenhof (p200)
» Hilde's Residence (p204)
» Gerald's Hotel (p206)
» Eden Hotel (p207)

Why Go?

Less visited than other parts of Romania, Moldavia rewards those intrepid enough to seek it out: from glorious medieval monasteries to rugged mountains ideal for skiing and hiking, this singular region combines natural and artistic beauty with plenty of action.

Moldavia's bucolic villages and oddly endearing towns feature some of Romania's friendliest locals. Beyond the hinterland's traditional ways, Moldavian modernity is fully displayed in Iaşi, Romania's second-largest city and a vibrant student town famous for its nightlife, shopping and exquisite, varied architecture.

Within Romania, Moldavia's known for its rolling plains, interrupted only by the accidental cluster of trees or grazing horse. These sweeping vistas are particularly hypnotic by evening, when fading sunlight spreads across the land and vast sky, suffusing both in tones and shapes as rich and varied as Moldavia's monastic art.

When to Go

Iaşi

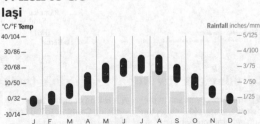

Apr & May Enjoy Iaşi when it's rejuvenated by spring flowers, boisterous students and live music.

Jul & Aug Escape the summer heat by hiking the Ceahlău and Rarău mountains.

Sep & Oct Visit the Bucovina painted monasteries minus crowds, as the autumn leaves change.

Moldavia & the Bucovina Monasteries Highlights

1 Immersing yourself in the cafe life, grand old architecture and general good vibes of university city **Iaşi** (p183)

2 Gazing heavenwards at soaring centuries-old frescoes at the sublime **Bucovina Monasteries** (p202)

3 Hiking or skiing the dizzying **Ceahlău** (p196) and **Rarău** (p207) mountains

4 Bearing down for some white-knuckle driving through the narrow, stupendously steep **Bicaz Gorges** (p197)

5 Skiing, swimming or drinking with the locals in mountain-ringed **Piatra Neamţ** (p192)

6 Saluting Moldavia's medieval might at the grandiose, refurbished **Târgu Neamţ fortress** (p194)

SOUTHERN MOLDAVIA

Iaşi

POP 263,410

Exuberant, cultured Iaşi (pronounced 'yash') clearly enjoys being Romania's second-biggest city. Once dubbed the 'city of the hundred churches', Iaşi is indeed bursting with centuries of architectural creations. Yet besides the monasteries, theatres and other historic buildings, this eclectic place has botanical parks, big squares and (for better or for worse) both communist-era concrete structures and gleaming modern shopping malls.

As with its shopping scene, Iaşi's innumerable eateries, drinking holes and lively clubs depend on the robust university population. You'll find international students here representing everywhere from Australia, Italy and Spain to Israel, Greece and Arab countries – making this little corner of Romania unexpectedly cosmopolitan.

Founded in the 14th century, Iaşi became Moldavia's capital in 1565. Its cultural tradition began with scholars clustering here in the early 17th century, and included a significant Jewish population, which was sadly decimated by WWII pogroms. Prominent literary luminaries immortalised here include Vasile Pogor, Ion Creangă and poet Mihai Eminescu. In 1862 Romania's first university, Ion Cuza, was established in Iaşi (it's still going strong today, along with several others).

The city's elaborate system of boulevards and squares centres on Piaţa Unirii, from which B-dul Ştefan cel Mare extends south to Piaţa Moldova. Between the two squares are some of the town's most famed historic buildings, like the Moldavian Metropolitan Cathedral and the Palace of Culture. Except for the outlying train and bus stations, most sights are within a 15-minute walk of this area.

◉ Sights

PIAŢA UNIRII TO PIAŢA PALATUL CULTURII

Piaţa Unirii (Union Sq) is a convenient landmark, filled with heritage buildings (including some of the upscale hotels).

Natural History Museum　　MUSEUM
(☎0232-201 339; B-dul Independenţei 16; admission 4 lei; ☺9am-3pm Tue, Thu & Sat, 9am-4pm Wed, Fri & Sun) The museum has over 300,000 exhibits, with a focus on Moldavia's endemic flora and fauna.

St Spiridon's Monastery　　MONASTERY
(☎0744-965 588; B-dul Independenţei 33) One block northeast of the square, this monastery contains the headless body of Grigore Ghica III, killed in 1777 for opposing the Turks. The present structure dates from 1807, after an 1802 earthquake damaged everything but the original steeple tower (1786). Interestingly, some church inscriptions were written in Romanian – but with Cyrillic letters.

Moldavian Metropolitan Cathedral　CHURCH
(Mitropolia Moldovei; B-dul Ştefan cel Mare) This cavernous cathedral, built between 1833 and 1839, was designed by architect Alexandru Orascu and decorated by painter Gheorghe Tattarescu. Since 1889, when the cathedral claimed the relics of Moldavia's patron saint, St Paraschiva, from the Church of the Three Hierarchs, the faithful have flocked here annually to see them displayed in mid-October.

Church of the Three Hierarchs　　CHURCH
(Biserica Sfinţilor Trei Ierarhi; B-dul Ştefan cel Mare; ☺9.30am-noon & 1-5.30pm) Built by Prince Vasile Lupu between 1637 and 1639, and restored between 1882 and 1904, this is one of Iaşi's most beautiful churches. Its exterior stone pattern-work is exquisite and reveals Turkish, Georgian and Armenian influences. It also contains the marble tombs of Prince Lupu and his family, plus those of Prince Alexandru Ioan Cuza and Moldavian prince Dimitrie Cantemir.

The **Museum of 17th-century Frescoes** (B-dul Ştefan cel Mare, Church of the Three Hierarchs; admission 3 lei; ☺10am-4pm Tue-Sun) occupies an adjacent Gothic-style hall.

Palace of Culture　　MUSEUM
(Palatul Culturii; B-dul Ştefan cel Mare) The grandiose neo-Gothic Palace of Culture was built between 1906 and 1925 over Prince Alexandru cel Bun's ruined 15th-century princely court. At the time of research, renovations were forecast to conclude by 2014. When open, you can enjoy the four small musuems within, plus the **Gheorghe Asachi Library**.

The palace's **Ethnographic Museum**, one of Romania's best, has exhibits ranging from agriculture, fishing and hunting

Iaşi

Copou Park
(Parcol Copou)

To Mihai Eminescu Museum of
Literature (530m); Obelisk
of Lions (530m); Botanical
Gardens (1.43km)

Str Sărăriei

Piaţa
Universităţii

Str M Kogălniceanu

Str N Istrati

Str Lascăr Catargi

Str H M Berthelot

To Jewish
Cemetery
(2km)

Str Toma Cosma

32

B-dul Carol I

13

Str Vasile
Pogor

Str Sf Atanasie

Str Păcurari

48

Str Florilor

36 43

Str Vasile Conta

Str N Bălcescu

Maxitaxis to
Chişinău

47

Str Fătu

17

Str Băcinschi

Ortadoğu Tur

Piaţa Mihai
Eminescu

Str Alexandru Lăpuşneanu

Piaţa
Independenţei

B-dul Independenţei

Piaţa
Academiei

Str Rece

To Bus
Station
(900m)

Str Străpungerea Silvestru

Str Gării

49

34

15

11

40

19

Str Arcu

Bus Station

Maxitaxis
to Cotnari

20

22

29

Str 14 Decembrie 1989

Piaţa
Unirii

Train
Station

Str Uzinei

Str Străpungerea Silvestru

Str Petru Rares

42

28

Str Cuza Vodă

23

Str C Brătianu

44

Sos Naţională

26

Str Săulescu

21

46

30

41

38

16

Str Agatha Bârsescu

Central
Park

Str Crişan

B-dul Ştefan cel Mare şi Sfânt

9

Str Răşcanu

Str Sf Andre

4

Piaţa
Palatul
Culturii

Bahl

To Gară Nicolina (800m);
Galata Monastery (2.5km);
Frumoasa & Cetăţuia
Monasteries (4km)

B-dul Nicolae Iorga

Str Funcţionarilor

Str Morilor

Str Ipsilante

To Lake Ciurbeşti (5km);
Bârnova (16km)

Str Palat

to winemaking, plus traditional costumes and rugs. The **Art Museum** is split into two: the Galeriade Artă Românească, with more than 20 works by Romanian artist Nicolae Grigorescu and others including Moldavian Petre Achiţemie; and the Galeria de Artă Universală, exhibiting foreign works. The **History Museum** highlights include portraits of Romania's rulers since AD 81. Various mechanical creations and musical instruments are displayed in the less colourful **Science & Technical Museum**.

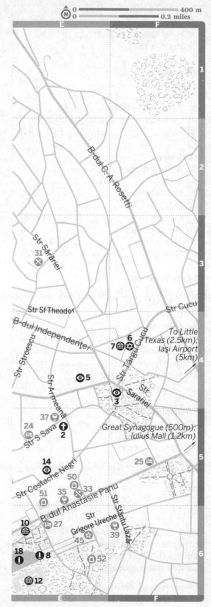

Museum of Old Moldavian Literature
MUSEUM

(☎0747-499 403; Str Anastasie Panu 54, Dosoftei House; adult/student 6/3 lei; ⊙10am-5pm Tue-Sun) This literary museum stands inside the 17th-century **Dosoftei House**. Dosoftei was Moldavia's metropolitan ruler between 1670 and 1686, and printed the first Romanian-language church liturgy in 1679.

MONASTERIES & CHURCHES
East of B-dul Ştefan cel Mare stand more of Iaşi's many Christian shrines: the city has 47 Orthodox churches alone, seven monasteries, three Catholic cathedrals and one Lippovan church. Entry to all is free.

Golia Monastery
MONASTERY

(Str Cuza Voda 51) This fortified late-Renaissance-style monastery is guarded by thick walls and the 30m-high Golia tower. The 17th-century church is notable for its vibrant Byzantine frescoes and intricately carved doorways, and features wall bastions from 1667. After repeated fires and closure from 1900 to 1947, the monastery was rejuvenated in 1992 and renovations continue. The complex also contains a house museum dedicated to writer and one-time resident Ion Creangă (1837–89), renowned for his Moldavian folklore-inspired short stories.

Armenian Church
CHURCH

(Biserica Armeană; ☎0232-214 893; Str Armeană 22) Considered Iaşi's oldest church, the stone-and-brick Armenian Church (1395) has been extensively renovated since 1803, eliminating most original architectural flourishes, though Armenian stone inscriptions from the 14th century remain.

St Sava's Monastery
MONASTERY

(Mănăstirea Sfântul Sava; Str Costache Negri 41) At Str Armeană's southern end, this 16th-century church was built on earlier foundations – records attest a wooden church consecrated here by a Byzantine bishop in 1330. Over ensuing centuries, it was refurbished by various princes (like the great Petru Rareş in 1534). With its two towers, large domes and iconostasis, today's church combines Byzantine, Gothic Moldavian, Wallachian and baroque styles.

Bărboi Monastery
MONASTERY

(Str Costache Negri) Built in 1841 over a 1615 church foundation, the Bărboi has an eccentric combination of Byzantine stone-and-brick interior and a neo-Classical portico

The palace is surrounded by historical reminders. On Piaţa Palatul Culturii is an equestrian **statue of Ştefan cel Mare** (1883). A **memorial** to Iaşi's heroes who died in 1989 stands by the palace grounds entrance.

Iaşi

supported by Doric columns – apparently a homage to similar churches at Greece's monastic commmunity of Mt Athos.

UNIVERSITY & AROUND

Piaţa Universităţii, northwest of the centre along B-dul Carol 1, is filled with crowded cafes and parks where students congregate.

Union Museum   MUSEUM

(Muzeul Unirii; ☎0232-314 614; Str Alexandru Lăpuşneanu 14; adult/student 4/2 lei; ☺10am-5pm Tue-Sun) This small, neoclassical palace was Alexandru Cuza's home for three years (1859–62), and later housed King Ferdinand during his WWI retreat from Bucharest. It displays the Cuza family's opulent furniture, pictures and personal effects.

Pogor House Literary Museum   MUSEUM

(Casă Pogor; ☎0232-410 340; Str Vasile Pogor 4; adult/student 6/3 lei; ☺10am-5pm Tue-Sun) This museum was originally Vasile Pogor's 1850s mansion, from 1871 hosting literary society meetings. On its grounds stand rows of busts of literary luminaries, including dramatist Ion Luca Caragiale (1852–1912) and poet Vasile Alecsandri (1821–90).

Copou Park   PARK

(Parcol Copou; B-dul Carol I) Designed between 1834 and 1848 under Prince Mihail Sturza, this 10-hectare park is allegedly where poet Mihai Eminescu (1850–89) wrote beneath a linden tree. The tree still stands behind the 13m-high Obelisk of Lions (supposedly modern Romania's oldest monument), which is opposite the main entrance. A bronze bust of Eminescu sits in front.

Mihai Eminescu
Museum of Literature   MUSEUM

(📞0232-144 759; Copou Park; adult/child 4/2 lei; 🕙10am-5pm Tue-Sun) This museum documents the writings, life and loves of Eminescu, Romania's favourite writer and poet. The great love of the married poet, Veronica Micle, was married also. They each outlived their spouses but never married due to Eminescu's deteriorating health. The busts of Veronica and Eminescu face each other by his favourite linden tree on Junimea Alea.

Botanical Gardens   GARDENS

(Grădină Botanică; 📞0232-201 373; Dumbrava Rosie 7-9, Parcul Exposiţiei; garden/greenhouse/photos 3/4/25 lei; 🕙9am-8pm) Iaşi's Botanical Gardens are Romania's first (1856) and largest (100 hectares). They sprawl across Parcul Exposiţiei's western side, and offer 21km of shady lanes, 800 rose varieties and orchid gardens, plus greenhouses with tropical flowers and carnivorous plants. Kids will enjoy the lawns and small lake. The gardens are popular for strolling and picnicking. They also host Vasile Lupu's Church of the Living (1638). The gardens are 3km northwest of the centre, so take a taxi (4 lei) or walk (20 minutes) up on B-dul Barol I – the gardens become visible about 500m past Copou Park, on the left.

🛏 Sleeping

Iaşi accommodation is business oriented and relatively expensive. Dedicated bargain hunters can find deals, however.

Advance booking is recommended for October 7 to 14, when both religious pilgrims and students returning to university (and their parents) occupy town.

TOP
CHOICE Hotel Unirea   HOTEL $$

(📞0232-205 006; www.hotelunirea.ro; Piaţa Unirii 5; s/d/ste 225/295/395 lei, parking 10 lei; P🐕❄ 📶🏊) Although several contenders around the main square vie for the title of Iaşi's best hotel, an indoor pool, spa centre and 13th-floor Panoramic Restaurant (with expansive views) sets the Unirea apart. Rooms are bright and business style, with comfortable beds and all amenities.

Grand Hotel Traian   HOTEL $$$

(📞0232-266 666; www.grandhoteltraian.ro; Piaţa Unirii 1; s/d 315/360 lei; P🐕❄📶) Right in the centre, the elegant Traian was designed by

JEWISH IAȘI

In the 15th century Jewish merchants from Poland and later Russia came to Iaşi, developing a vibrant community. By the 19th century the population was one-third Jewish, and Iaşi became important for Jewish culture and learning. In 1876 the first professional Jewish theatre opened here; a statue of Avram Goldfaden (1840–1908), a Polish composer and playwright and the theatre's founder, stands in the park on B-dul Ştefan cel Mare.

The Jewish community suffered devastating pogroms during WWII. Later on, the wily Ceauşescu extracted huge sums from the Israeli state by literally 'selling' many surviving families who chose to immigrate to the Jewish homeland.

Today only two of the original 127 synagogues exist for Iaşi's 1800 Jews. The Great Synagogue (📞0232-313 711; Str Sinagogilor 7), buit in 1671, is wedged between concrete apartment blocks. At the time of research, the synagogue was closed for renovation. Victims of the June 1941 pogroms are commemorated on a statue here. To see the small museum (📞0742-515 290; Str Sinagogilor; admission 5 lei) opposite, contact Avram Gatman, leader of Iaşi's Jewish community.

Many of the victims of the fascist Iron Guard's pogroms were buried in four concrete bunkers in the Jewish Cemetery (Cimitirul Evreiesc; admission 10 lei) on Mountain Hill (Dealul Munteni), west of the centre off Str Păcurari. There's a pogrom monument there and a small synagogue. A taxi from the centre costs about 7 lei.

ŞTEFAN CEL MARE: MOLDAVIA'S GREATEST PRINCE

It's a rare day when a Romanian doesn't say 'Ştefan cel Mare' (Stephen the Great, r 1457–1504): the name of Moldavia's greatest prince adorns squares, boulevards, streets, statues and landmarks nationwide. During his reign, Ştefan beat back Polish, Hungarian and Ottoman forces; his resistance to the latter won him admirers including Pope Sixtus IV, who declared Ştefan an *Athleta Christi* (Champion of Christ). Despite allegedly fathering over 20 illegitimate children, Ştefan's heroic deeds and church building won him canonisation by the Romanian Orthodox Church, as 'The Right-Believing Voivod Stephen the Great and the Saint'.

Although Ştefan is often overshadowed by his infamous cousin, Wallachian prince Vlad Ţepeş (Dracula), his battle record (34-2) speaks for itself, and he did erect 44 churches and monasteries – several now Unesco World Heritage sites. Both in battle and in church building, the prince kept up Romanian spirits and traditions, preventing the Ottomans from disrupting traditional cultures as they did almost everywhere else in the Balkans. Without Ştefan, Europe might well have turned out differently.

Gustave Eiffel himself. The rooms are appropriately outfitted with billowing curtains, high ceilings, big baths and a general old-world ambience prevails.

Iaşi Apartment
APARTMENT $
(☎0746-067 979; www.iasi-apartment.com; s/d/tr from 120/130/195 lei; ❄@☂) Run by a congenial local, Constantin Dunca, these downtown apartments have kitchens, air-con, internet and cable TV. Compare apartments, if possible, as quality and location differs, but price differences are minimal.

Hotel Select
HOTEL $$$
(Strada 14 Decembrie 1989 2; s/d/ste 330/360/420 lei; ❄☂) Considering the lack of extra services comparable to other Iaşi luxury hotels, Select seems overpriced, though the location's unbeatable and the rooms well-furnished. Even non-guests come to enjoy a coffee at the elegant outdoor corner cafe and patisserie.

Hotel Majestic
HOTEL $$$
(☎0232-255 557; www.hotel-majestic.ro; Str Petru Rareş 7; s/d from 155/220 lei; meals 12-60 lei; P❄❄☂☂) This formerly humble central pension has been renovated and expanded and its sharp rooms decorated with ornate furniture and billowing curtains. There's a new pool and the restaurant is excellent.

Hotel Continental
HOTEL $$
(☎0232-211 846; www.continental-iasi.ro; Str Cuza Voda 4; s/d with bathroom from 126/170 lei; ❄☂) The centrally located Continental occupies a listed historic building. Rooms have been freshened up, but remain almost budget-level quality. Some have private baths – avoid those overlooking the noisy street.

Hotel Moldova
HOTEL $$
(☎0232-260 240; www.hotelmoldovaiasi.ro; Str Anastasie Panu 31; s/d 130/170 lei; ❄@) Despite the dark and cavernous lobby, this old throwback has modern rooms at decent prices. It's about a 10-minute walk to Piata Unirii, and near several sights and malls.

Hotel Eden
HOTEL $$
(☎0332-144 486; www.hotels-eden.ro; Str S Sava 1; s/d 160/170 lei, breakfast 15 lei; ❄☂) An excellent new three-star option, the Eden is central and has a restaurant. The fresh-smelling rooms are spacious and some have balconies.

Best Western Hotel Astoria
HOTEL $$$
(☎0232-233 888; www.hotelastoria.ro; Str Alexandru Lăpuşneanu 1; s/d/apt 255/340/410; ❄☂) On Piata Unirii's western flank, this international chain has good business-class rooms.

Little Texas
HOTEL $$$
(☎0232-272 545; www.littletexas.org; Str Moara de Vant 31; s/d from 250/275 lei; P❄❄☂☂) On the airport road (a 10-minute drive from the centre), this four-star Texan-run hotel is outfitted in Americana decor and has business-class amenities, plus an authentic Tex-Mex restaurant. Free airport pick ups are offered.

Casa Bucovineana Hostel
HOSTEL $
(☎0232-222 913; Str Cuza Vodă 30; s/d/ste without bathroom 70/100/180 lei, d with bathroom 120 lei; ☂) Conditions have deteriorated at this old hostel, but shared bathrooms are clean enough and it's central.

Hotel Europa
BUSINESS HOTEL $$$
(☎0232-242 000; www.hoteleuropa.ro; Str Anastasie Panu 26; s/d/ste 275/350/415 lei; ❄☂) This slick new business hotel at the far end of

Str Anastasie Panu (a five-minute walk from Piaţa Moldova) is the furthest hotel from the central square, but it has pleasant rooms and professional service.

✗ Eating

La Castel
INTERNATIONAL $$

(☎0232-225 225; www.lacastel.com; Str Aleea M Sadoveanu 54, Copou; mains 17-36 lei; 🖶) With spacious, breezy lawns, La Castel incorporates French and Bavarian flourishes, a long wine list and sinful desserts. Restless youngsters will be appeased by the playground, and there's live music nightly. It's a 15-minute drive from town, or you can catch bus 6 (20-minute trip) from Piaţa Unirii or in front of Alexandru Ioan Cuza University in the Copou area.

La Rustica
ITALIAN $$

(☎0735-522 405; www.larustica.ro; Str Anastasie Panu 30; mains 17-30 lei; ⊙8am-11pm) Run by an Italian chef and his Romanian wife, this classy subterranean restaurant is Iaşi's best Italian eatery. It's on the ground floor of a shopping and apartment complex.

Buena Vista
SOUTH AMERICAN $

(☎0232-242 244; http://buena-vista.ro; Str Petru Movila 43; mains 12-20 lei; ⊙9am-midnight) This expansive bar and restaurant is a favourite with international students and a good choice for vegetarians too.

Casa Universitarilor
INTERNATIONAL $

(B-dul Carol I, 9; mains 6-15 lei; ⊙9am-midnight) Enjoy cheap but tasty bites on the terrace under the lime trees at this student joint.

Tuffli
CAFE, PATISSERIE $

(☎0721-290 812; www.tuffli.ro; Str Alexandru Lăpuşneanu 7B; cakes 5-12 lei; ⊙8am-11pm) This long-established cafe and patisserie with indoor and outdoor seating is a short walk from Piaţa Unirii.

Casa Lavric
ROMANIAN $$

(☎0232-229 960; Str Sf Atanasie 21; mains 10-40 lei) Decorated with classical musical instruments, Casa Lavric serves classic Romanian cuisine. Reserve ahead on weekends.

🍷 Drinking

Having failed as a commercial centre, the concrete expanse known as the Cub (The Cube; B-dul Ştefan cel Mare) now has a new lease on life – as host of subterranean student bars. To find it look for the giant side-long dice piece out front. Other happening places are near Piaţa Unirii.

^{TOP}_{CHOICE} Cafeneaua Acaju
BAR

(☎0733-027 588; Str S Sava 15; ⊙9am-2am) Easy to miss and hard to forget, this hip but unpretentious bar is barely signposted near the corner of Str Armeană. Its regulars include local artists, musicians and others of all ages. A small bar-top box reading 'nice things for nice people' purveys inexpensive handmade jewellery. Come for coffee by day.

La Baza
BAR

(B-dul Ştefan cel Mare, Cub; ⊙6pm-2am, to 6am Fri & Sat) This festive indie fave down in the Cub has outlandish aquarium-green walls, saffron-curtain ceilings and surrealist versions of Romanian monastic murals. The beer is cheap and the crowd is young; there's sometimes live music and film screenings.

Belfast
PUB

(Str Vasile Conta 30; ⊙10am-2am) This saloon-like pub features long benches separated by wood-framed sections, and plays '80s and '90s music; decent food is served 'til 10pm.

Terasa Corso
PUB

(www.corsoterasa.ro; Str Alexandru Lăpuşneanu 11; mains 15-30 lei; ⊙9am-2am; 🕿) Well-trimmed hedges and gardens adorn the centre of this expansive, amphitheatre-shaped pub with overlapping rows of long tables. It's good for coffee by day and drinks by night, and serves tasty pastas, pizzas and other fare.

Atelierul de Bere
PUB

(☎0232-452 557; B-dul Anastasie Panu 52; ⊙8am-midnight) Iaşi's speciality beer bar, the Atelierul offers brews from China to America (with strong European representation), served by affable bar staff.

Memories Cafe
BAR, CLUB

(Str Sfântu Lazăr 34; ⊙24hr) This blue-lit, late-night cocktail lounge has two levels throbbing with electro, techno and house music, sometimes spun by guest DJs.

The Gate
BAR

(B-dul Ştefan cel Mare, Cub; ⊙noon-1am) Metalheads unite! This dingy, compact Cub bar specialises in speed metal, death metal and all varieties of morose head-pounding music.

☆ Entertainment

24-Fun and Tot o Dată (www.totodata.ro) are widely available and free entertainment listings. **Vasile Alecsandri National Theatre** (www.teatrulnationaliasi.ro; Str Agatha Bârsescu 18) and **Opera Română** (☎0232-211 144; www.opera-romana-iasi.ro; Str Agatha Bârsescu 18) host important performances. Smaller performances at the national theatre are held in the black box known as the Cube Theatre (not to be confused with the Cub bar complex), Sala Mica (Small Hall) and Uzina cu Teatru (Factory Theatre).

The **Agenţia de Opera** (☎0232-255 999; B-dul Ştefan cel Mare 8; ⏰10am-5pm Mon-Sat) handles advance tickets, with tickets from 12 lei (50% student discounts).

Underground CLUB
(B-dul Ştefan cel Mare, Cub; DJ nights admission 15 lei; ⏰8pm-3am) Slightly posher than its neighbouring Cub bars, Underground does good live alternative music and DJ dance parties.

Dublin CLUB
(☎0729-802 765; www.dublinpub.ro; Str Vasile Conta 30; ⏰noon-4am) A cross between a large bar and a small club, the Dublin has plain wood floors but expensive drinks. Its weekend disco parties are frequented by stiletto-heeled gals and aspiring mafiosi who reserve tables with the compulsory bottle of whiskey. The burly black-clad security guards out front add a comic touch.

Luceafărul Theatre THEATRE
(☎0232-315 966; Str Grigore Ureche 5) Holds performances for children and young people.

Filarmonica CLASSICAL MUSIC
(www.filarmonicais.ro; Str Cuza Vodă 29; tickets 20 lei; ⏰box office 10am-1pm & 5-7pm Mon-Fri) The Iaşi State Philharmonic Orchestra's home hall is excellent for classical music; there's a 50% student discount.

Cinema Victoria CINEMA
(Piaţa Unirii 5; tickets 8 lei) Plays Hollywood blockbusters.

Shopping

Galeriile Anticariat ANTIQUES
(☎0748-515 374; Str Alexandru Lăpuşneanu 24) This long-time local antiques shop sells everything from folk heirlooms and jewellery to rare, expensive icons. It can provide authorised sale certificates for anything that might excite border-point customs agents.

Eurolibris BOOKS
(☎0232-210 858; B-dul Carol I, 3-4; ⏰9am-5pm) Sells useful maps and books on regional sites.

Palas Mall SHOPPING CENTRE
(www.palasiasi.ro/palas-mall; Str Palas; ⏰7am-midnight) If Moldavia is truly impoverished, you'd never know it from this sleek new hybrid of airport duty-free shops and American-style mega-mall.

Hala Centrala SHOPPING CENTRE
(Str Anastasie Panu) Kiosks selling jewellery, glass and knick-knacks.

Moldova Mall SHOPPING CENTRE
(Str Anastasie Panu) On the eponymous square, this modern mall has shops and a cinema; floor 5 offers nourishing, inexpensive prepared foods.

Information

Internet Access

The telephone centre, Piaţa Unirii, restaurants, bars and hotels have free wi-fi.

Forte Cafe (B-dul Independenţei 27; per hr 4 lei; ⏰24hr) Down a passage off the footpath.

Medical Services

Sfântu Spiridon University Hospital (☎ext 193 0232-240 822; B-dul Independenţei 1) Iaşi's largest hospital.

Money

ATMs and exchange offices abound in the centre.

Post

Post office (Str Cuza Vodă 10; ⏰9am-6pm Mon-Fri, to 1pm Sat)

Telephone

Telephone centre (Str Alexandru Lăpuşneanu; ⏰9am-6pm Mon-Fri, to 1pm Sat) Has fax and free wi-fi.

Tourist Information

Agenţia de Voiaj CFR (Piaţa Unirii 10; ⏰8am-8pm Mon-Fri, 9am-12.30pm Sat) Sells tickets for trains.

Cliven Turism (☎0232-258 326; www.cliven.ro; B-dul Ştefan cel Mare 8-12; ⏰9am-6pm Mon-Fri, to 2pm Sat) Arranges Antrec (National Association of Rural, Ecological & Cultural Tourism; www.antrec.ro) rural accommodation, wine tours, monastery tours and car hire.

Meridian Turism (☎0232-211 060; www.meridianturism.ro; B-dul Ştefan cel Mare 1C; ⏰9am-5.30pm Mon-Fri, 10am-2pm Sat) Rents cars and arranges Antrec (www.antrec.ro) rural accommodation.

Tourist information centre (☎0232-261 990; www.turism-iasi.ro; Piaţa Unirii 12; ⏰9am-6pm Mon-Fri, to 1pm Sat) Helpful staff provide city maps and activity brochures.

ℹ Getting There & Away

Air

Iaşi international airport (p264) is 5km east of the centre. **Tarom** (☎0232-267 768; www.tarom.com; Şos Arcu 3-5; ☉9am-7pm Mon-Fri, to 1pm Sat) has daily Bucharest flights (approximately 300 lei). **Carpatair** (☎0232-215 295; www.carpatair.com; Str Cuza Vodă 2; ☉9am-6pm Mon-Fri, to 1pm Sat) has flights to Timişoara (from 200 lei) and onwards from Monday to Saturday. **Malev** (www.malev.com) flies to Budapest five days weekly. **Austrian Airlines** (www.aua.com) flies to Vienna six days weekly.

Bus

The **bus station** (Str Moara de Foc 15A), behind the Auto Centre building, has innumerable daily buses and maxitaxis tor Târgu Neamţ (20 lei, two hours, eight daily), Suceava (30 lei, two hours, 12 daily), Bacău (20 lei, two hours, six daily), Piatra Neamţ (30 lei, three hours, 13 daily), Cluj-Napoca (70 lei, nine hours, one daily) and Chişinău (30 lei, five hours, nine daily). Six daily buses (daytime and overnight) serve Bucharest (60 lei) and its Otopeni Airport (64 lei, 7½ hours).

Maxitaxis to Cotnari leave hourly from the Old Customs Building (Vama Veche), across from the train station.

Speedier international **maxitaxis to Chişinău** (Fundac Bacinschi; 25 lei, about four hours, six daily) leave from outside **Billa supermarket** (Str Arcu 29; ☉8am-10pm Mon-Sat, 9am-6pm Sun).

Buy tickets for the daily Istanbul bus (170 lei, 16 hours), departing from Billa, at **Ortadoğu Tur** (☎0232-257 000; Str Bacinschi) across the street.

Train

Most trains use the **central train station** (Gara Centrală; Str Garii), which is also called Gara Mare and Gara du Nord. International trains to Chişinău depart from **Gara Nicolina** (Gare Nord; ☎0232 211 900; Bul Nicolae Iorga), also called Gara International, on B-dul Nicolae Iorga. The Agenţia de Voiaj CFR sells advance tickets. A **left-luggage office** (Bagaje de Mana; handbag/large bag 6/8 lei per 24hr) is by the car park.

Daily trains serve Bucharest (86 to 110 lei, seven hours, six daily), Brasov (86 lei, 8½ hours, one daily), while four slow, overcrowded trains lurch into Cluj-Napoca (86 lei, nine hours) and then Timişoara (78 lei, 16 hours) via Oradea – affectionately known as 'Horror Trains' by locals.

For Chişinău (55 lei, six hours) one train leaves at 3.13am on Thursday, Friday and Saturday only, crossing at Ungheni. As if that weren't awesome enough, you get to spend time watching the wheels be changed to fit Moldova's narrow-gauge track system.

Ungheni lacks visa-processing facilities. At the time of writing, American, Canadian, EU, Swiss and CIS states' citizens do not need visas. For those who do, visas must be pre-obtained at any Moldovan embassy; however, an original copy of your Moldovan hosts' invitation may be requested. Check the Moldovan Ministry of Foreign Affairs site (www.mfa.gov.md/entry-visas-moldova).

For the Bucovina Monasteries, take the Suceava train (21 lei to 39 lei, 2¾ hours, nine daily). For some monasteries, you must change trains, or take the train for Oradea, and disembark at Gura Humorului village. To reach Târgu Neamţ from Iaşi change at Paşcani.

ℹ Getting Around

TO/FROM THE AIRPORT

Only taxis connect Iaşi and its airport (20 to 30 lei).

CAR & MOTORCYCLE

Autonom (☎0748-110 557; www.autonom.ro; B-dul Ştefan cel Mare 8-12; per day 150 lei; ☉9am-6pm Mon-Fri, to 1pm Sat) rents cars and offers 24-hour assistance.

Around Iaşi

COTNARI

Cotnari is 54km northwest of Iaşi. Its vineyards, dating from 1448, are among the most famed in Romania, and its famous sweet white wines are exported worldwide.

Cotnari's Cătălina Hill (280m) hosted a 4th-century-BC Geto-Dacian stronghold. In 1491 Ştefan cel Mare built a small church, followed by a Latin college in 1562. Incoming French monks planted their own grape seeds and, by the late 19th century, Cotnari wine was prominent at international exhibitions. King Michael I's half-complete royal palace from 1947 (restored in 1966) today houses Cotnari Winery's administration.

Cotnari Winery (☎0744-532 426, 0232-730 393; www.cotnari.ro; tasting €50 per person, minimum five people per group; ☉7am-3.30pm) offers one-hour tours and wine-tasting sessions with food by appointment. Connoisseurs enjoy the 14 September harvest celebration here. Popular wines include white table wines like *frâncuşa* (dry), *cătălina* (semisweet), and the sweet, golden *grasă* and *tămâioasă* dessert wines.

By car from Cotnari's shop, follow the road towards Botoşani and turn left at the Cotnari warehouse – the visitor building is 200m further, down a right-hand dirt lane.

Three Iaşi–Hârlău buses stop at Cotnari daily (17 lei, 1¾ hours). Maxitaxis leave hourly opposite Iaşi's train station.

Piatra Neamţ

POP 77,393

Up-and-coming, easy-going Piatra Neamţ (German Rock) sprawls in three directions across a valley, gripped by forested mountains. Moldavia's third-biggest town, it clearly has grand ambitions. Recent civic improvements have included a summertime faux-sand beach and a new gondola line that merrily sways across the city skyline to Mt Cozla – site of a small but expanding ski centre. The energetic local authorities have been so efficient, in fact, that the Roma are now resettled out of town and mafia shootings occur only once every other year.

Piatra Neamţ lies 43km south of Târgu Neamţ, surrounded to the east by rocky Pietricica Mountain, to the southwest by Cernegura Mountain and the artificial Lake Bâtca Doamnei, and by Mt Cozla to the north. Locals are supremely proud of their burg, pointing out the distances that other Romanians will travel to partake in its nightlife, and that they (and not Iaşi) have hosted European Champions League football matches. The town's dotted with historic buildings attesting to its long and distinguished history (Ştefan cel Mare founded a princely court here).

The Romanian enthusiasm for boulevards and roundabouts is also visible here. B-dul Republicii leads north from Piaţa Mareşal Ion Antonescu towards Piaţa Ştefan cel Mare, the city's heart, where stands a statue of Ştefan cel Mare. The Telegondola running up to Mt Cozla is near the bus and train stations.

◉ Sights

Princely Court
Museum Complex   HISTORIC BUILDING
(Curtea Domnească; Piaţa Libertăţii; adult/child 4/2 lei; ⊙10am-6pm Tue-Sun) This small square houses museums and historical buildings comprising Ştefan cel Mare's 1497 Princely Court museum complex. Its headquarters, housed in the dank ruins of the Princely Court under the Petru Rareş School (Liceul Petru Rareş), has historical displays and archaeological finds like weapons, pottery and tool fragments.

Art Museum   MUSEUM
(Muzeul de Arta; ☑0233-216 808; Piaţa Libertăţii 1; adult/child 5/2 lei; ⊙8am-6pm Tue-Sun) This museum exhibits Romanian classic and modern art, including landscapes and still lifes, plus abstract art, modern cityscapes, and sculptures and tapestries. The building houses a small Ethnographic Museum.

St John's Church   CHURCH
(Biserica Sfântu Ioan; Piaţa Libertăţii) Opposite the Art Museum, towering over the square, the lovely, but sombre St John's Church (1498) has a 10m-high bell tower.

Museum of History
and Archaeology   MUSEUM
(Muzeul de Istorie şi Arheologie; ☑0233-226 471; Str Ştefan cel Mare 3; adult/child 4/2 lei; ⊙10am-6pm Tue-Sun) Well-executed displays on the Cucutenians, a neolithic culture with advanced pottery skills that lived in the area between 5500 BC and 2750 BC. A book on the Cucuteni, partly in English, is available (30 lei).

History Museum   MUSEUM
(☑0233-218 108; Str Mihai Eminescu 10; adult/child 5/2 lei; ⊙10am-6pm Tue-Sun) This museum documents local history from the Stone Age through the Moldavian princes and more recent developments.

Bal Shem Tov
Wooden Synagogue   SYNAGOGUE
(☑0233-223 815; Str Dr Dimitrie Ernici; tours per person 5 lei; ⊙by appointment) Just north of the Princely Court, this 1766 synagogue was built over the foundations of a 1490 predecessor. The tiny interior is decorated with Jewish artefacts, restored frescoes and paintings. If closed, walk 20m down the alley and around the corner to Str Petru Rareş 7 and inquire within. Alternatively, your hotel can phone the local Jewish community's leadership for you.

Natural History Museum   MUSEUM
(Muzeul de Ştiinţe Naturale; ☑0233-224 211; Str Petru Rareş 26; adult/child 3/2 lei; ⊙10am-6pm Tue-Sun) This museum exhibits local flora and fauna.

Parc Zoologic   ZOO
(Str Ştefan cel Mare; adult/child 2/1 lei; ⊙9am-8pm) Along Str Ştefan cel Mare, the tiny zoo has a seasonal outdoor minizoo.

Mt Cozla & Telegondola
Cozla Park is a sprawling, forested park at the base of the mountain. To get to the

Piatra Neamţ

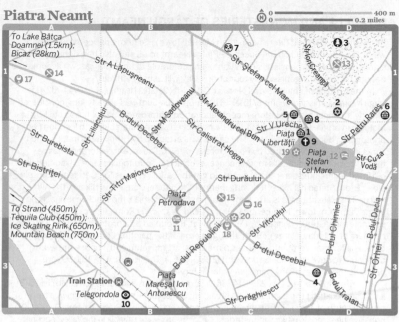

Piatra Neamţ

◉ Sights
1 Art Museum C2
2 Bal Shem Tov Wooden
   Synagogue D1
3 Cozla Park D1
4 History Museum D3
5 Museum of History and
   Archaeology C1
6 Natural History Museum D1
7 Parc Zoologic C1
8 Princely Court Museum Complex D1
9 St John's Church D2
10 Telegondola B3

◉ Sleeping
11 Central Plaza Hotel B3

12 Hotel Ceahlău D2

◉ Eating
13 Cercul Gospodinelor D1
14 Laguna A1
15 Pritiprod C2

◉ Drinking
16 Casablanca C2
17 Chaplin's Pub A1
18 Temple Pub C3

◉ Entertainment
19 Tineretului Theatre C2
20 Tonique Club C2

top and Mt Cozla (639m) take the aerial route with the new **Telegondola** (www. cozla.ro; adult/child 18/10 lei; ◷8am-11pm). Lift-off is achieved at a space-age structure by the train station. From here, self-contained eight-man gondolas run every few minutes, providing panoramic views of city, mountains and lake.

Note that besides the ticket price you must leave a 20-lei deposit for the lift card, which is refunded when you return down (only one deposit is required, regardless of group size). A sign at the ticket booth warns that drunks aren't allowed and that the lift is free for pensioners (it's unclear whether drunk pensioners just pay full price). In any case, being drunk is not a bad idea considering that the gondola tends to thud into the mountaintop lift area like a lost lunar probe.

CITADELS AND MONASTERIES OF TÂRGU NEAMŢ

Although Târgu Neamţ (literally, German Market Town) is a grim post-communist backwater, it's a transit hub on the Suceava–Piatra Neamţ road, and also has significant sights nearby. Rural *pensiunes* (pensions) are preferable to uninspiring town accommodation (though an organised day tour or drive-by will usually suffice).

In the town itself, the medieval **Neamţ Citadel** (Cetatea Neamţului; ☎0744-702 415; Târgu Neamţ; admission/photos 5/15 lei; ☉10am-6pm Tue-Sun) was already long considered Moldavia's finest fortress before recent renovations improved it again. It was built by Moldavian prince Petru I Muşat in 1359, who picked an impregnable, high location (very photogenic, but a tiring walk up). The castle was attacked by Hungarians in 1395 and by Turks in 1476, and conquered by Polish forces in 1691. The recent restoration has returned some of the citadel's magnificence, even adding odd touches like a traditionally outfitted mannequin ceremonial guard. To get there, follow signs for 'Cetatea Neamţului' along B-dul Ştefan cel Mare. If driving, park at the citadel's base and hike up the hill.

The Târgu Neamţ area is also known for hosting Romania's most active monasteries. Some 7km from town, 14th-century **Neamţ Monastery** is Romania's oldest and largest male monastery. Founded by Petru I Muşat, it doubled as a protective citadel. Ştefan cel Mare built today's large church, though some of the paintings date from Muşat's time. The fortified compound houses a medieval art museum and a house museum dedicated to novelist Mihail Sadoveanu (1880–1961). The library, with 18,000 rare books, is the largest of any Romanian monastery.

Agapia Monastery (☎0233-244 736; Agapia village; museum admission adult/child 5/3 lei, accommodation per person 30 lei, no breakfast; ☉museum 10am-7pm) lies down a turnoff 4km south of Târgu Neamţ, which is the main road towards Piatra Neamţ. Over 400 nuns live here today in two monasteries. **Agapia din Vale** (Agapia in the Valley; r per person 30 lei, no breakfast), at the end of Agapia village, was built between 1642 and 1644 by Gavril Coci (Vasile Lupu's brother). The church has relaxing gardens and an impressive neoclassical facade (dating from reconstructions between 1882 and 1903). The impressive frescoed interior was painted between 1858 and 1861 by a very young painter – the famous Nicolae Grigorescu (1838–1907). A small museum, off to the right, exhibits 16th- and 17th-century icons. Agapia din Vale offers accommodation for pilgrims. The second monastery, **Agapia din Deal** (Agapia on the Hill; Agapia village), also called Agapia Veche or Old Agapia, is 2.2km from the main monastery complex. Follow the right-hand road through Agapia to the signposted dirt road veering off to the right, though you'll need a sturdy car. Built by Petru Rareş' wife Elena between 1642 to 1647, it's more modern than its sister monastery but enjoys a peaceful ambience.

From here, a left-hand dirt road veers towards a small plateau and placid **Sihla Monastery** (Schitu Sihla; admission free), inhabited by 30 monks. Nearby, the venerated Cave of Pious St Teodora was where the eponymous nun lived for 60 years, sleeping on a rock slab. The hermitage is candlelit and visited by pilgrims (Kyiv's Pecherska Monastery now holds her relics). Sihla can house visitors (ask on site). Here you may observe *pustnici* (extreme hermit monks), who regularly kneel in prayer, sometimes remaining so for hours.

Some 7km south of Agapia on the main road is **Văratec Monastery** (admission free), inhabited by over 600 nuns. Founded in 1785, the complex houses an icon museum and small embroidery school. Whitewashed in 1841, the main church incorporates neoclassical elements and grounds featuring a small botanic garden. The lavishly decorated interior has numerous frescoes.

Getting to these monasteries from Târgu Neamţ on public transport is possible, though schedules don't allow for seeing them all in one day – it's much easier and more efficient to drive or take an organised tour. However, should you go by bus, seven daily buses make the 15km journey from Târgu Neamţ to Neamţ Monastery and from Târgu Neamţ to Agapia's lower monastery (listed on bus timetables as 'Complex Turistic Agapia'). You can hike to Văratec from Agapia (two hours) and to Secu, Sihăstria and Sihla Monasteries along clearly marked trails. There are maxitaxis to Văratec from Târgu Neamţ (10 daily). Buses from Suceava and Piatra also access some of the monasteries, but less frequently.

Atop the mountain, one can breathe cool, crisp air, have an atmospheric drink or lunch, and find (in winter) ski trails that double as hiking paths in summer; the adjoining wooded sections host ferocious paintball contests.

Ştrand

Just southwest of the centre, the Ştrand is a relaxed open promenade where locals go for an evening stroll; however, its other activities make it immensely popular throughout the year.

During winter, an outdoor ice-skating rink (admission with own skates 10 lei, incl skate rental 20 lei) operates, while in summer the fashionable Mountain Beach (admission 10 lei; ⊙10am-7pm Jun-Sep) consists of carted-in sand surrounding two swimming pools, and the obligatory 'beach bar'. It's a chic spot for the town's sunbathing young, and provides a warm-up for evening activities at the on-site nightclub, Tequila Club (p196), which operates as a cafe-bar by day. The complex can host up to 700 people.

Festivals & Events

The week-long International Theatre Festival occurs every May.

🛏 Sleeping

For a town its size, Piatra Neamţ lacks standout accommodation options. Visit the excellent English-language municipal tourism website, www.visitneamt.com, which has a long list of pensions. Alternatively, search Antrec (www.antrec.ro) for rural digs.

Hotel Ceahlău HOTEL $$
(☎0233-219 090; www.hotelceahlau.ro; Piaţa Ştefan cel Mare 3; s/d/ste 110/190/300 lei; ❄✳@🛜) This big, old three-star hotel has rooms that are slightly old-fashioned but perfectly fine, and some have balconies with excellent views. The restaurant chefs are kind to breakfast slackers and the menu is reasonably priced. The vulcan-tinted 12th-floor lounge bar becomes a desultory strip club after 10pm.

Central Plaza Hotel HOTEL $$$
(☎0233-216 230; www.centralplazahotel.ro; Piaţa Petrodava 1-3; s/d 270/360 lei; ❄✳🛜) Another large, old hotel, the Central Plaza's recent renovations have elevated it to four-star status (and sent prices up too). Rooms are well presented and sleek, though the hotel lacks a fitness centre or other amenities.

🍴 Eating & Drinking

Restaurant Popasul Haiducilor ROMANIAN $$
(☎0729-955133;www.restaurant-popasulhaiducilor.ro; Mt Cozla; mains 15-23 lei; ⊙8.30am-9pm) This traditionally decorated restaurant atop Mt Cozla by the Telegondola has great views from its upper floor (drinks only). The lower dining hall has good Romanian cuisine at great prices. It often hosts special parties and events so reserve on weekends.

Cercul Gospodinelor ROMANIAN $$
(☎0233-223 845; Str Ion Creangă; mains 10-24 lei; ⊙noon-10pm) Located at the top of the road to Cozla Park, this is another good pick for Romanian cuisine, with good views and nightly live music.

Laguna PIZZA $$
(☎0233-232 121; B-dul Decebal 80; mains 12-30 lei; ⊙10am-11pm) Essentially an unkempt student place above a supermarket, the Laguna does decent pizza and has billiard tables.

Pritiprod PATISSERIE $
(☎0233-234 330; B-dul Decebal 14; ⊙9am-9pm) This long-established patisserie does gelato and cakes.

Chaplin's Pub TOP CHOICE PUB
(Str Luceafarugui 22; ⊙9am-late) Created by charismatic owner and world traveller Cristian Dobrea, this nice pub consists of lots of weathered wood, historic photos, and small enclosed bars and tables with candles adding a touch of intimacy. It's very popular on Saturdays, when live bands perform.

Casablanca CAFE
(☎0233-213 214; B-dul Republicii 7; ⊙7am-11pm) An elegant Continental-style cafe, Casablanca has subdued decor with striped wallpaper and matching ornate chairs. Young lawyers, visiting television personalities and other socialites come for the good coffee, wines and beers.

Temple Pub PUB
(☎0233-215 215; B-dul Republicii 15; ⊙7am-late) This eclectic big bar at the B-dul Decebal intersection combines Greek fast food with Irish (and other) beer. It's a popular weekend nightspot.

☆ Entertainment

Tineretului Theatre THEATRE
(☎0233-211 036; Piaţa Ştefan cel Mare 1) Performances are usually held on weekend evenings. The adjoining Agenţia Teatrală sells tickets.

Tequila Club NIGHTCLUB
(Strand; ☺10am-3am) The town's most popular open-air summer club with a poolside location in the Strand, Tequila goes indoors in winter but remains popular for DJ parties, house, techno and R&B music.

Tonique Club CLUB
(B-dul Republicii 18; ☺24hr) There's something obscure bordering on the mysterious about this dark underground bar that works 24 hours a day. It has a few gambling video machines in the corner, and is frequented by muscular men singing traditional Romanian drinking songs, though weekend 'club nights' are more lively. Food is served until 10pm.

ℹ Information

ATMs line Piaţa Ştefan cel Mare and the central boulevards. At the time of research, a new tourist office was being built in the park next to Hotel Ceahlău; the hotel itself offers useful info and maps. The English-language municipal tourism website www.visitneamt.com is helpful. The **Agenţia de Voiaj CFR** (☎0233-211 034; Piaţa Ştefan cel Mare 10; ☺7.30am-8.30pm Mon-Fri) sells train tickets.

ℹ Getting There & Away

A night train heads to Bucharest (70.50 lei) and five daily trains serve Bicaz (4.40 lei). The **bus station** (☎0233-211 210; Str Bistriţei 1), near the train station, has 11 buses and maxitaxis to Târgu Neamţ (20 lei). Services run to Agapia (9 lei, two daily) and Gura Humorului (24 lei, one daily). Other buses serve Suceava (30 lei), Iaşi (42 lei), Braşov (50 lei) and Bicaz and Lacu Roşu (17 lei).

Bicaz & the Ceahlău Massif

The Ceahlău Massif offers great hiking and stunning mountain views; together with the Bicaz Gorges and Lacu Roşu, this general area offers an amazingly varied landscape.

Four kilometres west of unremarkable Bicaz village (population 9000), at the confluence of the Bicaz and Bistriţa Rivers, is the man-made **Bicaz Lake** (Lacu Izvorul Muntelui; Mountain Spring Lake), which sprawls northward for over 30 sq km. A hydroelectric dam (*baraj*) at the lake's southern end was built in 1950, with several villages submerged in the process. Near the dam, at the junction 4km north of Bicaz, a turn-off leads up a twisting mountain road to Ceahlău

(chek-*lau*). Turn right after the bridge, to the lake's western shore for picknicking or paddle-boat hire.

The next village, **Izvoru Muntelui**, has only hiking trails (so stock up on supplies in Bicaz): start here for the Ceahlău Massif, Moldavia's most spectacular mountain range. Enter the gated fence and after a five-minute climb a flat section with picnic tables emerges; the starting point for two trails, each going in opposite directions. A posted map illustrates how the trails meet at the peak, allowing for two unique hikes during ascent and descent. With an early start and the requisite fitness level, the Ceahlău Massif can be done in a single day. Placards detailing flora and fauna (in Romanian) stand along the trails. For those seeking to break up the trip, **Cabana Dochia** (☎0729-548 900; www.cabana-dochia.ro; dm 20 lei, d with bathroom 100 lei) at the peak has dorms and double rooms (with only cold-water showers) and a passable restaurant. This hike is also doable from Durău and Ceahlău.

Durău (elevation 800m), on the mountain's northwestern side, offers spa and winter sports. A steep track (red stripes, one hour) leads to Cabana Fântânele. From there, others lead towards the peak, Toaca. There is also the small **Durău Monastery** (1830), comprising two churches and nuns quarters. Visitors are welcome.

The **Ceahlău Folk Festival** is held annually on the second Sunday in August.

Ceahlău village (elevation 550m), 6km north of Durău, has 17th-century palace ruins, and an 18th-century wooden church. Bypassing the Bicaz mountain road, continue north for another 24km to **Grozăveşti**, with its Maramureş-like wooden church.

🛏 Sleeping

Camp freely outside Cabana Bicaz Baraj, the first cabana when entering Durău at the foot of the dam wall. The cabana itself is just a snack bar. Cabana Izvorul Muntelui (elevation 797m) has basic rooms. Durău has plenty of accommodation, including **Pensiuna Paulo** (☎0722-769 400; www.pensiunea-paulo.ro; Str Principala 266, Durau; d with/without bathroom 100/75 lei), on the road into Durău, with agreeable rooms in a yellow-and-red wooden chalet-style house. Some 50m further, **Pensiune Igor** (☎0233-256 503; Str Principala 268, Durau; r 85-100 lei) has five doubles with shared bathroom and a self-catering kitchen.

Ceahlău Massif

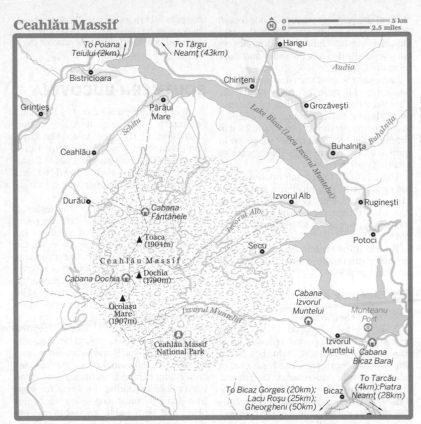

❶ Getting There & Away

For exploring, rent a car; however, trains reach Bicaz from Piatra Neamţ (11 lei, 40 minutes), and one of them (the red-eye) continues to Bucharest (78 lei, 6½ hours). Buses and maxitaxis link Bicaz with Piatra Neamţ (11 lei) throughout the day; buses run between Piatra Neamţ and Poiana and stop at Bicaz (six daily), Gheorgheni (one daily) and Braşov (two daily). All of these buses stop at Tarcău, and one daily bus continues to Izvoru Muntelui (otherwise it's a 4km hike). From Durău, buses serve Târgu Neamţ (18 lei, two daily) and maxitaxis reach Iaşi (36 lei, four daily).

Bicaz Gorges & Lacu Roşu

The winding road through the Bicaz Gorges (Cheile Bicazului), 20km west of Bicaz, is among Romania's most spectacular. The gorge twists and turns steeply uphill for 5km, cutting through sheer 300m-high limestone cliffs along which pine trees improbably cling. The narrow mountain road runs directly beneath the overhanging rocks in the 'neck of hell' (Gâtul Iadului) section, though it's never narrow enough to inspire claustrophobia.

Along the roadside, predatorial artisans hawk their crafts (some original, some mass-produced) from stalls beneath the rocks, at the points where it's wide enough for parking. The Bicaz Gorges belong to the Hăşmaş-Bicaz Gorges National Park (Parcul Naţional Hăşmaş-Cheile Bicazului).

A few kilometres west begins Transylvania's Harghita County (you'll notice the obligatory Hungarian-language signage) and Lacu Roşu (Red Lake; Gyilkos tó, in Hungarian) – in fairness, more a large pond. The murky waters here have no healing powers, but do conceal dead tree stumps that jut from the suface at odd angles. One cheerful lake legend attests that a picnicking group crushed by a fallen mountainside oozed their blood into the site where the lake amassed. (An 1838 landslide did in fact occur, eventually flooding the valley and damming the Bicaz River).

Lacu Roşu is most visited in summer for boating and hiking in the nearby woodlands. The village has only 60 full-time inhabitants, no ATMs, and one year-round supermarket. In summer, other shops operate, and even in autumn a few stubborn trinket sellers lay in wait. At time of research, the village was also awaiting wi-fi internet.

The lakefront tourist information kiosk has multilingual info brochures and organises boat hire. A flat scenic track circles the lake, while other more demanding trails ascend the various peaks, all offering stunning views.

The main road continues another 26km to Gheorgheni via the similarly scenic Bucin mountain pass.

🍴 Sleeping & Eating

Hotel Lacu Roşu
TOP CHOICE | HOTEL $

(☎0752-190 611; Str Principala 32; s/d 90/140 lei; 🌣) This well-signposted yellow-and-red structure is on the right, 100m before the lake (when entering from the Bicaz Gorges side), beyond the supermarket. Despite the slightly stodgy look, it does offer big bouncy beds with mirrored headboards. Nevertheless, the best attraction is the excellent restaurant. Try Transylvanian potatoes with onions, mountain trout, or chicken stuffed with mushrooms and cream (26 lei).

Hotel Turist
HOTEL $$

(☎0266-380 042; www.lacurosu.hostvision.ro; cabins per person 40 lei, s/d 120/150 lei; 🌣) Comfortable rooms with spacious bathrooms are offered at this old place, which is hidden by trees (look for the sign). Basic cabins with shared bathrooms are also available.

🍷 Drinking

Terasa Alpin Suhard
CAFE

(🕙9am-10pm Jul-Oct) This bamboo-backed lakefront cafe, 50m down past the souvenir stalls, serves everything from espresso and milkshakes to wine and cocktails.

ℹ️ Getting There & Away

Lacu Roşu is between Bicaz and Gheorgheni – every bus that goes from Piatra Neamţ to Braşov or Cluj-Napoca passes (quickly) through Lacu Roşu – arrive a little before the scheduled time so as not to miss the bus. Check departure times ahead. Hail down passing buses on the main road, near the supermarket or above the souvenir stalls.

SOUTHERN BUCOVINA

'Southern' Bucovina is located in Romania's very north – testimony to a long history of division. In 1775, the Austro-Hungarian Empire annexed Moldavia, keeping it until 1918, when Bucovina was returned to Romania. However, the Soviets annexed Northern Bucovina in 1940, incorporating it into the Ukraine.

Another historic aspect – the legacy of Prince Ştefan cel Mare and later successor Petru Rares – has endowed Southern Bucovina with several spectacular monasteries. The best of these fortified structures, painted both inside and out with exquisitely detailed frescoes in almost otherworldly tones, are also Unesco World Heritage sites.

Bucolic Bucovina is dotted with slant-roofed village houses and lovely groves of beech trees (indeed, the name 'Bucovina' comes from the German word for beech). As in Maramureş, you'll encounter old women in colourful traditional dress, fearless children riding bareback on horses, and enterprising locals scouring the forest for some truly massive mushrooms. It's an ornery place, and both public transport and foreign languages can be lacking, but Bucovina is nevertheless highly worthwhile for hill walks, cycling, rural idylls and, of course, the unforgettable monasteries.

Suceava

POP 86,282

Judging by its small centre alone, Suceava would hardly seem Moldavia's second-biggest town; however, it has sufficient urban sprawl to ensure runner-up status. While Suceava can't compete with Iaşi in things cultural or learned, it does make an incredibly useful and affordable base for visiting fortresses and the Bucovina painted monasteries, with myriad worthwhile tours offered. Suceava also has good eats and rudimentary nightlife.

As Moldavia's capital from 1388 to 1565, Suceava thrived commercially on the Lviv–Istanbul trading route. It boasted approximately 40 churches when Ştefan cel Mare's reign concluded in 1504. However, stagna-

Suceava

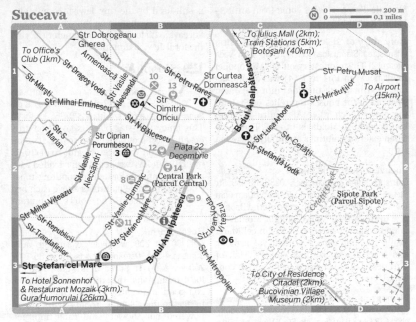

Suceava

Sights
1 Bucovina History Museum A3
2 Domnițelor Church C2
3 Ethnographic Museum B2
4 Gah Synagogue B1
5 Mirăuți Church C1
6 Monastery of St John the New C3
7 St Dumitru's Church B1

Sleeping
8 Hotel Gloria B2

tion followed a 1675 Turkish invasion. A century later, Austro-Hungary took over.

Patron St John is celebrated each 24 June; this open holiday (also called 'Suceava Days') involves beer, street food and music.

Services, restaurants and most sights are near the central Piața 22 Decembrie and nearby Str Ștefan cel Mare.

Sights

St Dumitru's Church CHURCH
(Biserica Sf Dumitru; Str Curtea Domnească) This impressive post-Byzantine church (1535) was built by Petru Rareș. Traces of original exterior frescoes are visible and the impressive interior frescoes are largely restored.

Mirăuți Church CHURCH
(Str Mirautilor 17) Suceava's oldest surviving church, Mirăuți is 500m northwest of the main square. Founded by Petru I Musa in 1375, it was Moldavia's original coronation church (Ștefan cel Mare was crowned here), and initial Moldavian bishops' seat. The church was largely restored between 1898 and 1901, preserving the original design.

Domnițelor Church CHURCH
(Princesses' Church; cnr B-dul Ana Ipătescu & Str Ștefăniță Vodă) Dedicated to St John the Baptist, this church was built by Vasile Lupu between 1632 and 1653. Its dedication inscription, from 1643, is in Old Church

Slavonic. Some frescoes come from an 1884 painting upgrade.

Monastery of St John the New   MONASTERY

(Mănăstirea Sfântu Ioan cel Nou; Str Ioan Voda Viteazul 2) This monastery off Str Mitropoliei (built between 1514 to 1554) was an important pilgrimage destination: in a decorated silver casket it houses the relics of St John the New, which ruler Alexandru cel Bun had brought to Moldavia in 1415. The badly faded exterior paintings exemplify Bucovina style.

Bucovina History Museum   MUSEUM

(Muzeul Naţional al Bucovinei; ☑0230-516 439; Str Ştefan cel Mare 33; adult/child 7/2 lei; ☺10am-6pm Tue-Sun) Displays here range from the Bronze Age to the present, but highlight Moldavia's famous rulers, particularly, Ştefan cel Mare. While the numismatics, medieval armour and tools are interesting, Ştefan's 'Hall of Thrones' court re-creation seems rather contrived.

Ethnographic Museum   MUSEUM

(☑0230-516 439; Str Ciprian Porumbescu 5; adult/child 6/3 lei; ☺9am-5pm Tue-Sun) West of Piaţa 22 Decembrie, Hanul Domnesc is an 18th-century guesthouse housing the Ethnographic Museum. It displays Moldavian folk costumes and household items.

Gah Synagogue   JEWISH

(☑Suceava Jewish Community 0230-213 084; Str Dimitrie Onciul 7) By the post office, this 1870 structure is Suceava's only surviving synagogue out of 18 original synagogues. The well preserved and elaborately decorated temple is still used by the tiny Jewish community. For more information on the synagogue and Suceava's historic Jewish cemeteries, ring the local Jewish Community.

🛏 Sleeping

⌂TOP CHOICE Hotel Sonnenhof   HOTEL $$$

(☑0230-220 033; www.hotelsonnenhof.ro; B-dul Sofia Vicoveanca 68; s/d from 220/265 lei; ❈🛜) This fancy four-star place is good for drivers and those not budget-conscious. It's 3km from town on the Târgu Neamţ road (10 lei by taxi), but has excellent rooms loaded with amenities and decorated in soothing tones (though, the huge paintings above each bed are rather gauche). The hotel's Restaurant Mosaik is well regarded.

Hotel Gloria   HOTEL $

(☑0230-521 209; www.hotelgloria.ro; Str Vasile Bumbac 4-8; s/d/ste incl breakfast from 85/140/260 lei; ❈@) If Suceava is your base for local excursions, this three-star throwback is a good and central budget choice; it has perfectly fine, simple rooms with super-powered hot showers and cable internet. Although English is hit-or-miss, staff are unfailingly polite. Omelette breakfasts are served in the cavernous adjoining hall.

Union Apartment   APARTMENT $

(☑0741-477 047; www.union-apartments.ro; B-dul Ana Ipatescu 7; apt 135-410 lei; ❈🛜) Run by local tour guide extraordinaire Gigi Traciu, this central apartment sleeping up to seven people provides an excellent budget option

---

DON'T MISS

CITY OF RESIDENCE CITADEL

Some 3km down Str Mitropoliei, the 1388 City of Residence Citadel (Cetatea de Scaun; adult/child 5/2 lei, photography 10 lei; ☺9am-6pm) is where an attack by Ottoman Sultan Mehmed II was halted in 1427, 23 years after his conquest of Constantinople (Istanbul). Without this defensive achievement against the Islamic empire, the Bucovina painted monasteries would not likely have been built.

Massive stretches of the rectangular structure remain. The original fortress was dubbed 'Muşat's Fortress' (after founder Petru I Muşat). Its eight square towers were surrounded by trenches. Ştefan cel Mare added 4m-thick, 33m-high walls, foiling archers outside.

The unconquerable fortress withstood multiple attacks. Exasperated Ottomans finally blew it up in 1675; a century later, home builders were still pillaging the ruins. Continuing restoration and excavation work began in 1944.

Nearby, the Bucovinian Village Museum (Muzeul Satului Bucovinean; City of Residence Citadel; adult/child 6/2 lei) displays relocated Bucovina traditional homes, with their original furnishings, accessories and tools.

and flexibility for self-caterers. Free airport pick up is offered for stays of over three days.

Eating

TOP CHOICE Latino ITALIAN **$$**
(Str Curtea Domnească 9; mains 12-45 lei, pizza 18-30 lei) Suceava's best Italian restaurant, this long-standing favourite has subdued class and prompt service. There are numerous pizza options, and the varied pasta mains are all excellent.

Restaurant Mozaik INTERNATIONAL **$$$**
(B-dul Sofia Vicoveanca 68, Hotel Sonnenhof; mains 25-45 lei) This upscale garden restaurant in the Hotel Sonnenhoff perhaps tries a bit too hard with its Romanian, French, Norwegian, German, Greek and Italian specialities, but hey, the cooks were trained by a Michelin-starred French chef. Among the pricier mains are beef in a doughy bread crust with mushrooms, pepper and cognac sauce, and honey-and-rosemary roasted lamb.

Restaurant Catalan INTERNATIONAL **$$**
(Str Vasile Bumbac 3; mains 15-28 lei; ⊘8am-11pm) This big local favourite serves hearty grills and salads, and has a good beer and liquor selection. Try the spicy roast chicken stuffed with potatoes, bacon and onions.

Drinking

From Thursday through Saturday nights, most bars become 'clubs' with DJ music, flashing lights and the works.

Salzburg Cafe CAFE
(Str Ştefan cel Mare 28; ⊘8am-10pm) This relaxing central cafe has a slightly Central European feel, plays pop-rock and even has live piano nights on Wednesday. It's good for coffees, with a small desserts selection.

Oscar Wilde PUB
(Str Ştefan cel Mare 26; ⊘8am-3am) Suceava's nearest thing to an Irish pub (look for the giant black Guinness canopies), Oscar Wilde's a big wood-floored bar with outdoor seating. It serves food until 10pm, and on weekends becomes a slightly chaotic 'club.'

No Limit BAR
(Str Curtea Domneasca 3; mains 10-26 lei; ⊘8am-4am) Doubles as a bar/restaurant cooking German, Romanian and Italian food.

Office's Club CLUB
(www.officesclub.ro; Str Viitorului 11; ⊘6pm-3am) Take a taxi (7 lei) to this big club on the out-skirts. Typical DJ parties and techno nights take place on weekends.

Eclipse Club CLUB
(☎0740-282 515; www.eclipseclub.ro; Str Ştefan cel Mare 20A) One of several similar clubs, Eclipse aims at a creamy FashionTV interior and appeals to local leather-jacketed toughs high on steroids and girls in miniskirts high on tabletops. There are DJ parties, karaoke nights and the like.

ⓘ Information

Internet Access
The telephone office, restaurants and bars have free wi-fi.

Money
ATMs and exchange offices line Piaţa 22 Decembrie and Str Ştefan cel Mare.

Post
Post office (Str Dimitrie Onciul)

Telephone
Telephone office (Romtelecom; cnr Str Nicolae Bălcescu & Str Dimitrie Onciu; ⊘9am-6pm Mon-Fri, 9am-1pm Sat) Has fax service and free wi-fi.

Tourist Information
Agenţia de Voiaj CFR (Str Nicolae Bălcescu 8; ⊘7.30am-8.30pm Mon-Fri) Sells train tickets.

AXA Travel (Str Sebastian Traciu; ☎0741-477 047; www.axatravel.ro) Quite possibly Moldavia's best tour agency, AXA is run by experienced local tour guide Sebastian 'Gigi' Traciu. One-day and multiday tours visit the Bucovina painted monasteries, Târgu Neamţ, Bicaz Gorges, Lacu Roşu and Maramureş. Monastery tour rates depend on participant numbers, but can be as cheap as 160 lei per person. Other day trips include rural horseback riding and river rafting.

Best Travel Bucovina (☎0230-521 094; www.travelbucovina.ro; Str Ştefan Cel Mare 48; ⊘9am-6pm Mon-Fri, 9am-2pm Sat) This well-informed central travel agency arranges monastery tours and accommodation.

Infoturism (☎0230-551 241; www.turism -suceava.ro; cnr B-dul Ana Ipătescu & Str Mitropoliei 4; ⊘8am-4pm Mon-Fri) Provides maps and information on local sites.

ⓘ Getting There & Away

Air
Ştefan cel Mare International Airport (www.aeroportsuceava.ro) is 15km northeast of Suceava, but has limited flights. **Tarom** (☎0230-214 686; www.tarom.ro; Str Nicolae

Bălcescu 2; ☉7am-5pm Mon-Fri, 9am-2pm Sat) has flights to Bucharest (two daily, except Saturday).

Bus

The central bus station is on Str Armenească. Bus and maxitaxi services include Gura Humorului (9 lei, one hour, 19 daily), Botoşani (12 lei, one hour, nine daily), Rădăuţi (8 lei, 45 minutes, 13 daily), Bucharest (70 lei, eight hours, four daily), Târgu Neamţ (20 lei, two hours, five daily) and Piatra Neamţ (29 lei, three hours, three daily). Maxitaxis to Iaşi (30 lei, 2½ hours, 12 daily) leave from a car park behind the bus station, dubbed 'Autogara Intertrans'.

Window 4 at the bus station sells international tickets. One daily bus theoretically serves Chernivtsi in the Ukraine (35 lei, three hours), though if it doesn't have enough passengers the bus may not even come from Chernivtsi. Alternatively, local tour operators like AXA Travel can arrange car transfer (450 lei for up to four people).

One daily bus at 6.30am serves Chişinău (60 lei, seven to eight hours).

Train

Buses to the train stations stop east of Piaţa 22 Decembrie, across B-dul Ana Ipătescu.

Suceava's two train stations, Gara Suceava (aka Gara Burdujeni, Gara Sud or Gara Principala) and Gara Nord (aka Gara Iţcani), are both roughly 5km north of the centre, and easily reached by bus or maxitaxi (7 lei). The Agenţia de Voiaj CFR (p201) sells advance tickets. Most trains originate or terminate at the Gara Suceava.

Train services include Gura Humorului (10 lei to 17 lei, 70 minutes, 10 daily) – disembark at the Gura Humorului Oraş stop – Iaşi (39 lei, two hours, nine daily), three to Timişoara (115 lei, 14 hours), four to Cluj-Napoca (71 lei, seven hours), one to Braşov (86 lei, 8½ hours) and Bucharest (86 lei to 107 lei, seven hours, six daily). The old train route to Moldoviţa via Vama was no longer running at the time of research.

❶ Getting Around

The central bus stops at the eastern end of Piaţa 22 Decembrie; all buses to and from the two train stations arrive and depart from here. Bus 2 runs between the centre and Gara Suceava. To reach Gara Nord, take Bus 5.

Autonom (☎0748-295 660; suceava@autonom.ro) offers good car-hire rates.

Bucovina Monasteries

Southern Bucovina's historic monasteries are among the most distinctive in all Christendom. Unusually, some have frescoes both outside and inside. While the region's prevailing winds and rains mean that north-facing exterior walls have largely lost their five-century-old paintings, frescoes facing other directions have survived – almost a miracle, considering that the plaster is only 5mm thick on some of the most impressive paintings.

There's no single explanation for this, though different reasons have been offered. Bucovina's clear and cold winters may have helped; historically speaking, long periods of disuse due to the Habsburgs' closures of many monasteries (after 1785) and Communist neglect may also have helped preserve the frescoes. Unfortunately, more senseless damage has also occurred – you'll note visitors' names (from both Austro-Hungarian and modern times) chiselled into paintings, along with the date; there's something deeply unsettling about seeing graffiti scrawled over a century ago, appearing to have been inscribed just yesterday.

While wall paintings and icons are common in Orthodox churches, external frescoes are more rare. Different explanations have been given for this too. Since these fortified monasteries were created when the Turks threatened, large numbers of soldiers would have been garrisoned within; they, like the villagers, were largely illiterate. Further, during services, these small churches could hold few parishioners (generally, the nobility). The edifying outdoor paintings thus helped explain biblical stories and ethical concepts to the masses – useful too, considering that liturgies in Old Church Slavonic were unintelligible to most Romanians. Majestic sacred art was also a potent symbol of Orthodoxy later, when the Habsburgs sought to Catholicise their subjects.

A guided tour is the most time-efficient and informative way to visit. Alternatively, renting a car allows you flexibility. Otherwise, public transport is possible, but difficult, requiring hopping around and backtracking. Hitching is not as safe as it was and isn't recommended. All monasteries operate from 8am to 7pm in summer, to 4pm in winter. In addition to accommodation options listed below, Suceava tour operators can book rural *pensiunes*; also see www.ruraltourism.ro or www.antrec.ro.

Note that most monasteries charge an entrance fee (5 lei for adults, 2 lei for students and children) and 10 or even 15 lei for photos and video; both are allowed on monastic grounds, but not inside the churches. Smoking is forbidden, and visitors should dress 'respectfully'; wearing shorts and hats (for men) is forbidden, and women are required to cover their shoulders and wear trousers or long skirts. If you strive for even more perfect Orthodox practice, don't put your hands in your pockets inside a church and always exit while facing indoors.

DRAGOMIRNA MONASTERY
Just 10km north of Suceava in Mitocul Dragomirnei, the 60-nun-strong Dragomirna Monastery (www.manastireadragomirna. ro; admission 5 lei) was founded between 1602 and 1609 by scholar, calligrapher, artist and bishop Anastasie Crimca. The intricate rope lacing around the main church's side (1609) represents the Holy Trinity, and the short-lived unification of the Moldavian, Wallachian and Transylvanian principalities in 1600.

Dragomirna's Museum of Medieval Art contains carved cedar crosses mounted in silver-gilt filigree and numerous religious texts.

The monastery hosts pilgrims. Drive or take a taxi from Suceava (20 to 30 lei).

HUMOR MONASTERY
Founded by Chancellor Theodor Bubuiog under Moldavian Prince Petru Rareş, Humor Monastery (Mănăstirea Humorului; admission adult/student 5/2 lei; ⊙8am-7pm summer, to 4pm winter), built in 1530, is surrounded by ramparts, with a three-level brick-and-wood lookout tower. Ascend it for views from the lookout deck. The narrow walls enclosing the last stretch of stairway were designed so that defending soldiers could kill off attacking Turks one by one.

Humor's predominantly red-and-brown exterior frescoes (1535) are divided topically. On the southern wall's left-hand side, patron saint the Virgin Mary is commemorated; on the right, St Nicholas' life and miracles are captured. A badly faded depiction of the 1453 siege of Constantinople, with a parable depicting the prodigal son's return, is on the right. St George appears on the northern wall. The porch contains a painting of the Last Judgment: the long bench on which the 12 Apostles sit, the patterned towel on the chair of judgment, and the long, hornlike *bucium* (pipe) announcing Christ's coming are all typical Moldavian elements. The three square images in red, white and black (on the bottom right) are unique to Humor: they represent the fire, the coldness and the darkness (or boiling tar) of hell.

Humor shelters five chambers. The middle one (the tomb room) hides a treasure room *(tainiţa)*, which safeguarded monastic riches. On the right-hand wall, a votive painting depicts Bubuiog offering (with the Virgin Mary's help) a miniature monastery replica to Christ, a common motif in the Byzantine artistic tradition. Bubuiog's tomb (1539) is on the room's right side, that of his wife on the left side; above the latter is a painting of his wife praying to the Virgin Mary.

KNOW YOUR MONASTERIES

You don't have to be an art-history snob to wow your friends with monastery fresco facts. Each Bucovina monastery is unique for its prevailing colour patterns and exemplary frescoes. While some have similar frescoes, the differing preservation qualities means that some 'versions' are most famous in one particular monastery. The following need-to-know details help keep things straight.

Humor Monastery
Representative colours: red and brown
Famous frescoes: *The Annunciation, The Life of St Nicholas*

Voroneţ Monastery
Representative colour: blue
Famous fresco: *Last Judgment*

Moldoviţa Monastery
Representative colour: yellow
Famous frescoes: *The Siege of Constantinople, The Story of Jesus' Life*

Suceviţa Monastery
Representative colour: green
Famous frescoes: *The Genealogy of Jesus, Ladder of Virtues, The Story of Moses' Life*

🛏 Sleeping

Dozens of homes here have rooms for rent, and nearby Gura Humorului is also a useful base.

Maison de Bucovine GUESTHOUSE $$
(☎0744-373 931; Str Mănăstirea Humor 172, Gura Humorului; s/d €30/50) This unassuming-looking home 30m from Humor Monastery is comfortable, with clean and modern rooms.

❶ Getting There & Away

Nine daily Suceava–Gura Humorului trains operate (10 lei to 17 lei, 50 minutes). Regular maxitaxis go the final 6km to the monastery.

VORONEȚ MONASTERY

Built in just three months and three weeks by Ștefan cel Mare following a key 1488 victory over the Turks, Voroneț Monastery (adult/child 5/2 lei; ⏰8am-7pm summer, to 4pm winter) is the only one to have a specific colour associated with it worldwide. 'Voroneț Blue', a vibrant cerulean colour created from lapis lazuli and other ingredients, is prominent in its frescoes.

A 2011 restoration of frescoes in the church's entryway has revealed the incredible quality of these paintings even more clearly. Today Voroneț is home to a small community of nuns.

The wondrous size, scope and detail of the *Last Judgment* fresco, which fills the entire exterior western wall of the Voroneț Monastery, has earned near-universal accolades as being the most marvellous Bucovina fresco. Angels at the top roll up the zodiac signs, indicating the end of time, while humanity is brought to judgment in the middle. On the left, St Paul escorts the believers, while a stern Moses takes the nonbelievers on the right. The Heaven and Garden of Eden is on the bottom left, the Resurrection is on the bottom right.

On the northern wall is *Genesis*, from Adam and Eve to Cain and Abel. The southern wall features the Tree of Jesse with the biblical genealogy. The first three rows portray St Nicholas' life and miracles. The next two rows recount the martyrdom of Suceava's St John the New. The bottom row, from left to right, features the monastery's patron saint, St George, fighting the dragon, St Daniel the Hermit with Metropolitan Grigorie, a Deisis icon, and the 1402 procession of St John the New's relics into Suceava.

In the narthex lies the tomb of Daniel the Hermit, the ascetic who encouraged Ștefan cel Mare to fight the Turks, and then became the monastery's first abbot.

The monastery is a 4km walk from the turn-off or 6km from Gura Humorului.

🛏 Sleeping & Eating

The following places are in Gura Humorului, which is a good base for both Humor and Voroneț Monasteries.

TOP CHOICE Hilde's Residence GUESTHOUSE $$
(☎0744-386 698; www.lucy.ro; Str Șipotului 2, Gura Humorului; s/d/ste from 180/200/290 lei; breakfast 24 lei; ⓟ🅿❋🅰) Among the village's more atmospheric and pricier guesthouses, the long-established Hilde's has nine uniquely designed rooms; it's just off the main road in Gura Humorului. The on-site Romanian restaurant is good too.

La Roata GUESTHOUSE $$
(☎0230-230 400; www.la-roata.ro; Str Wurzburg 21F, Gura Humorului; d/apt from 170/290 lei; ⓟ❋🅰) This new detached-guesthouses complex is 500m west of the town centre. It offers spacious rooms, a restaurant and kid-friendly attractions like a playground and table tennis.

Casa Doamnei GUESTHOUSE $$
(☎0735-530 753; www.casa-doamnei.ro; Str Voroneț 255, Gura Humorului; s/d from 120/150 lei; breakfast 20 lei) On the Voroneț road (500m after the train tracks, 3.5km before Voroneț Monastery), this guesthouse has stylish wooden furniture, balconies and nice bathrooms.

MOLDOVIȚA MONASTERY

Built in 1532 Moldovița Monastery (adult/student 5/2 lei; ⏰8am-7pm summer, to 4pm winter) occupies a fortified quadrangular enclosure with tower, gates and well-tended lawns. The central painted church has been partly restored and features impressive frescoes from 1537. The southern exterior wall depicts the Siege of Constantinople in AD 626, under a combined Persian-Avar attack. Interestingly, the besiegers are depicted in Turkish dress – keeping parishioners concentrated on the current enemy.

On the church's porch is another *Last Judgment* fresco. Inside the sanctuary, on a wall facing the carved iconostasis, a pious Prince Petru Rareș offers the church to Christ. The monastery's small museum displays Rareș' original throne.

🛏 Sleeping & Eating

Letitia Orsvischi Pension GUESTHOUSE $$
(☎0745-869 529; letita_orsvischi@yahoo.fr; Str Gării 20; s/d incl half-board 130/210, breakfast

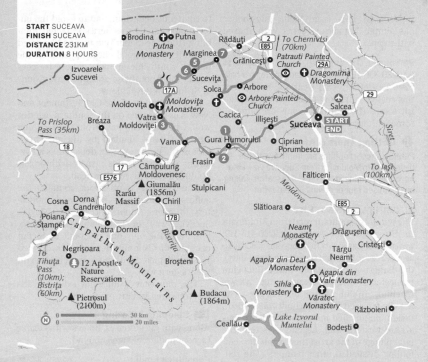

Driving Tour
Bucovina Monasteries

❯ Bucovina's painted monasteries are Moldavia's top cultural draw. Dazzling frescoes run from top to bottom in churches where monks and nuns follow traditional Orthodox vigils and services. On either a round-trip circuit or organised tour from Suceava, visiting the four most spectacular monasteries is achievable in a day. For a more leisurely tour and to visit additional monasteries like Putna, Arbore and Dragomirna, overnight at a rural guesthouse.

Leaving Suceava, take the southwest road for 50km (one hour) towards **Gura Humorului** village and ❶ **Humor Monastery**. Along with elaborate frescoes, this fortified monastery's tower offers nice views.

Continue on the south side of the Gura Humorului road for 10km (20 minutes) to ❷ **Voroneţ Monastery**, a spectacular structure known for its unique blue paint and detailed fresco of *Last Judgment*.

From here, head west and then northwest (35km, 45 minutes), passing through ❸ **Vatra Moldoviţei** for Moldoviţa Monastery, a pretty place known for its frescoes *The Story of Jesus' Life* and *The Siege of Constantinople*.

Backtrack to Vatra Moldoviţei and continue northeast on a winding mountain road, peaking at 1100m at ❹ **Ciumârna Pass**, dubbed 'Palma' (a giant human-palm statue stands here). You'll find great views, refreshing breezes and local vendors selling crafts and natural products.

Continue northeast for 10km to ❺ **Popas Turistic Bucovina**, an excellent lunch stop (it also has a hotel). Local forest mushrooms are used here in traditional sauces for chicken and pork dishes, and in hearty soups.

Another 4km north is ❻ **Suceviţa Monastery**, with paintings including the *Ladder of Virtues* and *The Miracles of Jesus*.

Travel 6km on the road back to Suceava to pass through ❼ **Marginea**, known for its unique black pottery, which is available at **AF Magopat Gheorghe**, where potters work on traditional wheels from Monday to Saturday. From here it's 50km (one hour) to Suceava.

15 lei; ✸🛏🛜) This large Vama guesthouse has simple but clean rooms with shared bathrooms.

Pensiunea Crizantema PENSION $$
(✆0230-336 116; www.vilacrizantema.ro; s/d half-board 140/180 lei; 🛏🛜) Near the monastery, this rustic eight-room place has cute, small-ish rooms (though bathrooms are simple), some with monastery views.

❶ Getting There & Away

Public transport options are limited, with the old train route to Moldoviţa from Suceava via Vama no longer running at the time of research. Taking an organised tour or driving is a safer bet.

SUCEVIŢA MONASTERY

The winding mountain road from Moldoviţa to Suceviţa Monastery (✆0230-417 110; www.manastireasucevita.ro; Suceviţa; adult/student 5/2 lei; ⏰8am-7pm summer, to 4pm winter), the largest and arguably finest Bucovina monastery, offers breathtaking views, reaching 1100m before descending. The heavily-frescoed church (built 1582–1601), inside the fortified monastic enclosure, has a bare western wall. Legend says that the fatal plunge of the artist there from the scaffolding dissuaded other painters. The red-and-green-based exterior frescoes date from around 1590.

Entering the complex, note the exterior *Ladder of Virtues* fresco, with its 32 steps to heaven. It exhorts priests, monks and nuns to righteous behaviour, and to avoid the unfortunate fate of the clerics depicted tumbling from the ladder due to sins like greed or vanity. More good cheer appears on the porch's south-side archway, where frescoes depict the Apocalypse and the dark visions of St John in Revelations.

The continuity of the Old Testament and New is emphasised on the southern exterior wall, where a tree grows from the reclining figure of Jesse, flanked by ancient Greek philosophers. The Virgin, depicted as a Byzantine princess, stands nearby, with angels holding a red veil over her head.

The church's tomb room contains the coffins of Moldavian nobles and monastery founders Simion and Ieremia Movilă. Suceviţa was the last painted monastery built, and the only one not built by Ştefan cel Mare or his family. Ieremia Movilă (died 1606) is depicted with his seven children on the western wall.

The monastery's museum exhibits various treasures and art pieces.

🛏 Sleeping & Eating

Along with guesthouses, homes with *cazare* (accommodation) signs abound.

Pensiunea Emilia GUESTHOUSE $$
(✆0743-117 827; Str Bercheza 173; r per person 80 lei, breakfast 10 lei) The most appealing local pension, Emilia has charming rooms and is 500m up the road opposite the monastery.

RĂDĂUŢI & MARGINEA

Side trips from the monastery trail include **Rădăuţi** (rah-*dah*-oots), a small market town with Moldavia's oldest church, the mid-14th-century **Bogdana Monastery**, built by Prince Bogdan I, which is also the mausoleum for eight Moldavian rulers and their families, including Bogdan I, Latcu, Roman Musat and Ştefan I.

Rădăuţi's square, Piaţa Unirii, features a multidomed **cathedral**. Opposite, the **Museum of Bucovina Folk Techniques** (✆0230-562 565; Str Piaţa Unirii 63; adult/child 5/2 lei; ⏰8am-5pm Mon-Fri, 8am-4pm Sat & Sun) is Moldavia's oldest ethnographic museum and displays over 1000 items, including regional pottery.

Tiny **Marginea**, 9km west of Rădăuţi, produces this unique black pottery, made with a technique dating to neolithic times. Here **AF Magopat Gheorghe** (Black Pottery Workshop; ✆0230-560 845; www.ceramicamarginea.ro; House 1265; ⏰7am-6pm Mon-Sat) displays and sells these items, and showcases the last traditional potters in action.

The area also has remarkably good guesthouses, many signposted, catering to all budgets. In Rădăuţi, **Gerald's Hotel** (✆0330-100 650; www.geraldshotel.com; Str Piaţa Unirii 3; s/d 350/400 lei; 🅿🛏✸@🛜) is among Moldavia's nicest hotels. It's loaded with business-class amenities, like a fitness centre and elegant bathrooms adorned with dark-wood furniture, plus a restaurant and bar.

Ieremia Movilă   GUESTHOUSE **$**

(☏0230-417 501; www.ieremiamovila.ro; Str Sucevita 459; r 110 lei; P☀✿🛜) This modern place has nice rooms with great bathrooms, balconies and wi-fi. Some rooms have monastery views. The on-site restaurant's tasty.

PUTNA

Some 28km northwest of Rădăuți, along a forested road dotted by traditional villages, **Putna Monastery** (☏0230 414-055; www. putna.ro; Putna; museum admission adult/student 5/2 lei), built 1466–1481, was built by Ştefan cel Mare following his victory over the Turks at Chilia (a large white cross indicates where he stood). About 60 monks live here. Simple accommodation is offered, ranging from dorm-type large rooms with five to 28 beds to en-suite doubles. Prices and availability change during the year so check ahead.

Putna Museum, behind the monastery, houses Eastern Europe's largest Byzantine items collection. Treasures include medieval manuscripts and the Holy Book that Ştefan cel Mare carried into battle. The largest of three bells inscribed in Old Church Slavonic outside dates from 1484, and was rung for royal deaths.

While Putna lacks spectacular frescoes, its royal inhabitants (Ştefan cel Mare is buried in the tomb room) keep it close to the Romanian heart. The graves of Ştefan's third wife, Maria Voichiţa, their two children, Bogdan and Petru, and Ştefan cel Mare's second wife, Maria are here too.

◎ Sights

Daniel the Hermit's Cave   CAVE

(Chilia lui Daniil Sihastrul) Just 2km from Putna, this cave contains a wooden table and memorial plaque to the 15th-century hermit and seer Daniel Dimitru. A monk by age 16, Daniel later dug and inhabited this rock cave; his fame was such that Ştefan cel Mare consulted him before doing battle.

From Putna, turn right off the main road following the sign for Cabana Putna. Bear left at the fork and continue to the second fork. Turn right, cross the railway tracks and continue over a small bridge, following the dirt road until you see the rock marked by a stone cross on your left.

🛏 Sleeping & Eating

Pensions abound and monastery lodging is available. Alternatively, seek enlightenment by camping opposite the Hermit's Cave.

Pensiunea Aga   GUESTHOUSE **$**

(☏0740-613 901; house 165; r with shared bathroom 70-90 lei, breakfast 15 lei) Right outside the monastery, Pensiunea Aga has 10 rooms, with those in the main house the best. No English spoken.

Pensiunea Muşatinii   GUESTHOUSE **$$**

(☏0744-503 536; www.pensiuneamusatinii.ro; Str Mănăstirii 513A; s/d/apt 140/170/220 lei; ☀✿🛜) This large, modern place behind the train station has the village's best rooms. There's a sauna and on-site restaurant.

❶ Getting There & Away

Putna is the furthest Bucovina monastery from Suceava, but reasonably close (28km northwest) to Rădăuți. The latter gets 13 daily buses from Suceava (8 lei, 45 minutes). Alternately, from Suceava, three or four daily trains make the three-hour trip to Putna (49 lei).

Câmpulung Moldovenesc

Situated at 621m, placid Câmpulung Moldovenesc dates from the 14th century. It's known for logging, fairs and outdoor sports – particularly cross-country and downhill skiing in winter (a short 800m ski slope employs a chairlift) and its annual winter sports festival occurs on the last Sunday in January.

Hotels and guesthouses abound. For comfort, try the **Eden Hotel** (☏0230-314 733; www.hotel-eden.ro; Calea Bucovinei 148; s/d/ste 150/200/340 lei; P☀✿🛜), an oasis-like complex with hotel, chalet and bungalow-style rooms. Its large bathrooms have hydro-massage tubs. Service is first-rate and the restaurant is excellent. Eden organises folk-dance shows and car hire. Unfussy budgeteers should try **Hotel Zimbru** (☏0230-314 356; www.rarau-turism.ro; Calea Bucovinei 1-3; r from 110 lei, breakfast 12 lei; @), a typical state-run place that actually offers clean rooms with great beds and friendly service. Zimbru's tourist office assists with monastery and horse-riding tours.

Câmpulung Moldovenesc is a good base for hiking the Rarău Massif, 15km south.

Rarău Massif

This Eastern Carpathian massif is snow-free from May to October. You can drive from Câmpulung Moldovenesc to its base station shelter **Cabana Rarău** (☏0720-538 197; www.rarau-turism.ro/cazare_cabana.html; d 80 lei).

Rarău Massif

Rooms here have comfy beds and basic bathrooms or shower. A small restaurant and provisions shop are nearby.

Entering Câmpulung Moldovenesc from the east, a left-hand road points to 'Cabana Rarău 14km': this narrow and rocky road is suitable only for 4WD vehicles. Alternatively, walk it in three to four hours (follow the red circles). A second and slightly better, but unmarked mountain road accesses the cabana from **Pojorâta** village, 3km west of Câmpulung Moldovenesc. Hiking takes four to five hours (follow the yellow crosses, and turn left at the fork after the post office, crossing the railway tracks; then turn left along the dirt road). Cabana Rarău is also accessible from the south, and **Chiril** village, 24km east of **Vatra Dornei** on the main Vatra Dornei–Durău road. This is the best road for drivers. Hiking takes three to four hours (blue circles).

Hiking from Cabana Rarău, a trail (30 minutes) leads to the foot of Rarău's most prized rocks, the **Lady's Stones** or Princess' Rocks (Pietrele Doamnei). Several crosses crown the highest one (1678m), a memorial for those who have died climbing here. Views from the top are superb. A trail marked by red stripes and red triangles (five hours) leads from the cabana to the **Slătioara Forest Reservation**. From here another trail (red triangles) leads to the **Todirescu Flower Reservation**.

The Danube Delta & Black Sea Coast

Best Places to Eat

» Chevalet (p224)

» Irish Pub (p222)

» Cherhana (p226)

» Pizzico (p222)

» Restaurant Select (p214)

Best Places to Stay

» Hotel Ferdinand (p222)

» Elga's Punk Rock Hotel (p225)

» Hotel Select (p214)

» Pensiunea Ana (p216)

» Club d'Or (p225)

Why Go?

Romania's 194km Black Sea coastline (*litoral*) is remarkably diverse, both from an environmental and a cultural standpoint. In the north, the mighty Danube River (Râul Dunărea) empties into the sea after completing its 2800km-long journey across the continent. The river's mouth, the Danube Delta, is a largely unspoilt wetland that draws bird lovers and seekers of solitude alike. It's a fantastic, tangled network of ever-eroding canals, riverbeds and marshlands with remote fishing villages and stretches of deserted coast. Further south, around Constanţa and below, a string of lively beach resorts draws a different kind of wildlife altogether. Everywhere you go you'll find evidence of Romania's long historical connections to ancient Greece and Rome, as well as surviving pockets of more recent Turkish, Tatar and Lippovani/Old Believer cultures.

When to Go

Tulcea

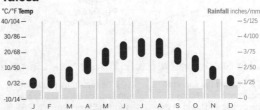

May & Jun The start of the season in the Danube Delta. Mornings are best for boating the wetlands.

Jul & Aug High season for Mamaia and Vama Veche. Book far in advance and get ready to party.

Sep & Oct Beach towns close and culture and clubbing action shifts back to Constanţa.

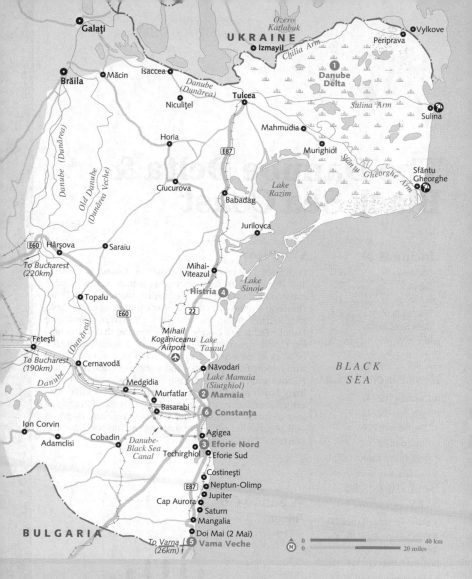

The Danube Delta & Black Sea Coast Highlights

1 Hearing the sound of thousands of pelicans in the canals and lakes of the **Danube Delta** (p211)

2 Testing the limits of sun, carousing and your beach modesty around **Mamaia** (p223)

3 Disregarding prudence and wallowing in stinky black mud in **Eforie Nord** (p226)

4 Reliving ancient Greece in **Histria** (p219)

5 Hitting a midsummer music fest and soaking up some counter-culture vibes at **Vama Veche** (p225)

6 Strolling **Constanţa's** (p217) lovely old port and marveling at the city's Greek and Roman roots

History

Archaeologists have discovered evidence of human civilisation dating back several thousand years all along the Black Sea coast. The ancient Greeks arrived around the 7th century BC. Histria, the oldest Greek settlement in Romania, was founded in 657 BC.

The Romans arrived around the 1st century BC and conquered the coastal region. The Romans considered the Black Sea to be on the very fringe of the empire. Indeed, it was to ancient Tomis – today's Constanța – where Emperor Augustus chose to banish the poet Ovid (43 BC–17 AD) in 8 AD for transgressions that remain unclear to this day.

In 1418 the coastal area was conquered by the Turks, who stayed for more than four centuries. The cultural impact of the Ottoman Empire was profound, as the presence of mosques to this day in Tulcea and Constanța testify.

In 1878, the territory became part of Romania when a combined Russo-Romanian army defeated the Turks. Once Romanian flags flew over the area, much was done to integrate it to the rest of the country as quickly as possible.

DANUBE DELTA

After passing through several countries and absorbing countless lesser waterways, the Danube empties into the Black Sea just south of the Ukrainian border. The Danube Delta (Delta Dunării), included on Unesco's World Heritage list, is one of Romania's leading tourist attractions. At Tulcea, the river splits into three separate channels: the Chilia, Sulina and Sfântu Gheorghe arms, creating a constantly evolving 4187-sq-km wetland of marshes, floating reed islets and sandbars. The region provides sanctuary for 300 species of bird and 160 species of fish. Reed marshes cover 156,300 hectares, constituting one of the largest single expanses of reed beds in the world. The delta is a haven for wildlife lovers, birdwatchers, fishers and anyone wanting to get away from it all for a few days. There are beautiful, secluded beaches at both Sulina and Sfântu Gheorghe, and the fish and seafood, particularly the fish soup, are the best in Romania.

National Parks

Much of the the delta is under the protection of the administration of the **Danube Delta Biosphere Reserve Authority** (DDBRA; ☎0240-518 945; www.ddbra.ro; Str Portului 34a, Tulcea), headquarted in Tulcea, with branch of-

Danube Delta

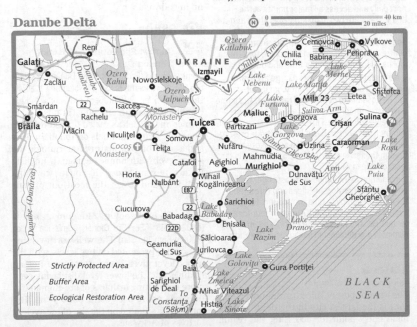

fices throughout the delta, including in Sulina (p216) and Sfântu Gheorghe (p217). There are around 20 strictly protected areas covering about 50,000 hectares that are off-limits to tourists, including the 500-year-old Leţea Forest and Europe's largest pelican colony. Visitation is limited in other areas. Note that visitors to the reserve are required to purchase an entry permit. Camping in the reserve is only allowed in official camping grounds.

Dangers & Annoyances

Mosquitoes and biting flies are a nuisance in summer, though they pose no danger to human health. Mosquito repellent is widely available in pharmacies and most hotels and pensions have window screens. If you're planning a day out in the delta, wear long pants and bring a long-sleeved shirt to wear in the evening.

Be sure to bring a hat and sunscreen if you're planning on spending any time out on a boat. The summer sun is relentless and just a brief exposure can result in a nasty burn.

ℹ Getting Around

There is no rail service in the delta and few paved roads, meaning the primary mode of transport is **ferry boat**. Regularly scheduled ferries, both traditional 'slow' ferries and faster (and more expensive) hydrofoils, leave from Tulcea's main port daily and access all major points in the delta. There are two main ferry operators and the ferry schedule can be bewildering on first glance. The helpful staff at the tourism information centre (p215) in Tulcea can help piece together a journey depending on your time and budget.

Note that the delta covers a large area, and depending on where you want to go it will usually not be possible to depart and return on the same day. Give yourself at least a few days for more leisurely exploration. Ferries can get crowded in summer, so try to arrive at least an hour prior to departure to secure yourself a seat. Note that, though the ferries run year-round, service is far less reliable in winter.

In addition to the scheduled passenger ferries, private boat operators in Tulcea and throughout the delta are happy to take you around, for a fee. Expect to pay upwards of 100 lei per hour for a water taxi. Be sure to negotiate everything up front to eliminate any unpleasant surprises at the end.

Tulcea

POP 92,380

The Danube port of Tulcea (pronounced tool-*cha*) is the largest city in the delta and the main entry point for accessing the region.

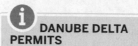

ℹ DANUBE DELTA PERMITS

All visitors to the protected areas of the delta, including those on hiking or boating excursions from Tulcea, Sulina or Sfântu Gheorghe, are required to purchase an entry permit. Permits are available for one day (5 lei), one week (15 lei) or one year (30 lei) from Danube Delta Biosphere Reserve Authority offices in Tulcea (p215), Sulina (p216) or Sfântu Gheorghe (p217). Boats are subject to spot inspections and if you're caught without a permit you could be fined. Note you need separate permits to fish or hunt.

It's got good bus and minibus connections to the rest of the country, and is home to the main passenger ferries. If you've only got a short amount of time (one to three days), you'll want to base yourself here and explore the delta via boating day trips. If you've got more time, you'll likely only transit through Tulcea on your way to deeper destinations like Sulina and Sfântu Gheorghe. There are plenty of good hotels and restaurants, and several interesting museums if you're caught up in bad weather.

◎ Sights

TOP CHOICE **Central Eco-Tourism Museum of the Danube Delta**   MUSEUM, AQUARIUM
(Centrul Muzeal Ecoturistic Delta Dunării; ☑0240-515 866; www.icemtl.ro; Str 14 Noiembrie 1; adult/student 15/5 lei; ⊙10am-6pm Tue-Sun; ▣) This combined museum and aquarium is a good primer on the delta's varied flora and fauna. There are stuffed animals on the main floor and a small but fascinating aquarium on the lower level, with ample signage in English. Highly recommended if you're travelling with kids and to get the most out of your visit.

History & Archaeology Museum   MUSEUM
(☑0240-513 626; Str Gloriei; admission 5 lei; ⊙10am-6pm Tue-Sun) The well-worth-visiting museum is presented on two levels, with the upper level given over to extensive Roman findings and the lower level displaying even more fascinating artifacts of pre-Roman civilisations going back some 6000 years. The museum is situated on the site of the ancient fortress of Aegyssus.

Folk Art & Ethnographic Museum   MUSEUM

(☑0240-516 204; Str 9 Mai 4; adult/student 6/3 lei; ☺10am-6pm Tue-Sun) This modest museum displays the ethnic and cultural diversity of the delta region over the centuries, and the interaction of Romanians with Turks, Russians, Ukrainians and Bulgarians. There is some signage in English, though you can get the general idea without linguistic help.

Fine Arts Museum   MUSEUM

(☑0240-513 249; Str Grigore Antipa 2; adult/child 6/3 lei; ☺10am-6pm Tue-Sun) The Fine Arts Museum has over 700 wood and glass icons and a large collection of Romanian paintings and sculptures, including some surrealist and avant-garde works.

🏃 Activities

Tulcea's main activities are boating, fishing and birdwatching. The port is lined with private boat operators offering a variety of excursions on slow boats, speedboats and pontoon boats; these can be tailored to accommodate special pursuits. Prices vary according to the operator, length of time, type of boat and number of passengers. Excursions are generally priced per person, assuming a minimum number. If the minimum is not reached, prices can go higher. Hotels and the tourism information centre (p215) can help plan trips and choose operators.

Safca   BOAT TOUR

(☑0744-143 336; www.egretamica.ro; port) This small father-and-son company offers a variety of boat excursions for individuals or groups up to around eight people. They have both faster boats and a pontoon boat. Among their tours is a popular all-day 'hyper' trip to Sulina, including a visit to the beach, for 250 lei per person.

Escape   BOAT TOUR

(☑0743-609 626; www.deltaescapetravel.ro) This private operator comes highly recommended. Offers a standard mix of four-, five- and eight-hour boat trips, on both slow and speed boats. Will tailor trips to accommodate special interests, such as fishing or birdwatching.

PASSENGER FERRY TIMETABLES

Two companies offer passenger-ferry service throughout the delta. State-run Navrom (☑0240-511 553; www.navromdelta.ro; Str Portului 26; ☺ticket office 11.30am-1.30pm) operates slower, traditional ferries (referred to as 'classic ships' on timetables) as well as faster catamarans. A second company, Nave Rapide (☑0726-774 074, 0742-544 068; www.naverapide.ro), offers only faster boats.

For the Navrom ferries, in Tulcea buy tickets on the day of departure at the Navrom passenger ferry terminal (Str Portului; ☺11.30am-1.30pm). Outside of Tulcea, buy tickets on departure at the entrance to the boat. For the Nave Rapide ferries, try booking at least a day in advance over the phone or turn to the tourism information centre (p215) in Tulcea for assistance.

While schedules vary from season to season, during the summer of 2012 boats were sailing according to the following timetable.

Navrom Services

» Slow ferries leave Tulcea for Sulina (via Crişan) at 1.30pm (34 lei, four to five hours) on Monday, Wednesday and Friday, and return at 7am on Tuesday, Thursday and Sunday. Fast ferries leave Tulcea at 1.30pm (42 lei, two to three hours) on Tuesday, Thursday and Saturday, returning at 7am on Monday, Wednesday and Friday.

» Slow ferries leave Tulcea for Sfântu Gheorghe (via Mahmudia) at 1.30pm (35 lei, five to six hours) on Monday and Friday, returning at 7am on Tuesday and Sunday. Fast ferries depart from Tulcea at 1.30pm (46 lei, three hours) on Wednesday and Thursday, returning at 7am on Thursday and Friday.

Nave Rapide Services

» Faster Nave Rapide boats depart Tulcea for Sulina (via Crişan) twice daily at 10am and 1pm (60 lei, 1½ hours), returning at 6.45am and noon.

» Boats departs from Tulcea for Sfântu Gheorghe (via Mahmudia) daily at 1.30pm (60 lei, 1½ hours), returning at 6.45am the next day.

Tulcea

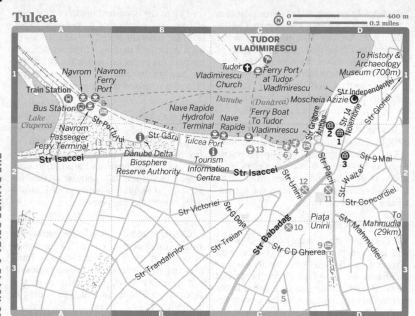

Ibis Tours
GUIDED TOUR

(☎0722-381 398, 0240-512 787; www.ibis-tours.ro; Str Dimitrie Sturza 6; ⊙9am-6pm Mon-Sat) Arranges wildlife and birdwatching tours in the delta and Dobrogea led by professional ornithologists.

🛏 Sleeping

TOP CHOICE Hotel Select
HOTEL $$

(☎0240-506 180; www.calypsosrl.ro; Str Păcii 6; s/d 140/170 lei; P⊕❋@🖲) Though we normally shy away from these boxy high-rises, this is our favourite hotel in Tulcea. The rooms are plain but very good value, with big and comfortable beds and light-blocking blinds on the windows. The staff could not be friendlier, and the restaurant is arguably the best in town.

Hotel Delta
HOTEL $$

(☎0240-514 720; www.deltahotelro.com; Str Isaccei 2; s/d 3-star 220/280 lei, 4-star 280/360 lei; ⊕❋🖲🕭) Landmark hotel situated toward the eastern end of the port offers both three- and four-star accommodation in adjoining buildings. The three-star rooms, with air-con and balcony views, are better value. The four-star side represents arguably Tulcea's most luxurious property. There's an indoor pool. The location is superb.

Hotel Esplanada
HOTEL $$

(☎0240-516 607; www.hotelesplanada.ro; Str Portului 1; s/d 280/360 lei; P⊕❋@🖲) This luxury property has smart rooms with contemporary furnishings and with excellent views out over the Danube. There's a good in-house restaurant. It's conveniently located next to the bus station.

Hotel Europolis
HOTEL $

(☎0240-512 443; www.europolis.ro; Str Păcii 20; s/d 120/180 lei; ❋@) Value-conscious travellers will enjoy these simple rooms with huge bathrooms. For even less money (single/ double 100/120 lei), you can stay at sister property the Complexul Touristic Europolis, a resort-like hotel by Lake Câşla, 2km outside of Tulcea.

✗ Eating & Drinking

There's a string of cafes, kebab places and fast-food joints as well as a big supermarket to pick up provisions along Str Unirii in the centre.

Restaurant Select
ROMANIAN $$

(www.calypsosrl.ro; Str Păcii 6; mains 15-30 lei; P🖲) Though it's a couple of blocks away from the port and lacks any buzz to speak of, this is still the best restaurant in town. The multilingual, varied menu offers fresh fish,

Tulcea

pizza and the local speciality, *tochitura dobrogeana* (pan-fried meat with spicy sauce).

Restaurant Central   ROMANIAN $$

(☎0240-515 020; Str Babadag 3; mains 15-20 lei; ⊙9am-11pm) Low-key terrace restaurant a couple of blocks away from the port draws a mostly local crowd for beers, well-done pork dishes and fresh fish.

Trident Pizzeria   PIZZA $$

(Str Babadag; mains 13-20 lei; 🛜) Excellent spot for good thin-crust pizza and fast pasta.

Istru   PUB

(☎0740-075 330; Str Gării 12; ⊙10am-midnight; 🛜) This is the best watering hole in the immediate port area, with great coffee drinks by day and Guinness and Skol wheat beer during the evening. Draws a mostly local student and arty (for Tulcea) crowd.

ⓘ Information

Banks and ATMs are found everywhere in the main commercial area around Str Babadag. There was no internet cafe at the time of research. The Hotel Select has a computer terminal off the lobby.

Danube Delta Biosphere Reserve Authority (☎0240-518 945; www.ddbra.ro; Str Portului 34a; permits per day 5 lei; ⊙8am-4pm Mon-Fri) This office is run by the national group charged with managing the delta. It's a good source of information on what to see and do. It publishes and distributes the helpful pamphlet *Guide of the Touristic Routes*, which lays out 19 aquatic routes. Sells delta visitors permits.

Post office (Str Babadag 5; ⊙7am-8pm Mon-Fri, 8am-noon Sat)

Raiffeisen Bank (Str Isaccei; ⊙8am-5pm Mon-Fri) Bank with ATM located directly across the small park from the entrance to the Hotel Delta.

Tourism information centre (☎0240-519 130; www.primariatulcea.ro; Str Gării 26; ⊙8am-7pm Mon-Fri, to noon Sat May-Sep) The helpful staff here can help sort through the confusing ferry schedules as well as advise on various travel agencies, hotels and restaurants. They also hand out an invaluable free map of Tulcea. It's hidden slightly back from the river promenade, next to the Căpitânia Portului building, halfway between the main port administration and the Hotel Delta.

ⓘ Getting There & Away

The **bus station** (☎0240-513 304; Str Portului 1) adjoins the main ferry terminal (p213). As many as 10 buses and maxitaxis head daily to Bucharest (55 lei, five hours); there are two daily buses to Iaşi (65 lei, four hours). Maxitaxis to Constanța (30 lei, two hours) leave every half-hour from 5.30am to 8pm. There's a smaller passenger ferry that runs every half-hour to the small village of **Tudor Vladimirescu**, across the Danube from Tulcea's port.

Sulina

POP 3600

The sleepy fishing port of Sulina is Romania's easternmost point and the highlight of any journey along the Danube's central arm. There's a beautiful, tranquil (during the day) here as well as a charming canal-side promenade. It's also an excellent base for forays deeper into the delta or on to the Black Sea.

🏃 Activities

Sulina is a quiet place. The main activities include strolling the main promenade (Str I), soaking up the sun at **Sulina Beach** (⊙May-Oct) or hiring the services of a local fisherman to take you around on the delta by small **boat** (☎0744-821 365; Str I; per person 30-50 lei).

🛏 Sleeping

There are several *cazares* and *pensiuneas* here: you can accept an offer from those who greet the boat, or ask around. Expect to pay around 100 lei per room, excluding board. Wild camping is possible on the beach, but there are no services and two discos blast dance music into the night air in summer until 3am.

Pensiunea Ana
PENSION $

(✆0727-001 569, 0724-421 976; pensiuneana@ yahoo.com; Str IV 144; r 80 lei) This charming family-run affair has four rooms and a beautifully shaded garden. The view from the street is not promising but once inside the blue gate things start to look up. To find it, walk 200m west from the ferry port along the main promenade, bear left on Str Mihail Kogălniceanu, and walk four blocks inland.

Hotel Casa Coral
HOTEL $$

(✆0742-974 016; www.casacoralsulina.ro; Str I 195; r 150 lei; ※🐾📶) This modern three-star property lacks character but is arguably the nicest hotel in Sulina centre. You'll have to book in advance in summer as it tends to fill up fast. You'll find it on the main promenade 100m west of the passenger ferry port.

✗ Eating & Drinking

Head to the main promenade (Str I) for all that tiny Sulina has to offer. Your pension is likely to cook better than any restaurant, so don't hesitate to book half- or full board if possible. In summer, nightlife shifts to the beach, where there are a couple of restaurants that transform into discos after sunset.

Restaurant Marea Neagră
ROMANIAN $$

(✆0240-543 130; Str I 178; mains 17-30 lei) This large and popular open-air terrace offers more than a dozen fish specialities, including sturgeon.

Irish Stoker Pub
PUB

(✆0744-696 842; Str I; ⊗9am-midnight; 📶) Popular watering hole on the river promenade with decent coffee and relatively rare nonfiltered Ciuc beer on tap for 5 lei per glass. It's about 300m west of the passenger ferry port, just next to the Sulina town hall (Primăria).

ⓘ Information

All of Sulina's services for visitors lie along the main promenade (Str I) that stretches about 2km west of the passenger ferry port.

BRD (Str I) Handy ATM located just east of the Hotel Casa Coral on the main promenade.

Danube Delta Biosphere Reserve Authority (www.ddbra.ro; Str I; ⊗8am-4pm Tue-Fri, noon-8pm Sat & Sun May-Oct) Sparsely furnished and funded information centre has basic information on the delta. Buy delta visitors permits here. Located on the main promenade.

Farmacie (Str I, cnr Str Mihail Kogălniceanu; ⊗8am-noon & 4-8pm Mon-Fri) Convenient pharmacy in the commercial complex next to the supermarket and post office.

Post Office (Str I, cnr Str Mihail Kogălniceanu; ⊗8am-7pm Mon-Fri) Situated in the commercial complex next to the supermarket.

ⓘ Getting There & Away

There's regular ferry and hydrofoil service between Tulcea and Sulina (see p213). The **ferry port** (Str I) is on the eastern end of the main promenade (Str I), about 100m east of the centre. While it's not possible to access Sulina by road from Tulcea, you can get to Sfântu Gheorghe (30km south) by dirt road. There's no commercial minibus service so you'll have to negotiate with a local taxi (around 250 lei). Sfântu Gheorghe is around three hours away by slow boat. There's no ferry service; instead try to deal with a local fisherman. Expect to pay anywhere from 300 to 500 lei for the trip.

Sfântu Gheorghe

POP 1000

First recorded in the mid-14th century by Visconti, a traveller from Genoa, the remote seaside village of Sfântu Gheorghe retains an ever-so-slight alternative vibe, fed by the town's lovely, lonely beach and its sleepy, noncommercial core. It's also one of the best places in the delta to sample traditional cooking (including some fabulous fish soup). Each August the village hosts what just might be the world's most remote film festival, the **Anonimul fest** (www.festival -anonimul.ro).

🏃 Activities

There's not much to do here and that's precisely the point. The **sandy beach** is 3km east of the centre. Hop the tractor-pulled **transport plaja** (Trocarici; ✆0740-572 269; Str Principala, Sfântu Gheorghe; 2 lei) that departs regularly during the day from the centre of the village. Several private **boat owners** (✆0755-415 219; Portul, Sfântu Gheorghe; per person 50 lei) offer excursions into the delta or to the Black Sea. Negotiate your itinerary and prices in advance. The Delta Marina hotel organises boat trips too. See the reception desk for details.

🛏 Sleeping

There are several *cazares* and pensions here: you can accept an offer from those who greet the boat, or ask around. Wild camping is possible on the beach, but it gets very windy and it's a long 3km hike in the dark.

Green Village   HOTEL, LUXURY BUNGALOWS **$$$**
(📞Bucharest head office 021-230 0507, local reception 0749-187 551; www.greenvillage.ro; Str Principala/Str I; s/d 340/420 lei; 🌊❄🛜🏊) Handsome four-star resort with a lovely pool as well as tastefully done-up bungalows built to harmonise with the delta setting. The location is near the beach, about 2km east of the village centre. Arrange transfers over the website or walk from the passenger ferry to the centre (100m) and take the *transport plaja* (beach transport) tractor.

Vila Petru & Marcela Stefanov   PENSION **$$**
(📞0763-088 859, 0240-546 811; near Str Principala/Str I; s/d half-board 120/150 lei) This family-run pension offers clean and comfortable accommodation just a few metres' walk from the town centre. Rates include half-board, often a delicious fish soup followed up by more grilled fish. The street is unmarked, but the pension is three houses north (on the left-hand side) of the *complex comercial* and supermarket, just beyond Str Principala (Str I).

Delta Marina   PENSION **$**
(📞0240-546 946; www.deltamarina.ro; Str Principala/Str I; r 130 lei; ❄🛜) This small, modern hotel is situated on the water about 200m west of the ferry port. The popular terrace restaurant is one of the few places in town to grab a sit-down meal (mains 17 to 20 lei).

Pensiunea Ovidiu   PENSION **$$**
(📞0744-507 164; www.pensiunea-ovidiu.ro; s/d incl full board 195/390 lei; ❄) The ramshackle exterior and dirt-road location hide what's actually a cosy, one-storey, motel-like setup. There are 10 units side by side, each with double bed, modern bath and air-conditioner. Quoted prices include full board (lunch and dinner). To find it make an immediate right (turn east) on exiting the ferry and follow a dirt road for 200m.

Dolphin Camping   CAMPGROUND **$**
(📞0749-187 551, Bucharest main office 021-230 0507; www.dolphincamping.ro; Str Principala/Str I; tents/cabins 15/75 lei) Boutique-style camping either in two-bed wooden cabins or with your own tent. There's a restaurant and club here and an open-air cinema.

🍴 Eating & Drinking

There are very few restaurants around, so you're best off booking full or half-board deals with your hotel or pension. The Delta Marina hotel has a decent terrace restaurant (mains 17 to 20 lei) that also opens at 7.30am for breakfast if necessary.

Supermarket   SUPERMARKET **$**
(Complex Comercial, Str Principala/Str I; ⊗8am-2pm & 4-10pm Mon-Sat, 8am-1pm Sun) This small but convenient minimarket is a good place to stock up on water, food and beer for the beach. Located in the centre of the village.

Bar Terasa   CAFE
(Str Principala/Str I; ⊘7am-3am May-Sep; 🛜) When it comes to evening drinking, this centrally located open-air terrace is the only game in town. Serves beer and coffee throughout the day to a pulsating pop soundtrack that changes over to live music around 9pm.

ℹ Information

There's a handy **ATM** (Str Principala, Complex Comercial; ⊗9am-5pm Mon-Fri) in the centre of the village.
Danube Delta Biosphere Reserve Authority (📞0240-518 926; www.ddbra.ro; Str I-a 39; permits day/week 5/15 lei; ⊗7am-noon & 4-7pm Tue-Fri, 9am-1pm Sat & Sun May-Oct) Decent source for what to see and do on the delta. Sells visitors permits. Located about 50m from the entrance to the passenger ferry port.

ℹ Getting There & Away

There's regular ferry and hydrofoil service between Tulcea and Sfântu Gheorghe. The **ferry port** is 100m south of the centre of the village. You can get here by road from Sulina (30km), but there is no commercial minibus service. You'll have to hire a taxi (about 250 lei for up to four people). It's also possible to travel by water taxi. Negotiate rates on the waterfront. Expect to pay upwards of 400 to 500 lei for the three-hour journey.

BLACK SEA COAST & LITTORAL

Constanţa

POP 260,000

Constanţa is Romania's largest and most important port city on the Black Sea; in summer, it's also the gateway to the country's

Black Sea Coast

Map labels:
To Histira (33km)
Mihail Kogălniceanu Airport
Lake Tasaul
To Hârsova (49km)
E60
2A
Năvodari
Staţiunea Năvodari
Mamaia Sat
Lake Mamaia (Siutghiol)
Ovidiu
Mamaia
BLACK SEA
Lake Tăbăcăriei
A2
Constanţa
Valu lui Traian
Palas
3
To Murfatlar (15km); Cernavodă (45km)
Cumpăna
Danube-Black Sea Canal
Agigea
Techirghiol
Eforie Nord
38
Lake Techirghiol
Eforie Sud
Tuzla
E87
39
To Negru Vodă (31km)
Costineşti
Lake Tatlageac
Pecineaga
Olimp
Neptun
Jupiter
Cap Aurora
Venus
To Negru Vodă (20km)
Saturn
Mangalia
Albeşti
Lake Mangalia
Limanu
Doi Mai (2 Mai)
Vama Veche
BLACK SEA
To Varna (24km)

seaside resorts. Accommodation here is cheaper than in Mamaia and maxi taxis cover the journey in about 15 minutes, so it may be worthwhile to consider basing yourself here even if you're only coming for Mamaia's beaches and discos. While the city shows obvious signs of neglect, especially around the port area, there are some very good museums, and a pretty portside walk. The restaurants are the best in this part of the country.

History

Constanţa has a rich history, bathed in legend, going back to the ancient Greeks. In the classical myth of Jason and the Argonauts, Jason is said to have fled here from King Aietes. Indeed, Constanţa's name in ancient Greece was 'Tomis', which means 'cut to pieces' – a reference to the story.

Under the Roman occupation, which began about 2000 years ago, Emperor Constantine fortified and developed the city and later renamed it after his sister. Constanţa's most important resident, doubtless, was the Roman poet Ovid (43 BC–AD 17), who was exiled here in AD 8 by Emperor Augustus. Ovid was one unhappy camper, apparently. He is said to have missed his beloved Rome greatly and died less than a decade later.

By the 8th century the city had been destroyed by invading Slavs and Avars and it fell into a long decline.

After Constanţa was taken by Romania in 1877, the town grew in importance as a Black Sea port, and a railway was built from Bucharest. By the early 1900s it was a fashionable seaside resort frequented by European royalty.

◉ Sights

CITY CENTRE & OVID SQUARE

The city centre and the area around Ovid Square (Piaţa Ovidiu) have the city's most important museums. Ovid Sq is easy to find. Just look for the statue of a rather unhappy-looking Ovid standing at the centre.

National History & Archaeological Museum   MUSEUM

(Muzeul de Istorie Nationala si Arheologie Constanta; ☎0241-618 763; www.minac.ro; Piaţa Ovidiu 12; adult/child 11/5 lei; ◷9am-8pm daily Jun-Sep, to 5pm Tue-Sun Oct-May) This museum is a minor disappointment. The stunning ground-floor exhibits of vases, jewellery and statuary from the Greek and Roman periods, lasting until about AD 500, justify the admission price, but the upper floors on more recent times

WORTH A TRIP

THE ANCIENT GREEK POLIS OF HISTRIA

Histria, or Istros, settled in 657 BC by Greek traders, is Romania's oldest town. Its founding by Greek colonists, through the Hellenic decline, the rise and fall of the Roman Empire and then the rise of Byzantium, forms a fascinating microcosm of early settlement in this part of the world.

Over the centuries, Histria became a key commercial port, superseding even that at Constanţa. But subsequent Goth attacks coupled with the gradual sand-locking of the harbour led to its equally rapid decline. By the 7th century AD the town was abandoned. Its ruins were discovered and excavated in the late 19th and early 20th centuries.

Relics uncovered at the site are displayed in the Histria **Archaeological Complex & Museum** (www.cimec.ro; Istria; admission 15 lei; ⊙9am-8pm). From the entrance to the site, paths lead visitors through the ancient city's remains, and pass by the big tower into the western sector, where most of the public buildings, the thermal baths and the civil basilica stood. Close by is the Christian basilica, built with stones from the old theatre in the 6th century AD.

On the cliffs in the eastern sector is the 'sacred zone' (*zona sacră*), where archaeologists have uncovered the remains of a Greek temple believed to have been built at the end of the 6th century BC.

and Romanian national history are poorly lit and lack signage in English. Skip the top floor altogether.

Roman Mosaic   RUINS
(Edificiul Roman cu Mozaic; Piaţa Ovidiu 12; adult/child 5/2.50 lei; ⊙9am-8pm Tue-Sun Jun-Sep, 10am-6pm Oct-May) Located just behind and south of the National History and Archaeological Museum, a modern building protects what's left of a Roman floor mosaic dating from the 4th century that was discovered in the 1960s. The site is near where the forum of ancient Tomis is thought to have existed.

Folk Art Museum   MUSEUM
(Muzeul de Artă Populară; ☎0241-616 133; B-dul Tomis 32; adult/child 10/5 lei; ⊙9am-7.30pm) This large and impressive collection features folk costumes, implements, household items and interiors of traditional homes from around Romania.

Great Mahmudiye Mosque   MOSQUE
(Moscheea Mare Mahmoud II; Str Arhiepiscopiei 5; adult/child 4/2 lei; ⊙9am-5pm) This impressive mosque is the seat of the mufti and was built in 1910 by King Carol I. It's the spiritual home of the 50,000 Muslims who inhabit the coastal region. The highlight is the enormous Persian rug, said to be the largest carpet in the country. You can climb the 140 steps of the minaret.

Geamia Hunchiar Mosque   MOSQUE
(B-dul Tomis 39; ⊙not open to the public) The city's second most important mosque was

built 1868 in Moorish style. Though it's not often open, if you get a chance, look inside to see an interior that remains little changed from the original design.

Great Synagogue   JEWISH
(Str Petru Rareş 2) Constanţa's once-glorious 19th-century synagogue is little more than a ruin these days, guarded by some mean dogs. Still, you can walk past the front to get a sense of the former majesty and significance of the place. Plans to restore the building have been put on indefinite hold due to funding problems.

Art Museum   MUSEUM
(Muzeul de Artă; ☎0241-617 012; B-dul Tomis 82-84; adult/child 10/5 lei; ⊙9am-7pm Mon-Fri) This airy museum in an atrium is heavy on 19th-century realism and landscapes, including those by Nicolae Grigorescu, whose pointillist and Impressionist paintings anticipated more modern movements. Our favourite has to be his *Study of a Cow*. The upper level is given over to the dark abstract modernist Ion Alin Gheorghiu.

Naval History Museum   MUSEUM
(Muzeul Marinei Române; ☎0241-619 035; Str Traian 53; adult/child 10/5 lei; ⊙9am-5pm Wed-Sun) Fascinating if slightly confusing stroll through 2000 years of maritime history on the Black Sea. The exhibit begins in the Greco-Roman period, with some intricate models of old Roman boats, but quickly moves to the 19th and 20th centuries. The garden is strewn with relics of real propellers, landmines and

Central Constanţa

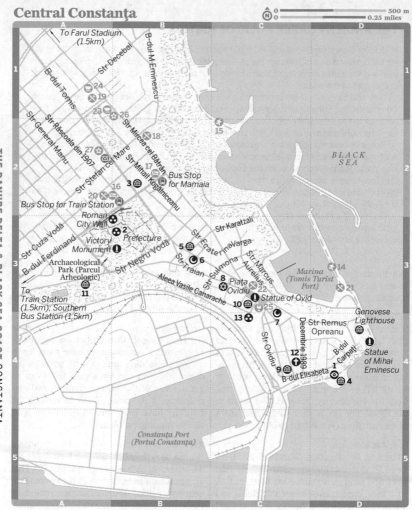

N
0 ——————— 500 m
0 ——————— 0.25 miles

THE DANUBE DELTA & BLACK SEA COAST CONSTANŢA

torpedoes that seem to be rusting into the ground.

Archaeological Park RUINS
(cnr B-duls Ferdinand & Tomis; ⊙24hr) Near the city's main intersection, B-dul Ferdinand and B-dul Tomis, is the Archaeological Park, which has remains of the 3rd-century **Roman city wall** and the 6th-century butchers' tower, loads of Roman sculptures and the modern **Victory Monument** (1968).

SEASIDE PROMENADE & AROUND
One of the city's finest assets is a peaceful promenade that meanders along the water-

front, offering sweeping views of the Black Sea. The crown jewel of the promenade is the gloriously derelict **casino**. There's also the evocative **Genovese Lighthouse** and a **Statue of Mihai Eminescu**.

Casino HISTORIC BUILDING
(Faleza Casino Constanţa; B-dul Elisabeta 1; admission free; ⊙10am-6pm Mon-Fri) Constanţa's amazing art nouveau casino, dating from 1910, was awaiting a long-overdue renovation at the time of research, but the city had opened the building to visitors to peek in and see some serious splendour (including

Central Constanţa

the world's most amazing chandeliers) in a perilous state of neglect.

Aquarium AQUARIUM
(Acvariu; ☎0241-611 277; ww.delfinariu.ro; B-dul Elisabeta 1, Faleza Casino Constanţa; adult/child 20/10 lei; ◎9am-8pm Tue-Sun Jun–mid-Sep, 10am-6pm Tue-Sun mid-Sep–May; ☖) This waterfront aquarium focuses on fish native to the Black Sea, including a large selection of endangered sturgeon, as well as local freshwater species.

Orthodox Cathedral CHURCH
(Catedrala Sf Apostol Petru si Pavel; ☎0241-611 408; Str Arhiepiscopiei 25; ◎8am-6pm) Constanţa's Orthodox cathedral, built in 1885 in Greco-Roman style, is a beautiful building and worth a peek to admire the dark, sombre interior. In front of the cathedral are some ruins of ancient Tomis.

Ion Jalea Sculpture Museum MUSEUM
(Muzeul Ion Jalea; ☎0241-618 602; Str Arhiepiscopiei 26; adult/child 5/2.50 lei; ◎10am-6pm Wed-Sun) This small museum, just at the entryway to the seaside promenade, features the works of Ion Jalea, a 20th-century sculptor often said to be a forefather of modern technique.

OUTSIDE THE CENTRE
Dolphinarium DOLPHIN SHOW
(Delfinariu; ☎0241-481 243; www.delfinariu.ro; B-dul Mamaia 255; adult/child 50/25 lei; ◎shows at 11am, 3pm, 7pm Mon-Fri, 10am, 1pm, 4pm, 7pm Sat & Sun) The country's first Dolphinarium (or Delfinarium) has been updated and modernised. Dolphin shows are held throughout the day in the large amphitheatre.

Planetarium PLANETARIUM
(www.delfinariu.ro; B-dul Mamaia; adult/child 10/5 lei; ◎shows at 10am, noon, 2pm, 4pm, 6pm, 7.30pm & 8.30pm Mon-Fri, 10.30am, noon, 1.30pm, 3pm, 4.30pm & 6.30pm Sat & Sun; ☖) Constanţa's planetarium is a fun rainy-day treat for kids.

 Activities

Not to be outdone by Mamaia, Constanţa has a small beach of its own, the **Plaja Modern**, situated at the eastern end of B-dul Ferdinand (walk down the steps). It's a pleasant place to get your feet wet, but the facilities at nearby Mamaia are nicer. You can take a short boat excursion aboard the **Condor Cruise Boat** (☎0742-174 296; Marina, Tomis Turist Port; per person per hr 25 lei, minimum of six people; ◎around 9am May-Sep), moored at the **Tomis Turist Port**.

Mistral Tours (p225) in Mamaia sells the **Constanţa City Pass** (www.mistraltours. ro; adult/child 135/70 lei), a discount card that offers reduced-entry prices for several attractions, including the National History & Archaeological Museum (p218), the Planetarium (p221), the Dolphinarium (p221), and the Aqua Magic (p224) water park.

THE DANUBE DELTA & BLACK SEA COAST CONSTANŢA

🛏 Sleeping

Hotel Ferdinand HOTEL $$
(📞0241-617 974; www.hotelferdinand.ro; B-dul Ferdinand 12; s/d 220/260 lei; P❄🛜) This is our favourite three-star hotel in town. Nothing fancy, just a very well-run hotel in a smart, nicely restored 1930s town house. Rooms have fridges and big, comfy beds. The hotel is within easy walking distance of virtually everything, including the city beach. Mamaia maxitaxis leave from across the street.

Hotel Class HOTEL $$
(📞0241-660 766; www.hotelclass.ro; Str Răscoala din 1907 1; s/d/ste 200/220/265 lei; P❄🛜) Well-managed three-star option, with clean rooms and comfortable beds with thick mattresses. Ask for a quiet room away from busy Str Răscoala.

Hotel Maria HOTEL $$
(📞0241-611 711; www.hotelmaria-ct.ro; B-dul 1 Decembrie 1918 2D; s/d 160/200 lei; ❄🛜) This modern, spotless option, across from the park facing the train station, has lots of glass, chrome and deep blues to soothe your sun-withered nerves.

Hotel Florentina HOTEL $
(📞0760-174 339, 0241-512 535; B-dul IC Brătianu 24; s 90 lei, d 100-120 lei; 🛜) A simple box of a hotel within walking distance of the bus/train station (about 10 to 15 minutes), and nothing else. Still, it's one of the better-value options in town, with clean rooms and a large breakfast (included in the price).

🍴 Eating

Stock up on fruit, cheese and vegetables at the central **market** (Str Răscoala din 1907). Just outside the market is a window serving classic Romanian snacks like cheese pies and *covrigi* (hot pretzels).

TOP CHOICE **Irish Pub** INTERNATIONAL $$
(📞0241-550 400; www.irishpub.ro; Str Ştefan cel Mare 1; mains 20-40 lei; ☺8am-midnight; 🛜) Several years after it opened to an enthusiastic reception, this is still *the* place to see and be seen, and one of the best meals in town. There are a couple of pub staples like burgers and fish and chips, but the menu has higher aspirations, with steaks and grilled fish. It's equally good for beer or coffee. Booking at meal times is essential.

Pizzico INTERNATIONAL $$
(📞0241-615 555; www.newpizzico.ro; Piaţa Ovidiu 7; mains 15-40 lei; 🛜) Pizzico has greatly expanded its range in the past couple of years, moving beyond very good wood-fired pizza to excellent grilled meats, seafood and chops. The location, on Ovid Sq, makes it easy to pair lunch here with a visit to a nearby museum.

On Plonge SEAFOOD $$
(📞0241-601 905; Portul Turistic Tomis; mains 15-40 lei; ☺9am-10pm) Brawny portside eatery with an informal, everyman vibe, specialising in fresh fish hauled in off the boat. Gets packed on summer nights and service suffers accordingly. The views out over the port and the old town are stunning.

Marco Polo ITALIAN $$$
(📞0241-617 357; Str Mircea cel Bătrân 103; mains 20-50 lei; 🛜) A swanky Italian restaurant where servers swarm to keep patrons happy. Portions are generous and the pizza, pasta, meat, fish and veg dishes are all delicious. You might consider dressing up for this one.

🍷 Drinking

Cafes usually do double duty as drinking establishments after sunset. In summer much of the drinking and clubbing action shifts to Mamaia, and Constanţa can feel like a ghost town.

Friends & Co CAFE
(Str Decebal 17; ☺10am-midnight Mon-Thu, 11am-1am Fri & Sat, 2-11pm Sun; 🛜) Relaxed student cafe with an alternative, indie vibe and a pretty, secluded terrace.

Café d'Art CAFE
(📞0241-615 092; www.cafedart.ro; B-dul Tomis 97; cocktails 15 lei; ☺9am-midnight; 🛜) Tree trunks sprout through the dining room and the terrace is lovely. Food is available (mains are 16 to 30 lei), but the long drinks menu makes it especially popular as an evening drinking hole.

Mozaic CAFE
(Piaţa Ovidiu 11; ☺8am-11pm; 🛜) The nearest cafe to the National History & Archaeological Museum (p218), where you can write postcards home while gazing out onto the statue of Ovid. Offers spotty free wi-fi, but you can sometimes cadge from the more reliable signal coming in from Pizzico across the square.

☆ Entertainment

Oleg Danovski National Theatre OPERA, BALLET
(Teatrul Naţional de Operă şi Balet 'Oleg Danovski'; 📞0241-481 460; www.opera-balet-constanta.ro; Str

Mircea cel Bătrân 97; tickets 30 lei; ⊘box office 10am-5pm Mon-Fri) The city's premier venue for opera and dance. Buy tickets at the theatre box office or the central ticket office (www.opera-balet-constanta.ro; B-dul Tomis 97; ⊘10am-3pm Mon-Fri, 10am-1pm Sat).

Farul Stadium FOOTBALL
(Stadionul Farul; www.fcfarul.ro; Str Primăverii 2) FC Farul Constanţa, the city's cherished football team, has its home ground at 15,000-seat Farul Stadium. Get tickets at the stadium on game days.

❶ Information

Internet Access
Forte-Games (☑0241-551 251; www.forte-games.ro; B-dul Tomis 235; per hr 6 lei; ⊘24hr)

Medical Services
Constanta Country Emergency Hospital (Spitalul Clinic Judeţean de Urgenţă Constanţa; ☑0241-662 222; www.spitalulconstanta.ro; B-dul Tomis 145)
Farmacia Miga (B-dul Tomis 80; ⊘8am-9pm Mon-Fri, 9am-2pm Sat & Sun) One of several pharmacies on this stretch near B-dul Tomis and B-dul Ferdinand.

Money
There are abundant banks and ATMs in the centre.
Banca Transilvania (B-dul Tomis 57; ⊘9am-5pm Mon-Fri) Issues cash advances on Visa and MasterCard and has a handy ATM.

Post & Telephone
Central post office (B-dul Tomis 79-81; ⊘7am-8pm Mon-Fri, 8am-1pm Sat)

Tourist Information
Constanţa has no tourist information office. One of the best sources of information on Constanţa is Mistral Tours (p225), located in Mamaia.
Contur Travel (☑0241-616 616; www.contur-travel.eu; Piaţa Ovidiu 14, block B; ⊘9am-5pm Mon-Fri) Contur's speciality is developing tailor-made tourist circuits around the coast, the delta and elsewhere in Romania. It can also get you discounts in some hotels.

❶ Getting There & Away

Bus
Constanţa, like many large Romanian cities, has several bus stations, depending on which bus line is operating the route. Buses to Bucharest (55 lei, three to four hours) depart from outside the train station. Many other buses, including

some travelling to the Black Sea resorts, use the large **southern bus station** (Autogara Sud; ☑0241-665 289; B-dul Ferdinand), about 200m north of the train station. Buses to Tulcea (30 lei, two to three hours) and points north often leave from other parts of town. Your best bet is to check the website www.autogari.ro to see times and departure points.

Train
Constanţa's **train station** (☑0241-614 960; www.cfrcalatori.ro; B-dul Ferdinand 45) is near the southern bus station, 2km from the centre. There are two fast Inter-City trains a day to Bucharest (60 lei, three to four hours). There are also daily services to Suceava, Cluj-Napoca, Timişoara and other destinations. In summer, several trains a day head from Constanţa south to Mangalia (7 lei, 1½ hours), with stops at resorts in between.
Agenţia de Voiaj CFR (www.cfr.ro; Aleea Vasile Canarache 14; ⊘8am-8pm Mon-Fri) Sells domestic and international train tickets and seat reservations as well as domestic air tickets.

Mamaia

Mamaia, a thin strip of sand extending north from Constanţa, is Romania's most popular and expensive beach resort. In season, from early June to early September, the 8km-long beachfront is lined end to end with sunbathers from all around Romania who compete for that precious patch of seaside real estate. By night, Mamaia morphs into party central, with dozens of high-adrenaline nightclubs and impromptu beach parties. It's a great time if you're in the mood for it, but not the best choice, perhaps, for a relaxing seaside holiday.

🏃 Activities

Mamaia's main activities are sunbathing and swimming. The beach stretches for 8km, with the southern end, towards Constanţa, being the most crowded and least appealing. The further north you go the more exclusive the resorts become, with correspondingly nicer sand and cleaner water. The beachfront is sectioned off into smaller private beaches, usually belonging to a hotel or sponsored by companies like Algida and Vodafone; entry is free but you'll usually be expected to rent a lounge chair (10 lei per day) or daybed bathing (s/d 35/50 lei per day). Our favourite bathing areas include **Nikkii Beach** (free admission, daybed single/double 30/60 lei), about 100m south of the northern telegondola (one way 10 lei; ⊘9am-

10pm Jun-Oct) station, or **Crush Beach** (www.clubcrush.ro); free admission, s/d daybed 35/50 lei), conveniently located opposite the northern end of the telegondola station.

Aqua Magic AMUSEMENT PARK
(www.aqua-magic.ro; adult/child 40/20 lei Jun & Sep, 60/30 lei Jul & Aug; ☉10am-6pm Jun & Sep, 9am-7pm Jul & Aug) This amazing water park (at the southern end of the telegondola station) has pools, slides and inner-tube rides galore. It can get very crowded on summer weekends, so try to arrive early to snag a decent chair, or go during the week.

Boats to Ovidiu Island BOATING
(Insula Ovidiu; B-dul Mamaia; per person return 20 lei; ☉boats 9am-midnight) In summer, boats ferry tourists across Lake Siutghiol to Ovidiu Island (Insula Ovidiu), with a good restaurant and where Ovid's tomb is said to be located. They depart every 30 minutes from the Tic-Tac wharf on the lake (*not* the beach) at about the midpoint of the Mamaia resort.

🛏 Sleeping

Mamaia is flush with resort complexes that are frankly more attuned to dealing with package tours than walk-ins. If you know your dates in advance and plan to stay at least three to four days, you're better off arranging a package through a travel agency like Mistral Tours. You'll save plenty on the rack rate and spare yourself the hassle of going from hotel to hotel trying to find a free room. You'll find a complete list of hotels in Mamaia on the website www.turistinfo.ro.

Frustratingly, hotels on the main strip don't have street addresses; instead, pick up a resort map from any hotel that shows the location of each hotel. Note that Mamaia pretty much shuts down in the low season (September to May) and only the biggest hotels stay open.

Camping is not permitted on the beach, though there are private campgrounds located at the northern end of the resort.

Hotel Splendid HOTEL $$$
(☎0341-412 541; www.splendidhotel.ro; B-dul Mamaia, Mamaia Nord; s/d 480/560 lei; P☻✳⚙@☎) This five-storey modern hotel, built in 2007, is a quieter option since it's on the western side of the main road (away from the beachfront, along Siutghiol Lake). The 31 rooms get high marks for cleanliness and the adjoining restaurant is a decent choice for a meal. You'll find it on the northern end of the resort.

Hotel Ovidiu HOTEL $$
(☎0241-831 590; www.hotelovidiu.ro; d/tr 250/350 lei; ☻✳☎) This simple two-star hotel offers basic, clean rooms at a good price and not much else. Request an upper-floor room to get a better sea view.

Hotel Perla HOTEL $$$
(☎0241-831 995; www.perlamamaia.ro; s/d 280/350 lei; ☻✳☎☎) Stationed at the resort's main entrance on the southern side of Mamaia, this huge hotel is both a landmark and a reliable service centre. Prices include breakfast, lunch and dinner. Wi-fi in reception.

GPM Campground CAMPGROUND $
(☎0241-831 001; www.gpm.ro; B-dul Mamaia Nord, Navodari; sites per person 20 lei, bungalows 140-460 lei; ✳) Attractive camping ground at the far northern end of Mamaia. Call or arrive early to reserve a site near the beach. Excellent self-serve restaurant is open to campers and noncampers alike.

🍴 Eating

Almost every hotel has its own adjoining restaurant and there are numerous fast-food stands and self-serve restaurants lining the boardwalk.

TOP CHOICE Chevalet INTERNATIONAL $$$
(☎0721-421 501; www.restaurantchevalet.com; B-dul Mamaia; mains 50-80 lei; ☉11am-11pm; ☎) Head chef Nelu Păucă trained around the world before opening this romantic terrace restaurant on Lake Siutghiol, near the southern end of Mamaia. Specialities include steak tartare, frog legs and a mouthwatering array of beef, pork and seafood. Book in advance to secure a table on the lake. Time your booking for sunset.

La Mama ROMANIAN $$
(☎0730-526 262; www.lamama.ro; Faleza Casino Mamaia; mains 17-30 lei; ☎) This branch of a reliable local chain serves up huge portions of traditional Romanian specialities at affordable, family-friendly prices. You'll find it on the main promenade about 200m south of the northern end of the telegondola.

☆ Entertainment

Mamaia is known around the country for its vibrant party scene. In season, the clubs decamp from Constanţa and reopen en masse on the coast, filling the air with the beat of dance music nightly, starting at around 10pm and continuing until the wee hours.

Crazy Beach
CLUB

(☑0726-779 292; www.crazybeach.ro; B-dul Mamaia Nord; ⏰8am-1am) One of the hottest clubs in Mamaia in 2012 was this open-air lounge and cocktail bar, situated in the extreme north of Mamaia, about 4km beyond the northern telegondola station. Take a taxi (about 10 lei from central Mamaia).

Megalos
CLUB

(☑0730-070 114; ⏰9pm-3am Jun-Sep) A perennial on the Mamaia summer scene, Megalos is situated in the centre of the resort, about 100m south of the northern telegondola station. If this club doesn't appeal, there are several others nearby.

ℹ Information

Mamaia lacks an official tourist information office, but stop in at Mistral Tours for basic information and to help book accommodation. There are plenty of **ATMs** and **pharmacies** along the main promenade.

Mistral Tours (☑0241-557 007; www.mistral tours.ro; ⏰9am-5pm Mon-Fri, to 1pm Sat) This helpful travel agency, located at the southern end of Mamaia's telegondola line, should be your first port of call. Staff can help find accommodation, plan day trips and excursions, including to the Danube Delta and Bulgarian Black Sea coast, and sell the Constanţa City Pass (p221).

Post office (Mamaia; ⏰8am-8pm Mon-Fri) Located 200m south of the northern telegondola station on the promenade.

ℹ Getting There & Away

Frequent maxitaxis (2 lei, 15 minutes) ply the route between central Constanţa and Mamaia from June to September. Maxitaxis 301 and 303 depart regularly from Constanţa's train station. You can wave them down conveniently on B-dul Ferdinand, across the street from both the Hotel Class (p222) and the Hotel Ferdinand (p222).

Once in Mamaia, stroll the boardwalk or take the **telegondola** (cable car; one way 10 lei; ⏰9am-10pm Jun-Oct) that runs from the southern end of the resort to approximately the midway point.

Vama Veche

If you've got time for just one Romanian resort, make it Vama Veche. While it lacks the polish of Mamaia and has fewer services, it's smaller, more relaxed and more rustic. Under the old communist regime, 'Vama' enjoyed a reputation as a haven for artists, hedonists and free thinkers. While it's slowly moving toward the mainstream –

these days the car park holds more than a few expensive SUVs from Bucharest – there's still something of a counter-culture vibe in the air. Don't come looking for luxury. There are no five-star resorts here. Instead, rent a bungalow, grab a beer, relax on the beach by day and party in the open air at night.

🏃 Activities

The main activities are swimming, sunbathing, drinking and partying, and not necessarily in that order. There's a 5km bike path to an adjoining seaside village called Doi Mai (2 Mai), that starts from the northern end of Vama Veche. The BazArt hostel rents bikes (☑0241-858 009; www.bazarthostel.ro; Str Ion Creangă; 2hr/day 10/30 lei.).

🛏 Sleeping

There's wild camping at both the far southern and northern ends of the beach. Club d'Or charges 10 lei per tent to camp (☑0743-335 114; www.clubdor.ro; Plaja Vama Veche) on a wide strip of beach toward the northern end and has showers and toilets.

In spite of Vama Veche's popularity, even in summer you can usually find a room. There's almost always someone standing by the road with a 'cazare' sign in hand. The **Dispencerat Cazare office** (☑0761-856 662; www.cazarevamaveche.net; Str Ion Creanga, cnr Hwy 87) can hook you up with a room in town for about 60 lei.

Club d'Or `[TOP CHOICE]`
HOTEL $$

(☑0743-335 114; www.clubdor.ro; Str Ion Creangă; r 160 lei; P☺🛜🏊) Clean, quiet and close enough to the beach to drift in and out when you want. The rooms resemble a motel and fan out around a gigantic, clean swimming pool. It's located 100m west of Hwy E87 at approximately the centre of the village.

Elga's Punk Rock Hotel
HOTEL $

(☑0722-366 711; www.punkrockhotel.com; Str Kogalniceanu, Hwy 87; r 80-100 lei; P☺❄🛜) This welcoming family-run hotel offers small but ultra-clean rooms with either double or twin beds in two price categories: A-level rooms are slightly larger and have air-conditioning, while category-B rooms are smaller and have fans. There's a shared kitchen on the premises.

BazArt
HOSTEL $

(☑0241-858 009; www.bazarthostel.ro; Str Ion Creangă; d 80-200 lei; q 150 lei; ❄❄🛜) This popular student choice on Vama Veche's main drag offers a variety of rooms, including comfortable private doubles with en suite

THE DANUBE DELTA & BLACK SEA COAST VAMA VECHE

WORTH A TRIP

BATHING IN THE MUD AT EFORIE NORD

Eforie Nord, 14km south of Constanţa, is a honky-tonk seaside resort, free of pretension, where families come to soak up the sun by day and gorge on junk food by night. That said, there's another reason for making a detour here: the amazing mud.

Lake Techirghiol, within walking distance of the centre of town, is famous for its dark *sapropel* mud. This black sediment is dense with organic matter and when slathered over your body is said to be restorative for skin and bones, and for treating ailments like rheumatism and other diseases.

Most of the big hotels in town offer some kind of mud-bath package, but the easiest – and cheapest – way to take the mud is to head to the public mud baths (Bai Reci; admission 10 lei; ☺8am-6pm) on the southern end of town, not far from the train station. At the baths, single-sex changing rooms lead to separate beaches, where convalescence seekers stand around nude, apply the glop and bask in the sun until the mud cracks.

After you've taken the mud, you can relax along the town's Black Sea beaches, just off Str Tudor Vladimirescu, which runs parallel to the main drag, B-dul Republicii.

Eforie Nord gets incredibly crowded in July and August, so advance hotel bookings are essential. There are tonnes of accommodation options in town. For budget travellers, we like Hotel Clas (☑0341-489 076; www.hotel-clas.ro; Str Armand Calinescu; r 120 lei; P✳☎). A decent midrange choice, close to the beach, is the Hotel Regal (☑0241-741 069; www.hotelregaleforie.ro; B-dul Ovidiu 20; d 230 lei; P✳☎). For top end, go for the Hotel Europa (☑0241-702 801; www.anahotels.ro; B-dul Republicii 13; s/d 240/450 lei; P➲✳@☎☒), which offers a full range of mud treatments and has a nice pool.

baths and air-conditioning, as well as budget twins and quads with shared facilities and no air-con. The location is convenient to the bars and clubs. Rents bikes (p225).

✗ Eating & Drinking

The main street, Str Ion Creangă, has plenty of fast-food stalls and mini-markets.

TOP CHOICE Cherhana   SEAFOOD $$
(mains 15-25 lei; ☺10am-11pm) This informal grill-and-picnic-tables beachfront place draws big crowds, particularly campers from the nearby wild campsites. The fresh fish is grilled on the spot. To find it, follow the main street, Str Ion Creangă, to the beach and turn left. It's situated on the northern edge of Vama Veche, beyond the Club d'Or camping (p225) area.

Terasa Lyana   ROMANIAN $$
(☑0744 671 213; mains 15-25 lei; ☺9am-midnight; ☎) Arguably the most upscale of Vama Veche's dining options, which means the picnic tables are a little cleaner than usual and the dining area is buffered from the beach by a stone wall. Open for breakfast for a quick omelette before the beach. It's near Str Ion Creangă.

Stuf   BEACH BAR
(Plaja Vama Veche; ☺9am-2am) This is the most likeable of several beachside drinking shacks with their signature thatched roofs and picnic tables. To find it, walk down the main drag, Str Ion Creangă, to the beach and turn left.

Molotov   BAR
(molotov_bar@yahoo.com; Str Falezei, Plaja Vama Veche; ☺10am-3am) This scruffily charming cocktail bar is one of the best places in town to sip your drink while you listen to the roar of the surf. It's located on the beach on the southern end of Vama Veche.

❶ Information

There's no tourist information office in Vama Veche, but it's small enough to negotiate on your own. The main street, Str Ion Creangă, which runs east from Hwy E87 to the beach, has everything you're likely to need, including a handy ATM (Str Ion Creangă) and a pharmacy (Str Ion Creangă).

❶ Getting There & Away

There are no trains to Vama Veche; instead take a maxitaxi from Constanţa (about 10 lei) or take a train to Mangalia and a maxi taxi from there (8km, 5 lei).

Understand Romania

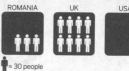

population per sq km

ROMANIA · UK · USA

≈ 30 people

Romania Today

EU Membership: Pros & Cons

After joining the European Union in 2007, Romania was told it could access up to €20 billion in aid until 2013 in order to catch up with more advanced fellow members. According to EU monitors much of that money has not been spent on the promised development programs and, five years after it joined the EU, Romania still has villages without electricity or running water, and a mere 300km of highway. Conversely, new EU regulations are also endangering classic aspects of Romanian life, such as free-range roaming of livestock and the selling of unpasteurised cheese by the roadside, but typically – like the 'no smoking' law, which has had little effect on the average Romanian who lights up pretty much all the time except during sleep – both still endure.

Pressure from the EU to address concerns such as pollution, corruption, destitute farmers and poor conditions for orphans has shown mixed results. Encouragingly at least, the number of children in public institutions has been significantly decreasing since foster-care facilities have been introduced, and many orphanages have been forced to close. Another plus, the presence of the EU stamp of approval has catapulted Romania to the top of consideration for European companies looking to relocate facilities in an effort to cut operating costs. Romania's abundance of multilingual, overeducated, underemployed college graduates make it a popular place for companies looking to outsource pan-European call centres. Employers can easily fill a telephone bank with agents that satisfactorily speak three languages (or more), with starting salaries as little as €300 per month.

> » Number of people bitten by stray dogs in Bucharest (2010): 8348

> » Average percentage of alcohol in Țuică (plum brandy), the national drink: 50%

> » EU country with the highest road mortality rate (2009): Romania

> » The average age a Romanian male/female marries is 31/27 years old.

Superstitions

» Don't sit at the corner of a table or you'll never marry.

» If your right hand itches, you're about to lose some money.

» If you spill your coffee, you're in for some good luck.

» If you spill your salt, you'll receive bad luck.

Social Faux Pas

» Don't sit down while a woman is standing up.

» Men shouldn't shake hands with gloves on.

» Don't accidentally imply Transylvania belongs to Hungary – you'll open a Pandora's box.

» Don't call someone in Romania after 10pm.

» Don't point at someone with your index finger.

» Don't enter someone's house with shoes or a hat on.

belief systems
(% of population)

86.8 Eastern Orthodox

7.5 Protestant

4.7 Roman Catholic

1 Other

if Romania were 100 people

89 would be Romanian
7 would be Hungarian
3 would be Roma
1 would be Other

Romanian Politics Today

To the international community it seemed like a spat between two overgrown boys. At a critical juncture in Romania's economy and recent accession to the EU, a row between its prime minister and president could not be more ill-timed. Victor Ponta promised his reign would usher in generational change, a final breakaway from the cloying legacy of communism. In December 2012 Ponta's Social Liberal Union (USL) won nearly 60% of the vote, while Băsescu's Right Romania Alliance (ARD) limped in second with about 17%. The result threatened to lead to a constitutional crisis; with President Basescu having previously hinted he might refuse to reappoint his arch-rival Ponta.

Since coming to office in May 2012, Ponta has issued two-dozen emergency decrees – among them dismissing the speakers of both chambers of parliament (considered by many as illegal) – greatly alarming Western diplomats. In another Machiavellian move the ombudsman was also conveniently dismissed, leaving a vacuum for someone to challenge legislation and granting Ponta free reign. Amid a sea of public distrust and impatience with politicians, Ponta was also accused of plagiarism in his doctoral thesis, a claim that was upheld by the University of Bucharest. Amid the confusion, a concerned Washington dispatched its envoy to Bucharest to hold immediate talks with the feuding politicians. Meanwhile Traian Băsescu has kept a very low profile since his near impeachment. The sparring continues, to the anger of most Romanians, who are desperate for their country to move forwards, and not backwards because of internecine squabbling.

» Population:
21.8 million

» Area: 238,391 sq km

» GDP growth (2011): 2.5%

» Inflation rate (2011): 3.4%

» Official unemployment rate (2012): 7.5%

» Average monthly salary (2012): 1296 lei (€340)

Top Books

Along the Enchanted Way (William Blacker) Looks at life among the Roma and peasants, through an English traveller's eye.

The Historian (Elizabeth Kostova) Brilliantly reanimates the Dracula myth focusing on Vlad Țepeș.

Best Films

4 Months, 3 Weeks & 2 Days (Cristian Mungiu) Moving drama about an illegal abortion in 1980s Romania.

Filantopica (Nae Caranfil) Dark comedy about an impoverished writer who learns to create an alternative income.

California Dreamin' (Cristian Nemescu) Gentle comedy about NATO soldiers stuck in Romania.

History

Often referred to as 'Europe's great survivor', this melting pot of Romanians, Hungarians, Germans and Roma has been constantly invaded and occupied throughout its existence. The name 'Romania' didn't refer to Wallachia or Moldavia until 1859 and, in fact, Transylvania remained part of the Austro-Hungarian empire until 1918 – even 'Dracula' (Vlad Țepeș) was actually a Magyar (Hungarian) – so what is 'Romania'? Understanding its ancient past and the surrounding empires and countries who influenced it is probably the best way to get a grip on this fascinating enigma.

Roman Dacia

Ancient Romania was inhabited by Thracian tribes. From the 7th century BC the Greeks established trading colonies along the Black Sea at Callatis (Mangalia), Tomis (Constanța) and Histria. In the 1st century BC, a strong Dacian state was established by King Burebista to counter the Roman threat. The last Dacian king, Decebal (r AD 87–106), consolidated this state but was unable to stave off attacks led by the Roman emperor Trajan between AD 101 and 102, and Dacia became a province of the Roman Empire.

The slave-owning Romans mixed with the conquered tribes to form a Daco-Roman people who spoke Latin. The reflected glory of Rome was short-lived when, after increasing Goth attacks in AD 271, Emperor Aurelian (r 270–75) decided to withdraw the Roman legions south of the Danube, meaning Rome governed here for fewer than 175 years. Romanised peasants remained in Dacia and mixed with the locals; hence the Roman heritage of contemporary Romanians. To this day, machismo-driven Romanian men are fiercely proud of this short yet formative chapter in their country's history.

TIMELINE

650 BC

Dacians are first recorded in the area of present-day Transylvania from their trade with Greeks, who established colonies at Callatis, Tomis (now Constanța) and Histria.

AD 106

Dacia becomes a Roman province for 175 years, until Goth attacks (AD 271) force Emperor Aurelian to withdraw Roman legions south of the Danube.

896

Magyars settle in the Carpathian Basin integrating Transylvania into Hungary.

Medieval Principalities

Waves of migrating peoples, including the Goths, Huns, Avars, Slavs, Bulgars and Magyars, swept across this territory from the 4th to the 10th centuries, each one leaving its mark on the local culture, language and gene pool. By the 10th century, a fragmented feudal system ruled by a military class appeared. From then on the Magyars expanded into Transylvania, and by the 13th century it had become an autonomous principality under the Hungarian crown. Following devastating Tartar raids on Transylvania in 1241 and 1242, King Bela IV of Hungary persuaded German Saxons to settle in Transylvania with free land and tax incentives. He also granted the Székelys – a Hungarian ethnic group who had earlier migrated to the region with the Magyars – autonomy in return for their military support.

In the 14th century, Prince Basarab I (r 1310–52) united various political formations in the region south of the Carpathians to create the first Romanian principality – Wallachia, dubbed Ţara Românească (Romanian Land). Its indigenous peasantry became known as Vlachs. Peasants dominated the populations of these medieval principalities. In Wallachia and Moldavia peasants were subjugated as serfs to the landed aristocracy (Boyars), a hereditary class. There were some free land-owning peasants (moşneni) too. The two principalities were ruled by a prince who was also the military leader. Most noblemen were Hungarian; the peasants were Romanians. After a 1437 peasant uprising in Transylvania, Magyar nobles formed a political alliance with the Székely and Saxon leaders.

The name 'Romania' supposedly comes from Romanus (Latin for 'Roman') but others argue it's also from rumân (dependent peasant).

Ottoman Expansion

Throughout the 14th and 15th centuries Wallachia and Moldavia offered strong resistance against the Ottoman's northward expansion. Mircea cel Bătrân (Mircea the Old; r 1386–1418), Vlad Ţepeş ('The Impaler'; r 1448, 1456–62, 1476) and Ştefan cel Mare (Stephen the Great; r 1457–1504) were legendary figures in this struggle. When the Turks conquered Hungary in the 16th century, Transylvania became a vassal of the Ottoman Empire, retaining its autonomy by paying tribute to the sultan, as did Wallachia and Moldavia. In 1600 these three principalities were briefly united at Alba Iulia under the leadership of Mihai Viteazul (Michael the Brave; r 1593–1601), who shortly after was defeated by a joint Habsburg-Transylvanian noble army and beheaded.

Following the defeat of the Turks, in 1687 Transylvania came under Habsburg rule. The 18th century marked the start of the Transylvanian Romanians' fight for political emancipation. Romanian peasants constituted 60% of the population, yet continued to be excluded from political life. In 1784 three serfs called Horea, Cloşca and Crişan led a major uprising.

AD 1000	1241	14th century	1431
Byzantine, Slavic, Hungarian and Oriental records first mention the existence of Romanians under the name of Vlachs.	After the Mongols invade Transylvania, King Bela IV of Hungary offers free land to entice German Saxons to Transylvania, fortifying defence.	Prince Basarab I creates the first Romanian principality – Wallachia. The region is known as Ţara Românească (Romanian Land).	Vlad Ţepeş (Vlad the Impaler) is born. He grows a handlebar moustache then spends much of his cumulative eight years in power terrorising and slaughtering invading Turks.

WALLACHIA UNDER VLAD THE IMPALER

If you were a Boyar (nobleman), Saxon merchant, unchaste woman or Turk during the time of Vlad Ţepeş (r 1448, 1456–1462 and 1476), your life was in the balance. Throughout his reign Vlad finessed his torture methods – which included flaying, strangulation, burning, blinding and amputation – to a frightening degree. Legend has it, that as a test of respect to him, a gold cup could be placed in any town square; and while anyone could drink freely of its contents, the cup had to remain. Not surprisingly, it never strayed.

In 1462 the famous 'Forest of the Impaled' incident occurred, which immortalised Vlad's infamy in history books. In a daring bid to drive out Turkish invaders from the Danube River valley, Vlad burnt the crops and poisoned the wells, while his soldiers, disguised as Turks, sneaked into their camp to surprise them. To add gore to injury, when the Turkish sultan marched on Ţepeş' city, Târgovişte, he discovered 20,000 of his men impaled outside the city walls in a forest of flesh. The wooden stakes were driven through the victims' anuses, emerging from the body just below the shoulder, in such a way as not to pierce any vital organs. This ensured at least 48 hours of unimaginable suffering before death.

Tellingly, it transpires that many of Vlad's youthful years were spent in a Turkish prison, where he was allegedly raped by members of the Turkish court. Revenge? For an individual soaked in others' blood, it seems fitting he himself was beheaded in 1462, his head preserved in honey and taken to the sultan in Constantinople.

Their death wasn't without some success, for in 1785 the Habsburg emperor, Joseph II, abolished serfdom in Transylvania. The 17th century in Wallachia, under the reign of Constantin Brâncoveanu (r 1688–1714), brought a period of prosperity characterised by a cultural and artistic renaissance. In 1775 part of Moldavia's northern territory – Bucovina – was annexed by Austria-Hungary. This was followed in 1812 by the loss of its eastern territory – Bessarabia (most of which is in present-day Moldova) – to Russia. After the Russo-Turkish War of 1828–29, Wallachia and Moldavia became Russian protectorates while remaining in the Ottoman Empire.

Romanians are proud, proud, proud that the Turks never completely conquered their land, but – in quiet tones – some admit that Bucharest wasn't even on the way between Constantinople and the Ottomans' main goal, Vienna.

One State

The revolutionary spirit that gripped much of Europe in the years leading up to 1848 was entangled with the Hungarian revolution in Transylvania, led by Hungarian poet Sándor Petőfi. Romanian revolutionaries demanded their political emancipation, equality and the abolition of serfdom. The Austrian authorities struck a deal with Transylvania's Romanians, promising them national recognition in return for joining forces with them against the Hungarian revolutionaries in Transylvania. Thus Transylva-

1437
After a 1437 peasant uprising in Transylvania, Magyar nobles form a political alliance with Székely and Saxon leaders, dubbed the Union of the Three Nations.

1453
The fall of Constantinople. The Ottomans block trade on the Black Sea, deepening Romania's isolation.

1467
Stephen the Great (Ştefan cel Mare) defeats the Hungarian army (Hungary's last attempt to conquer Moldavia), then defeats Tartar forces at Lipnic and finally invades Wallachia (1471) to repel the Ottomans.

GETTY IMAGES ©

» Vlad Ţepeş

nian Romanians fought against and enacted revenge upon Transylvanian Hungarians for what was seen as centuries of mistreatment. Russian intervention finally quashed the Hungarian revolutionaries, ending a revolution that had shocked all sides by its escalation to civil war.

In the aftermath, the region fell under the direct rule of Austria-Hungary from Budapest. Ruthless 'Magyarisation' followed: Hungarian was established as the official language and any Romanians who dared oppose the regime were severely punished. By contrast Wallachia and Moldavia prospered. In 1859, with French support, Alexandru Ioan Cuza was elected to the thrones of Moldavia and Wallachia, which created a national state known as the United Romanian Principalities on 11 December 1861. This was renamed Romania in 1862.

The reform-minded Cuza was forced to abdicate in 1866 by mutinous army officers, and his place was taken by the Prussian prince Carol I. With Russian assistance, Romania declared independence from the Ottoman Empire in 1877. In 1881 it was declared a kingdom and on 22 May 1881 Carol I was crowned the first king of Romania.

WWI & Greater Romania

Through shrewd political manoeuvring, Romania greatly benefited from WWI. Despite having formed a secret alliance with Austria-Hungary in 1883, it began WWI with neutrality. In 1916 the government, under pressure from the Western allies, declared war on Austria-Hungary, with the ultimate prize being to annex Transylvania from Austria-Hungary. The defeat of Austria-Hungary in 1918 paved the way for the formation of modern Romania. Bessarabia, the area east of the Prut River that had been part of Moldavia until 1812 when it was taken by the Russians, was joined to Romania. Likewise, Bucovina, which had been in Austro-Hungarian hands since 1775, was also reunited with Romania. Part of the Austro-Hungarian Banat, which had been incorporated in Romania, was also handed over. Furthermore, Transylvania was finally united with Romania. Hence, at the end of WWI, Romania – now known as Greater Romania – more than *doubled* its territory (from 120,000 to 295,000 sq km) and its population (from 7.5 to 16 million). The acquisition of this new territory was ratified by the Triple Entente powers in 1920 under the Treaty of Trianon.

On 8 January 1923, George Enescu makes his American debut as a conductor at Carnegie Hall in New York City.

Carol II & The Iron Guard

In the years leading up to WWII, Romania sought an alliance with France and Britain, and joined Yugoslavia and Czechoslovakia in the Little Entente. Romania also signed a Balkan Pact with Yugoslavia, Turkey and Greece, and later established diplomatic relations with the USSR. These efforts were weakened by the Western powers' appease-

16th century	1600	1606	1683
The Turks conquer Hungary, and Transylvania becomes a vassal of the Ottoman Empire.	Wallachia, Transylvania and Moldavia are united for 15 months under Mihai Viteazul.	The Treaty of Vienna gives religious and constitutional rights to Hungarian-speaking Transylvanians but none to Romanian-speaking people.	The Ottomans' siege of Vienna ends in the defeat of the Turks; then the Habsburg empire moves in to take control of Transylvania.

ment of Hitler and by Romania's own King Carol II, who succeeded his father Ferdinand I to the throne. Extreme right-wing parties opposed to a democratic regime emerged, notably the anti-Semitic League of the National Christian Defence, which consequently gave birth to the Legion of the Archangel Michael in 1927. This notorious breakaway faction, better known as the fascist Iron Guard, was led by Corneliu Codreanu, and by 1935 it dominated the political scene.

Finding himself unable to manipulate the political parties, Carol II declared a royal dictatorship in February 1938. All political parties were dissolved and laws were passed to halve the size of the electorate. Between 1939 and 1940 alone, Romania had no fewer than nine different governments. In 1939 Carol II clamped down on the Iron Guard, which he had supported until 1937. Codreanu and 13 other legionaries were arrested, sentenced to 10 years' imprisonment and then assassinated. In revenge for their leader's death, Iron Guard members murdered Carol II's prime minister, Armand Călinescu, leading to the butchering of 252 Iron Guard members by Carol II's forces. In accordance with the king's wishes, the corpses were strung up in public squares. Only with the collapse of the Axis powers at the end of WWII did the Iron Guard disintegrate (in 1999 Codreanu's nephew, Nicador Zelea Codreanu, tried unsuccessfully to revive the reviled group).

Romania was isolated after the fall of France in May 1940, and in June 1940 Greater Romania collapsed in accordance with the Molotov–Ribbentrop Pact. The USSR re-occupied Bessarabia. On 30 August 1940 Romania was forced to cede northern Transylvania to Hungary by order of Nazi Germany and fascist Italy. In September 1940 Southern Dobrogea was given to Bulgaria. Not surprisingly, the loss of territories sparked widespread popular demonstrations. Even Carol II realised he could not quash the increasing mass hysteria, and on the advice of one of his councillors, the king called in General Marshall Ion Antonescu. To defend the interests of the ruling classes, Antonescu forced King Carol II to abdicate in favour of the king's 19-year-old son Michael. Antonescu then imposed a fascist dictatorship, with himself as *conducător* (supreme leader).

Romanian–Nazi Alliance

German troops were allowed to enter Romania in October 1940, and in June 1941 Antonescu joined Hitler's anti-Soviet war. The results of this Romanian–Nazi alliance were gruesome, with over 200,000 Romanian Jews – mainly from newly regained Bessarabia – and 40,000 Roma deported to transit camps in Transdniestr and later murdered. After the war, Antonescu was turned over to the Soviet authorities who condemned him to death in a show trial.

Fifty years after his death, Carol II's remains were transferred back to Romania from Portugal, where he died. He was interred in Curtea de Argeş.

On Clowns (1993) is a cutting rant on Romanian dictatorship by Jewish Romanian writer Norman Manea (b 1936), who was deported to the Transdniestr concentration camp in 1941 when he was only five years old.

1784	1812	1819–34	1864
A peasant uprising results in Habsburg emperor, Joseph II, abolishing serfdom in Transylvania the following year.	Treaty of Bucharest, signed at the conclusion of the Russo-Turkish War, grants Russia control of eastern Moldavia, and the Ottoman Empire gains control of western Moldavia.	Wallachia and Moldavia are occupied by Russia.	In retaliation, after Romanian Jews refuse to provide financial support, Alexandru Ioan Cuza inserts a clause to deny suffrage to all non-Christians in his draft of a constitution. Jews are forbidden to practice law.

As the war went badly and the Soviet army approached Romania's borders, on 23 August 1944 an opportunistic Romania suddenly changed sides again by capturing the 53,159 German soldiers stationed in Romania and declaring war on Nazi Germany. By this dramatic act, Romania salvaged its independence and shortened the war. By 25 October the Romanian and Soviet armies had driven the Hungarian and German forces from Transylvania, replacing the valued territory back under Romanian control. And the cost? About 500,000 Romanian soldiers died fighting for the Axis powers, and another 170,000 died after Romania joined the Allies.

Romanian People's Republic

Of all the countries that burst forward into the mass-industrialised, communist experiment in the 20th century, Romania and Russia were the least prepared, both being overwhelmingly rural, agricultural countries. Prior to 1945, Romania's Communist Party had no more than 1000 members. Its postwar ascendancy, which saw membership soar to 710,000 by 1947, was a consequence of backing from Moscow. The Soviet-engineered return of Transylvania greatly enhanced the prestige of the left-wing parties, which won the parliamentary elections in November 1946. A year later, Prime Minister Petru Groza forced King Michael to abdicate (allegedly by holding the queen mother at gunpoint), the monarchy was abolished and a Romanian People's Republic was proclaimed. Then 1948 saw a shift to collectivisation; the process by which industry was redesigned as a state farm, and villagers were ripped from their ancestral land and forced to live in dehumanising city high-rises.

A period of terror ensued in which all the prewar leaders, prominent intellectuals and suspected dissidents were imprisoned or interned in hard-labour camps. The most notorious prisons were in Piteşti, Gherla, Sighetu Marmaţiei and Aiud. Factories and businesses were nationalised, and in 1953 a new Slavicised orthography was introduced to obliterate all Latin roots of the Romanian language, while street and town names were changed to honour Soviet figures. Braşov was renamed Oraşul Stalin. Romania's loyalty to Moscow continued until Soviet troops withdrew in 1958, and after 1960 the country adopted an independent foreign policy under two 'national' communist leaders, Gheorghe Gheorghiu-Dej (leader from 1952 to 1965) and his protégé Nicolae Ceauşescu (leader from 1965 to 1989). By 1962 the communist state controlled 77% of Romania's land.

Ceauşescu refused to assist the Soviets in their 1968 'intervention' in Czechoslovakia, his public condemnation earning him more than US$1 billion in US-backed credits in the decade that followed. And when Romania condemned the Soviet invasion in Afghanistan and participated

HISTORY

The US Holocaust Memorial Museum paints a harrowing portrait of anti-Semitic horror in Romania during WWII, chronicling how the state used various brutal methods – aside from organised murder – to rid itself of Roma and Jews.

1881

Prince since 1866, Carol I is crowned the first king of Romania.

1897

Bram Stoker's *Dracula* is published.

JONATHAN SMITH / GETTY IMAGES ©

» Statue of King Carol I, Peleş Castle (p73)

in the 1984 Los Angeles Olympic Games despite a Soviet-bloc boycott, Ceauşescu was officially decorated by Great Britain's Queen Elizabeth II.

Ceauşescu and The Grand Delusion

It's all but impossible for us to fully appreciate how hard life became under the megalomaniacal 25-year dictatorship of Nicolae Ceauşescu and his wife, Elena. Political freedom was *verboten*, as was freedom of the media (ownership of a typewriter could be punishable by death). TV and radio programs entirely revolved around the personality cult of their venerable leader; the brainwashing of the population even stretched its tentacles into schools. In the 1980s in his attempts to eliminate a $10 billion foreign debt and impress the world, Ceauşescu exported Romania's food while his own people were forced to ration even staple goods. Unless you were a high-ranking member of the Communist Party you had to queue for two hours for basics such as milk and potatoes, returning to a house where electricity was turned off to save energy.

Along with bugged phones and recorded conversations there were strict curfews. Few of the dictator's sinister schemes were more frightening than the pro-birth campaign, designed to increase the working population from 23 to 30 million. In 1966 it was decreed: 'The fetus is the property of the entire society...' A celibacy tax was charged on offenders with up to 10% of their monthly wages docked until they had children. Romania's birth rate predictably swelled, with the country's infant-mortality rate soaring to 83 deaths in every 1000 births. Women under the age of 45 were rounded up at their workplaces and examined for signs of pregnancy (in the presence of government agents – dubbed the 'menstrual police'). Many fled to Hungary, leaving a legacy of millions of hungry orphans – many with serious developmental problems – to the outrage of the international community when the story broke in 1990.

The Securitate (Secret Police) was Ceauşescu's chief instrument and it ruled with an iron hand, proliferating paranoia and fear, delivering torture and threatening to place people on its infamous 'blacklist'. Estimates suggest that as many as one person in 30 had been recruited as a Securitate by the 1980s – many Romanians couldn't trust their own families for fear of them being informers. Worse still, many of them were children. In March 1987 Ceauşescu embarked on 'Systematisation', a rural urbanisation program that would see the total destruction of 8000 villages (mainly in Transylvania) and the resettlement of their (mainly Hungarian) inhabitants into ugly apartment blocks.

The 1989 Revolution

In late 1989, as the world watched the collapse of one communist regime after another, it seemed only a matter of time before Romania's turn would

For an in-depth look at Romania since communism, check out Tom Gallagher's *Modern Romania: The End of Communism, the Failure of Democratic Reform, and the Theft of a Nation* (2005).

1916	February 1938	1940	1944
Romania relinquishes its WWI neutrality and declares war on Austria-Hungary in order to annexe Transylvania.	King Carol II declares a royal dictatorship. All political parties are dissolved.	Romania is forced to cede northern Transylvania to Hungary by order of Nazi Germany.	Following secret talks between Stalin, Churchill and Roosevelt, the Soviet Union gains a 90% share of 'influence' in Romania.

come. The Romanian revolution was carried out with Latin passion and intensity – of all the Soviet bloc countries, only Romania experienced a government transfer that ended with a dead leader. The spark that ignited Romania occurred on 15 December 1989 when Father László Tökés publicly condemned the dictator from his Hungarian church in Timişoara, prompting the Reformed Church of Romania to remove him from his post. Police attempts to arrest demonstrating parishioners failed and within days the unrest had spread across the city, leading to some 115 deaths. Ceauşescu proclaimed martial law in Timiş County and dispatched trainloads of troops to crush the rebellion. The turning point came on 19 December when the army in Timişoara went over to the side of the demonstrators.

On 21 December in Bucharest an address made by Ceauşescu during a mass rally was interrupted by anti-Ceauşescu demonstrators in the 100,000-strong crowd who booed the dictator and shouted 'murderer'. The demonstrators retreated to the wide boulevard between Piaţa Universităţii and Piaţa Romană – only to be crushed a couple of hours later by police gunfire and armoured cars. Drenched by ice-cold water from fire hoses, they refused to submit, erecting barricades under the eyes of Western journalists in the adjacent Hotel Inter-Continental. At 11pm the police began their assault, using a tank to smash through the barricades, and by dawn the square had been cleared of debris and the corpses of insurgents. Estimates vary, but at least 1033 were killed.

The following morning thousands more demonstrators took to the streets, and a state of emergency was announced. At noon Ceauşescu reappeared on the balcony of the Central Committee building to try to speak again, only to be forced to flee by helicopter from the roof of the building. Ceauşescu and his wife, Elena, were arrested near Târgovişte and taken to a military base there. On 25 December, they were condemned by an anonymous court and executed by a firing squad. Footage of the Ceauşescu family's luxury apartments broadcast on TV showed pure-gold food scales in the kitchen and rows of diamond-studded shoes in Elena's bedroom.

While these events had all the earmarks of a people's revolution, many scholars have advanced the notion that they were just as much the result of a coup d'état: the Communist Party, tired of having to bow down to Ceauşescu, had been planning an overthrow for months. Communist bystanders quickly came to power following Ceauşescu's fall, calling themselves the 'National Salvation Front'. Not until 2004 did Romania have a president who was not a former high-ranking communist.

Following spats between Băsescu and Ponta, the EU postponed Romania's bid to join the European Union's coveted visa-free zone, scheduled for September 2012.

Attempts at Democracy

The National Salvation Front (FSN) took immediate control of the country. In May 1990 it won the country's first democratic elections since

1947	1968	1976	1989
The monarchy is abolished and a Romanian People's Republic is proclaimed.	Nicolae Ceauşescu's public condemnation of the soviet 'intervention' in Czechoslovakia is lauded by the West, which rewards him with economic aid.	Fourteen-year-old Nadia Comăneci wins three gold medals and scores a perfect '10' at the Montreal Summer Olympics, the first '10' awarded in modern Olympic gymnastics history.	After 25 years in power, Nicolae Ceauşescu and his wife Elena are executed on Christmas Day in Târgovişte.

Best Places to Catch the Ghost of Vlad Ţepeş

» Head to his birthplace in Sighişoara and have a coffee outside his house.

» Imprison yourself for an hour in Bran Castle where the bloodthirsty Ţepeş was interned.

» Climb up to ghostly Poienari Citadel, Vlad's stronghold, en route to the Transfăgărăşan Road.

» In Târgovişte, where Vlad had 20,000 Turks impaled.

1946, placing Ion Iliescu, a Communist Party member since the age of 14, at the helm as president. Protests ensued, but Iliescu sent in 20,000 coal miners to violently quash them. Iliescu was nonetheless re-elected in 1992 as the head of a coalition government under the banner of the Party of Social Democracy. New name, same policies. Market reforms remained nowhere in sight. In 1993 subsidies on food, transportation and energy were scrapped, prompting prices to fly sky-high and employment to plummet to an all-time low.

Iliescu was finally ousted in the 1996 presidential elections by an impoverished populace, who ushered in Emil Constantinescu, leader of the right-of-centre election alliance Democratic Convention of Romania (CDR), as president. Constantinescu's reform-minded government made entry into NATO and the European Union (EU) its stated priorities, together with fast-paced structural economic reform, the fight against corruption and improved relations with Romania's neighbours, especially Hungary.

Scandal and corruption surrounded the November 2000 electoral race. In May of that year the National Fund for Investment (NFI) collapsed. Thousands of investors – mainly pensioners who'd deposited their life savings into the government fund – took to the streets to demand their cash back (US$47.4 million, long squandered by the NFI).

After Constantinescu refused to run in the 2000 'Mafia-style' elections, Iliescu retook the helm as the country's president and his Social Democrat Party (PSD) formed a minority government, with Adrian Nastase as prime minister. The 2004 elections were marred by accusations of electoral fraud, and there were two rounds of voting before Traian Băsescu was announced the winner, with 51% of the votes. The PNL (National Liberal Party) leader, Călin Popescu Tăriceanu, became prime minister and swore in a new coalition that excluded the PSD.

The government's main goal, aside from addressing the many domestic issues, was integration with international bodies, most notably the EU. In 2002 Romania was invited to join NATO. Romania (and Bulgaria) finally joined the EU in 2007, their membership having been delayed by Romania's record of organised crime, corruption and food safety. The EU has been a big supporter of Romania's EU cause, with Brussels granting billions of euros to infrastructure, business development, environmental protection and social services. In 2009, though minor progress had been noted, it was reproached for lack of momentum.

Băsescu re-nominated Emil Boc as prime minister in December 2009, following which a coalition government of the centre-right Democrat Liberals and UDMR was formed. Boc resigned in 2012 following street protests and increasing pressure from the Opposition to call early elections. He was followed briefly by Mihai Razvan Ungureanu, and later

1990

The National Salvation Front, led by Communist Party member Ion Iliescu, wins the first democratic elections held in Romania since 1946. Protests follow but are violently quashed.

1993

The government removes its subsidies on food, transport and energy causing prices to skyrocket and employment figures to fall to an all-time low.

1994

Eugène Ionesco (b 1909), the celebrated Romanian playwright, dies. Ionesco was half French and didn't write his first play until his late thirties.

PHOTO RESEARCHERS / GETTY IMAGES ©

» Eugène Ionesco

trounced by Victor Ponta, leader of the Social Democratic Party, who formed a coalition with National Liberal Party.

Battle of The Titans

In July 2012 President Băsescu was accused by newly installed Prime Minister Victor Ponta of breaching the constitution – among his assertions Ponta accused him of pressuring prosecutors in legal cases, and using his reach with the secret service – and parliament voted to suspend him. Băsescu in turn accused Ponta of engineering a coup d'état. The attempt to oust him might have failed, but the upshot of this bitter spat has had toxic ripples that are still being felt at the time of research.

The Securitate was finally abolished in late 1989, after Ceauşescu was ousted, leaving behind a damaging footprint of paranoia and mistrust that is still not entirely gone from the Romanian psyche today.

HISTORY

1997	**2004**	**2007**	**2012**
The number of stray dogs in Bucharest reaches between 150,000 and 200,000 – twice as many as New York City, which is three times larger. The Associated Press reports that they bite 50 people per day.	Romania joins NATO, a major step in guaranteeing security, external stability and eventual EU membership.	On 1 January, Romania and Bulgaria become the 26th and 27th members of the European Union.	Parliament, urged by new prime minister, Victor Ponta, votes to impeach Traian Băsescu as president of Romania.

The Dracula Myth

Love it or loathe it, visit Romania and you can't ignore the omnipresence of Dracula; from mugs to T-shirts, and bat and blood-themed menus to vampire-costumed waiters. But what's really chilling is that a blueprint for the pale, shape-shifting count we were reared on in horror films actually existed – though not in a black cape and cloud of fog, rather as a Wallachian warrior king with a predilection for extreme cruelty. In equal measure to a face of fangs staring back at you at every turn, you'll also see the moustached visage of Vlad Ţepeş (later known as Vlad the Impaler).

The Impaler

Fifteenth-century prince Vlad Ţepeş is often credited with being Dracula, the vampire-count featured in the classic Gothic horror story *Dracula* (1897). His princely father, Vlad III, was called Vlad Dracul. Dracul(a) actually means 'son of the house of Dracul', which itself translates as 'devil' or 'dragon'. Add to this diabolical moniker the fact that Vlad used to impale his victims – from which you get his other surname: Ţepeş (Impaler) – and it's easy to see why Dracula's creator, Irishman Bram Stoker, tapped into his bloodline. Even though Romanian shops are quick to bunch merchandise of the 19th-century vampire and 15th-century leader together, Vlad Ţepeş is still a much respected figure in Romania today; a symbol of independence and resistance, for his stand against the Ottoman empire.

Legend has it that Ţepeş was born in 1431 opposite the clock tower in Sighişoara, and at the age of 17 he ascended to the throne of Wallachia. In 1459 his first act of murderous renown was against the Boyars of Târgovişte for the murder of his father and brother. The older among the Boyars were brutally impaled on spikes while the remainder were frogmarched 80km to Poienari where they were ordered to build an 850m-high fortress guarding the pass. You can still visit the ruins today via 1500 steps.

The Vampire

Bram Stoker's literary Dracula, by contrast, was a bloodsucking vampire – an undead corpse reliant on the blood of the living to sustain his own immortality. But who would have thought this oftentimes hyperbole-blown epistolary-style yarn about a lawyer visiting a megalomaniac aristocrat would almost single-handedly spawn a literary genre? Forget your *Vampire Chronicles* and *Twilight* series, because arguably neither would have been written without *Dracula*. And Victorian dramatics aside, this late-19th-century Gothic epic is a master-class in thriller writing, and so beautifully crafted in places it leaves an indelible impression on the

Best Dracula Films

» *Bram Stoker's Dracula* (Francis Ford Coppola, 1992)

» *Nosferatu the Vampyre* (Werner Herzog, 1979)

» *Horror of Dracula* (Terence Fisher, 1958)

Stoker undoubtedly read Emily de Laszowska Gerard's *Transylvanian Superstitions*, detailing how to kill vampires.

More than 200 films have been made featuring the character Dracula. The first movie, *Dracula*, was released n 1931 and starred Hungarian actor, Bela Lugosi.

IN THE FOOTSTEPS OF DRACULA

For diehard *Dracula* fans, the good news is that the Transylvania chapters of the book are rooted in pure geographical fact, so you can actually see the places visited by its hero, Jonathan Harker. Despite visiting much of the world in his capacity as actor Henry Irving's manager, Irish-born Bram Stoker never actually set foot in Eastern Europe. Instead, he relied on exhaustive research from afar. Follow this itinerary to squeeze as many drops from both legends.

To catch the trail of the real Dracula, head to the remote Poienari Citadel on the Transylvania–Wallachia border where the Impaler's wife committed suicide. Not far from Brasov – where he also had people impaled – is Bran Castle, where Țepeș was briefly imprisoned. The pretty Saxon citadel of Sighişoara may look to be straight out of a fairytale, but it's also the birthplace of Vlad the Impaler. Visit the spooky Casa Dracula (p100) restaurant for lunch.

Next follow Jonathan Harker's footsteps to northern Transylvania's Bistriţa – known in the book as Bistritz – the medieval town he visited on the eve of St George's Day where locals pleaded with him to turn back from his destination at Castle Dracula. From here it's a short drive up the lonely, forested Tihuţa Pass (which in the book is described as the Borgo Pass). Perched on top of the pass, in exactly the spot Harker described the castle as being, is the Hotel Castle Dracula (p145). This hotel is loosely Gothic with blood-red carpets and stuffed animals in reception (not forgetting its occasional heart-attack-inducing crypt). The real reason to come, however, is the view. The rest is up to your imagination!

reader's mind; none more so than the eerie passages following Harker's journey and imprisonment in Transylvania.

Countless films have loosely followed its storyline, and the novel has never been out of print.

Writer's Block

While he might have hit on the idea of writing a vampire story, initially Stoker couldn't think of where to locate it. He was also lost for a name for his bloodthirsty nobleman. But then he found a book on Vlad Dracula in Whitby Library whilst on holiday, and met a Hungarian who told him at length about Transylvania (meaning 'the land beyond the forests'), and suddenly his story slotted together. It was only then that Stoker immersed himself in the Reading Room at the British Museum Library, swotting up on everything from geography to Romanian folklore and the mythology of vampires.

In the 1980s the original manuscript of *Dracula* was found in a barn in northwestern Pennsylvania.

Outdoor Activities & Wildlife

The Land

When the gods were doling out unspoilt wildernesses they seem to have been extra generous with Romania; covering 237,500 sq km this oval-shaped country offers a panorama of mountains, pristine forests, lakes and rolling meadows unparallelled in the rest of Europe. And thanks to traditional methods of farming, incursions into the habitats of wild animals have been relatively low. In fact it's the other way around if you speak to shepherds bemoaning dogs and sheep lost to wolves, or donkeys feasted upon by the country's healthy population of brown bears.

Increasingly, travellers on the hunt for isolated locations abundant with nature and wildlife are coming to Romania. It's also a great time for ecotourism, with an association of 30 companies with green credentials under the umbrella of Discover Eco-Romania (www.eco-romania.ro). Be it birdwatching in the Danube Delta, wolf tracking in the Carpathians, musical visits to Roma camps, crouching in a hide watching brown bears, or mountain climbing and hiking with a reliable guide, you should find what you need in the way of expertise and information.

Following is a list of some of the activities you can do in Romania, and where and how to go about doing them.

> The proportion of forested land in Romania is 26.3%. Within these dark spaces, according to the Romanian General Association of Hunters and Anglers, lurk around 4000 wolves.

Hiking

Transylvania, Moldavia, Crişana and Maramures boast breathtaking landscapes to warrant strapping on a pair of walking boots. A sense of

---

A WORD FROM A PRO

Dan Marin, Best Guide of the Year 2007, *Wanderlust* magazine, shares his favourite treks in Romania.

The Carpathian Mountains are one of Europe's great wonders. Where can you still go tracking wolves, bears and lynx and see 50 species of wild orchids blooming, while crossing some of the best-preserved old forests and alpine meadows in Europe?

For trekking, I recommend Piatra Craiului National Park near Braşov. Short of time and not the eight-hours-a-day-hiker type? Go up to the shepherds' villages of Măgura and Peştera for some of the most beautiful countryside in Romania, and then down to the spectacular Zărneşti Gorges. Not in a rush and pretty fit? Cross the same gorges on the way up to Cabana Curmătura and then to the main ridge (for many Romanians the greatest walk in the country) or to the secondary ridge (Piatra Mică).

adventure and a decent map are all you need to get you started in Romania as there are well-marked trails in most parts of the Carpathian Mountains, and cabanas (huts or chalets) dotted throughout the ranges catering to the weary trekker. If you want to really discover and understand the area, its history, culture, traditions, wildlife and nature, then local guides are recommended; they can take you to places no other tourists go, find tracks of wild animals, and tell you about villagers' use of local plants in traditional cooking, medicine and even folk magic. There are some very solid guides and tours working out of Braşov and Cluj-Napoca. Some youth hostels (like the Retro Hostel, p136, in Cluj-Napoca) offer fun guided excursions too. Another credible source of guides can be found at www.alpineguide.ro.

If you're looking for cultural, wildlife-immersive treks, again check out Discover Eco-Romania for a list of eco-approved guides.

WHERE TO HIKE

The Carpathians (aka Transylvanian Alps) offer endless opportunities for hikers, the most popular areas being the Bucegi and Făgăraş ranges, south and west of Braşov. The Bucegi has a flat top plateau that can be reached by cable cars from Sinaia. Well known for their karst formations and underground caves, the Apuseni Mountains, southwest of Cluj-Napoca are at last on the adventurer's radar. Other zones include the Retezat National Park, Romania's first national park, which lies northwest of Târgu Jiu and south of Deva in Transylvania; around Păltiniş, south of Sibiu; and, in Romania's Moldavian region, the less-visited Rarău and Ceahlău mountains near the Bicaz Gorges.

Skiing & Snowboarding

Romania is finally on the winter adrenalin map, with boarders and skiers fed up with remortgaging to pay for a vodka–Red Bull heading out here for bargain accommodation, powder snow and uncluttered slopes. Recent investments have also seen many of the country's resorts getting state-of-the-art gondolas and new pistes added. Beginner, intermediate and expert slopes are marked as blue, red and black, respectively. The ski season runs generally from December to March, with some slopes opening by mid-November and staying open into April.

WHERE TO SKI

The most popular places are reached as day trips from Braşov. Meanwhile, Sinaia in the Prahova Valley offers scope to the experienced skier with wide bowls at its summit that funnel to gullies and half-pipes. Poiana Braşov – recently voted one of Europe's best-value resorts – is more of a beginner/intermediate option and is a 20-minute bus ride west of

The proportion of agricultural land in Romania is up to 60%. One third of Romania is constituted by mountains, another third hills and plateaus, while the remainder is plains.

SURVIVAL TIPS IN THE CARPATHIANS

Eco specialists Carpathian Nature Tours (www.cntours.eu), who operate trips to a bear hide, share a few common-sense tips to keep you safe:

» Stay on marked trails – especially in national parks.

» Have a decent map with you, and don't end up trekking in the dark (most decent maps detail walk durations on their reverse).

» Always wear sturdy shoes and make sure you're carrying enough water.

» Carry the telephone number of Salvamont (p244), the emergency rescue service, and check the weather forecast before setting out.

» Never attempt a difficult trail alone.

Braşov. Also nearby is the ski resort Predeal. And south of Sibiu, you can find smaller lifts at pretty Păltiniș.

Outside Transylvania, there are some fun smaller ski hills in Maramureş, at Izvoare and Borsa, though the latter has no rentals. The south side of the Apuseni Mountains has a couple of ski hills at Stâna de Vale and Gârda de Sus. In Moldavia, you can ski at Vatra Dornei.

> Check out www.mountainguide.ro for tips on lesser-known ski locations.

TICKETS AND GEAR

Check out www.ski-in-romania.com for images, webcams and information on resorts and snowfall forecasts, and also www.surmont.ro (in Romanian only) for listings of snowboarding, skiing and mountain-biking events in the Bucegi Mountains.

Horse Riding

Throughout the Carpathians a network of horse-riding trails snake through beautiful and remote areas. Cross-Country Farm (p98), outside Sighişoara, offers day rides from 70 lei per person.

Mountain Biking

The best place to mountain bike is the plateau atop the Bucegi Mountains. From Sinaia (the town below) you can hire bikes; pay for an extra ticket on the gondola lift and go up for the day and work your way back down.

HIRING A BIKE

Aside from Sinaia and Buşteni, other bike-hire options are in Sibiu, Sighişoara, Sovata and, up in Maramureş, Botiza in the Izei Valley or in Bucharest from 60 to 100 lei per day. Ask staff at a hostel or *pensiune* (pension), who can sometimes track down a bike for you.

For multiday mountain-bike adventures to the Danube Delta or Transylvania check out the excellent website Cycling Romania (www.cyclingromania.ro).

Caving, Rock Climbing & Paragliding

In 2002 cavers found a 35,000-year-old human jawbone while digging around in the Peştera cu Oase (Cave with Bones) in the southwestern Carpathians; it turned out to be the oldest-known human fossil in Europe.

Romania has more than 12,000 caves *(peştera)*. Two of the best are reached from south of the Apuseni Mountains: the spectacular Ice Cave,

MOUNTAIN RESCUE

Emergency rescue is provided by Salvamont (☎0-SALVAMONT; www.salvamont.org), a voluntary mountain-rescue organisation with 20 stations countrywide. Its members are skilled climbers, skiers and medics. They are also an invaluable source of weather warnings and practical advice.

The national Salvamont contact number will automatically route your call to the office nearest your location. In an emergency dial 112.

Some of Salvamont's major contact points:

» Braşov (p89)
» Buşteni (☎0-SALVAMONT, 0244-321 656; Str Telecabinei 22)
» Sibiu (p112)
» Sinaia (p78)
» Vatra Dornei (☎0-SALVAMONT, 0726-686 687; salvamontdorna@yahoo.com)
» Zărneşti (p94)

which is one of Romania's five glacier caves, and the Bear Cave (Peştera Urşilor).

Check with Apuseni Experience (p143), based in Oradea, for caving tours. Green Mountain Holidays (p143) also generates great reports for its caving trips in the Apuseni Mountains. The **Emil Racoviţa Institute of Speleology** (☑0264-595 954; www.speleological-institute-cluj.org), based in Cluj-Napoca, can offer a guided tour to the otherwise-closed 45km Wind Cave – Romania's largest.

For climbs around Braşov check the new title, *Rock Climbing in Romania* by Ciprian Draghici, available in Sport Virus (p138) shops. Rock climbers take to the walls at the Piatra Craiului National Park, not far from Bran. The Bicaz Gorges offer spectacular challenges too, and there's some climbing near Băile Herculane.

Paragliding is gaining in popularity in Romania. You can arrange classes through Braşov Traveller. **Extreme Wings** (☑0723-887 459; www.extremewings.ro; tandem paraglide 250 lei) also offers tandem one-hour motorised paragliding tours of Braşov and beyond, as well as training. Finally, check out www.azlr.ro for a full index of paragliding instructors across Romania.

Health Spas

Those with illnesses including kidney, liver and heart diseases, as well as metabolism, gynaecological and nutrition disorders, can find relief in a number of spas across the country; check the map provided by the National Organisation of Spas (www.spas.ro).

Treatment goes underground at popular salt mines at Turda (p140) and Praid (p121).

Some standout spas:

Băile Tuşnad A *pensiune*-filled valley in Transylvania with mineral baths and pools in the Harghita Mountains.

Covasna spa resort Feels like an untouched, communist-era resort; popular with an older set who roam the halls in pink and sky-blue robes.

Eforie Nord's mud baths Bathers (some nude) slop mud on themselves and bake under the Black Sea sun.

Sovata Between Târgu Mureş and Sighişoara in Transylvania. Famed for a curative dip in a bear-shaped lake.

Wildlife

For the nature lover keen to get off the beaten track and see animals in their natural environment, Romania delivers on all fronts; not just because of its pristine forests but also for its offering of experienced wildlife guides. Romania's splendid nature teems with enough life to keep enthusiasts busy: there are 33,802 species of animals here (32 of these are endangered), and the Carpathians has the highest concentration of large carnivores in Europe.

Romania is also home to roughly 3700 species of plants (39 of which are endangered). The Carpathian Mountains are among the least-spoilt mountains in Europe, with alpine pastures above and thick beech, fir, spruce and oak forests below.

The country has more than 500 protected areas, including a dozen national parks, three biosphere reserves and one World Heritage site (the Danube Delta), totalling over 12,000 sq km. Most of these areas are located in the Carpathians. Except for the Danube Delta Biosphere Reserve (DDBR), the Retezat National Park and the Piatra Craiului National Park, none of the reserves or national parks have organised visitor facilities.

THE BEAR AND THE TRAVELLER

Thanks to its megalomaniac dictator (under Ceauşescu no one but he was allowed to hunt bears) 60% of Europe's brown bears are today found in Romania – a staggering 5500 bears. The chances of seeing one are high if you're trekking with a guide or going to a bear hide. A cousin of the grizzly bear, Romanian bears are smaller but have the same powerful hump of muscle on their back. They can also move at almost 50km/h.

Hikers have been killed by bears in recent years, usually because of accidentally surprising them, so here's a few tips to be mindful of. Try to pitch your tent in an open spot so bears can see you, and any used sanitary material or rubbish should be kept in a sealed bag. When walking through dense forest, talk loudly to announce your presence – the last thing a bear wants is to engage with you.

Birdwatching in the Danube Delta

The Danube Delta provides a major transit hub for birds migrating from as far off as the Russian Arctic to the Nile Delta. Here birdwatchers can hire boats or take tours or ferries on one of three channels through Romania's 3446-sq-km wetland. Almost the entire world's population of red-breasted geese (up to 70,000) winter here, as does 60% of the world's small pygmy cormorant population. In the summer white pelicans along with birds from up to 300 other species can also be seen.

Though you are guaranteed to see some birds on any of the boat excursions you take, Tulcea's Ibis Tours (p214) can organise specialised tours guided by ornithologists. Otherwise, the Information & Ecological Education Centre (www.ddbra.ro) can suggest other ways to spot the flying beauties.

There are also birdwatching excursions in Transylvania's mountains. Roving România (p86) in Braşov runs well-regarded bird trips.

Migration season in spring runs from March to May, in autumn August to October. It's particularly good in mid-April and October.

The Romanian government has issued an ambitious plan to cut energy use by at least 30% by 2015, partly by introducing renewable energy sources.

The Environment

Two key EU criticisms of Romania included waste management and water pollution. For NGOs like ProNatura and the Transylvania Ecological Club (p136) in Cluj-Napoca, educating an apathetic public about how to diminish the impact of tourism on the environment is a main priority.

In spring 2006, the Danube River rose to its highest level in over a century. Various engineering projects have resulted in up to 20,000 sq km of floodplains being cut off from the river, which has endangered many species in this area. Though the pollution bellowing out of Romania's factories has been halved, air pollution still exceeds acceptable levels in some areas, and the Danube Delta has a long way to go before it can be pronounced a healthy environment. In 2006 tension built up over the mining of Roşia Montană and, in the same year, Romania took out a €55 million loan to modernise its water supply to meet EU standards; the project is still in progress.

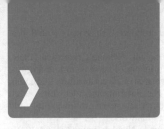

Visual Arts & Folk Culture

Visual Arts

Painting

Medieval painting in Romania was marked by a strong Byzantine influence. Devised to educate illiterate peasants, paintings took the form of frescoes depicting scenes from the Bible on the outside walls of churches; they also appeared on iconostases inside churches and in miniature form as decorative frames for religious manuscripts.

The Bucovina monasteries, dating from the 15th and 16th centuries, are home to Romania's loveliest and liveliest frescoes. The works are prized not only for their composition, but perhaps even more for their inventive application of colour and harmony.

Renaissance influences were muted in many areas by the cultural influence of the Ottoman Empire, but can be seen here and there in western areas, and even in parts of Wallachia, which served initially as a vassal state of the Hungarian kingdom. The beautifully preserved frescoes on the wall of the 14th-century St Nicholas Church in Curtea de Argeş represent a rare synthesis of Byzantine themes, such as portraits of saints given a fleshier, three-dimensional cast, more characteristic of the Renaissance.

As art entered its modern phase in the 19th century, Romania trailed behind Western Europe. France, as the arbiter of painting styles, exerted a disproportionate influence. While many early Romanian attempts were

> In 2009 one of Brâncuşi's works, *A Portrait of Mme LR*, sold for US$37 million at a Christie's auction in Paris.

LITERATURE: ROMANIA'S NOBEL LAUREATES

In literature, few modern Romanian writers have managed to break through to a wider international public, but one notable exception is the German-speaking author Herta Müller (b 1953), who won the Nobel Prize for Literature in 2009. Müller grew up in a German-speaking village in the Banat during a time when the German minority was subject to harsh oppression and deportation. Unsurprisingly, her work centres on the severity of life in communist Romania. She left Romania in 1987 and lives in Berlin. Her books are anything but easy reads, but several are available in English, including *The Land of Green Plums* (1998), *The Appointment* (2002) and *The Hunger Angel* (2012).

Any discussion of Romanian Nobel laureates would not be complete without mention of the Holocaust survivor and acclaimed writer Elie Wiesel, who was born in the northern city of Sighetu Marmaţiei in 1928 and who was awarded the Nobel Peace Prize in 1986. Wiesel has written 57 books, but he's best known for *Night*, a moving depiction of his experiences as a prisoner at the Auschwitz-Birkenau and Buchenwald concentration camps during WWII.

knock offs of French styles, by the mid- and late-19th century, true Romanian masters were emerging.

The best of these masters, arguably, was Nicolae Grigorescu (1838–1907). Grigorescu absorbed French influences like realism and Impressionism, but brought them home with scenes celebrating Romanian landscapes, peasantry and soldiers. His portraits included unexpected subjects, like the Roma and Jewish women. He was a prolific painter, and art museums around the country carry his work.

Another modern painter to look for is Nicolae Tonitza (1886–1940), who was greatly influenced by Impressionism and early modern movements, but whose subject matter is less nationalistic than Grigorescu. The symbolist movement was represented by Ion Ţuculescu (1910–62), who incorporated decorative motifs of Moldavian carpets in his work.

Sculpture

Sculpture has been an active art form on the territory of modern Romania since the days of the ancient Greeks along the Black Sea, and the history and archaeology museums in Tulcea and Constanţa are filled with these works of antiquity. In more modern times, in the 19th and 20th centuries, sculpture often took the form of statues of national heroes.

This rigid, didactic statue-making, however, was blown away in the 20th century by the abstract works of Romanian master Constantin Brâncuşi (1876–1957). Brâncuşi turned the world of modern sculpture on its head with his dictum of using sculpture not to focus on an object's form, but rather its inner essence. His work is featured at Craiova's Art Museum and Bucharest's National Art Museum, as well as in a series of open-air public works at Târgu Jiu, not far from where he was born.

Contemporary Romanian sculpture got a boost – or perhaps a setback (depending on your point of view) – by a controversial work unveiled in 2012 at Bucharest's National History Museum. The bronze statue, by Vasile Gorduz (1931–2008), depicts a fully nude (and anatomically correct but not particularly well-endowed) Roman emperor Trajan holding a wolf to symbolise the synthesis of Roman and Dacian cultures. It provoked derision on all sides, but tellingly has emerged as the city's most-photographed work of art.

Folk Culture

Romanian folk traditions have come under increasing threat from modern life, but remain surprisingly strong, particularly in Maramureş, parts of Transylvania and in the western region of Wallachia, called Oltenia. Folk crafts sit alongside the fine arts and have exerted strong influence over the centuries on Romanian painting, sculpture and music.

Arts & Crafts

Folk culture continues to thrive in traditional crafts such as pottery making, weaving and woodworking. Romanian pottery is incredibly diverse. Materials and patterns vary according to the area where the pottery was made. The ethnographic museum in Craiova has an excellent display of regional pottery. Other important areas include Miercurea-Ciuc and Baia Mare.

Similarly, textile weaving carries on into the modern age; many private homes in smaller towns and villages still have looms, and the embroidery, patterns and materials can differ greatly from region to region. Weaving is used to produce bed clothing and towels as well as curtains and rugs. Romanian carpet tradition, not surprisingly, shares much in common with the Ottoman Turks. Even today, one of the most common carpets you'll see are the thin-weave, oblong rugs called *kilims*.

CINEMA: THE ROMANIAN 'NEW WAVE'

Romanian film has not traditionally commanded worldwide attention, but that changed 10 years ago with the emergence of a brilliant younger generation of directors making films in a style that has come to be known as the Romanian 'New Wave'. While the films differ greatly in theme, they share a low-budget, low-key, hyper-realistic aesthetic that feels refreshing at a time when much of world cinema is dominated by big-budget blockbusters.

One of the early big hits was director Cristi Puiu's (b 1967) *Death of Mr Lăzărescu* in 2005. That film tells the tragi-comic story of an old man and his futile efforts to get hospital care in Romania's dysfunctional medical system. It won the top prize at Cannes for young and upcoming directors.

That was followed up in 2007 by Cristian Mungiu's (b 1968) amazing *Four Months, Three Weeks and Two Days*. Set in Ceauşescu-era Romania, the film explores the frightening world of backstreet abortions, but more generally the limits of friendship and the inability of society to cope with basic problems. It won the Palme d'Or at Cannes for best film.

Other well-known directors working in this style include the late Cristian Nemescu (1979–2006), who was tragically killed in a car crash, Corneliu Porumboiu (b 1975) and Radu Muntean (b 1971).

One other recent film has won numerous international awards, but is not normally regarded as part of the 'New Wave'. Andrei Ujică's *Autobiography of Nicolae Ceauşescu*, from 2010, tells a convincing story of the former dictator's descent into madness using nothing more than hours and hours of official footage, edited and spliced together. It's mesmerising.

Maramureş is the centre of the country's woodworking expertise. Over the centuries, the inhabitants have used the abundant forests to create fabulous wooden churches. Traditionally, every family's woodworking skills are on display on the enormous, elaborately carved wooden gates that front the family house. Wood was often used in making cooking utensils, and spoon carving is still carried on throughout Maramureş and parts of Transylvania.

Folk Music

You won't travel far without hearing Romanian folk music, which is still common at family celebrations, holidays and weddings.

Traditional Romanian folk instruments include the *bucium* (alphorn), the *cimpoi* (bagpipes), the *cobză* (a pear-shaped lute) and the *nai* (a panpipe of about 20 cane tubes). Many kinds of flute are used, including the ocarina (a ceramic flute) and the *tilinca* (a flute without finger holes).

Folk music can take many forms. A *doină* is a solo, improvised love song, a sort of Romanian blues with a social or romantic theme that is sung in a number of contexts (at home, at work or during wakes). The *doină* was added to the Unesco World Heritage list of intangible cultural elements in 2009. Another common form, the *baladă* (ballad), is a collective narrative song steeped with feeling.

Couples may dance in a circle, a semicircle or a line. In the *sârbă*, males and females dance quickly in a closed circle with their hands on each other's shoulders. The *hora* is another fast circle dance. In the *brâu* (belt dance), dancers form a chain by grasping their neighbour's belt.

When they perform, Roma musicians circulate through their village, inviting neighbours to join in weddings, births, baptisms, funerals and harvest festivals. Improvised songs are often directed at a specific individual and are designed to elicit an emotional response (and a tip).

VISUAL ARTS & FOLK CULTURE

Best Folk CDs

» *Band of Gypsies* by Taraf de Haidouks

» *Art of the Bratsch* by Anatol Ştefăneţ

» *Baro Biao* by Fanfare Ciocarlia

» *World Library of Folk & Primitive Music, Vol XVII*

The Romanian People

An Island of Latins

Today's Romanian often describes his country as being 'an island of Latins surrounded by a sea of Slavs', and though this statement relies on a short period in Romanian history two millenia past, when the country was occupied for 175 years by the Romans, it's certainly fair to call them Latin. For Romanians are a warm, passionate people who often raise their voices in conversation, are family-oriented, opinionated, display machismo and are highly impatient behind the wheel!

One thing you can rely on with a Romanian is getting the truth from them. Newcomers to the country are often amazed by the candour of their host's inquiries as to their salary, views on homosexuality, the Roma, and anything else usually deemed off-limits conversation in other countries.

Ethnicity
Romanian: 89.5%
Hungarian: 6.6%
Roma: 2.5%
Other: 1.4%

The Birth of Bling!

As Westernisation accelerates, Romanians are lapping up the shiny brands foreign advertisers are hawking to them: mobile phones, prestige-brand cars, cosmetics and clothes. Indeed a whole new class has evolved, the *fitosi* (nouveau riche), obsessed with gadgetry and personal appearance. To an outsider this might seem a bit shallow, but in truth many of those flashy cars return not to expensive houses but modest flats – image these days is everything. After so many years of their parents suffering limited choice, paranoia and oppression, it's no wonder young Romanians live by a *carpe diem* creed; for they seem to delight in parking where they like, smoking in places they shouldn't, nattering to one another in cinemas and enjoying late nights out midweek as if the world might end tomorrow.

It's not just aesthetic changes taking place; slowly, the national psyche is also shifting from one of '*Asta e*' ('that's the way it is') mute acceptance, toward a voice of disgruntlement at the corrupt status quo. Funding for SMURD, the emergency medical-rescue service, was due to be severely reduced in 2012 until murmurs of disagreement surfaced, with demos against the cuts. Hardly a revolution at 2500 people admittedly, but a seismic shift from passive to active in a country ghosted by the mantle of communism – in former times you would have been sent to prison, Siberia, or simply shot for raising your voice.

In 2001 Romania finally repealed the criminalisation of homosexuality.

Hot Potatoes: Issues You May Come Across

The most apparent undercurrent of racial tension is between Romanians and Hungarian Romanians (the nation's second-largest ethnic group). Each views the other with suspicion justified by their misdeeds against

WOMEN IN ROMANIAN SOCIETY

Romanian media portrayals of women can seem outdated, with TV shows peppered with dancing girls in barely a strip of clothing and anchor women on news channels doled up like beauty queens. Juxtaposed to this celebration of the female form is a worrying domestic-abuse record. Typically Latin, this is very much a man's country where women are expected to conform to being gentle and submissive, and males dominant and strong.

Surveys suggest that as many as one in five women have been abused by their partner. In 2003 the Law on Preventing and Combating Domestic Violence was adopted, and two years later an initiative to get bridegrooms to attend a course to deter them from future violence was announced. The fight against human trafficking – particularly of females – also remains a work in progress. That said, Romania's developing economy is seeing an increasing number of female professionals taking their place in management positions within the workplace.

one another throughout the country's history. Meanwhile, right-wing groups such as Noua Dreaptă (New Right) organising anti-gay banners during GayFest in Bucharest, TV talk shows unblushingly discussing anti-Semitic views, and groups denying the Holocaust are, sadly, other signs of negative nationalism.

Finally, you're likely to hear tirades from usually mild-mannered Romanians about the Roma. Rightly or wrongly, the average Romanian blames his country's besmirched image as a crime-ridden country on the practices of the Roma.

The Comeback Kid

Romanians remain extremely open and friendly to visitors. Younger people in particular are tolerant, highly educated, multilingual and prepared to give you detailed directions when you're lost. And despite the country's unfair reputation for crime you'll find inner cities largely safe and locals more interested in getting to know you than filching your wallet.

The doors that EU membership opened have arguably made the lure of jobs abroad even more powerful, exacerbating the country's 'brain drain'. Romanians working in construction or the service industry in Greece, Spain or Italy stand to make far more money than university professors or engineers at home.

Since the country's 2007 EU ascension, leaps forward have included strong gains by the lei against the euro and a dizzying real-estate boom that attracted investors from around the world. In 2006 the Romanian Statistics Office reported a GDP growth of 7.7%, one of the highest rates in Europe. After an eye-widening GDP growth of 8.9% in the first nine months of 2008, Romania joined the rest of the globe under the dark cloud of the financial crisis. But at a time when other EU countries' GDP was sliding backwards, in 2011 and 2012 Romania's was on the rise. Slowly and surely this most complex of countries is making a comeback.

Number of medals Romania has won in all the Summer Olympics: 301.

Rapes are still difficult to convict in Romania because a witness and medical certificate are required, and most women are too scared to report the crime to police.

The Romanian Table

Romanian dishes have a delightful, homemade character to them, incorporating the fertile land's fresh, organic produce into relatively uncomplicated but delicious meals. Many dishes use pork in some form, paired with a staple like polenta, potatoes or cooked cabbage. The recipes derive from peasant cooking going back hundreds of years, with a liberal dose of borrowings from neighbouring (and occasionally occupying) cultures like Turkish, Hungarian, German and Slav.

If you want to make your own *mămăligă*, a couple of good books include Galia Sperber's *The Art of Romanian Cooking* and Nicolae Klepper's *Taste of Romania*.

Comfort Food

Romanian food wasn't bred so much to dazzle as to satisfy. *Mămăligă*, a corn-meal mush (often translated as 'polenta' on English menus), seemingly was designed to warm and fill the stomach. You'll find it at restaurants, inns and family homes around the country – it can be disappointingly bland or stodgy in restaurants, but when homemade and served with fresh *smântână* (sour cream), it certainly hits the spot.

Mămăligă pairs beautifully with *sarmale*, the country's de facto national dish (though it's actually an import from the days of Ottoman rule) and comfort-food extraordinaire. *Sarmale* are cabbage or vine leaves that are stuffed with spiced meat and rice; the *mămăligă* here provides an excellent backstop for soaking up the juices.

Soups & Stews

Romanian meals always begin with soup, usually a 'sour' soup called *ciorbă*. The sour taste derives from lemon, vinegar, cabbage juice or fermented wheat bran added during preparation. Sour soups come in several varieties – the local favourite is *ciorbă de burtă*, a light garlicky tripe soup. Others worth looking for include *ciorbă de perişoare* (spicy soup with meatballs and vegetables) and *ciorbă de legume* (vegetable soup cooked with meat stock).

Dare To Try

» *răcituri* – jelly made from pig's hooves

» *ciorbă de potroace* – soup made from chicken entrails

» *brânză în coajă de brad* – cheese wrapped in tree bark

The fish soup (*ciorbă de peşte*) served in and around the Danube Delta is some of the best in the world. It's typically made from several types of fresh fish, including trout, pike-perch, sturgeon, carp and a giant Black Sea catfish known as *somn*, plus lots of fresh vegetables, garlic and other spices, all simmered in a cast-iron kettle.

Tochitură, another menu staple, is a hearty stew that could easily be filed away under the 'comfort food' category too. There are regional varieties, but it's usually comprised of pan-fried pork, sometimes mixed with other meats, in a spicy tomato sauce or wine sauce, served with *mămăligă*, cheese and – this is the rub – topped with an egg cooked sunny-side up. How can it go wrong?

Street Eats

Romanians love to eat on the go. Look out for:

» *covrigi* – hot pretzels sprinkled with salt or sesame or poppy seeds

» *gogoşi* – doughnuts, dusted with sugar or stuffed with fruit

» *plăcinte* – warm sweet or savoury pastries, stuffed with fruit, curd cheese or meat

» *mici* – grilled rolls of spiced minced pork or beef, served with mustard

» *shoarma* – like a shawarma, though usually made from chicken or pork, with toppings like cabbage and tomato sauce

Going Meatless

Devout Orthodox Christians observe a vegan diet on Wednesdays and Fridays and for extended periods during religious holidays. That said, the quantity and quality of meatless offerings at most restaurants on most days is not what it ought to be. During religious holidays, some restaurants will offer a *meniu de post* (menu without meat or dairy). This menu could include mains such as *cartofi piure cu şniţele de soia* (mashed potatoes with soy schnitzels), *sarmale de post* (vegan cabbage rolls), *zacuscă de vinete cu ciuperci* (eggplant and mushroom dip) and *tocăniţă de legume de post* (vegan vegetable stew).

Aside from that, nearly every restaurant will have a list of vegetarian salads. *Salată de roşii* (tomato salad) is sliced tomatoes doused in olive oil and vinegar, and covered in chopped parsley and onion. Also popular is *salată de castraveţi* (cucumber salad), or tomatoes and cucumbers combined in a *salată asortată* (mixed salad).

On entree lists, look for *murături* (pickled vegetables, such as cucumbers or cauliflower), *ciuperci umplute* (stuffed mushrooms), and potato dishes, including *cartofi ţărăneşti* (country-style potatoes), which is often served alongside meats.

Leave Room for Dessert

Romanian cooking excels in the sweets department, so be sure to leave plenty of room for a 'second' main course. More pedestrian – but still delicious – desserts include strudels, crepes (*clătite*) and ice cream (*îngheţată*). Our favourite, though, has to be *papanaşi*. This is fried dough, stuffed with sweetened curd cheese and covered with jam and heavy cream.

Romanian Drink

The Hard Stuff

Sure, Romanians enjoy a good beer or glass of wine, but when it comes to serious drinking, the only real contender is fruit brandy – schnapps,

THE ROMANIAN TABLE

Soups are often served with a small pepper on the side. Don't put the pepper in the soup; instead take a nibble of it along with a spoonful of soup. You might also be served a dish of clear or creamy garlic sauce. The local habit is to take a spoonful of the garlic and mix it with the soup.

Not all *ţuică* is the real deal. If you're wondering if your drink is genuine or merely fruit-flavoured alcohol, rub a bit on your arm and give it a sniff. If you smell the fruit and not the alcohol, it's the genuine article.

COOKING COURSES

A trip to Romania is a rare opportunity to learn the basics of Romanian cooking. While there are not many cooking schools or programmes to choose from yet, the list is growing every year.

» **Mobile Cooking Romania** (http://mobile-cooking-romania.com) A travel company offering package tours to major tourist destinations, combined with themed gourmet cooking classes and dining events with international chefs and sommeliers.

» **Société Gourmet** (www.societegourmet.ro) This Bucharest-based outfit offers themed cooking classes. Most of the courses feature international cuisines, but there are also regional courses, such as regular weekend truffle hunts in Transylvania. It also has kid's programmes.

HOLIDAY TREATS

Romanian celebrations and rituals are intricately bound up with food.

All Saints Day (9 March) Little *mucenici* (martyrs) are baked on this day; in most of Romania they are pieces of unleavened dough in a figure eight. However, in Moldavia they're brushed with honey and sprinkled with walnuts, and in Wallachia they're boiled with sugar then covered with crushed walnuts and cinnamon.

Easter The high point of the Orthodox calendar. The main meal revolves around lamb; especially delicious is *stufat de miel*, a lamb stew made with green onions and garlic. Breads play an important side role, particularly *pască*, a traditional Easter sweet cake, and a sweet egg bread called *cozonac*.

Christmas Dinner centres on pork, starting with a soup of smoked pork, and ham or pork chops as the main course. *Sarmale* will also be served. Sweets include *cozonac*, walnut cake and even pumpkin pie. In Transylvania, you will find *singeretta*, sausages made with pig's blood, liver, kidneys and fat.

Outside of the main wine-making regions, Drăgăşani in Wallachia is home to one of the country's most promising new wineries, Casa Isărescu, owned by the governor of the national bank. Also new and highly regarded is the Nachbil winery in the northwest near Satu Mare.

---

eau de vie – or as the Romanians say, *ţuică*. Typically, *ţuică* is made from plums (surveys say three-quarters of the nation's plums end up in a bottle), though we've also seen apricots and pears applied to this nefarious craft.

The best batches are from the backyard still, and nearly everyone has an uncle or grandpa who makes the 'best in Romania'. You'll often find *ţuică* sold in plastic bottles at roadside fruit stands, sitting there innocently next to the apples and watermelons.

A shot of *ţuică* before a meal is a great way to break the ice, and Romanians say it does wonders for the appetite. Unless you're a seasoned drinker, though, we'd hold the line at one or two shots. Homemade batches can run as high as 50% to 60% alcohol (100 to 120 proof).

Palincă (called *horincă* in Maramureş and *jinars* in the Cluj-Napoca region) is similar, only it's filtered twice and can be even stronger.

Wine & Beer

Though it definitely flies under the radar screen for wine production, Romania is the 9th-biggest winemaker in the world and produces many wines that are world class.

The country's wineries turn out both reds (*negru* and *roşu*) and whites (*alb*). There are five traditional wine-making regions: Târnave plateau (outside Alba Iulia; whites), Cotnari (outside Iaşi in Moldavia; whites), Murfatlar (near the Black Sea coast, whites and reds), Dealu Mare (south of the Carpathians; reds) and Odobeşti (in southern Moldavia; whites and reds).

Wines to Watch

» Cotnari's Fetească neagră (slightly sweet red)

» Grasă de Cotnari (a sweet white)

» Fetească Regală (sparkling wine)

» Murfatlar (quality reds)

For day-to-day tippling, though, Romanians are beer drinkers at heart, with quality ranging from passable to pretty good. Most breweries are owned by international brewers and it's sometimes easier to find a Tuborg or a Heineken in a pub than a Romanian label. That said, some of the better Romanian brands to look for include Ciuc, Ursus, Silva and Timişoara's local favourite, Timişoreana. All are broadly similar pilsner-style pale lagers, but each has its passionate defenders. Ursus and Silva both produce highly regarded darks.

In Bucharest, be sure to stop at the Caru' cu Bere (p46) restaurant. Not only does it cook traditional Romanian food uncommonly well, it brews its own beer – and it's very good.

Survival Guide

Directory A-Z

Accommodation

Romania has a wide choice of accommodation options to suit most budgets, including hotels, pensions and private rooms, hostels and camping grounds. Prices across these categories have risen in recent years, but are still generally lower than comparable facilities in Western Europe.

This book divides accommodation options into three categories based on price: budget, midrange and top end (see boxed text, opposite page). Budget properties normally include hostels, camping grounds and some cheaper guesthouses. Midrange accommodation includes three-star hotels, pensions and better guesthouses. Top end usually means four- and five-star hotels, corporate chains and high-end boutiques.

» Bucharest is the most expensive place to stay, followed by other large cities. The further away from the cities you go, the cheaper the accommodation gets.

» Watch for seasonal fluctuations on rates. Summer resorts, particularly on the Black Sea, have much higher prices in July and August.

» We've quoted prices in this guide in lei, though many hotels quote rates in euro. Regardless of the quote, you'll still have to pay in lei and your credit card will be debited in lei at the current exchange rate.

Hotels

Romanian hotels are rated according to a 'star' system, which provides a rough approximation of what you can expect – though stars are awarded according to a property's facilities and not on intangibles like appearance, location and value.

» The top end (four and five stars) is usually a guarantee of Western European levels of comfort and luxury. Expect in-room refrigerators, flat-screen TVs, climate control and key-card door locks. Five-stars will usually have a pool or sauna. A double in a four- or five-star hotel will run anywhere from 300 to 500 lei (higher in Bucharest).

» Three-star hotels hit the sweet spot between comfort and price. While three-star properties may not have pools or fancy fitness rooms, you can expect a well-managed property, with well-proportioned, clean rooms, air-conditioning, en suite baths and in-room wi-fi. A three-star double typically costs around 200 to 250 lei per night outside of the capital; 300 to 400 lei in Bucharest.

» Two-star and lower properties are usually only acceptable if saving money is the main criterion. In many cases, these are unreconstructed holdovers from former communist times. Furnishings and carpets are likely to appear frayed; beds will be uncomfortable and appear worn. A double room at a two-star property runs anywhere from 140 to 200 lei per night, depending on the location.

Pensions & Private Rooms

» A pension (*pensiune*) is a small, privately run guesthouse where you'll normally get a clean, comfortable room and breakfast. Occasionally, you'll have the option to take half- or full board (one or both main meals). These are usually good value and represent a more atmospheric alternative to staying in two- or three-star hotels. Singles/doubles typically run around 100 to 120 lei per room.

BOOK YOUR STAY ONLINE

For more accommodation reviews by Lonely Planet authors, check out http://hotels.lonelyplanet.com. You'll find independent reviews, as well as recommendations on the best places to stay. Best of all, you can book online.

PRICE RANGES

The following price ranges refer to a double room with a bathroom, including breakfast (Bucharest prices tend to be higher):

Budget $ Under 150 lei for a double

Midrange $$ 150 to 300 lei for a double

Top End $$$ Over 300 lei for a double

» One rung down from a pension is a room (*cazare*) in a private home. Many families rent spare rooms in their homes as a way of supplementing income. You can spot these places by a *'cazare'* sign in the window or by the homeowner holding a sign at the side of the road or at the train station. While stays here can lend great insights into the lives of ordinary people, they often also mean sharing a bathroom with the family and having little privacy.

» Private rooms, in our experience, work best in a rural or farm setting, where the homes are decorated in traditional rural style and where the stays can include hearty meals and authentic extras like visits with shepherds, hikes or horseback rides.

» Several organisations operate throughout Romania to promote agritourism schemes. We've listed the websites of the best ones here (see boxed text, this page). Expect to pay 50 to 80 lei per person per night, not including meals.

Hostels

Hostels in Romania are not as well developed as in other European countries. Large cities, like Bucharest and Braşov, do have several, good-quality private hostels. These typically have group kitchens, laundry facilities, computers or wi-fi, and engaged, English-speaking staff to answer questions. We're big fans of these places and have listed the best of them as per destination.

Outside a handful of big cities, though, the concept of a youth hostel means something quite different. These hostels are often open only from June to August and are located in university dormitories or other institutional spaces that have been repurposed as seasonal lodgings. Don't expect kitchens, internet connections or English-speaking receptionists. What you'll usually get is a student dorm with a shower down the hall, and that's about it. We've included the best of these in this guide. Local tourist information offices will also be able to provide information.

Camping & Mountain Huts

» Camping grounds (*popas turistic*) run the gamut between a handful of nicely maintained properties in scenic areas to grungy affairs, with wooden huts packed unattractively side-by-side like sardines. Bare mattresses are generally provided and sometimes you have to bring your own sleeping bag. We've listed the best of these, but have omitted properties that don't meet basic standards.

» Often a better bet is camping rough. Wild camping is technically prohibited in parks and legally protected zones, but outside these areas you will rarely be disturbed, provided you exercise discretion, stay quiet and leave the area pristine when you leave. Wild camping can be great along the Black Sea coast, particularly in places like Sfântu Gheorghe or Vama Veche that attract a younger crowd looking to escape the big resorts.

» In most mountain areas there's a network of cabins or chalets (cabanas) with dormitories and occasionally restaurants. Prices are lower than those of hotels (about 30 to 40 lei for a bed) and no reservations are required, but arrive early if the cabana is in a popular location such as next to a cable-car terminus. It's often possible to camp on the grounds surrounding mountain huts.

Business Hours

Reviews only list opening hours if they don't adhere to the standard opening hours listed here. Shopping centres and malls generally have longer hours and are open from 9am to 8pm Saturday to Sunday. Museums are almost invariably closed on Mondays, and have shorter hours outside high season.

Banks 9am to 5pm Monday to Friday; 9am to 1pm Saturday (varies)

Museums 10am to 5pm Tuesday to Friday; 10am to 4pm Saturday to Sunday

Offices 8am to 5pm Monday to Friday; 9am to 1pm Saturday (varies)

USEFUL ACCOMMODATION WEBSITES

» **www.pensiuni.info.ro** Homestays and farmstays in Maramureş.

» **www.ruralturism.ro** Scenic guesthouses and farmstays around the country.

» **www.hihostels-romania.ro** Local Hostelling International site.

Post offices 8am to 7pm Monday to Friday; 8am to 1pm Saturday (cities)

Restaurants 9am to 11pm Monday to Friday; 10am to 11pm Saturday to Sunday

Shops 9am to 6pm Monday to Friday; 8am to 2pm Saturday

Children

» Travelling with children in Romania doesn't create any specific problems: children often enjoy privileges on local transport and with accommodation and entertainment; age limits for particular freebies or discounts vary from place to place, but are not often rigidly enforced; and basic supplies for children are easily available in cities.

» For general suggestions on how to make a trip with kids easier, pick up a copy of Lonely Planet's *Travel with Children*.

Customs Regulations

» You're allowed to import hard currency up to a maximum of €10,000 or the equivalent.

» Goods valued over €1000 should be declared upon arrival.

» For foreigners, duty-free allowances for items purchased *outside* of the EU are 4L of wine, 2L of spirits and 200 cigarettes. For more information, go to www.customs.ro.

Discount Cards

» A Hostelling International (HI) card yields a token discount in some hostels. You can become a member by joining your own national Youth Hostel Association (YHA) or IYHF (International Youth Hostel Federation); see **www.hihostels.com** for details.

» Holders of an **International Student Identity Card (ISIC)** are privy to many discounts in Romania. A full list (in Romanian) of ISIC discounts as well as many helpful hints for student travellers in Romania can be found at the local ISIC website: **www.isic-romania.ro**.

Electricity

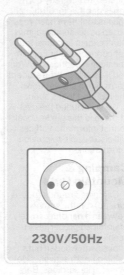

230V/50Hz

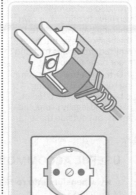

230V/50Hz

Embassies & Consulates

The website http://embassy-finder.com maintains an up-to-date list of consulates and embassies around the world. Embassies are located in Bucharest, while several countries maintain consulates at other cities around the country. New Zealand does not maintain an embassy in Romania; official affairs are handled through the country's embassy in Belgium.

Australia (☏021-307 5000; www.dfat.gov.au; Str Tuberozelor 1-3) At the time of research, Australian consular services were being handled temporarily by the Embassy of Canada.

Canada (☏021-307 5000; www.canadainternational.gc.ca/romania-roumanie; Str Tuberozelor 1-3)

France (☏021-303 1000; www.ambafrance-ro.org; Str Biserica Amzei 13-15)

Germany (☏021-202 9830; www.bukarest.diplo.de; Str Gheorghe Demetriade 6-8)

Ireland (☏021-310 2131; www.embassyofireland.ro; Str Buzeşti 50-52)

Netherlands (☏021-208 6030; http://romania.nlembassy.org; Aleea Alexandru 20)

UK (☏021-201 7200; www.ukinromania.fco.gov.uk; Str Jules Michelet 24)

Ukraine (☏021-230 3660; www.mfa.gov.ua/romania; B-dul Aviatorilor 24)

US (☏Consulate 021-270 6000, embassy 021-200 3300; http://romania.usembassy.gov; B-dul Dr Liviu Librescu 4-6)

Food

For an in-depth discussion of Romanian food and drink, see p252.

Gay & Lesbian Travellers

Public attitudes toward homosexuality remain

PRICE RANGES

In this guide we have broken down the eating listings into three price categories – budget, midrange and top end – depending on the price of an average main-course item.

Budget $ Under 15 lei

Midrange $$ 15 to 30 lei

Top End $$$ Over 30 lei

relatively negative. In spite of this, Romania has made significant legal progress in decriminalising homosexual acts and adopting antidiscrimination laws.

» There is no legal provision for same-sex partnerships.

» Bucharest remains the most tolerant city in the country, though here too open displays of affection between same-sex couples are rare.

» The Bucharest-based **Accept Association** (☏021-252 9000; www.accept -romania.ro) is an NGO that defends and promotes the rights of gays and lesbians at a national level. Each year in June the group organises a six-day **GayFest** in the capital, with films, parties, conferences and a parade.

Health

Romania is a relatively safe country and visitors are not subject to any major health dangers that one wouldn't find in any other European country. There are no vaccinations required to enter Romania.

Health Insurance

» EU citizens are entitled to free emergency medical care provided that they have a European Health Insurance Card (EHIC), available from health centres or via www. dh.gov.uk in the UK.

» Citizens from other countries will likely have to pay cash upfront for any medical treatment and then seek reimbursement later from their private or public health insurers.

» Be sure to save any and all paperwork provided by the hospital to present to your insurance company along with any reimbursement claim.

Availability & Cost of Health Care

Every Romanian city or large town will have a hospital or polyclinic that handles emergencies. In rural areas, the nearest hospital may be quite some distance away, though local people will be able to advise the best course of action.

» Romanian hospitals and medical centres may not look very promising from the outside, but rest assured if something does go wrong, you will receive relatively prompt, professional care.

» If you need to go to the hospital, be sure to bring your passport, credit card and cash, as you may be required to prepay for services. You'll likely have to pay out of pocket for any medications, bandages or crutches etc.

» Romanian health care, particularly in public hospitals, is generally affordable by Western European (and certainly American) standards. Rates can be much higher in private clinics, though the quality of the care may be better as well.

Infectious Diseases
RABIES
Rabies cases are thankfully rare but still a concern given

TIPS FOR GETTING BETTER RESTAURANT SERVICE

Don't get us wrong, we know waiting tables can be a bear, and we have nothing but respect for those who do it night-in, night-out. It's back-breaking work with few rewards besides a (small) tip. Still, it should be said that service at some restaurants can be absolutely exasperating, slow, inept, indifferent, even rude. Here are a few pointers to improve the dining-out experience.

» Greet the staff as you enter. A nicely timed 'bună ziua' (literally 'good day') can go a long way towards breaking the ice. It lets the staff know you're there and gets things going on the right footing.

» Don't linger over the menu. If a menu is posted outside, give it a quick perusal to see what you might want before entering. The waiter will usually take a drinks order first. When he or she brings the beverages, this is the time to order the food.

» Keep some small bills handy. These can be a lifesaver when it comes to paying and getting out fast. You'll need to signal the server that you want your bill, which will be brought in a folder or pouch. You're then free to stick the money in and go. Paying with a big bill inevitably means another delay as you wait for change.

» Enjoy your meal and take your time. After all, you're on holiday. Unless you've got a train to catch, there's usually no need to rush.

PRACTICALITIES

» Catch up on current affairs with the *Nine O'Clock* (www.nineoclock.ro), a daily available online and from newsagents. Foreign papers can be found at some bookshops and gift stores of upmarket hotels.

» State-run Romanian Radio is the main broadcaster, operating on AM and FM; programmes are in Romanian.

» Romania lags behind much of Europe in enacting limits on public smoking. In theory, all restaurants have a nonsmoking section, but in practice this is spottily enforced.

» Televiziunea Română (TVR) is the state broadcaster, with six channels and regional studios in large cities. There are several private channels, including Pro TV and Antena 1. Programmes are in Romanian, though movies are often broadcast in their original language and subtitled.

» Romania uses the metric system for weights and measures.

---

the number of stray dogs on the streets. If bitten by a homeless dog, seek medical attention within 72 hours (most main hospitals will have a rabies clinic).

TICK-BORNE ENCEPHALITIS

Ticks are common in Romania's grasslands and open areas. Tick-borne encephalitis is a rare but debilitating virus that attacks parts of the brain. If you're planning on spending time hiking and camping in the open air, consider a vaccination.

Water Quality

» Tap water is generally considered safe to drink in Romania.

» Any water found in the mountains should be treated with suspicion – never drink it without purifying (with filters, iodine or chlorine) or boiling it first, unless assured that it's safe to drink by a guide or local authority.

Insurance

» Insurance is not compulsory to enter Romania but a decent policy that covers

medical expenses, theft or loss is always a good idea.

» Worldwide travel insurance is available at www.lonely planet.com/travel_services. You can buy, extend and claim online anytime – even if you're already on the road.

Internet Access

Wi-Fi

Romania is well-wired, and the majority of hotels, above a basic pension or guestroom, usually offer some form of internet access, normally wi-fi, for you to use with your own laptop, smartphone or tablet device.

» Many bars, cafes and restaurants offer free wi-fi for customers, though the strength and reliability of the signal can vary considerably. McDonald's and KFC outlets nationwide offer free wi-fi for customers.

» In this guide, we've used 🛜 to identify hotels, restaurants, cafes and bars that have wi-fi access for guests.

Finding a Computer

Finding a computer to use for a few minutes of internet access has gotten harder as

many hotels have dropped the former practice of making a computer terminal available for guests.

» Larger hotels will sometimes have a 'business centre', though this may incur an added fee.

» The situation with internet cafes is much the same. As more Romanians purchase their own computers, the number of internet cafes has dropped. We've listed internet cafes in this guide in areas where we could find them.

» Internet cafes normally charge 3 to 5 lei per hour.

» Other options include the tourist information office, which may have a terminal for a few minutes of gratis surfing, or the local library.

» In this guide, we've used @ to indicate hotels that have computers available for guests.

Legal Matters

Foreigners in Romania, as elsewhere, are subject to the laws of the host country. While your embassy or consulate is the best stop in any emergency, bear in mind there are some things it cannot do for you, like getting local laws or regulations waived because you're a foreigner, investigating a crime, providing legal advice or representation in civil or criminal cases, getting you out of jail, or lending you money.

» A consul can issue emergency passports, contact relatives and friends, advise on how to transfer funds, provide lists of reliable local doctors, lawyers and interpreters, and visit you if you've been arrested or jailed.

» Romanian police take a dim view toward illegal drug use of any kind, including cannabis, as well as obvious displays of public drunkenness.

Money

The official Romanian currency is the leu (plural: lei), noted in this guide as 'lei' but listed in some banks and currency exchange offices as RON. One leu is divided into 100 bani. Banknotes come in denominations of 1 leu, 5 lei,10 lei, 50 lei, 100 lei, 200 lei and 500 lei. The coins come in 50 bani and, relatively useless, 10 bani pieces. For current exchange rates see p19.

» The leu is a stable currency that has more or less held its own with respect to the euro and US dollar in recent years.

» Despite the fact that Romania is a member of the European Union, the euro does not circulate. There is no point in converting your money into euro prior to arrival, since you will have to convert it to lei anyway.

» Try to keep small-denomination (1 leu and 5 lei) notes on hand for shops, transport tickets, cafes and tips for waiters. Getting change for 100 lei notes and higher that ATMs often spit out can be a problem.

ATMs

ATMs (cash points) are everywhere and give 24-hour withdrawals in lei on a variety of international bank cards, including Visa and MasterCard.

» Romanian ATMs require a four-digit PIN.

» Before leaving home, inform your bank where you're going, so the card security company does not (protectively) block your card once your Romanian transactions start coming through.

Cash

The best place to exchange money is at a bank. You'll pay a small commission, but get a decent rate.

» You can also change money at a private exchange booth (casa de schimb) but be wary of commission charges and always ask how many lei you will receive before handing over your bills.

» You will usually need to show a passport to change money, so always have it handy.

» Never change money on the street with strangers; it's almost always a rip-off.

Credit Cards

International credit and debit cards, including Visa and MasterCard, are widely accepted at hotels, restaurants and shops in cities and large towns. In rural areas, you'll usually need to pay with cash.

» American Express cards are typically accepted at larger hotels and restaurants, though they are not as widely recognised as other cards.

» Credit card transactions may also require a PIN number, so it's best to work that out with your bank prior to departure and to have that number handy.

» You will need to have a valid credit card if you plan to hire a car.

» Credit cards can be used to get cash advances at most banks.

Tipping

In restaurants, tip 10% of the bill to reward good service. Leave the tip in the pouch that the bill is delivered in or hand the money directly to the waiter.

» Tip hairdressers and other personal services around 10% of the total.

WHO'S ON THE BILLS

One strike against the EU is the standardised currency, which makes cross-Europe travel a little less exciting than it once was. For now, the portraits on Romania's money still tell a tale of the country's history.

1 leu: Nicolae Iorga (1871–1940) The cofounder of the Democratic National Party was renowned as a rare voice against fascism as WWII loomed. He was eventually tortured and executed.

5 lei: George Enescu (1881–1955) Famous for composing 'Romanian Rhapsodies' (1903), he left Romania after communism took over.

10 lei: Nicolae Grigorescu (1838–1907) Romania's best-known painter progressed from Ruben copies to originals of traditional scenes around Romania.

50 lei: Aurel Vlaicu (1882–1913) The first Romanian to excel in flight (vampires included), he died in the crash of his *Vlaicu II* in 1913.

100 lei: Ion Luca Caragiale (1852–1912) This playwright was happy to mock everyone with his rather ironic stabs at the modernising of Romania at the end of the 19th century.

200 lei: Lucian Blaga (1895–1961) Poet, playwright, essayist, philosopher, professor and diplomat.

500 lei: Mihai Eminescu (1850–89) The mere mention of this national poet inspires Romanian pride. He suffered from manic-depressive psychosis and died at age 38.

» Taxis drivers won't expect a tip, but it's fine to round the fare up to reward special service.

» Tip hotel cleaning staff 3 to 5 lei per night or 20 lei per week to reward good service. In luxury hotels, tip doormen and concierges 5 to 10 lei for special assistance as warranted.

Post

The **Romanian Postal Service** (www.posta-romana.ro) is slow but reliable and fine for sending letters and nonessential parcels home. Buy stamps in post offices, as letters must normally be weighed to determine correct postage.

» Delivery time within Europe is one week; overseas letters will take seven to 10 days.

Public Holidays

If you travel during public holidays it's wise to book ahead, as some hotels in popular destinations may be full.

New Year (1 and 2 January)

Orthodox Easter Monday (April/May)

Labour Day (1 May)

Pentecost (May/June, 50 days after Easter Sunday)

Assumption of Mary (15 August)

Feast of St Andrew (30 November)

Romanian National Day (1 December)

Christmas (25 and 26 December)

Telephone

Domestic & International Calls

Romania has a modern telephone network of landlines and mobile (cell) phones. It's possible to receive and make direct international calls from anywhere in the country. Romania's country code is 40.

» All Romanian landline numbers have 10 digits, consisting of a zero, plus a city code and the number.

» The formula differs slightly depending on whether the number is in Bucharest or outside of Bucharest. Bucharest numbers take the form: 0 + two-digit city code (21 or 31) + seven-digit number. Outside of Bucharest, numbers take the form: 0 + three-digit city code + six-digit number.

» Mobile-phone numbers can be identified by a three-digit prefix starting with 7. All mobile numbers have 10 digits: 0 + three-digit prefix (7xx) + six-digit number.

CALLING WITHIN ROMANIA

» If you are calling from within Romania, to reach a landline outside of Bucharest, dial 0 + three-digit city code + six-digit number.

» To reach a landline in Bucharest, dial 0 + 21 (or 31) + seven-digit number.

» To reach any mobile number, dial 0 + three-digit mobile prefix + six-digit number.

DIALING FROM ABROAD

To reach a Romanian landline from abroad, dial your country's international access code, then 40 (Romanian country code), then the city code (minus the zero) and the six- (or seven-) digit local number. For example, a call to a landline in Bucharest from abroad would take the form: international access code + 40 (country code) + 21 + seven-digit number.

» For a mobile number, use the three-digit mobile prefix instead of the city code. A call to a mobile number from abroad would follow the form: international access code + 40 (country code) + three-digit mobile prefix + six-digit number.

» To call abroad from Romania, dial the international access code in Romania (00), then the code for the country you want to call, then the area code and number.

Mobile Phones & Smartphones

Romanian mobile (cell) phones use the GSM 900/1800 network, which is the standard throughout much of Europe as well as in Australia and New Zealand and many other parts of the world. This band is not compatible with most mobile phones in North America or Japan (though some multi-band phones do work across regions). Ask your provider if you're uncertain whether your phone will work.

» Using your own phone and SIM card in Romania could expose you to expensive roaming fees, particularly for long calls or data downloads. A cheaper option is to buy a prepaid Romanian SIM card, which gives you a temporary local number and charges local (cheaper) rates for calls, texts and data transfers. These cards only work with phones that are 'unlocked' (able to accept foreign SIM cards).

» Prepaid SIM plans start at about 20 lei per card and usually include some bonus minutes. They are offered by all three of Romania's main carriers: **Vodafone** (www.vodafone.ro), **Cosmote** (www.cosmote.ro) and **Orange** (www.orange.ro).

» Buy prepaid SIM cards at any provider shop or independent phone seller. You can top up the card at phone shops, newspaper kiosks and even some ATMs. Shops around the country also sell new or used phones that can be used in conjunction with local prepaid SIM cards.

» The situation is more complicated if you have a smartphone like an iPhone, Android or Blackberry that cannot easily be unlocked. With these phones, it's best to contact your home provider to consider short-term international calling and data plans appropriate to your needs.

» Even if you are not using your smartphone as a phone, it still makes a handy wi-fi device. Be sure to switch off the 'data roaming' setting to avoid unwanted roaming fees.

Payphones & Phonecards

» Public phones usually require a magnetic-stripe phonecard, which you can buy from post offices, newspaper kiosks, and some tourist offices and hotel reception desks.

» Phonecard rates start at about 10 lei and allow for a certain number of impulses (minutes).

» It's possible to dial abroad from a pay telephone.

Time

» All of Romania lies within the Eastern European time zone, GMT/UTC+2, one hour ahead of most of continental Europe. Romanian local time is two hours ahead of London and seven hours ahead of New York.

» Romania observes daylight saving time, and puts the clock forward one hour at 2am on the last Sunday in March and back again at 3am on the last Sunday in October.

» The 24-hour clock is used for official purposes, including transport schedules. In everyday conversation, people commonly use the 12-hour clock.

Toilets

» Public toilets are few and far between and often not very clean. Use better facilities in restaurants or hotels when you have the chance.

» Toilets are labelled *toaletă* or simply 'WC'.

» Men should look for 'B' (*bărbaţi*). Women's toilets are marked with an 'F' (*femei*).

» The fee for a public toilet is usually 1 or 2 lei, collected by a toilet attendant sitting at the door. Have coins or small bills ready.

» Some toilets have a plastic bin by their side – this is for used toilet paper.

Tourist Information

» The **Romanian National Tourist Office** (www.romania tourism.com) maintains a wonderful website with a trove of useful information. There's a large English-language section on festivals and events, accommodation and tips on what to see and do all around the country.

» Romania's national network of tourist offices has made encouraging strides in recent years. Nearly all big cities (with the notable exception of urban centres in Wallachia like Craiova, Ploieşti and Piteşti) have decent tourist offices. Tourist information can still be tough to track down in rural areas.

» If you turn up in a city without a tourist office, you're pretty much on your own. Local bookstores or newsagents can sometimes sell a local map, but don't expect much help from local travel agencies. They are far more preoccupied with outbound travel by Romanians than by assisting visiting foreigners.

Travellers with Disabilities

» Romania is not well equipped for people with disabilities, even though there has been some improvement over recent years.

» Wheelchair ramps are available only at some upmarket hotels and restaurants, and public transport will be a challenge for anyone with mobility problems.

» One resource is the **Romania Motivation Foundation** (☑021-448 0242; www.motiva tion.ro), which has worked hard since its foundation in 1995 to provide access to wheelchairs for locals in need. They run wheelchair sports leagues and camps, with a focus on helping people improve their wheelchair skills.

Visas

Citizens of EU countries do not need visas to visit Romania and can stay indefinitely. Citizens of the USA, Canada, Australia, New Zealand, Israel, Japan and many other countries can stay for up to 90 days without a visa. Other nationalities should check current requirements with the Romanian embassy or consulate in their home country. As visa requirements can change, check with the **Ministry of Foreign Affairs** (www.mae.ro) before departure.

Note that Romania, while a member of the European Union, is not part of the EU's common border and customs area known as the Schengen area. In practice, this means that regardless of nationality you will have to show a passport or EU identity card when entering from EU member states Hungary and Bulgaria, as well as from from non-EU states Ukraine and Serbia. Romania's Schengen status was under review at the time of research and may have changed by the time you are reading this.

Transport

GETTING THERE & AWAY

Travel to Romania does not pose any unusual problems. Bucharest has air connections with many European capitals and large cities, and train and long-haul bus service is frequent. Flights, cars and tours can be booked online at lonelyplanet.com.

Entering Romania

Travellers entering Romania should not experience any trouble at customs and immigration, particularly if they come from a country that does not require a visa.

Passport

For a discussion of which nationals require a visa to travel to Romania, see p263. The expiry date of your passport should not be less than three months after the date of your departure from Romania. Additionally, some airlines may deny travel to passengers whose passports are within six months of expiration.

Air

Romania has good air connections to Europe and the Middle East. At the time of research there were no direct flights to Romania from North America or Southeast Asia.

Airports

The majority of international flights to Romania arrive at Bucharest's **Henri Coandă International Airport** (OTP/Otopeni; ☎021-204 1000; www.otp-airport.ro; Şos Bucureşti-Ploieşti). Several other cities have international airports that service mostly domestic flights and those to and from European cities. The largest of these include the following:

Cluj Airport (☎0264-416 702; www.airportcluj.ro; Str Traian Vuia 149)

Iaşi Airport (☎info 0733-261 111; www.aeroport.ro; Str Moara de Vant 34)

Sibiu Airport (☎0269-253 135; www.sibiuairport.ro; Sos Alba Iulia 73)

Târgu Mureş Airport (☎0265-328 259; www.targumuresairport.ro; Str Ludus, km 14.5)

Timişoara Airport (Traian Vuia Timişoara Airport; ☎0256-493 639; www.aerotim.ro; Str Aeroport 2, Ghiroda)

Airlines

Romania's national carrier is Bucharest-based **Tarom** (☎call centre 021-204 6464; www.tarom.ro). While the airline was previously the butt of jokes, in recent years it has transformed itself into a safe and reliable carrier. It operates an extensive network of domestic flights to cities around Romania. It also flies to major cities in Europe, including London and Paris, and the Middle East.

Many other national carriers, particularly from Europe

CLIMATE CHANGE & TRAVEL

Every form of transport that relies on carbon-based fuel generates CO_2, the main cause of human-induced climate change. Modern travel is dependent on aeroplanes, which might use less fuel per kilometre per person than most cars but travel much greater distances. The altitude at which aircraft emit gases (including CO_2) and particles also contributes to their climate-change impact. Many websites offer 'carbon calculators' that allow people to estimate the carbon emissions generated by their journey and, for those who wish to do so, to offset the impact of the greenhouse gases emitted with contributions to portfolios of climate-friendly initiatives throughout the world. Lonely Planet offsets the carbon footprint of all staff and author travel.

and the Middle East, operate regular flights to Romania, normally between their respective capitals and/or major cities and Bucharest.

Additionally, many budget carriers service the Romanian market, mainly to and from destinations in Italy, Spain, Germany and the UK. These include Bucharest-based **WizzAir** and **Blue Air**, Timişoara-based **Carpatair**, as well as **GermanWings** and **Ryanair**. Check the airline websites for the latest information on flights and routes.

MAJOR CARRIERS

Air France (☑021-206 9200; www.airfrance.com)

Austrian Airlines (☑021-204 4560; www.austrian.com)

British Airways (☑reservations 021-303 2222; www.britishairways.com)

Lufthansa (☑021-204 8410; www.lufthansa.com)

Swiss Airlines (☑021-312 0238; www.swiss.com)

Turkish Airlines (☑+90-212 444 0849; www.turkishairlines.com)

BUDGET CARRIERS

Blue Air (☑mobile 1499; www.blueairweb.com)

Carpatair (☑0256-300 900; www.carpatair.com)

Germanwings (☑toll 0903-760 101; www.germanwings.com)

Ryan Air (☑UK + 44 871 246 0002; www.ryanair.com)

WizzAir (☑toll 0903-760 160; www.wizzair.com)

Tickets

Fares vary depending on the route, the time of year, and the day of the week. Romania's high season is summer (June to August) and a short period around Christmas. The rest of the year is quieter and cheaper. Weekday flights tend to be more expensive than weekends, or trips that include a weekend stay.

For flights within Europe, travellers have the choice of several major, full-fare carriers as well as budget carriers. Budget options from Britain, Italy and Spain are particularly good.

On transatlantic and long-haul flights your travel agent is probably still the best source of cheap tickets, although there is an increasing number of online booking agencies. One feasible option is to find the best deal to a European hub, like London, and then try to find a budget flight from there. That might land you the cheapest deal, but bear in mind budget airlines rarely use main airports, and you're likely to have to change not just planes en route but airports too.

Land

Border Crossings

» Romania shares a border with five countries: Bulgaria, Hungary, Moldova, Serbia and Ukraine. Most crossings follow international highways or national roads. Romania has four car-ferry crossings with Bulgaria (see the boxed text, this page). Highway border posts are normally open 24 hours; though some smaller crossings may only be open from 8am to 8pm. Ferries run during daylight and may have reduced operating hours.

» At the time of research, Romania was not a member of the EU's common customs and border area, the Schengen area, so even if you're entering from an EU member state (Bulgaria or Hungary), you'll still have to show a passport or valid EU identity card.

» Border crossings can get crowded, particularly during weekends, so prepare for delays.

» For information on visas, see p263.

Bus

Long-haul bus services remain a popular way of travelling from Romania to Western Europe as well as to parts of southeastern Europe and Turkey. Bus travel is comparable in price to train travel, but can be faster and require fewer connections.

WESTERN EUROPE

» Bus services to and from Western European destinations are dominated by two companies: **Eurolines** (www.eurolines.ro) and **Atlassib** (www.atlassib.ro; Soseaua Alexandriei 164, Bucharest). Both maintain vast networks from cities throughout Europe to destinations all around Romania. Check the companies' websites for the latest schedules, prices and departure points.

» For sample prices, a one-way ticket from Vienna to

MAJOR INTERNATIONAL ROAD & FERRY CROSSINGS

Major international road and car-ferry crossings are located at or near the following Romanian towns.

To/from Bulgaria Road crossings at Giurgiu, Vama Veche, Calafat (planned for 2013); ferry crossings at Calafat, Bechet, Turnu Măgerele, Călăraşi

Hungary Road crossings at Nădlac, Borş, Cenad, Valea lui Mihai, Urziceni

Moldova Road crossings at Rădăuţi-Prut, Albiţa, Galaţi, Ştefăneşti, Sculeni

Serbia Road crossings at Moraviţa, Comloşu Mare, Jimbolia, Porţile de Fier

Ukraine Road crossings at Siret, Sighetu Marmaţiei

Bucharest in 2012 would cost roughly €70. From Paris, the trip would cost about €100.

SOUTHEASTERN EUROPE

» Bucharest is the hub for coach travel to Bulgaria, Greece and Turkey. Given Bucharest's position in the southeast of Romania, buses are often quicker and cheaper than trains.

» One bus departs daily from Bucharest's Filaret bus station to **Sofia** (€18, seven hours).

» Bucharest-based **Murat Turism & Transport** (☎021-316 5520; www.muratturism.ro; Soseaua Viilor 33) offers a daily bus service from the Romanian capital to **Istanbul** (€40, 14 hours) and to **Athens** (€50, 18 hours).

Car & Motorcycle

» Romania has decent road and car-ferry connections to neighbouring countries, and entering the country by car or motorcycle will present no unexpected difficulties.

» At all border crossings, drivers should be prepared to show the vehicle's registration, proof of insurance (a 'green' card) and a valid driver's license. All visiting foreigners, including EU nationals, are required to show a valid passport (or EU identity card).

» From Western Europe, the best road crossings are via Hungary at Nădlac (near Arad), along Hwy E68; and Borş (near Oradea), on Hwy E60. Both are major international transit corridors and are open 24 hours.

» The main road connection to Bulgaria is south of Giurgiu on Hwy E85, across the Danube River. A second car bridge traverses the Danube at Calafat along Hwy E79, connecting to the Bulgarian city of Vidin.

» For road rules and more information see p268.

Train

Romania is integrated into the European rail grid, and there are decent connections to Western Europe and neighbouring countries. Nearly all of these arrive at and depart from Bucharest's main station, **Gara de Nord** (☎021-319 9539, phone reservations 021-9521/2; www.cfr.ro; Piaţa Gara de Nord 1).

» Budapest is the main rail gateway in and out of Romania from Western Europe. There are two daily direct trains between Budapest and Bucharest, with regular onward direct connections from Budapest to Prague, Munich and Vienna.

» Buy international train tickets at major train stations or at CFR (Romanian State Railways) in-town ticket offices (identified by an 'Agenţia de Voiaj CFR' sign).

» For longer overnight journeys, book a couchette (cuşetă) or a berth in a sleeping car (vagon de dormit). The former are cheaper but less comfortable; they are standard second-class rail cars with seats that convert to makeshift beds at night. Sleeping cars have dedicated beds, though you're not actually likely to get much sleep since you'll still be awoken at border crossings to show tickets and passports. Book sleeping-car berths well in advance at train ticket windows or CFR offices.

RAIL PASSES

» If you plan on doing a lot of rail travel or combining travel to Romania with neighbouring countries, you might consider an international rail pass. Romania is part of both the **InterRail** (www.interrailnet.com) and **Eurail** (www.eurail.com) networks, and several passes offered by both include rail travel in Romania.

» Passes typically allow for a number of train travel days within a period of 15 days or a month. Some passes allow for unlimited travel. InterRail passes are cheaper but can only be purchased by EU nationals or anyone living in Europe at least six months prior to travel. Eurail passes are open to anyone. Check the websites for specific details and prices. Another rail-pass company worth checking is **Rail Europe** (www.raileurope.com).

» Romanian rail travel is included on InterRail's GlobalPass, which includes 30 European countries, and the Romanian country pass. Eurail passholders can choose from the Hungary–Romania Pass or the Eurail Balkan Flexipass. This latter option allows for unlimited train travel in Romania as well as Bulgaria, Greece, Turkey, and much of former Yugoslavia.

POPULAR INTERNATIONAL RAIL JOURNEYS

Most long-haul international rail trips arrive at and depart from Bucharest's main station, Gara de Nord. Travel times and the approximate cost of a second-class ticket are as follows (accurate at the time of research but subject to change):

Bucharest–Budapest (via Arad; 210 lei, 14 hours, two daily)

Bucharest–Belgrade (via Timişoara; 200 lei, 12 hours, one daily)

Bucharest–Sofia (180 lei, nine hours, two daily)

Bucharest–Kyiv (280 lei, 26 hours, one daily)

Bucharest–Chişinău (200 lei, 13 hours, one daily)

Tours

It's generally cheaper to use a Romanian-based operator if you want a prebooked tour. Here are a couple of recommended international tour agencies offering Romania tours:

Quest Tours (☎800-621 8687; www.romtour.com) US-based operator offers several themed tours of Romania, ranging from two to 10 days, with the 10-day Romanian Experience tour priced at around US$2200 per person, not including flights.

Transylvania Uncovered (☎+44-1-539-531258; www. beyondtheforest.com) UK-based operator books a variety of inclusive trips, including themed travel to the painted monasteries, and travel to Transylvania and Maramureş. Check the website or email for an up-to-date list of excursions and prices.

GETTING AROUND

Air

Given the distances and poor state of the roads, flying between cities is a feasible option if time is a primary concern.

The Romanian national carrier **Tarom** (☎call centre 021-204 6464; www.tarom.ro) operates a comprehensive network of domestic routes. The airline flies regularly between Bucharest and Baia Mare, Cluj-Napoca, Iaşi, Oradea, Satu Mare, Sibiu, Suceava, Târgu Mureş and Timişoara.

» Flights between regional cities usually involve travel via Bucharest and connections aren't always convenient.

» Timişoara-based **Carpatair** (☎0256-300 900; www. carpatair.com) also runs many domestic flights. The carrier flies from Timişoara to Iaşi, Craiova and Bacău.

Bicycle

Romania has great potential as a cycling destination, though cycling has not yet caught on to the extent it has in other European countries.

On the positive side, cycling offers an excellent way of seeing the country and meeting locals. Off the main highways, Romania is criss-crossed by thousands of kilometres of secondary roads that are relatively little trafficked and ideal for cycling.

On the negative side, there's not much cycling infrastructure in place, such as dedicated cycling trails and a network of bike-rental and repair shops. Many cities, including Bucharest, do have some cycling trails, but these are half-hearted efforts and frequently leave cyclists at the mercy of often-ignorant and aggressive drivers.

It's possible to hire or buy bicycles in many major towns, though not all. The group **i'velo** (☎021-310 6397; www.ivelo.ro) is trying to popularise cycling and has opened bike-hire outlets in several cities, including Bucharest, Timişoara, Braşov, Constanţa, Iaşi and Sibiu. Rates average about 5 lei per hour or 30 to 50 lei per day.

Taking Your Bike on the Train

» Bicycles can usually be transported on trains, though not every train will have room for bikes, including many newer IC trains. Check the timetable at www.cfr.ro. Trains that accommodate cyclists are marked with a bicycle sign.

» If you are travelling with your bike, try to arrive at the train station early and inform the ticket seller you have a bike. You may have to buy a separate ticket for the bike, usually a flat fee of 10 lei, and be instructed to hand the bike over to the baggage window.

» Even if the ticket seller says it's not possible, it's always worth taking your bike to the platform and trying to negotiate with the conductor. Frequently, if the train is not full he or she may allow you to board.

Bus

A mix of buses, minibuses and 'maxitaxis' – private vans holding anywhere from 10 to 20 passengers – form the backbone of the Romanian national transport system. If you understand how the system works – and that's a big if – you can move around regions and even across the country easily and cheaply.

Unfortunately, there appears to be little logic behind how the system is organised and how it functions. Buses and maxitaxi routes change frequently; often these changes are communicated between people by word of mouth. Towns and cities will sometimes have a half-dozen different bus stations (*autogara*) and maxitaxi stops, depending on which company is operating a particular route and the destination in question.

In this guide, we've tried our best to identify bus stations and routes for towns and cities where that is possible. In other areas, we've identified common bus routes but directed readers to the website www.autogari. ro. This is an up-to-date timetable that is relatively easy to use and lists routes, times, fares and departure points. Another tried-and-true method is simply to ask around.

Once you've located the bus station and your bus, buy tickets directly from the driver. Have small bills handy, as drivers cannot usually provide change for big bills.

Fares vary according to the demand and number of competing bus companies, but are usually cheap. Figure on about 3 to 4 lei for every 20km travelled.

Car & Motorcycle

Driving around Romania has some compelling advantages. With your own wheels, you're free to explore off-the-beaten-track destinations and tiny villages. Additionally, you're no longer at the whim of capricious local bus schedules and inconvenient, early morning train departures.

That said, driving in Romania is not ideal, and if you have the chance to use alternatives like the train and bus, we strongly recommend considering this option.

Roads are generally crowded and in poor condition. The country has only a few short stretches of motorway (autostrada), meaning that most of your travel will be along two-lane national highways (drum naţional) or secondary roads (drum judeţean). These pass through every village en route and are choked with cars and trucks, and even occasionally horse carts and tractors pulling hay racks. It's white-knuckle driving made worse by aggressive motorists in fast cars trying to overtake on every hill and blind curve. When calculating arrival times, figure on covering about 50km per hour.

Western-style petrol stations are plentiful, but be sure to fill up before heading on long trips through the mountains or in remote areas. A litre of unleaded 95 octane costs about 6 lei. Most stations accept credit cards, but you'll need to have a PIN to use them.

Hire

International companies like Avis, Budget, Hertz and Europcar have offices in large cities and at Henri Coandă International Airport in Bucharest (see p52 for a list of car-hire companies in the capital). Book cars in advance over company websites to get the best rates. Drivers must normally be at least 21 years old, and the renter must hold a valid credit card.

Hitching

Hitching is never entirely safe in any country in the world. People who choose to hitch will be safer if they travel in pairs and let someone know where they are going. That said, hitching is popular in Romania, where people usually stand along the main roads out of a city or town.

An arm-length, pat-the-dog motion is the prevailing gesture used to indicate a ride is desired, though the thumbs-up signal is becoming more widespread. It's common practice to pay the equivalent of the bus fare to the driver (about 1 to 2 lei for every 10km).

Local Transport

Bus, Tram, Trolleybus & 'Maxitaxi'

Romanian cities generally have very good public transport systems comprised of buses, trams, trolleybuses and, in some cases, maxitaxis. Bucharest is the only Romanian city with an underground metro. The method for accessing the systems is broadly similar. Purchase bus or tram tickets at newsagents or street kiosks marked bilete or casă de bilete before boarding, and validate the ticket once aboard. For maxitaxis, you usually buy a ticket directly from the driver. Tickets generally cost from 2 to 3 lei per ride.

Taxi

» Taxis are cheap and reliable and a useful supplement to the public transport systems. Drivers are required by law to post their rates on their doors or windscreens. The going rate varies from city to city, but during our research in 2012 was anywhere from 1.39 to 1.89 lei per kilometre. Any driver posting a higher fare is likely looking to rip-off unsuspecting passengers.

» While it's usually okay to use a taxi parked at a taxi rank (provided the taxi is not at Bucharest's airport or main train station) or to hail one from the street, we strongly recommend ordering taxis by phone from reputable companies or asking hotels or restaurants to order taxis for you. In Bucharest,

---

ROAD RULES

Motorists are required to buy and display a sticker, called a rovinieta, that can be purchased on the border or at petrol stations. A vignette valid for one week costs about 15 lei, for 30 days, 30 lei. Other common traffic rules are as follows:

» Standard speed limits are 50km/h in town; 90km/h on national roads; 130km/h on four-lane expressways.

» The minimum driving age is 18.

» The blood-alcohol limit is zero.

» The use of seat belts is compulsory for front-seat passengers. Children under 12 are prohibited from sitting in the front seat.

» Headlights must be always on, even in bright daylight.

» Give way to traffic entering a roundabout.

ROMANIA ROAD DISTANCES (KM)

	Arad	Baia Mare	Bistriţa	Braşov	Bucharest	Cluj-Napoca	Constanţa	Deva	Iaşi	Miercurea Ciuc	Oradea	Piatra Neamţ	Piteşti	Ploieşti	Satu Mare	Sibiu	Suceava	Târgu Mureş	Timişoara	Tulcea
Timişoara																				825
Târgu Mureş																			377	558
Suceava																		284	648	437
Sibiu																	406	124	279	540
Satu Mare																343	403	282	297	846
Ploieşti															573	271	392	289	550	262
Piteşti														119	497	188	475	282	440	401
Piatra Neamţ													383	300	456	295	107	201	578	345
Oradea												463	478	549	129	320	467	260	168	817
Miercurea Ciuc											411	140	246	214	433	255	247	151	534	406
Iaşi										258	581	118	422	454	347	413	140	321	742	335
Deva									586	378	190	422	281	349	319	126	492	221	156	666
Constanţa								631	432	486	815	425	349	291	822	538	562	554	829	147
Cluj-Napoca							662	178	428	261	153	310	325	396	175	167	300	106	334	665
Bucharest						432	243	388	389	272	528	342	107	58	607	265	434	347	545	304
Braşov					175	281	383	279	307	99	434	236	147	115	458	156	328	174	435	384
Bistriţa				267	439	123	648	301	355	209	276	244	375	382	226	271	191	93	457	591
Baia Mare			151	429	538	142	781	290	508	349	117	383	431	544	67	322	318	227	370	777
Arad		236	393	392	574	270	809	150	686	522	117	620	431	544	251	274	588	378	52	813
Alba Iulia	236	319	217	229	340	94	581	84	458	288	247	358	231	344	264	73	408	137	240	600

try **Cobalcescu** (☏021-9451; www.autocobalcescu.ro), **CrisTaxi** (☏021-9461; www.cristaxi.ro) or **Meridian** (☏021-9444; www.meridiantaxi.ro).

Tours

Considering how remote much of Romania remains, it's not always a bad idea to consider arranging a tour with local agencies. Here are some of the standouts.

Green Mountain Holidays (☏0744-637 227; www.greenmountainholidays.ro) Excellent hiking, cycling and caving trips, chiefly around the Apuseni Mountains.

Pan Travel (☏0264-420 516; www.pantravel.ro; Cluj-Napoca) These engaging guides lead personalised, customised trips around Transylvania, Maramureş and Moldavia.

RoCultours/CTI (Map p38; ☏021-650 8145; www.rotravel.com/cti) Reliable agent with many cultural tours, and personalised itineraries listed on the website. It's best to contact it in advance.

Roving Romania (☏0724-348 272; www.roving-romania.co.uk) Run by an Englishman based near Braşov, this is an out-of-home agency for personalised, usually small-scale tours – great for birdwatching and 4WD trips. Email for sample itineraries.

Train

Trains are a slow but reliable way of getting around Romania. The extensive network covers much of the country, including most of the main tourist sights and key destinations.

» The national rail system is run by **Căile Ferate Române** (Romanian State Railways; www.cfr.ro), universally abbreviated as 'CFR'. The CFR website has a handy online timetable (*mersul trenurilor*).

» Buy tickets at train-station windows, specialised Agenţia de Voiaj CFR ticket offices, private travel agencies, or online at www.cfrcalatori.ro.

» *Sosire* means 'arrivals' and *plecare*, 'departures'.

On posted timetables, the number of the platform from which the train departs is listed under *linia*.

Classes & Types

Romania has three different types of trains that travel at different speeds, offer varying levels of comfort and charge different fares for the same destination.

» **InterCity**, listed in blue or green as 'IC' on timetables, are the most expensive and most comfortable but are not always much faster than 'IR' trains (see below). IC trains often travel outside the country.

» **InterRegional**, listed in red as 'IR' on timetables, are the next rung down. These are cheaper and nearly as fast as 'IC' trains, but may not be as modern.

» **Regional**, listed in black as 'R' on timetables, are typically the oldest and slowest trains in the system, often sporting historic rolling stock.

Language

WANT MORE?

For in-depth language information and handy phrases, check out Lonely Planet's *Eastern Europe Phrasebook*. You'll find it at **shop.lonelyplanet.com**, or you can buy Lonely Planet's iPhone phrasebooks at the Apple App Store.

Romanian is a member of the Romance language family – as a descendant of Latin, it shares a common heritage with French, Italian, Spanish and Portuguese. Today, Romanian is the official language of Romania and Moldova (where it's called Moldovan), with about 24 million speakers.

Romanian pronunciation is pretty straightforward for English speakers, and if you read our coloured pronunciation guides as if they were English, you'll be understood. Note that ai is pronounced as in 'aisle', ew as the 'ee' in 'see' but with rounded lips, oh as in 'note', ow as in 'how', uh as the 'a' in 'ago', zh as the 's' in 'measure', and that the apostrophe (') indicates a very short, unstressed i sound. The stressed syllables are indicated with italics.

BASICS

Hello.	Bună ziua.	boo·nuh zee·wa
Goodbye.	La revedere.	la re·ve·de·re
Yes.	Da.	da
No.	Nu.	noo
Please.	Vă rog.	vuh rog
Thank you.	Mulţumesc.	mool·tsoo·mesk
You're welcome.	Cu plăcere.	koo pluh·che·re
Excuse me.	Scuzaţi-mă.	skoo·za·tsee·muh
Sorry.	Îmi pare rău.	ewm' pa·re ruh·oo

How are you?
Ce mai faceţi?   che mai fa·chets'

Fine. And you?
Bine. Dumneavoastră?   bee·ne doom·ne·a·vo·as·truh

What's your name?
Cum vă numiţi?   koom vuh noo·*meets'*

My name is ...
Numele meu este ...   noo·me·le me·oo yes·te ...

Do you speak English?
Vorbiţi engleza?   vor·*beets'* en·gle·za

I don't understand.
Eu nu înţeleg.   ye·oo noo ewn·tse·*leg*

ACCOMMODATION

Where's a ...?	*Unde se află ...?*	oon·de se a·fluh ...
campsite	un teren de camping	oon te·ren de kem·peeng
guesthouse	o pensiune	o pen·syoo·ne
hotel	un hotel	oon ho·tel
youth hostel	un hostel	oon hos·tel

Do you have a ... room?	*Aveţi o cameră ...?*	a·vets' o ka·me·ruh ...
single	de o persoană	de o per·so·a·nuh
double	dublă	doo·bluh

How much is it per ...?	*Cît costă ...?*	kewt kos·tuh ...
night	pe noapte	pe no·ap·te
person	de persoană	de per·so·a·nuh

DIRECTIONS

Where's the (market)?
Unde este (piaţa)?   oon·de yes·te (pya·tsa)

What's the address?
Care este adresa? ka·re yes·te a·dre·sa

Can you show me (on the map)?
Puteţi să-mi arătaţi poo·te·tsi suh·mi a·ruh·tats'
(pe hartă)? (pe har·tuh)

How far is it?
Cît e de departe? kewt ye de de·par·te

EATING & DRINKING

I'd like (the) ..., please.	Vă rog, aş dori ...	vuh rog ash do·ree ...
bill	nota de plată	no·ta de pla·tuh
drink list	lista de băuturi	lees·ta de buh·oo·too·ri
menu	meniul	me·nee·ool
that dish	acel fel de mâncare	a·chel fel de mewn·ka·re

What would you recommend?
Ce recomandaţi? che re·ko·man·dats'

Do you have vegetarian food?
Aveţi mâncare a·ve·tsi mewn·ka·re
vegetariană? ve·je·ta·rya·nuh

I'll have ...	Aş dori ...	ash do·ree ...
Cheers!	Noroc!	no·rok
beer	bere	be·re
bottle	sticlă	stee·kluh
breakfast	micul dejun	mee·kool de·zhoon
cafe	cafenea	ka·fe·ne·a
coffee	cafea	ka·fe·a
cup	cană	ka·nuh
dinner	cină	chee·nuh
eggs	ouă	o·wuh
fish	peşte	pesh·te
fork	furculiţă	foor·koo·lee·tsuh
fruit	fructe	frook·te
glass	pahar	pa·har
juice	suc	sook
knife	cuţit	koo·tseet
lunch	dejun	de·zhoon
meat	carne	kar·ne
milk	lapte	lap·te
restaurant	restaurant	res·tow·rant
spoon	lingură	leen·goo·ruh
tea	ceai	che·ai
vegetable	legumă	le·goo·muh
water	apă	a·puh
wine	vin	veen

EMERGENCIES

Help!	Ajutor!	a·zhoo·tor
Go away!	Pleacă!	ple·a·kuh

Call ...!	Chemaţi ...!	ke·mats' ...
a doctor	un doctor	oon dok·tor
the police	poliţia	po·lee·tsya

I'm lost.
M-am rătăcit. mam ruh·tuh·cheet

Where are the toilets?
Unde este o toaletă? oon·de yes·te o to·a·le·tuh

I'm sick.
Mă simt rău. muh seemt ruh·oo

I'm allergic to ...
Am alergie la ... am a·ler·jee·ye ya la ...

SHOPPING & SERVICES

Where's the ...?	Unde este ...?	oon·yes·te ...
ATM	bancomat	ban·ko·mat
bank	bancă	ban·kuh
department store	magazin universal	ma·ga·zeen oo·nee·ver·sal
grocery store	magazin alimentar	ma·ga·zeen a·lee·men·tar
local internet cafe	un internet café în apropiere	oon een·ter·net ka·fe ewn a·pro·pye·re
newsagency	stand de ziare	stand de zee·a·re
post office	poşta	posh·ta
tourist office	biroul de informaţii turistice	bee·ro·ool de een·for·ma·tsee too·rees·tee·che

I'd like to buy (a phonecard).
Aş dori să cumpăr ash do·ree suh koom·puhr
(o cartelă de telefon). (o kar·te·luh de te·le·fon)

Can I look at it?
Pot să mă uit? pot suh muh ooyt

Do you have any others?
Mai aveţi şi altele? mai a·*vets*' shee *al*·te·le

How much is it?
Cât costă? kewt *kos*·tuh

That's too expensive.
E prea scump. ye pre·a skoomp

There's a mistake in the bill.
Chitanţa conţine kee·*tan*·tsa kon·*tsee*·ne
o greşeală. o gre·she·a·luh

TIME & DATES

What time is it?
Cât e ceasul? kewt ye che·a·sool

It's (two) o'clock.
E ora (două). ye o·ra (*do*·wuh)

Half past (one).
(Unu) şi (oo·noo) shee
jumătate. zhoo·muh·*ta*·te

At what time ...?
La ce oră ...? la che o·ruh ...

At ...
La ora ... la o·ra ...

yesterday ...	*ieri* ...	ye·ri ...
tomorrow ...	*mâine* ...	mew·ee·ne ...
morning	*dimineaţă*	dee·mee·ne·a·tsuh
afternoon	*după amiază*	doo·puh a·*mya*·zuh
evening	*seară*	se·a·ruh
Monday	*luni*	*loo*·ni
Tuesday	*marţi*	*muhr*·tsi
Wednesday	*miercuri*	*myer*·koo·ri
Thursday	*joi*	zhoy
Friday	*vineri*	*vee*·ne·ri
Saturday	*sâmbătă*	*sewm*·buh·tuh
Sunday	*duminică*	doo·*mee*·nee·kuh
January	*ianuarie*	ya·*nwa*·rye
February	*februarie*	fe·*brwa*·rye
March	*martie*	*mar*·tye
April	*aprilie*	a·*pree*·lye
May	*mai*	mai
June	*iunie*	*yoo*·nye
July	*iulie*	*yoo*·lye
August	*august*	*ow*·goost
September	*septembrie*	sep·*tem*·brye
October	*octombrie*	ok·*tom*·brye
November	*noiembrie*	no·*yem*·brye
December	*decembrie*	de·*chem*·brye

TRANSPORT

Public Transport

Is this the ... to (Cluj)?	*Acesta e ... de (Cluj)?*	a·*ches*·ta ye ... de (kloozh)
boat	*vaporul*	va·*po*·rool
bus	*autobuzul*	ow·to·*boo*·zool
plane	*avionul*	a·*vyo*·nool
train	*trenul*	*tre*·nool

What time's the ... bus?	*Când este ... autobuz?*	kewnd *yes*·te ... ow·to·*booz*
first	*primul*	*pree*·mool
last	*ultimul*	*ool*·tee·mool
next	*următorul*	oor·muh·*to*·rool

Where can I buy a ticket?
Unde pot cumpăra oon·de pot koom·puh·*ra*
un bilet? oon bee·*let*

One ... ticket (to Cluj), please.	*Un bilet ... (până la Cluj), vă rog.*	oon bee·*let* ... (*pew*·nuh la kloozh) vuh rog
one-way	*dus*	doos
return	*dus-întors*	doos ewn·*tors*

How long does the trip take?
Cât durează kewt doo·re·a·zuh
călătoria? kuh·luh·to·*ree*·a

Is it a direct route?
E o rută directă? ye o *roo*·tuh dee·*rek*·tuh

At what time does it arrive/leave?
La ce oră soseşte/ la che o·ruh so·*sesh*·te/
pleacă? ple·a·kuh

How long will it be delayed?
Cât întârzie? kewt ewn·*tewr*·zye

Does it stop at (Galaţi)?
Opreşte la (Galaţi)? o·*presh*·te la (ga·*la*·tsi)

How long do we stop here?
Cât stăm aici? kewt stuhm a·*eech*

What station/stop is this?
Ce gară/staţie e che ga·ruh/*sta*·tsye ye
aceasta? a·che·*as*·ta

Question Words		
How?	*Cum?*	koom
What?	*Ce?*	che
When?	*Când?*	kewnd
Where?	*Unde?*	*oon*·de
Who?	*Cine?*	*chee*·ne
Why?	*De ce?*	de che

LANGUAGE TIME & DATES

Numbers

1	unu	oo·noo
2	doi	doy
3	trei	trey
4	patru	pa·troo
5	cinci	cheench'
6	şase	sha·se
7	şapte	shap·te
8	opt	opt
9	nouă	no·wuh
10	zece	ze·che
20	douăzeci	do·wuh·ze·chi
30	treizeci	trey·ze·chi
40	patruzeci	pa·troo·ze·chi
50	cincizeci	cheench·ze·chi
60	şaizeci	shai·ze·chi
70	şaptezeci	shap·te·ze·chi
80	optzeci	opt·ze·chi
90	nouăzeci	no·wuh·ze·chi
100	o sută	o soo·tuh

What's the next station/stop?
Care este următoarea   ca·re yes·te oor·muh·to·a·re·a
gară/staţie?   ga·ruh/sta·tsye

Please tell me when we get to (Iaşi).
Vă rog, când   vuh rog kewnd
ajungem la (Iaşi)?   a·zhoon·jem la (ya·shi)

I'd like a taxi ...	Aş dori un taxi ...	ash do·ree oon tak·see ...
at (9am)	la ora (nouă dimineaţa)	la o·ra (no·wuh dee·mee·ne·a·tsa)
now	acum	a·koom
tomorrow	mâine	mew·ee·ne

How much is it to ...?
Cât costă până la ...?   kewt kos·tuh pew·nuh la ...

Please take me to (this address).
Vă rog, duceţi-mă la   vuh rog doo·chets'·muh la
(această adresă).   (a·che·as·tuh a·dre·suh)

Please ...	Vă rog, ...	vuh rog ...
slow down	încetiniţi	ewn·che·tee·neets'
stop here	opriţi aici	o·preets' a·eech
wait here	aşteptaţi aici	ash·tep·tats' a·eech

Driving & Cycling

I'd like to hire a ...	Aş dori să închiriez o ...	ash do·ree suh ewn·kee·ryez o ...
bicycle	bicicletă	bee·chee·kle·tuh
car	maşină	ma·shee·nuh
motorbike	motocicletă	mo·to·chee·kle·tuh

How much for ... hire?	Cât costă chiria pe ...?	kewt kos·tuh kee·ree·a pe ...
hourly	oră	o·ruh
daily	zi	zee
weekly	săptămână	suhp·tuh·mew·nuh

air	aer	a·er
oil	ulei	oo·ley
petrol	benzină	ben·zee·nuh
tyres	cauciucuri	kow·choo·koo·ri

I need a mechanic.
Am nevoie de un   am ne·vo·ye de oon
mecanic.   me·ka·neek

I've run out of petrol.
Am rămas fără   am ruh·mas fuh·ruh
benzină.   ben·zee·nuh

I have a flat tyre.
Am un cauciuc   am oon kow·chook
dezumflat.   de·zoom·flat

Is this the road to (Arad)?
Acesta e drumul   a·ches·ta ye droo·mool
spre (Arad)?   spre (a·rad)

GLOSSARY

The following are handy Romanian words. Hungarian (Hun) is included for key words.

Agenţia Teatrală – theatre ticket office (Hun: színház jegyiroda)

Agenţia de Voiaj CFR – train ticket office (Hun: vasúti jegyiroda)

Antrec – National Association of Rural, Ecological & Cultural Tourism

autogara – bus station (Hun: távolsági autóbusz pályaudvar)

bagaje de mână – left-luggage office (Hun: csomagmegőrző)

biserică – church (Hun: templom)

biserică de lemn – wooden church

cabana – mountain cabin or chalet

casă de bilete – ticket office (Hun: jegyiroda)

cascadă – waterfall

cazare – accommodation

CFR – Romanian State Railways

cheile – gorge

de jos – at the bottom

de sus – at the top

drum – road, trip

gara – train station (Hun: vasútállomás)

mănăstire – monastery (Hun: kolostor)

metropolitan – the head of a province of the church

pensiune – usually denotes a modern building or refurbished home, privately owned, that's been turned into accommodation for tourists

pensiunea – see *pensiune*

piaţa – square or market (Hun: főtér or piac)

plecare – departure (Hun: indulás)

sosire – arrival (Hun: érkezés)

ţară – land, country

Bulgaria

Bulgaria

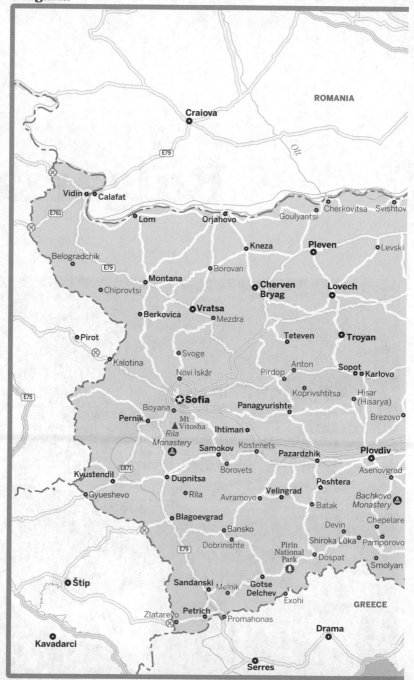

welcome to Bulgaria

Black Sea Beaches

It isn't hard to see why so many foreign – and Bulgarian – holidaymakers descend on the Black Sea coastline each summer. The long, professionally maintained sandy beaches at the big resorts are the equal of some of the most popular Mediterranean destinations, and, if you just want to relax, top up your tan or try out some water sports, there's nowhere better. Away from the parasols and jet skis you'll find smaller, more traditional seaside towns ideal for young families, as well as ancient settlements with cobbled lanes, quaint wooden houses and long, fascinating histories. Even the coast's two big cities, Varna and Burgas, have attractive beaches within minutes of their busy urban hearts.

Churches & Icons

Bulgaria has a long tradition of religious art, and wherever you go, you can't fail to notice the beautiful, timeless icons appearing in museums and, of course, countless churches and monasteries. The luminous images of saints are at their most evocative and powerful inside candlelit Orthodox churches, often set into a gilded wooden screen known as an iconostasis. Engaging religious murals were created in the 19th century and adorn the walls of Bulgaria's most important monasteries. Older churches built during the Ottoman occu-

From wild, wooded mountain ranges speckled with remote villages and enchanting monasteries to vibrant modern cities and long sandy beaches hugging the Black Sea coast, Bulgaria rewards exploration.

(left) Canyon near Veliko Tărnovo (p373)
(below) Traditional dancing

pation can be identified by their sunken and deliberately unobtrusive appearance.

Mountains & Forests

With no fewer than seven diverse mountain ranges criss-crossing the country, Bulgaria is a true haven for hikers, mountaineers and anyone interested in wildlife and the great outdoors. An extensive system of hiking trails and huts makes it easy for walkers to enjoy the country's rich and varied landscapes. Unspoiled alpine forests, lakes, waterfalls and bubbling streams are all there to explore; bears, lynx and wolves still roam and activities from skiing and snowshoeing to caving and kayaking are all available.

Ancient Ruins

With such a long and tumultuous history, it's hardly surprising to find that Bulgaria still harbours impressive stony reminders of the ancient peoples and civilisations that have risen, fallen, conquered and passed through this land. The fearsome Thracians left their mark across the southern and central areas of Bulgaria, and the tombs of some of their kings and nobility can still be seen today. Signs of 2500-year-old Greek and Hellenistic colonisation are evident along the coast, while elsewhere, fortifications, bathhouses and theatres indicate the reach and resources of the Roman Empire at its zenith.

need to know

Currency
» The lev (lv), divided into 100 stotinki

Language
» Bulgarian

When to Go

■ Dry climate
■ Warm to hot summers, mild winters
■ Mild to hot summers, cold winters
■ Mild summers, cold winters

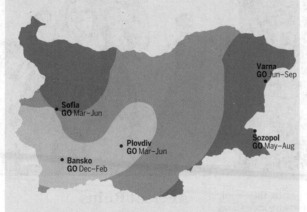

Varna
GO Jun–Sep

Sofia
GO Mar–Jun

Plovdiv
GO Mar–Jun

Sozopol
GO May–Aug

Bansko
GO Dec–Feb

High Season
(Jun–Aug)

» Expect high temperatures, bright sunny days and warm evenings throughout Bulgaria during high season.

» The Black Sea coast, especially, is at its busiest and most expensive at this time.

Shoulder
(Apr–May)

» Spring is a great time to visit Bulgaria. The weather is warm, though evenings may still be chilly.

» All the sights and attractions are open again after winter, and there are fewer tourists around. September is also pleasant.

Low Season
(Oct–Mar)

» Temperatures fall rapidly in autumn, and snow is common over much of the country in winter.

» Many coastal resorts close down completely, but the ski resorts are in full swing between December and February.

Your Daily Budget

Budget: Less than
60 lv

» Dorm beds: 18–22 lv

» Street markets for self-caterers and meals from great-value cafeterias: 5–10 lv

» Cheap public transport tickets: around 1 lv

Midrange:
60–120 lv

» Double room in a midrange hotel: 60–80 lv

» Lunch and dinner in decent restaurants: 20–30 lv per person

Top end: More than
120 lv

» Double room in top-end hotel: 150–300 lv

» Three-course meals with wine in top-end restaurants: 40–60 lv per person

Money

» ATMs are widely available. Credit cards are accepted in most hotels and restaurants.

Visas

» Visas are not required for EU citizens. Citizens of Australia, Canada, New Zealand and the USA can visit visa-free for up to 90 days.

Mobile Phones

» Visitors from elsewhere in Europe will be able to use their mobile phones in Bulgaria. Local SIM cards can be used in most phones.

Transport

» Drive on the right; the steering wheel is on the left side of the car. Buses link most towns, trains are slower.

Websites

» **Bulgaria Travel** (www.bulgariatravel. org) Official tourism portal.

» **Vagabond** (www. vagabond.bg) Features on culture and politics.

» **Anglo Info** (www. bulgaria.angloinfo. com) Expat site with useful general information.

» **Beach Bulgaria** (www.beachbulgaria. com) Seaside information.

» **Bulgarian Ministry of Foreign Affairs** (www.mfa.government. bg) Practical basic information.

» **Lonely Planet** (www. lonelyplanet.com/ bulgaria) Get a quick overview of Bulgaria and see our hotel and hostel reviews.

Exchange Rates

Australia	A$1	1.54 lv
Canada	C$1	1.54 lv
Europe	€1	1.95 lv
Japan	¥100	1.92 lv
New Zealand	NZ$1	1.23 lv
Romania	1 lei	0.40 lv
UK	£1	2.43 lv
USA	US$1	1.51 lv

For current exchange rates see www.xe.com

Important Numbers

Bulgarian area codes have between two and five numerals. When dialing a local number, drop the initial '0'.

Country Code	☏359
Ambulance	☏150
Fire	☏160
Police	☏166
24-hour Pharmacy Information	☏178

Arriving in Bulgaria

» **Sofia Airport**
Minibus – 1.50 lv; minibus 30 to the city centre; 30–40 minutes
Bus – 1 lv; bus 384 to Mladost Metro Station from Terminal 2 or bus 84 to Sofia University from Terminal 1; 40–50 minutes
Taxi –10–12 lv to centre; 30–40 minutes

» **Varna Airport**
Bus – 1 lv; bus 409 to the city centre; 30 minutes
Taxi – 10 lv to centre; 20–30 minutes

Yes or No?

One cultural oddity that foreign visitors may find confusing at first is that Bulgarians shake their head from side to side in a curved, almost wobbly motion to indicate 'yes' and gently jerk their heads up and backwards when they want to say 'no'. To add to the confusion, if Bulgarians know they are addressing a foreigner, they may reverse these gestures in an attempt to be helpful. If you are in any doubt about their real meaning, asking 'Da ili ne?' (Yes or no?) will soon set you straight.

if you like...

Churches & Religious Art

Luminous icons and wonderful murals adorn churches, monasteries and museums all around the country. Many of the older churches are themselves worth seeking out – here you can appreciate the art as it was meant to be seen.

Boyana Church Dating back to the 13th century, this is one of the best-preserved medieval churches in the country, housing rare, colourful murals of saints, kings and queens (p304)

Rila Monastery Founded in the 10th century, Rila is Bulgaria's most important religious site, and features large frescoes by the 19th-century master, Zahari Zograf (p322)

Aleksander Nevski Crypt Bulgaria's biggest and most comprehensive collection of icons and religious art, collected from churches all over the country, is on show at this fascinating Sofia museum (p303)

Sveti Stefan Church In the heart of Nesebâr, this medieval church is famous for its beautiful 16th-to-18th century murals, which cover virtually the whole interior (p410)

Beaches

If you're looking for sandy beaches, the Black Sea coastline has something for everyone, from organised water sports and nightlife to cheaper seaside towns favoured by Bulgarian families. You could also combine a beach holiday with a city break in Burgas or Varna.

Sunny Beach Bulgaria's most popular destination for foreign visitors, with a soft, sandy beach, countless organised activities and plenty of clubs and pubs (p411)

Primorsko Popular with young Bulgarians and families, this small resort town has two long, attractive beaches and shallow water ideal for paddling (p404)

Sinemorets White sandy beaches, clean water and a slower pace of life make this remote seaside village in the far south an appealing choice (p406)

Varna Experience the best of both worlds in Bulgaria's 'maritime capital', with its long sandy beach within walking distance of bars, clubs, shops and big-city buzz (p412)

Castles

Bulgaria's long and often violent history has left the countryside peppered with crumbling reminders of the civilisations which crossed, fought over, settled and conquered this land. Romans, Byzantines, Bulgars and Ottoman Turks have all left their mark.

Tsarevets Fortress The seat of Bulgaria's medieval tsars in Veliko Târnovo still impresses, with its mighty walls and towers and almost palpable sense of history(p364)

Kaleto Fortress Almost blending into the natural rockface in Belogradchik, this awe-inspiring citadel was largely built by the Turks over older foundations stretching back to the Romans (p429)

Baba Vida Museum Fortress One of the best-preserved castles in Bulgaria watches over the Danube at Vidin. Originally a Roman fort, it was built up by medieval Bulgarians and 17th-century Turks (p430)

Shumen Fortress With origins going back to the Thracians, this vast fortress was expanded under the Byzantines and became an important military and industrial centre under the Second Bulgarian Empire (p359)

PETER SCHOLEY / GETTY IMAGES ©

» Roman Amphitheatre (p339), Plovdiv

Skiing & Snowboarding

Skiers and snowboarders from all over Europe, as well as plenty of Bulgarian snow bunnies, descend on the country's slopes in winter, and whether you're a seasoned pro or a nervous novice, you're sure to find somewhere that meets your needs.

Bansko Bulgaria's biggest and most popular resort with international visitors, Bansko also has the best après-ski fun; you can also try cross-country skiing here (p330)

Pamporovo Another big, modern resort, with good facilities including easier slopes for learners and cross-country trails, though there's not much to the town itself (p352)

Chepelare The smaller, quieter resort in the Rodopi Mountains is great for families; as well as some long, challenging trails, it also has gentler slopes and is good for snowboarding (p350)

Mt Vitosha Just a short ride from the nation's capital, the six slopes here are the highest in Bulgaria, and ideal if you just fancy an afternoon's skiing before heading back to town (p318)

Roman Remains

The Roman Empire extended its reach into Thracian territory, and the land we know today as Bulgaria, in the 1st century AD, and soon made itself at home, building towns, theatres and bathhouses, as well as heavily defended fortifications.

Hisar Bulgaria's most extensive and impressive Roman ruins dominate this little spa town, including vast gateways and city walls (p381)

Roman Thermae In the Black Sea port of Odessos (Varna), you can still see the bathing areas and furnaces at these huge public baths (p412)

Roman Amphitheatre Plovdiv's magnificent theatre was built in the 2nd century AD, and still hosts drama and music performances today (p339)

Roman Fortress of Sexaginta Prista Dating back to the 1st century AD, this Roman outpost in Ruse once commanded river traffic on the Danube (p433)

Hiking & Climbing

With seven mountain ranges and a remarkable 37,000km of marked hiking trails and numerous mountain huts for overnight stays, Bulgaria truly is a paradise for the outdoors enthusiast. Experienced rock climbers will also be in their element.

Rila Mountains The rugged and heavily wooded range in southern Bulgaria has walking routes to suit all abilities, one heading past the lovely Rila Monastery (p321)

Pirin Mountains In the southwest corner of the country, this alpine landscape of glacial lakes and valleys is picturesque walking country, and has tough rock-climbing routes suitable for experienced climbers (p327)

Rodopi Mountains Towards the Greek border, the forested Rodopi Mountains offer a variety of walks and fine views taking in lush countryside, pretty villages and natural wonders such as the Trigrad Cave (p350)

Stara Planina Cutting Bulgaria in two, the 'Old Mountains' offer breathtakingly beautiful scenery and a wide variety of peaks and valleys (p379)

month by month

January

New Year festivities in Bulgaria can be colourful affairs, especially in rural areas where old customs are still followed. Snow covers much of the country and it's the peak time for skiing.

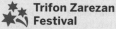
St Vasil's Day
Traditionally, New Year's Day in the country-side is marked by young boys, known as *sourvakari*, tapping people with deco-rated twigs to wish them luck for the year ahead. The day ends with traditional festive music and partying.

February

Cold and crisp, February is a quiet time of year in the cities, but the skiing season continues in the mountains. It's a good time for snowboarding and snowshoeing, too.

Trifon Zarezan Festival
To celebrate the patron saint of wine in Melnik and other winemaking areas, vines are pruned, sprinkled with wine and blessed by a priest on the first day of February.

March

March sees the start of spring in Bulgaria, though weather can be unpredictable. Snowfall is still possible in the mountains. Tourist sites open up again after winter.

Baba Marta
'Granny March' signifies the beginning of spring, and Bulgarians present each other with red and white woollen tassels on 1 March, known as *martinitsi,* as good-luck tokens.

March Days of Music Festival
One of Bulgaria's best clas-sical music festivals, held in Ruse. Concerts take place over the last two weeks of the month (www.march musicdays.eu).

April

The weather warms up in April, the skiing season ends, and, depending on the year, Orthodox Easter celebrations usually take place towards the end of the month.

Easter
Easter is the most important festival of the Bulgarian Orthodox Church, and incense-and-music-filled services take place in churches everywhere. Painted eggs and ritual loaves and cakes are part of the celebrations.

May

May is often wet and warm, and is a good time to visit the coast, before the crowds descend and prices rise. Some of the big festivals begin this month.

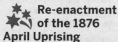
Re-enactment of the 1876 April Uprising
The momentous events surrounding the 1876 April Uprising are remembered by patriotic locals in Ko-privshtitsa, who dress in period costume. Curiously, it's held around 1 and 2 May.

Varna Summer International Festival
Kicking off in May and last-ing all summer in Varna, this is one of the oldest and biggest festivals (p416) in

Bulgaria, comprising music, theatre and other cultural events (www.varnasummer fest.org).

June

Summer is well under way, temperatures are rising and the tourist season on the coast begins. A great time for hiking, climbing and birdwatching.

Flower for Gosho Festival

Rock and blues bands from all over Bulgaria come to Sofia's vast Yuzhen Park in early June for a high-decibel music festival (p305) held among the trees.

 Festival of Roses

Cheery community festival in Kazanlâk, honouring the local flower crop on the first weekend in June, with street parades, dancing, concerts and the crowning of the Rose Queen (www. rose-festival.com).

July

High temperatures are recorded across the country in July. Both Bulgarian and foreign tourists flock to the coastal resorts while the cities bake.

Sand Sculpture Festival

Come to the beach in Burgas to admire the fantastic sand sculptures (p396) created by visiting artists. There's a different theme each year and the sculptures remain all summer.

August

Temperatures are at their highest in August, with long, hot sunny days, warm evenings and little or no rain. Music festivals are in full swing.

Bansko International Jazz Festival

Top jazz musicians from across Europe and beyond come to Bansko (p333). Free concerts are held in the main square over a week in early August.

Spirit of Burgas Festival

A popular Black Sea music event, Spirit of Burgas (p397) brings in international rock and jazz acts for a three-day beach party in early August.

September

Days are still hot in September, but begin to cool later in the month. A good time for birdwatching, as the Via Pontica migration begins.

Plovdiv Night of Museums

Plovdiv's museums and art galleries open their doors for free entry on one Friday evening late in the month, with exhibitions, performances and film screenings around town (www.night.bg).

Apollonia Arts Festival

A huge festival (p402) of music, drama and dance in the seaside town of Sozopol, attracting big names over the first week of the month (www.apollonia.bg).

October

Cooler days across Bulgaria come in October but temperatures are still pleasant. Harvest and cultural festivals take place around the country.

Days of Ruse

Yearly cultural festival (p433) in Ruse focusing on music, dancing and drama performances. Held at various locations around town in early October.

November

Winter approaches and temperatures drop. Expect rain and cold, shorter days. The pace of life slows down, but there's always something to see and do in the cities.

Young Wine Festival

Plovdiv celebrates the new wine vintage with parades, music and dance performances as well as lots of opportunities to sample local wines in the streets and houses of the old town.

December

Cold weather descends on Bulgaria in December, with snowfall on higher ground. The skiing season begins. Christmas services in Orthodox churches are truly atmospheric.

Christmas Festival of Arts

Folk music ensembles, dancers and singers perform for the crowds in Sofia's chilly Ploshtad Bulgaria, held over a few days just after Christmas.

itineraries

Whether you've got six days or 60, these itineraries provide the starting point for a trip of a lifetime. Want more inspiration? Head online to lonelyplanet.com/thorntree to chat with other travellers.

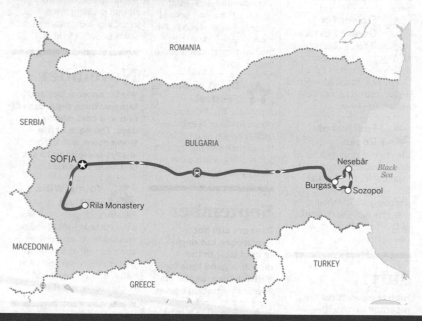

Two Weeks
From Sofia to the Coast

> Start off with a few days in the capital, **Sofia**, taking time to visit a couple of the fascinating museums, galleries and churches. From Sofia, you can take a day trip out to the beautiful **Rila Monastery**, Bulgaria's most important pilgrimage site and one of the country's real highlights.

Take the bus – or train, if you prefer – from Sofia to **Burgas** on the southern Black Sea coast. Spend at least one night in this laid-back city, and take a stroll through the lovely Maritime Park down to the beach. Take the bus for the short trip southwards along the coast to the ancient town of **Sozopol**, with its quaint cobbled lanes and attractive sandy beaches. Spend three or four days here, relaxing by the seaside, sampling the fresh local seafood and maybe enjoying one of the free outdoor concerts or a yacht trip around the peninsula. If you're here in summer, catch the ferry up to **Nesebâr**, famed for its numerous medieval churches, and spend the day sightseeing.

Return to Burgas to get the bus or train back to Sofia.

ROMANIA

Silistra

Ruse
Rusenski Lom
Nature Park

Pleven

Varna

SERBIA

Vratsa

Veliko
Târnovo

Shipka Pass

SOFIA

Karlovo

Shipka
Kazanlâk

Hisar (Hisarya)

BULGARIA

Black
Sea

Plovdiv

Bansko

Bachkovo
Monastery

TURKEY

MACEDONIA

Rozhen Monastery

Melnik

GREECE

Along the Danube to the Sea
Southern & Central Bulgaria

Two Weeks
Along the Danube to the Sea

> From Sofia, head north by bus to the little town of **Vratsa**, where you can spend a couple of days walking in the mountains or visiting the interesting museums. From here, travel by bus to **Pleven** where you can pick up another bus to **Ruse**, for your first glimpse of the mighty Danube. One of Bulgaria's most elegant and appealing cities, Ruse is known for its grand Viennese-style architecture and boasts several diverting museums, extensive parkland and a lively cafe scene.

Spend three or four days in Ruse, taking a day trip south of the city to the **Rusenski Lom Nature Park** to visit the remarkable rock churches and caves, and maybe spot some of the rare local wildlife.

From Ruse head eastwards to **Silistra**, a quiet town on the Danube, for a relaxing day or two before continuing to the Black Sea coast at **Varna**. You could easily spend several days in Bulgaria's 'maritime capital'. Relax on the long, sandy city beach, enjoy a show or concert at one of the city's many cultural venues, or go clubbing along the vibrant seafront.

Three Weeks
Southern & Central Bulgaria

> From Sofia, catch a bus south to tranquil **Melnik**, famous for its wine, chalky 'pyramids' and National Revival–era mansions. Soak up the sunshine for a couple of days and visit historic **Rozhen Monastery** nearby. Continue by bus to **Bansko**, for two or three days of summer hikes or winter skiing.

From Bansko, take the train as it meanders on a narrow-gauge rail through mountainous forests before reaching Septemvri, on the main line to **Plovdiv**; this city boasts a sublime old town with clustered, classic architecture, ancient sites, art galleries and cafes – it deserves three or four days, especially if you'll also visit nearby **Bachkovo Monastery**. Head north to **Hisar**, famous since antiquity for its healing waters.

Continue to quiet **Karlovo** for more traditional ambience before visiting **Kazanlâk**, famous for its ancient Thracian Tomb. Cross the mountains at the gorgeous **Shipka Pass**, stopping first in **Shipka** village, to see its gleaming, golden onion-domed church. Finally, unwind for a few days in **Veliko Târnovo**, Bulgaria's medieval capital. In the shadow of its impressive fortress, this university city offers elegant eating and vivacious nightlife.

regions at a glance

Sofia

Culture ✓✓✓
Parks & Gardens ✓✓
Dining ✓✓

Culture
The Bulgarian capital is the country's cultural heart, and home to an abundance of museums and galleries, ranging from serious old-school collections to more engaging modern exhibition spaces. Whether your taste is for archaeology, religious art, natural history or socialist realism, you'll have plenty of choice. The National Museum of History will take up half a day and give you a solid overview of the nation's past, while you could spend several more days exploring the diverse museums spread across the city centre. Pore over a century of Bulgarian paintings at the National Art Gallery, or visit a battalion of stone Lenins at the Museum of Socialist Art.

Parks & Gardens
Get away from the urban hustle and bustle, and head to one of the city's many parks. The vast welcoming greenery of Borisova Gradina, with its shady pathways and simple little cafes is the perfect place for an afternoon stroll and is great for kids, with plenty of open spaces and play areas. Smaller, neater city gardens are the place to go to watch the world go by.

Dining
Sofia has some of the best and most varied restaurants in Bulgaria. Sample the highest-quality traditional Bulgarian cuisine, or try something new – Italian, French, Greek or Moroccan perhaps – or shop for fresh fruit, pastries and tasty local snacks.

p294

Plovdiv & Southern Mountains

Art Galleries ✓✓✓
Skiing ✓✓✓
Entertainment ✓✓

Art Galleries
Plovdiv's elegant old town is an impeccable host for some of the Balkans' top art galleries. The best Bulgarian painters, including contemporary artists, are on display; free city-wide exhibitions each September are prominent events on the cultural calendar.

Skiing
The Rila, Pirin and Rodopi Mountains sprawl across southern Bulgaria and offer the country's best skiing. Bansko offers unexplored terrain for off-piste adventures and raucous après-ski partying; smaller places like Chepelare are family-friendly, with idyllic cross-country trails.

Entertainment
From alternative bars, rock concerts and slick Bulgarian discos to classical and opera performances held in ancient Roman theatres, student-oriented Plovdiv offers some of Bulgaria's most dynamic and diverse nightlife.

p319

Veliko Târnovo & Central Mountains

Churches ✓✓✓
Architecture ✓✓✓
Hiking ✓✓

Churches
Central Bulgaria's Orthodox churches, many dating to Byzantine times, are among the Balkans' most historically and aesthetically significant. Fantastically carved iconostases and masterful frescoes comprise the treasures that have survived centuries of upheaval.

Architecture
Bulgaria's central heartland was crucial to the National Revival of the 18th and 19th centuries, and there's no better place to see these lavishly decorated and ornate period mansions, many now museums or B&Bs.

Hiking
The Stara Planina mountain range stretches across Bulgaria's central spine for almost 550km. This rolling deciduous-and-pine range is dotted with marked trails – perfect both for easy ambling on a forested path and arduous long-haul trekking.

p357

Black Sea Coast

Beaches ✓✓✓
Ancient Towns ✓✓
Nightlife ✓✓✓

Beaches
Bulgaria's Black Sea coastline is the country's biggest tourist draw, boasting long and inviting sandy beaches. Top up your tan, try a spot of jet skiing or parasailing at the big resorts, or find a hidden cove in the far north or south.

Ancient Towns
With histories stretching back millennia, the Black Sea's quaint historic towns are a joy to explore. Take a trip back in time through the cobbled lanes of Sozopol and explore the ruined medieval churches of Nesebâr.

Nightlife
The Black Sea coast has many of Bulgaria's best clubs. The big package resorts have the pick of the bunch, attracting international DJs and acts, while Varna is summertime party central for young Bulgarians.

p393

The Danube & Northern Plains

The Great Outdoors ✓✓✓
Fortresses & Ruins ✓✓✓
Urban Charm ✓✓

The Great Outdoors
Northern Bulgaria encompasses a wide variety of landscapes, from the wild, mountainous northwest, ideal for hiking and rock climbing, to the diverse beauty of the Rusenski Lom Nature Park, famed for its wildlife.

Fortresses & Ruins
The remains of ancient fortresses abound in this historic frontier zone. The Roman fort of Sexaginta Prista in Ruse, Byzantine city walls in Silistra and Ottoman fortifications in Vidin and Belogradchik show how much this region was prized.

Urban Charm
The Danubian city of Ruse boasts elegant architecture, excellent restaurants and the region's best museums. It's also a great base for exploring the surrounding countryside.

p425

> **Every listing is recommended by our authors, and their favourite places are listed first**

> **Look out for these icons:**

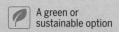 Our author's top recommendation

 A green or sustainable option

FREE No payment required

On the Road

Sofia

📄 02 / POP 1.3 MILLION

Includes »

Best Places to Eat

» Manastirska Magernitsa (p307)

» Annette (p308)

» Pastorant (p307)

» Olive Garden (p308)

» Before & After (p308)

Best Places to Stay

» Hotel Niky (p305)

» Residence Oborishte (p306)

» Hotel Les Fleurs (p306)

» Arena di Serdica (p306)

» Canapé Connection (p306)

Why Go?

Bulgaria's pleasingly laid-back capital, Sofia (*So*-fia) is often overlooked by tourists heading straight to the coast or the ski resorts, but they're missing something special. It's no grand metropolis, true, but it's a largely modern, youthful city, while its old East-meets-West atmosphere is still very much evident, with a scattering of onion-domed churches, Ottoman mosques and stubborn Red Army monuments sharing the skyline with vast shopping malls and glassy five-star hotels. Sofia's grey, blocky civic architecture lends a lingering Soviet tinge to the place, but it's also a surprisingly green city. Vast parks and manicured gardens offer welcome respite from the busy city streets, and the ski slopes and hiking trails of mighty Mt Vitosha are just a short bus ride from the city centre. Home to many of Bulgaria's finest museums, galleries, restaurants and entertainment venues, Sofia may persuade you to stick around and explore further.

When to Go
Sofia

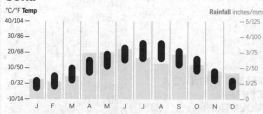

Mar–May Spring is warm and wet, and Easter is a colourful time to visit.

Jun–Aug Summer is very hot and dry, especially August, but there's plenty to see and do in the city.

Nov–Feb Winters in Sofia are often icy cold, with heavy snowfalls, but January is perfect for skiing.

Sofia Highlights

1 Visiting impressive **Aleksander Nevski Memorial Church** (p303)

2 Viewing the paintings and artwork on show at the two **museums** (p297) inside the former Royal Palace

3 Looking over ancient treasures at the **Archaeological Museum** (p297)

4 Taking a leisurely walk around leafy **Borisova Gradina** (p302), with its statues, fountains and cafes

5 Exploring history at the **National Museum of Military History** (p303)

6 Taking a trip out to visit the lovely **Boyana Church** (p316), famous for its medieval murals

7 Getting lost in the wild landscape of **Yuzhen Park** (p303)

8 Uncovering the past at the **Museum of Socialist Art** (p303)

9 Experiencing Sofia's spiritual side in **Sveta Nedelya Cathedral** (p296)

10 Buying fruit and veg at the bustling **Ladies' Market** (p312)

History

The Thracian Serdi tribe originally settled the Sofia region as far back as the 8th century BC, but the city as we know it today was founded by the Romans, who conquered the region in AD 29 and built the town of Ulpia Serdica. In the late 3rd century AD Serdica became a major regional imperial capital, reaching a zenith in the early 4th century under Emperor Constantine the Great. The Sveti Georgi Rotunda is the most prominent reminder of the Roman era still standing.

The city passed back and forth between the Bulgarians and the Byzantine Empire during the early Middle Ages, until the Ottomans, sweeping through the Balkans, captured it in 1382, and held it for nearly 500 years. The Ottomans built baths and mosques, such as the Banya Bashi Mosque, but many churches were destroyed or abandoned; the tiny Church of Sveta Petka Samardzhiiska is a very rare survivor.

It was in Sofia that the celebrated anti-Turkish rebel Vasil Levski was hanged in 1873, after first being interrogated and tortured in the building that later became the Royal Palace. After the liberation of the city from the Turks in early 1878, Sofia officially became the capital of Bulgaria on 4 April 1879.

Much of Sofia was destroyed in bombing during WWII and postwar Socialist architects set to work rebuilding the heavily damaged city on the Soviet model, complete with high-rise housing blocks in the suburbs and monstrous monuments in the city centre, such as the old Party House, which dominates pl Nezavisimost.

◉ Sights

Most of Sofia's sights are handily located in the compact city centre, and you won't have to do too much walking to get round them all. Further afield, the suburb of Boyana is the location of the city's biggest museum and its most revered church.

AROUND PLOSHTAD SVETA NEDELYA

Sveta Nedelya Cathedral CHURCH
(pl Sveta Nedelya; Ⓜ Serdika) Completed in 1863, this magnificent domed church is one of the city's major landmarks, noted for its rich, Byzantine-style murals. It was blown up by communists on 16 April 1925 in an attempt to assassinate Tsar Boris III. Over 120 people were killed in the attack, including most of the cabinet, but Boris escaped unharmed.

NORTH OF PLOSHTAD SVETA NEDELYA

Sveta Petka Samardzhiiska Church CHURCH
(bul Maria Luisa; Ⓜ Serdika) Closed due to surrounding excavations at the time of research, this tiny church was built during the early years of Ottoman rule (late 14th century), which explains its sunken profile and inconspicuous exterior. Inside are some 16th-century murals. It's rumoured that the Bulgarian national hero Vasil Levski is buried here.

Sofia Synagogue JEWISH
(www.sofiasynagogue.com; ul Ekzarh Yosif 16; ☺9am-4pm Mon-Fri, 10am-2pm Sun; 🚌20) Sofia's Moorish-style synagogue was designed

---

SOFIA IN...

One Day

Head straight to Sofia's most impressive sight, the Aleksander Nevski Memorial Church (p303). While you're there, visit the Aleksander Nevski Crypt to see the Museum of Icons. Go along to the nearby Royal Palace, and take a look over the paintings and sculptures in the National Art Gallery (p297). In the evening, drop by Pri Kmeta (p309) for a beer or two.

Three Days

Follow the above itinerary, and on the second day admire the treasures on show at the Archaeological Museum (p297) and take the opportunity to watch the changing of the guard at the neighbouring President's Building (p301). On the next day, take a relaxing stroll around Borisova Gradina (p302) and have dinner at the excellent Manastirska Magernitsa (p307).

One Week

After the above itinerary, go to Boyana to see the National Museum of History (p316) and the lovely Boyana Church (p316). Take a look round the Museum of Socialist Art (p303) and take a day trip out to Koprivshtitsa.

SOFIA'S BEST FREE ATTRACTIONS

» Aleksander Nevski Memorial Church (p303)
» Borisova Gradina (p302)
» Last Monday of the month at the National Gallery for Foreign Art (p301)
» The preserved ruins of the Roman amphitheatre in the Arena di Serdica (p306) hotel.
» Sofia City Art Gallery (p300)

by Austrian architect Friedrich Gruenanger, and was consecrated in 1909. Built to accommodate up to 1170 worshippers, it is the second-largest Sephardic synagogue in Europe, and its 2250kg brass chandelier is the biggest in Bulgaria.

Banya Bashi Mosque   MOSQUE
(bul Maria Luisa; admission free; ☉dawn-dusk; 🚍20) Sofia's only working mosque was built in 1576. It's certainly an eye-catching edifice and the red-brick minaret makes a convenient landmark. Visitors are welcome outside prayer times if modestly dressed.

Mineral Baths   HISTORIC BUILDING
(ul Triaditsa; 🚍20) The Mineral Baths – also known as the Turkish Baths – was completed in 1913. Its elegant striped facade and ceramic decorations recall the designs of Nesebâr's medieval churches. Following lengthy restoration, the building now hosts occasional art exhibitions, advertised in *Programata* magazine.

National Polytechnic Museum   MUSEUM
(ul Opalchenska 66; adult/student 5/2 lv; ☉9am-5pm Mon-Fri; 🚍1, 5) A treasure trove for anyone interested in the history of technology, this low-key museum displays an intriguing (though not always well labelled) collection covering such subjects as photography, radio and time measurement. Exhibits include atomic clocks, early movie cameras, mechanical pianos and a gleaming 1928 Ford Model A.

AROUND PLOSHTAD BATTENBERG
Originally built as the headquarters of the Ottoman governor and his police force, it was at the **Royal Palace** that Bulgaria's national hero, Vasil Levski, was tried and tortured before his public execution in 1873. After the liberation the building was remodelled in Viennese style and in 1887, apparently undeterred by its grisly recent past, Prince Alexander Battenberg moved in and it became the official residence of Bulgaria's royal family until the communist takeover.

These days it provides a grand setting for the National Art Gallery and the Ethnographical Museum. There are gardens at the back of the palace, with a number of statues and a pleasant little cafe, Toba & Co.

National Art Gallery   GALLERY
(pl Battenberg, Royal Palace; adult/student 6/3 lv; ☉10am-6pm Tue-Sun; 🚍20) This gallery holds one of the country's most important collections of Bulgarian art, with several galleries full of mainly 19th- and 20th-century paintings. All the big names are represented, including the ubiquitous Vladimir Dimitrov, whose orange, Madonna-like *Harvester* hangs in the former music room. Upstairs, a warren of corridors and small rooms forms a display space for Bulgarian sculpture.

Ethnographical Museum   MUSEUM
(pl Battenberg, Royal Palace; adult/student 3/1 lv; ☉10am-4pm Tue-Sun; 🚍20) Displays on regional costumes, crafts and folklore are spread over two floors of the palace, and many of the rooms, with their marble fireplaces, mirrors and ornate plasterwork, are worth pausing over themselves; note the lobster, fish and dead duck on the ceiling of what was once presumably a royal dining room. There are regular temporary exhibitions.

Archaeological Museum   MUSEUM
(www.naim.bg; pl Nezavisimost; adult/student 10/2 lv; ☉10am-6pm May-Oct, 10am-5pm Tue-Sun Nov-Apr; 🚍10) Housed in a former mosque, built in 1496, this museum displays a wealth of Thracian, Roman and medieval artefacts. Highlights include a mosaic floor from the Church of Sveta Sofia, the 4th-century BC Thracian gold burial mask, and a magnificent bronze head, thought to represent a Thracian king. Also here are icons and frescoes removed from churches around Bulgaria.

National Museum of
Natural History   MUSEUM
(www.nmnhs.com; bul Tsar Osvoboditel 1; adult/student 4/2 lv; ☉10am-6pm; 🚍9) You can

Central Sofia

0   400 m
0   0.2 miles

To National Polytechnic Museum (370m)

Hristo Botev

Silvnitsa

Silvnitsa

General Danail Nikolaev

Vladaiska River

Silvnitsa

To Central Bus Station, Matpu-96 & Trafik Market (550m)

Lion Bridge

46

44

Maria Luisa

Pop Bogomil

Immigration Office

Struma

Sv Kiril i Methodii

Pop Bogomil

Budapeshta

48

Vasil Levski

Chumerna

Dunav

11 Avgust

Rakovski

Benkovski

Tsar Simeon

Ekzarh Yosif

Iskăr

Bacho Kiro

Veslets

Rostza

Parizh

Stara Planina

Vrabcha

Dondukov

Dondukov

To Poduyane Bus Station (2km)

17

Vasil Levski Memorial

Yanko Sakazov

To Residence Oborishte (440m); Bistro Landau (440m)

Krakra

Oborishte

15

19 Fevruari

14

25

pl Aleksander Nevski

1

Holy Synod Church

Vasil Levski

Oborishte

41

92

28

99

Parizh

85

76

37

Georgi Benkovski

30

16

13

Moskovska

pl Battenberg

Tsar Osvoboditel

77

Djakon Ignaty

80

22

Knyaz Al Battenberg

2

Party House

Nezavisimost

Minibus 30

53

101

39

Serdika

82

6

10

65

3

27

91

52

24

Serdika Metro Station

Todor Aleksandrov

23

Trapezitsa

Ekzarh Yosif

Knyaz Boris I

Tsar Simeon

Pirotska

96

Stefan Stambolov

George Washington

Veslets

69

Sv Kiril i Methodii

Stamboliyski

33

Tsar Samuil

Bratya Miladinovi

72

100

To easyHotel (1km)

To Mall Of Sofia (450m); Cinema City (450m)

20

29

Săborna

pl Sveta Nedelya

Sv Sofia

National Tourist Information Centre

26

Lăvele

71

Pozitano

Palace of Justice

73

32

Lege

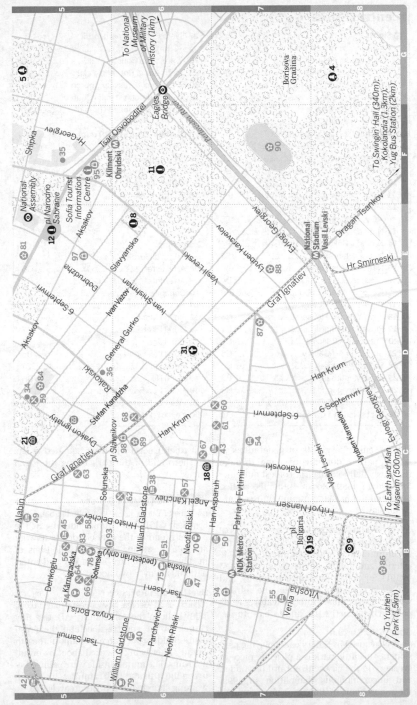

SOFIA

Central Sofia

almost sense the ghosts of generations of school parties dutifully trooping through the musty halls of Bulgaria's oldest museum, founded in 1889. Rocks, minerals, stuffed birds and animals and mounted insects are on display.

Sveti Nikolai Russian Church   CHURCH
(ul Tsar Osvoboditel; ⊙7.45am-6.30pm; ⊟9) This beautiful church, with its glittering mosaic exterior and golden domes, was completed in 1914 for Sofia's Russian community, and named in honour of St Nikolai, the 'miracle worker'. The cramped interior features icons painted between the 11th and 14th centuries.

Sofia City Garden   PARK
(⊟10) Favoured by Sofia's chess-playing pensioners, this little park is a pleasing piece of greenery in the city centre. Until its sudden and unceremonious demolition in 1999, the mausoleum of Bulgaria's first commu-nist ruler, Georgi Dimitrov, squatted at the northern end of the park facing the Royal Palace.

FREE Sofia City Art Gallery   GALLERY
(ul General Gurko 1; ⊙10am-7pm Tue-Sat, 11am-6pm Sun; ⊟10) This chunky building at the southern end of the City Garden is now an art gallery, staging rotating exhibitions of mostly contemporary Bulgarian and international art over two floors.

Sveti Georgi Rotunda   CHURCH
(Church of St George; www.svgeorgi-rotonda.com; ⊟10) Built in the 4th century AD, this tiny church in the courtyard behind the President's Building was largely rebuilt in the 6th century after being knocked about by invading Huns. The murals inside were painted between the 10th and 14th centuries. It's a busy, working church, but tourists are welcome.

President's Building   NOTABLE BUILDING
(pl Nezavisimost; 🚇10) The Bulgarian president's office isn't open to the public, but the **changing of the guard** ceremony (on the hour) is a spectacle not to be missed, as soldiers in raffish Ruritanian uniforms stomp their way to their sentry boxes outside.

Party House   NOTABLE BUILDING
(pl Nezavisimost; 🚇20) This domineering Stalinist monolith, built in 1953, was once the headquarters of the Bulgarian Communist Party. It is now used as government offices. The red star perched on top of the building is now in the Museum of Socialist Art (p303).

AROUND PLOSHTAD ALEKSANDER NEVSKI

Sveta Sofia Church   CHURCH
(ul Parizh; ⏱7am-7pm summer, 7am-6pm winter; 🚇9) Sveta Sofia Church is the capital's oldest, and gave the city its name. Inside the much-restored red-brick church, you can see evidence of its earlier incarnations through glass panels in the floor. Outside are the Tomb of the Unknown Soldier and an eternal flame, and the grave of Ivan Vazov, Bulgaria's most revered writer.

Sofia University Botanic Garden   GARDENS
(ul Moskovska; admission 2 lv; ⏱10am-5pm; 🚇1, 2) Sofia's small Botanic Garden includes a glasshouse filled with palms and cacti, a rose garden and various trees and flowers (labelled in Bulgarian and Latin). The entrance is through what looks like a flower shop on bul Vasil Levski.

National Gallery for Foreign Art   GALLERY
(www.foreignartmuseum.bg; ul 19 Fevruari 1; adult/student 6/3 lv, last Mon of month free; ⏱11am-6.30pm Wed-Mon; 🚇1, 2) An eclectic assemblage of international artworks is exhibited in this huge, squeaky-floored gallery,

ranging from Indian woodcarvings and African tribal masks to countless 19th- and 20th-century paintings, mostly by lesser-known artists. Minor sketches by Renoir and Matisse and works by Gustave Courbet are on show too.

SOUTH OF PLOSHTAD ALEKSANDER NEVSKI

Monument to the Soviet Army MONUMENT
(**M**Kliment Ohridski) Near the entrance to Borisova Gradina, this gigantic monument was built in 1954 and is a prime example of the forceful socialist-realism of the period. The place of honour goes to a Red Army soldier atop a column, surrounded by animated cast-iron sculptural groups depicting determined, gun-waving soldiers and grateful, child-caressing members of the proletariat.

Borisova Gradina PARK
(🚌5, 76, **M**National Stadium Vasil Levski, Kliment Ohridski) Lying southeast of the city centre, Sofia's most attractive park is filled with countless statues and flowerbeds and is a relaxing place for a stroll. It's a vast place, and is home to the **Vasil Levski Stadium** and **CSKA Stadium**, as well as several cafes and children's play areas.

The eastern end of the park is dominated by a gigantic communist monument built in 1956 and known as the **Mound of Brotherhood**, featuring a 42m-high obelisk and socialist-realist icons including a pair of partisan fighters, dramatically gesturing comrades clutching Kalashnikovs, and smiling, stoic workers. It has long been neglected by the authorities, and several of the socialist heroes are now missing limbs and gaining coats of graffiti, but small groups of pensioners come on occasion to lay flowers in remembrance of the red old days.

Ploshtad Bulgaria PARK
(pl Bulgaria; 🚌1, 2, 5, **M**NDK) Watched over by the polygonal concrete bulk of the **National Palace of Culture** (NDK; pl Bulgaria), this elongated park, with its fountain, ice-cream kiosks and bars, is popular with promenading locals, skateboarding teens and buskers. At the southern end is a tiny memorial chapel dedicated to the victims of communism.

Sveti Sedmochislenitsi Church CHURCH
(Church of the Seven Saints; ul Graf Ignatiev; ⏰7am-7pm; 🚌10) Set in a leafy garden, this church, dedicated to Sts Cyril and Methodius and their five disciples, was originally built as a mosque in 1528; it later became an arms depot and a prison, before being consecrated as a church in 1903. Inside, there's a gilded iconostasis with icons painted by Anton Mitov.

PRINCE ALEXANDER BATTENBERG

Emerging from five centuries of Ottoman rule, the leaders of the nascent state of Bulgaria decided they would rather like their country to be a monarchy. With no obvious native claimant to the throne, the Russian tsar suggested his 22-year-old nephew, a minor German prince named Alexander of Battenberg, to take up the position, and he was duly installed as Prince of Bulgaria in 1879, modern Bulgaria's first head of state. The young ex-army officer was feted on his arrival in the country, but Alexander soon found that governing the fractious new state was anything but easy, and in 1881 he suspended the constitution to rule as an absolute monarch, though in effect, it was the prince's Russian backers who were really running the show.

Democracy was restored in 1883, and Alexander dismissed the Russian generals who had been controlling the country. In 1885, without the approval of the Russian tsar, the province of Eastern Rumelia was reunited with the rest of Bulgaria. Alexander had made many enemies in his pro-Russian military, and in 1886, a group of army officers forced him to abdicate and handed him over to the Russian authorities. There was a swift counter-revolution, and the prince was soon recalled to Sofia. However, without Russian support, Alexander's position was untenable, and he formally abdicated in September 1886. A new prince, Ferdinand of Saxe-Coburg-Gotha, was elected in his place.

Alexander left Bulgaria for the last time and headed for Austria, where he took the title Count von Hartenau and married an actress called Johanna Loisinger. He died in 1893, aged just 36. Alexander retained a deep affection for the country he had briefly ruled and, according to his wishes, his remains were brought back to Sofia and interred in an elegant **mausoleum** (bul Vasil Levski; **M**Kliment Ohridski) on bul Vasil Levski, which has been carefully restored and is open to the public.

ALEKSANDER NEVSKI MEMORIAL CHURCH

One of *the* symbols not just of Sofia but of Bulgaria itself, this massive, awe-inspiring **church** (pl Aleksander Nevski; admission free; ⊙7am-7pm) dominating pl Aleksander Nevski was built between 1882 and 1912 in memory of the 200,000 Russian soldiers who died fighting for Bulgaria's independence during the Russo-Turkish War (1877–78). It is named in honour of a 13th-century Russian warrior-prince.

Designed by Russian architect AN Pomerantsev, the church was built in the neo-Byzantine style favoured in Russia at the time and is adorned with mosaics and gold-laden domes. The cavernous, incense-scented interior is decorated with naturalistic, though now rather faded, murals, pendulous chandeliers and elaborate onyx and alabaster thrones.

Visitors are welcome and there are daily services where you can hear evocative Orthodox chants and prayers.

A door to the left of the main entrance leads down to the **Aleksander Nevski Crypt** (Museum of Icons; pl Aleksander Nevski; adult/student 6/3 lv; ⊙10am-6pm Tue-Sun; 🚍1). It displays Bulgaria's biggest and best collection of religious icons dating from between the 5th and 19th centuries, brought here from churches all over the country.

Earth and Man Museum
MUSEUM
(www.earthandman.org; bul Cherni Vrâh 4; adult/student 4/2 lv; ⊙10am-6pm Tue-Sun; 🚍6) This rather old-fashioned museum is dedicated to geology, with two floors' worth of minerals, crystals, ores and the like. There are some big, impressive geodes on show.

Yuzhen Park
PARK
(🚍74) South of the city centre, Yuzhen Park is a vast, wild green sprawl, filled with trees and shady pathways. A sparkling stream bubbles through it, and there is a handful of discreet bars and cafes that are not always easy to find, but it's a satisfying place to get lost in and explore for yourself.

Peyo Yavorov House-Museum
HISTORIC BUILDING
(🖉987 3414; ul Rakovski 136, 2nd fl; adult/student 3/2 lv; ⊙10am-5pm Mon-Wed & Fri, 1-5pm Thu; 🚍9) The Romantic poet and revolutionary Peyo Yavorov (1878–1914) briefly lived in a small apartment here; the three rooms here have been restored to their original appearance, while ghoulish mementos include the dress Yavorov's wife, Lora, was wearing when she killed herself in the study and Yavorov's death-mask. Ring the doorbell for admittance.

EAST OF PLOSHTAD ALEKSANDER NEVSKI
Doctors' Garden
PARK
(ul Shipka; 🚍9) Behind the National Library, this neat, secluded park features a big, pyramidal monument dedicated to the medics who died in the Russo-Turkish War (1877–78). Also here is an outdoor lapidarium, with lots of Roman architectural fragments dug up around Sofia.

Oborishte Park
PARK
(Vladimir Zaimov Park; bul Yanko Sakazov; 🚍20) This attractive park, with its fountains, lovely rose beds, cafes and popcorn vendors, is especially popular with young families, and there are some attractions for younger kids, including electric cars and a bouncy castle. There are also ping-pong tables that are free to use.

National Museum of Military History
MUSEUM
(www.militarymuseum.bg; ul Cherkovna 92; admission 3 lv; ⊙10am-6pm Wed-Sun; 🚍9, 72, 🚍20) This slightly out-of-the-way museum tells the story of warfare in Bulgaria, with most space given to the period from the 1876 April Uprising through to WWI. Weaponry, rebel flags, uniforms and decorations are on show, while outside is an impressive collection of Soviet-made military hardware including Scud missile launchers, tanks and MiG fighters.

Museum of Socialist Art
MUSEUM
(ul Lachezar Stanchev 7, Iztok; admission 6 lv; ⊙10am-5.30pm Tue-Sun; Ⓜ GM Dimitrov) If you wondered where all those unwanted statues of Lenin ended up, you'll find some here, along with the red star from atop Sofia's Party House (p301). There's a gallery of paintings, rejoicing in such catchy titles as 'Youth Meeting at Kilifarevo Village to Send Worker-Peasant Delegation to the

PEYO YAVOROV

One of Bulgaria's most admired lyric poets, Peyo Yavorov's turbulent life story sounds like it could have come from the pages of a lost Puccini opera. He was born in Chirpan in 1878 and by his early twenties his moody writing style had won many admirers. He was already a celebrated literary figure in Sofia when he joined the guerrillas fighting the Turks in Macedonia. His girlfriend Mina Todorova (whose parents had forbidden her relationship with the restless poet) died of consumption in Paris in 1910, and it was at her funeral that he met his next lover, Lora Karavelova, who lived with him at the house on ul Rakovski that now holds a museum dedicated to his memory. However, theirs was a stormy marriage and Lora, jealous of her husband's supposed affairs with other women, shot herself in 1913. Yavorov, a now broken and penniless man, shot himself a year later.

USSR,' and stirring old propaganda films are shown.

The museum isn't the easiest place to find. Catch the metro to the GM Dimitrov station, in the Iztok suburb, walk north up bul Tsankov and then turn right onto ul Lachezar Stanchev. The museum is housed in a gated Ministry of Culture building next to the Sopharma Business Towers. There is no sign anywhere, but you can see the big red star in the garden.

🏃 Activities

There are a number of gyms, pools and sports centres around Sofia. For details about hiking, skiing and other popular activities, see Vitosha Nature Park (p316).

🐎 Courses

Sofia University   LANGUAGE COURSE
(☑971 7162; www.deo.uni-sofia.bg; bul Tsar Osvoboditel) Bulgarian-language courses for foreigners are offered by the university. One-to-one courses cost 380 lv for 20 hours' tuition; group courses cost from 340 lv per person for 20 hours. Summertime classes in Bulgarian language and folklore are also offered; the intensive two-week course costs 549 lv. Accommodation is available.

Study in BG   LANGUAGE COURSE
(☑986 6973; www.studyinbg.com; ul Rakovski 145; 🚇9) Modern language centre offering Bulgarian-language lessons to foreigners. Private, one-to-one lessons cost 20 lv per hour on site, or 30 lv elsewhere. Longer group courses are available.

👉 Tours

There are a number of free tours you can join to explore Sofia and the surrounds, run by enthusiastic local volunteers; donations, to keep these enterprises going, are much appreciated. Some hostels organise day trips for guests.

Rila Monastery is awkward to visit in one day by public transport from Sofia, so an organised tour may be more convenient. However, renting a car or even chartering a taxi for the day may be cheaper for a group of two to four people.

FREE **Free Sofia Tour**   WALKING TOUR
(☑0886 993 977; www.freesofiatour.com; ⊙11am & 6pm) Explore Sofia's sights in the company of friendly and enthusiastic English-speaking young locals on this guided walk. No reservation is needed, just show up at the meeting place, outside the Palace of Justice on bul Vitosha, at 11am or 6pm. Walks take around two hours.

FREE **Sofia Bike Tour**   CYCLING
(☑0885 523 630; www.sofiagreentour.com; ⊙10am, 11am & 5pm Apr-Nov) Discover Sofia on two wheels, on free one-hour tours led by English-speaking guides, departing from the front of the Ivan Vazov National Theatre (p310) at 10am. Bring your own bike, or borrow one free of charge. Three-hour tours depart at 11am and 5pm, and cost 10 lv for bike rental.

Boyana Hiking Tour   HIKING
(☑0885 523 630; www.sofiagreentour.com; tours 10 lv; ⊙11am Apr-Nov) The same people who run the bike tours (and with the same meeting point) also run this guided four-hour hike, taking in the wild countryside around Boyana Church. The fee covers the return minibus to Boyana. Longer hikes are also offered.

Zig Zag Holidays   OUTDOORS
(☑02-980 5102; www.zigzagbg.com; bul Stamboliyski 20-V; ⊙9.30am-6.30pm Mon-Fri) Offers all sorts of tailor-made outdoor activities, in-

cluding hiking, climbing, caving and biking trips. It offers day trips to Rila Monastery (96 lv) and Koprivshtitsa (96 lv) as well as one-day hiking trips to Mount Vitosha (98 lv). Prices are per person, for groups of up to six. Entrance is on ul Lavele.

⭐ Festivals & Events

Sofia International Film Festival   CINEMA
(www.siff.bg; ☉Mar) Movie buffs descend on the capital each March for a celebration of international independent films.

Flower for Gosho Festival   LIVE MUSIC
(Yuzhen Park; ☉Jun) This two-day event in early/mid-June takes place in Yuzhen Park (p303) and features blues musicians and rock bands from across Bulgaria.

A to JazZ   JAZZ
(www.atojazz.bg; Doctors' Garden; ☉late Jun) Live jazz performances take place in the Doctors' Garden (p303) over a few days in late June.

Sofia International   TRADITIONAL DANCE,
Folklore Festival   TRADITIONAL MUSIC
(☉mid-Jul) Takes place in and around the city for three days in mid-July.

St Sofia's Day   CHRISTIAN
(☉Sep) The city's patron saint is honoured with services at churches across the capital on 17 September.

Sofia Dance Week   DANCE
(NDK; ☉late Sep-early Oct) A varied program of modern dance, held over two weeks at the NDK (p302).

Cinemania   CINEMA
(☉Nov-Dec) A month-long, non-competitive celebration of independent film-making held in the National Palace of Culture (NDK; p302) in November and December.

🛏 Sleeping

Unsurprisingly, accommodation in Sofia tends to be more expensive than anywhere else in Bulgaria, with prices comparable to those in Western European cities.

Good-quality budget hotels are a bit of a rarity in Sofia, and the cheaper places that do exist are often either squalid dives best avoided or in awkward-to-reach locations; hostels are a much better deal.

The dependable **Wasteels** (☑931 0636; www.wasteels.bg; central train station; ☉9am-6pm Mon-Fri; 🖫1) accommodation bureau at the train station can book you into hotel rooms in Sofia and elsewhere, from 50 lv per night.

TOP CHOICE **Hotel Niky**   HOTEL **$$**
(☑953 0110; www.hotel-niky.com; ul Neofit Rilski 16; r/ste from 80/120 lv; 🅿☺❄🛜; 🖫1) Offering excellent value and a good city-centre location, Niky has comfortable rooms and gleaming bathrooms, while the smart little

---

SOFIA FOR CHILDREN

Lions, tigers, elephants and bears are among the animals at **Sofia Zoo** (www.zoosofia. eu; Borisova Gradina; adult/child 4/2 lv; ☉8.30am-5pm; 🖫120), which also has play areas for children, and a couple of simple cafes. It's free for children under seven years old.

Young speed fans (over eight years old) can take the wheel of a motorised go-kart and zoom around the twisting, 1km-long track at **Karting Sport** (☑920 1447; www. karting-bg.com; bul Vardar 3a; per lap 2 lv; ☉9am-9pm May-Sep, 10am-6pm Oct-Apr; 🖫11,77, 🖫4, 11, 22), a modern speedway circuit in the Krasna Polyana district.

Kids and adults can enjoy active, outdoorsy fun at **Kokolandia** (www.kokolandia.com; ul Nezabravka, Borisova Gradina; admission 3-5 lv; ☉9am-9pm May-Oct; 🖫84, 413), an adventure park inside Borisova Gradina. Divided into three increasingly challenging areas, it offers rope-climbing, tree-top obstacle courses (harnesses provided) and rock-climbing walls. The first zone is suitable for children aged five to 10, while the third is for over-18s only.

Play areas can be found in Borisova Gradina (p302), which has wide open green spaces that young children might enjoy. Sofia City Garden (p300) and Oborishte Park (p303) also have playgrounds and attractions like electric cars. Older siblings might prefer a game of bowls at **Mega Xtreme Bowling** (www.mega-xtreme.com; ul Kosta Lulchev 52, SkyCity Mall; price per game 2.50-4.50 lv; ☉24hr; 🚻; 🖫9) or a spot of tennis at the **Maleeva Tennis Club** (☑962 2288; www.maleevaclub.com; bul Nikola Vaptsarov; 🖫88).

Sofia has several English-speaking nurseries and day-care centres, aimed more at expat families, but there are no reliable babysitting agencies working with foreign tourists. However, some top-end hotels may be able to provide such services.

suites all come with kitchenettes with microwave ovens, fridges and tea- and coffee-making facilities. It's a very popular place and frequently full. Advance reservations are recommended.

Residence Oborishte
BOUTIQUE HOTEL $$$

(☏0885 006 810; www.residence-oborishte.com; ul Oborishte 63; s/d/ste from 180/200/220lv; 🌐✖️❄️🛜; 🚌9, 72) A salmon-pink 1930s home with its own bistro, the Residence has nine rooms and sumptuous suites with cherry-wood flooring, antique-style furnishings and lots of space. The penthouse (260 lv) has a view over the Aleksander Nevski Church. Prices drop by 20% at weekends.

Arena di Serdica
LUXURY HOTEL $$$

(☏819 9191; www.arenadiserdica.com; ul Budapeshta 2-4; r from 220 lv; P🌐❄️🛜) Rooms in this modern five-star hotel are plush but understated. The hotel's name comes from the remains of the 4th-century Roman amphitheatre, which were uncovered during construction and are now preserved below the foyer. There's also a 'Roman-style' spa.

Visitors are welcome to gaze over the remains of the Roman amphitheatre inside the hotel (free; 10am to 4pm).

Arte Hotel
HOTEL $$

(☏402 7100; www.artehotelbg.com; bul Dondukov 5; r/ste from 110/220 lv; ❄️🛜; 🚌20) Welcoming city-centre hotel with bright, modern rooms and contemporary artworks adorning the walls. Prices drop slightly at weekends, and breakfast is an additional 20 lv.

Sheraton Sofia
Hotel Balkan
LUXURY HOTEL $$$

(☏981 6541; www.sheratonsofia.com; pl Sveta Nedelya 5; r/ste from 320/470 lv; P🌐❄️🛜; Ⓜ️Serdika) Marble floors, glittering chandeliers and large, plush rooms provide a level of comfort that should please the most demanding of guests at this landmark hotel. The official rates are rather high, but discounts are frequently available.

Hotel Les Fleurs
BOUTIQUE HOTEL $$$

(☏810 0800; www.lesfleurshotel.com; bul Vitosha 21; r from 270 lv; P🌐❄️🛜; 🚌10) You can hardly miss this very central hotel, with gigantic blooms on its facade. The flowery motif is continued in the large, carefully styled rooms and there's a very good restaurant on site.

Canapé Connection
HOSTEL $

(☏441 6373; www.canapeconnection.com; ul William Gladstone 12a; dm/s/d from 20/46/60 lv; @;

🚌1) Run by three young travellers, Canapé is a homely place with eight- and four-bed dorms featuring smart wooden bunks and wooden floors, as well as private rooms. Homemade *banitsa*, pancakes and croissants are on the breakfast menu.

Hostel Gulliver
HOSTEL $

(☏987 5210; www.gulliver1947-bg.com; bul Dondukov 48; dm/s/d 18/38/48 lv; 🛜; 🚌20) Just a couple of blocks north of pl Aleksander Nevski, Gulliver is a clean and brightly furnished place with a couple of five-bed dorms and three doubles. All rooms have TVs and fridges.

The House
BOUTIQUE HOTEL $$

(☏952 0830; www.hotelthehouse.com; ul Verila 4; s/d from 45/55 lv; P🌐❄️🛜; 🚌1) On a quiet sidestreet off bul Vitosha, this attractively renovated townhouse has a wide choice of rooms, some quite small, but it's good value for central Sofia. Some might find the narrow wooden stairs awkward.

Hostel Mostel
HOSTEL $

(☏0889 223 296; www.hostelmostel.com; bul Makedoniya 2; dm/s/d from 20/50/60 lv; P🛜; 🚌6, 9, 12) Popular Mostel occupies a renovated 19th-century house, and has six- and eight-bed dorms, with either shared or private bathrooms, as well as a single and a couple of doubles; guests have use of a kitchen and cosy lounge.

Red House
B&B $$

(☏988 8188; www.redbandb.com; ul Lyuben Karavelov 15; s/d from 50/80 lv; @; Ⓜ️Vasil Levski, 🚌10) Attached to the Red House cultural centre, in an unusual Italianate building partly designed by sculptor Andrei Nikolov, who lived here in the 1930s, this six-room hotel is a unique place to stay. All rooms are individually decorated, though none have private bathrooms and some are a bit basic.

Art Hostel
HOSTEL $

(☏987 0545; www.art-hostel.com; ul Angel Kânchev 21a; dm/s/d 20/44/60 lv; 🛜; 🚌12) This bohemian hostel stands out from the crowd with its summertime art exhibitions, live music, dance performances and more. Accommodation consists of a attractive, brightly painted three- to eight-bed dorms as well as some airy private rooms, and there's a peaceful little garden at the back.

Kolikovski Hotel
BUSINESS HOTEL $$$

(☏933 3000; www.kolikovski.com; ul Hristo Belchev 46; s/d/ste 110/130/200 lv; ❄️@🛜; 🚌1) On a side street near the National Palace of Culture (NDK), the Kolikovski offers a range of elegant rooms, including 'business class' (with a free bottle of wine thrown in) and some spacious suites – the one on the 5th floor comes with kitchenette and terrace.

Hotel Lion HOTEL $$$
(917 8400; www.sofia.hotelslion.bg; bul Maria Luisa 60; s/d from 115/135 lv; 🌐🛜; 🅿7) Facing the Lions Bridge, this is a grand old building in a lively location. Rooms are large, modern and a variety of shapes and styles, and all come with fridges,TVs and bathtubs.

Internet Hostel Sofia HOSTEL $
(0889 138 298; www.internethostelsofia.hostel.com; ul Alabin 50a, 2nd fl; dm/s/d/apt from 16/40/50/70 lv; @🛜; 🅿12) Centrally located hostel with a wide choice of large, clean rooms, with four- and six-bed dorms, singles, doubles, and private studios with separate entrances. Not immediately obvious from street level, the entrance is inside an arcade a couple of doors down from a McDonald's.

Sofia Guesthouse HOSTEL $
(403 0100; www.sofiaguest.com; bul Patriarh Evtimii 27; dm/d 18/56 lv; 🅿🌐🛜; 🅿12) Set in a private garden off the main road, this place has basic but clean dorms and a few private twin and double rooms. Staff can organise various day trips and activities, as well as longer excursions to the mountains.

Levitt Hostel HOSTEL $
(0885 640 012; www.levitthostel.com; bul Vitosha 55; dm/s/d from 20/40/60 lv; 🛜🛜) Certainly one of Sofia's best-located hostels, this welcoming American-run place has 12 smart rooms, all with cable TV, and the friendly, multilingual staff can organise day trips. Apparently, it's the only place in Sofia to serve kosher breakfast, too.

Scotty's Boutique Hotel BOUTIQUE HOTEL $$
(983 6777; www.scottyshotel.info; ul Ekzarh Yosif 11; s/d from 85/100 lv; 🅿🌐🛜; 🅿20) Opposite the synagogue, Scotty's is a small, stylish, gay-friendly hotel with just nine rooms, all individually designed and named after international cities, such as the Cape Town Room, kitted out with zebra-print details.

Hotel Diter HOTEL $$$
(989 8998; www.diterhotel.com; ul Han Asparuh 65; s/d 110/130 lv; 🅿🌐🛜; 🅿9) Occupying a restored, bright-blue 19th-century townhouse on a quiet street within easy walking distance of the centre, the Diter is a cosy place with a variety of bright rooms. There's also an on-site restaurant, bar and garden.

Hotel Pop Bogomil HOTEL $
(983 1165; www.popbogomil.com; ul Pop Bogomil 5; r 45-80 lv; 🅿🛜; 🅿9) This small hotel has 10 comfortable rooms, all individually decorated and variously priced. It's handy for the central train and bus stations, though a little out of the way for anything else.

easyHotel HOTEL $
(920 1654; www.easyhotel-sofia.bg; ul Aldomirovska 108; r 40-70 lv; 🅿🌐🛜; MKonstantin Velichkov, 🅿3) This modern, orange-hued hotel, part of the easyJet empire, has 57 clean and clinical rooms, but they are very compact. Not one for the claustrophobic.

Hotel Enny HOTEL $
(983 4395; www.enyhotel.com; ul Pop Bogomil 46; s/d from 30/40 lv; 🅿7) This quiet place offers reasonable value for budget-conscious travellers, although some rooms are small and you don't even get a fan for this price. En-suite rooms cost slightly more.

🍴 Eating

Compared with the rest of Bulgaria, Sofia is gourmet heaven, with an unrivalled range of international cuisines represented and new, quality restaurants springing up all the time.

In summer, cafes seem to occupy every piece of garden and footpath in Sofia. Some are just basic spots for a coffee and a sandwich, while others offer a more refined setting for cocktails and cakes. Most cafes are open from about 8am to midnight.

There are plenty of kiosks around town where you can buy tasty local fast food such as *banitsa* (cheese pasties) and *palachinki* (pancakes), as well as pizzas and burgers.

TOP CHOICE Manastirska Magernitsa BULGARIAN $$
(980 3883; www.magernitsa.com; ul Han Asparuh 67; mains 5-10 lv; ⏰11am-2am) This traditional *mehana* (tavern) is among the best places in Sofia to sample authentic Bulgarian cuisine. The enormous menu features recipes collected from monasteries across the country, with such dishes as 'drunken rabbit' stewed in wine as well as salads, fish, pork and game options. Portions are generous and service attentive.

Pastorant ITALIAN $$$
(981 4482; www.pastorant.eu; ul Tsar Assen 16; mains 11-26 lv; ⏰noon-10.30pm; 🖊) This charming

MAKING A DIFFERENCE

Like any other big European city, Sofia has its social problems, and beggars are a common feature of the streets. Many are elderly, struggling to exist on very low pensions, who have resorted to selling flowers, singing, playing an instrument or simply sitting beside a battered old pair of bathroom scales where passers-by can weigh themselves for a few stotinki. Anything you can spare will be greatly appreciated. Beware, though, the professional beggars who pretend to be mentally or physically disabled, and gangs of children.

pea-green restaurant provides an intimate setting for high-quality Italian cuisine, including some inventive pasta and risotto dishes as well as traditional favourites like saltimbocca and pesto chicken.

Annette   MOROCCAN $$

(☑0885 139 676; www.annette.bg; ul Angel Kânchev 27; mains 8-18 lv; 🛜) With its cushion-filled couches, glowing candles and lanterns and spicy aromas, this is a great place for authentic Moroccan cooking, including a big selection of tasty meze, and tagine meals like lamb with figs and apricots, and chicken in wine sauce.

Olive Garden   MEDITERRANEAN $$

(☑481 1214; www.olivegardensofia.com; ul Angel Kânchev 18; mains 10-22 lv; ⊙11am-11pm; 🛜🍴) Expertly cooked roast lamb, trout, salmon, pasta and risotto are served here. There's a smart indoor dining room, or you can sit in the little garden with its mulberry tree. A cheaper lunch menu is also offered.

Bistro Landau   BISTRO $$$

(☑814 4888; www.bistrolandau.com; ul Oborishte 63; mains 12-30 lv; ⊙7am-10.30pm; 🛜; 🚌9, 72) Attached to the Residence Oborishte (p306), this romantic bistro offers an eclectic menu of interesting dishes such as beef entrecote, breaded tilapia, trout and sausages in curry sauce.

Before & After   CAFE $$

(☑981 6088; ul Hristo Belchev 12; mains 5-15 lv; ⊙10am-midnight; 🛜; 🚌8) With its stylish art-nouveau interior, this is an agreeable spot for light meals and drinks. Pasta, risotto, fish and steaks feature on the menu.

Olive's   INTERNATIONAL $$

(ul Graf Ignatiev 12; mains 7-18lv; 🍴🛜; 🚌10) Walls splashed with vintage advertising posters and mock newspapers for menus give Olive's a quirky twist, and the international cuisine on offer is excellent, featuring dishes such as chicken skewers, pasta, steaks and burgers.

Trops Kâshta   CAFETERIA $

(bul Maria Luisa 26; mains from 3 lv; ⊙8am-8.30pm; 🍴) There are several branches of this budget cafeteria around town, offering Bulgarian favourites such as *kebabche* (grilled spicy meat sausages), soups and moussaka. There's no menu; just point at whatever takes your fancy. Best to get here early as popular items get snapped up and the remainder get cold.

Soupateria   BUFFET $

(pl Slaveikov 6; mains 3-5 lv; ⊙24hr; 🍴) If you're just looking for a quick bite, this bright cafeteria offers a variety of freshly made, filling and very tasty soups, as well as sandwiches and drinks. There's no English menu, but friendly staff will help you choose.

Afreddo   ICE CREAM $

(bul Vitosha 12; tubs & cones 2-4 lv) For the best ice cream in Sofia, come to Afreddo, and try one (or more) of the dozens of flavours on display; the pistachio is good. There are seats upstairs, too, and coffee and sandwiches are also available.

Krâchme Divaka   BULGARIAN $

(ul 6 Septemvri 41a; mains 3-7 lv; ⊙24hr; 🍴; 🚌10) In an appealing old house, this restaurant is a good choice for traditional Bulgarian food. Dishes include wine-soaked kebab with mashed potatoes, a filling potato cream soup, and grilled trout, and there are plenty of vegetarian options.

Pri Yafata   BULGARIAN $$

(☑980 1727; www.pri-yafata.com; ul Solunska 28; mains 7-20 lv; ⊙10am-midnight; 🛜🍴; 🚌1) Done out like a traditional *mehana*, with agricultural tools, rifles and rugs adorning the walls, Pri Yafata serves hearty dishes of duck, rabbit, pork and chicken and plenty of vegetarian options. It's very popular, and reservations are advisable for the evenings, which regularly feature live music.

Sofi French Bakery   BAKERY $

(ul Rakovski 161; sandwiches 3-6 lv; ⊙8.30am-8pm Mon-Sat, 9am-6pm Sun; 🚌9) This takeaway bakery offers a tempting range of sandwiches, baguettes, croissants and the like, and some of the best pastries in town. There are a couple of stand-up tables inside.

Dream House   VEGETARIAN $

(www.dreamhouse-bg.com; ul Alabin 50a, 1st fl; mains 4-8 lv; ✎; 🖫10, 12) This informal vegetarian restaurant is up some grubby stairs, in an arcade just off the street. Options include stir-fries, curries, pancakes and homemade lemonade. There's an all-you-can-eat buffet on Sundays (10 lv).

Cafe Theatre   CAFE

(Dyakon Ignatiy; cakes from 3 lv) Beside the imposing Ivan Vazov National Theatre, this summer-only pavement cafe is a pleasant spot for drinks and cakes.

Central Hali Shopping Centre   FAST FOOD $

(bul Maria Luisa 25; ⊘7am-9pm) There are several outlets in the upstairs food court in this market hall that sell cheap fast food such as kebabs, pizzas and ice cream, as well as beer.

Self-Catering

An abundance of fresh fruit and veg can be yours at the Central Hali, the Ladies' Market and the **stalls** along ul Graf Ignatiev (outside the Sveti Sedmochislenitsi Church). For everything else, try branches of Piccadilly Supermarket, which can be found in the basements of the Mall of Sofia and the City Center Sofia shopping malls.

Piccadilly   SELF CATERING

(bul Maria Luisa 2, Tsum Retail Centre; ⊘8am-10pm; MSerdika) With a separate entrance at the side of the Tsum Retail Centre, this is the most central branch of the nationwide supermarket chain, with a selection of chilled foods, snacks, drinks and a deli counter. There's a much bigger branch in the Mall of Sofia.

🍷 Drinking

There's a seemingly inexhaustible supply of watering holes all over Sofia. The cheapest places to grab a beer are the kiosks in the city's parks; if you're looking for a more sophisticated ambience, the city centre has plenty of swish new bars.

Pri Kmeta   PUB

(www.prikmeta.com; ul Parizh 2; ⊘noon-4am; 🛜; 🖫20) 'At the Mayor's' is a microbrewery serving its own 'Kmetsko' beer, available in litre and, for the very thirsty, metre-length measures. There are seats at ground level, but the cellar beer hall, with its gleaming copper

vats, is more atmospheric, and hosts regular live music events.

Ale House   BEER HALL

(www.alehouse.bg; ul Hristo Belchev 42; ⊘11am-midnight; 🖫9) No need to queue at the bar at this convivial beer hall – the tables have their own beer taps. Food is also served, and there's live music on Fridays and Saturdays.

Lavazza Espression   CAFE

(bul Vitosha 44; ⊘8am-10pm; 🛜) This trendy little cafe brings a touch of Italian style to the city centre, with a long list of coffees to choose from, and a brief menu of bruschetta and sandwiches.

Toba & Co   COCKTAIL BAR

(ul Moskovska 6; ⊘8.30am-6am) Ensconced in what was once Tsar Ferdinand's butterfly house, in the gardens at the rear of the Royal Palace, this discreet cafe is a charming spot to sip cocktails or indulge in ice cream and cakes.

Veda House   TEAHOUSE

(ul William Gladstone 2; teas from 3 lv; ⊘10.30am-11pm; 🖫1) This sociable, vaguely Indian-themed teahouse has a lengthy (Bulgarian-only) menu of black and green teas, served in pretty little teapots. Light vegetarian meals are available, too.

Upstairs   COCKTAIL BAR

(bul Vitosha 18; ⊘10am-2am) Join the 'in-crowd' on the 1st-floor terrace stools of Upstairs and look down on the shoppers along bull Vitosha over cocktails, or lounge on the sofas inside.

Buddha Bar   LOUNGE

(ul Lege 15a; ⊘24hr; 🛜; 🖫10) Very hip, very trendy and very crowded, this Buddha-bedecked drinking spot also serves food, and has a nightly disco from around 9pm.

Café-Club Tintin   GAY

(ul Bratya Miladinovi 12; ⊘9am-11pm; 🛜; 🖫1) Spread over two floors, this is a chic bar attracting a mixed crowd. There's outdoor seating in the garden in summer.

Exit   GAY

(📞0887 965 026; ul Lavele 16; ⊘8am-2am; 🛜; 🖫8) This modern and fashionable bar–diner is a popular gay venue, with a DJ party every evening.

JJ Murphy's   PUB

(www.jjmurphys.net; ul Kârnigradska 6; ⊘noon-12.30am; 🖫1) Popular city-centre Irish pub frequented by expats, with live music at weekends.

 Entertainment

If you read Bulgarian, or at least can decipher some of the Cyrillic, *Programata* is the most comprehensive source of entertainment listings; otherwise check out its excellent English-language website, www.programata.bg. You can book tickets online at www.ticketpro.bg.

Nightclubs

Some clubs charge admission fees of anywhere between 2 lv and 15 lv, mostly late at night and at weekends when live bands are playing. Studentski Grad is home to several of Sofia's trendier clubs; ask around for the latest venues.

Swingin' Hall   LIVE MUSIC
(963 0059; bul Dragan Tsankov 8; 9pm-4am; 10) Huge club offering an eclectic program of live music each night, ranging from jazz and blues to rock and folk pop.

Social Jazz Club   JAZZ
(0884 622 220; pl Slaveikov 4; 10pm-4am Mon-Sat; 10) The place to go to catch some quality live jazz, with a program of leading international acts.

Avenue   CLUB
(0898 553 085; ul Atanas Manchev 1a, Studentski Grad; 24hr; 94) One of the more popular student joints, Avenue plays both Western songs and Bulgarian *chalga* (folk pop) music.

ID Club   GAY
(www.idclub.bg; ul Kârnigradska 19b; 9pm-5am Tue-Sat;) ID is a big, glittering gay club with three bars, theme nights, cabaret and a playlist including everything from house to *chalga*.

Chervilo   CLUB
(www.chervilo.com; bul Tsar Osvoboditel 9; 10.30pm-6am Tue-Sat; 9) The live music, guest DJs and themed party nights at 'Lipstick' draw in Sofia's young and fashionable set at night, and it also has a pleasant terrace for sitting out with a drink or two.

Cinemas

As well as a couple of modern multiplexes, Sofia has several smaller cinemas dotted around town. Most screen recent English-language films with Bulgarian subtitles, although cartoons and children's films are normally dubbed into Bulgarian.

Cinema City   CINEMA
(www.cinemacity.bg; bul Stamboliyski 101; tickets 6-12 lv; Opalchenska) Modern, multiscreen cinema on the top floor of the Mall of Sofia, showing the latest Hollywood releases.

Dom Na Kinoto   CINEMA
(www.domnakinoto.com; ul Ekzarh Yosif 37; tickets 4-7 lv; 20) Shows a varied program of Bulgarian-language, independent and vintage foreign films.

Odeon   CINEMA
(989 2469; bul Patriarh Evtimii 1; tickets 4-6 lv; 10) Snubs modernity by showing only classic old films, which run for months at a time.

Theatre & Music

Ticket prices at these venues vary enormously. For the Opera House or the National Theatre, they might cost anything from 10 lv to 30 lv; shows at the NDK vary much more, with tickets costing from 30 lv to 70 lv for international acts and around 10 lv to 30 lv for local ones.

National Opera House   OPERA
(987 1366; www.operasofia.com; bul Dondukov 30, entrance on ul Vrabcha; ticket office 9am-2pm & 2.30-7pm Mon-Fri, 11am-7pm Sat, 11am-4pm Sun; 9, 20) Opened in 1953, this monumental edifice is the venue for grand opera and ballet performances, as well as concerts.

National Palace of Culture   CONCERT VENUE
(NDK; 916 6368; www.ndk.bg; pl Bulgaria; ticket office 9am-7pm; ; NDK) The NDK (as it's usually called) has 15 halls and is the country's largest cultural complex. It maintains a regular program of events throughout the year, ranging from film screenings and trade shows to big-name international music acts.

Bulgaria Hall   CLASSICAL MUSIC
(987 7656; ul Aksakov 1; ticket office 9am-6pm; 9) The home of the excellent Sofia Philharmonic Orchestra, this is the place to come for classical music concerts.

Ivan Vazov National Theatre   THEATRE
(811 9219; www.nationaltheatre.bg; ul Dyakon Ignatiy 5; ticket office 9.30am-7.30pm Mon-Fri, 11.30am-7.30pm Sat & Sun; 9) One of Sofia's most elegant buildings, the Viennese-style National Theatre opened in 1907, and is the city's main stage for Bulgarian drama.

Red House   ARTS CENTRE
(988 8188; www.redhouse-sofia.org; ul Lyuben Karavelov 15; ; 10) Occupying a unique,

early 20th-century mansion, this avant-garde institution hosts everything from political and cultural debates (in various languages) to poetry readings and dance performances. Many events are free; check the website for the current program. There's also a hotel here.

Sport

Football (soccer) is Bulgaria's main sporting passion, and Sofia alone has four teams. The main clubs are **CSKA** (www.cska.bg), which plays at the CSKA Stadium in Borisova Gradina, and **PFC Levski**, (www.levski.bg) based at the Georgi Asparoukhov Stadium (bul Vladimir Vazov, Poduyane). Lokomotiv and Slavia are Sofia's two smaller teams.

No other spectator sport comes close to the popularity enjoyed by football, although basketball has a keen, if relatively small, following. The main teams are **Lukoil Academic** (www.lukoilacademic.net) and **Levski** (www.levskibasket.com).

Vasil Levski Stadium   STADIUM
(Borisova Gradina; Ⓜ National Stadium Vasil Levski) This is the main venue for international football matches, athletics and other big sporting events.

🔒 Shopping

Bul Vitosha is Sofia's main shopping street, mostly featuring international brand-name boutiques interspersed with restaurants. More shops cluster along ul Graf Ignatiev, while ul Pirotska is a central pedestrian mall lined with cheaper shops selling clothes, shoes and household goods. There are also a few big modern shopping malls, housing international fashion chains, cinemas and supermarkets. Street stalls and markets are the best places to seek souvenirs.

Artists sell paintings, mainly of traditional rural scenes, near the Mineral Baths and around pl Aleksander Nevski, where you'll also find stalls selling reproduction religious icons, jewellery, souvenirs and embroidery. But be wary of the 'antiques': there are some genuine items here, but much of it's fake, and prices are very much aimed at tourists. The underpass below pl Nezavisimost has souvenir shops selling the usual array of postcards, paintings and books.

Stenata   OUTDOOR EQUIPMENT
(✆980 5491; www.stenata.com; ul Bratia Miladinovi 5; ⊙10am-8pm Mon-Fri, 10am-6pm Sat, 11am-6pm Sun; 🚇4) The best place in town to buy hiking, climbing and camping equipment, including backpacks, tents and sleeping bags.

Alpin Sport   OUTDOOR EQUIPMENT
(✆0886 456 600; www.alpinsport-bg.com; off ul Geo Milev, Slatina; ⊙10am-7pm Mon-Fri, 10am-5pm Sat; 🚇72) Slightly out of the way, near the Akademik Stadium in the eastern Slatina neighbourhood, this shop has an excellent stock of skiing, snowboarding, camping and climbing equipment.

Helikon   BOOKS
(bul Patriarh Evtimii 68; ⊙9.30am-8.30pm Mon-Sat, 10am-8.30pm Sun; 🚇1) Good range of English-language fiction plus books on Bulgaria in various languages.

Knizharnitsa   BOOKS
(Sofia University underpass; ⊙8.30am-8.30pm Mon-Fri, 9am-8.30pm Sat, 10am-8.30pm Sun; Ⓜ Kliment Ohridski) One of the better selections of English-, French- and German-language novels, with a little cafe on site.

Greenwich Book Center   BOOKS
(bul Vitosha 37; ⊙10am-10pm Mon-Sat, 10am-9pm Sun; ☎; 🚇10) Offers a small selection of foreign-language souvenir books about Bulgaria, as well as guidebooks, maps and music CDs. There's a cafe in the basement.

Mirela Bratova   WOMEN'S CLOTHING
(ul Ivan Shishman 4; ⊙10.30am-7pm Mon-Fri, 10.30am-6pm Sat; 🚇94) Stylish women's fashions designed by Sofia couturier Mirela Bratova are on display at this little shop, including knitwear, jewellery and accessories.

Centre of Folk Arts & Crafts   SOUVENIRS
(www.craftshop-bg.com; ul Parizh 4; ⊙9.30am-6.30pm Mon-Sat; 🚇20) Typical Bulgarian souvenirs such as hand-woven rugs, pottery, silver jewellery, woodcarvings and CDs of Bulgarian music are available in this crowded shop, though prices are rather high. There's another branch inside the Royal Palace, at the exit from the Ethnographic Museum.

Central Hali
Shopping Centre   SHOPPING CENTRE
(bul Maria Luisa 25; ⊙7am-9pm; 🚇20) This elegant market hall, built in 1911, has three floors of shops and cafes. Stalls on the ground floor sell fruit, vegetables, pastries, wine and cheese. Upstairs there's a cheap food court and more shops. The centre also holds a pharmacy, post office, bank and ATMs.

Mall of Sofia
SHOPPING CENTRE

(www.mallofsofia.com; bul Stamboliyski 101; ⊙10am-10pm; MOpalchenska) Sofia's biggest and busiest shopping centre, filled with international brand-name stores and coffee bars. There's a big supermarket in the basement, and a cinema, IMAX screen and food court on the top floor.

Tsum Retail Centre
SHOPPING CENTRE

(bul Maria Luisa 2; ⊙10am-8pm Mon-Sat, 11am-7pm Sun; MSerdika) The monumental former state department store, built in 1956, is now an upmarket, five-floor shopping mall, with clothing, jewellery, perfume and homeware shops. It's eerily quiet, often seeming to have more staff than customers, but it does have some smart free public toilets.

Open-Air Bookmarket
BOOKS

(pl Slaveikov; ⊙dawn-dusk; ⊑10) Dozens of bookstalls crowd this square daily, selling mostly Bulgarian novels, but plenty of books on Bulgarian history, culture and cuisine are available in foreign languages, as well as some secondhand English novels, maps and dictionaries.

Ladies' Market
MARKET

(ul Stefan Stambolov; ⊙dawn-dusk; ⊑20) Stretching several blocks between ul Ekzarh Yosif and bul Slivnitsa, this is Sofia's biggest fresh-produce market. Fruit and vegetables, cheap clothes, shoes, car parts, kitchen utensils and pretty much anything else you can think of can be bought here. It does get very crowded, so watch your belongings.

ℹ️ Information

Dangers & Annoyances

The main danger you are likely to face in Sofia comes from the often dreadful traffic; pedestrian crossings and traffic lights don't mean much to many drivers, so be extra careful when crossing roads. Note that traffic lanes and pedestrian areas are marked only by faint painted lines on the cobbles around pl Aleksander Nevski and pl Narodno Sabranie, and although the central section of bul Vitosha, between ul Alabin and bul Patriarh Evtimii, is now pedestrianised, you should still watch out for vehicles zipping out of the side streets.

Sofia has a large, and increasing, population of stray dogs – it is estimated that as many as 10,000 animals roam the city's streets, and there have been instances of people being attacked, seriously injured and even killed. You are unlikely to encounter packs of stray dogs in the city centre, but exercise caution and do not approach feral dogs.

As always, be careful with bags, wallets and purses on crowded public transport and particularly in busy areas such as the Ladies' Market and around pl Sveta Nedelya.

Emergency

Ambulance (☑150)

Fire (☑160)

Mountain Rescue (☑0886 404122, 926 5112)

Police (☑166)

Traffic Police (☑982 2723)

Media

Programata (www.programata.bg; free) A useful, widely available weekly listings magazine, with details of cinemas, restaurants and clubs. It's only in Bulgarian, but the website is in English.

Sofia City Info Guide (www.cityinfoguide.net; free) Published monthly, this includes basic practical information and reviews of hotels, restaurants and clubs and comes with a free city map. Available at hotel reception desks.

Sofia - The Insider's Guide (www.insidesofia. com; free) A pleasingly opinionated quarterly publication featuring background information and advice for visitors, as well as restaurant and entertainment reviews. Available at some hotels and travel agencies.

Medical Services

Neomed Pharmacy (☑951 5539; bul General Totleben 2B; ⊙24hr; ⊑4) Twenty-four-hour pharmacy.

Dr Ivan Dimitrov Dental Practice (☑952 2328; www.drivandimitrov.com; ul Dragshan 5; ⊑4) English-speaking dentist.

International Medical Centre (☑944 9326; www.imc-sofia.com; ul Gogol 28; ⊑9, 306) The IMC has English- and French-speaking doctors who will make house calls at any time. It also deals with dental care.

Pirogov Hospital (www.pirogov.bg; bul General Totleben 21; ⊑4) Sofia's main public hospital for emergencies.

Tokuda Hospital (☑403 4000; www.tokuda bolnica.bg; bul Nikola Vaptsarov 51b; ⊙24hr; ⊑88) Modern, Japanese-run private hospital with English-speaking staff.

Money

There are several foreign exchange offices on bul Vitosha, bul Maria Luisa and bul Stamboliyski.

Biochim Commercial Bank (ul Alabin)

Unicredit Bulbank (cnr ul Lavele & ul Todor Alexandrov)

United Bulgarian Bank (ul Sveta Sofia)

Post

Central Post Office (ul General Gurko 6; ⊙7.30am-8.30pm)

Tourist Information

National Tourist Information Centre (☎987 9778; www.bulgariatravel.org; ul Sveta Sofia; ⊗9am-5pm Mon-Fri; 🚌5) Helpful, English-speaking staff and glossy brochures for destinations around Bulgaria.

Sofia Tourist Information Centre (☎491 8345; Sofia University underpass; ⊗8am-8pm Mon-Fri, 10am-6pm Sat-Sun; Ⓜ Kliment Ohridski) Lots of free leaflets and maps, and helpful English-speaking staff.

Travel Agencies

Alexander Tour (☎983 5258; www.travelin bulgaria.eu; ul Pop Bogomil 40; ⊗9.30am-6pm Mon-Fri; 🚌6) Offers tours all over Bulgaria, including day trips and longer, tailor-made tours, as well as excursions to Romania and Turkey.

Odysseia-In Travel Agency (☎989 0538; www.odysseia-in.com; bul Stamboliyski 20-V, 1st fl, enter from ul Lavele; Ⓜ Serdika) Odysseia-In can book you on hiking, skiing, climbing, birdwatching and numerous other trips across the country. It deals with groups; individuals should contact the associated Zig Zag Holidays (p304) on the ground floor of the same building.

Zig Zag Holidays (☎980 5102; www.zigzagbg. com; bul Stamboliyski 20-V, enter from ul Lavele; ⊗9.30am-6.30pm Mon-Fri; Ⓜ Serdika) This private travel agency sells a range of maps and books, and has some free leaflets.

Websites

www.programata.bg Comprehensive eating, drinking and clubbing information.

www.sofia.bg Official municipal website, with business information.

www.sofiaecho.com Online news from Bulgaria and overseas, plus reviews and features.

www.sofia-life.com Bar and restaurant reviews, as well as practical advice.

www.sofiatraffic.bg Information on public transport.

ⓘ Getting There & Away

Air

The only domestic flights within Bulgaria are between Sofia and the Black Sea coast. **Bulgaria Air** (☎402 0405; www.air.bg; bul Dondukov 13; ⊗8.30am-5pm Mon-Fri; 🚌20) flies daily to Varna, with two or three daily flights between July and September. Bulgaria Air also flies between the capital and Burgas.

Bus

Sofia's **Central Bus Station** (Tsentralna Avtogara; www.centralnaavtogara.bg; bul Maria Luisa 100; 24hr; 🚌7), right beside the train station, handles services to most big towns in Bulgaria as well as international destinations. There are

dozens of counters for individual private companies, as well as an information desk and an **OK-Supertrans taxi desk** (⊗6am-10pm).

Departures are less frequent between November and April. These schedules are for the summer:

DESTINATION	FARE	DURATION (HR)	FREQUENCY
Albena	36 lv	8	4-5 daily
Bansko	16 lv	3	5-6 daily
Blagoevgrad	11 lv	2	about hourly
Burgas	30 lv	7-8	6-10 daily
Gabrovo	22 lv	3-4	7 daily
Haskovo	22 lv	6	12-14 daily
Kazanlâk	16 lv	3½	4-5 daily
Lovech	14 lv	3	2-3 daily
Nesebâr	37 lv	7	5-10 daily
Pleven	16 lv	2½	hourly
Plovdiv	14 lv	2½	several hourly
Ruse	29 lv	5	hourly
Sandanski	14 lv	3½	10-12 daily
Shumen	31 lv	6	7 daily
Sliven	24 lv	5	8 daily
Smolyan	25 lv	3½	6-7 daily
Sozopol	32 lv	7	6-8 daily
Stara Zagora	22 lv	4	8 daily
Varna	33 lv	7-8	every 30-45min
Veliko Târnovo	22 lv	4	hourly
Vidin	20 lv	5	6-7 daily

From the far smaller **Ovcha Kupel bus station** (☎955 5362; bul Tsar Boris III, Zapad; 🚌5) – sometimes called Zapad (West) station – a few buses head south, eg to Bansko, Blagoevgrad and Sandanski (although more buses to these places leave from the Central Bus Station).

From tiny **Yug bus station** (☎872 2345; bul Dragan Tsankov 23; 🚌413, Ⓜ Joliot-Curie), buses and minibuses leave for Samokov (6 lv, one hour, every 30 minutes).

From the ramshackle **Poduyane bus station** (☎847 4262; ul Todorini Kukli; 🚌79) – aka Iztok (East) station – buses leave infrequently for small towns in central Bulgaria.

DESTINATION	FARE	DURATION (HR)	FREQUENCY
Gabrovo	22 lv	3½	1-2 daily
Lovech	14 lv	3	1-2 daily
Troyan	15 lv	3	2 daily

International

Some agencies operate at the Central Bus Station, offering services to Istanbul (50 to 60 lv, 18 hours), Athens (108 lv, 12 hours) and elsewhere, although most are now found at the **Trafik Market** (Avtogara Serdika; www.avtogara-serdika. com; bul Maria Luisa; ⛟1, 7), also known as **Serdika Bus Station**, immediately in front of the central train station. There are numerous kiosks here representing all the major companies such as **Eurolines** (www.eurolines.bg) and **Union-Ivkoni** (www.union-ivkoni.bg), which sell tickets on buses to destinations all over Europe.

Eurotours (☑932 2310; www.eurotours.bg; basement, central train station) also sells tickets for international destinations, including daily trips to Belgrade (39 lv, eight hours), Bucharest (52 lv, eight to nine hours) and Skopje (32 lv, six hours)

Matpu-96 (www.matpu.com; Trafik Market) offers some of the best services to Greece and other Balkan countries, including Macedonia and Serbia. There is another office at ul Damyan Gruev 23.

It pays to shop around, though, as different companies offer different prices.

Train

The **central train station** (bul Maria Luisa; ⛟1, 7) is a massive, rather cheerless concrete hive, built in the 'Brutalist' style in the 1970s.

Destinations for all domestic and international services are listed on timetables in Cyrillic, but departures (for the following two hours) and arrivals (for the previous two hours) are listed in English on a large computer screen on the ground floor. Directions and signs around the station are sometimes translated into French. Other facilities include a post office, **left luggage** (central train station; per bag per day 2lv; ⏱6am-11pm) office, cafes, a supermarket and accommodation agencies. The rates at the foreign exchange offices are very poor indeed, so best wait until you get into town.

Same-day tickets are sold at counters on the ground floor, while advance tickets are sold in the gloomy basement, accessed via an unsigned flight of stairs obscured by another set of stairs that heads up to some snack bars. Counters are open 24 hours, but normally only a few are staffed and queues are long, so don't turn up at the last moment to purchase your ticket, and allow some extra time to work out the confusing system of platforms (indicated with Roman numerals) and tracks.

All tickets for international trains, and advance tickets for domestic services, can be bought at one of several Rila Bureau including at the **central train station** (☑932 3346; ⏱8.30am-8.20pm) and on **ul General Gurko** (☑987 0777; ul General Gurko 5; ⏱7am-7.30pm Mon-Fri, 7am-6.30pm Sat). Staff at these offices usually speak some English.

❶ Getting Around

To/From the Airport

Sofia airport (☑937 2211; www.sofia-airport. bg; off bul Brussels) is located 12km east of the city centre. Minibus 30 shuttles between the airport and pl Nezavisimost for a flat fare of 1.50 lv; you can pick it up outside the Sheraton Hotel. Less convenient are bus 84 from Terminal 1 and bus 284 from Terminal 2 (which handles the bulk of international flights), both of which take a slow and meandering route before depositing you opposite Sofia University.

When you emerge into the arrivals hall you will immediately be greeted by taxi drivers offering you a ride into town, at often ridiculously inflated rates; bypass these and instead head to the reputable **OK-Supertrans taxi** (☑973 2121; www.oktaxi.net) office counter, where you can book an official, meter-equipped taxi. They will give you a slip of paper with the three-digit code of your cab, which will normally be immediately available. If there happen to be none available, you can try to negotiate an unmetered rate with one of the other taxis, but check the price carefully first. A taxi (using the meter) from the airport to the city centre should cost no more than 15 lv.

Car

Frequent public transport, cheap taxis and horrendous traffic all provide little or no incentive to drive a private or rented car around Sofia. If you wish to explore further afield, though, a car would certainly come in handy. Rental outlets include the following:

Avis (☑945 9224; www.avis.bg; Sofia airport, terminal 2; ⏱9am-9pm)

Hertz (☑439 0222; www.hertz.bg; bul Nikola Vaptsarov 53; ⏱9am-5.30pm Mon-Fri, 10am-2pm Sat; ⛟88)

Sixt (☑945 9276; www.tsrentacar.com; Sofia Airport, terminal 2; ⏱8am-11pm)

Public Transport

Trams, buses, minibuses, trolleybuses and the underground metro run from 5.30am to 11pm every day. Tickets within Sofia cost 1 lv, and can often be bought at on-board ticket machines. But it's far easier and quicker, especially during peak times, to buy tickets from kiosks at stops before boarding. Metro tickets can only by bought from counters inside the station.One day/five day/one month transit cards (4/15/50 lv) are valid for all trams, buses and trolleybuses (but not the metro), and must be validated on board. There's a 10 lv fine if you don't have a ticket; unwary foreigners are a favourite target. An extra ticket is required for each piece of

DOMESTIC TRAIN SERVICES TO/FROM SOFIA

DESTINATION	1ST-/2ND-CLASS FARE	DURATION (HR)	NUMBER OF TRAINS (DAILY)
Burgas	23.60/18.90 lv (fast), 28.80/23.10 lv (express)	7-8	4 fast & 2 express
Gorna Oryakhovitsa	18.30/14.60 lv (fast), 21.40/17.20 lv (express)	4-4½	6 fast & 2 express (for Veliko Târnovo)
Plovdiv	11.30/9 lv (fast), 14.30/11.50 lv (express)	2½-3	6 fast, 3 express & 4 slow
Ruse	23.60/18.90 lv	6	3 fast
Sandanski	12.80/10.20 lv	4	3 fast
Varna	29.50/23.60 lv (fast), 36.90/29.60 lv (express)	7½-9	5 fast & 1 express
Vidin	17.30/13.30 lv (fast)	5	3 fast

oversized luggage, which officially is anything exceeding 60cm x 40cm x 40 cm.

Useful trams for visitors include 1 and 7, which link the central train station with bul Vitosha (near the NDK) via bul Hristo Botev and tram 10, which runs across the city from bul Stamboliyski to ul Graf Ignatiev

Buses for Boyana, Zlatni Mostove and Aleko depart from the Hladilnika bus terminal. It is near the southern terminus of Trams 2, 4, 9 and 12 from pl Sveta Nedelya. (From the final tram stop, walk through the tiny park to the bus stop on the main road.)

Marshroutki (private minibuses; 1.50 lv) are a popular and efficient alternative to public transport. Pay the driver upon boarding. Route 30 goes to the airport; 5 goes to the central train station; 21 runs to Boyana; 41 goes to Simeonovo.

Sofia's metro system (www.metropolitan.bg) is expanding rapidly, and at the time of research, much of the city centre was being dug up for new lines. Tickets cost 1 lv, but cannot be used on other forms of public transport. Useful central stations include Serdika, near pl Sveta Nedelya, Kliment Ohridski, close to Sofia University, and NDK, at the southern end of bulevard Vitosha.

Taxi

Taxis are an affordable and easier alternative to public transport. By law, taxis must use meters, but those that wait around the airport, luxury hotels and within 100m of pl Sveta Nedelya will often try to negotiate an unmetered fare – which, of course, will be considerably more than the metered fare. All official taxis are yellow,

have fares per kilometre displayed in the window, and have obvious taxi signs (in English or Bulgarian) on top. Never accept a lift in a private, unlicensed vehicle, because you will (at best) pay too much or (at worst) be robbed.

The rates per kilometre may range enormously from one taxi company to another, but the standard rate is 0.59 lv per minute in the daytime, 0.70 lv per minute at night.

In the very unlikely event that you can't find a taxi, you can order one by ringing **OK-Supertrans** (p314) or **Yellow Taxi** (☎911 19). You will need to speak Bulgarian.

AROUND SOFIA

The places mentioned here are accessible from Sofia by public transport, but beyond Boyana, it's worth staying at least one night to avoid excessive travel and to really appreciate the surroundings.

Boyana   Бояна
☎02

Boyana is a peaceful and prosperous suburb of Sofia, lying around 8km south of the city centre. Once a favourite retreat for communist leaders and apparatchiks, these days it's home to Sofia's wealthy elite and two of the capital's major attractions. However, besides these there's little else to detain you.

◉ Sights

National Museum of History MUSEUM
(www.historymuseum.org; ul Vitoshko Lale 16; admission 10 lv, with Boyana Church 12 lv; ⊘9.30am-6pm; ▣21) Housed in the former communist presidential palace, this museum occupies a stunning, if inconvenient, setting; unless a coach party turns up, you may have the place to yourself. The exhaustive collection includes Thracian gold treasures, Roman statuary, folk costumes, weaponry and icons, while outside you can see some Russian MiG fighters. There are regular temporary exhibitions, too.

Boyana Church CHURCH
(www.boyanachurch.org; ul Boyansko Ezero 3; adult/student 10/1 lv, combined ticket with National Historical Museum 12 lv, guide 10 lv; ⊘9.30am-5.30pm Apr-Oct, 9am-5pm Nov-Mar; ▣64, 21) The tiny, 13th-century Boyana Church is around 2km south of the National Museum of History. It's on Unesco's World Heritage list and its 90 murals are rare survivors from that period, and are among the very finest examples of Bulgarian medieval artwork. They include the oldest known portrait of St John of Rila, along with representations of King Konstantin Asen and Queen Irina.

❶ Getting There & Away

Minibus 21 runs to Boyana from Sofia's city centre (pick it up on bul Vasil Levski). It will drop you right outside the gates of the National Museum of History and also connects the museum with Boyana Church. You can also take bus 63 from pl Ruski Pametnik, or bus 64 from the Hladilnika terminal. Signs advertising the museum line the motorway, but it's not easy to spot the building, which is set back from the road behind a screen of trees. A taxi (about 8 lv one way) from the city centre to the museum is probably the easiest option of all; for the museum, ask for the 'Residentsia Boyana'.

Vitosha Nature Park
Природен Парк Витоша

♪02
The Mt Vitosha range, 23km long and 13km wide, lies just south of Sofia; it's sometimes referred to as the 'lungs of Sofia' for the refreshing breezes it deflects onto the often polluted capital. The mountain is part of the 22,726-hectare **Vitosha Nature Park** (www.park-vitosha.org), the oldest of its kind in Bulgaria (created in 1934). The highest point is Mt Cherni Vrâh (Black Peak; 2290m), the fourth-highest peak in Bulgaria, where temperatures in January can fall to -8°C.

As well as being a popular ski resort in winter, the nature park is popular with hikers, picnickers and sightseers on summer weekends, and receives around 1.5 million visitors a year. There are dozens of clearly marked hiking trails, a few hotels, cafes and restaurants and numerous huts and chalets that can be booked through the Bulgarian Tourist Union.

ALEKO АЛЕКО
ELEV 1800M
Aleko was named in honour of the renowned writer Aleko Konstantinov, who kick-started the hiking craze back in 1895 when he led a party of 300 fellow outdoors enthusiasts to the top of Mt Cherni Vrâh. On summer weekends the area is crammed with picnicking families and hikers.

ZLATNI MOSTOVE ЗЛАТНИ МОСТОВЕ
ELEV 1400M
Zlatni Mostove (Golden Bridges) takes its name from the bubbly little stream here, known as the Stone River, which was once a popular site for gold-panning. The trail of mammoth boulders running along its length was dumped here by glaciers during the Ice Age. It's another very popular spot on summer weekends, but at other times you may have the place to yourself. Minibus 10 runs between Sofia's pl Ruski Pametnik and Zlatni Mostove (1.50 lv); otherwise a taxi from the city centre will cost about 20 lv one way.

DRAGALEVTSI ДРАГАЛЕВЦИ
A two-person **chairlift** starts about 5km (by road) up from the centre of Dragalevtsi village (it's about 3km on foot if you take the obvious short cut up the hill). One chairlift (2 lv, 20 minutes) goes as far as Bai Krâstyo, from where another (2 lv, 15 minutes) carries on to Goli Vrâh (1837m). Both lifts operate year-round, but most reliably from about 8.30am to 6.30pm Friday to Sunday.

A pleasant option is to take the chairlift to Goli Vrâh, walk to Aleko (30 minutes) and catch the gondola down to Simeonovo (or vice versa).

From the start of the chairlift, a well-marked trail (about 1km) leads to **Dragalevtsi Monastery**. Probably the oldest extant monastery in Bulgaria, it was built around 1345, but abandoned only 40 years later. The monastery contains colourful mu-

Vitosha Nature Park

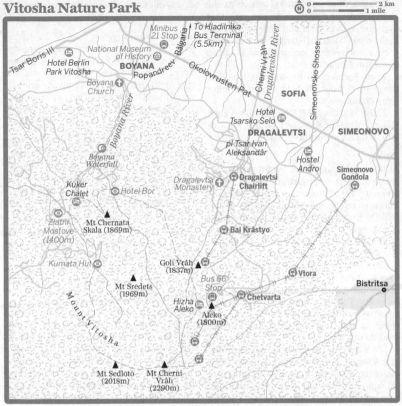

rals and is revered as one of the many hiding places of the ubiquitous anti-Turkish rebel leader Vasil Levski.

Pl Tsar Ivan Aleksandâr in Dragalevtsi village has a number of cafes and traditional restaurants. There are also places to eat and drink along the road from the village to the chairlift.

Buses 64 and 93 from the Hladilnika terminal go to the village centre; bus 93 continues on to the chairlift.

SIMEONOVO СИМЕОНОВО
Take a gondola to the mountains from Simeonovo (3/5 lv one way/return, 30 minutes). It operates Friday to Sunday from 9am to 6.30pm 1 October to 31 March, and 8.30am to 6pm 1 May to 30 September. You can jump off at the junctions of Vtora or Chetvarta, from where hiking trails lead deep into the park, and then continue the trip later with the same ticket. Bus 123 from the

Hladilnika terminal goes directly to the gondola station.

 Activities

Hiking

The best map is probably *Vitosha Turisticheska Karta* (1:50,000), printed in Cyrillic and available at bookshops around central Sofia.

Some of the shorter and more popular hikes around the park:

Aleko–Goli Vrâh A short trail (30 minutes) between the top of the gondola from Simeonovo and the chairlift from Dragalevtsi.

Aleko–Mt Cherni Vrâh A popular, but steep, 90 minutes on foot. Alternatively, take the chairlift from Aleko to within 30 minutes' walk of the summit.

Aleko–Zlatni Mostove Follow the trail to Goli Vrâh, skirt around Mt Sredets (1969m) and pass Hotel Bor; about three hours.

Boyana Church–Zlatni Mostove At the church, ask for directions to the path that hugs the Boyana River and leads to the 15m-high Boyana Waterfall (best in winter). From there, obvious paths lead to Zlatni Mostove; about three hours in total.

Dragalevtsi chairlift–Goli Vrâh Follow the chairlift from the bottom; a three-hour steep climb.

Zlatni Mostove–Mt Cherni Vrâh A challenging hike, via Kumata Hut and Mt Sedloto (2018m); about three hours.

Skiing

At 1800m above sea level, Mt Vitosha is Bulgaria's highest ski resort and its six slopes are only 22km from the centre of Sofia. There is rarely enough snow here before mid-December, but the season can often last into April.

The 29km of alpine ski runs (the longest is about 5km) range from easy to very difficult, and start as high as Mt Cherni Vrâh. Cross-country skiing is ideal along the 15km of trails, and snowboarding is also possible. As well as the Simeonovo gondola and Dragalevtsi chairlift there is a handful of other chairlifts and draglifts. A one-day lift pass costs 25 lv.

However, Mt Vitosha gets very crowded at weekends, the slopes are not always well maintained and the quantity and quality of ski equipment for hire is not great because so many locals use their own gear. The ski-rental shop at the start of the Simeonovo gondola and the Aleko Ski Centre at Aleko both charge about 20 lv to 30 lv per day for a set of ski gear. A snowboard and boots cost 25 lv per day.

The ski school at Aleko caters mainly to Bulgarians but instructors are multilingual. Five-day ski courses (four hours per day) are offered for 135 lv. The website www. skivitosha.com may be useful for those who read Bulgarian.

🛏 Sleeping & Eating

In Vitosha Nature Park there are several modern hotels, which are usually much cheaper than those in the city centre. Ideally, though, you'll have your own transport

to stay out here. Hikers can stay at any of the numerous mountain huts.

Hizha Aleko HOSTEL $
(☑967 1113; www.motensport.com; Aleko; dm/apt from 10/48 lv; 🅿🛜) This long-established *hizha* offers a number of dorm rooms with two to 10 beds, and three apartments, all with shared bathrooms. There's a restaurant and tea room, and skiing gear is available to rent.

Kuker Chalet CHALET $
(☑955 4955; www.kukerbg.com; Zlatne Mostove; r 36-48 lv; 🅿; 🛏10) One of the more comfortable 'huts', Kuker has 10 double rooms with TVs and bathrooms and an on-site restaurant. Prices are slightly higher on Friday and Saturday.

Hostel Andro PENSION $
(☑961 1506; www.hostel-andro.free.bg; ul Bor 10, Simeonovo; s/d from 30/50 lv; 🅿@; 🛏41) There's just one room and two apartments at this homely little place, each with TVs, fridges and sparkling modern bathrooms.

Hotel Berlin Park Vitosha LUXURY HOTEL $$$
(☑895 000; www.berlinparkvitosha.com; ul Georgi Rilski, Boyana; r/ste from 140/210 lv; 🅿🏊❄🛜) This bright modern hotel in the Boyana neighbourhood is ideally located for exploring Vitosha Nature Park, and has a spa centre, indoor pool and excellent restaurant. A shuttle service from the airport is available, and there are various package deals.

Tsarsko Selo Spa Hotel LUXURY HOTEL $$$
(☑816 0101; www.tsarskoselo.com; Oklovrusten Pat, Dragalevtsi; s/d/ste from 110/130/170; 🅿❄🛜♨) At the base of Mt Vitosha, this hotel offers a variety of large rooms, while facilities include a restaurant, gym, Turkish bath and indoor and outdoor pools. Suites come with private saunas. There's even a football pitch and a casino.

ⓘ Getting There & Away

To Aleko, bus 66 departs from Sofia's Hladilnika terminal 10 times a day between 8am and 7.45pm on Saturday and Sunday, and four times a day on weekdays. Minibus 41 runs from Sofia city centre to Simeonovo (1.50 lv).

Plovdiv & the Southern Mountains

Best Places to Eat

» Puldin Restaurant (p345)

» Hebros Hotel Restaurant (p345)

» Mehana Mencheva Kâshta (p336)

» Pelelanovska Konak (p351)

Best Places to Stay

» Hotel Renaissance (p344)

» Park Hotel Gardenia (p333)

» Hotel Bolyarka (p336)

» Spa Hotel Evridika (p355)

Why Go?

With spectacular and infinitely varied nature, and some of Bulgaria's greatest spiritual and cultural attractions, the south is a fascinating region that should be high on every traveller's itinerary. From the stunning Rila Monastery and the fabled Seven Rila Lakes, strung out like jewels in the mountains beyond it, to dynamic cultural capital Plovdiv, southern Bulgaria offers something for everyone. Its striking landscapes range from the sandstone 'pyramids' of Melnik, where you can sample the country's best wine in splendid serenity, to the rugged Pirin Mountains and the gentler Rodopi range, together hosting Bulgaria's best ski resorts.

The legacy of southern Bulgaria's colourful and complex history of ancient civilisations – from the mysterious Thracians and the Macedonians to the Romans, Slavs, Byzantines and Turks – is also abundantly evident, in Plovdiv's grand Roman amphitheatre, the enthralling medieval monastery of Bachkovo, numerous Ottoman mosques and other sites attesting to a glorious past.

When to Go
Plovdiv

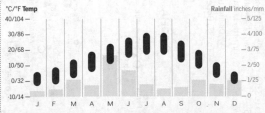

May & Jun Hike in the Rila and Pirin mountains while spring flowers are in full bloom and the air is cool.

Sep & Oct Indulge in Plovdiv's month of culture, and spa bliss in the nearby Rodopi Mountains.

Dec & Jan Ski by day and party by night over winter holidays in Bansko.

Plovdiv & the Southern Mountains Highlights

1 Skiing at **Bansko** (p330) and **Borovets** (p325). Bulgaria's baddest winter resorts

2 Sampling Bulgaria's best wine beneath sandstone cliffs in little **Melnik** (p334)

3 Diving into **Plovdiv's** (p337) Bohemian old town

and partaking of its vibrant nightlife

4 Making a pilgrimage to the spellbinding **Rila** and **Bachkovo Monasteries** p349), and considering their

vivid frescoes of eternal damnation

5 Cleansing yourself with the spa waters and massage therapies of **Devin spa**

resort (p355) in the Rodopi Mountains

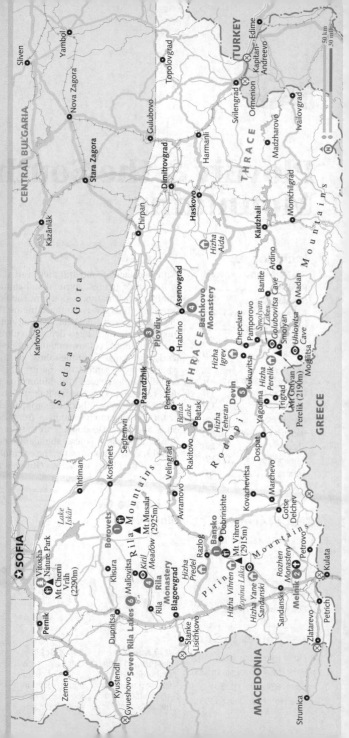
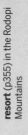

History

The vastness of southern Bulgaria and its mountainous geography have graced it with great historical diversity. It was the stomping ground of the ancient Thracians, an enigmatic, warlike group of tribes that left no written records in their own language, but once dominated large parts of modern-day Bulgaria, northeastern Greece and today's European Turkey. Thracian customs and beliefs have been passed down to us in Greek. Their mystery religion found its supreme expression at the Temple of the Great Gods on the Greek island of Samothraki, influenced antique religion, attracting initiates even from Macedonian and Egyptian royalty.

Today's 'Bulgarian Thrace' – the section between the Sredna Gora Mountains, the Rodopi Mountains and the Black Sea coast – was the birthplace of the legendary slave leader Spartacus, and Orpheus, the tragic, semimythical inventor of music. Some two-thirds of historical Thrace lie in Bulgaria, with Greece and Turkey splitting the remainder. Although the Thracians have long died out, there is a certain proud, earthy toughness common to the different inhabitants of these three parts of Thrace that might, just perhaps, express the spirit of that long-lost civilisation.

In the deep south of Bulgaria, the sparsely populated Rodopi Mountains, dotted with tiny, untouristed villages, attest to the more recent Ottoman legacy. The Muslim populations of Turks and Pomaks (Bulgarian Slavs who converted to Islam to win special benefits during Ottoman times) are evidenced here by minarets that pierce the boundless sky in villages unchanged over the centuries.

On the other side, in the western region of Pirin, towns such as Sandanski and Gotse Delchev preserve the names of heroic revolutionaries who fought the Ottomans at the turn of the 20th century to free Macedonia from Turkish rule. The issue of the similarities and differences between Bulgarian and Macedonian national identities and history remain controversial topics to this day, something you may experience while travelling in this region.

RILA MOUNTAINS
РИЛА ПЛАНИНА

'Mountains of Water' was the ancient Thracian name for this compact, majestic set of peaks covering 2629 sq km – a reference to the 180 lakes, streams and springs gushing with pure alpine aqua. These waters give the range famous attractions such as the small but stunning Sedemte Ezera (Seven Lakes), and entice hikers and day-tripping travellers from Sofia. A hiking trail from the lakes also leads to Bulgaria's most important religious shrine, the captivating Rila Monastery, which draws throngs of devout Bulgarians and curious foreigners to gaze upon its dramatic architecture and vivid, wall-to-wall frescoes and icons.

The Rila Mountains also include Bulgaria's biggest ski resorts, Bansko and Borovets, and new access roads that will substantially reduce the driving time to Sofia are sure to expedite their expansion. Now increasingly popular for skiing (and partying) with groups from Britain, Israel, Russia and beyond, these resorts are growing at the expense of the natural environment; lovers of untouched natural beauty are encouraged to come before Bulgaria catches up with more developed winter resort countries.

Despite the inevitable incursions of modern development, the permanently open Rila National Park remains a sanctuary for wildlife and flora, comprising 144 sq km of forest and 130 sq km of alpine pastures. Its fir trees, beechwoods and other conifers provide a peaceful habitat for deer, wild goats, eagles, falcons and more. Mt Musala (2925m), near Borovets, is Bulgaria's (and the Balkans') highest peak, and offers excellent hiking. Mountain huts *(hizhas)* provide simple accommodation (from about 10 lv per person), sometimes serving meals (but do bring extra food).

Invaluable for hikers is Julian Perry's *Mountains of Bulgaria*, which details an extensive north–south trek (part of the trans-European E4 trek) across the Rila Mountains. It starts at Klisura and finishes at Hizha Predel, near Razlog, and takes from seven to 10 days. For serious hiking, you'll need Kartografia's *Rila* map (1:55,000), with place names in Cyrillic.

Rila Village   Рила
POP 3044

The jumping-off point for Bulgaria's most sacred Orthodox shrine, this village 22km east of Rila Monastery is a sleepy place kept awake by its small faculty of tourism. Most monastery-bound buses connect here, however, and Rila does offer more inexpensive accommodation options than the monastery.

Rila Mountains

The town post office (which, amusingly, sells Christmas cards, not Rila postcards!) is behind the bus station. But the action, such as there is, centres on the main square, pl Vazhrajdane. Here you'll find ATMs, cafes and restaurants, plus the Rila Tourist Information Center, which has bus timetables, monastery and hiking info, and maps.

🛏 Sleeping & Eating

Hotel Orbita   HOTEL $
(📞07054-2167; s/d 26/40 lv; 🅿✸🛜🏊) The village's old standby has basic but clean rooms with good-size bathrooms, though the communist-era facade and lobby are rather glum. If staying out after 10pm, you'll have to ring the bell to get someone to open up. The Orbita is 30m to the right when walking upwards (a northeasterly direction) on the square.

Bistro 169   GRILLS $
(mains 4-7 lv; 🛜) Despite its unpromising interior, this little place just right of the square serves decent salads, light grills and local fish. Tables are on the footpath.

Kafe Djoana   CAFE
(pl Vazhrajdane 2; ⊙7am-1am; 🛜) A small, bright place on the square, good for an evening drink, and attracting a young local crowd.

ℹ Information

Rila Tourist Information Center (📞0887 848 439; rilatur@gmail.com; pl Vazharajdane; ⊙7am-1pm & 2-7pm) Rila village's small tourist information office has bus timetables, monastery and hiking information, maps, and large placards with local information.

ℹ Getting There & Away

Blagoevgrad-Rila buses operate hourly, the last returning to Blagoevgrad around 8pm (3 lv, 45 minutes). Two daily buses also serve Sofia. If connecting from elsewhere, use Dupnitsa-Rila buses (three daily).

Three daily buses (2 lv) also connect Rila village to Rila Monastery. If you're making a day trip from somewhere other than Rila village, start early to leave enough time for all the connections.

Rila Monastery
📞07054 / ELEV 1147M

Bulgaria's largest and most renowned monastery emerges abruptly out of a forested valley in the Rila Mountains. It's a major attraction for both Bulgarian pilgrims and foreign tourists. On summer weekends the site is especially busy, though at other times it provides more solitude. Stay at a nearby hotel or camping ground, or even at the monastery itself to experience Rila's photogenic early mornings and late evenings. You can also hike the surrounding mountains.

The monastery was founded in AD 927 by hermit monk Ivan Rilski. Originally built 3km to the northeast, it came to its current location in 1335. By the 14th century's end, it had become a powerful feudal fiefdom. Though it was plundered early in the 15th century, the monastery was restored in 1469, when Rilski's relics were returned from Veliko Tărnovo. Rila Monastery was vital to the preservation of Bulgarian culture and religion under Ottoman rule, even though the Ottomans sacked it several times.

Rila's greatest modern catastrophe was an 1833 fire that nearly engulfed all monastic buildings. An inundation of funds from Bulgarian and foreign donors allowed reconstruction to commence within a year. In 1961 the communust regime proclaimed Rila a national museum, and 22 years later it became a Unesco World Heritage Site.

MONASTERY GROUNDS

The monastery compound (open 6am to 10pm) includes a main church and two museums, guest rooms and a post office. Photos are prohibited inside the church. Souvenir shops sell religious paraphernalia and holy water.

Drivers usually park near the western Dupnitsa gate; the eastern entrance is called the Samokov gate. At both you'll find multilingual placards with historical details.

Within the monastery's walls, four levels of colourful balconies – with monastic cells, storerooms, refectory and kitchen – surround the large courtyard and its magnificent **Church of Rozhdestvo Bogorodichno** (Church of the Nativity; Rila Monastery), Bulgaria's grandest monastery church. Built between 1834 and 1837, the structure is crowned by three domes. Its outside walls are covered with frescoes both vivid and harrowing (or humorous, depending on your disposition): demons with whips, chains and pitchforks torture damned sinners in various states of woe and undress. The happier paintings depict the virtuous, accompanied by angels and saints. Some are autographed by Zahari Zograf, most eminent of Rila's painters. The gilded, intricately carved wooden iconostasis was created by master artisans from Samokov and Bansko.

Note the need for proper attire. Long shorts are fine, but more revealing dress is forbidden. Luckily, a few sporting green tunics lie at the ready.

The monastery's **museum** (Rila Monastery; admission 8 lv; ◷8am-5pm), in the compound's southeastern corner, contains collected 18th- and 19th-century ecclesiastical paraphernalia, prints and bibles. The centrepiece is the astonishing **Rila Cross**, a double-sided crucifix carved by a certain Brother Raphael between 1790 and 1802. It's incised in miniature with 140 biblical scenes and inscriptions, and about 650 human figures. Not surprisingly, Raphael ended up beatifically blind after so much staring through a magnifying glass. To protect visitors from the same fate the monastery exhibits blown-up photos, revealing the cross's incredible detail. Labelling is in Bulgarian only, but an English-language booklet is available.

Beside the Samokov gate in the northeast of the monastic compound is the **Ethnographic Museum** (admission 8 lv; ◷8am-5pm), displaying regional folk costumes, textiles and crafts. Again, labelling is in Bulgarian.

The nearby 23m-high stone **Hreliova Tower** (1335), named after a significant benefactor, is the only 14th-century structure remaining here. The monastery's **kitchen** (1816) is in the northern wing's courtyard. The 22m-high chimney, caked with centuries' worth of soot, cuts through all storeys, with 10 arched rows crowned by a small dome. Thousands of pilgrims formerly dined here simultaneously, with food prepared in giant cauldrons -- a single cauldron could fit an entire cow.

The **upper balcony** offers outstanding views over Rila Mountains.

🛏 Sleeping

External accommodation is within 100m of Samokov gate. The monastery provides relatively spartan accommodation for those desiring the full Rila experience.

Zodiak CAMPGROUND $
(☎0888 216 527; www.camping-zodiac.com; camp sites 10 lv, d from 30 lv) This forested camping ground is a bit run-down but enjoys an idyllic setting along the river, 1.6km past Rila Monastery towards Kiril Meadow. The Zodiak's restaurant is decent, and in summer it does outdoor barbeques. There's also space for 30 camper vans (30 lv).

Hotel Rilets HOTEL $
(☎2106; s/d incl breakfast from 25/35 lv; 🅿) Located down a 500m-long access road

starting 1.2km past Rila Monastery, on the road to Kiril Meadow, the large and somewhat lacklustre Rilets offers basic rooms and an average on-site restaurant.

Rila Monastery's Rooms   MONASTERY $

(☎0896 872-010; www.rilamonastery.pmg-blg.com; Rila Monastery; r 30-60 lv) The monastery offers older, dorm-style western-wing rooms (the communal facilities have toilets but no showers), and some nicer en suite rooms. In summer, the latter rooms can be booked by midday, so call ahead or arrive early. The reception office (in the southern wing) handles bookings.

Hotel Tsarev Vrah   HOTEL $

(☎2280; www.tzarevvrah.com; s/d/tr 35/45/60 lv) On land owned by Rila Monastery, the renovated Tsarev Vrah has clean, though not terribly well-lit rooms; most balconies offer forest views, but you can request a monastery-view room. The hotel cooks up tasty Bulgarian cuisine (mains 6 lv to 11 lv), and the leafy garden tables are popular for a summer repast. It's signposted about 150m from the monastery's Samokov gate.

✖ Eating

Most restaurants are near Samokov gate. Rila's local delicacy is *pasturvka* (trout); prices are usually per 100g.

Rila Restaurant   BULGARIAN $

(mains 7-12 lv; ☺8am-midnight) This restaurant specialising in Bulgarian grills and local fish is the area's most atmospheric, set in a traditionally decorated 19th-century building.

Bakery   BAKERY $

(☺dawn-dusk) This popular little bakery near Rila Monastery's Samokov gate is good for a mid-morning snack of hot, deep-fried doughnuts, bread and all-natural sheep's-milk yoghurt.

Restaurant Drushlyavitsa   BULGARIAN $

(☎0888278756; mains 6-13 lv; ☺8am-10pm) Outside Rila Monastery's Samokov gate, this fine place has outdoor tables overlooking a brook, and serves traditional Bulgarian cuisine.

ⓘ Getting There & Away

Most travellers visit Rila Monastery from Sofia (to the north) or Blagoevgrad (to the south). One daily morning bus (17 lv, 2½ hours) goes from Sofia's Ovcha Kupel bus station, returning in the afternoon. However, the monastery gets five daily buses from Rila village (4 lv), making the latter a better transport hub. If you somehow get stranded in Dupnitsa, two daily buses from there serve Rila Monastery directly.

Monastery day trips from Sofia by bus require leaving before 8am to travel to Dupnitsa (1½ hours) from the central bus station or Ovcha Kupel bus station. Then grab the next bus to Rila village or monastery, and repeat the process back to Dupnitsa, which also has train connections to Sofia.

Five daily buses (9 lv, 45 minutes) run between Rila village and Blagoevgrad. A monastery day trip from Blagoevgrad also requires starting early (leaving around 7am).

Alternatively, a taxi from Rila village to the monastery costs 20 lv. Taxis are available at both village and monastery, so there's no need to pay the driver extra to wait for you to finish your sightseeing.

Prices vary for organised full-day monastery tours from Sofia, but they're generally around 100 lv per person. Bansko and Borovets resorts may also offer day trips, though prices fluctuate considerably.

Around Rila Monastery

KIRIL MEADOW

Situated 7km northeast of Rila Monastery is Kiril Meadow, a gorgeous area with pine trees, picnic spots, cafes and stunning views of the craggy cliffs. It's an easy, and mostly shady, walk, and there's a guesthouse offering simple rooms with shared bathrooms, and bungalows with five beds and a private bathroom. It's an excellent alternative for those seeking spiritual reflection amidst tranquil nature rather than at the busy monastery.

ST LUKE'S HERMITAGE & ST IVAN'S CAVE

About 3.7km northeast of Rila Monastery, a left-hand trail leads to St Luke's Hermitage (1798); look for Sveti Ivan's picture here. (Considered a saint in his own lifetime, the 10th-century Sveti Ivan remains Bulgaria's patron saint today.) The hermitage features a large courtyard and the Church of Sveti Luka. A footpath leads, after about 15 minutes, to St Ivan's Cave, where Rila Monastery founder Ivan Rilski lived and is buried. According to legend, anyone able to pass through the aperture in the cave's roof has not sinned; the generous size of the hole would seem to indicate that gluttony is the only significant one of the seven deadly sins.

TOP PICKS: BULGARIAN SKI RESORTS

» Bansko
» Borovets
» Pamporovo
» Chepelare
» Malîovitsa

Borovets   Боровец

📞 07503 / ELEV 1350M

Although it's been overtaken by Bansko as Bulgaria's biggest ski resort, Borovets still draws both locals and foreign package tourists. The improved road has cut driving time from Sofia to about 40 minutes. However, at the time of research there was no traction on the long-promised 'Super Borovets' project, which would increase the skiable terrain to 90km.

Borovets is among Bulgaria's oldest ski resorts, as the slightly faded and worn structures and lifts attest. However, unlike built-up and populated Bansko, Borovets is simply a resort; most accommodation and services spill off the mountain. Out of ski season, when the shuttered restaurants offer only last season's chalk-scrawled menus out the front, it can feel eerily empty. However, the thick pine forests here are excellent for summer hikes, and the mountain air is crisp and refreshing.

🏃 Activities

Skiing

Only 70km from Sofia, and accessed locally by the transport-hub town of Samokov, Borovets sits under Mt Musala (2925m). It has twice hosted World Cup alpine skiing

rounds, and generally enjoys 1.5m of snow in winter. The 45km of ski runs, which include Bulgaria's longest, occupy the main areas of Markudjika, Yastrebets and Sitnyakovo-Martinovi Baraki. Four cross-country trails (totalling about 19km) start about 2km from Borovets.

Shops here rent out ski equipment (50 lv to 60 lv per day). Well-qualified, multilingual instructors provide training for 300 lv (four hours per day for six days, including a lift pass and ski gear). Guests at the big hotels can get cheaper training from in-house instructors.

Borovets has three chairlifts, 10 draglifts and a gondola from the Borosports complex in Borovets to Yastrebets, costing 10/15 lv one way/return. A one-day lift pass (60 lv) gets you free minibus access to the slopes from the main hotels. Borovets also has decent snowboarding – equipment runs about 50 lv per day, and lessons cost about 120 lv for six hours.

Other Activities

Horse riding in summer is organised outside the Hotel Rila, and costs around 40 lv for two hours, while Hotel Samokov has an indoor swimming pool (admission 5 lv), bowling alley and fitness and spa centre. These facilities are open daily in winter, and at weekends in summer.

The major hotels all offer excursions to Plovdiv, Sofia and Rila Monastery (at varying prices).

🛏 Sleeping

Independent travellers planning to ski (and sleep in) Borovets should book three to six months ahead for midrange or top-end hotels. The rates listed here increase by 25% in winter. Borovets' streets are unnamed and few, so addresses don't really exist.

HIKING

From Borovets marked hiking trails – some simply following established ski runs – provide access to the eastern Rila Mountains. The hiking trails around Borovets aren't marked on Kartografia's *Rila* map.

Some short and popular hikes:

Borovets–Chernata Skala Take the road towards Kostenets, and follow the signs pointing south to Hizha Maritsa; three hours (easy).

Borovets–Hizha Maritsa From the Borovets to Chernata Skala road, continue along the southern road; 4½ hours (moderately difficult).

Borovets–Hizha Sokolets Follow the road south through Borovets; 2½ hours (easy). Another trail (1½ hours) from Hizha Sokolets heads south to Mt Sokolets (2021m).

WORTH A TRIP

SKIING MALÎOVITSA & HIKING THE SEVEN RILA LAKES

For more low-key skiing than at Borovets or Bansko, try Malîovitsa (Mali-ov-itsa), located 13km southwest of Govedartsi at the foot of the Rila Mountains. Malîovitsa is ideal for beginner and intermediate skiers; its relatively placid atmosphere makes it more family-friendly too. In summer, it's popular for rock climbing, mountain climbing, hiking and birdwatching.

In winter, the **Central Mountain School** (☏07125-2270; Maliovitsa) rents out equipment (5 lv to 10 lv per person per day, depending on quality). Malîovitsa's one draglift costs 12 lv per person per day. In summer, the same outfit offers rock climbing and mountain climbing (30 lv to 50 lv per person per day). This includes a guide, but not transport or equipment (they're available at the school). Between March and June, and in September and October, the school runs kayaking and rafting trips on local rivers. The **Central Mountain School** (☏07125-2270; d from 25 lv; P) pension also offers simple accommodation from 25 lev per person.

Malîovitsa's also the base for one of Bulgaria's most popular hiking destinations: the **Seven Rila Lakes** (Sedemte Rilski Ezera). These glittering turquoise lakes, small but exquisitely beautiful, are strung out like jewels across rolling meadows in the central Rila Mountains.

From Malîovitsa, well-marked hiking trails access the lakes (Kartografia's detailed *Rila* map is useful too); along the trails, several *hizhas* (mountain huts) provide accommodation. From the village, first hike (about one hour) to Hizha Malîovitsa (2050m). The barracks-like rooms have between four and 20 beds. There's cheap camping too. The cafe has basic meals and a kitchen.

From Hizha Malîovitsa, it's a seven-hour hike to Hizha Sedemte Ezera, an older hut with simple dormitories. Alternatively, a little further north is **Hizha Rilski Ezera** (☏0701-50 513; dm/r with shared/private bathroom from 40/50 lv per person), at 2150m. The Rila Mountains' best *hizha*, it offers dorm beds and rooms with shared/private bathroom from 40/50 lv per person, including breakfast and dinner, plus a cafe. Reservations aren't necessary, except during August.

From the Seven Lakes, it's an easy one-hour walk downhill to **Hizha Skakavitsa** (☏0701-50 513; dm from 25 lev), at 1985m, and its lovely waterfall; alternatively, head for Rila Monastery (a six- to seven-hour hike).

Another route to the Seven Rila Lakes from Malîovitsa is via Hizha Vada and Hizha Lovna, bypassing Hizha Malîovitsa.

In nearby Govedartsi village, **Guesthouse Djambazki** (☏0888 573-133; www. house-djambazki.com; bul Iskar 53, Govedartsi; s/d/apt from €35/50/75; P❀≋) is a cosy place with comfortable rooms, some with balconies, plus a sauna and bike rental. Otherwise, the bigger **Hotel Malîovitsa** (☏07125-2222; Malîovitsa; d/tr/q incl breakfast from 25/40/60 lv; P), above the central car park, has clean rooms at good rates, plus restaurant, bar, ski school and kids' playground.

From Sofia's Yug bus station, one daily direct minibus (10 lv, two hours) departs for Malîovitsa in the morning. Otherwise, go via Samokov, from where a minibus runs to Malîovitsa (5 lv, 45 minutes). Minibuses return to Samokov twice daily, and once daily to Sofia. From Blagoevgrad, take any bus passing through Samokov, then catch the Malîovitsa minibus.

For cheaper accommodation, try Samokov, or nearby villages like Govedartsi and Malîovitsa.

Borovets' hotels spread over several kilometres of the resort; the following year-round places all occupy the small, curving main street (starting from the Samokov–Kostenets road and ending at the mountain's base). Ask about hiking, guided tours and other activities through the big hotels or ski shops.

Flora Hotel
HOTEL $$
(☏33 100; www.flora-hotel.net; s/d/ste from 45/70/95 lv; P❀≋≋) The four-star Flora boasts a swimming pool, spa and 'Irish pub'.

It's a more intimate alternative to the larger local resort hotels, while boasting similar amenities. Rooms are plain but clean, with balconies, and the restaurant's good. Kids under two sleep free, as do those under 11 (when accompanied by two adults).

Alpin Hotel HOTEL $$
(☎32 201; www.alpin-hotel.bg; d/ste from 96/135 lv; P❄️🅿️) On the mountain's base by the winter sports action, this modern place has small but comfortable rooms with all mod cons, and a sparkling lobby bar.

Hotel Rila HOTEL $$$
(☎32 295; www.rilaborovets.com; s/d/apt 90/120/160 lv; P❄️🅿️🛋️) The gigantic Rila, opposite the mountain near the main road's upper end, has impressive facilities including fitness centre, tennis court, two restaurants, shops and nightclub. The once very modern rooms are faded but fine. Those on the upper floor facing the mountain offer wonderful views from their balconies.

Hotel Samokov HOTEL $$
(☎323 09; www.samokov.com; s/d/ste from 60/80/120 lv; P❄️🛋️) Halfway down the main road from the mountain, the gargantuan Samokov has three restaurants, nightclub, shopping centre, gym, bowling alley and ski school. The comfortable modern rooms are somewhat more bland than those of other local resorts, but the prices are considerably lower for a similar range of services.

Villa Stresov VILLA $$$
(☎02-980 4292; www.villastresov.com; Borovets; d from €90, villa from €480; P🅿️) This large Swiss-style villa has four double rooms sleeping up to eight people, a full kitchen, a garden and all mod cons. Rent it all, or just pay for one, two or three bedrooms. There's a two-night minimum stay.

✖️ Eating

Borovets' main streets feature cafes, bars and restaurants heavy on 'English steaks' and cocktails reminiscent of gauche seaside summer holidays. Without the package tourists after winter, however, most close.

La Bomba INTERNATIONAL $$
(☎483; mains 5-9 lv; ⏱️8am-1am; 🅿️) Opposite the big hotels on the mountainside, La Bomba serves pizzas and dishes like steak and chips.

Black Tiger BULGARIAN $
(☎0899150304; mains 8-12 lv; ⏱️9am-1am; 🅿️) A simple place playing punchy Bulgarian music, the Black Tiger goes for the well-lacquered ski lodge look, and is popular with locals year-round, serving good Bulgarian fare. It's on the mountain's base amidst the other restaurants and hotels.

Alpin Restaurant INTERNATIONAL $
(mains 9-12 lv; 🅿️) The Alpin's cosy, pub-style restaurant offers a varied, if touristy, menu of pizzas, grills and barbecue meals.

ℹ️ Information

Central Borovets has exchange offices and ATMs, as do some of the larger hotels' lobbies.

Bulgariaski.com informs on snow conditions, accommodation and news on Bulgaria's ski resorts; the **Bulgarian Extreme & Freestyle Skiing Association** (www.befsa.com) lists organised competitions, demonstrations and excursions in Borovets and elsewhere.

ℹ️ Getting There & Away

There's not (yet) direct public transport between Sofia and Borovets, but that will probably change with the Sofia–Borovets road's completion.

For now, take a bus from Sofia to Samokov (4 lv, one hour) and then a minibus to Borovets (1.20 lv, 20 minutes). Minibuses from Samokov leave every 30 to 45 minutes between 7am and 7pm. Borovets has no bus station; minibuses from Samokov stop outside Borovets' Hotel Samokov.

Alternatively, if you're coming on a long-haul bus passing by Borovets, such as the Blagoevgrad–Plovdiv service, the driver may leave you on the side of the road; from here, it's a 1km uphill walk into town.

Taxis are good for out-of-town travel; note, however, that taxi rides within Borovets itself during ski season start at a staggering 10 lv. For out-of-town journeys, normal rates apply. Sample rates include 100 lv to Sofia and 125 lv to Plovdiv.

PIRIN MOUNTAINS
ПИРИН ПЛАНИНА

The stark Pirin Mountains, with peaks surpassing 2900m, rise dramatically out of Bulgaria's southwest; their dark, portentous appearance has affected the human imagination since well before the ancient Slavic tribes named the mountains after their god

DON'T MISS

HIKING IN THE PIRIN MOUNTAINS

A network of marked hiking trails (13 primary and 17 secondary) links 13 huts and shelters throughout the park. The primary trails are described and mapped in the Bulgarian Ministry of Environment's detailed map (1:55,000) in the *National Park Pirin* leaflet printed in English, available at the National Park office, or from souvenir shops.

Kartografia's *Pirin* map (1:55,000) is the only accurate and detailed hiking map of the whole range. Also, Domino's *Bansko* map includes a small but detailed map in English of 12 hiking trails. These trails include Bansko to **Hizha Banderitsa** (☑07443-8279; dm from 20 lev), 2km southwest of Shiligarnika, and Bansko to **Hizha Vihren** (☑07443-8279; dm 20 lev), 2km further up. Both offer convenient bases for hikes to nearby caves and lakes, such as Hizha Vihren to Mt Vihren (about three hours one way).

From Sandanski, a popular three-hour hike leads to the glorious **Popina Lûka** region, with lakes, waterfalls and pine forests. Hikers can stay at Hizha Kamenitsa or Hizha Yane Sandanski (25 lv including half-board). Julian Perry's *Mountains of Bulgaria* describes a hike across the entire Pirin Mountains from Hizha Predel to Petrovo village near the Greek border. It's a tough, seven- to 10-day hike (longer in bad weather), so the maps really help.

of thunder and storms, Perun. These mountains and their life-giving waters – some 230 springs and 186 lakes – have attracted Macedonians, Greeks, Slavs and Turks, among others. While their average height is just 1033m, more than a hundred Pirin peaks exceed 2000m, and 12 are higher than 2700m. The highest, Mt Vihren (2915m), is near Bansko.

Pirin National Park, Bulgaria's largest, occupies 40,447 hectares of the Pirin range. It's permanently open and free. The gate is 1.8km southwest of Bansko, Bulgaria's premier ski resort. A Unesco World Heritage Site since 1983, the park's varied and unique landscape is home to 1100 species of flora, 102 types of birds and 42 mammal species, such as bears, deer and wild goats. The Bansko-based **Pirin National Park office** (☑07443-2428; ul Bulgaria 4) offers information for longer hikes.

Besides skiing at Bansko and hiking, visitors to the Pirin region can enjoy fine wine at Melnik, a village clustered with 18th- and 19th-century houses, and even indulge in some nightlife at Pirin's provincial capital and a major university town, Blagoevgrad.

Blagoevgrad   Благоевград

☑073 / POP 70,656

About 100km straight south of Sofia, Blagoevgrad (Bla-*go*-evgrad) is a friendly, liveable place bisected by a small river and filled with grand squares, vibrant cafes and clubs

frequented by the 16,000 Bulgarian (and foreign) students at the Neofit Rilski Southwest University and American University of Bulgaria. On road and rail lines between Sofia, Sandanski and Greece, Blagoevgrad makes a useful base for day trips or longer forays to Rila Monastery, Bansko, the mountains and Melnik.

Blagoevgrad in Ottoman times was called Gorna Dzhumaya, but its large Turkish population was displaced after the Balkan Wars of 1912–13. It was renamed by the communists in 1950, after the 19th- century Bulgarian Marxist Dimitar Blagoev.

The town's services and most popular eating and drinking spots are on or near the three large and pedestrianised adjoining squares, pl Bulgaria, pl Makedonia and pl Georgi Izmirliev Makedoncheto.

◉ Sights

Between Forest Park and bul Aleksandâr Stamboliyski, which runs parallel to the river on its eastern bank, is the old quarter, Varosha. Here there are renovated Bulgarian National Revival–period homes, including the **Georgi Izmirliev Makedoncheto House-Museum**, and art galleries such as the **Stanislav Art Gallery**. Opening hours are erratic and unpredictable, however.

A steep road (700m) from Varosha accesses **Forest Park** (*Loven Dom*), a shady and popular place with good views. Towards the southern edge are the small **Botanical Gardens**.

History Museum
MUSEUM

(☎823 557; bul Aleksandâr Stamboliyski; admission 3 lv; ☺9am-noon & 3-6pm Mon-Fri) The History Museum, located near the Varosha old quarter, exhibits roughly 160,000 religious relics, archaeological artefacts and traditional costumes, and has displays on Macedonian military history (from the Bulgarian point of view). The natural-history section contains Bulgaria's biggest stuffed bird and animal collection.

Church of Vavedenie Presvetiya Bogoroditsi
CHURCH

(Church of the Annunciation of the Virgin; ☎884 795; ul Komitrov; ☺6.30am-8pm) In a small, serene garden, the Church of Vavedenie Presvetiya Bogoroditsi (1844) has a richly frescoed portico and a unique black-and-white chequered facade, with an extraordinary painting of the circle of life that includes continents and astrological symbols. There are more murals and icons inside.

🛏 Sleeping

Kristo Hotel
HOTEL $$

(☎880 444; hotel_kristo@abv.bg; ul Komitrov; s/d/apt incl breakfast 50/70/75 lv; P✳) Probably Blagoevgrad's most atmospheric place, the Kristo features white walls bedecked with wood-framed windows and flowering balconies. The cosy, well-furnished rooms have nice views; many have fireplaces. The hotel's excellent *mehana* (tavern) is popular for weekend weddings – book ahead.

Hotel Korona
HOTEL $

(☎831 350; www.hotelkorona.info; ul Nikola Vaptsarov 16; s/d/apt incl breakfast from 35/40/50 lv; P✳🖥) Located a five-minute walk from the centre, in a quieter residential area, the Korona is popular as much for its restaurant as for anything else. But it's good value, and the spacious, modern rooms have all mod cons; however, only the larger ones have bathtubs (the others have showers aimed at the floor).

Hotel Alpha
HOTEL $

(☎831 122; www.hotelalpha.net; ul Kukush 7; s/d/apt 36/45/50 lv; P✳🖥) One of Blagoevgrad's backstreet favourites, this popular place has modern, though slightly cramped rooms, and the carpeting seems glum. Still, service is friendly and professional. It's a five-minute walk from the centre.

Hotel Alenmak
HOTEL $$

(☎884 076; pl Georgi Izmirliev Makedoncheto; s/d 35/60 lv; P✳🖥) This renovated, formerly communist hotel has certainly improved on its appeal, with slick modern rooms and a central location, though service remains indifferent.

Hotel Bor
HOTEL $

(☎0887 932 313; hotel_bor@yahoo.com; Loven Dom; s/d 30/35 lv; P✳) In the forested hills above Varosha, Bor offers small indoor and outdoor restaurants, a lobby bar, and a small (and chilly!) indoor pool with Jacuzzi, sauna, steam bath and miniature fitness room. The peaceful location is, however, the best asset. Drive or take a taxi (3 lv) over the bridge and up the steep and winding ul Pirin (about 1km).

🍴 Eating

Blagoevgrad's eateries line the main square, along with the cafes, bars and clubs popular with students.

Kristo Restaurant
BULGARIAN $

(☎880 444; ul Komitrov; mains 4-8.50 lv; 🖥) The Kristo Hotel's restaurant has outdoor seating overlooking Vavedenie Presvetiya Bogoroditsi church, and serves good salads and grilled meats – try the chicken shashlik.

Pizza Napoli
PIZZERIA $

(☎34 649; pl Hristo Botev 4; mains 5-8 lv; ☺8am-midnight; 🖥) This place has an attractive square-side setting, and serves good pizzas, pasta and grills.

Restaurant Korona
BULGARIAN $

(☎831 350; ul Nikola Vaptsarov 16; mains 6-9 lv; ☺7am-midnight; 🖥) Although the shiny lobbyside setting lacks ambience, the Hotel Korona's restaurant does good grills like *tatarsko kiofte* (minced hamburger stuffed with melted cheese), and is popular with locals.

🍸 Drinking & Entertainment

For Hollywood blockbusters, visit the widescreen **Movie Max** (pl Georgi Izmirliev Makedoncheto). The respected **Vaptsarov Theatre** (☎823 475; pl Georgi Izmirliev Makedoncheto) and the **Vaptsarov Chamber Opera** (☎820 703; pl Makedonia) offer more edifying entertainment, but they close during August.

Old Dublin Irish Pub
PUB

(ul Trakiya 3; ☺8am-2am; 🖥) What a Bulgarian university town would be without an

Irish pub finds no definitive answer in this big, well-furnished establishment playing techno-pop instead of jigs and reels. Nevertheless, it's popular with students, and its long, wrap-around bar gives it some pub ambience. It has friendly service, and serves snacks and full meals (mains 7 to 15 lv).

Underground   BAR
(☎0888552578; pl Bulgaria; ☺9pm-4am; ☎) This very popular student place serves unusual cocktails and features a dimly lit and subterranean brick-walled bar. Usually house music and R&B are played.

Kristal Bar   BAR
(Mizia 14; ☺8am-2am; ☎) This small, central cafe-bar has indoor and outdoor seats that spill across the pedestrian drag. It's good for coffee by day and cocktails by night.

Piano Bar   BAR
(☎0898828828; ul Petko Petkov; ☺10pm-4am; ☎) Although the drinks are expensive at this stylish after-hours club, the live rock or jazz bands are usually worthwhile.

Nightclub Extreme   CLUB
(☎832 340; ul Koritarov; ☺11pm-5am; ☎) Blagoevgrad's most popular club. It's near the central square and the river.

ℹ Information

Foreign-exchange offices line ul Tsar Ivan Shishman, on the western riverbank. ATMs are near the main square and central pedestrian streets.
Escapenet (☎0899879042; ul Petko Petkov 2; per hr 2 lv; ☺10.30am-11pm Mon-Sat) Centrally located internet cafe.
Post Office (ul Mitropolit Boris) Includes telephone centre.

ℹ Getting There & Away

Blagoevgrad's adjoining train station and two bus stations are on ul Sveti Dimităr Solunski, about 2km from the centre (taxis cost around 4 lv).

The **main bus station** (Tsentralna Aftogara; ☎884 009) and nearby **Chastna Aftogara** (☎831 132), serve Sofia, Sandanski, Gotse Delchev, Petrich, Dupnitsa and Plovdiv. The main bus station has a left-luggage office.

Blagoevgrad serves Sofia hourly (11 lv, two hours) via Dupnitsa, though more connections arrive en route to/from Kulata or Sandanski. The latter gets 10 daily buses (6 lv, 1½ hours). Another six buses serve Bansko (6 lv, two hours). One direct bus goes to Melnik daily at 11am (10 lv, two hours). Buses to Rila village (3 lv, 45 minutes) leave hourly until about 8pm. Two daily buses serve Plovdiv (10 lv, three hours).

The **train station** (☎885 695) is near the bus stations. Blagoevgrad's on the line between Sofia and Kulata (for Greece). From/to Sofia there are five daily fast trains (1st/2nd class 11/9 lv, 2½ hours), and one slow train, via Dupnitsa (9 lv). Three of the fast trains continue to Sandanski (1st/2nd class 7.50/6 lv, two hours) and Kulata (1st/2nd class 9/7 lv, 2½ hours). At the time of research, the two trains that would normally continue to Thessaloniki from Blagoevgrad had been suspended by a cash-strapped Greek government, but check again when you're there.

Bansko   Банско

☎0749 / POP 8562 / ELEV 930M

Bansko is the big daddy of Bulgarian ski resorts. With trails starting from 900m high to 2600m, and more than a hundred hotels and *pensions*, the once-quiet village has more beds than permanent residents. In winter, Brits, Russians, Bulgarians and others come to ski (and party) in this sunny yet snow-filled resort. In summer things are quieter (except for August's jazz festival), and the action shifts to the leafy central square, while elderly women in traditional dress sit chatting on the doorsteps of lovely stone-built homes in Bansko's old quarter.

Built in the 10th century over an ancient Thracian settlement, Bansko became wealthy by the mid-18th century, well positioned on the caravan route between the Aegean coast and Danubian Europe. It spawned eminent traders, artisans, icon painters and woodcarvers, plus Otets Paisii Hilendarski, the 18th-century monk who fuelled Bulgarian ethnic nationalism with his literary work and travels.

Bansko's historic significance is attested to in several museums and over 150 cultural monuments, most from the 19th-century National Revival period. These stone-and-timber houses were buttressed by fortress-style walls, with hidden escape routes, protecting their inhabitants from the Turks. As elsewhere, many have been reincarnated as *mehanas* (taverns) or guesthouses, and there's an old quarter with cobblestone lanes.

Bansko's adjacent bus and train stations are right on the main road north of the centre, a 15-minute walk (or 3 lv taxi ride) to the main square, pl Nikola Vaptsarov, and then nearby pl Vâzhrazhdane. This 'summer centre' features shops and cafes on the pedestrian mall, ul Tsar Simeon. In winter, however, the slopeside ski gondola and its terminus up at Baderishka Polyana become the real centre.

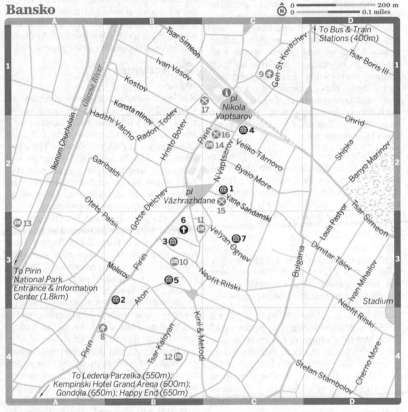

Bansko

◉ Sights

1 Bansko Permanent Icon
   Exhibition C2
2 Historical Museum B3
3 House Museum of Neofit Rilski B3
4 House Museum of Nikola
   Vaptsarov C2
5 Museum of Otets Paisii
   Hilendarski B3
6 Sveta Troitsa Church B3
7 Velyanov's House C3

◉ Activities, Courses & Tours

8 Intersport A4

9 Pirin Sport C1

◉ Sleeping

10 Alpin Hotel B3
11 Duata Smarcha B3
12 Hotel Avalon B4
13 Hotel Glazne A3
14 Hotel Rodina C2

◉ Eating

15 Mehana Kasapinova Kâshta C2
16 Mehana Tumbeva Kâshta C2
17 Mehana Vodenitsata C1

◉ Sights

House Museum of
Nikola Vaptsarov   MUSEUM
(☑8304; pl Nikola Vaptsarov; admission 3 lv; ⊘8am-noon & 2-5.30pm) This house museum was the birthplace of Nikola Vaptsarov (1909–42), a respected antifascist poet and activist, influenced by communist ideology while a student. His populist writings caused his arrest and torture by the war-time fascist government; he wrote his most famous poem while awaiting execution. Period decor, plus photographs, documents and Vaptsarov's personal belongings are exhibited, while a short video, followed by an audio tape (English, French or German), provides background.

Velyanov's House   MUSEUM
(☑4181; ul Velyan Ognev 5; admission 3 lv; ⊘9am-noon & 2-5pm Mon-Fri) Velyanov's House features elaborately painted scenes and woodcarvings from the 'Bansko School' of carving, icon and fresco painting.

Bansko Permanent Icon
Exhibition   MUSEUM
(☑88 273; ul Yane Sandanski 3; admission 3 lv; ⊘9am-noon & 2-5pm Mon-Fri) This museum has more Bansko School creations, and houses the most valuable historic icons.

House Museum of Neofit Rilski   MUSEUM
(☑2540; ul Pirin 17; admission 3 lv; ⊘9am-noon & 2-5pm Mon-Fri) Occupying a former school-house, this house museum exhibits manuscripts by, and photos of, Rilski (1793–1881), the father of Bulgarian secular education, who created an early Bulgarian grammar textbook (1835) and a Bulgarian–Greek dictionary.

Sveta Troitsa Church   CHURCH
(pl Vâzhrazhdane; ⊘7am-7pm) Sveta Troitsa Church (1835) is surrounded by a 1m thick and 4m high stone wall, and features magnificent wooden floors and faded murals. It also hosts Bansko's major landmark: the 30m-high clock tower (1850). Until Sofia's Alexander Nevsky Cathedral was completed in 1912, it was Bulgaria's largest church.

Historical Museum   MUSEUM
(☑88 304; ul Aton 3; admission 3 lv; ⊘9am-noon & 2-5pm) The Historical Museum, also called 'Radonova Kâshta' after the building in which it's housed, contains finds dating back to 6000 BC, plus antique, medieval and 19th-century National Revival–period items.

Museum of Otets Paisii
Hilendarski   MUSEUM
(☑88 304; ul Otets Paisii 21; ⊘9am-noon & 2-5pm) Commemorating the eponymous local monk, author and instigator of Bulgarian nationalism, this museum contains a chapel with a replica of the room at the Serbian Hilandarski Monastery on Greece's Mt Athos, where Paisii wrote his seminal and fulsome narrative of the history of the Slavs.

⚡ Activities

Skiing

Nestled at 1000m, at the base of rugged Mt Vihren (2915m), Bansko enjoys long, snowy winters. With trailhead peaks ranging from 900m to 2560m, Bansko boasts Bulgaria's most consistent skiing conditions. The snow, often 2m thick between mid-December and mid-April, sometimes lasts until mid-May. Lifts and slopes are modern and well maintained, while snowmaking equipment works during above-freezing temperatures.

Bansko also boasts a state-of-the-art gondola (carrying eight persons). The trip lasts 20 minutes and takes skiers directly from town and onto the slopes at Baderishka Polyana, with pubs, restaurants and ski schools. At the time of research, a second gondola was expected to open here in 2013. From Baderishka Polyana, another chairlift accesses more trails at Shiligarnika, which has four chairlifts and five draglifts. Bansko has 10 chairlifts and 16 draglifts.

Chalin Vrag I and II are the most famous of Bansko's 15 (and counting) ski runs, which total 67km, along with 8km of cross-country trails. The total trail coverage comprises 35% for beginners, 40% for intermediates and 25% for advanced skiiers. There's no freestyle helicopter skiing at Bansko, though veering off some trails accesses wide open, untouched mountainside where you're essentially taking your life into your hands. There's also a half-pipe for snowboarders.

An all-day Bansko lift pass costs 70 lv, though prices rise yearly.

Pirin Sport (☑8537; ul Gen St Kovachev 8) rents out ski equipment (from about 55 lv per day) and snowboarding gear, and provides instructors for both sports. Similar services are provided by Intersport (☑4876) and some hotels near the gondola. Intersport rents out mountain bikes in summer.

Other Activities

There's a hot mineral water bath in Dobrinishte, 6km south of Bansko, and summertime hiking; see the Bansko Tourist Information Center (p334) for more information.

Ledena Parzelka
SKATING

(ul Pirin; ⊙9am-10pm Dec-Apr) Try ice skating at the new skating rink, Ledena Parzelka in Bulgarian. Skate rental is 10 lv; another 5 lv gets you 90 minutes of skating time. Alternatively, an all-day skating pass is 15 lv.

✿ Festivals & Events

St Theodor's Day
RELIGIOUS

(⊙First Sat of Lent) Celebrated with horse racing; in Dobrinishte.

Celebration of Bansko Traditions
FOLK

(⊙17-24 May) Folklore, dancing and the like.

International Jazz Festival
JAZZ

(www.banskojazzfest.com; ⊙around 7-15 August) This very popular international fest attracts Bulgarian and foreign artists. Most events are held on an open-air stage at pl Nikola Vaptsarov and in the Theatre Zhelev.

Bansko Day
HOLIDAY

(⊙5 Oct) Folklore performances, commemoration ceremonies and public celebrations marking Bansko's date of liberation from the Ottomans.

🛏 Sleeping

Bansko accommodation ranges from simple private rooms to five-star luxury hotels. Discreet camping is possible in the Pirin National Park. Most foreigners come on package tours, but independent bookings are possible; the Bansko Tourist Information Center (p334) can recommend rooms for all budgets. Book ahead for ski season, when rates are 25% higher than listed here (highest during the Christmas–New Year holidays).

TOP CHOICE Park Hotel Gardenia
HOTEL $$

(☑86 900; www.parkhotelgardenia.com; ul tsar Simeon 72; s/d incl breakfast 49/65 lv; ✳🛜🏊) Right down from the post office and main square, the Gardenia has an excellent central location during the non-ski season. The ample, attractive modern rooms are more business than traditional, with flat-screen TVs and big baths. There's a swank lobby-terrace bar, two restaurants, and a small spa centre with a coolly lit elliptical pool, sauna and massage treatments (from 35 lv).

Kempinski Hotel Grand Arena
LUXURY HOTEL $$$

(☑88 565, 88 888; www.kempinski-bansko.com; ul Pirin 96; s/d/ste from 260/320/360 lv; P✳🏊@) Bansko's most lux accommodation (and priced accordingly), the Kempinski is close to the gondola and winter nightlife – it's the place to be in ski season. It boasts luxurious rooms with all expected amenities, prompt, efficient service and excellent facilities.

Duata Smarcha
PENSION $

(☑2632; ul Velyan Ognev 2; s/d incl breakfast from 25/35 lv) The lovely garden of this popular and reasonably priced *pension* encloses a well-run, friendly place with airy rooms and traditional home-cooked meals. It's just south of the main square.

Hotel Avalon
HOTEL $$

(☑88 399; www.avalonhotel-bulgaria.com; ul Eltepe 4; s/d/tr/ste €20/30/40/55; P@) A friendly, British-run place popular with budget travellers, the Avalon has airy rooms, some with Jacuzzi, plus a restaurant serving French and Italian fare. The owners also organise local excursions. It's in the backstreets before the centre, to the left if coming from the bus/train stations (a five-minute walk).

Alpin Hotel
HOTEL $

(☑88075; ul Neofit Rilski 6; s/d from 30/40 lv; 🛜) This small hotel south of the main square and opposite the Hilendarski monument offers clean, simple rooms and friendly local service.

Hotel Rodina
HOTEL $$

(☑8106; ul Pirin 7; s/d/apt 50/64/120 lv) The Rodina is a cosy and central place that, despite the lacklustre lobby area, has nice, simple rooms. The hotel offers sauna and massage from 30 lv, plus a restaurant and tavern.

Hotel Glazne
HOTEL $$

(☑88 022; www.glazne-bansko.eu; ul Panayot Hitov 2; s/d 60/80 lv; ✳🛜🏊) On the river's western bank towards the south of town, the Glazne offers smart, well-done rooms, and the service and restaurant are excellent. A 'sky bar', pool, sauna and massage are on offer here.

🍴 Eating & Drinking

Bansko's traditional *mehanas* (taverns) offer regional delicacies and excellent local wine. Some close in summer.

Mehana Pri Dedo
BULGARIAN $$

(pl Nikola Vaptsarov; mains 6-9 lv; ⊙8am-midnight; 🛜) This main-square *mehana* (tavern) serves good international and Bulgarian fare at prices half those of the bigger restaurants (rates don't increase in winter, either). There's an airy deck in summer and in winter a cosy interior where a live guitarist croons pop classics. The laid-back owner will drive guests to their hotel for free if they've had too much to drink.

Mehana Tumbeva Kâshta   BULGARIAN $$
(☑0899888993; ul Pirin 7; mains 5-11 lv; ⊙8am-midnight) A small and friendly bar and grill offering meat specialities and lighter fare, the Tumbeva Kâshta rests in a secluded garden (the cosy interior functions in winter) between the two central squares.

Mehana Kasapinova Kâshta   BULGARIAN $$
(☑3500; ul Yane Sandanski 4; mains 6-12 lv; ⊙8am-1am) Excellent local food and wine mark the Kasapinova, just southeast of the main square. Nice touches include the colourful local rugs, clay pitchers of wine and cosy fireplace.

Mehana Vodenitsata   BULGARIAN $$
(☑84 019; cnr ul Hristo Botev & ul Ivan Vazov; mains 8-13 lv; ⊙11am-midnight) A traditional Bulgarian restaurant just west of pl Vaptsarov, the Vodenitsata offers hearty portions and live music, and is popular with locals and visitors alike. It's open irregularly in summer.

Happy End   BAR
(⊙11am-late; 🛜) They forgot the '-ing', but never mind: this grand bar–disco, capable of containing 400 ruddy skiers for après-ski activity, is a wintertime favourite, opposite the gondola. Numerous other bars and nightclubs are in the general area as well.

Club   CLUB
(pl Vâzhrazhdane; entry 5 lv; ⊙11pm-4am) Worth mentioning for its sheer weirdness, this modest nightspot has Vegas-like walls that morph into coloured cubes; the ceiling's strung out on Christmassy lights and revolving disco balls, while robotic patrol boys grimly prowl the periphery dressed in ridiculous grey blazers. This is what being inside an Atari game must be like.

❶ Information
Wi-fi is available in most hotels and cafes, and the town library on the main square (opposite the tourist information center) offers free internet access for visitors.

www.bansko.bg Official municipal website; also in English.

www.bulgariaski.com Invaluable resource on skiing in Bansko and all other Bulgarian resorts.
Bansko Tourist Information Center (☑88 580; infocenter@bansko.bg; pl Nikola Vaptsarov 1; ⊙9am-5pm daily) The centrally located Tourist Information Center has friendly and informed staff who can advise on accommodation, cultural and outdoors activities, and upcoming events. They sell Bansko town maps (4 lv), with hotels, restaurants and banks listed on the front, and the Pirin National Park map on the back; the similarly priced winter map features Bansko's ski trails, gondola and lifts too.
Pirin National Park Office (☑/fax 88 202; www.pirin-np.com; ul Bulgaria 4) Info about long Pirin Mountain treks.

❶ Getting There & Away
From Sofia (17 lv, three hours), 15 daily **buses** serve Bansko, most via Blagoevgrad; from the latter to Bansko, it's 6 lv. Several more buses travelling to Gotse Delchev stop at Bansko.

From Bansko, four or five daily buses serve Blagoevgrad (two hours). Two morning buses serve Plovdiv (16 lv, 3½ hours). Between mid-June and mid-September, three daily minibuses (4 lv) serve Hizha Banderitsa.

The coolest route to Bansko, however, is by **narrow-gauge railway**; the last such route in Bulgaria, the train goes from Bansko to Septemvri station in five hours (5 lv, four daily), from where you continue west to Sofia or east to Plovdiv and beyond.

At the two-hour mark after leaving Bansko is **Avramovo Station**, the highest Balkan train station at 1267m. The leisurely, visually stunning ride passes through narrow tunnels and dense forests and past bubbling rivers. It's highly recommended for those not in a rush, and the train is as modern on the inside as it is lovably antiquated on the outside. Word is that the government keeps this unprofitable route open only for the nostalgic value and touristic enjoyment, so do consider patronising it.

Three daily trains depart Bansko for Septemvri. The ticket office sells tickets only 10 minutes before departure time, so ascertain these times ahead.

Melnik   Мелник
☑07437 / POP 385
Tiny Melnik is one of Bulgaria's most distinctive villages due to its traditional architecture, local wine, and location (about 20km north of Greece). Tucked beneath imposing sandstone cliffs. the village has historically been a wine-production centre, and you'll find plenty to sample at restaurants

and even at National Revival–era house museums where vintners once lived.

The yellow-white mixture of clay and sand in the backing hills has, over centuries, eroded into bizarre formations resembling pyramids and giant mushrooms. (The village's name probably comes from the Old Slavonic *mel*, 'sandy chalk'.)

Melnik has seen Thracian, Roman, Byzantine and early Bulgarian rule. After an Ottoman doldrums, it had a resurgence during the National Revival period. Melnik's once-notable Greek population among its 20,000 inhabitants was forcibly relocated by the Greek army in the 1912–13 Balkan Wars, when the village was largely burned.

Melnik's good for exploring the southern Pirin Mountains and, though seeing the village requires just one day, you may enjoy lingering on in the sunshine and quietude. Nice places to stay and eat abound.

Melnik is very easy to navigate on foot as it only stretches for 1km. The bus stop is right at the village's entrance (on the road connecting Sandanski and Rozhen); opposite is the municipal building, site of the tourist office. Here begin the two streets that run into town, alongside the dried-up river.

⊙ Sights & Activities

Wineries

Melnik's wines, celebrated for more than 600 years, include the signature dark red, Shiroka Mehichka Loza. Shops and stands dot Melnik's cobblestone paths, with reds and whites for 3 to 4 lv and up. Try to sample first, and buy from the refrigerator – avoid the bottles displayed in the sun all day.

Numerous hotels and restaurants advertise wine tasting.

Mitko Manolev Winery WINE TASTING
(☑0887545795; ☺9am-midnight) For the most atmospheric adventure in *degustatsia* (wine tasting), clamber up the slippery cobblestones to the Mitko Manolev Winery. Also called Mitko Sheshtaka ('the Six-Fingered') it's basically a cellar dug into the rocks, and an informal hut with tables and chairs outside, with both reds and whites available. It's along the hillside trail between the Bolyaskata Kâshta ruins and the Kordopulov House. There are certainly worse things than whiling away the hours in the sunshine with a glass of Melnik red, and the views from above are wonderful.

Museums

Melnik's grand old houses, many jutting out from cliffs, feature handsome wood balconies and spacious upper quarters, with cool stone basements for wine storage. Officially, all buildings must be built and/or renovated in the Bulgarian National Revival–period style, and painted brown and white.

Not always open and without many attractions, the **City Museum** (☑229; admission by donation; ☺9am-7pm Mon-Fri) features local traditional costumes, ceramics and jewellery, plus early 20th-century photos of Melnik.

Kordopulov House MUSEUM
(☑265; admission 2 lv; ☺8am-8pm) According to the proud caretaker, it's the Balkans' biggest house museum; in any case, the Kordopulov House (1754), former home of one of Melnik's foremost wine merchants, is a truly impressive structure. The sitting rooms have been carefully restored, and boast 19th-century murals, stained-glass windows and exquisite carved wooden ceilings, plus couches bedecked with colourful pillows.

Downstairs, the house's enormous wine cellar includes 180m of illuminated labyrinthine passageways; look out for the wall full of glittering coins, which well-wishers have managed to stick into the soft cave surface – a gesture of goodwill and hope that the rains will fall and the crops will be good. If you share these sentiments, stick a stotinka of your own into the wall. You can taste, and buy, the house wine here. The Kordopulov House is the four-storey building on the cliff face at the street's end, south of the creek.

Ruins

The 10th-century **Bolyaskata Kâshta**, one of Bulgaria's oldest homes, is ruined except for some partially standing walls. You can peer in and enjoy great views too. Nearby is the ruined 19th-century **Sveti Antoni Church** (also not signposted).

Of Melnik's original 70 churches only 40, mostly ruined ones, survive. A signposted path leads to the ruined **Sveti Nikolai Church** (1756), and to the Despot Slav's ruined **Slavova Krepost Fortress**. Both are visible from the Bolyaskata Kâshta ruins, or from near the Lumparova Kâshta Hotel. The trail veers east along the ridge about 300m to the ruined **Sveta Zona Chapel**.

The **Turkish Baths** are difficult to recognise, standing just before the Mehana Mencheva Kâshta tavern. **Sveti Petâr &**

Pavel Church (1840) is down from the Hotel Melnik's car park. Just below the Kordopulov House, the 15th-century **Sveta Varvara Church** has retained its walls and floor, and displays icons where visitors light candles. The caretaker at Sveti Nikolai Church can open the closed churches.

✱ Festivals & Events

The **Trifon Zarezan Festival** (1 February) is dedicated to Sveti Trifon, patron saint of the vine. Events occur during grape-picking season (first two weeks of October). There's a **folklore festival** on 1 April.

🛏 Sleeping

Private rooms (15 lv to 20 lv per person) usually come with shared bathrooms. Look for the English-language 'Rooms to Sleep' signs.

TOP CHOICE Hotel Bolyarka   HOTEL $$
(☑2383; www.bolyarka.hit.bg; s/d/apt incl breakfast 40/60/130 lv; P❊✿) The spiffy Bolyarka has elegant and well-decorated rooms, and apartments with fireplaces. Sauna and massage treatments are available, but the authentic Ottoman-era hamam (Turkish bath) is for viewing only. The on-site restaurant is excellent. Bolyarka's about 300m straight down the main street on the right-hand side.

Chavkova Kâshta   PENSION $
(☑0893 505-090; www.themelnikhouse.com; ul Melnik 12; s/d 30/40 lv; ✿) This friendly pension, a two-minute walk straight in from the bus on the left, under the square's giant plane tree, has airy and clean rooms (the only drawback being the shower shoots onto the floor). There's a tasty *mehana* (tavern) attached for dinner or drinks.

Hotel Bulgari   HOTEL $
(☑2215; www.hotelbulgari.net; s/d 30/50 lv; ✿) This imposing new hotel, located after the square on the left, seems out of place – but considering the shiny, sleek and spacious rooms, it would be well suited to guests anywhere and is surprisingly good value. The cavernous restaurant is more suitable for banquets than intimate dining, though.

Lumparova Kâshta   PENSION $
(☑0888 804-512; r per person 25 lv; P) The Lumparova has cosy rooms with balconies that enjoy fantastic cliff views, and attractive decor and beds. There's traditional food and wine tasting, too. It's up a steep path starting behind the village.

St Nicola Hotel   HOTEL $
(☑2286; stnicola@datacom.bg; d/apt from 50/90 lv; P❊✿) At Melnik's far end near the history museum, the St Nicola offers excellent value. Rooms are large, cheery and tastefully furnished, and the apartment has sun terrace, lounge, kitchen and big bathroom. There's a tasty restaurant, serving the famous house wine.

✗ Eating

Melnik's best eats are at hotel or pension restaurants, though other worthy spots abound. Aside from the local wine, try the traditional *banitsa* (a flaky cheese pasty), a local speciality, and the mountain river trout.

TOP CHOICE Mehana Mencheva Kâshta   BULGARIAN $
(☑339; mains 6-11 lv; ⊙10am-11.30pm) This tiny tavern has an atmospheric upper porch overlooking the main street down towards the end of the village. It's popular with locals and does the full run of Bulgarian dishes – sometimes venison, wild boar and local snails are available.

Chinarite Restaurant   BULGARIAN $$
(☑0887992191; mains 5-8 lv; ✿) Midway up the main road, by the bridge, Chinarite serves Bulgarian dishes and homemade Melnik *banitsa*. It also has a small wine cellar for tasting.

Loznitsite Tavern   BULGARIAN $$
(☑283; mains 5-8 lv) Loznitsite Tavern has an inviting, vine-covered outdoor setting, and good Bulgarian fare.

ℹ Information

Melnik is hassle-free and new services have made it a more convenient base. Wi-fi is now available at most hotels, and there's a new ATM by the Hotel Bulgari, past the central square, where the post office and phone centre stands.

Melnik Tourist Information Center (☑0884282705; gradmelniktic@abv.bg; obshtina building; ⊙9am-5pm) Located behind the bus stop, on the *obshtina* (municipality) building's upper floor, this friendly centre advises on accommodation and local activities, including hikes and visiting Rozhen Monastery.

ℹ Getting There & Away

One daily direct bus connects Melnik with Sofia (17 lv, four hours); times vary. One daily direct bus serves Blagoevgrad (9 lv, two hours). Three daily minibuses go from Sandanski to Melnik, continuing to Rozhen.

Note that, if you're travelling in a group by this minibus, there may be insufficient seats if the village elders are en route to shopping in Sandanski. Melnik has no taxis.

Rozhen Monastery

The **Rozhen Monastery** (admission free; 7am-7pm), also called Birth of the Virgin Mary Monastery, stands 7km north of Melnik. Built in 1217, it was reconstructed in the late 16th century, though the Turks soon destroyed it. Today's monastery, mostly built between 1732 and the late 18th century, has undergone significant modern renovations. Photography and video cameras are prohibited inside.

The **Nativity of the Virgin Church** (1600) contains stained-glass windows, 200-year-old murals, woodcarvings and iconostases. Murals also occupy the 2nd-floor refectory. The monastery enjoys a great setting atop Melnik's cliffs and has a vine-covered courtyard.

About 200m before the monastery car park is the (closed) **Sveti Kiril & Metodii Church**; here too is the grave of Yane Sandanski (1872–1915), one of the most important Macedonian revolutionary leaders.

The **Rozhen Fair** of traditional culture is held on 8 September.

Hotel Rozhena (0878 832-192; www.hotel rojena.net/; Rozhen; s/d.apt incl breakfast from 50/80/140 lv; P) has simple but comfortable rooms with TV and bathroom, and more luxurious double apartments, plus sauna, gym and restaurant.

There are *mehanas* (taverns) near the bus stop, and a cafe by the car park.

ⓘ Getting There & Away

It's 7.2km from Melnik to the monastery, including the steep 800m uphill bit from Rozhen. Buses from Sandanski to Melnik continue to Rozhen. Alternatively, hike (6.5km) from Melnik up the track by the Bolyaskata Kâshta ruins along the creek bed, then look for the English-language signs. The trail is shadeless – avoid midday walking, wear a hat and take water.

BULGARIAN THRACE

The vast territory of the ancient Thracian tribes, now encompassed by modern Bulgaria, Greece and Turkey, remains a wild region of varied and dramatic landscapes and remote villages. However, its one major urban centre, Plovdiv, is Bulgaria's second-biggest – and, arguably, its best – city, and an important transport hub. Just south of it, striking Bachkovo Monastery lies among wooded hills and vineyards. The largely unvisited east features a strong Turkish presence.

Plovdiv Пловдив

032 / POP 338,184

With its art galleries, winding cobbled streets and bohemian cafes, Plovdiv (*Plovdiv*) equals Sofia in things cultural and is a determined rival in nightlife as well – it has a lively, exuberant spirit befitting its status as a major university town. Being a smaller and less stressful city than Sofia, Plovdiv is also great for walking.

Plovdiv's appeal derives from its lovely old town, largely restored to its mid-19th-century appearance. It's packed with atmospheric house museums and art galleries and – unlike many other cities with 'old towns' – has eminent artists still living and working within its tranquil confines. The neighbourhood boasts Thracian, Roman, Byzantine and Bulgarian antiquities, the most impressive being the Roman amphitheatre – the best preserved in the Balkans, it's still used for performances.

Plovdiv's modern centre, on the south side of the Maritsa River, features a shop-lined pedestrian mall, ul Knyaz Aleksandâr, which passes over the Roman Stadium and up to a splendid square with gushing fountain. The nearby Tsar Simeon Garden is a shady, popular spot for relaxing. Plovdiv's cafes and bars are widespread, though one concentration of popular places is in the Kapana district, northwest of the old town.

Like Rome, Plovdiv boasts seven hills, though one was flattened by communists and only four impress: Nebet Tepe, with Thracian fort ruins above the old town; Sahat Tepe (Clock Hill), crowned with a clock tower; Bunardjika (the 'Hill of the Liberators') to the west; and Djendem ('Hill of the Youth') in the southwest.

Plovdiv's always been one of Bulgaria's wealthiest and most cosmopolitan cities, and it's also Bulgaria's second-largest road and railway hub and economic centre. Although travellers often merely regard it as a stopover point between Bulgaria and Greece

Plovdiv

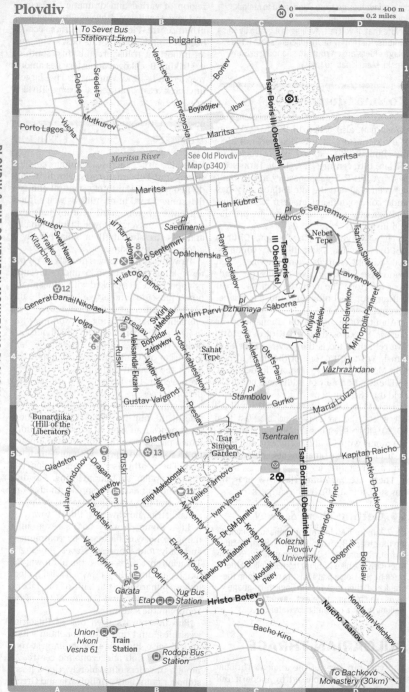

N
0 _____ 400 m
0 _____ 0.2 miles

To Sever Bus
Station (1.5km)

Bulgaria

Vasil Levski

Bonev

Boyadjiev

Ibar

Sredets

Pobeda

Vucha

Mutkurov

Brezovska

Porto Lagos

Maritsa

Maritsa River

See Old Plovdiv
Map (p340)

Maritsa

Maritsa

Han Kubrat

Yakuzov

Sveti Naum

Traiko Kitanchev

ul Tsar Kaloyan

pl Saedinenie

6 Septemvri

Opalchenska

pl Hebros

6 Septemvri

Nebet Tepe

Tsar Ivan Shishman

7

8

HristoG Danov

Rayko Daskalov

Tsar Boris III Obedinitel

Lavrenov

12

General Danail Nikolaev

Volga

Sv Kiril I Metodii

Bozhidar Zdravkov

Antim Parvi

Dzhumaya

pl Saborna

PR Slaveikov

Mitropolit Panaret

6

Preslav

4

Aleksandar Ekzarh

Viktor Jugo

Todor Kableshkov

Sahat Tepe

Knyaz Aleksandar

Otets Paisi

Knyaz Tseretelev

pl Vazhrazhdane

Ruski

Gustav Vaigand

Preslav

pl Stambolov

Gurko

Maria Luiza

Bunardjika
(Hill of the
Liberators)

Gladston

Tsar Simeon Garden

pl Tsentralen

Kapitan Raicho

13

Ruski

9

Dragan

Filip Makedonski

Veliko Tarnovo

11

Ivan Vazov

2

Tsar Boris III Obedinitel

Petko D Petkov

Gladston

ul Ivan Andonov

Karavelov

3

Radetski

Vasil Aprilov

Odrin

Aksentiy Veleshki

Ekzarh Yosif

Tsanko Dyustabanov

Dr GM Dimitov

Kristo Pastuhov

Tsar Asen

Bulair

Kostaki Peev

pl Kolezha

Plovdiv University

Leonardo da Vinci

Bogomil

Borislav

5

pl Garata

Etap

Yug Bus Station

Hristo Botev

10

Bacho Kiro

Naicho Tsanov

Konstantin Velichkov

Union-Ivkoni
Vesna 61

Train Station

Rodopi Bus Station

To Bachkovo
Monastery (30km)

Plovdiv

od. In 1855, Hristo Danov founded Bulgaria's first publishing house in the city.

While most of Bulgaria was freed following the Russo-Turkish War of 1877, the ensuing Congress of Berlin left Plovdiv and the south in Turkish hands. Only in 1885 did it join the Bulgarian state. Probably for the better, Plovdiv thus missed the opportunity of becoming Bulgaria's capital.

◎ Sights

Plovdiv's 19th-century 'baroque' style house involves an overhanging upper storey with jutting eaves, columned portico and brightly painted facade. The interior rooms feature finely carved woodwork, painted wall decorations and ornamental niches. Most display art or other exhibits.

Plovdiv's artistic community enriches the city's many galleries, already bursting with 200 years of Bulgarian painting.

Each September the magical **Night of the Galleries** sees every Plovdiv gallery open, for free, from 8pm to 3am.

Roman Amphitheatre　　ANCIENT THEATRE
(Map p340; ul Hemus; admission 3 lv; ⊙8am-6pm) Plovdiv's magnificent 2nd-century-AD amphitheatre, built by Emperor Trajan, was uncovered only during a freak landslide in 1972. It once held about 6000 spectators. Now largely restored, it again hosts large-scale special events and concerts. Visitors can admire the amphitheatre from several lookouts along ul Hemus, or from the cafes situated above.

An unmarked shortcut from above the Church of Sveta Bogoroditsa leads along ul T Samodomov; enter through the passageway into the Academy of Music, Dance and Fine Arts on the right-hand side. Alternatively, pay the entrance fee and explore the marble seats and stage.

Roman Stadium　　ANCIENT STADIUM
(Map p340) While the once huge Roman Stadium is mostly hidden under the pedestrian mall, in 2012 the subterranean southern back end was further renovated, with stairways from different sides now allowing entrance into the gleaming rows up close. A small shop down below provides some info and souvenirs.

At the time of research, the city was planning further reconstructions, with the modern bronze statue of the city's founder, Macedonian King Philip II, removed and awaiting a permanent home elsewhere.

or Turkey, Plovdiv repays a longer visit and will certainly draw you in if you let it.

History

Thracians settled here around 5000 BC, building a fortress at Nebet Tepe in the old town, called Eumolpias. Philip II of Macedon (father of Alexander the Great) extended the settlement, humbly naming it Philipopolis in 342 BC. He refortified the existing fortress, making Philipopolis an important military centre. However, the ruins that survive today largely come from the Roman annexation (AD 46) and thereafter. The Romans built streets, towers and aqueducts for the new city, Trimontium. Unfortunately, Goths and Huns plundered and destroyed it in the mid-3rd century and in AD 447 respectively, and Trimontium languished. The Bulgar Khan Krum seized it in 815 and renamed it Pupulden, making it an important strategic outpost of the First Bulgarian Empire (681–1018).

Pupulden, or Philipopolis as the Byzantines called it, was controlled by Constantinople, Bulgars and even Latin Crusaders over the following centuries. The Ottomans conquered it in 1365, renaming the city Filibe (a bastardisation of the Greek Philipopolis). The city thrived and its merchants grew wealthy. Some of Bulgaria's finest and most lavish town houses were built here during the Bulgarian National Revival peri-

Old Plovdiv

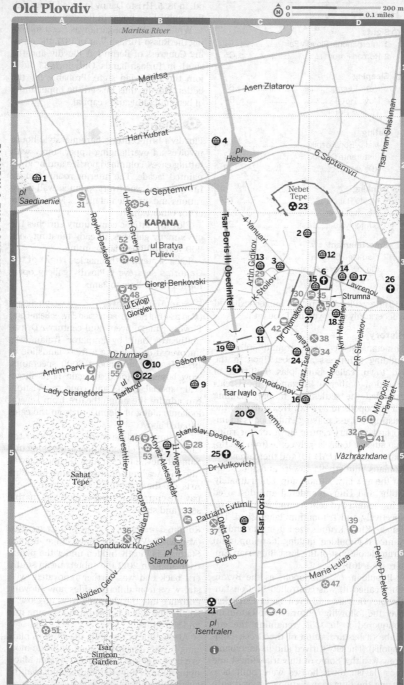

Maritsa River

0 _____ 200 m
0 _____ 0.1 miles

Maritsa

Asen Zlatarov

Han Kubrat

4

pl Hebros

6 Septemvri

Tsar Ivan Shishman

1

pl Saedinenie

31

ul Ioakim Gruev

54

KAPANA

Nebet Tepe

23

6 Septemvri

Rayko Daskalov

52

49

ul Bratya Pulievi

2

12

Artin Gidikov

4 Yanuari

13

3

29

14

17

26

Giorgi Benkovski

45

48

ul Evlogi Giorgiev

K. Stoilov

15

6

30

35

Strumna

Lavrenov

Tsar Boris III Obedinitel

25

27

50

18

Kiril Nektariev

11

42

Dr Chomakov

19

Knyaz Tserein

38

PR Slaveikov

Antim Parvi

44

55

10

Sáborna

5

T Samodomov

24

34

Pulden

22

ul Tsanbrod

9

Tsar Ivaylo

16

Mitropolit Panaret

Lady Strangford

A. Bukureshtliev

pl Dzhumaya

20

Hermus

56

32

41

Sahat Tepe

46

53

Knyaz Aleksandăr

11 Avgust

28

Stanislav Dospevski

25

Dr Vulkovich

pl Vâzhrazhdane

Naiden Gerov

36

Dondukov Korsakov

33

43

pl Stambolov

Patriarh Evtimii

37

Otets Paisii

8

Tsar Boris

Gurko

39

Naiden Gerov

51

21

pl Tsentralen

40

Maria Luiza

47

Petko D Petkov

Tsar Simeon Garden

Old Plovdiv

Roman Forum RUIN

(Map p338) Just down the steps at the overpass near pl Tsentralen, ruins of the Roman Forum are still being excavated; peer over the fence along the road.

Roman Odeon RUIN

(Map p340) Adjacent to the tourist information centre, the remains of a Roman Odeon have been partially restored. There's a tiny, reconstructed amphitheatre that's used for occasional performances, and some original columns.

Ruins of Eumolpias RUINS

(Map p340; ul Dr Chomakov; admission free; ⊗24hr) Some 203m high in the old town, a hill contains the sparse ruins of Eumolpias, a Thracian settlement in 5000 BC. The fortress and surrounding town enjoyed a strategic position, later bolstered by Macedonians, Romans, Byzantines, Bulgarians and Turks, who named it Nebet Tepe (Prayer Hill).

While the remaining rubble is rather formless, the site does offer great views. Get there from ul Dr Chomakov (the continuation of ul Sâborna). Partially restored remains of a 13th-century reservoir are also here.

Ethnographical Museum
MUSEUM

(Map p340; ☑625 654; ul Dr Chomakov 2; adult/student 5/1lv; ⊙9am-noon & 2-5.30pm Tue-Thu, Sat & Sun, 2-5.30pm Fri) This intriguing museum houses 40,000 exhibits, including folk costumes and musical instruments, jewellery and traditional craftworks like weaving, metalworking, winemaking and beekeeping. Traditional tools displayed range from grape-crushers and wine-measures to apparatuses used for distilling attar of roses.

Restored 19th-century rooms upstairs have carved wooden ceilings. Plovdiv's most renowned National Revival–period home, it was built in 1847 and owned by the eminent Agir Koyoumdjioglou, later becoming a girls boarding school and a tobacco and flour warehouse.

Historical Museum
MUSEUM

(Map p340; ☑623 378; ul Lavrenov 1; admission 2 lv; ⊙9am-noon & 1-5.30pm Mon-Sat) The Historical Museum concentrates on the 1876 April Uprising and the massacre of Bulgarians at Batak, which directly led to the Russian declaration of war on Turkey the next year. Built in 1848 by Dimitâr Georgiadi, it's also called the Georgiadi Kâshta.

Archaeological Museum
MUSEUM

(Map p340; ☑624 339; pl Saedinenie 1) Thracian and Roman pottery and jewellery, and ecclesiastical artefacts, icons and liturgical paraphernalia are on display here, along with a collection of 60,000 archaeological items.

Museum of History
MUSEUM

(Map p340; ☑629 409; pl Saedinenie 1; admission 2 lv; ⊙9am-5pm Mon-Sat) Housed within the Archaeological Museum, this museum chronicles the 1885 Unification of Bulgaria through documents, photographs and belongings of the protagonists.

Cultural Center Thrakart
MUSEUM

(Map p340; ☑631 303; Podlez Arhaeologiski; ⊙9am-5pm Mon-Sat) Visible through floor-to-ceiling windows in the Tsar Obedinitel underpass, Cultural Center Thrakart contains extensive Roman floor mosaics and various artefacts from Roman (and earlier) times. Concerts are performed on the centre's small stage.

Hindlian House
MUSEUM

(Map p340; ☑628 998; ul Artin Gidikov 4; adult/student 5/1 lv; ⊙9am-5pm Mon-Fri) Once owned by merchant Stepan Hindlian, Hindlian House, built in 1835, is one of Plovdiv's most opulent. It's full of exquisite period furniture and walls painted with real and imaginary landscapes of Venice, Alexandria and Constantinople.

These scenes, which took six months to complete, impressed visitors by showing the locales of the owner's overseas trading empire. The magnificent panelled ceilings and 'Oriental' marble bathroom, with its high, domed ceiling and skylight, are other highlights. The small courtyard garden is lovely, too.

Danov House
MUSEUM

(Map p340; ☑629 405; ul Mitropolit Paisii 2; admission 2 lv; ⊙9am-12.30pm & 2-5pm Mon-Sat) Danov House, dedicated to renowned writer and publisher Hristo Danov and several other Bulgarian authors, contains a re-creation of a bookshop and a National Revival–era classroom. There's an old printing press, and the **gardens** offer wonderful views. Enter through a wall up the laneway leading to the Church of Sveta Bogoroditsa.

Balabanov House
MUSEUM

(Map p340; ☑627 082; ul K Stoilov 57; admission 3 lv; ⊙9am-7.30pm) Once owned by Luka Balabanov, a wealthy 19th-century merchant, the Balabanov House was completely rebuilt in 1980 according to the original blueprints. It contains modern paintings and antique furniture.

Lamartine House
MUSEUM

(Map p340; ☑631 776; ul Knyaz Tseretelev 19; ⊙open by special arrangement) Built in 1830, the Lamartine House, also called the Georgi Mavridi House, belongs to the Union of Bulgarian Writers. The building is named after French poet Alphonse de Lamartine, who stayed for three days in 1833, during his 'travels in the Orient'.

Nedkovich House
MUSEUM

(Map p340; ☑626 216; ul Lavrenov; admission 3 lv; ⊙9.30am-noon & 1-6pm) The Nedkovich House, dating from 1863, has a lovely, leafy courtyard that sometimes hosts art shows, but alas, the house is poorly lit inside. The highlights are the ornate wood ceiling and flowery wall paintings.

Permanent Exhibition of Dimitar Kirov
GALLERY

(Map p340; ☑635-381; Kiril Nektariev 17; adult/student 5/1lv; ⊙9am-5pm Mon-Fri) Housed in a grand old-town mansion where Plovdiv's budding artists worked in the 1960s, this special place celebrates the life and works of Dimitar Kirov, who died in 2008 at the age of 73. Arguably Plovdiv's most original artist, Kirov produced work marked by bold and vivid uses of colour, from mosaics to abstracts.

Encho Pironkov City Gallery of Fine Arts
GALLERY

(Map p340; ul Vasil Konchev 1; admission 1 lv; ⊙9am-12.30pm & 1-5.30pm Mon-Fri, 10am-5.30pm Sat) Bulgarian modern art is displayed at this gallery down a small laneway downhill from ul Sâborna.

Zlatyu Boyadjiev House
GALLERY

(Map p340; ☑635 308; ul Sâborna 18; admission 3 lv; ⊙9am-noon & 1-6pm Apr-Sep, 8.30am-noon & 12.30-5pm Mon-Fri Oct-Mar) Zlatyu Boyadjiev House, on ul Sâborna in the old town, contains paintings by Plovdiv native Zlatyu Boyadjiev (1903–76), many idealising the Bulgarian peasantry; some cover entire walls.

State Gallery of Fine Arts
GALLERY

(Map p340; ☑635 322; ul Sâborna 14; admission 3lv, Thu free; ⊙9.30am-12.30pm & 1-5.30pm Mon-Fri, from 10am Sat & Sun) The State Gallery of Fine Arts, occupying a mansion from 1846, contains outstanding works by 19th- and 20th-century masters such as Goshka Datsov, Konstantin Velichkov and Nikolai Rainov. Look out also for works by Georgi Mashev and Vladimir Dimitrov.

Philippopolis Art Gallery
GALLERY

(Map p340; ☑622 742; ul Sâborna 29; admission 3lv; ⊙10am-6pm) Bulgaria's first private art gallery, this occupies the well-restored Hadzhi Aleko house (1865). It boasts works by 19th- and 20th-century Bulgarian masters such as Vladimir Dimitrov, Anton Mitov and Dimitar Gyudzhenov.

City Art Gallery
GALLERY

(Map p340; ☑624 221; ul Knyaz Aleksandâr 15; admission 2 lv; ⊙9am-12.30pm & 1-5.30pm Mon-Fri, 10am-5.30pm Sat) The City Art Gallery, another branch of the State Gallery of Fine Arts, holds small, temporary exhibitions of abstract art.

Atanas Krastev House
GALLERY

(Red Pony Art Gallery; Map p340; ☑625 792; ul Dr Chomakov 5a; admission 1 lv; ⊙10am-6pm Mar-Nov) This was where local painter and conservationist Atanas Krastev lived until his death in 2003. His self-portraits and personal collection of (mostly) abstract 20th-century Bulgarian paintings are displayed. The cosy, well-furnished house is strewn with personal mementos, and the terrace offers superb views. The garden also houses exhibits.

Center for Contemporary Art
GALLERY

(Map p340; ☑638 868; Chifte Banya, pl Hebros; admission 3 lv; ⊙1-6pm Tue-Sun) The Center for Contemporary Art is housed on in the Chifte Banya, an old Turkish bath, and hosts contemporary works.

Church of Sveta Bogoroditsa
CHURCH

(Map p340; ☑623 265; ul Sâborna 40; ⊙7am-7pm) This huge, three-aisle church stands atop a series of stone stairs at the old town's base. With its unmistakable pink and blue bell tower, this church (built in 1844 on the site of a 9th-century shrine) contains icons and murals, including one depicting a sword-wielding Turkish soldier harassing chained and lamenting Bulgarian peasants.

Church of Sveti Konstantin & Elena
CHURCH

(Map p340; ul Sâborna 24) Plovdiv's oldest church, this was built over a late Roman church. It's dedicated to Constantine the Great, the 4th-century emperor who made Orthodox Christianity the state religion, and his mother, Sveta Helena. The current church, however, dates to 1832. The wonderful iconostasis was painted by Zahari Zograf between 1836 and 1840. The covered portico features sumptuous frescoes.

Icon Gallery
MUSEUM

(Map p340; ul Sâborna 22; adult/student 2/1lv; ⊙9.30am-12.30pm & 1-5.30pm Mon-Fri, from 10am Sat & Sun) Beside the Church of Sveti Konstantin & Elena, this small museum has a sublime display of icons from the 15th century onwards.

Sveta Marina Church
CHURCH

(Map p340; ul Dr Vulkovich 7) Built in 1561, Sveta Marina Church was burnt down 50 years later, rebuilt in 1783, and repaired in 1856. Note the 17m-high pagoda-shaped wooden bell tower (1870), and the intricate, 170-year-old iconostasis.

Sveta Nedelya Church
CHURCH

(Map p340; ☑623 270; ul PR Slaveikov 40; ⊙8am-5pm) The grand, reopened Sveta Nedelya Church, built in 1578 and renovated in the 1830s, contains exquisite carved-walnut iconostases and faded wall murals from the mid-1800s.

Dzhumaya Mosque
MOSQUE

(Map p340; pl Dzhumaya) The largely renovated Dzhumaya Mosque, one of the Balkans' oldest, dates from the mid-15th century. With a 23m-high minaret, it was the largest of Plovdiv's more than 50 Ottoman mosques, though its thunder has slightly been stolen by the renovated Roman Stadium remains just opposite.

✦ Festivals & Events

International Plovdiv Fair
TRADE

(Map p338; ✏️fairgrounds 553 146; bul Tsar Boris III Obedinitel 37; ☺mid-May & late Sep) Week-long trade fair held in the massive north-side fairgrounds.

Cultural Month Festival
CULTURE

(☺late May–mid-Jul) Performances and exhibits of opera, literature, painting and events celebrating the greatness of Bulgarian history.

Verdi Festival
OPERA

(☺early Jun) Two-week festival of opera concerts in the Roman amphitheatre.

International Festival of Chamber Music
MUSIC

(☺mid-June) Popular 10-day festival of chamber music.

International Folklore Festival
FOLKLORE

(☺end Jul–early Aug) Folklore groups perform on the pedestrian mall for free in the afternoon; evening shows performed in amphitheatre.

Thracia Summer Music Festival
MUSIC

(☺Aug) Regional traditional music.

City Holiday
HOLIDAY

(☺6 Sep) Celebration of the Day of National Unification (Narodni Saedinenie), ratified in Plovdiv in 1885. Unusually, officials shampoo the city's monument before the event.

Jazz Festival
MUSIC

(☺Sep) Acclaimed international festival.

🛏️ Sleeping

While the fairs are on, in May and September, prices increase substantially.

Campers have the **Complex 4th Kilometre** (✏️951 360; sites per person 3 lv, bungalows 28-38 lv; ☺year-round; 🖥🎐) and the **9th Kilometre Complex** (✏️632 992; www.leipzig.

bg; bul Pazardzhikoshose; sites per person 3 lv, tents 3 lv, bungalows 20 lv, r renovated/unrenovated 32/25 lv; ☺year-round; 🎐🖥). The former (also called Gorski Kat Camping) is a shady, loud place about 4km west on the old Sofia Hwy, and includes a restaurant–bar and water park. Take bus 4, 18 or 44 west along bul Bulgaria, or bus 222 from the train station to its terminus and walk another 200m. The latter camping ground, owned by Plovdiv's Hotel Leipzig, is snazzier, with a restaurant and 24-hour bar. There's also a large outdoor swimming pool. Take a taxi (12 lv).

🔝 Hotel Renaissance
BOUTIQUE HOTEL $$

(Map p340; ✏️266 966; www.renaissance-bg.com; pl Vâzhrazhdane 1; s/d incl breakfast from 115/145 lv; 🅿🖥@🎐) This lovely boutique hotel between the old town and the main shopping streets aims to recreate a National Revival-era home through its intricate Plovdiv-style floral wall and ceiling paintings. Each room is unique, with handsome wood floors. Some boast period furniture. (Note the Arabic-language property document from 1878). Friendly, English-speaking owner Dimitar Vassilev is a font of local knowledge.

Hikers Hostel
HOSTEL $

(Map p340; ✏️0896764854; www.hikers-hostel. org; ul Sâborna 53; incl breakfast tent/dm/s/d with shared bathroom 12/20/43/48 lv; @🎐) The ideal place for independent travellers to chill in Plovdiv's old town, Hikers has comfy couches, outside tables, and sleeping choices ranging from tents and dorms to lofts and private rooms. There's free wi-fi, a computer, lockers for luggage, and laundry service (5 lv). If full, they offer (less appealing) private rooms and dorms near Dzhumaya Mosque.

Hebros Hotel
BOUTIQUE HOTEL $$$

(Map p340; ✏️260 180; www.hebros-hotel.com; ul K Stoilov 51; s/apt incl breakfast €99/119; 🖥🎐) This two-century-old mansion in the old town has a subdued elegance in its 10 well-furnished, spacious rooms. It's a bit pricier than others, but tremendously atmospheric. There's a back courtyard, spa and sauna (25 lv extra), plus a great restaurant.

Dali Art Hotel
BOUTIQUE HOTEL $$$

(Map p340; ✏️621 530; ul Otets Paisii 11; d/ste/apt incl breakfast 100/130/150 lv; 🖥🎐) This intimate boutique hotel off the mall has eight subtly little and airy rooms, including two apartments, with appropriately minimalist decor. However, it's most distinguished by its friendly and relaxed staff – not to mention the original works by Dali.

Plovdiv Guest House HOSTEL $
(Map p340; ☑622 432; www.plovdivguest.com; ul Sâborna 20; dm/s/d/q €9/25/30/45; ❄@🐾) Another backpacker option on Sâborna, this offers clean and bright dorms with 10, eight or four beds, and there's one spacious attic double. Dorms feature their own self-contained and modern bathroom or shower. There's an outdoor cafe out the back, above the ancient Roman wall.

Old Town Residence BOUTIQUE HOTEL $$$
(Map p340; ☑639 988; ul Knyaz Tseretelev 11; d 100 lv, apt from 160 lv; 🐾) The Residence has commanding old-town views and well-appointed rooms, with ornate reproduction furniture invoking the National Revival period. It offers six doubles and three sumptuous apartments, and has a posh restaurant and bar (light sleepers, note that noisy weddings are sometimes held at weekends).

Hotel Elite HOTEL $$
(Map p340; ☑624 537; ul Rayko Daskalov 53; d/ste 60/100 lv; ❄) The modern and reasonably central Elite is on the corner of bul 6 Septemvri, just west of the Kapana bar district. Rooms are insulated from road noise, and it's clean and comfortable. The suites, however, are really glorified doubles.

Hotel Leipzig HOTEL $$
(Map p338; ☑654 000; www.leipzig.bg; bul Ruski 70; s/d/apt from 82/100/124 lv; P❄🐾) This sharply renovated fixture has more than 60 appealing modern rooms and apartments designed with eclectic, colourful decor uncommon in a place that basically doubles as a business hotel and wedding-banquet venue. Some rooms have great views of the Hill of the Liberators, and there's a restaurant, lobby bar and casino.

Hotel Star HOTEL $$$
(Map p340; ☑633 599; www.starhotel.bg; ul Patriarh Evtimii 13; s/d incl breakfast from 70/130 lv; P❄@🐾) On the central pl Stambolov, the star (formerly known as Hotel Bulgaria) has rebranded itself as a 'budget hotel', with different-sized rooms priced accordingly. Rooms are bright and modern, with good bathrooms and double-glazed windows that block street noise.

Trakiya Hotel HOTEL $
(Map p338; ☑624 101; ul Ivan Vazov 84; s/d 35/60 lv; 🐾) This small hotel 100m from the train station has basic, clean rooms (with fan), and they are quiet, despite the noisy location and popular bar downstairs.

Noviz Hotel HOTEL $$$
(Map p338; ☑631 281; www.noviz.com; bul Ruski 55; s/d/ste 100/140/170 lv; P❄🐾) While the Noviz is small, it's friendly and the rooms are large and well furnished. It offers excellent and inexpensive massage therapy (from 30 lv); there's also a sauna and a refreshing cold pool.

🍴 Eating

Puldin Restaurant INTERNATIONAL $$$
(Map p340; ☑631 720; ul Knyaz Tseretelev 8; mains 8-15 lv; ⏱9am-midnight; 🐾) The magical Puldin is one of Plovdiv's most atmospheric restaurants. In one dining room, the famous whirling dervishes of the Ottoman Empire once whirled themselves into ecstatic exhaustion, while in the cellar hall Byzantine walls and Roman artefacts predominate. Although it's expensive, the decor alone makes it worthwhile.

Hebros Hotel Restaurant BULGARIAN $$$
(Map p340; ☑625 929; ul K Stoilov 51; mains 11-22 lv; 🐾) The upscale restaurant of the eponymous hotel enjoys a secluded garden setting and does excellent, innovative Bulgarian cuisine, such as rabbit with plums, braised trout, pork with blue cheese and more.

Restaurant Renaissance INTERNATIONAL $$
(pl Vâzhrazhdane 1; mains 9-17 lv; ⏱10am-10:30pm Tue-Sun) The restaurant of the Hotel Renaissance cooks up a wide range of inventive appetizers (duck lung stuffed with apple, anyone?), plus grills, risottos and fresh fish from the Aegean. The local wine list is particularly strong, the service friendly and attentive.

Dayana GRILLS $$
(Map p340; ☑623 027; ul Dondukov Korsakov 3; mains 5-9 lv; ⏱9am-late; 🐾) This big place off the pedestrian mall, popular with locals and foreigners alike, has a huge (and colourful) menu strong on grilled meats.

Gusto ITALIAN $$
(Map p340; ☑623 711; ul Otets Paisii 26; mains 5-9 lv; ⏱9am-1am) Across from the boulevard's pedestrian underpass, the friendly Gusto has diner-style booths upstairs and cosy tables downstairs, both with classy decor. While it's arguably not even the best

offering, pasta accompanied by wine seems the most popular choice.

Philippopolis
Restaurant & Café   INTERNATIONAL $$$
(Map p340; ☏624 851; ul Sâborna 29; mains 13-24 lv; ◷10am-midnight; ⌂) Formerly just a cafe, this restaurant belonging to the eponymous art gallery has a garden section with views, and indoor dining too. They've gone up-market now, however, complementing an extensive array of meat and fish dishes with a long wine list – at prices to match.

Ristorante Da Lino   ITALIAN $$$
(Map p338; ☏631 751; bul 6 Septemvri 135; mains 9-15 lv; ⌂) Plovdiv's best place for Italian food, Da Lino occupies a converted monastery; however, prices are high and portions small.

Malâk Bunardzhik   BULGARIAN $$
(Map p338; ☏446 140; ul Volga 1; mains 5-10 lv; ⌂) Quality Bulgarian cuisine is served at this popular place with garden dining and live music most nights.

XIX Vek   BULGARIAN $$
(19th Century; Map p338; ☏653 882; ul Tsar Kaloyan 1; mains 6-10 lv; ◷7am-midnight; ⌂) Pronounced *devetnaystee vek,* this local favourite in a garden near the pedestrian mall offers traditional *satch* (stew baked in a clay pots) dishes, charcoal-grilled shish kebabs and more. Its walls are decorated with 19th-century village decor.

🍷 Drinking

Plovdiv's nightspots are widespread. However, several good places occupy the district called Kapana, meaning 'the trap', referring to its tight streets (the areas north of pl Dzhumaya, between ul Rayko Daskalov to the west and bul Tsar Boris Obedinitel to the east).

Note that clubs undergo sporadic name changes, sometimes closing and reopening under new management – double-check locally with a free nightlife booklet like *Programata.*

⌂TOP CHOICE Naylona   BAR
(Map p340; ☏0889496750; ul Giorgi Benkovski 8, Kapana; ◷noon-4am; ⌂) They say that the owners of this Kapana dive bar purposely didn't fix the roof, so that the rain would trickle in; whatever the story, this damp, bare-bones place usually playing classic (and other) rock remains the unwashed, long-haired antithesis of Plovdiv style.

Art Bar Maria Luiza   BAR
(Map p340; bul Maria Luiza 15; ◷8am-4am; ⌂) Too pretty to be just a dive bar, the Maria Luiza has dedicated owners who keep adapting the décor to suit their whims. The colourful downstairs is particularly stylish, vaguely reminiscent of 1920s Paris. There's a dedicated local following.

Dreams   CAFE
(Map p340; ☏627 142; pl Stambolov; sandwiches around 2 lv; ◷9am-11pm; ⌂) This excellent and very popular cafe on pl Stambolov is the perfect place to relax before the square's giant gushing fountain on a balmy summer's day. It serves good cakes, along with numerous alcoholic and nonalcoholic drinks. There's also a spacious upstairs hall.

Sky Bar   BAR
(Map p340; ☏633 377; ul Knyaz Aleksandâr 30; ◷24hr; ⌂) You can't beat the Sky Bar, located atop one of Plovdiv's tallest buildings, for panoramic evening or night-time views in the company of a cold drink.

Mojito Bar   BAR
(Map p338; ☏643 221; ul Ivan Andonov 5; ◷9am-2am; ⌂) Mojito specialises in cocktails, and has carried over the same sharp-dressed slick Bulgarian crowd from its previous incarnation as Club Planet.

Fashion Café   BAR
(Map p340; ☏632 131; ul Antim Parvi; ◷8am-4pm; ⌂) In the shopping centre west of Dzhumaya Mosque, this popular place offers mixed musical styles and is popular with students by night.

Café Starino   CAFE
(Map p340; pl Vâzhrazhdane; ◷8am-2am; ⌂) One of Plovdiv's oldest and most atmospheric cafes, this dark, weathered place on the old town's southern edge has pillowy, Ottoman-style bench-tables on the upper section. Behind the antique, handpainted walls are even older, Turkish-era sections. The Starino attracts mostly a subdued, local crowd.

Plazma Light   BAR
(Map p338; ☏033 055; Hristo Botev 82; ◷24hr; ⌂) This chic local favourite with the house-music crowd has a nightclub behind, and features detached, island-like bars set in a sea of cream-and-black decor. Shiny screens

and shiny people complete the mesmerising effect.

Café Taksim Tepe
CAFE

(Map p340; ul Sâborna 47; ⊙10am-midnight; 🛜) With its patio setting overlooking Plovdiv's red roofs, this tiny place has a relaxing vibe and (sometimes) plays ragtime and jazz. Despite the allusive name, it doesn't serve Turkish coffee.

Café Avenue
CAFE

(Map p340; ☑626 526; bul Maria Luiza 12; ⊙7.30am-1.30am; 🛜) Very popular with local celebrities (and the youngsters desirous of them), this fashionable, dressed-up cafe plays retro, house and dance music.

Simfoniya
CAFE

(Map p338; ☑630 333; Tsar Simeon Garden; ⊙24hr; 🛜) At the park's western end, Simfoniya is a busy bar–cafe with drinks (and cakes).

☆ Entertainment

Nightclubs

Petnoto
CLUB

(Map p340; ☑0898542787; ul Ioakim Gruev 36, Kapana; ⊙8am-6am; 🛜) The pinstriped Petnoto combines a bar, a small restaurant and a music stage where Bulgarian bands and DJs perform.

Marmalad
LIVE MUSIC

(Map p340; ul Bratya Pulievi 3; cocktails 3 lv; ⊙9am-2am) This two-floor place is one of Kapana's best for live music. The upper floor is a bar, the lower one a club where nationally known rock bands perform on Thursday. Other weekly features include piano bar, karaoke, tribute nights and DJ action.

City Place
CLUB

(Map p340; ☑0888715657; bul Maria Luiza 43; ⊙11pm-6am; 🛜) Plovdiv's longest-running nightclub was formerly called Paparazi, but in its current incarnation it has seen some slick renovations – though the DJ-driven house music, *chalga* (Bulgarian pop music) and hip-hop playlist remains the same in this cavernous place composed of three large halls.

Enjoy Club 69
CLUB

(Map p340; ☑0888699688; Evlogi Giorgiev 1; ⊙11pm-6am; 🛜) This scantily clad *chalga* (Bulgarian folk-pop) club somehow combines brick-wall decor and plasma video screens, attracting students and wannabe mafiosi.

King's Stables Café
LIVE MUSIC

(Map p340; ul Sâborna; cocktails 3.50 lv; ⊙8.30am-2am Apr-Sep) This summer-only outdoor cafe has a lower area beside the restaurant, with live music stage, and a funky upper bar (the 'second stage'), offering a short list of well-made cocktails. A DJ here spins chilled-out tracks, sometimes accompanied by wafting, pungent incense.

Caligula
GAY

(Map p340; ☑626 867; ul Knyaz Aleksandâr 30; ⊙10am-8am; 🛜) Plovdiv's only gay club is, Bulgarian men only half-jokingly say, a nice place to meet girls. Whatever the case, the mixed crowd comes not only for the greased-up male pole dancers but also for the live music, DJs and neighbouring facilities (the Sky Bar is in the same complex).

Infinity
CLUB

(Map p340; ☑0888281431; Bratya Pulievi 4, Kapana; ⊙10am-late; 🛜) Varied music, from pop to dance, is played at this student late club in Kapana.

Cinemas

See recent foreign films in original languages (with Bulgarian subtitles) at **Luki Cinema** (Map p340; ☑629 070; ul Gladston 1), **Flamingo Cinema** (Map p338; ☑644 004; bul 6 Septemvri 128) or **Faces Cinema** (☑683 310; bul Saedinenie, Trakiya District).

Theatre & Opera

Roman Amphitheatre
ANCIENT THEATRE

(Map p340; ul Hemus) The amphitheatre hosts Plovdiv's annual Verdi Festival (June), plus other summertime opera, ballet and music performances.

Nikolai Masalitinov Dramatic Theatre
THEATRE

(Map p340; ☑224 867; ul Knyaz Aleksandâr 38) One of Bulgaria's top theatres, it features anything from Shakespeare to Ibsen (usually in Bulgarian).

Plovdiv Opera House
OPERA

(Map p338; ☑632 231; opera@thracia.net; ul Avksentiy Veleshki) Classic and modern European operas are performed in Bulgarian at this venerable hall.

🛍 Shopping

Trendy clothes and shoe stores line the pedestrian mall ul Knyaz Aleksandâr. Continuing up ul Sâborna, you'll find several antique shops. Paintings by Bulgarian artists are sold in various cafes and galleries – considering the quality and increasing prominence of the Plovdiv school of painting, this can also be a shrewd investment.

Ponedelnik Pazar
MARKET
(Monday Market; Map p340; pl Vazhrajdane) Busy fruit-and-veg market between old town and main shopping streets.

Litera
BOOKS
(Map p340; ☑625 300; ul Tsaribrod 1; ◷8.30am-8.30pm Mon-Fri, 10am-7pm Sat & Sun) A bookshop opposite Dzhumaya Mosque; has English-language travel books about Bulgaria.

 Information

Internet access
Free wi-fi is widespread. Internet centres around pedestrianised ul Knyaz Aleksandâr operate 24 hours (1 lv to 2 lv per hour).
Internet Café Speed (2nd fl, bul Maria Luiza 1) Internet centre.

Medical Services
Klinika Medicus Alpha (☑634 463; www.medicusalpha.com; ul Veliko Târnovo 21; ◷24hr) A modern medical centre with many different specialists.

Money
Exchange offices line ul Knyaz Aleksandâr and ul Ivan Vazov. Most close on Sunday. ATMs are widespread, including around pl Dzhumaya and ul Knyaz Aleksandâr, though not in the old town's upper reaches.

Post
Main Post Office (pl Tsentralen; ◷7am-7pm Mon-Sat, to 11am Sun) Has several computers with online access, and phone booths on the ground floor (open 7am to 10pm).

Telephone
Telephone Centre (pl Tsentralen; ◷6am-11pm) Inside the post office.

Tourist information
The *Plovdiv Guide* and *Programata* are free weekly magazines listing local bars, restaurants and clubs. The latter is Bulgarian-only, though its website (www.programata.bg) is in English too. The municipal website www.plovdiv.bg and www.plovdivcityguide.com also are useful.

Although bookshops sell city maps like Domino's *Plovdiv* (1:11,500), free maps from hotels, hostels and tourist information centres should suffice.

Tourist Information Centre (☑/fax 656 794; tic@plovdiv.bg; pl Tsentralen 1; ◷9am-7pm)

This helpful centre by the post office provides maps and finds local accommodation.

Patrick Penov Personal Trips & Tours
(☑0887 364-711; www.guide-bg.com) Licensed tour guide Svetlomir 'Patrick' Penov has two decades of experience leading individual and small-group tours all over Bulgaria, covering everything from gastronomy and wine to churches and culture – not to mention mountain biking, snorkeling and extreme sports.

Since the tours he offers are wide-ranging and can be modified to suit demand, prices vary, but an average daily rate (as many hours as it takes!) is 200 lv.

 Getting There & Away

Air
Approximately 12km from town, formerly neglected Plovdiv Airport is seeing more international flights, especially in summer. At the time of research, Ryanair was offering flights to Frankfurt and London, with talk of other carriers to come; check ahead. There's no airport shuttle bus; a taxi to the centre runs 12 lv to 15 lv.

Bus
Plovdiv's three bus stations include the **Yug bus station** (☑626 937, 626 916) diagonally opposite the train station and a 15-minute walk from the centre (a taxi costs 5 lv to 7 lv). Alternatively, local buses (0.80 lv) stop across the main street outside the station, on bul Hristo Botev. From the Yug bus station, public and private buses serve the destinations listed. Note that there's often no way of predicting whether you'll be getting a big, modern bus or a cramped minibus – the latter is particularly likely for rural destinations but can even be encountered for longer intercity trips.

DESTINATION	FARE	DURATION	FREQUENCY
Bansko	14 lv	3½hr	2 daily
Blagoevgrad	13-15 lv	3hr	3 daily
Burgas (private)	19 lv	4hr	2 daily
Karlovo	8 lv	1½hr	half-hourly
Ruse (private)	19 lv	6hr	1 daily
Sliven	14 lv	3hr	5 daily
Sofia	9 lv	2½hr	half-hourly
Stara Zagora	8 lv	1½hr	4 daily
Varna	22 lv	7hr	2 daily
Veliko Târnovo (private)	17 lv	4½hr	3 daily

In summer, one or two daily buses leave for the Black Sea (Kiten, Ahtopol, Albena and Nesebâr).

From **Rodopi bus station** (☎657 828), through the train station underpass, 13 daily buses serve Karlovo and hourly buses (between 6am and 7pm) go to Smolyan (10 lv, 2½ hours), via Bachkovo (4 lv, one hour), Chepelare (8.50 lv), Devin (12 lv), and Pamporovo.

The **Sever bus station** (☎953 011), in the northern suburbs, has one daily bus to Kazanlâk (9 lv), Pleven (23 lv), Ruse (12 lv), Troyan (15 lv), Koprivshtitsa (6 lv) and Veliko Târnovo (20 lv).

Union-Ivkoni Vesna 61 (☎628 365; train station underpass; ⊗8am-6pm) serves international destinations, including Paris (220 lv), Rome (220 lv), Vienna (170 lv) and Amsterdam (200 lv).

Etap (☎632 082; Yug bus station) sells bus tickets to Istanbul (40 lv), Athens (140 lv) and more.

Train

Plovdiv, along the major Sofia–Burgas line, has many trains; the main ones are given here.

DESTINATION	1ST-/2ND-CLASS FARE	DURATION	NUMBER OF TRAINS (DAILY)
Burgas	14.60 lv	6hr	6
Stara Zagora	6 lv	2hr	6
Sliven	11.40 lv	4 hr	2
Bansko (via Septemvri)	8.20 lv	6 hr	2
Karlovo	3.90 lv	2hr	5
Sofia	9/7 lv*	2½hr*	14
Svilengrad	7.40 lv	3½hr	3

*denotes express trains

Plovdiv's **train station** (bul Hristo Botev) is well organised, though the staff don't speak English. Computer screens at the station entrance and in the underpass leading to the platforms list recent arrivals and upcoming departures. The luggage-storage (2 lv per bag for 24 hours) office is always open.

For international tickets see the **Rila Bureau** (☎446 120; ⊗8am-6.30pm Mon-Sat), on a side street paralleling bul Hristo Botev.

❶ Getting Around

Plovdiv is best experienced on foot. Much of the old town is off-limits to cars anyway, so with a taxi your 'final destination' will be outside the Church of Sveta Bogoroditsa on ul Sâborna, where all cars must turn back (at night the street is usually open). Although taxi drivers conscientiously use meters, a few offenders charge rates as opprobrious as 4 lv per kilometre; the daytime base rate should be around 0.93 lv per kilometre, slightly higher at night.

For car rental, **Tourist Service Rent-a-Car** (☎623 496; Trimontium Princess Hotel) and **Avis** (☎934 481; Novotel) are well known but expensive; travel agencies along the mall or the tourist information centre can find better prices.

Around Plovdiv

BACHKOVO MONASTERY

About 30km south of Plovdiv, the magnificent **Bachkovo Monastery** (Bachkovo; admission free; ⊗6am-10pm) was founded in 1083 by Georgian brothers Gregory and Abasius Bakuriani, aristocrats in Byzantine military service. The monastery flourished during the Second Bulgarian Empire (1185–1396) but was ransacked by Turks in the 15th and 16th centuries. Major reconstructions began in the mid-17th century. Bachkovo's now Bulgaria's second-largest monastery, after Rila.

In the courtyard, the **Church of Sveta Bogoroditsa** (1604) contains frescoes by Zahari Zograf from the early 1850s. Other highlights include the 17th-century iconostasis, more 19th-century murals and a much-cherished icon of the Virgin, allegedly painted by St Luke, though actually dating from the 14th century. Pilgrims regularly pray before the silver-encased icon.

The monastery's southern side houses the former **refectory** (1601). The walls are filled with stunning frescoes relating the monastery's history. A gate beside the refectory leads to a (rarely open) courtyard; this leads to the **Church of Sveti Nikolai** (1836). During the 1840s, Zograf painted the superb *Last Judgment* inside the chapel; note the condemned, nervous-looking Turks on the right and Zograf's self-portrait (no beard) in the upper-left corner.

Around 50m from the monastery entrance, the restored **Ossuary** features wonderful medieval murals, but it remains closed.

A prominent explanation board provides monastic history (in English, French and German), and a map of **hiking trails** to nearby villages. The helpful guidebook (15 lv) is available too.

🛏 Sleeping & Eating

Bachkovo Monastery offers austere older rooms with shared bathrooms, and newer ones with their own bathrooms, for 20 lv per person and 40 lv per person, respectively. Enquire upstairs in the reception office.

Echo Hotel   HOTEL **$**
(☏048-981 068; d incl breakfast 50 lv; ❄) On the other side of the road, and river, from the Bachkovo Monastery turn-off, this small place offers quiet, comfortable rooms.

Restaurant Vodopada   BULGARIAN **$**
(mains 4-9 lv; ⊙9am-10pm) The best place to eat near Bachkovo Monastery, this charming courtyard restaurant, ranged around a waterfall and fish pool, serves good grills and salads.

❶ Getting There & Away

Take any bus to Smolyan from Plovdiv's Rodopi bus station (3 lv), disembark at the turn-off about 1.2km south of Bachkovo village and walk about 500m uphill. There are also direct buses half-hourly.

RODOPI MOUNTAINS
РОДОПИ ПЛАНИНА

Vast stretches of serene pine forests, perilously steep gorges and hundreds of remarkable caves characterise the enthralling Rodopi (rod-*oh*-pee) Mountains, which cover some 15,000 sq km of territory, spilling across into Greece. Much of the border between the two countries is determined by the Rodopi range (85% of which is Bulgarian).

Being relatively remote compared with the Rila and Pirin mountain ranges further west, the Rodopi Mountains see far fewer foreign visitors, with the exception of the ski resorts of Pamporovo and Chepelare, and the spa town of Devin. Outside these areas, however, the region remains one of Bulgaria's wildest, an endless expanse of majestic, thickly packed conifer forests where more than 200 bird species and brown bears, wild goats and wolves dwell. The Rodopi Mountains are exceptionally rich in wildflowers, including indigenous violets, tulips and the unique *silivriak* – a fragile white flower said to have sprung up from the blood of Orpheus, the semidivine father of music, after he was torn to pieces by the frenzied Bacchantes.

Despite being sparsely populated, this mountain range named after a Thracian god, Rhodopa, is dotted with hundreds of tiny, traditional villages. This is particularly so for the Muslim villages populated by Turks and Pomaks (Slavic Christians who converted to Islam to win benefits during the Ottoman occupation). The Rodopi area fell to the Turks in 1371 and suffered harshly under their rule, which saw a massacre at Batak in 1876. Today, relations between the various ethnic and religious groups are normal, though Bulgarians are nervous about rising Turkish nationalism.

Along with winter skiing, summertime outdoor activities such as hiking, horse riding and caving are all excellent here. There are more than 700 mapped caves in the Rodopi Mountains, the most spectacular being near Trigrad and Yagodina, though others, such as the partly underwater Golubovitsa, are still being discovered. While the range's average height is only 785m, the highest peak – Mt Golyan Perelik, near Smolyan – rises to 2190m.

Chepelare   Чепеларе
☏03051 / POP 5412 / ELEV 1150M
A laid-back village and ski centre with 20km of runs, modest Chepelare has plans to (someday) link up to the far larger and louder Pamporovo, 6km down the road. Till then, it makes a perfect getaway for family-friendly skiing (downhill and cross-country) without the nightlife and other distractions of Bansko. In summer, the nearby mountains offer excellent hiking.

🏃 Activities
Skiing
Chepelare is a humbler, more family-friendly place than Bulgaria's big ski resorts. However, it does offer world-class skiing: the two most famous trails, Mechi Chal I (3150m), a black-level super giant slalom course, and Mechi Chal II (5250m) are among Bulgaria's longest, and have hosted international competitions.

Heights of total ski terrain range from 1150m to 1873m. Chepelare's three main trails equal 11.4km; a fourth, gently sloping trail is, so the tourist office humorously states, 'suitable for women and children'.

In fact, Chepelare's most famous native is a female athlete: Ekaterina Dafovska, biathlon gold medallist of 1998's Nagano Winter Olympics. Her success prompted local leaders to open an academy for skiing, snowboarding and, oddly enough, table tennis. The school (not for tourists) aims to train future Olympians.

The chairlift, 1.5km south on the Pamporovo road, is signposted. Chepelare also offers 30km of cross-country skiing. Hire

DON'T MISS

HIKING IN THE RODOPI MOUNTAINS

Exploring the idyllic forested region around Chepelare, Smolyan, Shiroka Lûka and Devin is the high point for nature lovers here. First, get the English-language *West Rhodopean Region* or *Western Rhodope Mountains* maps (1:100,000) from the Pamporovo, Chepelare or Smolyan tourist offices. They detail hiking trails of three to five hours, plus five mountain-biking routes. Kartografia also has an excellent *Rodopi* map (1:100,000).

Julian Perry's *Mountains of Bulgaria* describes (but with poor maps) a five- to seven-day trek from Hizha Studenents, near Pamporovo, to Hizha Rodoposki Partizanin, near Hrabrino, about 14km southwest of Plovdiv. *Hizhas* are available.

For shorter hikes, base yourself in Devin. Nine marked trails, including one to Chepelare, via Kukuvitsa (two to three hours one way) and another to Mt Golyam Perelik (five to six hours), begin here. Other excellent hikes along marked trails:

Batak to Hizha Teheran About four hours.

Chepelare to Hizha Igrev About three hours. From there, continue to Shiroka Lûka (three hours) or Pamporovo (seven hours).

Pamporovo to Progled An (easy) five-hour return trip across the lovely Rozhen fields.

Smolyan to Hizha Smolyanski Ezera About three hours one way.

---

gear at **Orion Ski** (☑2142; Chepelare), by the lift, note that few instructors are available. Chepelare has a ski factory, and you can buy cheap, good-quality ski gear.

🛏 Sleeping & Eating

The tourist offices in Chepelare or Smolyan can book private rooms in Chepelare (from 20 lv per person with shared bathroom). Hotel prices increase significantly in winter.

More Chepelare hotels, signposted along the Plovdiv–Smolyan road, require private transport to reach.

Hotel Phoenix HOTEL $
(☑3408; ul Murgavets 4; s/d 25/30 lv) About 200m up ul Vasil Dechev from the town square, the Phoenix offers simple, spotless rooms with TV, along with a traditional restaurant.

Hotel Savov HOTEL $
(☑2036; ul Vasil Dechev 7; d/tr/apt from 30/40/50 lv; P) Opposite the Hebros Bank, this comfortable place offers large, airy doubles, and apartments with sitting areas. The restaurant is popular and good.

Hotel Gergana HOTEL $
(☑4201; ul Hristo Botev 75; d incl breakfast from 35 lv; P) The Gergana, along the Plovdiv road, is a cosy, family-run place with simple, clean rooms. Home-cooked traditional cuisine is served at the hotel restaurant.

TOP CHOICE Pelelanovska Konak BULGARIAN $$
(☑2176; ul Dimitar Chichovski 10; mains 5-9 lv; ☺11am-1am Mon-Sat) This traditional Rodopean *mehana* (tavern) is in the backstreets, across the river. Tucked inside a little enclosure, it has outdoor seating and a spacious, hunting-lodge interior with hanging pelts and antlers. The enormous traditional menu includes the 'chef's special' *satch*, a riotous mixture of various meats, cheese and vegetables baked in a clay pot. Service is friendly and attentive.

ℹ Information

The combined post office and telephone centre, near the town square, has internet, and there's a nearby bank and ATM. The informative municipal website, **www.chepelare.com**, has ski information.

Tourist Information Centre (☑2110; tic@chepelare.bg; ul Dicho Petrov 1A; ☺8.30am-12.30pm & 1.30-6pm) A helpful place 100m up from the square, on a side street, the centre provides detailed brochures about hiking routes, skiing and other activities.

ℹ Getting There & Away

The bus station is across a footbridge, 200m northeast of the square. Buses leave hourly for Smolyan (5 lv, one hour), via Pamporovo. Regular services between Plovdiv (11 lv, 90 minutes) and Madan, and Plovdiv and Smolyan, also stop in Chepelare.

Pamporovo Пампорово

☑ 3095 / ELEV 1650M

Pamporovo (Pam-*por*-ovo), 6km south of Chepelare, is one of Bulgaria's four major ski resorts. As with Bansko, rampant expansion has left the place – full of cranes, stacked building supplies and the skeletons of characterless, identical luxury apartments – looking like one monstrous construction site. However, unlike Bansko, there's no settlement, just a decentralised resort. Pamporovo is increasingly popular and thus more expensive; it's also expanding deeper into the forests, with almost 30km of new trails connecting Pamporovo with Chepelare (the 35,000-sq-km 'Perelik project') and dismaying local environmentalists.

Although there's good nearby hiking, most of the town closes in summer. Other nearby villages have more atmospheric accommodation, which means that Pamporovo is recommended only if you're on a planned ski holiday. Otherwise, you can pass it by without feeling much guilt. The main cultural event for locals, the **Rozhen Folk Festival** (☺ late August) occurs in the Rozhen fields between Pamporovo and Progled.

🏃 Activities

Skiing

Nestled in Bulgaria's deep south, Pamporovo and Chepelare boast over 250 days of sunshine a year. With significant snowfall between mid-December and mid-April, skiing conditions are often ideal.

Pamporovo's facilities are comparatively new and the slopes well maintained; however, the resort sprawls, so private transport is helpful. In winter, accommodation for independent skiers and travellers is scarce. If you're skiing here, consider cheaper accommodation options in Chepelare, Momchilovtsi, Smolyan and Shiroka Lûka.

Pamporovo's eight downhill ski runs total 25km and are complemented by 25km of cross-country trails and four training slopes. At least three new trails are being gouged out of the mountains between Pamporovo and Stoykite. The resort is at 1620m, with the highest trailhead rising to 1937m. Of Pamporovo's original five chairlifts and nine draglifts, a few operate during summer. Chairlifts cost 15/20 lv one way/return and a day pass costs about 60 lv. Minibuses from the hotels to the lifts are free if you have a lift pass.

Pamporovo offers trails for beginners, and instructors speak English or German. There's also a children's ski kindergarten. Most instructors charge about 220 lv per person for 12 to 24 hours group training, spread over six to 12 days.

More than a dozen ski shops rent gear, including the **Sport Shop** (☑ 0888552354) in the Hotel Perelik complex. A full set of equipment costs 50 lv to 80 lv per day. Pamporovo is ideal for snowboarding; visit the popular British-run **Snow Shack** (snowshack_uk@ yahoo.co.uk) in the Hotel Markony complex for snowboarding gear and/or training courses.

Other Activities

In summer local providers rent out mountain bikes (from 8 lv per hour), and hiking guides (from 25 lv per hour) are usually available. Horse riding (40 to 50 lv per hour) is offered around the central T-junction. Tennis courts are also nearby.

🛏 Sleeping & Eating

In winter hotel rates are 25% higher than those quoted here.

Hotel Perelik   HOTEL **$$$**
(☑ 8405; www.perelikhotel.com; s/d from 114/184 lv; P✳🛜♨) The sharply renovated Perelik has good, if not spectacular rooms, but people come for the extras. Facilities include a big indoor pool, spa centre, sauna, billiards, shops, restaurants, bar and disco. It has all manner of special-price packages (some include lift ticket in ski season), so check ahead.

Grand Hotel Murgavets   HOTEL **$$$**
(☑ 58310; www.murgavets-bg.com; s/d/apt from 120/170/250 lv; P✳🛜♨) This Pamporovo giant was snapped up by a nationwide chain, improving its look and already formidable services, which include a gym, spa centre, playground, pool, bar and restaurant. The rooms are spiffy and the single beds surprisingly large.

Hotel Finlandia   HOTEL **$$**
(☑ 58367; www.hotelfinlandia.com; s/d from 90/120 lv; P♨) The four-star Finlandia has clean, classy rooms plus a nightclub, health centre and ski school with English- and German-speaking instructors; there's also a kindergarten for depositing surplus baggage while on the slopes. The hotel's Bulgarian-specialties restaurant is excellent.

ℹ Information

Try www.bulgariaski.com for updated snow reports, advice and accommodation information for all Bulgarian ski resorts.

Most hotels, restaurants and shops in remote parts are closed from May to October, but everything around the central Hotel Perelik is open year-round.

ℹ Getting There & Away

The hourly Smolyan–Chepelare buses pass Pamporovo, as do the regular Smolyan–Plovdiv and Smolyan–Sofia buses. A few daily buses from Sofia go directly to Pamporovo (24 lv, four hours) and up to eight leave from Plovdiv (12 lv, two hours). The bus stop is at the Ski Lift No 1 chairlift at the central T-junction.

This junction unites the roads to Smolyan, Chepelare and Devin (via Shiroka Lŭka) and is also Pamporovo's central point. From here, the amoeba-like resort spreads for 4km along several roads.

Smolyan   Смолян

📞0301 / POP 30,283 / ELEV 1000M

The longest (10km) and highest town in Bulgaria (1010m), Smolyan is actually an amalgamation of four villages, and is the southern Rodopi Mountains' administrative centre. The steep and forested mountains rise abruptly on its southern flank, lending a lovely backdrop to a town that's otherwise slightly timeworn and gritty. As in most of the Rodopi region, there's a notable Pomak Muslim population here.

First settled by Thracians around 700 BC, the town is an alternative place to stay for skiing Pamporovo and Chepelare, though certainly not the most beautiful one. It's the transport hub for villages such as Shiroka Lŭka and Devin. Smolyan is also a base for exploring the seven Smolyan Lakes, the caves of Golubovitsa, partly underwater, and Uhlovitsa, with its bizarre rock formations.

Although Smolyan is 10km long, the centre is essentially the partly pedestrianised bul Bulgaria, which has ATMs, a post office, and cafes and restaurants on its western end.

◉ Sights

Historical Museum   MUSEUM

(📞62 727; Dicho Petrov 3; admission 5 lv; ◷9amnoon & 1-5pm Mon-Sat) Smolyan's Historical Museum, up behind the civic centre, has exhibits including Palaeolithic artefacts and Thracian armour and weaponry. Rodopi weaving and woodcarving, plus numerous traditional musical instruments and folk costumes (most notably the fantastical Kuker outfits worn at New Year celebrations) are also shown. Upstairs are photos and models of traditional buildings.

Smolyan Art Gallery   GALLERY

(📞62 328; Dicho Petrov 7; admission 5 lv; ◷9amnoon & 1.30-5pm Tue-Sun) The gallery boasts some 1800 paintings, sketches and sculptures by local, national and foreign artists.

Planetarium   PLANETARIUM

(📞83 074; bul Bulgaria 20; admission 5 lv) Bulgaria's biggest planetarium, about 200m west of Hotel Smolyan, offers a spectacular show (35 to 40 minutes) with commentary in English, French or German at 2pm from Monday to Saturday, and in Bulgarian at other times. The foreign-language shows are for groups of five or more; otherwise, you'll pay 25 lv for a solo viewing.

WORTH A TRIP

SMOLYAN'S MYSTERIOUS CAVES

In ancient times, the road to hell was paved with water; so, too, in today's Bulgaria. Although not exactly replicating the voyage to Hades along the River Styx, the journey into the recently discovered Golubovitsa Cave is a thrilling and similarly aquatic one. Located 3km south of Uhlovitsa Cave, off the road between Smolyan and Mogilitsa, the cave is accessible by boat, as the first 25m or so is completely underwater. After that, you walk, accompanied by a lantern and a guide. For daredevils, there's even a way down by rope.

The more established Uhlovitsa Cave (admission 4 lv; ◷10am-4pm daily summer, Wed-Sun winter), about 3km northeast of Mogilitsa, boasts numerous waterfalls (most spectacular in winter) and some bizarre formations, but it requires private transport; check with the Smolyan Tourist Information Center for more details.

🛏 Sleeping

The tourist office finds private rooms (about 20 lv per person).

Hotel Kiparis A
HOTEL $$

(☑64 040; www.hotelkiparis.eu; bul Bulgaria 3a; s/d/apt incl breakfast 50/75/110 lv; ❄️🔊) This comfortable hotel with an excellent spa centre has plush and light-toned rooms, plus all mod cons.

Three Fir Trees House
PENSION $

(☑81 028; www.trieli.hit.bg; ul Srednogorets 1; s/d/apt with shared bathroom 30/40/80lv; @🔊) Some 200m east of the main bus station, this relaxed family-run place has well-maintained rooms. It's signposted down the steps from bul Bulgaria. There's an excellent, varied breakfast (5 lv), and the helpful, multilingual owner arranges tours and rental cars, plus a cheap laundry service.

Hotel Babylon
HOTEL $

(☑63 268; ul Han Presian 22; d/tw/apt 36/52/70 lv) This central place offers large, two-room apartments with comfortable lounge, plus a downstairs bar and restaurant. It's behind the little park, above bul Bulgaria.

Hotel Smolyan
$$

(☑62 053; www.hotelsmolyan.com; bul Bulgaria 3; s/d/apt from 36/60/90 lv; P@🔊) This still unrenovated ex-communist hotel facing the civic centre has clean but forlorn rooms; some have balconies overlooking Smolyan's lovely forests.

🍴 Eating & Drinking

Starata Kâshta
BULGARIAN $$

(ul Studenska 2; mains 6-9 lv; ⊙4.30pm-midnight) Also known as the Pamporovata Kâshta, this place offers a short menu of grills and salads. The attractive National Revival–style house (built in 1840) has a few rough-hewn outdoor tables and benches. It's up the steps from bul Bulgaria.

Rodopski Kat
BULGARIAN $$

(bul Bulgaria 3; mains 5-8 lv; ⊙7am-2am) This nice restaurant, wedged between hotels in the centre, is excellent for traditional Rodopean fare.

Riben Dar
SEAFOOD $$

(☑63 220; ul Snezhanka 16; mains 6-12lv) In the western neighbourhood of Nevyasta, this is great for delicious fresh fish, such as Rodopi Mountain trout. Take a taxi (3 lv to 5 lv).

Club Venus
BAR

(bul Bulgaria 11; ⊙24hr) Sleepy Smolyan's best entertainment spot, the Venus is popular at night, and serves good food. There's a wi-fi hot spot, too.

ℹ Information

Regional Association of Rhodope Municipalities (☑62 056; bul Bulgaria 14) Represents the 20 local districts. Has arts and crafts information and organises tours or guides.

Tourist Office (☑62 530; www.smolyan.com; bul Bulgaria 5; ⊙9am-5.30pm Mon-Fri) The major Rodopi-villages tourism office; a good source of info for Smolyan and nearby towns and outdoor activities.

ℹ Getting There & Away

Most buses to/from Smolyan use the **main bus station** (☑63 104; bul Bulgaria) at Smolyan's western end. Four daily buses serve Sofia (28 lv, 3½ hours) and hourly buses serve Plovdiv (17 lv, 2½ to three hours), via Chepelare (6 lv, one hour) and Pamporovo (4 lv, 30 minutes). From this station, buses also serve Shiroka Lûka and Devin (8 lv, 90 minutes, three to four daily), for Trigrad and Yagodina Caves.

From near the station, local buses 2 and 3 (0.80 lv, every 20 minutes) serve the centre. Walk left out of the station and turn left up a double set of stairs; after 50m, you'll see the stop on the left. The taxi rank is further down the street. By taxi, it's around 3 lv to the tourist office.

Alternatively, if you're heading out on the Smolyan–Pamporovo–Chepelare–Plovdiv road, minibuses go from Hotel Smolyan's car park. They leave every hour on the hour between 8am and 5pm.

Devin
Девин

☑03041

One of Bulgaria's best spa towns, placid Devin is somewhat dated, though it does offer solitude, services and one or two cafebars. Still, it's the kind of place where unworried mothers leave their baby carriages outside the shop while browsing, and the only noise you'll hear at night is the far-off baying of hounds.

Devin's famous for producing Bulgaria's premier brand of bottled mineral water, and for its balneological resort; indeed, plenty of wealthy Sofians (driven in black Jeeps with tinted windows) frequently come for discreet, five-star luxury treatment. However, the slightly faded town hardly resembles a resort, and you can take in the waters inexpensively outdoors, hike the lovely local eco-path and stay in budget accommodation. Devin also makes a handy base for visiting nearby caves.

⊙ Sights & Activities

The lovely **Devin eco-path** follows the Vacha River through lush countryside, eventually winding uphill into the mountain. A sort of triangular loop, beginning and ending at Devin's mineral baths, takes in the ruined **Devinsko Kale** (Devin Castle), where locals once made a desperate last stand against the Turkish onslaught. The whole hike takes about three hours. There are a couple of picnic tables along the way.

🛏 Sleeping

TOP CHOICE **Spa Hotel Evridika**   HOTEL $$
(☑0888137222; www.spahotelevridika.com; s/d/apt 65/79/92 lv; ✳🛜🏊) This warm, intimate place has a handful of doubles and apartments, handsomely done up and provided with all amenities. Service is personalised and friendly, and there's a restaurant with Bulgarian and international fare, a summer garden, and the (literal) topper: a sky bar with mineral bar and jacuzzi, affording sweeping views of the Rodopi forests.

The spa centre offers a range of restorative and relaxing treatments. All in all, this is hard to beat for the price.

Spa Hotel Devin   HOTEL $$$
(☑2513; www.spadevin.com; ul Druzhba 2; s/d/apt from 90/130/170 lv; 🅿@🏊) One of Devin's most popular places, this hotel has breezy and cheerful rooms, friendly staff and a very good restaurant. The hydrotherapy centre includes swimming pools, Jacuzzis and massage (from 40 lv). There are also a cafe–*sladkarnitsa* (sweet shop) and a casino. During summer various outdoor activities are organised.

Orpheus Spa & Resort   HOTEL $$$
(☑2041; www.orpheus-spa.com; Tzvetan Zangov 14; s/d/ste 125/140/225 lv) Devin's poshest address is this giant gingerbread mansion, its centre dominated by a huge pool over which an enormous faux crystal improbably rises. Rooms are luxurious but have traditional features in the wood-framed windows and decor, so that the place doesn't seem like a misplaced business hotel.

Spa-centre treatments involve gold dust, diamonds and caviar. There's a fitness centre, Jacuzzi, pool, tennis courts and football pitch. The hotel's two restaurants include a lavishly decorated Turkish one.

Hotel Elite   HOTEL $$
(☑2240; www.elite-devin.com; ul Undola 2; s/d/apt 50/65/80 lv; 🅿) On the central pedestrian street, the Elite has large, well-kept rooms with gleaming modern bathrooms; doubles have bathtubs. The basement mini-spa includes sauna, Jacuzzi and massage (from 25 lv). Note that there is an extra 15 lv charge for children aged two to 14.

Villa Ismena   GUESTHOUSE $$
(☑4872; www.ismena.bg; ul Goritsa 441; s/d/apt 55/85/160 lv; 🅿🏊) At the top of a steep road, the signposted Ismena is a modern villa offering quality rooms with smart decor, balconies and sparkling bathrooms. The restaurant's terrace has views, and the modest spa centre does various therapeutic programs.

✗ Eating & Drinking

In town, the Royal Café, within the unmissable *obshtina* (municipality) building, is good for a drink. The nightclub below it attracts a fairly juvenile crowd.

Oriental Restaurant   TURKISH $$
(☑2041; www.orpheus-spa.com; Tzvetan Zangov 14; mains 8-16 lv; 🛜) In the Orpheus resort, the Oriental serves Turkish kebabs and is decorated with the requisite couches, pillows and gauze.

Complex Struilitsa   BULGARIAN $
(☑0888838971; ⊙10.30am-midnight) This restaurant by the public mineral baths is up a short trail that veers left above the car park, in the forest. It does Bulgarian grills and salads and has a lovely terrace.

Bulgarsko Selo Restaurant   BULGARIAN $$
(☑2513; www.spadevin.com; ul Druzhba; mains 7-16 lv; ⊙8am-midnight) Inside Spa Hotel Devin, this place does reasonably priced meat dishes and more expensive regional specialities. The cosy folk decor is enhanced by the open oven, where you can watch the chef baking huge, crunchy slabs of bread.

❶ Information

At the time of research, the municipal tourist office remained closed. Enquiring at your hotel or at the regional tourist office (p354) back in Smolyan is your best bet.

THE CAVES OF TRIGRAD & YAGODINA

The most accessible and developed Rodopi caves are south of Devin, near Trigrad and Yagodina. Admission to both caves includes a guided tour, in Bulgarian only.

The **Trigrad Cave** (Dyavolskoto Gurlo Peshtera; ☏0889052208; admission 3 lv; ⊙9am-5pm May-Sep, shorter hr rest of year), also called the Devil's Throat Cave (Dyavolskoto Gurlo Peshtera) has extensive and speleologically significant grottoes. The mandatory 20-minute guided tour requires three or four tourists; you can stay longer, under the caretaker's supervision. As you descend, you can hear (but unfortunately not see) a 45m-high waterfall. Exiting involves a somewhat daunting set of steep steps. You may see a (harmless) bat or two flitting about.

The spectacular 8km **Yagodina Cave** (☏03419-200; admission 4 lv; ⊙9am-5pm May-Sep, shorter hr rest of yr) is the longest known Rodopi cave and, with its many abysses and labyrinthine tunnels, also one of Bulgaria's deepest. The 45-minute tour highlights the remarkable stalagmites and stalactites, which resemble curtains, and mentions the neolithic settlers who lived here 8000 years ago. Visitor numbers permitting, tours leave on the hour every hour between 9am and 4pm, except at midday. From 1 October to 1 May, at least six visitors are required for the tour; otherwise, you pay 15 lv. In summer, 10 visitors (or 25 lv) are required. Remember that no matter how hot it may be, caves are chilly, so pack extra clothes.

Trigrad village is 2.3km south of the road from the cave entrance. The cave is 6.4km south of the turn-off along the Smolyan–Dospat road, and 3km south of Yagodina.

You can hike to Trigrad, or ask for directions in Yagodina to the **South Rodopi Ecotrail**; contact Smolyan's tourist office (p354) for details.

Hotels and restaurants have wi-fi. ATMs are along the main street, by the House of Culture, and at Orpheas Spa & Resort.

❶ Getting There & Away

From **Devin bus station** (☏2077) buses serve Smolyan (4.60 lv, 1½ hours, six daily), Plovdiv (7 lv, three hours, four daily) and Yagodina (3.80 lv, 40 minutes, 8am Monday to Saturday). A daily bus to Sofia (12 lv, four hours) leaves at 6.45am. Alternatively, catch a bus to Plovdiv, which has numerous bus and train connections to the capital. All Smolyan-bound buses stop in Shiroka Lûka.

Veliko Târnovo & Central Mountains

Includes »

Why Go?

Bulgaria's central heartland is vital to the national consciousness, for its role in the 18th- and 19th-century National Revival; this legacy lingers in the period architecture of Lovech and Koprivshtitsa, and at battle sites such as the forested Shipka Pass. Other historic highlights include the vivid church frescoes of Dryanovo and Troyan monasteries, and the incredibly detailed 19th-century Tryavna School woodcarvings.

The area around the Central Mountains is ideal for hiking, climbing, caving, horseback riding and other outdoor activities in its mountain ranges: the Stara Planina and the Sredna Gora, sprawling just to the southeast. The lowlands are famous too for the Valley of Roses, near Kazanlâk, an important producer of rose oil.

Most impressive, however, is Veliko Târnovo, once capital of the Bulgarian tsars. Built into steep hills and bisected by a river, its fortress is among Europe's most impressive. Târnovo's exuberant existence as a university town translates into fine dining and fun nightlife.

Best Places to Eat

» Han Hadji Nikoli (p370)
» Hotel-Mehana Gurko (p370)
» Minaliat Vek Restauran (p361)
» Pri Hadjiyata (p392)

Best Places to Stay

» Hotel Bolyarski (p368)
» Hotel Merien Palace (p388)
» Hotel IT Shipka (p387)
» Hotel Varosha 2003 (p378)

When to Go
Veliko Târnovo

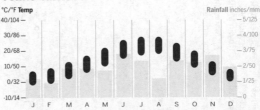

May-Jun Experience the Kazanlâk Rose Festival and Koprivshtitsa's 1877 uprising re-enactment.

Aug-Sep Escape the heat in cooler climes, while hiking the Stara Planina.

Oct Enjoy Veliko Târnovo's Sound & Light Show under clear skies, along with nightlife.

Veliko Târnovo & Central Mountains Highlights

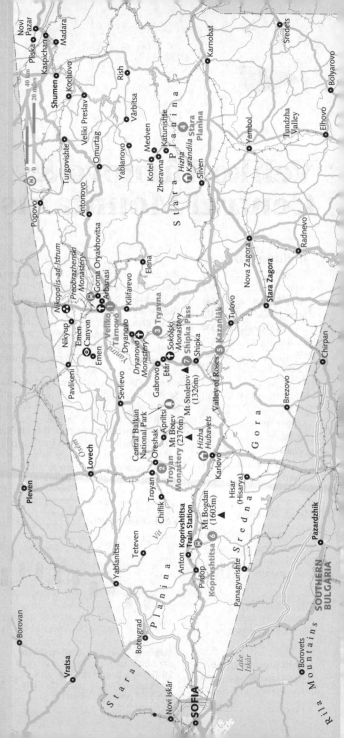

1 Taking in the illuminated castle, churches and old quarters of **Veliko Târnovo** (p363)

2 Seeing the frescoes of legendary Zahari Zograf at **Troyan Monastery** (p380)

3 Marvelling at the hand-carved wood iconostases of

the 'Tryavna school' in pretty **Tryavna** (p374)

4 Hiking Bulgaria's grand 'old mountain', **Stara Planina** (p379)

5 Diving into the garrulous open market in ethnically mixed **Kazanlâk** (p383)

6 Stepping back in time at the lovingly preserved

historical village of **Koprivshtitsa** (p382)

7 Crossing thickly forested **Shipka Pass** (p387), site of a key 19th-century battle, bedecked with a church

Shumen Шумен

📞054 / POP 80,511

History

Thracians, and then Romans, settled and fortified today's Shumen. After the Turkic Bulgar migrations in the 6th century, nearby Veliki Preslav and Pliska became the centres of the medieval Bulgarian kingdom. In 1388 the Ottomans captured Shumen, renaming it Chumla. It became an important market town and, in the final days of Ottoman domination, part of the Turks' strategic quadrangle (with Ruse, Silistra and Varna) of towns fortified against Russian advances in 1877. Reminders of Ottoman multi-ethnicity remain with Shumen's minority Jewish, Armenian and Muslim communities.

👁 Sights

Shumen Fortress FORTRESS

(adult/student 3/1 lv; ☺9am-5pm Mon-Fri) Towering over the city from a steep hillside, the Shumen Fortress dates originally to the early Iron Age. It was augmented and reinforced by the Thracians (5th century BC). Between the 2nd and 4th centuries AD, the Romans added towers and walls. It was refortified later by the Byzantines, who made it an important garrison.

During the Second Bulgarian Empire (1185–1396) the fortress was one of northeast Bulgaria's most significant settlements, renowned for its pottery and metalwork. However, invading Ottomans in the late 14th century burnt and looted it.

Placards are dotted around the site and a yellowing information booklet (2 lv) is available at the gate. The fortress is 5.5km up from the mosque. A taxi costs about 5 lv.

From the fortress entrance, a 3km path leads to the gigantic Creators of the Bulgarian State Monument, from where you return to the centre.

Creators of the Bulgarian State Monument MONUMENT

This massive, Soviet-era hilltop monument was built in 1981 to commemorate the First Bulgarian Empire's 1300th anniversary. Climb the staircase behind the History Museum for the 3km path leading from the equally communist Partisan's Monument. The circuitous 5km road going there starts along ul Sv Karel Shkorpil at the History Museum. Go by taxi (5 lv one way), and then just walk back down the steps to the centre.

The Information Centre (📞852 598; admission 3 lv; ☺8.30am-5pm winter, 8am-7pm summer), about 300m from the Creators of the Bulgarian State Monument, has information about the structure and surrounding flora. A 3km path passes the Information Centre and car park, finishing at Shumen Fortress.

Tombul Mosque MOSQUE

(📞802 875; ul Rakovski 21; admission 2 lv; ☺9am-6pm) Arguably Bulgaria's most beautiful mosque, and definitely the largest still used, Shumen's Tombul Mosque (1744) is also called the Sherif Halili Pasha Mosque. Its Turkish nickname, *tombul* (plump), refers to its 25m-high dome. The 40m-high minaret has 99 steps. Local Muslim belief says that the courtyard fountain gushes sacred water. Take the informative leaflet (English and French).

History Museum MUSEUM

(📞857 487; bul Slavyanski 17; admission 2 lv; ☺9am-5pm Mon-Fri) This brick museum on the main road exhibits Thracian and Roman artefacts from Madara, Veliki Preslav and Pliska. Also displayed are ancient coins, icons and a Shumen Fortress scale model as it was in its heyday.

Museum Complex of Pancho Vladigerov MUSEUM

(📞852 123; ul Tsar Osvoboditel 136; admission 3 lv; ☺9am-5pm Mon-Fri) One of several National Revival and early 20th-century baroque houses dotted along ul Tsar Osvoboditel's cobblestone western section, this museum commemorates Bulgaria's most renowned composer and pianist. The handsome structures include a library, set around a shady courtyard garden.

Pripoden Park PARK

Also known as Kyoshkovete Park, this 3930-hectare park on Shumen's western edge has modest, shaded hiking trails. You'll see and hear the humming of the city's most famous product being made at the nearby Shumensko Brewery.

🎭 Festivals & Events

Days of Shumen Cultural Festival CULTURAL FESTIVAL

(☺Mid-May) Annual cultural festival.

Folklore Festival CULTURAL FESTIVAL

(☺Aug) Summertime festival of folklore.

Shumen

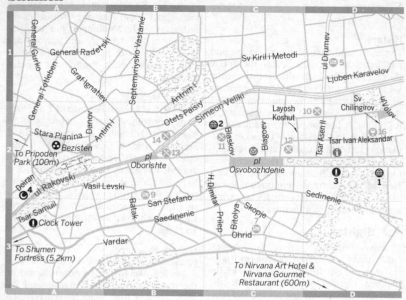

Shumen

⊙ Sights
1 History Museum D2
2 Museum Complex of Pancho
   Vladigerov C2
3 Partisan's Monument D2
4 Tombul Mosque A2

🛏 Sleeping
5 Acktion Center D1
6 Hotel Prolet E1
7 Hotel Rai C3
8 Hotel Solo E2
9 Hotel Zamaka B2
   Hotel-Restaurant Minaliat Vek ..... (see 14)

🍴 Eating
10 Biraria Regal D2
11 Dom na Architekta C2
12 Katmi C2
13 Mehana Popsheitanova Kushta B2
14 Minaliat Vek Restaurant B2

🍷 Drinking
15 Cocktail Bar Arizona E2
16 Zino D2

★ Entertainment
17 Club Retro F2
18 Nightclub Colosseum F1

Watermelon Festival   FOOD FESTIVAL
(⊙Last Sunday in August) Free watermelons! What's not to love?

🛏 Sleeping

Hotel-Restaurant Minaliat Vek   HOTEL $
(✆801 615; www.minaliatvek.com; bul Simeon Veliki 81; s/d/apt 30/45/55; ❄⊚) This new hotel in the western part of town is remarkably popular with foreign travellers, and represents good value; rooms are clean and spacious (though not as terrific as the on-site restaurant). Staff are friendly and helpful.

Nirvana Art Hotel   HOTEL $$
(✆800 127; www.hotelnirvana.bg; ul Nezavisimost 25; s/d/apt from 75/85/130 lv; ❄⊚⊛) While there is something distinctly odd about this new hotel set in a dusty residential part of south Shumen, it does boast the city's most distinctive rooms. Each is painted in various soothing tones and with minimalist decor and the occasional canopy bed. Sauna, Jacuzzi and massage (from 25 lv) are offered, and Nirvana's 'gourmet' restaurant is remarkably good.

To Bus Station (500m)

To Veliki Preslav (18km)

Acktion Center
BUSINESS HOTEL $

(☏801 081; www.acktioncenter.com; ul Drumev 12; s/d/tr/apt 42/49/60/69 lv) Despite the name, the Acktion Center is a modern business hotel with 11 rooms and five apartments, all done up in handsome modern style. It's reasonably central and offers a manicurist, hairdresser and cosmetics salon.

Hotel Prolet
HOTEL $

(☏0897 849 220; www.hotelprolet.eu; ul Marin Drinov 11; s/d/tr/apt 22/32/45/60 lv; ❄️🛜) This tiny side-street 'family hotel' is a 10-minute walk west of the bus station and offers clean, simple rooms, though the apartments are not enormous. There's a relaxing cafe at ground level and staff are kind.

Hotel Solo
HOTEL $$

(☏981 571; www.hotelsolo-bg.com; ul Volov 2; s/d incl breakfast €20/35; ❄️@🛜) This friendly small hotel run by a helpful local couple has an excellent central location above the pedestrian street. Rooms vary in size but are clean and well kept (the larger ones have better showers). The photo-sensitive should note, however, that the annoying flashing lights from the casino opposite can't be completely blocked out by the curtains.

Hotel Rai
HOTEL $$

(☏802 670; www.hotel-rai.eu; ul Ohrid 26a; s/d €20/28; ❄️@) The Rai has a quiet setting near the Shumensko Plato Nature Park. Rooms are spacious and well done, with all amenities including hydromassage showers, a fitness centre and solarium.

Hotel Zamaka
HOTEL $$

(☏800 409; www.zamakbg.eu; ul Vasil Levski 17; s/d/apt 40/60/85 lv; ❄️🛜) This lovely new hotel in a quiet residential neighbourhood just west from the main square has friendly staff and cosy rooms, set around a garden courtyard with a traditional restaurant.

✖ Eating

TOP CHOICE Minaliat Vek Restaurant
BULGARIAN $$$

(☏801-615; bul Simeon Veliki 81; mains 9-17 lv; 🛜) This local favourite, and part of the Minaliat Vek hotel, seeks to re-create the 'old time' tastes its name suggests. There's a long (and colourfully described!) list of Bulgarian specialities, ranging from filling *satch* (a stew baked in clay pots) to shashliks and a variety of tasty salads, plus numerous Bulgarian wines.

Katmi
PANCAKES $

(pl Osvobozhdenie 12; pancakes 2 lv; ⊙7.30am-8pm) This local takeaway institution, off a side entrance on the square, offers delicious *palachinki* (pancakes) – much better than the usual Balkan crepe – with a choice of 122 different combinations. A pancake with all-natural blueberry and strawberry jam is especially tasty.

Nirvana Gourmet Restaurant
INTERNATIONAL $$$

(☏300 127; ul Nezavisinost 25; mains 11-23 lv; 🛜) For those seeking relatively elegant international dining, it's worth the 10-minute drive to the lonely quarter where this restaurant exists above the eponymous hotel. The so-called 'gourmet' Nirvana does more sophisticated grills and Italian fare (try the rich pasta carbonara) than usual for Shumen, and there's a long wine list.

Mehana Popsheitanova Kushta
BULGARIAN $$

(☏802 222; ul Tsar Osvoboditel 158; mains 4-11 lv; ⊙11am-2am; 🛜) This wood-framed traditional restaurant has big outdoor benches and big portions, too. Try the chicken *shishle* 'special' (skewered chicken with cooked red peppers, onions, tomatoes and mushroom on the side).

Biraria Regal
BULGARIAN $$

(☑802 301; ul Tsar Osvoboditel 108; mains 5-7 lv; ⏱8am-2am; 🛜) This traditional *mehana* (tavern) on ul Tsar Osvoboditel enjoys a leafy garden setting and offers a good selection of grills and salads.

Dom na Architekta
BULGARIAN $$

(ul Tsar Osvoboditel 145; mains 5-9 lv; ⏱8am-1am; 🛜) This wood-and-stone traditional tavern has great Bulgarian specialities, served in a balmy back garden in summer, moving indoors in front of a crackling fire in winter.

Drinking & Entertainment

Numerous good cafes line the leafy pedestrian mall of ul Slavyanski.

Cocktail Bar Arizona
BAR

(ul Kliment Ohridski 7; ⏱10am-2am; 🛜) This sharp new bar and club has two interior (for winter) floors and more atmospheric outdoor terraces with canopied tables during warmer times of the year. There's an inventive list of long drinks for the mostly local 20-something patrons, and generally chilled-out pop and electronic music played.

Zino
BAR

(Tsar Ivan Aleksandar 81; 🛜) One of several adjoining bars on the ul Slavyanski pedestrian mall, Zino has a slightly less frenetic vibe than its neighbours and has both indoor and relaxing outside couches.

Nightclub Colosseum
CLUB

(☑830 444; ul Simeon Veliki; admission 2 lv; ⏱10pm-4am Mon-Sat; 🛜) Still Shumen's most popular full-on club, this cavernous disco features theme nights that range from student nights to DJ parties and retro.

Club Retro
CLUB

(☑832 742; City Park; ⏱8am-1am; 🛜) This cafe in the park is good for a relaxing coffee by day, or for cocktails at night. There's salsa dancing on Fridays.

Information

Post Office (pl Osvobozhdenie; ⏱7am-10pm Mon-Fri)

Telephone Centre Inside the post office.

Tourist Information Centre (☑857 773; www.shumen.bg/en/tourism; bul Slavyanski 17; ⏱9am-5pm Mon-Fri) Helpful info centre provides maps and details on local sights, in and around town.

Getting There & Away

The bus and train stations are adjacent at Shumen's eastern end. From the **bus station** (☑830 890; ul Rilski Pohod), buses serve Burgas (14 lv, three hours, four daily), Ruse (11 lv, two hours, three daily), Dobrich (13 lv, two hours, four daily), Silistra (13 lv, 2½ hours, three daily), Veliko Târnovo (11 lv, two hours, several daily), Madara (2 lv, 20 minutes, five daily), Veliki Preslav (2 lv, 30 to 60 minutes, three daily), Sofia (31 lv, six hours, hourly) and Varna (11 lv, 1½ hours, nine daily). Private buses, such as those operated by **Etap Adress** (☑830 670), also stop (at the same station) in Shumen on the Sofia–Varna route.

From the **train station** (☑860 155; pl Garov) daily trains (including one express) serve Varna (7 lv, two hours, nine daily), and fast trains reach Sofia (19 lv, four to seven hours, two daily). Trains serve Ruse (12 lv, three hours, daily) and Plovdiv (18 lv, six hours, daily). Two trains stop at Madara. The station has a left-luggage office.

Taxis wait at the bus and train stations, and are easily found downtown.

Madara
Мадара

☑05313 / POP 1400

An important town for the mysterious Thracians around 7000 years ago, this village, 16km east of Shumen, was also settled during the Roman occupation. It's most famous today for the Madara Horseman, a grand rock carving from the 8th-century Bulgar khanate.

Sights

Madara National Historical & Archaeological Reserve
HISTORIC SITE

(admission 4 lv; ⏱8am-7.30pm summer, to 5pm winter) This reserve surrounds the so-called Madara Horseman (*Madarski Konnik*). Carved into a cliff 23m high, the bas-relief features a mounted figure spearing a lion, followed by a dog.

This early 8th-century creation was made to commemorate the victorious Khan Tervel, and the creation of the First Bulgarian Empire (681–1018). Bulgaria's only known medieval rock carving, it's a Unesco heritage site.

At the reserve's entrance gate, the Madara booklet (2 lv, in English or German) explains the site and gives information on the popular hiking trails to nearby tombs and caves. Since the permanent scaffolding hides more of the bas-relief the closer you get, it's not necessary to climb up to the figure for the best views.

North of the horseman, a 373-step rock stairway leads to the 130m-high clifftop and the ruined Madara Fortress, built during the Second Bulgarian Empire (1185–1396). There are sweeping views from above.

✨ Festivals & Events

Madara Horseman Music Days Festival   MUSIC FESTIVAL
(⊙mid-Jun–mid-Jul) Held in the reserve on four successive Thursdays from mid-June to mid-July.

🛏 Sleeping & Eating

Camping Madara   CAMPGROUND $
(✆5313; camp site per person 7 lv, cabins 20 lv) A shady and peaceful camping spot 500m from the horseman, with a small restaurant.

Hizha Madarski Konnik   MOUNTAIN LODGE $
(✆2091; dm 18 lv) Offers dorm rooms.

ℹ Getting There & Away

Public transport to Madara's limited, and the horseman is 3km up a steep road from the village. Several daily Shumen–Varna trains stop at Madara, but Shumen–Madara buses are infrequent; better to catch the bus from Shumen to Kaspichan (five daily), and then a minibus to Madara from there. A taxi from Shumen costs 30 lv return, including waiting time. Madara has no taxis.

Veliko Târnovo
Велико Търново

✆062 / POP 68,735
The evocative capital of the medieval Bulgarian tsars, sublime Veliko Târnovo is dramatically set amidst an amphitheatre of forested hills, divided by the ribboning Yantra River. Commanding pride of place is the magisterial, well-restored Tsarevets Fortress, citadel of the Second Bulgarian Empire. It's complemented by scores of churches and other ruins, many still being unearthed.

As the site of Bulgaria's most prestigious university, Veliko Târnovo also boasts a revved-up nightlife of which many larger towns would be jealous. There's great food and drink, too, in restaurants offering commanding views of the river and castle, or the old-world ambience of the Varosha quarter, with its terracotta rooftops and lounging cats.

As a major stop on the Bucharest–Istanbul express train, Veliko Târnovo is also a backpackers' fave. However, it's also popular with weekending Bulgarians drawn by its romantic ambience and European tour groups peering over the sites. Certainly, it's one of the 'obligatory' destinations for getting the full Bulgarian experience, but Târnovo is well worth it, and will keep you entranced for at least a few days.

Veliko Târnovo is stacked upwards along a ridge above the Yantra River – try to think vertical to make sense of city maps. The river winds in a horseshoe bend between four hills: Tsarevets, site of the fortress; Momina Krepost, several kilometres to the east; Trapezitsa; and Sveta Gora (Holy Mountain).

The centre of town runs along ul Nezavisimost and ul Stefan Stambolov, between the post office and a huge underpass. Follow ul Rakovski as it branches up from Stambolov for the traditional crafts shopping quarter, Samovodska Charshiya, and beyond it the quiet and cobblestoned old town, Varosha. Târnovo's nondescript modern part is west and southwest from ul Vasil Levski.

History
The strategic geography of Târnovo's hills attracted settlers from early times. Neolithic people in 5500 BC, and Thracian tribes three millennia later, inhabited Tsarevets Hill (on which the fortress stands today) and Trapezitsa Hill opposite. The Romans built the fortress's first walls and, in the 6th century Byzantine Emperor Justinian created a citadel. Slavic tribes captured it in the 7th century, but it soon was fought over in the interminable wars between Byzantium and the First Bulgarian Empire.

In 1185, under brothers Asen and Petâr, Târnovgrad became a hotspot for rebellion against weakening Byzantine rule. With their foundation of the Second Bulgarian Empire, it replaced the destroyed Pliska and Veliki Preslav as the new capital, becoming second only to Constantinople in importance. Trade and culture flourished for the next 200 years.

On 17 July 1393 the Ottomans captured Târnovgrad, destroying the citadel. No longer very strategic in the middle of a vast empire, the town stagnated through Ottoman times until Bulgarian nationalism asserted itself during the mid-19th century. In 1877, during the Russo-Turkish War, Russian General Gurko liberated Târnovgrad.

Because of its importance during the Second Bulgarian Empire, Veliko Târnovo (as it was renamed) was the location for writing

VELIKO TÂRNOVO & CENTRAL MOUNTAINS VELIKO TÂRNOVO

Bulgaria's Constitution in 1879, and was where the independence of the Bulgarian state was officially proclaimed in 1908. In 2012 it was the site of spectacular fireworks and speeches from top leaders during a huge celebration of 140 years of independence.

⊙ Sights

Most churches are closed on Wednesdays.

Tsarevets Fortress   MEDIEVAL FORTRESS
(adult/student 6/2 lv, scenic elevator 2 lv; ⊙8am-7pm Apr-Sep, 9am-5pm Oct-Mar) The inescap-

Veliko Târnovo

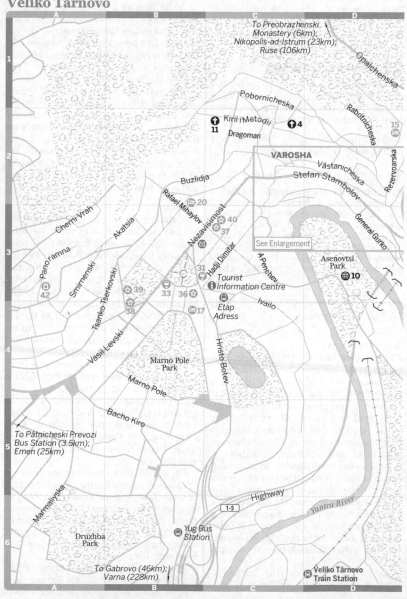

able symbol of this proud medieval town, this reconstructed fortress dominates the skyline, and is one of Bulgaria's most beloved monuments. It features remains of more than 400 houses, 18 churches and numerous monasteries, dwellings, shops, gates and towers.

Tsarevets Museum-Reserve is located on Tsarevets Hill, which has been settled since time immemorial due to its strategic location. Thracians and Romans used it as a

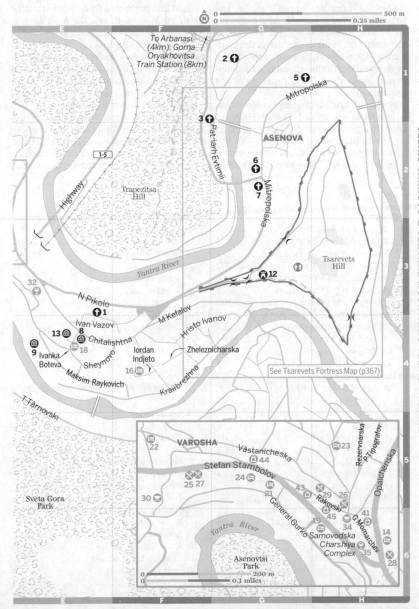

defensive position, but the Byzantines built the first significant fortress here between the 5th and 7th centuries. The fortress was rebuilt and fortified by the Slavs and Bulgars between the 8th and 10th centuries, and again by the Byzantines in the early 12th century. When Târnovgrad became the Second Bulgarian Empire's capital, the fortress was truly magnificent, but with the Turkish invasion in 1393, it was sacked and destroyed. Tourists can thank the communists for returning it to a semblance of its former glory (although some archaeologists grumble about the faithfulness of the restoration).

Not much English-language information is provided, but guided English-language tours (10 lv) can be arranged by enquiring in the Tourist Information Centre.

Entering the structure, pass through two gates and veer left (northeast) for the fortress walls – some were once 12m high and 10m thick. Further along the walls are the unrecognisable remains of a 12th-century monastery, various dwellings and workshops and two churches. To the north lie remains of a 13th-century monastery, and Execution Rock, from which traitors were pushed into the Yantra River. Alleged traitor Patriarch Joachim III was the most famous figure to take the plunge, in 1300.

The complex's eastern path is unremarkable; return to the middle, using the hill-top Patriarch's Complex as a landmark. Past one of several modern bells (used in the Sound & Light show) are a ruined nobleman's dwelling and two churches to the left (east).

Below the Patriarch's Complex are the foundations of the Royal Palace, from where 22 successive kings ruled Bulgaria. Once covering 4500 sq m, the palace included an appropriately enormous throne (measuring

Veliko Târnovo

◎ Sights
1 Church of Sveta Bogoroditsa................E3
2 Church of Sveti Dimitâr G1
3 Church of Sveti Georgi.......................... F1
4 Church of Sveti Nikolai........................ C2
5 Church of Sveti Petr & Pavel.................G1
6 Church of the Assumption G2
7 Forty Martyrs Church............................ G2
8 Museum of National Revival &
   Constituent Assembly........................E4
9 Sarafkina Kâshta................................E4
10 State Art Museum D3
11 Sveti Kiril & Metodii Church C2
12 Tsarevets Fortress G3
13 Veliko Târnovo Archaeological
   Museum E4

▣ Sleeping
14 Grand Hotel Yantra............................... H6
15 Hikers Hostel...D2
16 Hostel Mostel F4
17 Hotel Allegro.. B4
18 Hotel Boliari..E4
19 Hotel Bolyarski....................................... H6
20 Hotel Premier... B2
21 Hotel-Mehana Gurko............................. G5
22 Kâshata Private Flats F5
23 Slavyanska Dusha................................. H5
24 Villa Tashkov G5

✗ Eating
25 Ego Pizza & Grill.................................... F5
26 Han Hadji Nikoli H5
   Hotel-Mehana Gurko ....(see 21)
27 Shtastlivetsa F5
28 Starata Mehana H6
29 Stratilat...H5

◉ Drinking
30 Café Aqua F5
31 City Pub B3
32 Dada Bar E3
33 Geronimo Bar..B3
34 Shekerdzinitsa H6
35 Tequila Bar H6

✪ Entertainment
36 Bally...B3
37 Deep Café Club C3
38 Jack B4
39 Konstantin Kisimov Dramatic
   Theatre B3
40 Melon Live Music Club...........................C3

▩ Shopping
41 Book Cave H6
42 Gorgona A3
43 Icons Krasimir Ivanov G5
44 Knisharnitsa Apoloniya.........................G5
45 Samovodska Charshiya
   Complex.. H6

Tsarevets Fortress

about 30m by 10m) and Roman columns, probably transferred from nearby Nikopolis-ad-Istrum.

From the palace, head west to the main path and up the steps to the Patriarch's Complex, also called the Church of the Blessed Saviour. Once about 3000 sq m in size, it was probably built about 1235, and has been extensively restored. The city views from the front steps are more impressive than the modern murals inside, depicting 14th- and 15th-century Bulgarian history.

Returning towards the main entrance, veer left along the path hugging the southern wall. At its end is the restored Baldwin Tower, where Baldwin I of Flanders – the perfidious Crusader who led the sack of Christian Byzantium in 1204 – got his just desserts, imprisoned and executed after his defeat by the Bulgarians a year later. There are great views from the top.

Sarafkina Kâshta
MUSEUM

(ul General Gurko 88; adult/student 6/2 lv; ⊙9am-6pm Mon-Fri) Built in 1861 by a rich Turkish merchant and moneylender, this fine five-storey National Revival–style house-museum displays antique ceramics, metalwork, woodcarvings and jewellery, and has some fascinating exhibits about traditional

costumes and breadmaking. Revival-period furniture fills the upper floor, along with vintage family photos.

Museum of National Revival & Constituent Assembly
MUSEUM

(ul Ivan Vazov; adult/student 6/2 lv; ⊙9am-6pm Wed-Mon) This museum, in a former Turkish town hall built in 1872, was where Bulgaria's first National Assembly was held to write the country's first constitution in 1879.

The ground floor contains costumes, books and photos about Veliko Târnovo's history. The former assembly hall, upstairs, displays portraits of local personalities. The basement has classic old-town photos, and some valuable icons.

Veliko Târnovo Archaeological Museum
MUSEUM

(ul Ivan Vazov; adult/student 6/2 lv; ⊙9am-6pm Tue-Sun) Housed in a grand old building with a colonnaded terrace and courtyard full of Roman sculptures, the archaeological museum contains Roman artefacts from Nikopolis-ad-Istrum, and more Roman pottery and statues from elsewhere. Medieval Bulgarian exhibits include huge murals of the tsars, while there's also some ancient gold from nearby neolithic settlements.

Forty Martyrs Church
CHURCH

(ul Mitropolska; adult/student 5/1 lv; ⊙9am-5.30pm) The Forty Martyrs Church, in the old Asenova quarter, was built in 1230 to celebrate Tsar Asen II's victory over the Byzantines. It was used as a royal mausoleum, and then as a mosque by the Turks.

Church of the Assumption
CHURCH

Across from Forty Martyrs Church is the tiny Church of the Assumption, built in 1923 over a ruined 14th-century church. It's usually closed, but is very pretty, with blue-painted bas-reliefs decorating its sides.

Church of Sveti Petr & Pavel
CHURCH

(ul Mitropolska; adult/student 4/2 lv; ⊙9am-6pm) The St Peter & St Paul Church, located just past the bridge, contains fragments of murals from the 14th to 17th centuries.

Church of Sveti Dimitâr
CHURCH

(ul Patriarh Evtimii) Across the river, enclosed by a high wall, is Târnovo's oldest church, the beautifully proportioned Church of Sveti Dimitâr. Built in the so-called Târnovo style, it was named after St Dimitrios, patron saint of Thessaloniki (Greece). During its

1185 consecration, Tsars Asen and Petår proclaimed an uprising against Byzantine rule, which would create the Second Bulgarian Empire (1185–1396).

It's often closed, but the Church of Sveti Petar & Pavel's caretaker can open it on request.

Church of Sveti Georgi
CHURCH

(☎620 481; ul Patriarh Evtimii; admission 4 lv; ⊙by arrangement) This church, probably built in 1612 on medieval church ruins, was destroyed by Ottoman invaders, but restored during their rule in the early 18th century. It boats impressive murals inside. The Tsarevets Fortress ticket office arranges visits.

Church of Sveta Bogoroditsa
CHURCH

(⊙9am-5pm) Notable frescoes are the main draw at the Church of Sveta Bogoroditsa, the town's main cathedral. Located just off ul Ivan Vazov, the church's large green neo-Byzantine domes distinguish it on the old town's skyline.

State Art Museum
ART GALLERY

(Asenovtsi Park; adult/student 4/2 lv, Thu free; ⊙10am-6pm Tue-Sun) Dramatically situated in a tight bend of the Yantra River, the State Art Museum contains paintings of Veliko Tårnovo and the region by numerous artists. The 2nd floor exhibits more artworks, mostly on permanent loan from galleries in Silistra, Dobrich and Ruse. Guided tours (English and French) are available for about 5 lv extra per person; entry's free on Thursdays.

Up in Varosha, visit the 1879 Church of Sveti Nikolai (ul Våstanicheska; ⊙9am-5pm). After, follow the steps on the left (western) side, and turn left along ul Kiril i Metodii to the Sveti Kiril & Metodii Church (⊙9am-5pm), which has an elegant tower.

🏃 Activities

Numerous local operators offer hiking, mountain biking, horse riding and caving; ask the Tourist Information Centre for hiking maps and contacts. The Centre also offers the useful *Climbing Guide,* for serious rock climbers.

🎉 Festivals & Events

Holiday of Amateur Art Activities
CULTURAL FESTIVAL

(⊙early May) Also called the Balkan Folk Festival, it's held over 10 days.

International Festival of Religious Music
MUSIC FESTIVAL

(⊙Jun) This festival presents Bulgarian, Romanian and other choral singers in the fortress; ask at the Tourist Information Centre for a schedule of performances.

International Folklore Festival
CULTURAL FESTIVAL

(☎630 223; ⊙late Jun–mid-Juy) Three-week festival with over 300 acts from Bulgaria and other Balkan countries. Details available from mid-April.

🛏 Sleeping

At time of writing, Veliko Tårnovo's once-plentiful accommodation scene had been hit hard by the global economic crisis, with fewer tourists venturing to Bulgaria. This is not necessarily bad for travellers, however, as surviving hotels have stepped up services while keeping prices competitive.

The Tourist Information Centre finds private rooms (25/35 lv for a single/double). For atmosphere, stay near the Samovodska Charshiya Complex in the Varosha district, along the lower (southeastern) end of ul Gurko, or near Tsarevets Fortress, though the latter is a considerable walk from town.

TOP CHOICE Hotel Bolyarski
HOTEL $$

(☎613 200; www.bolyarski.com; ul Stefan Stambolov 53a; s/d incl breakfast from 80/130 lv; P❄🅿🛜🏊) One of the town's best hotels, the Bolyarski has a phenomenal location on the bluff on ul Stambolov, with magical views of the town and river from its long cafe patio and rooms, and close proximity to all the local restaurants and bars. Its modern, well-kept rooms are pitched at business travellers.

Nevertheless, single rooms (without a view) are just 40 lv. There's a fitness centre, a swimming pool and a Jacuzzi too.

Hikers Hostel
HOSTEL $

(☎0889 691661; www.hikers-hostel.org; ul Rezevoarska 91; campsites/dm/d incl breakfast 14/20/52 lv; @🛜) Still Tårnovo's most laid-back hostel, Hikers has an unassuming location high in Varosha's old quarter (a 10-minute walk from downtown). Charismatic owner Toshe Hristov does free bus/train station pick-ups and runs trips. The two dorms (one with four beds, the other with 10) are spartan but clean, and there's one double room, a kitchen and two shared bathrooms.

The windowed upstairs patio also has couches and space for tents, and offers

THE SOUND & LIGHT SHOW

Târnovo rocks out with medieval flair during the Sound & Light Show, a nocturnal event that sees Tsarevets Hill lit up in great flashes of colour and rumbling music, a spectacular homage to the Second Bulgarian Empire. The show doesn't happen unless a certain number of people have bought tickets, but during the summer expect it most nights. The show's 40 minutes long and apparently relates the rise and fall of the Second Bulgarian Empire (for most people it will just be a pretty array of flashing lights set to music).

To see if the show is happening, ring the organisers on ☎636 828 or ask at the Tourist Information Centre or your hotel. Alternatively, turn up at the fortress and hope for the best. Otherwise, simply listen for the bells, and look for the laser beams. Starting time is anywhere from 8pm to 9.30pm depending on the time of year.

great views of the Sound & Light Show. The friendly little spot offers laundry service, wi-fi, computers, three hostel guitars and beer. Good times, good times.

Slavyanska Dusha GUESTHOUSE $
(☎625 182; www.slavianska-dusha.com; ul Nikola Zlatarski 21; s/d/tr/apt from 25/35/45/60 lv; ✳☎) Very affordable and clean, this cheery guesthouse is run by a local couple who grow their own veg for the on-site restaurant. The place offers simple but nice rooms decked out in traditional decor.

Hostel Mostel HOSTEL $
(☎0897 859 359; www.hostelmostel.com; ul Iordan Indjeto 10; campsites/dm/s/d incl breakfast 18/20/46/60lv; @☎) The famous Sofia-based Hostel Mostel has become Târnovo's biggest, with clean, very modern dorm rooms and doubles with sparkling bathrooms. It's just 150m from Tsarevets Fortress – good for exploring there, but a long walk from downtown (free bus/train pickup is possible). As in Sofia, there's free spaghetti and a glass of beer thrown in.

Hotel-Mehana Gurko HOTEL $$
(☎627 838; www.hotel-gurko.com; ul General Gurko 33; s/d/apt 80/110/135 lv; ✳@☎) The Gurko is one of the best places to sleep (and eat) in town, located under the old town. Rooms are spacious and soothing, each individually decorated and with great views. There aren't any extras, but service is friendly.

Grand Hotel Yantra HOTEL $$$
(☎600 607; www.yantrabg.com; ul Opalchenska 2; s/d/ste 100/156/180 lv; ✳☎) The Yantra, spreading across the base of Varosha, is one of Târnovo's most opulent hotels. Service is excellent and rooms are sumptuously decorated; some suites even have fireplaces. It lacks

the intimacy of smaller places and attracts business conferences, though. There's also an art gallery and casino.

Kâshata Private Flats APARTMENT $$
(☎604 129; www.the-house.hit.bg; pl Slaveikov 4; 1-/2-/4-person apt 35/50/80 lv) Kâshata (The House) provides a centrally located solution for those who want the flexibility of a self-catering apartment. The flats are well equipped and of good quality.

Hotel Boliari HOTEL $$
(☎606 002; www.boliarihotel.com; ul Ivanka Boteva 2; s/d/ste 72/90/109 lv; ✳☎) This boutique hotel has attractive rooms with handsome wood furnishings. It has a small reception cafe and is a friendly, quiet place, with a small spa centre.

Villa Tashkov VILLA $$
(☎635 801; ul General Gurko 19; d from 80 lv, entire villa 200 lv; ✳☎) This gorgeous, centrally located villa can be rented in part or in full – book ahead. The rooms are fully equipped, and there's a daily cleaning service. Reception is at ul Stambolisky 13.

Hotel Allegro HOTEL $$
(☎602 332; www.hotelalegro.co; ul Todor Svetoslav 15; s 80-100/ d 109-130 lv; ✳@☎) The Allegro, located between Marno Pole Park and the Tourist Information Centre, is a 10-minute walk from the old town. It has friendly service and spotless rooms, some quite large, with all mod cons and modern art. There's a breezy garden restaurant.

Hotel Premier HOTEL $$$
(☎615 555; www.hotelpremier-bg.com; ul Sava Penev 1; s/d 160/220 lv, ste 240-480 lv; P✳☎✎) Târnovo's Hotel Premier (part of the Best Western chain) is a smart option, located on a side street near the post office. Facilities include a

rooftop pool, sauna, spa treatments and (they claim) Bulgaria's biggest Jacuzzi. Spa treatments veer more towards cosmetics.

✗ Eating

Veliko Tărnovo has excellent restaurants and cafes for all budgets; for atmosphere, try those with terraces overlooking the river and gorge, or some up in Varosha.

TOP CHOICE Han Hadji Nikoli INTERNATIONAL $$$

(☎651 291; www.hanhadjinikoli.com; ul GS Rakovski 19; mains 25-30 lv; 🕸) Without doubt Veliko Tărnovo's finest restaurant, Han Hadji Nikoli occupies a beautifully restored 1858 building with an upstairs art gallery. Winner of Bulgaria's 'building of the year' in 2010, this former inn, crafted by National Revival architect Kolyo Ficheto, resembles a Venetian mansion with its curving arches, secluded courtyard and refined halls – architecture befitting its excellent international fare.

Start off with escargots bourguignon, move on to roast chicken with cranberry and rosé wine sauce, and finish with chocolate mousse flecked with raspberries and Cointreau. Oh, and by the way, these are just from the 'regular' menu (there's also a discreet 'gourmet room' in the back, which has its own special menu!).

Hotel-Mehana Gurko BULGARIAN $$

(☎627 838; ul General Gurko 33; mains 5-11 lv; 🕸) This traditional-style *mehana* of the Hotel Gurko is a cosy place with great views and tasty Bulgarian specialities. Portions are hearty and service is prompt and friendly.

Shtastlivetsa BULGARIAN $$

(☎600 656; ul Stefan Stambolov 79; mains 7-14 lv; 🕸11am-1am; 🕸) A local institution, the 'Lucky Man' (as the almost unpronounceable name means in Bulgarian) has an ideal location overlooking the river's bend and a great menu of inventive meat dishes, baked-pot specials, nourishing pizzas and (at lunchtime) delicious soups – every visitor to Veliko Tărnovo comes here at least once.

Stratilat INTERNATIONAL $$

(☎635 313; ul Rakovski 11; mains 5-9 lv; 🕸) The large outside terrace makes this a very popular place for a coffee, a light meal or dessert from the morning till night for students and visitors alike.

Starata Mehana BULGARIAN $$

(ul Stefan Stambolov; mains 5-11 lv) The Starata Mehana offers great views and traditional, good-value Bulgarian cooking. Try the mouth-watering chicken shashlik.

Ego Pizza & Grill PIZZA $$

(☎601 804; ul Nezavisimost 17; mains 5-12 lv; 🕸9am-midnight; 🕸) Probably Tărnovo's best pizza place, Ego has a new location overlooking the river's bend. It's a spacious restaurant with outdoor and indoor seating with excellent views. Service can be hit-or-miss.

🍷 Drinking

Dada Bar BAR

(ul Velcho Dzhamdzhiyata 12; 🕸10pm-4am) This funky place has a subterranean bar and outdoor enclosed courtyard beyond. Good prices, good music, and gets busy after midnight – just watch your head when going down the (rather low and steep) stairway.

Geronimo Bar BAR

(ul Vasil Levski 1; 🕸7am-2am) Coffee bar by day, drinks and cocktails bar by night, this stylish, popular place along the main road has a vaguely American Southwest decor.

Tequila Bar BAR

(ul Stefan Stambolov 30; 🕸12pm-3am) Overlooking the main street and near th Samovodska Charshiya Compex, Tequila Bar is a festively painted student bar with good cocktails and cheap beer.

City Pub PUB

(ul Hristo Botev 15; 🕸noon-1am) This popular, big British-style pub near the post office and Tourist Information Centre is somewhat gimmicky, but still a hit with local students and expats.

Shekerdzinitsa CAFE

(☎0898 563 490; ul Giorgi Momarchev 13; 🕸9am-6pm Tue-Sun) This lovely little cafe with traditional furnishings in the old market serves real Turkish coffee: as per tradition, prepared in a diminutive copper pot run across a basin of heated sand.

Café Aqua CAFE

(☎623 567; ul Nezavisimost 3) Lounge over a coffee and *slatka* (sweet) until late in the evening at this central cafe, which has a breezy balcony overlooking the gorge.

☆ Entertainment

Veliko Tărnovo's nightlife is buzzing year-round; in summer, backpackers and other foreign travellers pass through, while September summons back the town's 20,000 university students.

The little-visited new town, where many students reside, also has some popular little bars and clubs from autumn to spring.

Melon Live Music Club   CLUB
(☑0895 424 427; bul Nezavistnost 21; ⊗6pm-4am) This great new spot for live music (ranging from rock to R&B and Latin Jazz) is tucked halfway up the main street, between the post office and Varosha.

Jack   CLUB
(☑0887 203 016; ul Magistraka 5; ⊗10pm-4am) This pumping student club is especially popular at weekends, with house music and dancing. Entry usually 3 lv.

Bally   CLUB
(☑0885 565 666; ul Hristo Botev 2; ⊗10pm-5am Mon-Sat) This two-part club has rooms for Bulgarian folk-pop and more international pop fare, respectively. Monday's student night with special offers.

Deep Café Club   CLUB
(☑321 645; ul Nezavisimost 23; ⊗8am-1am) This small, eccentrically lit subterranean bar-verging-on-club caters to a young crowd with hip-hop and house music.

Cinema Arena   CINEMA
(tickets 6 lv; ⊗10am-midnight) The latest Hollywood films are on at Cinema Arena in the Central Mall, which also has a nightclub, a bowling alley and a casino. (Take a taxi, 3 to 5 lv.)

Konstantin Kisimov Dramatic Theatre   THEATRE
(☑623 526; ul Vasil Levski) This theatre has regular performances from the international pantheon and Bulgarian plays. Ask the Tourist Information Centre what's on.

🔒 Shopping

Roughly opposite the Hotel Bolyarski, ul Rakovski veers upwards from the main road, ul Stambolov. On and behind it is the Samovodska Charshiya Complex (ul Rakovski), the town's historic centre of craftsmanship, with blacksmiths, potters and gunsmiths, among other artisans. Numerous bookshops and purveyors of antiques, jewellery and art are also housed in appealing Bulgarian National Revival houses. It's good for shopping, or just a stroll, as is the equally appealing old residential quarter of Varosha just above it.

At the beginning of ul Rakovski, a prominent map signposts the name and location of each shop in the *charshiya*, in both Bulgarian and English.

Icons Krasimir Ivanov   ICONS
(☑0885 060 544; cnr ul Rakovski & ul Kapitan Diado Nikola; icons 60-400 lv; ⊗10am-7pm) Lovely hand-painted icons by elder artist Krasimir Ivanov, and detailed ink sketches of old Tårnovo (20 lv), are sold at this store–workshop.

Gorgona   OUTDOORS GEAR
(☑601 400; www.gorgona-shop.com; ul Zelenka 2; ⊗10am-1pm & 2-7pm Mon-Fri, 10am-2pm Sat) For camping, climbing, skiing and biking gear

Knisharnitsa Apoloniya   BOOKSHOP
(☑620 287; ul Stefan Stambolov 65; ⊗9am-7.30pm Mon-Sat, 10am-6.30pm Sun) Central bookstore with maps, Lonely Planet guides and other English-language travel books.

If you're interested in local monasteries, look for *The V Turnovo Monasteries: A Guide* (4 lv). Domino's Veliko Tårnovo map also includes maps of Tsarevets Fortress and Arbanasi.

Book Cave   BOOKSTORE
(☑0898 229 910; ul Opalchenska 9) This bookstore at the bottom of the Varosha district is a cosy place for buying, exchanging or donating books. The friendly English expat owner is a fount of local information.

Central Mall   SHOPPING
(☑674 040; www.mallvt.eu; ul Oborishte 18; ⊗10am-8pm) The eastside Central Mall has shiny and modern shopping opportunities.

ℹ️ Information

INTERNET ACCESS Most hotels and hostels have wi-fi connections, and sometimes computers.
I-Net Internet Centre (off ul Hristo Botev; per hr 1.50 lv)
MEDICAL SERVICES Hospital Stefan Cherkezov (☑626 841; ul Nish 1) Modern hospital with an emergency room and English-speaking doctors.
MONEY Foreign exchange offices and ATMs are plentiful on the main drag and in the shopping malls.
POST Main Post Office (ul Nezavisimost)
TELEPHONE Telephone Centre (ul Hristo Botev 1) Inside the post office.
TOURIST INFORMATION Tourist Information Centre (☑622 148; www.velikoturnovo.info; ul Hristo Botev 5; ⊗9am-6pm Mon-Fri,

Mon-Sat summer) Helpful English-speaking staff can help book accommodation and rent cars.

ⓘ Getting There & Away

Bus

Two (non-central) bus stations serve Veliko Târnovo. **Pâtnicheski Prevozi bus station** (Zapad Bus Station; ☑640 908; ul Nikola Gabrovski 74), about 4km from the centre, is the main intercity one. Local buses 10, 12, 14, 70 and 110 go there, along ul Vasil Levski. There's also a left-luggage office. From here, buses serve Kazanlâk (9 lv, 2½ hours, five daily), Ruse (8 lv, two hours, eight daily), Sliven (8 lv, two hours, seven daily), Burgas (18 lv, four hours, four daily) and Plovdiv (19 lv, four hours, four daily). Daily buses serve Troyan (10 lv, two hours), Karlovo (19 lv, four hours) and Pleven (14 lv, two hours).

The somewhat more central **Yug bus station** (☑620 014; ul Hristo Botev) has many daily buses to Sofia (21 lv, four hours), Varna (19 lv, four hours) and Burgas (23 lv, 3½ hours). From here, several daily buses also serve Shumen (13 lv, three hours) and Ruse (11 lv, two hours).

Etap Adress (☑630 564; ul Ivailo 2, Hotel Etâr) has hourly buses to Sofia (22 lv, 3½ hours) and Varna (18 lv, four hours), plus two daily buses to Dobrich (20 lv, four hours), one to Kavarna (21 lv, 4½ hours) via Albena and Balchik and one to Shumen (13 lv, two hours).

To reach Romania by bus, go first to Ruse: from its main bus station, three daily minibuses make the three-hour trip to Bucharest (20 lv), as do taxis (90 lv).

Train

The remarkably unhelpful **Veliko Târnovo train station** (☑620 065), 1.5km west of town, has been known to ask for a 'fee' to provide train information. Three daily trains serve Plovdiv (21 lv, five hours) via Stara Zagora (11 lv, two hours). Trains also serve Sliven (15 lv, three hours, six daily), Burgas (21 lv, five hours, three daily), Varna (20 lv, five hours, three daily) and Sofia (21 lv, 4½ hours, six daily). Regular trains serve Târnovo's other train station, at Gorna Oryakhovitsa. From the Veliko Târnovo station, buses 10, 12, 14, 70 and 110 go to the centre. Alternatively, take a taxi (3 lv to 6 lv).

Gorna Oryakhovitsa train station (☑826 118), 8.5km from town, is along the Sofia–Varna line. It has daily services to/from Sofia, via Pleven (18 lv, five hours, eight daily) and Varna (17 lv, four hours, three daily) and 11 trains to Ruse (9 lv, two hours). There are also six daily connections to Stara Zagora (14 lv, four hours), and 10 to Shumen (14 lv, four hours).

From Târnovo, minibuses wait opposite the market along ul Vasil Levski to get here, as do bus 14 from the Pâtnicheski Prevozi bus station and bus 10 from the centre. Taxis cost about 12 lv.

A daily train for Bucharest leaves Veliko Târnovo train station, stops at Gorna Oryakhovitsa and continues from there. A Târnovo–Istanbul night train (56 lv, 70 lv with sleeper car, 11 hours) usually runs.

ⓘ Getting Around

Walking is ideal for seeing Târnovo.Taxis are good for zipping around the central areas, but sometimes refuse to drive in the old quarters, especially Varosha, due to the narrow streets. If staying in such a neighbourhood, therefore, take advantage of any free pick-up services offered. If driving, park in the central Varosha car park: avoid the narrow lanes higher up. Hiring taxis (at fixed metered rates) for local destinations like Arbanasi, or chartering them (for negotiable rates) to places further afield is more feasible.

For car rental, ask at the Tourist Information Centre for the best offers (usually around 40 lv per day, including insurance, but not petrol).

Around Veliko Târnovo

PREOBRAZHENSKI MONASTERY

Preobrazhenski Monastir (Monastery of the Transfiguration; monastery admission 2lv), originally dating from 1360, is located high in a forest 7km north of Veliko Târnovo. Bulgaria's fourth-largest monastery, it offers fantastic views. Despite being destroyed by the Turks in the late 14th century, it was rebuilt in 1825, about 500m from the original site, but was later damaged by landslides. On both sides of the main church, note the massive rocks: they tumbled down the hill and miraculously just missed the building.

The monastery's churches boast murals painted between 1849 and 1851 by the renowned Zahari Zograf. While the best inhabit Veliko Târnovo's Archaeological Museum, a restoration program has brightened up the remaining age-blackened frescoes, making a visit here very worthwhile. You may also see (and hear!) the enormous barrels of fermenting plum brandy in the courtyard being made by the rascally monks.

Bus 10 from Veliko Târnovo passes the monastery. It will leave you at a turn-off on the road headed to Ruse. From here, it's a shady, uphill 3km walk. A taxi from Veliko Târnovo costs about 8 lv one way.

EMEN   EMEH

The 3km-long Emen Canyon, along the Negovanka River, is unique in Bulgaria. Some 25 hectares of land here exist as a protected reserve for species of butterflies, fish, birds and bats. The reserve also includes the 10m-

high Momin Skok Waterfall, most impressive in spring.

Hiking the Negovanka Ecotrail, which runs in a loop in and around the canyon, is Emen's main attraction. The trail is signposted from Emen village. Veliko Târnovo's

WORTH A TRIP

ARBANASI

Arbanasi is a historic village known for its monasteries and activities, like horse riding and hiking. Although it has always attracted moneyed visitors to its clifftop 'resort' hotels, today this sleepy village of just 1500 souls is mostly visited by big tour buses on day trips. If based in Veliko Târnovo (4km away), it's easy to visit the main attractions, take in the views and enjoy a relaxed lunch, and still be back in town for dinner, whether you drive (taxis are 5 lv) or even hike up (90 minutes).

Nearly 90 of the village's churches, homes and monasteries are state-protected cultural monuments. During the 16th century and thereafter, it generally flourished under the Ottomans who rather unusually encouraged church-building here.

Arbanasi's three major sites, two churches and one house-museum, are all covered by the same ticket (5 lv). Each operates from 9.30am to 6pm daily, though they're usually closed between 1 October and 31 March.

First in precedence is the Nativity Church (adult/student 6/2 l), the oldest surviving one here. It features a kaleidoscopic frescoed interior, with paintings (created between 1632 and 1649) covering its five chambers. The church's hand-carved central iconostasis is also magnificent. Over 3500 figures are depicted in some 2000 scenes throughout the church, which also boasts lavish wood iconostases created by Tryavna School carvers.

The 16th-century Church of Sveti Arhangeli Mikhail & Gavril, built over a ruined medieval church, also contains impressive frescoes. The wooden iconostases were also carved by Tryavna artisans. Arbanasi's final major site, the 17th-century Konstant-salieva House (admission 5 lev), was later rebuilt in National Revival style. It contains period furniture (and a souvenir shop with embroidery and other handicrafts). Arbanasi also hosts three 17th-century working monasteries: Sveti Georgi Church, the Sveta Bogoroditsa Monastery (☑620 322) and the Sveti Nikolai Monastery (☑650 345; Arbanasi). All are usually open.

For equestrians, the Arbanasi Horse Base (☑623 668), on the village's eastern edge, provides a nice opportunity to enjoy guided horse riding trips in the lush hills around Arbanasi. Phone for programs and prices, or consult Veliko Târnovo's Tourist Information Centre. It also hosts a riding tournament each June.

There's no need to linger after seeing the sights, but should you seek some pampering the Hotel Arbanassi Palace (☑630 176; www.arbanassipalace.bg; s/d/ste from 90/125/170 lv; P✲@⊠✿) is the most venerable of several clifftop resorts. This grandly aging structure (once Todor Zhivkov's local residence) has great views over the valley towards Veliko Târnovo from the restaurant balcony, and from many of the rooms. Despite its dishevelled appearance, the place nevertheless has an elegant marble interior and smart modern rooms. The resort activities include horse riding, tennis, swimming and spa centre.

For humbler but still decent digs, the central Rooms Mehana Arbat (☑631 811; s/d incl breakfast 35/50 lv) offers doubles with weathered wood floors and traditional furnishings. Bathrooms are simple but modern. It's just above the similarly named Mehana Arbat (☑631 811; mains 6-12 lv), which does great Bulgarian fare at reasonable prices.

The Arbanasi municipal website (www.arbanassi.org) contains information about local history, accommodation, eating and activities. With only a couple of streets, it's impossible to get lost, and ATMs exist in the centre.

Tourist Information Office can provide more details and/or maps.

Emen village and the canyon are 25km west of Veliko Tărnovo, and are accessible by the bus from Veliko Tărnovo to Pavlikeni, which leaves Tărnovo's Pătnicheski Prevozi bus station twice daily.

Dryanovo Monastery

☑0676

Originally dating from the 12th century, this monastery (admission free; ⏱9am-6pm) lies tucked beneath limestone cliffs about 6km from Dryanovo (Dry-*an*-ovo) village. It was alternately destroyed by the Turks and rebuilt by Bulgarians over a 500-year period. Like many other monasteries, it provided sanctuary to the revolutionary leader, Vasil Levski, and his men. Later, during the Russo-Turkish War (1877–78), more than a hundred locals made a valiant last stand against the Turks, for some nine days. The Turks eventually won, burning the place down yet again. The villagers' bravery is commemorated with a mausoleum in the monastery grounds.

Dryanovo's monks have a reputation for friendliness and are happy to chat with visitors. Accommodation is usually available, but call in advance if possible.

Inside the Komplex Vodopadi is a Historical Museum (☑2097; Dryanovo Monastery; admission 3 lv; ⏱9am-noon & 12.30-3.30pm Mon-Fri, 9.45am-3.45pm Sat & Sun), devoted mostly to the 1876 April Uprising and the Russo-Turkish War. The macabre collection of skulls is remarkable. Downstairs are artefacts from nearby caves, including Bacho Kiro, and some icons.

From the bridge near the car park, a 400m path leads through lush forest to the 1200m-long Bacho Kiro Cave (short/long tour 2/4 lv; ⏱9am-6pm Apr-Oct, 10am-4pm Nov-Mar), inhabited during the Palaeolithic era. It's a long, well-lit cave, and guided tours are offered, though aren't really necessary.

Hikers have the Dryanovo Ecotrail, a well-marked, circular path that starts and finishes near the monastery. The hike takes about four hours, and passes through lush, hilly forests. To find the trailhead, ask at the Bacho Kiro cave or at the Mehana Mecha Dupka, which is in the woods just behind the monastery, about 50m from the start of the trail leading to the cave.

WORTH A TRIP

NIKOPOLIS-AD-ISTRUM
НИКОПОЛИС-АД-ИСТРУМ

Originally a Roman city built in AD 102 by Emperor Trajan, Nikopolis-ad-Istrum was destroyed by Slavs in the late 6th century; the extensive ruins include streets, towers, gates, the city square and town hall. Veliko Tărnovo's Archaeological Museum displays the site's best surviving artefacts.

If driving from Veliko Tărnovo, head north towards Ruse and take the sign-posted turn-off to the left (west) after about 20km. This access road is rough in parts. By bus, take the same northerly route, and dismount at the turn-off to Nikyup; from there, it's a 4km sign-posted walk. In summer, check opening hours ahead in the Veliko Tărnovo TIC.

🛏 Sleeping & Eating

The monastery (☑5253; Dryanovo Monastery; per person with shared bathroom 15 lv) offers simple rooms.

Komplex Vodopadi　　　　　HOTEL $
(☑2314; d/apt 40/50 lv) This place, virtually attached to the monastery, offers several small but clean rooms. Many have balconies overlooking the monastery.

Mehana Andyka　　　　BULGARIAN $
(☑2230; mains 5-9 lv; ⏱9am-1am) This relaxing restaurant has a lovely wooded setting between cliffs, about 300m before the cave entrance, and does good grilled meats and salads.

❶ Getting There & Away

Buses travelling between Veliko Tărnovo and Gabrovo can leave you at the turn-off to the monastery (4km south of Dryanovo), from where you'll have to walk the last 1.5km. Car parking costs 2 lv.

Tryavna　　　　　Трявна
☑0677 / POP 12,200

Once just a day trip and now a tourist draw, Tryavna (40km southwest of Veliko Tărnovo) has been impressively renovated thanks to EU largesse. The National Revival homes, stone bridges and cobblestone streets are all aesthetically appealing, as is the sight of the main church selectively floodlit at night. Tryavna is most famous for its craftsmanship, and particularly for the eminent Tryavna school of religious woodcarving. However, despite its plethora of exhibitions and churches, Tryavna has not become simply a museum town; a school for woodcarving still exists, attended by young Bulgarians continuing this aspect of their national heritage.

◉ Sights

A two- to three-hour walking tour suffices for Tryavna's sights. From the bus station, head east (away from the train line) and then turn right along ul Angel Kânchev to reach the impressive 1852 Church of Sveti Georgi (ul Angel Kânchev 128; ⊙7.30am-12.30pm & 2.30-5.30pm) on the left; it features some beautiful icons and carvings. Further on the right is the Angel Kânchev House-Museum (☑2278; ul Angel Kânchev 39; admission 2 lv; ⊙8am-6pm Apr-Oct, to 5pm Nov-Mar). Built in 1805, it contains exhibits about revolutionary hero Kânchev, and the liberation of Tryavna during the Russo-Turkish War.

Walk over the bridge, past the shady park and head right (still along ul Angel Kânchev) to pl Kapitan Dyado Nikola. First built in 1814 in National Revival style, this large square is dominated by a clock tower (1844) that chimes loudly on the hour. Facing this square is Staroto Shkolo (ul Angel Kânchev 7; admission 3 lv; ⊙9am-6pm), the town's old school. Built in 1836, it's now been fully restored and houses the Tryavna Museum School of Painting (☑2039, 2517; adult/student 2/1 lv; ⊙9am-7pm). Also overlooking the square is the slate-roofed Church of

Sveti Arhangel Mihail (admission 1lv), Tryavna's oldest church, which is magically lit at night. Burnt down by the Turks but rebuilt in 1819, it boasts intricate Tryavna School woodcarvings. Its Museum of Icons illustrates the history of Bulgarian icon painting.

Across the stone Arch Bridge (1844) is ul PR Slaveikov, one of Bulgaria's nicest cobblestone streets. On the left-hand side is Daskalov House (ul Slaveikov 27; admission 3 lv; ⊙9am-6pm). This walled home with garden also contains the intriguing and unique Museum of Woodcarving & Icon Painting, which features superb examples of the Tryavna school of woodcarving, plus icons and antique copper implements.

Housed in a former chapel, Tryavna's second, larger Museum of Icons (☑3753; ul Breza 1; admission 2 lv; ⊙9am-4.30pm summer, 10am-6pm winter) contains more than 160 icons from the erstwhile collections of famous local families. The museum is beyond the train line, and signposted from ul PR Slaveikov.

On ul Slaveikov, the Slaveikov House-Museum (☑2166; ul PR Slaveikov 50; admission 2 lv; ⊙8am-noon & 1-6pm Wed-Sun) is dedicated to Petko Slaveikov and his son Pencho, renowned poets who once lived here. Further down on the left is the 1830 Summer Garden Kalinchev House (☑3694; ul PR Slaveikov 45; admission 3 lv; ⊙9am-1pm & 2-6pm Mon-Fri), which features a charming courtyard cafe (open 8am to 11pm) and contains, but does not exhibit, 500 works by Bulgarian artists, including Kalinchev. More paintings, drawings and sculptures are displayed at the next-door Ivan Kolev House (☑3777; ul PR Slaveikov 47; admission 2 lv; ⊙9am-1pm & 2-6pm Mon-Fri).

VELIKO TÂRNOVO & CENTRAL MOUNTAINS TRYAVNA

WOODCARVING

During the Bulgarian National Revival period, Tryavna became renowned for its woodcarvings, intricately chiselled from local walnut, birch, poplar and oak trees. Many were used to decorate monasteries in Gabrovo, Veliko Târnovo, Arbanasi and Rila. Tryavna carvers were sought after by builders and house owners as far away as Serbia, Turkey and modern-day Iran.

By the early 19th century more than 40 Tryavna workshops were producing wooden cradles, frames, icons, friezes, doors and crosses, each individually designed. Ornate and detailed flower motifs became particularly associated with the Tryavna School. Some beautiful exhibits include the 'sun ceiling' inside Tryavna's Daskalov House, home to the Museum of Woodcarving & Icon Painting.

Carving courses for tourists are available: one/two/three days (six hours per day) cost 50/70/90 lv. Every even-numbered year, the school also hosts the International Woodcarving Competition. See the local TIC for details on both.

🛏 Sleeping

Along the first 200m of ul Angel Kânchev after the bus station rooms-for-rent are signposted. The tourist office arranges private rooms for about 20 lv to 25 lv per person, including breakfast.

Hotel Tigara   HOTEL $
(☎0889 393 154; www.tigara.tryavna.biz; ul D Gorov 7a; s/d 30/40 lv) The Tiger Hotel is a friendly, family-run place in the centre, near the History Museum. The best of the clean and comfortable rooms are the newer ones at the back. Breakfast costs 5 lv.

Kompleks Tryavna   HOTEL $$
(☎63448; http://complex.tryavna.biz/; ul Angel Kânchev 46; s/d 50/70 lv; ❈🛜) The shiny Kompleks Tryavna has an excellent central location and very modern, though fairly standard, accommodation. There are two restaurants, a fitness centre, a spa centre, a bar and a garden cafe.

Zograf Inn   GUESTHOUSE $$
(☎64970; http://zograf.tryavna.biz; ul PR Slaveikov 1; s/d/apt 40/65/90 lv) In the heart of historic Tryavna near the clocktower, the Zograf occupies a renovated historic building. The rooms are spotless and good value, though (unlike the National Revival building) are simply modern. Breakfasts are hearty at the recommended traditional *mehana* attached.

Hotel Seasons   HOTEL $$
(☎2285; http://seasons.tryavna.biz; ul Kâncho Skorchev 11; s/d/ste from 50/70/100 lv; 🅿@🛜❄) Tryavna's luxury option includes a large outdoor pool, sauna and Jacuzzi. The breezy, spacious rooms are the town's best, though the 'superior' doubles are not considerably better than the regular ones. It's up a steep hill, so better for drivers. The professional staff organise walking tours in the nearby hills.

🍴 Eating & Drinking

Zograf Mehana   BULGARIAN $$
(ul PR Slaveikov 1; mains 5-11 lv) The traditional-style restaurant in the hotel of the same name is just off the main square and serves reliable Bulgarian staples.

Restaurant Tryavienski Kut   BULGARIAN $$
(☎2033; ul Angel Kânchev; mains 5-10 lv; ⊘8am-midnight) This atmospheric restaurant in an imposing National Revival house has worn wooden floors and carved ceilings, and a good range of homemade Bulgarian cooking.

Starata Loza   BULGARIAN $$
(☎4501; ul PR Slaveikov 44; mains 6-15 lv; 🛜) The Old Vine features eccentric traditional decor (wood carvings on the interior, wine casks sticking out of the walls) and has a big menu of inventive Bulgarian fare, plus 27 kinds of *rakia* (fruit brandy). The specials, such as pork stuffed with onions, sausage, mushrooms and walnut (11 lv) are expensive, but worth it. It's on the cobblestone street opposite the entrance to Daskalov House.

Bar Kokoracia   BAR
(☎6811; ul Han Asparuh 1; ⊘6pm-2am weekdays, to 4am weekends; 🛜) This cool place with red paper lanterns and house music is the best watering hole in town.

ℹ Information

Get local maps at Tryavna train station or at shops. An ATM and some restaurants are around the square.

Internet Centre (ul Angel Kânchev 15; 2 lv per hour) Internet cafe.

Tourist Information Centre (☎2247; www.tryavna.bg; ul Angel Kânchev 33; ⊘9am-noon & 2-5pm Mon-Fri) In the post office building; can help with bus and train schedules, and arrange private rooms.

ℹ Getting There & Away

The bus and train stations are 100m apart, west of ul Angel Kânchev, the main road through the old town.

Most public transport to Tryavna goes via Gabrovo; frequent minibuses connect the two (4 lv, 30 minutes). From other points of origin, connect in Gabrovo. By train, Tryavna is along a spur track, and has nine passenger trains daily (7 lv, 50 minutes). It's one of the closest stops to Veliko Târnovo and hence easy to see before or after visiting that town.

Etâr   Етър
☎066

This complex of traditional artisans just 8km southeast of Gabrovo is fun for shopping, or just wandering and watching the artisans at work. It also offers nearby hiking.

Cumulatively known as the **Etâr Ethnographic Village Museum** (☎801 831; www.etar.hit.bg; admission 7 lv; ⊘8.30am-6pm), the market complex contains nearly 50 shops and workshops clustered along narrow lanes. It's set all by itself in a 7-hectare, tree-lined spot along the Gabrovo–Shipka road.

Etâr's 19th-century National Revival buildings house the workshops of bakers, cartwrights, cobblers, furriers, glass workers, hatters, jewellers, leather workers, millers, potters, weavers and more. True, it's all a bit precious, but there are quality goods produced, and if you're looking to take home a memento of bygone days in the Balkans, this is the place. Intriguingly, some of the workshops are powered by water from a stream running through the complex.

Enter the complex either on the northern side (near the Hotel Strannopriemnitsa), at the central administration building, or on the far southern side, near the large car park. A multi-entry, one-day ticket is usually required, and guided tours (in English, French or German) are available for another 7 lv per person (minimum of five people).

Fair Day (14 October) features traditional dance and music, played on instruments such as locally made *kavals* (wooden flutes).

Besides the market, there's also excellent hiking in the lush, hilly forests around Etâr. A large map standing opposite the entrance to the ethnographic village details some 15 different trails through the nearby Bulgarka Natural Park, plus the time required to hike them. Some trails can be done as day hikes, allowing you to park at Etâr and return there afterwards.

🛏 Sleeping

Hotel Strannopriemnitsa　　　　HOTEL $
(☏801 831; s/d incl breakfast 36/60 lv) At the northern (Gabrovo) end of the market complex, this hotel is decent value, though singles are tiny. The doubles have balconies with views (of the less interesting part of the complex).

Hotel Perla　　　　　　　　　　HOTEL $
(☏801 984; d 45 lv) This friendly place offers the best value around, with spacious rooms that boast shiny bathrooms and balconies. Breakfast is 5 lv extra.

🍴 Eating

Restaurant Strannopriemnitsa BULGARIAN $$
(mains 6-11 lv) Part of the Hotel Strannopriemnitsa, this hunting-lodge-style *mehana* (replete with wall-mounted deer antlers) has better decor than food. The service is good, however, and the outdoor tables overlook the grass and trees.

Renaissance Tavern　　　　　BULGARIAN $$
(mains 8-10 lv) With an atmospherically touristy location within the market complex, the Renaissance has reasonably good Bulgarian fare. The complex's little bakery sells takeaway food, such as glazed *simit* buns (a local speciality) and cheese pies, while the *sladkarnitsa* (sweet shop) offers a tempting and very colourful range of traditional sweets, including *lokum* (Turkish delight) and halvas.

ℹ Getting There & Away

Etâr is best served from the nondescript town of Gabrovo, which has local buses for the 15-minute trip. Alternatively, any Gabrovo–Kazanlâk bus will leave you at the turn-off, from where it's a 2km-walk. A taxi from Gabrovo costs about 8 lv. From Etâr, a taxi to Tryavna (about 25 lv) saves the trouble of bussing via Gabrovo.

If driving, Etâr makes a good day trip from Veliko Târnovo, Arbanasi, Trayvna or Dryanovo.

Lovech　　　　　　　　　Ловеч
☏068 / POP 36,200

Popular with weekending locals but less visited by foreign travellers, Lovech is a quiet, well-restored traditional village along the Osêm River, 35km south of Pleven. The old quarter of Varosha hosts more than 150 restored National Revival structures, while the photogenic covered bridge over the river is a symbol of the town.

Lovech was a significant military outpost and trade centre during Thracian and Roman eras, and again during the Second Bulgarian Empire. During the Ottoman occupation, however, it would reach its peak, though precariously playing with fire as the surreptitious headquarters of the Bulgarian Central Revolutionary Committee during the mid-19th century.

The main square, pl Dimitrov, has banks, exchange offices and post office.

◉ Sights

Just past the Hotel Lovech is the Pokritiyat Most (covered footbridge) – the Balkans' only such structure. Built in 1872, and completely restored twice since, it once again features its original wooden design. Arts and crafts shops, as well as cafes, are found within. Passing the square beyond the bridge brings you to the Art Gallery (☏23 937; ul Vasil Levski 9; admission free; ⊙9am-noon &

1-6pm Mon-Sat), with works by local and other Bulgarian artists exhibited.

Extensive ruins of the Hisar Fortress (admission free; ☺8am-6pm) are visible from the old town. Here was signed the treaty with the Turks that ushered in the Second Bulgarian Empire. The fortress is fun to explore and offers great views. From Varosha, it's a 10- to 15-minute uphill walk.

From near the art gallery, follow the cobblestoned ul Hristo Ivanov Golemia uphill about 100m to the Ethnographical Museum (☎27 720; ul Hristo Ivanov Golemia; admission 3 lv; ☺8am-noon & 2-5pm Mon-Sat). The two mid-19th-century buildings contain fascinating exhibits and period furniture, plus a cellar full of wine-making equipment. Leaflets in English, French or German are available.

About 50m further up, the Vasil Levski Museum (☎27 990; admission 2 lv; ☺9am-5pm Mon-Fri) contains extensive displays about the revered revolutionary. Another 50m uphill is the Byzantine Sveta Bogoroditsa Church – renovated, but not always open.

From the church, follow the steps past more renovated National Revival homes leading to Stratesh Hill, where lilacs blossom and a stern Vasil Levski statue stands.

🛏 Sleeping

TOP CHOICE Hotel Varosha 2003   GUESTHOUSE $$
(☎22 277; www.varosha2003.com; ul Ivan Drasov 23; s/d/ste/apt incl breakfast €30/45/50/60; P❄🐾📶) Certainly the most atmospheric guesthouse in town, this friendly, family-run place on the river is marked by its National Revival architecture and flowery, woodtrim balconies. The five spacious and well-equipped rooms lend a feeling of cosiness with their smooth wood floors and comfortable beds. The kind owners serve breakfast in the garden and offer nourishing evening meals.

Hotel Lovech   HOTEL $
(☎604 717; www.hotellovech.com; ul Târgovska 12; s/d/tr/apt 30/44/54/100 lv; ❄🐾📶) In Lovech centre by the footbridge, this renovated boxy structure surprises with its many options (including restaurant, casino and spa centre), and has well-maintained and spacious rooms too.

Hotel Tsariana   PENSION $
(☎600 995; tsariana@mbox.digsys.bg; pl Todor Kirkov 10; s/d 230/38 lv) The two-star Tsariana, set on Varosha's square, occupies a lovely refurbished National Revival home (though the general structure has more ambience than the actual rooms).

Hotel Oasis   HOTEL $
(☎26 239; ul NV Drasov 17; s/d 35/50 lv) Another riverfront hotel, the well-furnished Oasis is signposted 100m from the vehicle bridge. A decent restaurant, often featuring live music, is attached.

🍴 Eating

Cafes and brasseries line pl Todor Kirkov in Varosha.

Mehana Gallereya   BULGARIAN $
(ul Vasil Levski; mains 4-9 lv) Located beside the eponymous Art Gallery, this *mehana* features a large courtyard, good service and very tasty food.

Mehana Billaya   BULGARIAN $$
(ul Marni Poplukanov; mains 5-8 lv) Up the cobblestoned street downtown, the Billaya has atmosphere and good Bulgarian traditional food (though on most evenings there's loud live music).

ℹ Getting There & Away

From the adjacent bus and train stations, take a taxi (preferable) or walk along ul Tsacho Shishkov, veer right and follow the signs to the centre.

From the bus station (☎603 618), hourly buses serve Troyan (6 lv, 45 minutes). Three daily buses serve Burgas (30 lv, six hours), Sliven (29 lv, four to five hours) and Veliko Târnovo (7 lv, two hours); more frequent buses cross the Stara Planina to Shipka (15 lv, 2½ hours, four daily) and Kazanlâk (14 lv, 3½ hours, four daily). Hourly buses also serve Pleven (8 lv, one hour) and Sofia (20 lv, three hours, six daily).

From the train station (☎634 935), three daily trains serve both Troyan (4 lv, one hour) and Levski (4 lv, 1 hour); from the latter, change for Sofia and the important railway hub of Gorna Oryakhovitsa for Veliko Târnovo and beyond.

Troyan   Троян
☎0670 / POP 21,003

Troyan, associated mostly with its famous nearby monastery, is a laid-back, slightly faded town enjoying crisp, clean mountain air. The grand, communist-era square has a relaxed atmosphere and several well-frequented cafes. There's also a notable Pomak Muslim population. Although there's not much to do, it makes a good base for

HIKING IN THE STARA PLANINA

With an average height of little over 700m, the Stara Planina (Old Mountain) range is not high, particularly compared with the Rila and Pirin Mountains. Nonetheless it is vast, covering 11,500 sq km (about 10% of Bulgaria) and, at close to 550km long, it extends almost the entire length of the country. Nearly 30 peaks are more than 2000m high and the mountains feed a third of Bulgaria's major rivers. The highest point is Mt Botev (2376m), north of Karlovo.

Julian Perry's *Mountains of Bulgaria* describes the strenuous 25-day (650km to 700km) trek across the entire range. This trek – which starts at Berkovitsa, near the border with Serbia, and finishes at Emine Cape, about 20km northeast of Nesebâr on the Black Sea coast – is on the trans-European E3 trek. The book's text is detailed, but maps are poor; buy Kartografia's widely available *Stara Planina* map.

Some of the more interesting hikes along marked trails:

Cherni Osêm to Hizha Ambaritsa Four hours.

Dryanovo Ecotrail Four hours.

Etâr to Sokolski Monastery One hour, then continue to Shipka Pass (extra two to three hours; steep).

Gabrovo to Hizha Uzana Four hours.

Karlovo to Hizha Hubavets Two hours, or continue to Hizha Vasil Levski (another two to three hours) and Mt Botev (further two to three hours).

Shipka Monastery to Shipka Pass Two hours.

Sliven to Hizha Karandila Three hours.

seeing the Troyan Monastery, Lovech and Karlovo. Troyan's also close to some excellent Stara Planina hiking paths.

Millennia ago, the Thracians first made Troyan strategically significant. During the Bulgarian National Revival period, it became famous for woodcarving, metalwork and particularly pottery. Examples of these crafts can be admired at Troyan's museum.

Sights

The **Museum of Folk Craft & Applied Arts** (☎62 063; pl Vûzhrazhdane; admission 2 lv; ⏲9am-5pm Mon-Fri) by the bridge exhibits local textiles, woodcarving, metalwork, weaving, pottery and ceramics, plus archaeological artefacts. The adjoining **History Museum** is included in the admission cost.

Activities

Horse riding (20 lv per person per hour) at local villages is arranged by the tourist centre, which also helps rent **mountain bikes** (per hour/day 2/14 lv); there are five designated mountain-bike routes, including to Troyan Monastery. Guides (50 lv per day) speaking French, German or English are available for local tours and **hikes**.

Sleeping & Eating

The tourist office finds private rooms for about 15 lv per person, usually with breakfast. It also offers central Troyan apartments with kitchen facilities, sitting room and bathroom (40 lv to 60 lv per double).

Cafes and pizza places are on the corner of ul Vasil Levski and pl Vûzhrazhdane.

Troyan Plaza Hotel HOTEL $$
(☎64 399; www.troyanplaza.com; ul PR Slaveykov 54; s/d/ste incl breakfast 80/110/130 lv; P@) Troyan's classiest place, the four-star Troyan Plaza has all the expected amenities, including two restaurants and a spa centre. It can arrange activities such as horse riding, archery and shooting.

Hotel Panorama HOTEL $$
(☎622 930; hotelpanoramatr@mail.bg; Park Kâpincho; s/d/apt 48/68/120 lv; ❄📶) The renovated Panorama, located in the hillside park above town, offers clean and decent rooms in a relaxed setting. Along with sauna and massage, there are various sports courts and a kids' playground. Take a taxi (about 2 lv from the bus station or town centre).

Café Antik BULGARIAN $$
(☎60 910; Ploshtad Vûzhrazhdane; mains 7-12 lv; ⏲7am-midnight) This cafe-restaurant, located

HIKING IN THE SREDNA GORA

The Sredna Gora (Central Range) mountains comprise more than 6000 sq km from Iskâr Gorge (near Sofia) to the Tundzha Valley (south of Yambol), peaking at Mt Bogdan (1603m) near Koprivshtitsa.

The Mountains of Bulgaria by Julian Perry provides a detailed description of the two- or three-day hike from Hisar (Hisarya) to Koprivshtitsa. No dedicated Sredna Gora map exists, but most hiking routes are in Kartografia's Stara Planina map.

Domino's Koprivshtitsa map includes a small but clear map with five local hiking routes. One four-hour route leads to Mt Bogdan, and a hut for overnight stays.

behind the folk museum and with relaxing views of the river, is a good bet for coffee on the terrace when it's warm out, or a shot of strong Troyan brandy when it's cold. It also does some inventive (though relatively expensive) meat dishes.

ℹ Information

The Troyan **tourist office** (✆35 064; infotroyan @yahoo.com; ul Vasil Levski 133; ⊗8am-8pm summer, 9am-5pm Mon-Fri winter) finds private accommodation, provides maps and arranges activities such as riding, as well as car rental from about 60 lv per day.

ℹ Getting There & Around

From the bus/train stations, walk 300m along ul Zahari Stoyanov and cross the Bely Osâm River's footbridge for the centre. From here, turn right and walk along the mall, ul General Kartsov, to Troyan's main square, pl Vûzhrazhdane.

From the Troyan **bus station** (✆62 172), one daily bus serves Sofia (18 lv, three hours); buses passing through Lovech (3.50 lv, 45 minutes, hourly) have immediate connections to Pleven. For Troyan Monastery, take the hourly bus for Cherny Osâm and ask to disembark at the gates.

Troyan Monastery

Only 10km southeast of Troyan is Bulgaria's third-largest monastery, after Rila and Bachkovo. Troyan Monastery (admission free, photos 5 lv, video 15 lv; ⊗6am-10pm) boasts powerful and searching frescoes, painted by Zahari Zograf, the leading mural artist of the Bulgarian National Revival period. One of the highlights in the area around the Central Mountains, it can be seen in an hour or two.

Some of this 16th-century monastery survived numerous attacks by the Turks between the 16th and 18th centuries, but most of today's monastery dates to 1835. All of the striking murals inside the Church of the Holy Virgin were painted in the 1840s by Zahari Zograf. The church is poorly lit, so it's hard to see the detail of the frescoes inside, though they are slowly being restored. Zograf's finest frescoes, however, are outside on the back wall. They depict Judgment Day, the apocalypse and hell, including a seven-headed fire-breathing dragon and demonic torture of sinners.

The monastery's also renowned for its hand-carved wood altar and iconostasis, crafted in the mid-19th century by Tryavna woodcarvers. The highlight for most, though, is the legendary Three-Handed Holy Virgin, only seen in public during the annual monastery celebrations on Virgin Mary's Day (15 August).

The 19th-century revolutionary leader, Vasil Levski, formed and trained insurgents here, and urged the monks themselves to fight the Turks in 1876. This history is highlighted in the small 3rd-floor museum (Trojan Monastery; admission 4 lv; ⊗Open on request). The door is usually locked, but reception office staff can open it.

Troyan Monastery is not as touristy as Rila Monastery, though it does have several cafes, restaurants, souvenir shops and art galleries around it.

Ask at the reception office for rooms; basic but expensive (doubles 60 lv), they sometimes require advance booking.

Monastirska Bara (✆0888798591; mains 2-8 lv; ⊗8am-midnight) is a simple *mehana* next to the monastery for quick eats.

ℹ Getting There & Away

The hourly Troyan–Cherni Osêm bus stops at the monastery gates. A taxi from Troyan to the monastery costs about 10 lv one way. Most taxi drivers will return at a specified time to bring you back.

Hisar   Хисар

📞0337 / POP 7691

Therapeutic mineral springs have been Hisar's (also known as Hisarya) main claim to fame ever since Roman times, when it was named Diokletianopolis, after the Emperor Diocletian. The 22 mineral-water springs here are said to cure many ailments, and the popularity of these springs even today has ensured this sleepy mountain town's livelihood. The main street has some unique ruins from the days of ancient Rome, though the major reason to visit today, as then, is for the indolent spa therapy.

There's an ATM on the corner of the central ul Hristo Botev.

◎ Sights

Hisar's Roman walls, refortified by the Byzantines, are more than 5m high and up to 3m thick, and among Bulgaria's best-preserved Roman ruins. Built to protect a 30-hectare span of the town and its mineral baths from invaders, the walls were too formidable for 6th-century Slavic raiders. The most-visited section is near the bus and train stations.

More ruins lie along unnamed roads heading towards the centre from the main road. These unfenced, unsupervised ruins include remains of an amphitheatre, baths and some dwellings.

Archaeological Museum   MUSEUM
(📞62 012; ul Stamboliyiski 8; admission 3 lv; ◎8-11.30am & 1-4.30pm Tue-Sun) The Archaeological Museum features an original city walls scale model, and photos of early excavations. The traditional regional costumes and agricultural and weaving equipment displays are arguably more interesting. The poorly signposted museum is after the post office, and accessible from the main road through a pretty courtyard.

🛏 Sleeping & Eating

Both Hisar hotels are about 1km down bul General Gurko, which starts about 700m along the main road from the bus and train stations; look for the sign (in English) to the Augusta Spa Hotel. Both are close to the mineral springs.

Private rooms are on bul General Gurko (look for signs reading *stay pod naem*).

Besides the good hotel restaurants, several hearty, home-style *mehanas* line bul General Gurko; try the Evropa (bul General Gurko; Mains 5-9 lv; ◎8a,-11pm) or the National (bul General Gurko; Mains 4-9 lv; ◎9am-12am). Also, the Tsesar (ul Hristo Botev; Mains 5-9 lv; ◎9am-11pm) serves up excellent Bulgarian grills in a rustic courtyard, decorated by a faux windmill. Chinar (📞62288; www.hotelchinar.bg; ul Vasil Petrovich 5; s/d/apt from 80/90/175 lv; ❄🖥), near the town's church, is also popular.

Augusta Spa Hotel   SPA HOTEL $$$
(📞63 821; www.augustaspahotel.com; ul General Gurko 3; s/d from €41/58; 🅿@🏊) Try for one of the fully refurbished rooms in this central place: they are attractive, but not particularly glorious for the price. The hotel is known for its spa facilities, which include a mineral-rich outdoor pool, an indoor one, a gym and a solarium. However, given the wide range of illnesses and conditions treated here, one might be hesitant to test the waters.

Hotel Hisar   HOTEL $$$
(📞62 717; ul General Gurko; s/d 100/125 lv; 🅿❄@🏊) The post-renovation prices at the Hisar have risen, but get you handsome, well-maintained rooms, several restaurants, a great outdoor pool, a sauna and fitness centre, plus the modern balneological complex.

ℹ Getting There & Away

The train station and bus station (📞62 069) are adjacent. Six daily buses serve Karlovo (4 lv, 30 minutes), while three serve Sofia (21 lv, three hours). Buses also go to Veliko Târnovo (22 lv, 3½ hours, four daily) via Kazanlâk (14 lv, two hours, one daily). Several daily trains connect Hisar with Plovdiv (3.80 lv, 30 minutes).

From the bus and train stations, walk (300m) to the main road, ul Hristo Botev, leaving the ruins on your right. Then turn right onto bul Ivan Vazov to reach the centre and park.

Karlovo   Карлово

📞0335 / POP 22.931

Historic Karlovo, nestled in the foothills of the Stara Planina roughly equidistant from Koprivshtitsa and Kazanlâk, is not just another appealing mountain town full of National Revival architecture and antiquated churches; it's also venerated as the birthplace of Vasil Levski, the leader of the revolution against the Turks in the early 1870s. Although this historic link is everywhere in Karlovo, most (non-Bulgarian, at least) visitors will be rather more inspired by the town's placid atmosphere, churches and classic architecture.

WORTH A TRIP

KOPRIVSHTITSA

Quiet Koprivshtitsa (Ko-priv-shti-tsa) is a well-preserved 'museum village' filled with gorgeous National Revival mansions. Although it's much more accessible from Sofia than from other central or southern Bulgarian hubs, the village is very definitely part of the central heartland; it was the place where revolutionary Todor Kableshkov declared an uprising against the Turks on 20 April 1876, from Kalachev Bridge (also called Kableshkov Bridge).

Koprivshtitsa once had 12,000 residents, rivalling Sofia, but after 1878 and independence, many of its merchants, sheepherders and intellectuals left for the cities; the village remained essentially unchanged, and the post-WWII communist governments declared it variously a 'town-museum' and a 'historical reserve'.

Today, Koprivshtitsa's few streets are dotted with historic homes interrpersed with rambling, overgrown lanes, making it a romantic getaway and a safe and fun place for children.

Koprivshtitsa boasts six house-museums. Some are closed either on Monday or Tuesday (all operate Wednesday through Sunday). To buy a combined ticket for all (adults/students 5/3 lv) visit the souvenir shop **Kupchinitsa** (near the Tourist Information Centre).

Of these house-museums, the most worthwhile include the **Oslekov House** (ul Gereniloto 4; ☉closed Mon), built 1853–56, arguably the town's best example of Bulgarian National Revival architecture, with a triple-arched entrance, spacious interior, stylish furniture and brightly coloured walls. See also the **Kableshkov House** (ul Todor Kableshkov 8; ☉closed Mon), built by the famous revolutionary who (probably) fired the 1876 April Uprising's first shot. His former home (1845) has exhibits about the revolt.

Each 1 May, costumed locals perform the Re-enactment of the April 1876 Uprising. In mid-August, the Folklore Days Festival features traditional music and dance.

Except for during such events, accommodation's plentiful. The squarefront **Tourist Information Centre** (www.koprivshtitsa.info; pl 20 April; ☉10am-1pm & 2-7pm) arranges rooms from 25 lv per person in summer (it can also organise local tours). Hotel Trayanov Kâshta is arguably Koprivshtitsa's most atmospheric guesthouse, with traditionally furnished, colourful rooms inside an enclosed courtyard with garden, and relaxing upstairs balcony for an evening drink. Also, the **Bonchova House** (☎2614; ul Tumangelova Cheta 26; d/apt 30/50 lv), close to the Kalachev Bridge, offers two bright, modern rooms and an apartment; the relaxing common room features a working fireplace. (Breakfast 5 lv extra.)

Traditional fare is served at **Dyado Liben** (☎2109; ul Hadzhi Nencho Palaveev 47; mains 4-9 lv; ☉11am-midnight; ☎), an atmospheric 1852 mansion with tables set in a warren of halls, graced with ornate painted walls and heavy, worn wood floors. Find it just across the bridge leading from the main square inside the facing courtyard.

The village's helpful and friendly Tourist Information Centre, located in a small maroon building on the main square, provides local information and can organise private accommodation. There's ATM machines and a post office/telephone centre inside the village centre.

Getting to Koprivshtitsa is a bit of a challege. Being 9km north of the village, the train station requires a shuttle bus (2 lv, 15 minutes), which isn't always dependably timed for meeting incoming and outgoing trains. Trains do come from Sofia (11 lv, 2½ hours, four daily) and connections can be made for Plovdiv and other points, like Burgas, which gets a daily train (18 lv, five hours). Alternatively, Koprivshtitsa's bus stop is central and has more frequent connections including five daily buses to Sofia (13 llv, two hours), and one daily to Plovdiv (12 lv, two hours).

👁 Sights & Activities

Karlovo's main sights are accessed by walking up ul Vasil Levski to pl 20 Yuli. Stop first at pl Vasil Levski, where the revolutionary's **statue** depicts him with a lion (his nickname among rebel peers). Turn right two times for **Sveta Bogoroditsa Church** (admission free; ⏱7am-7pm) with intricate wooden iconostases. Opposite, the similarly coloured **History Museum** (📋4728; ul Vûzrozhdenska 4; admission 0.50 lv; ⏱9am-noon & 1-5pm Tue-Sun) features ethnological displays.

Further up ul Vasil Levski, the closed 1485 **Kurshum Mosque** (ul Vasil Levski) occupies the park. Continue up the mall to the square, then head left (west) for about 300m, past the **clock tower**, to Vasil Levski Museum.

Vasil Levski Museum　　MUSEUM
(📋3489; www.vlevskimuseum-bg.org; ul Gen Kartzov 57; admission 1 lv; ⏱8.30am-1pm & 2-5pm Mon-Fri) This set of rooms around a cobblestone courtyard contains exhibits about Levski with English explanations. Ask to see the modern shrine, where a lock of Levski's hair is displayed while Bulgarian religious chants waft up. A guided tour in English costs 3 lv per person.

🛏 Sleeping

Hotel Fani　　HOTEL $
(📋2894; ul Vasil Levski 73; r per person 15 lv) This small, family-run place by a popular lunch-spot offers two rooms, which are basic, but clean and tidy. They share a bathroom; nevertheless it's still great value.

Hemus Hotel　　PENSION $
(📋94 597; ul Vasil Levski 87; s/d from 22/28 lv; ❄) Another small family-run hotel, the Hemus has eight comfortable rooms and friendly owners. Since it's not obvious, follow the street numbers or ask around.

Sherev Hotel　　HOTEL $$
(📋93 380; pl 20 Yuli; s 30-40 lv, d 60-115 lv) Enjoying Karlovo's best location, overlooking the square and its popular cafes and restaurants, the Sherev is somewhat overpriced. The unrenovated rooms are run-down, and in general it's not great value.

🍴 Eating

Pl 20 Yuli has restaurants and cafes.

Restaurant Dionisi　　BULGARIAN $
(ul Evlogi Georgiev; mains 4-9 lv) Over near pl Sveti Nikolai, Restaurant Dionisi does hearty, home-cooked fare including a range of meat and veg soups.

Voenen Klub　　BULGARIAN $
(pl 20 Yuli; mains 4-9 lv; ⏱9am-11pm) A good place for salads and grills, as well as evening drinks, is the Voenen Klub bar–restaurant on the opposite side of the square.

ℹ Getting There & Around

Karlovo sprawls across a long hill. The bus and train stations are at its base. From the train station, cross the small park to where three roads go up the hill; the central one, ul Vasil Levski stretches for 2km to the town's main square, pl 20 Yuli.

The bus station, 100m up left of the three roads from the train station, is past the yellowish block of flats and to the right.

The **bus station** (📋93 155) has services to Hisar (4 lv, 30 minutes, eight daily), Sofia (18 lv, three hours, two daily) and Veliko Târnovo (16 lv, 2½ hours, two daily). About every hour, a bus travelling to or from Plovdiv (7 lv, one hour) stops in Karlovo, near the Vasil Levski Museum.

The **train station** (📋94 641) has trains going on the Sofia–Burgas line, via Kazanlâk and Sliven. Trains serve Sofia (11 lv, 2¼ hours, two daily), Burgas (19 lv, four hours, one daily) and Plovdiv (8 lv, two hours, three daily), though the bus is quicker and more frequent.

Kazanlâk　　Казанлък

📋0431 / POP 46,990

A bit rough around the edges, Kazanlâk is nevertheless a fascinating town where Bulgaria's various ethnic and religious groups commingle amicably. Life revolves around the loud central square, pl Sevtopolis (good accommodation, eating and drinking are there or nearby). Most famous, however, are the archaeological remains from the area's ancient Thracian civilisation. The major site, the Thracian Tomb, is a 15-minute walk northeast of the central square, across the small Stara Reka (Old River).

Kazanlâk is also the jumping-off point for journeys across the Valley of Roses (Rozovata Dolina), a wide plain blooming with roses, responsible for more than 60% of the world's supply of fragrant rose oil. Crossi... the plain, one ascends to Shipka villag... Shipka Pass, site of a decisive sho... the 1877–78 Russo-Turkish War

Kazanlâk

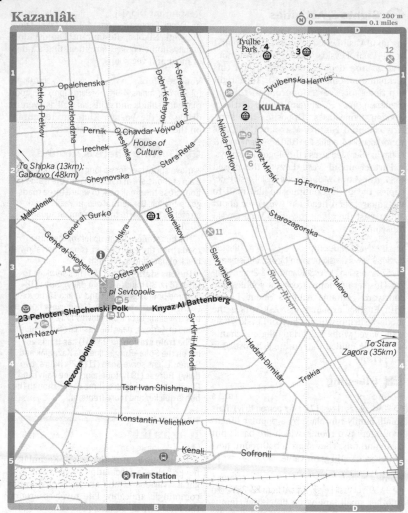

VELIKO TÂRNOVO & CENTRAL MOUNTAINS KAZANLÂK

Kazanlâk

town retains considerable Ottoman spirit, with a working mosque and notable Turkish and Pomak Muslim minorities.

◉ Sights

Thracian Tomb of Kazanlâk
MUSEUM

(Tyulbe Park; admission 20 lv; ☉10am-5pm) In hilly Tyulbe Park, just up from the Kulata Ethnological Complex, is a very large and very locked tomb: built in the 4th century BC for a Thracian ruler, it was discovered in 1944 during a bomb shelter construction, and is now a Unesco World Heritage site.

Along the *dromos* (vaulted entry corridor), a double frieze depicts battle scenes. The burial chamber is 12m in diameter, and covered by a beehive dome typical of Thracian 3rd to 5th centuries BC design. The dome's murals depict events such as a funeral feast and chariot race.

Museum
MUSEUM

(☑64 750; Tyulbe Park; admission 2 lv; ☉10am-6pm) Considering that you get basically the same experience from seeing the full-scale tomb replica in this museum, most visitors choose not to spend the 20 lv required to see the real thing. The staff guiding you around the faux tomb are friendly and speak good English.

Iskra Museum & Art Gallery
MUSEUM

(☑23 741; ul Sv Kiril i Metodii; adult/student 2/1 lv; ☉9am-6pm Mon-Fri) This gallery displays extensive archaeological finds including pottery, jewellery and tools from excavations of Thracian tombs like that in Tyulbe Park. All explanations are in Bulgarian, so the brochure (2 lv) in English, French or German is helpful.

Upstairs, numerous paintings are displayed, including by renowned local artists such as Ivan Milev and Vasil Barakov. Purchase the printed catalogue (in English and French; 3 lv).

Kulata Ethnological Complex
ETHNO-MUSEUM

(☑621 733; ul Knyaz Mirski; admission 3 lv, with rose-liquor tasting 4 lv; ☉8am-noon & 1-6pm) Just down from Tyulbe Park and the Thracian tomb, you'll find the appealing Kulata (Tower) district, site of the Kulata Ethnological Complex. A replica of a one-storey peasant's home and wooden sheds with agricultural implements and carts are among the rustic exhibits.

A courtyard leads to the two-storey House of Hadzhi Eno, built by a wealthy rose merchant in Bulgarian National Revival style. Some explanations in German and English are given, and you may be invited by the caretaker to sample some rose tea, liquor or jam.

FREE Museum of the Roses
MUSEUM

(☑23 741; ul Osvobozhdenie; admission free; ☉9am-5pm summer) The grandly named Research Institute for Roses, Aromatic & Medicinal Plants houses this tiny museum. It's 3km north of centre up ul Osvobozhdenie; take a taxi (3 lv one way), or bus 3 from Kazanlâk's main square. The photos and displays explain (in Bulgarian only) the 300-year-old method of cultivating the roses, picking their petals and processing the oil.

The attached shop sells rose oils, perfumes, shampoos, liqueurs, tea bags and jams. Guided tours (rates negotiable) are available in English and French, but ring first about opening times in winter.

Open Market
BAZAAR

Kazanlâk's *pazar* (open market) is a very entertaining, dusty, all-purpose place that offers a truly characteristic Balkan shopping experience: if you happen to be around on a Tuesday or Friday, the market's busiest days, be sure to stop by.

🛏 Sleeping

Hotel Palas
HOTEL $$

(☑62 311; www.hotel-palas.com; ul Petko Stajnov 9; s/d/ste incl breakfast 82/96/120 lv; P🌢🛜) This posh place opposite the post office and near the main square offers spacious, classy rooms. The suites are enticing and great value (prices can be negotiable for multinight stays). The restaurant is respectable, though service is slow when busy. The buffet breakfast is better-than-average, though the 'spa centre' is opened only on request and its Jacuzzi usually bereft of water.

Hadzhi Eminova Kâshta
GUESTHOUSE $

(☑62 595; bul Nikola Petkov 22; s/d/apt 20/30/40 lv) This established guesthouse offers big, traditionally furnished rooms featuring woollen quilts, and overlooking an authentic 19th-century walled compound. The one apartment is huge, and worth booking ahead. All rooms feature bathrooms, though they tend to be small, and the restaurant is excellent.

Roza Hotel
HOTEL $$

(✆50 105; www.hotelrozabg.com; ul Rozova Dolina 2; s/d from 50/70 lv; ❄@🖥) Set atop an office complex opposite the square, the Roza has a small collection of rooms and a giant, astro-turfed terrace with panoramic views. The rooms on the hall's right-hand side are smaller, with beds jammed in lengthways, whereas the slightly larger ones on the left are more normal (and slightly pricier).

Staff are very friendly and free tea, coffee and fruits are available throughout the day in the breakfast nook.

Hotel-Restaurant Chiflika
HOTEL $

(✆21 411; www.chiflika-bg.com; ul Knyaz Mirski 38; s/d 35/50 lv; ❄@🖥) Over by the Church of Sveti Ilias, the Chiflika has a faux-traditional look, though rooms are of a relatively high standard and the restaurant does good Bulgarian standbys.

Hotel Teres
HOTEL $

(✆64 272; www.hotelteres.com; ul Nikola Petkov; s/d incl breakfast 48/54; P❄@) This friendly hotel is located directly below the hill of the Thracian Tomb, opposite the river. It has clean, modern and cosy rooms, a lobby bar and an adjacent restaurant.

Grand Hotel Kazanlâk
HOTEL $$

(✆63 210; hotel_kazanlak@abv.bg; pl Sevtopolis; s/d 50/80 lv; ❄🖥) Although its communist origins will never really be extirpated, the renovated Grand Hotel Kazanlâk has good-enough rooms and a great location on the main square. There's a restaurant, a late-night bar upstairs (weekend nights only), and the popular Cocktail Bar Hollywood attached on the square.

✗ Eating

New York Bar & Grill
INTERNATIONAL $$

(pl Sevtopolis; mains 5-10 lv; 🖥) When in Kazanlâk... This eternally popular restaurant-pub on the square has a big menu (with pictures), serving everything from pizza to fish and grills. It's not gourmet, but the locals love it.

Hadzhi Eminova Kâshta
BULGARIAN $$

(✆62595; bul Nikola Petkov 22; mains 5-9 lv) Set in the courtyard of the hotel of the same name, this well-regarded restaurant does some of Kazanlâk's best traditional cooking.

Bulgaran
BULGARIAN $$

(✆64 920; Tyulbe Park; mains 6-15 lv; 🖥) This 'traditional' place up on Kazalanlak's north-eastern edge, just past Tyulbe Park, goes a bit over the the top with the costumed mu-

sic nights, but the Bulgarian specialities are undeniably good. It's a 15-minute walk from centre.

Banicharnitsa Violeta Asenova
BAKERY $

(Otets Paisii 33; banitsa 0.80 lv; ⏲6.30am-9.30pm) Kazanlâk's best breakfast nook is this tiny hole-in-the-wall place opposite the open market, serving a variety of flaky cheese (and other) pies from the *banitsa* and *byurek* family of Balkan pastry.

🍺 Drinking

Cocktail Bar Hollywood
BAR

(✆0886 316 604; pl Sevtopolis; ⏲10am-1am; 🖥) This slick and very popular curbside bar on the square has two rooms, disco balls, strobe lights and tiger-skin couches. At time of research it was closed for renovation, so doubtless it will come back twice as swank.

Kafe Kredo
CAFE

(ul General Skobelev; ⏲6.30am-10.30pm; 🖥) Most popular by day, this cafe is good for a relaxed drink; it's set outdoors on a pedestrian street northwest from the square.

ℹ Information

ATMs are on the square and especially on the section of ul 23 Pehoten Shipchenski Polk that runs between the square and ul Petko Stajnov. A **Telephone Centre** is inside the post office.

Internet Centre (ul Otets Paisii; 1 lv per hour; ⏲9am-11pm) Under a video-rental store.

Post Office (ul 23 Pehoten Shipchenski Polk)

Tourist Information Centre (✆62817; ul Iskra 4; ⏲8am-1pm & 2-6pm Mon-Fri) Assists with hotels, excursions and general information about the town.

ℹ Getting There & Away

From the bus and train stations, it's a 10-minute walk (or 2 lv cab ride) northwards to the square. Kazanlâk's **bus station** (✆62 383; ul Kenali) has connections to Sofia (18 lv, 2½ hours, six daily), Veliko Târnovo (17 lv, 2½ hours), Lovech (18 lv, three hours), Plovdiv (13 lv, two hours) and Karlovo. An hourly bus serves Gabrovo (9 lv, 60 minutes to 90 minutes) via Shipka.

Minibuses for Stara Zagora (6 lv, 45 minutes) run half-hourly from just outside the main station. Along the road by the roundabout, town bus 6 (1 lv, 25 minutes, half-hourly) runs to Shipka; the central stop for this bus is at the corner of Knyaz Al Battenberg and Sveti Kiril & Metodii.

The Kazanlâk **train station** (✆662 012; ul Sofronii) serves Sofia (21 lv, 3½ hours, three daily) and Burgas (19 lv, three hours, four daily), via Karlovo (5 lv, one hour, six daily). Trains to or from Plovdiv often involve changing at the Tulovo station, just before Kazanlâk station.

Shipka · Шипка

📞04324 / POP 2300

The tiny mountain village of Shipka, impressively set in the foothills of steep mountains, lies near the famous Shipka Pass. The one good route through the Stara Planina, the pass was where the Russian army and Bulgarian volunteers decisively thwarted an Ottoman counterattack in the 1877 Russo-Turkish War. Aside from the bucolic peacefulness here, the exquisite Shipka Monastery with its golden dome, and the Freedom Monument (dedicated to the soldiers who died fighting the Turks), make Shipka a great day trip from Kazanlâk. While it's easiest done by car, regular minibuses also go.

Shipka is now also world famous for some amazing archaeological remains. In 2004 a 2400-year-old burial shrine for Thracian King Seutus III was uncovered nearby, containing vast amounts of Thracian gold and a unique golden mask, which were promptly sent on triumphant tours of world museums. The tomb's physical remains can be seen, but the gold resides in Sofia.

◉ Sights

Shipka Monastery   MONASTERY
(Shipka Pass) Even before arriving in Shipka, you'll see the splendid, onion-shaped golden domes of the **Nativity Memorial Church** (admission 2 lv, photography permit 5 lv; ⊙8.30am-7pm) glittering from amidst verdure above the village, framed against the mountain. Part of the Shipka Monastery, and also called the Church of St Nikolai, the magnificent structure was built in 1902 to honour soldiers who died at the Shipka Pass battle.

The design is deliberately influenced by Russian architecture, and features five golden domes and 17 church bells that resound for several kilometres. Inside the crypt Russian soldiers who perished are interred, and frescoes depict scenes from Russian history. If it's not cloudy, the church offers marvellous views of the Valley of Roses. To get there, follow the sign labelled Hram Pametnik for 1.2km through the village, or walk 300m up from the restaurant along the Kazanlâk–Gabrovo road.

Shipka Pass
(Mountain) About 13km along a winding road north of Shipka village is the Shipka Pass (1306m). Some 900 steps lead to the top of Mt Stoletov (1326m), dominated by the impressive, 32m-high **Freedom Monument** (admission free; ⊙9am-5pm). It was built in 1934 as a Russo-Turkish War memorial.

The monument pays tribute to the 7000 Russian troops and Bulgarian volunteers who, in August 1877, died while successfully repelling numerous attacks by some 27,000 Turkish soldiers desperately trying to relieve their besieged comrades in Pleven. To reach the pass from Kazanlâk or Shipka, take any bus to Haskovo, Gabrovo or Veliko Târnovo and ask to get off at the Shipka Pass (Shipchensky prokhod).

🛏 Sleeping & Eating

TOP CHOICE **Hotel IT Shipka**   GUESTHOUSE $
(📞0896 755 090; www.shipkaithotel.com; ul Kolyo Adjara 12; s/d/apt40/50/70 lv; ❋🛜🏊) In a quiet residential area 500m east of the square, this friendly, family-run guesthouse has attractive, modern rooms with great views of either the Valley of Roses, or up to the mountain and the gleaming domes of the Russian-style church. The hotel's little restaurant serves home-cooked Bulgarian fare, and there's a small outdoor swimming pool and infrared sauna and steamroom.

Ring ahead and English-speaking owner Ivan will collect you from the bus stop on the main square. He can also arrange local hiking and other outdoor activities.

Hotel-Restaurant Shipka   HOTEL $
(📞2730; Shipka Pass; r 50 lv) The best bet for those wishing to stay atop the pass, the hotel features well-furnished rooms, some quite large. It's 50m up from the car park at the top of the pass.

ℹ Getting There & Away

Bus 6 runs half-hourly between the local bus stop near the Kazanlâk bus station and Shipka village (1 lv, 25 minutes). Alternatively, the hourly bus between Kazanlâk and Gabrovo stops at the village, and Shipka Pass, as do buses to Veliko Târnovo.

Stara Zagora · Стара Загора

📞042 / POP 137,416

Stara Zagora (literally 'old behind the mountain') is a businessy city, and an important national road and rail connection point. However, it also boasts one of Bulgaria's nicest central parks and is a surprisingly stylish place filled with beautiful young people luxuriating in cafes along the pedestrian malls.

Stara Zagora has a few more edifying ancient sites and a museum, but is best known for Zagorka, a leading Bulgarian beer. The brewery is visible when entering from the west (though unfortunately it doesn't conduct tours).

History

Throughout history, the salubrious climate and fertile land here attracted many invaders and settlers, including the Thracians (from the 4th century BC), who called it Beroe. Around 100 AD Romans came, creating the prosperous Ulpia Augusta Trayana. Stara Zagora's strategic location made it important during Byzantine and medieval Bulgarian times.

Unfortunately, rampaging Turks frequently destroyed the city, which was abandoned in the mid-13th century. After eventually regrouping, it saw fierce fighting during the Russo-Turkish War, again being completely demolished by the Turks in 1877. The few surviving remnants of Thracian and Roman ruins are now largely hidden beneath the modern city.

Today, Stara Zagora's very much a living city, and a thriving educational and cultural centre.

◉ Sights

Old City   RUINS
Built on the grid of an ancient Roman city, Stara Zagora has yielded some amazing discoveries. One, a massive **floor mosaic** (4th to 5th centuries AD), is in the post office's eastern entrance. The room relies on natural light: see it on a sunny day.

Roman Theatre   ANCIENT SITE
(ul Mitropolit Metodii Kusev) The 3rd-century AD Roman Theatre, often called the Antique Forum Augusta Trayana, is well preserved and hosts summertime concerts. As wandering around isn't allowed, peer in from the roadside. Other ruins opposite are accessible too.

Neolithic Dwellings Museum   MUSEUM
(☑600 299; admission 3 lv; ⊙9am-noon & 2-5pm Mon-Sat) Two 8000-year-old Stone Age houses are partially preserved in a secure and airtight environment at the Neolithic Dwellings Museum. These modest one-room homes were abandoned after a fire several millennia ago, making them among the Balkans' best preserved neolithic dwellings.

Guided tours (5 lv per group, minimum of five people) are available, and are useful for distinguishing the doors, walls and chimneys from one another. Remains of handmade pottery used by the houses' prehistoric residents exist. The *Neolithic Dwellings: Stara Zagora* booklet (2 lv), available at the museum, offers details.

The museum basement features exhibits of pottery, tools and jewellery from this and other excavations; nothing is labelled in English, so the tour and/or booklet are worthwhile. One of the strangest displays (here or anywhere) is the 6000-year-old headless hedgehog.

To find the museum enter the hospital gates, walk straight down about 100m and up the staircase; the museum is at the top.

Geo Milev House-Museum   MUSEUM
(☑23 450; ul Geo Milev 37; admission 4 lv; ⊙9am-noon & 2-5pm Mon-Sat) Set around a garden, this house-museum contains manuscripts and paintings by locally born Milev (1895–1925). Despite losing an eye in WWI, Milev wrote poetry dealing with social issues, such as *Septemvri*, about the September 1923 agrarian revolution. His politics led Milev's work to be confiscated. Milev was arrested, put on trial, and then kidnapped by the police and murdered.

Contemporary artists also sell their work in the museum, which has a relaxing cafe in the garden courtyard.

Eski Mosque   MOSQUE
(ul Tsar Simeon Veliki) One of Bulgaria's oldest Muslim shrines, the 15th-century Eski Mosque stands along the mall. Although decidedly abandoned, it remains an interesting sight from outside and a special addition to Stara Zagora's skyline.

City Garden   GARDENS
The City Garden is one of Bulgaria's best: clean, with plenty of shade, new seats and functioning fountains.

Park   PARK
This small park that stands between the train station and the central square features a placid pond lined with weeping willows. You can rent paddle boats here.

🛏 Sleeping

TOP
CHOICE **Hotel Merien Palace**   HOTEL $$
(☑611 100; www.merianpalace.com; bul Ruski 8; s/d/apt incl breakfast 95/115/150 lv; P❋🐾❄)

This impressive new place near the train and bus stations has ultra-modern rooms (some fitted for disabled travellers) and uniquely designed 'VIP' apartments with surround-sound stereo. There's a restaurant, a bar and a swimming pool with a spa centre. While the gaudy exterior will not win any style awards, it offers great location and attentive service.

Hotel Zhelezhnik
HOTEL $

(☎629 063; www.zhelezhnikhotel.com; ul Parchevich 1; s/d 40/50 lv; ❄️✳️🛜) This former communist place is less elegant than the others but a good budget option, near the train and bus stations. It has clean, renovated rooms, though these are quite small.

Hotel Ezeroto
HOTEL $$

(☎600 103; www.ezeroto-sz.com; ul Bratya Zhekovi 60; s/d/ste from 46/60/69 lv; 🅿️✳️🛜) Located along the northern shore of a curving pond flanked by willows, the tasteful and well-furnished Ezeroto offers excellent value in its 24 rooms and suites, which are well furnished with all mod cons. There's a restaurant, a bar, and underground parking.

Hotel Vereya
HOTEL $$

(☎919 373; www.hotel-vereya.com; ul Tsar Simeon Veliki 100; d/apt from 70/110 lv; ✳️🛜) A posh place geared to business travellers, the Vereya offers sleek modern rooms with bathtubs while two of the suites have Jacuzzis. It's well situated on the town's liveliest square, the so-called 'Complex', full of cafes and restaurants.

✖ Eating & Drinking

Most restaurants and cafes are on the pedestrian sections of ul Metropolit Metodii Kusev and ul Tsar Simeon Veliki, which cross one block west of the City Garden.

Mehana Chevermeto
BULGARIAN $$

(☎630 331; ul Bratya Zhekovi 60; mains 7-12 lv; ⊙7am-2am; 🛜) With its traditional decor and soothing setting along a leafy pond, this restaurant of the Hotel Ezeroto has a family ambience and great traditional Bulgarian fare.

Restaurant Vereya
INTERNATIONAL $$$

(☎630 666; cnr ul Metropolit Metodii Kusev & ul Tsar Simeon Veliki; mains 11-18 lv; ⊙9am-midnight; 🛜) Close to but not part of the eponymous hotel, the Vereya aims at gourmet status and offers specialities ranging from pizzas to unusual meat dishes, and some innovative

vegetarian options as well. Seating is both indoors and outdoors on the lively square.

Sobieski LABB
BAR

(ul Tsar Simeon Veliki 102; ⊙7am-midnight; 🛜) The most visually alluring cafe on ul Tsar Simeon Veliki is also the first after turning right from the square (from ul Metropolit Metodii Kusev). Its stylish black-and-white decor extends to the outside benches facing the park. Pop and house music are played.

Bacardi Cocktail Bar
BAR

(☎621 096; ul Bratya Zhekovi 60; ⊙7am-11pm; 🛜) This cute cocktail bar attached to the Hotel Ezeroto has a shiny interior and plays candy pop music to complement the sweet cocktails; you can also sit outdoors and gaze out onto the pond.

☆ Entertainment

Geo Milev Drama Theatre
THEATRE

(☎627 331; http://dtgeomilev.com; 28 Mitropolit Metodii Kusev; adults 4-14 lv, concession 4-5 lv) Popular performances are still held behind the City Garden, at the Geo Milev Drama Theatre, which was built in 1914.

ℹ Information

Post Office (ul Sv Knyaz Boris I; ⊙9am-noon & 2-5pm Mon-Fri)

Telephone Centre (⊙6am-midnight) Inside the post office.

ℹ Getting There & Away

From the **bus station** (☎605 349; ul Slavyanski) buses serve Sofia (28 lv, four hours, hourly), Plovdiv (12 lv, 1½ hours), Burgas (21 lv, three hours, every hour), Sliven (10 lv, 1¼ hours, hourly), Varna (34 lv, five hours, five daily), Veliko Târnovo (21 lv, three hours, seven daily) and Ruse (32 lv, five hours, four daily).

For Kazanlâk (5 lv, 45 minutes), catch a bus towards Veliko Târnovo, or get a direct minibus from the bus station. Minibuses from Kazanlâk stop in Stara Zagora's centre. Private companies offer different prices and international destinations such as Athens and Istanbul.

Stara Zagora's **train station** (☎626 752) is located at the southern end of ul Mitropolit Metodii Kusev, a five-minute walk from the bus station. It's on the Sofia–Burgas line. Trains for Sofia (26 lv, four hours) go via Plovdiv (13 lv, two hours). Eastwards, five daily trains serve Burgas (11 lv, two hours). Kazanlâk (9 lv, one hour), Veliko Târnovo (13 lv, three hours) and Ruse (30 lv, six hours); note that changing trains at Tulovo station (about 45 minutes east of Stara Zagora) is often required. There are also three daily services to Varna (20 lv, five hours).

Rila Bureau (📋 622 724), at the train station, sells advance tickets for domestic trains and tickets for all international services.

Sliven
Сливен

📋044 / POP 101.300

Sitting in a sort of bowl around rocky hills of up to 1000m in height, Sliven is well known historically for its role in the 19th-century revolution. While the most famous nearby sight (the so-called 'Blue Rocks') is somewhat lacklustre, Sliven is still a laid-back and authentic small city with unique museums and good accommodation.

Thracians, Romans and Greeks all settled in the Sliven area, but little evidence of their civilisations remains. Sliven's modern history is inextricably linked to the *haidouks,* the anti-Turkish rebels who lived in the rocky hills nearby from the early 18th to the mid-19th centuries. Eventually uniting under Hadzhi Dimitâr and the revered Vasil Levski, they rose up successfully against their Turkish overlords.

Despite the plenitude of communist concrete and decrepit apartment blocks, Sliven has friendly citizens and a foreign presence appropriate to its martial past – Western military contingents from the nearby NATO training base, who sometimes liven up local restaurants and bars.

Sliven's main square, pl Hadzhi Dimitâr, has most services, including ATMs and the post office/telephone centre. The appealing **Deboya Church** is south of it.

⊙ Sights & Activities

Blue Rocks   NATURAL ATTRACTION
(chairlift one way/return 5/10 lv; ⊙ chairlift 8.30am-5.30pm Tue-Sun, 12.30-5.30pm Mon) Within the folds of these magnificent rocks once hid the *haidouks,* bedevilling the Turks and making armed mischief. However, these craggy peaks a few kilometres out of town are not exactly blue, and not particularly different from other craggy peaks encountered around the world, though the air is crisp and clean and the views from above are marvellous.

A chairlift can get you up there, or you can walk (one to 1½ hours) up the hill following the chairlift. From the top of the chairlift, a path leads down about 300m to the main road; cross it and proceed 500m through the woods to Hizha Poveda, which serves drinks and meals.

To reach the chairlift from Sliven, catch minibus 13 outside the train station or Hotel Sliven. Alternatively, walk about 1km uphill from the end of the route for trolleybus 18

Sliven

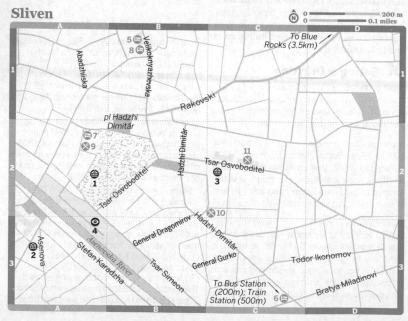

or 20 from the centre. Taxis are about 6 lv one way.

Hadzhi Dimitâr Museum MUSEUM
(☏622 496; ul Asenova 2; admission 2 lv; ⊙9am-noon & 2-5pm Mon-Fri) This museum dedicated to the 19th-century rebel movement leader is set in a lovely building and features several rooms of furniture (including antique weaving equipment) set around a cobblestone courtyard.

History Museum MUSEUM
(Museum; ☏622 495; ul Tsar Osvoboditel 18; admission 2 lv; ⊙9am-noon & 2-5pm Mon-Sat) Along the mall, the History Museum occupies a grand old building of three floors that house archaeological and ethnological items such as coins, weapons and books. The best exhibits concern the Turkish struggle.

FREE Galeriya Dimitâr Dobrovich ART GALLERY
(☏622 083; ul Tsar Osvoboditel 13; admission free; ⊙9am-12.45pm & 2-4.45pm Mon-Sat) Galeriya Dimitâr Dobrovich is signposted from the centre as 'Sirak Skirnik'. This art gallery in the park displays paintings by 19th- and 20th-century Bulgarian artists, including many by its namesake, Sliven-born painter Dimitâr Dobrovich. Among the works, which display French and Italian influences, are portraits of local luminaries and ordinary people, plus impressionistic landscapes (including an evocative portrayal of Veliko Târnovo).

Sliven

⊙ Sights

⊜ Sleeping

⊗ Eating

The gallery's most intriguing section, however, belongs to the Museum of Christian Art on the lower floor, which has many 18th- and 19th- century icons, some from the Tryavna school of icon painting. Works range from monumental wall icons to unique small pieces, the most unusual being an almost Oriental icon of the Virgin Mary surrounded by roses (1836).

Obshtinski Pazar (Municipal Market) OPEN MARKET
Shop with the locals at this large warren of shops, which sells everything from fruits and vegetables to clothes and electronics supplies. The market's entrance is located opposite ul Tsar Simeon where it meets the park's southwestern edge.

Hiking
From the oft-closed information centre set along the road to the Blue Rocks chairlift, marked trails head through the hills to the signposted caves used by the *haidouks*. Information (in English) about the trails is included in a mapless leaflet (1.50 lv), available at the chairlift.

For more general information about local hikes, consult the local **National Park Authority** (☏22 926; dpp.skamani@sl.bia-bg.com).

⊨ Sleeping

Hotel Ricas HOTEL $
(☏510 800; www.ricas.eu; cnr bul Hadzi Dimitar & bul Brayya Miladinovi 23; s/d/tr 40/50/60; ✳☎) This giant glassy structure 10 minutes by foot from the square has the town's poshest rooms, though the attached lounge-bar is rather Vegas and even the elevator floor is glittery. But it's undeniably great value, with big, well-decorated rooms and gleaming baths.

Hotel Imperia HOTEL $
(☏667 599; www.hotelimperia.net; ul Panaiot Hitov; s/d/apt 40/50/60 lv; P✳☎) The price drop at this welcoming place some 3km from Sliven's centre (and about 1km from the chairlift) makes it a great find. The Imperia has sophisticated, colourful rooms with individual character and decor, along with exemplary bathrooms. With a swimming pool and tennis courts, it's a good option for those with transport and concentrating on Sliven's outdoor attractions.

Hotel Toma GUESTHOUSE $
(☏623 333; www.hoteltoma.com; ul Velikoknyazhevska 27; d incl breakfast 50-60 lv; ✳@☎) Once an 18th-century residence, the Toma

is a small guesthouse (with a big and sometimes loud adjoining restaurant) up on a side street north of the square. The decor ranges from animal-trophy to ornate woodcarvings. Rooms on the upper floor are slightly more spacious than the ground-floor ones, but bathrooms are cramped in both cases.

Try for room 4, which has an ornate painted cupola and 18th-century handcarved wooden ceiling.

Hotel National Palace
BUSINESS HOTEL $$
(☏662 929; www.nationalpalace.bg; ul Velikoknyazhevska 29; s/d/ste/apt from 68/90/100/135 lv; ✸☎) Sliven's best business hotel, this gleaming place just north of the square offers classy, clean rooms with all expected amenities. Nice touches include contemporary art in the hallways and rainbow-hued floor lighting opposite the elevators. The well-stocked restaurant, Pri Fabrikadzhiyata, in a courtyard setting is another plus.

Hotel Sliven
HOTEL $
(☏624 0446; www.hotel.sliven.net; pl Hadzhi Dimitâr; s/d/tr 20/34/45 lv; ✸☎) This (still unrenovated) communist throwback rises high on the central skyline, and looms high in the centre of town and offers uninspiring but clean rooms. The upstairs bar works weekends only. Air conditioning is 10 lv extra.

✕ Eating

TOP CHOICE Pri Hadjiyata
BULGARIAN $$
(☏0878 553 222; ul Yordan Kyuvliev 11; mains 8-13 lv; ☎) This festive local favourite set around a leafy courtyard, with indoor seating for winter, does excellent Bulgarian foods prepared and served in the traditional way. *Satch,* ribs, and river fish deserve special recommendations. The friendly owner, Nasko, can advise on daily specials and wine combinations.

Restaurant Maki
BULGARIAN $$
(ul Tsar Osvoboditel; mains 4-8 lv; ☎) A large and popular restaurant just off the square, this place has a huge outdoor section for summer dining, though the interior is somewhat bland. It does good grills and salads, among other fare.

Deboya Restaurant
BULGARIAN $$
(☏625 427; pl Hadzhi Dimitâr; mains 5-7 lv; ⏱10am-midnight; ☎) The fairly cavernous Deboya is very central, and a popular place for pizza and traditional Bulgarian dishes.

Restaurant Toma
BULGARIAN $$
(☏0886 836 263; ul Velikoknyazhevska 27; mains 5-9 lv) This lively *mehana* outside the Hotel Toma has a typically large menu of traditional Bulgarian specialities. The live Bulgarian music performed nightly often caters to special events, which can get loud but end by 12.30am. When busy service can be a bit gruff.

Pri Fabrikadzhiyata
BULGARIAN $$
(☏662 929; ul K Irecheck 14; mains 8-14 lv; ☎) With a curious name that literally means 'at the manufacturer's place', this somewhat posh restaurant in the courtyard of the Hotel National Palace serves an extensive range of good Bulgarian dishes and features bland live pop music.

There's seating indoors, outdoors and (when there's enough of a crowd) in an atmospheric 18th-century house next door. The restaurant's prices are relatively steep, though the food is good, with the roast lamb being downright succulent.

ℹ Getting There & Away

From the small **bus station** (☏662 629; ul Hadzhi Dimitâr), just past the massive Bila Supermarket, many daily buses and minibuses go to Stara Zagora (11 lv, one hour) and Plovdiv (19 lv, three hours). Regular buses serve Veliko Târnovo (16 lv, two hours, eight daily) and Sofia (29 lv, five hours, 10 daily). Two daily buses serve Kazanlâk (13 lv, one hour), and one serves Ruse (26 lv, four hours).

Sliven's **train station** (☏622 614) is on the Sofia–Burgas line. Trains serve Sofia (35 lv, 5½ hours, three daily), Burgas (10 lv, 1½ hours, seven daily), Kazanlâk (12 lv, two hours, six daily), Stara Zagora (12 lv, two hours, five daily), Plovdiv (21 lv, four hours, three daily), Ruse (41 lv, seven hours, three daily) and Varna (14 lv, four hours, three daily).

Black Sea Coast

Best Places to Eat

» Tanasi (p417)

» Roma (p398)

» Francis Drake (p422)

» Panorama (p403)

» Restaurant Chaika (p404)

Best Places to Stay

» Art Hotel (p402)

» Hotel California (p397)

» Hotel Lalov Egrek (p406)

Why Go?

Bulgaria's long Black Sea coastline is the country's summertime playground, attracting tourists from across Europe and beyond, as well as Bulgarians themselves. The big, purpose-built resorts here are becoming serious rivals to those of Spain and Greece, while independent travellers will find plenty to explore away from the parasols and jet skis. Sparsely populated sandy beaches to the far south and north, the bird-filled Burgas Lakes and picturesque ancient towns such as Nesebâr and Sozopol are rewarding destinations, and the 'maritime capital' of Varna is one of Bulgaria's most vibrant cities, famous for its summer festival and nightlife as well as its many museums and galleries. Those with their own transport will have even greater choice, with the wild Strandzha Nature Park in the south and the picturesque Kaliakra Cape and Dobrudzha region in the north theirs to discover.

When to Go
Burgas

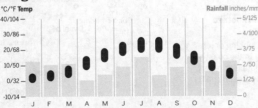

Apr & May Spring on the coast is pleasantly warm and relaxed, with fewer tourists around.

Jun–Aug Reliably hot, dry, sunny days in summer bring the crowds to the beaches.

Nov–Mar Winters are chilly, resort hotels close for the season, but it's a good time for birdwatching.

Black Sea Coast Highlights

1 Enjoying **Sozopol**'s (p400) sandy beaches and exploring the cobbled lanes of the lovely old town

2 Visiting Queen Marie's seaside palace and gardens in **Balchik** (p421)

3 Enjoying the long, sandy beach, great nightlife and excellent museums in **Varna** (p412)

4 Taking in the marvellous sight of **Nesebâr's** (p407) medieval churches

5 Walking in the diverse landscapes of **Strandzha Nature Park** (p406)

6 Taking a boat trip or following hiking trails though the **Ropotamo Nature Reserve** (p404)

7 Getting away from it all and soaking up the sun in remote **Sinemorets** (p406)

8 Lazing on the uncrowded city beach in **Burgas** (p395) or taking a walk through the seaside park

9 Paddling in the shallow sea at laid-back **Primorsko** (p404)

10 Clubbing or jet skiing in the coast's most popular resort, **Sunny Beach** (p411)

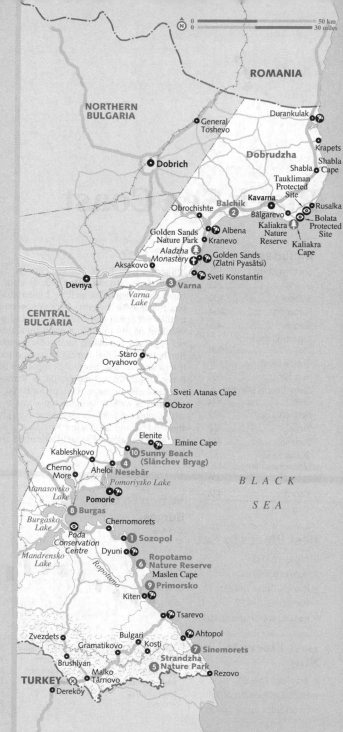

SOUTHERN COAST

Burgas   Бургас

♪056 / POP 212,000

For most visitors, the port city of Burgas (sometimes written as 'Bourgas') is no more than a transit point for the more obviously appealing resorts and historic towns further up and down the coast. If you do decide to stop over, you'll find a lively, well-kept city with a neat, pedestrianised centre, a long, uncrowded beach and some interesting museums. A clutch of reasonably priced hotels, as well as some decent restaurants, makes it a practical base for exploring the southern coast, too.

Almost everything of interest in Burgas is within the compact city centre. The train station and the main Yug bus station are both located just south of the main pedestrian thoroughfare, ul Aleksandrovska, which runs northwards, via pl Troikata, to bul San Stefano. A few blocks up from the stations, another pedestrian street, bul Aleko Bogoridi, heads eastwards towards Maritime Park.

Nature lovers also come to Burgas for the four lakes just outside the city, which are havens for abundant bird life.

History

Greek colonists from Apollonia (modern-day Sozopol) expanded their territory into the Burgas region as far back as the 6th century BC. Later, the Romans came along and Emperor Vespasian founded a city here, named Deultum, in the 1st century AD. The name Burgas first appeared on maps in the 17th century, when fisher folk from the wider region settled here. The city grew quickly after the completion of the railway from Plovdiv (1890) and the development of the port (1903). Today it's a major industrial and commercial centre, home to the largest oil refinery in the Balkans.

◉ Sights

Archaeological Museum   MUSEUM
(bul Aleko Bogoridi 21; adult/student 4/2 lv; ⊙10am-6pm Mon-Sat) This small museum houses a diverting collection of local finds, including neolithic flint tools, a wooden canoe from the 5th century BC, Greek statuary and the remarkably well-preserved wooden coffin of a Thracian chieftain.

Natural History Museum   MUSEUM
(ul Konstantin Fotinov 20; adult/student 4/2 lv; ⊙10am-6pm Mon-Sat) Old-fashioned but informative displays on local flora, fauna and geology are on view here. Exhibits of rocks, seashells, butterflies and beetles occupy the ground floor, while upstairs there's a collection of stuffed birds and animals.

Ethnographical Museum   MUSEUM
(ul Slavyanska 69; adult/student 4/2 lv; ⊙10am-6pm Mon-Sat) Regional folk costumes, jewellery and furniture are on show at this museum, as well as displays covering the local weaving and fishing industries. Everything is labelled in Bulgarian.

Sv Cyril & Methodius Cathedral   CHURCH
(ul Vûzhrazhdane; ⊙8am-5pm) Completed in 1907, the city's main church boasts an especially fine, intricately carved iconostasis and colourful murals.

Soviet Army Monument   MONUMENT
(pl Troikata) Standing sentinel over pl Troikata is this towering Red Army memorial. Comprising a column surmounted by a saluting Russian soldier and figurative panels, it remains a major city focal point.

Maritime Park   PARK
(◳8, 12) Stretching lazily along the Black Sea coast and filled with manicured flower beds, fountains, busts of Bulgarian worthies, abstract sculptures and cafes, this park is the pride of Burgas. There are spectacular views over the sea from the terraces, and steps lead down from here towards the beach.

Beach   BEACH
(◳8, 12) Although it can't compare with beaches at the nearby resorts, Burgas beach still attracts plenty of locals on a hot

---

LIFE'S A BEACH

Every day during summer, lifeguards work between 8am and 6pm at the resorts and popular beaches; they usually rescue a few tourists who ignore the warnings and don't swim between the flags. It is extremely important to pay attention to these warnings on the Black Sea – there are often very strong currents at play and there are fatalities every year.

Topless bathing is acceptable at the major resorts, but less so elsewhere.

summer day. It's a bit grubby at the southern end, with its long concrete pier used as a diving platform by teenage boys and a fishing station by old men, but further on there are beach bars and restaurants.

★ Festivals & Events

Burgas Sand Sculpture Festival
(www.sandfestburgas.com; ⏰early Jul) International artists create fantastic sand sculptures on Burgas beach each July, following

Burgas

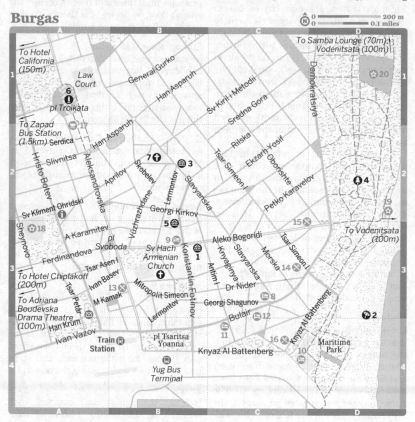

BLACK SEA COAST BURGAS

Burgas

◉ Sights

1 Archaeological Museum	B3
2 Beach	D3
3 Ethnographical Museum	B2
4 Maritime Park	D2
5 Natural History Museum	B3
6 Soviet Army Monument	A1
7 Sv Cyril & Methodius Cathedral	B2

⊜ Sleeping

8 Burgas Hostel	C3
9 Fotinov Guest House	B3
10 Grand Hotel Primoretz	C4
11 Hotel Bulair	C4
12 Hotel Luxor	C3

⊗ Eating

13 BMS	B3
14 London Pub & Restaurant	C3
15 Roma	C3
16 Sorrento	C4

⊜ Drinking

17 China Tea House	A2

✪ Entertainment

18 Burgas Opera House	A3
19 Sea Casino Cultural Centre	D2
20 Summer Theatre	D1

TOP BEACHES FOR...

» Water sports: Albena

» Urban swimming: Varna

» Safe, shallow water: Primorsko

» 24-hour fun: Sunny Beach (Slânchev Bryag)

» A low-key hideaway: Sinemorets

different themes each year. The works usually stay on show until September.

International Folklore Festival
TRADITIONAL MUSIC

(☺late Aug) Burgas' main festival, with shows during the evening at the Summer Theatre in Maritime Park and various locations around the city centre.

Spirit of Burgas Festival
LIVE MUSIC

(www.spiritofburgas.com; ☺Aug) One of the biggest music events in Bulgaria, attracting top national and international rock, jazz, hip-hop and experimental acts and DJs. Takes place on the beach for a few days in early to mid-August.

Emil Chakarov Music Festival
CLASSICAL MUSIC

(☺early Jul) Internationally attended classical-music festival.

Burgas Sea Song Festival
LIVE MUSIC

(☺Jul & Aug) Showcases up-and-coming popular-music acts from around the country and offers new talents a chance to perform. Held in Maritime Park.

Flora Flower Exhibition

(☺Apr & Sep) The Black Sea coast's biannual flower show.

🛏 Sleeping

Few foreign tourists hang around in Burgas for longer than it takes to get the next bus or train out again, but there's a good choice of mostly midrange hotels. Private rooms are another option – look out for pensioners carrying signs at the train station.

TOP CHOICE Hotel California
BOUTIQUE HOTEL $$

(☑531 000; www.burgashotel.com; ul Lyuben Karavelov 36; s/d 60/70 lv; P⊝✴🛜; 🖵4) This appealing boutique hotel on a quiet side street about five minutes' walk west of the city cen-

tre is a winner, with large rooms featuring colourful wall prints and especially soft mattresses. Guests get a 20% reduction in the excellent restaurant.

Hotel Chiplakoff
BOUTIQUE HOTEL $$

(☑829 325; www.chiplakoff.com; ul Ferdinandova 88; s/d 50/60 lv; P✴@) A 10-minute walk west of the centre, this hotel occupies an attractively restored mansion, designed by the same architect who built the city's grand train station. Rooms are large and contemporary in style, and the original spiral staircases have been retained; there's no lift, however. There's a popular pizza restaurant downstairs.

Grand Hotel Primoretz
LUXURY HOTEL $$$

(☑812 345; www.hotelprimoretz.bg; ul Knyaz Al Battenberg 2; s/d/ste from 216/236/296 lv; P⊝✴🛜🏊; 🖵12) This huge, five-star complex at the southern end of the city beach looks out of scale in Burgas, but its excellent facilities include a spa and indoor and outdoor pools. Sea views cost a little extra, as does the wi-fi and parking, which seems a bit cheeky at these prices.

Fotinov Guest House
HOTEL $$

(☑0878 974 703; www.hotelfotinov.com; ul Konstantin Fotinov 22; s/d 72/82 lv; ✴🛜) Conveniently located right in the city centre, with a selection of brightly coloured rooms featuring fridges, kettles and cable TV. The multilingual staff are friendly and helpful, and there's even a small sauna.

Hotel Bulair
HOTEL $

(☑844 389; www.hotelbulair.com; ul Bulair 7; r 55 lv; P✴🛜; 🖵12) In a converted town house on a busy road, the 14-room Bulair is very handy for the bus and train stations.

HOTEL PRICES

All accommodation prices listed in this chapter (unless stated otherwise) are what you should expect to pay during the high season (July and August). During the shoulder season (May, June, September and October), room prices drop by up to 50%, so along with the continually good weather and greatly reduced crowds, this is the best time to visit. Note that many hotels and restaurants in the resort towns only open for the summer season.

BLACK SEA COAST BURGAS

Hotel Luxor HOTEL $$

(☎847 670; www.luxor-bs.com; ul Bulair 27; s/d 65/75 lv; P❋@; ▯12) This vaguely Egyptian-inspired place has comfortable, three-star rooms and an Italian restaurant.

Burgas Hostel HOSTEL $

(☎825 854; hostelburgas@gmail.com; ul Slavyanska 14; dm incl breakfast 20 lv; @; ▯12) The only hostel in town didn't bother with a fancy name. It sports five- and eight-bed dorms, plus a small lounge and kitchen.

🍴 Eating & Drinking

Outlets along bul Aleko Bogoridi sell pizza, kebabs and ice cream, and there are several summertime bars along the beach, most of which also serve food.

Roma ITALIAN $$

(☎825 467; bul Aleko Bogoridi 60; mains 6-20 lv; ▯8) This trendy Italian place has a wide menu, ranging from simple pasta and risotto dishes (5 to 6 lv) up to pricier options such as grilled sea bass (20 lv). Steaks, grills and various fish dishes are available. Reservations are advisable in the evenings.

Vodenitsata BULGARIAN $

(Water Mill; ☎0899174715; mains from 3 lv; ◷10am-2am; ▯12) Standing on the seafront overlooking the beach, this is a traditional wood-cabin affair, which is always packed out with locals. Specialities include grilled fish, barbecues, steaks and salads.

London Pub & Restaurant BRITISH $$

(ul Tsar Simeon 4a; mains 8-20 lv; ◷10am-1am; 🕾; ▯12) Caters to homesick British expats and visitors. Come here for all-day English breakfasts, as well as mixed grills and steak-and-onion pie. The kitchen closes at 9pm, but drinks are served until 1am, and there's karaoke on Friday evening.

BMS CAFETERIA $

(ul Aleksandrovska 20; mains 3-6 lv; ◷8am-10pm) Cheap, self-service, cafeteria-style chain offering simple but filling fare such as sausages, salads and stews. There are some outdoor tables and it also serves beer.

Sorrento ITALIAN $$

(ul Knyaz Al Battenberg 14; mains 7-20 lv; ▯8) Set in the leafy courtyard of a grand century-old house, Sorrento is a good choice for pizza, pasta, risotto and salads. It also has an extensive wine list.

TOP CHOICE China Tea House TEAHOUSE

(pl Troikata 4; tea from 2 lv; ◷8.30am-10pm Mon-Fri, 11am-10pm Sat; 🕾) Oil paintings by local artists decorate this chilled-out little teahouse, which offers a big menu of black, green and herbal teas, as well as a few freshly prepared vegetarian dishes.

Samba Lounge BAR

(◷8am-midnight) One of the more attractive beach bars, set on decking over the sand and surrounded by potted flowers. It's a pleasant spot just to relax with a beer (2 lv) and it also serves light meals like salads and soups throughout the day.

☆ Entertainment

In summer, nightclubs and bars materialise among the trees of Maritime Park.

Alibi CLUB

(☎0897962262; Maritime Park; ◷11pm-late) Among the more reliable summertime clubs, with a varied program including 'retro nights', dance and Latino music.

Summer Theatre THEATRE

(Maritime Park) Live music, dance and drama performances often take place here.

Sea Casino Cultural Centre CULTURAL BUILDING

(Maritime Park) The city's renovated 1930s casino is now a cultural centre, hosting a varied program of concerts and exhibitions.

Adriana Boudevska Drama Theatre THEATRE

(☎842 266; ul Tsar Asen I 36A) This stylish venue stages classic and contemporary Bulgarian drama.

Burgas Opera House OPERA

(☎840 762; www.operabourgas.com; ul Sv Kliment Ohridski 2) A regular program of opera, ballet and concerts is held at the city's opera house.

ℹ Information

Numerous banks with ATMs can be found along ul Aleksandrovska and ul Aleko Bogorid, including **Unicredit Bulbank** (ul Aleksandrovska), **Central Cooperative Bank** (ul Aleksandrovska) and **Raiffeisen Bank** (ul Ferdinandova).

Tourist information centre (☎825 772; www. tic.burgas.bg; ul Hristo Botev; ◷8.30am-5.30pm Mon-Fri; ▯12) At the entrance to the underpass below ul Hristo Botev, the city's tourist office has English-speaking staff and plenty of brochures.

❶ Getting There & Away

Air

Bulgaria Air links **Burgas Airport** (☎870 248; www.bourgas-airport.com; 📮15), 10km north-east of town, with Sofia three times every day (April to October). In summer, **Wizz Air** (www.wizzair.com) connects Burgas with London Luton, Budapest, Prague and Warsaw. Other carriers fly to destinations in Germany and Russia.

Bus

Yug bus station (cnr ul Aleksandrovska & ul Bulair), outside the train station at the southern end of ul Aleksandrovska, is where most travellers will arrive or leave. There are regular buses to coastal destinations. Departures are less frequent outside summer.

Sozopol (4.50 lv, 40 minutes, every 30 minutes)

Nesebâr (6 lv, 40 minutes, every 30 to 40 minutes)

Sunny Beach (Slânchev Bryag; 6 lv, 45 minutes, every 30 to 40 minutes)

Primorsko (7 lv, one hour, every 30 minutes)

Kiten (8 lv, one hour, every one to 1½ hours)

Tsarevo (9 lv, two hours, several daily)

Pomorie (Поморие Център; 3 lv, 25 minutes, every one to 1½ hours)

Sinemorets (13 lv, 2½ to three hours, one daily)

Sofia (30 lv, seven to eight hours, several daily)

Plovdiv (17 lv, four hours, several daily)

Varna (14 lv, two hours, every 30 to 40 minutes)

A number of agencies around Yug bus station, including **Union-Ivkoni** (☎840 986), run coaches to Istanbul each day (55 lv, seven hours). **Nışıklı Turızm** (☎841 261; ul Bulair) has several daily departures (55 to 60 lv) from outside its office. Union-Ivkoni also runs daily buses to destinations in Greece, including Thessaloniki (80 lv, 13 hours).

From the less convenient **Zapad bus station** (☎20 521; ul Maritsa 2), 2km northwest of pl Troikata, buses leave for Malko Târnovo (7.50 lv, three hours, four or five daily) in the Strandzha Nature Park and Veliko Târnovo (25 lv, four hours, three daily). Take city bus 4 from Yug bus station to get there.

Train

The historic **train station** (ul Ivan Vazov) was built in 1902. Through the **ticket windows** (◷8am-6pm) on the right you can buy advance tickets for domestic and international services, while same-day tickets can be bought at the **windows** (◷24hr) on the left. The **left-luggage office** (train station; ◷6am-10.45pm) is outside the station.

Sofia (23.10 lv, seven to eight hours, six daily)

Plovdiv (19 lv, five to six hours, seven daily)

Kazanlâk (14.40 lv, three hours, two daily)

Stara Zagora (15.80 lv, three hours, four daily)

Sliven (9.50 lv, 1 hour 40 minutes, five daily)

International tickets are also available at the **Rila Bureau** (◷8am-5.30pm Mon-Thu, 8am-4pm Fri, 8am-3.30pm Sat) inside the station.

❶ Getting Around

TS Travel (☎0888622658, 845 060; www.tstravel.net; ul Bulair 1; ◷9am-6pm Mon-Fri, to 2pm Sat & Sun; 📮12) This English-speaking car-rental agency offers various models, from 80 lv per day in summer, including unlimited kilometres and insurance.

Burgas Lakes

Бургаски Езера

The four lakes surrounding Burgas are Pomoriysko (or Pomorie), Atanasovsko, Mandrensko (Mandra) and Burgasko (Burgas). These are collectively known as the Burgas Lakes. Comprising over 9500 hectares, it's the largest wetland system in Bulgaria, and is home to some 255 bird species, representing around 67% of the country's total.

The **Poda Conservation Centre** (☎056-500 560; www.bspb-poda.de; adult/student 3.60/1.20 lv; ◷8am-6pm) opened in 1998 under the auspices of the Bulgarian Society for the Protection of Birds (BSPB) and is an admirable effort at wildlife conservation so close to the urban sprawl of Burgas.

In the **Poda Protected Area**, which surrounds the centre, bird lovers will delight in spotting numerous scarce and endangered birds, including Dalmatian pelicans, five species of herons, avocets, little terns and red-breasted geese. Most birds can be seen year-round, while others are migratory, stopping over only to breed or see out the winter. The 15 kinds of mammal include Europe's smallest native species, the pygmy shrew. Several reptile species, such as the Balkan green lizard, can also be seen.

To really admire the bird life up close, go on a walk along the signposted, 2.5km **nature trail** (admission up to 6 people 10 lv). It takes about three hours to complete and there's an explanatory leaflet in English available from the centre. It's recommended that you get a guide (English- or German-speaking), which will cost an extra 20 lv per group.

East of Burgas, the 28-sq-km **Burgasko Lake** (or Lake Vaya) is the largest sea lake in Bulgaria. It is home to pelicans throughout the year, but the best time to see them is between April and October. A 1½-hour **boat trip** around this lake costs about 5 lv per person, but a minimum of six passengers is required. A guide is recommended and costs extra. For details, contact the **conservation office** (☎056-500 560) in Burgas, or the Poda Conservation Centre. More information is available at www.burgaslakes.org.

The conservation centre is poorly signposted on the left, about 8km south of Burgas on the road to Sozopol. It's accessible by taxi (about 10 lv one way), or catch bus 15 from Yug bus station (p399).

Sozopol · Созопол

☎0550 / POP 5000

Ancient Sozopol, with its charming old town of meandering cobbled streets and pretty wooden houses huddled together on a narrow peninsula, is one of the coast's real highlights. With two superb beaches, a genial atmosphere, plentiful accommodation

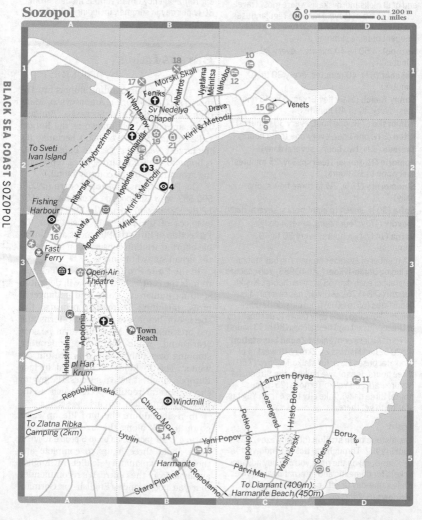

Sozopol

0 — 200 m
0 — 0.1 miles

and good transport links, it has long been a popular seaside resort and makes an excellent base for exploring the area. Although not quite as crowded as Nesebâr, it is becoming ever more popular with international visitors. There's a lively cultural scene, too, with plenty of free concerts and other events in summer.

The new town, or 'Harmanite' as it's known, lies south of the tiny bus station. The best beach is in this part of town, but otherwise, it's mainly modern hotels and residential areas.

History

Sozopol is the oldest settlement on the Bulgarian Black Sea coast, founded in an area belonging to the Thracian Skyrmianoi tribe in 611 BC by Greek colonists from Miletus, who called their home Apollonia Pontica, in honour of the god Apollo. One of these early settlers was the philosopher and astronomer Anaximander.

Apollonia, ruled by an elected Council of Archons, flourished as a major trading hub, but in 72 BC the town was sacked and mostly destroyed. Its famous bronze statue of Apollo was taken to Rome as booty.

Under the Byzantine Empire, and renamed Sozopolis (City of Salvation), the town was an important religious centre. It fell to Khan Tervel in 705, was recaptured by the Byzantines in 759 and finally reverted to the First Bulgarian Empire (681–1018) in 969. Under Turkish rule, ship building and fishing were mainstays of the economy.

During the communist era, the town was promoted as a holiday resort, although not until the 1990s did it really take off, with Russians and Germans being among the more numerous foreign visitors.

◉ Sights

The town's two beaches are attractive, though waves can be quite high. The 1km-long **Harmanite Beach** is wide and clean and offers a water slide, paddle boats, volleyball nets and beach bars. At the southern end, incongruously, archaeological excavations have uncovered stone sarcophagi on the site of the ancient **Apollonia necropolis**. The **Town Beach** (or Northern Beach) is another pleasant curve of sand, but it's smaller, gets *very* crowded, and doesn't offer the same number of beachside cafes, restaurants and bars.

Archaeological Museum MUSEUM
(ul Han Krum 2; admission 4 lv; ◷9am-6pm, closed Sat & Sun winter) Housed in a drab concrete box near the port, this museum has a small collection of local finds. The high-quality imported Athenian ceramics, dating from the 5th century BC, give an indication of the wealth and sophistication of Apollonia's classical-era citizens, and there are lots of anchors and amphorae dredged up from ancient shipwrecks.

Southern Fortress Wall & Tower Museum ANCIENT SITE
(ul Milet 40; adult/student 4/3 lv; ◷9.30am-8pm Jul & Aug, 9.30am-5pm May, Jun, Sep & Oct) The reconstructed walls and walkways along the

BLACK SEA COAST SOZOPOL

Sozopol

rocky coastline, and a 4th-century BC well that was once part of a temple to Aphrodite here are free to explore – the few, mostly empty, rooms you get to see for your four leva are something of an anticlimax.

Church of Sveta Bogoroditsa
CHURCH

(ul Anaksimandâr 13; admission 1 lv; ☺10am-1pm & 2-6pm) This 15th-century church was built below street level, as required at the time by the Ottoman rulers. Set in a courtyard with a giant fig tree, it is one of the most picturesque in town, with an exquisite wooden iconostasis and a pulpit carved with bunches of grapes.

Church of Sveti Georgi
CHURCH

(ul Apolonia; ☺9am-1pm & 3-8pm Mon-Sat, 7am-1pm & 3-8pm Sun) This is another attractive church, with a fine painting of St George and the Dragon over the entrance and an impressive 19th-century iconostasis. The custodians here are rather keen to enforce the dress code (no shorts).

Sveti Zossim Chapel
CHURCH

(☺4.30-9pm) This small working church in the shady gardens opposite the bus station was built in 1837, on the foundations of a much older structure. Dedicated to the the patron saint of sailors, it houses several icons.

 ## Activities

Sailing Boats
SAILING

(Sozopol Harbour) Sailing boats moored in the port offer cruises around the peninsula every evening in summer (adult/child 10/6 lv).

Aqua Sub
DIVING

(☎0899408020; www.aqua-sub.com; ul Odessa 22) Aqua Sub offers one/two beginner dives from 80/140 lv, as well as a range of specialist dives such as wreck dives (130 lv) and PADI courses. It also has a kiosk at the fishing harbour in the old town.

Festivals & Events

Live music, dancing and other shows are often staged through the summer at the modern open-air **theatre** near the Archaeological Museum.

Apollonia Arts Festival
MUSIC, ART

(www.apollonia.bg) Held in the first half of September, this is the highlight of Sozopol's cultural calendar, featuring jazz, pop and alternative music at various venues in the old and new towns, as well as art exhibitions.

Sleeping

Sozopol has countless private homes offering rooms. Look for signs along Republikanska in the new town and pretty much anywhere in the old town.

TOP CHOICE Art Hotel
HOTEL $$

(☎24 081; www.arthotel-sbh.com; ul Kiril & Metodii 72; d Jul-Sep 75 lv, Oct-Jun from 40 lv; ❄@☎) This peaceful old-town house, belonging to the Union of Bulgarian Artists, is located within a walled courtyard towards the tip of the peninsula, away from the crowds. It has a small selection of bright and comfortable rooms with balconies, most with sea views, and breakfast is served on the terraces directly over the sea.

Hotel Villa List
HOTEL $$

(☎22 235; www.hotellist-bg.com; ul Yani Popov 5; s/d from 65/92 lv; ❄@☎) With a superb setting just off the town beach, big rooms with balconies and an outdoor pool with a view over the sea, Villa List is understandably very popular, and frequently fully booked in summer. There's even a 'nude terrace' for that all-over tan.

Hotel Diamanti
HOTEL $$

(☎22 640; www.hoteldiamanti.com; ul Morski Skali; d/apt 80/120 lv; ☺❄☎) Old-town Diamanti has a variety of rooms, some with sea views, including apartments with kitchenettes; larger apartments are available in a second building nearby. There's also a terrace restaurant, with live music in summer.

Doctor's House
HOTEL $$

(☎22 731; www.doctorshousesozopol.com; ul Morski Skali 35; r 55-70 lv, apt 100-140 lv; ❄) Perched over the sea at the northern tip of the peninsula, the Doctor's House has basic twin-bedded rooms and larger apartments, sleeping up to four people. All rooms have balconies and sea views. It has a restaurant and even its own chapel.

Sasha Khristov's Private Rooms
PENSION $

(☎23 434; ul Venets 17; s/d 20/30 lv) This lovely family home in the old town faces the art gallery at the end of the Sozopol peninsula. It comprises good-sized rooms and a large apartment. Book ahead in summer.

Ani Dimitrova's Rooms
PENSION $$

(☎0886804915, 22 753; ul Anaksimandâr 12a; r 50-100 lv; ❄☎) There are 12 large, clean rooms, sleeping up to four people, in this comfortable home run by the friendly, German-speaking Ani, all with TVs, fridges and private bathrooms. Look for the hairdresser's sign reading 'Friseur Ani'.

Hotel Anaxemander
HOTEL $$

(☎0882683361; www.hotel-anaxemander.com; ul Odessa 38; d/tr/apt 66/80/100 lv; � Apr-Sep; P✱) On a rocky promontory in a quiet corner of the new town, the Anaxemander has light and airy rooms, all with sea views and terraces, while the larger, two-bedroom apartments come with small kitchens and bathtubs. The hotel runs various excursions, including yacht trips.

Hotel Orka
HOTEL $

(☎23 977; hotel_orka@abv.bg; ul Pârvi Mai 2; d/tr/apt 50/65/80 lv; ✱@) In the centre of the new town, this is a neat, family-run hotel not far from the beach. Rooms are plain but clean, with balconies, TVs and fridges.

Zlatna Ribka Camping
CAMPGROUND $

(☎22 534; www.zlatnaribka.bgcamping.com; Tsarski Beach; tent/caravan spaces from 25/30 lv; ☉Jun-Sep; P🚗) Around 2km west of Sozopol's old town, Zlatna Ribka is a well-ordered campsite on its own private beach, with guarded spaces for 150 caravans and tents. On-site facilities include a restaurant, shops, a bakery, a surf school and other water sports, while lifegards patrol the beach. Buses between Sozopol and Burgas stop outside the gates.

Eating

Fish, naturally enough, is the local speciality, and several reasonably priced restaurants are strung out along the port area. The best restaurants in town are on ul Morksi Skali, and are large and traditional affairs with some spectacular views.

The pedestrianised section of ul Ropotamo, alongside Harmanite Beach, is packed with cafes, restaurants and bars. They're all pretty much the same.

TOP CHOICE Panorama
SEAFOOD $$$

(ul Morski Skali 21; mains 8-20 lv) As the name suggests, this place has an open terrace with a fantastic view towards Sveti Ivan Island. Fresh, locally caught fish is a mainstay of the menu, and service is quick and friendly.

Bizhou
SEAFOOD $$

(ul Kraybrezhna; mains 4-9 lv) This simple harbourside restaurant is good value, specialising in a variety of fresh fish dishes. Bulgarian staples like *kebabcheta*

(spicy grilled sausages) and salads are also available.

Ksantana
SEAFOOD $$$

(☎22 454; ul Morski Skali 7; mains 8-15 lv) The split-level terraces of this traditional fish restaurant afford a bird's-eye view of Sveti Ivan Island from the courtyard balcony. The restaurant can be entered at both the top and bottom of the steps and can be easy to miss.

Diamant
BULGARIAN $$

(ul Ropotamo; mains 4-9 lv) One of the better Harmanite beachfront restaurants, serving traditional grills, soups, fish and cheap three-course lunch deals from around 5 lv.

☆ Entertainment

Art Club Michel
LIVE MUSIC

(☎0883352622; ul Apolonia 39; tickets 3-5 lv) With its walled garden just off one of the old town's main streets, this is a mellow place to go for live music, especially jazz.

🛍 Shopping

In summer, the streets in the old town are lined with stalls selling the usual array of tourist tat, but there are some better-quality souvenirs to be found.

Art Gallery Laskaridi
SOUVENIRS

(ul Kiril & Metodii) Sells contemporary art, jewellery and pottery, as well as souvenir books about Sozopol.

Gallery Bissera
SOUVENIRS

(ul Apolonia 52) Set up in an old wooden barn behind the cinema, Gallery Bissera offers a range of local paintings and ceramics, as well as some antique oddments.

ℹ Information

Many banks with ATMs can be found along the old town's main streets, and around the new town's main square.

ℹ Getting There & Away

The small public **bus station** (ul Han Krum) is just south of the old town walls. Buses leave for Burgas (4.50 lv, 40 minutes) about every 30 minutes between 6am and 9pm in summer, and about once an hour in the low season.

In summer, hourly buses go to Primorsko (4.50 lv, 35 minutes) and Kiten (5 lv, 45 minutes). Public buses leave up to three times a day for Sofia.

Buses arrive and depart from spots around the new town's main square. Three or four buses go to Sofia daily and one or two depart for Plovdiv.

Fast Ferry (www.fastferry.bg), operating from a kiosk at the harbour, runs ferries at least four days a week to Nesebâr (single/return from 27/54 lv, 30 minutes) between June and September.

ⓘ Getting Around

Sozopol is easy to get around on foot. If you need a car, there are several agencies around pl Harmanite and ul Ropotamo in the new town, which can arrange car rental from about 60 lv per day.

Ropotamo Nature Reserve
Национален Резерват Ропотамо

This reserve was established in 1940 to protect fragile landscapes of extensive marshes and the largest sand dunes in Bulgaria, as well as rare flora such as the endemic sand lily. The reserve also protects some 257 species of birds, reptiles and mammals, including white-tailed eagles, wild boars, jackals and 10 species of bat.

At several well-signposted places along the road between Burgas and Primorsko, visitors can stop and admire some of the reserve, and wander along short **walking trails** where explanations (in English) about the local flora, fauna and natural landscapes are provided. The reserve also encompasses Thracian megaliths and tiny Sveti Toma Island, which hosts Bulgaria's only wild cacti. (It's also known as Snake Island, after the indigenous water snakes that live hereabouts.)

Where the main road between Sozopol and Primorsko crosses the Ropotamo River is the major entrance to a stretch of **parkland** (admission free, parking 3 lv; ☺dawn-dusk). There are a couple of cafes and picnic spots, and some short **hiking trails**, but most visitors come for a **boat ride** (40/70min trips per person 8/10 lv) along the river. To get to the parkland entrance by public transport, take any bus south of Sozopol, and get off at the prominent, well-signposted bridge, found around 10km or 15 minutes beyond Sozopol.

Primorsko   Приморско
☏0550 / POP 3700

Primorsko (meaning 'by the sea') is a busy resort 52km southeast of Burgas and popular mainly with Bulgarian families. It's far less developed than resorts to the north, although the two long, sandy beaches are attractive, with warm, shallow water.

The bus station is at the western end of town, from where it's around 1km along ul Treti Mart into the centre. Most shops are along ul Cherno More, which heads southeast from the central square. The popular South Beach is a short walk from here. The quieter North Beach is several blocks to the north.

🛏 Sleeping

Hotel Prima Vera   HOTEL $$
(☏33 488; hotel_primavera@abv.bg; ul Cherno More 46; d/apt 60/100 lv; ▣) A good town-centre choice with clean and spacious rooms, all with balconies, and a good restaurant downstairs. It's right in the thick of the action, and around 50m from South Beach. Cheaper rates are offered for longer stays.

Spektar Palace   HOTEL $
(☏31 043; www.spektar-palace.com; ul Treti Mart 82; d/tr 55/65 lv; ☺May-Oct; ▣▣▣▣) Closer to the bus station than the beaches, Spektar has large rooms and excellent facilities, including a small pool and gym. The hotel also arranges trips to Istanbul.

Hotel Plovdiv   HOTEL $$
(☏32 372; www.hotel-primorsko.com; ul Briz 9; s/d Jul & Aug from 36/72 lv; ▣▣▣) On a quiet street overlooking North Beach, the Plovdiv is excellent value. Rooms are basic but bright and perfectly comfortable. There's a restaurant and a children's pool. Prices vary throughout the year.

✖ Eating

Kebabs, pizzas and burgers from stalls around town seem to be standard fare for most visitors. Some of the better restaurants are on ul Cherno More.

 Bistro Silva   CAFE $
(South Beach; mains from 3 lv) Set right on the beach, this is a great place for a quick, cheap lunch. You can sit on the wooden terrace or in one of the old fishing boats alongside that are fitted out with tables, and tuck into dishes such as moussaka, pizza, and chicken and rice.

Restaurant Chaika   BULGARIAN $$
(☏32 990; ul Cherno More 40; mains 5-20 lv; ☺8am-midnight) Grilled octopus, mackerel and other fishy dishes feature here; other options include stuffed peppers and goulash. There's outdoor seating in the shady little park behind the restaurant.

Birariya Dionisii BULGARIAN $

(cnr ul Cherno More & ul Hristo Botev; mains from 3.50 lv; 🍽) This small, traditional tavern in a quieter part of town serves up the usual range of Bulgarian specialities as well as pizzas, salads and locally caught fish.

ℹ️ Getting There & Away

Primorsko's bus station, 1km from the town centre, is where all public transport arrives and leaves. From here there are buses to Kiten (1 lv, 10 minutes, roughly every 30 minutes). There are six buses a day to Tsarevo (2.50 lv, 30 minutes) and several to Sozopol (4.50 lv, 35 minutes). In addition, buses travel daily to Burgas (7 lv, one hour, every 30 minutes between 6am and 7pm). Around five buses a day also go to Sofia (30 lv, eight hours).

Kiten Китен

📞 0550 / POP 950

Little Kiten, 5km south of Primorsko, is popular with Bulgarian tourists, and numerous hotel complexes have risen up in recent years. There's no town centre as such, so all shops, restaurants and hotels are dotted along the roads between the two beaches; the biggest concentration is on ul Atliman, which is lined with restaurants and bars. Prices are higher here than in Primorsko.

The northern **Atliman Beach** is along a horseshoe-shaped bay, one of the prettiest along the Black Sea coast. **Morski Beach** to the south is sheltered and ideal for swimming and has plenty of beachside cafes.

🛏 Sleeping & Eating

All the hotels listed have restaurants; try **Eos Restaurant** (mains 2-3 lv) for cheap grills and salads.

Dodo Beach HOTEL $$$

(📞 36 294; www.dodo-beach.com; ul Urdoviza 8; s/d incl full board 156/210 lv; ⊙Jun-Sep; 🅿❄🛜🏊) With superb views over the coast, this big glass box has some of the best rooms and facilities in town, although the seemingly obligatory full-board arrangement won't be ideal for everyone.

Hotel Marina HOTEL $$

(📞 36 984; www.marinakiten.com; Kiten Marina; r/apt from 70/110 lv; 🅿❄) Overlooking Kiten's mini marina and with its own scrap of private beach, this fresh-looking hotel has spacious rooms, most with sea views.

Eos Hotel HOTEL $$

(📞 36 205; www.eoskiten.com; ul Petrova niva 7; r/apt 65/100 lv; ⊙Jun-Sep; ❄🛜🏊) A short walk from the bus stop, though a little further from the beaches, Eos is a friendly hotel with a tiny pool. Rooms are standard fare: plain and comfortable.

ℹ️ Getting There & Away

The bus station is at the top end of ul Strandzha, at the junction of the roads to Primorsko and Ahtopol. Daily buses to Burgas (8 lv, one hour, hourly) travel via Primorsko and Sozopol (5 lv, 40 minutes). In summer, buses to Sofia (35 lv, seven to eight hours) leave throughout the day.

Tsarevo Царево

📞 0550 / POP 5800

Spread lazily over two small peninsulas jutting out into the Black Sea, Tsarevo is a quiet, elegant little town, once a popular holiday spot for the Bulgarian royal family. Called Vasiliko until 1934, it was renamed Tsarevo ('royal place') in honour of Tsar Boris III; the communists then renamed it Michurin (after a Soviet botanist) in 1950, and it reverted once again in 1991. The centre, on the northern peninsula, has a calm, affluent atmosphere and feels more like a real town than some of Tsarevo's seaside-resort neighbours.

◎ Sights

Overlooking the rocky headland at the end of the main road, ul Han Asparuh, are the peaceful **Sea Gardens**, offering dramatic panoramic views across the Black Sea. Other sights of interest include the **Church of Sveti Tsar Boris-Mikhail**, dedicated to the former king, and the tiny **Church of the Holy Trinity**, built in 1810 above the beach, accessed by steps on the northern side of the headland. It's a small but picturesque scrap of sand with a couple of bars.

Across the wide bay, the southern peninsula is of less interest, dominated by modern apartments and holiday homes, although the headland, reached by scrambling over rocks, has Tsarevo's best **beach**. Sadly, this is no secret cove, though, as it's also occupied by the giant Serenity Bay hotel.

🛏 Sleeping & Eating

Hotel Zebra HOTEL $$

(📞 55 111; www.hotel-zebra.com; ul Han Asparuh 10; s/d Jul & Aug 60/76 lv, s/d Sep-Jun from 46/56 lv;

P✳@≋) Near the scenic Sea Gardens, this modern complex offers superb value. The large, comfortable rooms all have balconies and sparkling bathrooms, and there's an outdoor pool and a restaurant.

Hotel Ribarska Sreshta HOTEL $

(📞52 455; www.hotelribarska.com; Tsarevo Harbour; d/tr 50/65 lv; ✳✳🖥) Looking like a small, stranded cruise liner right on the fishing harbour, this place has attractive rooms with sea-facing balconies. There's an excellent fish restaurant downstairs.

Hotel Chaika HOTEL $

(📞0888249125; www.chaika.in; ul Han Asparuh 21; d 25-40 lv) In the centre of town, the Chaika is an older hotel that has been renovated. Most of the brightly painted rooms have balconies with sea views, and are great value for this price.

Hotel Lalov Egrek RESORT $$

(📞056-916784; www.hotel.lalov.net; s/d/apt 70/112/ 134 lv; P➲✳🖥≋) Around 3km north of Tsarevo, on the outskirts of Lozenets, this beachfront complex enjoys stunning sea views and has an excellent restaurant. At the heart of the resort is a top-class diving centre – there's a dedicated training pool on site, and a wide variety of diving courses are offered.

Ribarska Sreshta SEAFOOD $$

(mains 5-12 lv; ⊙7am-midnight; 🖥) Fresh fish is on the menu at the harbourside restaurant of the hotel of the same name.

❶ Getting There & Away

Tsarevo's bus station is at the top of ul Mikhail Gerdzhikov, about 2km west of the centre. Minibuses to Burgas (9 lv, 50 minutes) run roughly every 30 minutes to one hour between 6am and 8pm via Kiten and Primorsko, and there are two daily buses to Sofia (37 lv, eight hours).

Strandzha Nature Park
Природен Парк Странджа

📞05952

In Bulgaria's southeastern corner is the remote Strandzha Nature Park, established in 1995. The 1161 sq km of rolling hills protect the country's most diverse vegetation, including vast forests of oak and beech, as well as 40 species of fish, 134 breeding bird species, 65 species of mammals, including golden jackals, wildcats and otters, and various ancient ruins.

The park's ecotourism potential is slowly being developed, but visiting the area is not easy without private transport. Be sure you don't stray too close to the Turkish border: this is an area of smugglers and suspicious border-patrol guards.

The park is ideal for **hiking** because it's sparsely populated and relatively flat. Several short hikes (1km to 8km long), and longer treks (about 20km) between the coast and the centre of the park, are detailed in the colourful *Nature Park Strandzha* map (1:70,000; 4 lv), available at bookshops in Burgas. The park also contains what are probably the most undeveloped stretches of sandy **beach** along the Bulgarian Black Sea coast. If you visit in early June, make sure you witness the **fire-dancing festival** in Bulgari. There is some useful information online, at www.discoverstrandja.com and www.visitstrandja.com, if you intend exploring.

The administrative centre of the park is Malko Târnovo, a small, dusty town in the southwest. The **History Museum** (ul Konstantin Petkanov; 2 lv; ⊙8am-noon & 1-4pm Mon-Fri) has some local archaeological finds, and the **Ethnographical Museum** (📞2126) contains displays about the park. For more details, contact the **park office** (📞tel/fax 05952-3635; www.strandja.bg; ul Yanko Maslinov 1, Malko Târnovo).

From the Zapad bus station in Burgas, buses leave for Malko Târnovo (7.50 lv, three hours, four or five a day) via Bulgari, but transport to other villages in the park is infrequent.

Sinemorets Синеморец

📞0550 / POP 300

If you have your own transport, tiny Sinemorets (Si-ne-*mor*-ets), with its lovely white beaches, is a relaxing place to escape the crowds. Its attractions haven't escaped the attention of the developers, sadly, but despite the presence of an enormous hotel on the best beach, the atmosphere of remote, slow-paced village life remains, and it's a superb base for visiting the nearby Strandzha Nature Park and **hiking** and **birdwatching** in the surrounding countryside.

🛏 Sleeping & Eating

Asti Arthotel HOTEL $$

(📞65 504; www.asti-bg.com; ul Silistar 8; d/ apt 84/136 lv; ⊙Apr-Oct; P✳🖥≋) All 26 apartments here have terraces and tiny kitchenettes, and there are also three smaller double rooms. There's a tennis court, pool, playground and restaurant, and bikes are available for rent.

Casa Domingo   HOTEL **$**
(☑66 093; www.casadomingo.info; ul Dunav 73; s/d/apt from 40/50/120 lv; 🛜🗷) This attractive modern complex has a range of rooms, studios and apartments, set in a pretty garden with an open-air pool and restaurant. Breakfast is 6 lv extra and there are reductions for children under 12 years old.

Dayana Beach Hotel   HOTEL **$$**
(☑65 502; www.dayanabeach.com; s/d 50/70 lv; ⊙May-Oct; 🅿✳🛜🗷) Close to the central beach, this modern family hotel has bright rooms with verandahs, TVs and fridges.

❶ Getting There & Away

Public transport to/from Sinemorets is very poor. There's one daily bus leaving Burgas in summer (13 lv, 2½ to three hours). Otherwise, you'll need to travel to Ahtopol and change there for one of the four daily minibuses to Sinemorets (1 lv, 15 minutes). There are no taxis in Sinemorets.

CENTRAL COAST

Pomorie   Поморие
☑0596 / POP 13,500

Like neighbouring Nesebâr, Pomorie sits on a narrow peninsula, and until it was ravaged by fire in 1906 it was almost as picturesque. There, however, the similarities end. The modern town centre has a lazy charm, and there's a serviceable though unspectacular beach. Known for its salt lakes and therapeutic mud treatments, Pomorie is very much a Bulgarian resort and is almost entirely bypassed by foreign tourists.

◉ Sights & Activities

There are a few churches worth a look, including the **Preobrazhenie Gospodne Church**, dating from 1765.

It's often windy at the beach, making it ideal for **windsurfing**. Mud baths, hydrotherapy and countless other treatments are available at many hotels.

Sveti Georgi Monastery   MONASTERY
(ul Knyaz Boris I) On a dusty road about 2km out of town, heading towards the main bus station, is Sveti Georgi Monastery. Built in 1856, it's a small complex set in pretty gardens with a quaint, icon-filled church and a bell tower covered in saintly frescoes. It's also possible to stay here.

🛏 Sleeping & Eating

Pensioners holding cardboard signs gather near the main bus station and further along ul Knyaz Boris I, offering private rooms from around 10 lv per person, and many houses on this road have accommodation signs for *svobodni stai* (Свободни Стаи) in their windows.

The beachfront promenade, ul Kraybrezhna, is lined with restaurants, while better options (with multilingual menus) are found near the Preobrazhenie Gospodne Church, including **Restaurant Tsarevets** (ul Knyaz Boris I; mains 4-10 lv), which offers grilled pork, chicken and fish dishes.

Hotel Pri Amerikaneca   HOTEL **$$**
(☑22 824; www.attheamericans.com; ul Knyaz Boris I 9; r 100 lv; 🅿✳@) The curiously named 'At the Americans' is a modern seafront hotel in the old town, with its own private little beach. The 12 spacious studios all have balconies and panoramic sea views, and there's a restaurant and cocktail bar on site.

Zeus Hotel   HOTEL **$$**
(☑22 770; www.zeus-hotel.com; ul Rakovska 9; s/d 65/80 lv; ✳) The town-centre Zeus has a variety of cosy rooms, all with balconies, fridges and TVs. Prices drop by up to 50% outside the summer season.

❶ Getting There & Away

There are two bus stations in Pomorie: the main bus station is about 3km outside the town centre (accessible by local bus 1); regular buses and minibuses between Burgas and Nesebâr and/or Sunny Beach (Slânchev Bryag) invariably stop only at the main bus station. Roughly hourly minibuses marked 'Pomorie Central' (Поморие Център) leave from Burgas (3 lv, 30 minutes) and Sunny Beach (2 lv, 30 minutes), stopping at Pomorie's small central bus station.

Nesebâr   Несебър
☑0554 / POP 10,300

On a small rocky outcrop 37km northeast of Burgas, connected to the mainland by a narrow, artificial isthmus, pretty-as-a-postcard

BLACK SEA COAST POMORIE

Nesebâr

200 m
0.1 miles

BLACK SEA

Emona
Neptun
Kraybrezhna
Sadala
Slavyanska
Han Asparuh
Neptun
Vrachhavski
Mitropolitska
Il Asen
Ivan Asen II
Mesembria
Ivan Alexander
Hemus
Hemus
Venera
Aheloi
Hemus
Tervel
Mesembria
Ribarska
Tsar Simeon
Mitropolitska
Kraybrezhna
Mena
Mesembria
Chaika

Russalka

19
20
3
13
15
14
8
2
9
6
17
10
5
4
11
7
18
1
16
12

Water Taxis
to Sunny Beach

Town Gate

Trolleybus to Sunny
Beach (Slánchev
Bryag) (summer only)

To Nesebâr New
Town (400m);
South Beach (1km)

Bus
Station

Harbour

To Fast
Ferry (50m)

Nesebâr

◎ Sights
1 Archaeological Museum B3
2 Archangels Michael & Gabriel
   Church..D2
3 Basilica of the Merciful Virgin E1
4 Christ Pantokrator Church.................C3
5 Church of St John the Baptist.............C2
6 Ethnographical Museum......................D3
7 St John Aliturgetos Church C4
8 Sveta Paraskeva Church D2
9 Sveta Sofia Church.............................D2
10 Sveti Spas Church C2
11 Sveti Stefan Church C3

⨁ Activities, Courses & Tours
12 Angel Divers.......................................B4

▣ Sleeping
13 Hotel Tony E1
14 Hotel Trinity Sea Residence D2
15 Prince Cyril Hotel D2
16 Rony Hotel B3
17 Royal Palace Hotel.............................C2

⊗ Eating
18 Old Nesebâr..C3
19 Pri Shopite E2
20 Zlatnoto Runo....................................E3

Nesebâr (Ne-*se*-bar) is famous for its surprisingly numerous, albeit mostly ruined, medieval churches. It has, inevitably, become heavily commercialised, and transforms into one huge, open-air souvenir market during the high season; outside summer, it's a ghost town. Designated by Unesco as a World Heritage site, Nesebâr has its charms, but in summer these can be overpowered by the crowds and the relentless parade of tacky shops. With Sunny Beach (Slânchev Bryag) just across the bay, meanwhile, you have every conceivable water sport on hand. The 'new town' on the other side of the isthmus has the newest and biggest hotels and the main beach, but the sights are all in the old town.

History
Greek colonists founded what became the thriving trading port of Mesembria in 512 BC, although most of their temples and towers were submerged after the level of the Black Sea rose around 2000 years ago.

Under Byzantine rule, during the 5th and 6th centuries, several grand churches were erected and the fortifications extended.

After the Bulgar invasion in 812, the town was renamed Nesebâr; over the following centuries, it passed back and forth between Byzantium and the First Bulgarian Empire (681–1018) but remained largely unscathed, finally falling to the Turks in 1453.

During the Bulgarian National Revival of the 18th and 19th centuries, Nesebâr prospered, and wealthy merchants built grand villas here, some of which remain today. Nesebâr ceased to be an active trading town from the early 20th century, and these days it survives almost entirely on tourism.

◎ Sights
A multiticket (adult/child 10/5 lv), sold at the Archaeological Museum, gives access to Sveti Stefan Church, Sveti Spas Church and the Archaeological Museum. Combined tickets for the Archaeological Museum and Sveti Stefan Church cost 8/4 lv. Opening times below are for July and August; slightly shorter hours will apply for the rest of the year.

Nesebâr was once home to about 80 churches, but most are now in ruins. Characteristic of the Nesebâr style are the horizontal strips of white stone and red brick, and facades decorated with green ceramic discs. Except where indicated, each church is open daily during daylight hours and admission is free.

Around 1.5km west of the old town is South Beach. All the usual water sports are available, including jet skiing and waterskiing. The longer sandy shores of Sunny Beach (Slânchev Bryag), just a few kilometres up the coast, are an alternative option.

Sveta Sofia Church   CHURCH
(Old Metropolitan Church; ul Mitropolitska) No visitor can help but be impressed by the ruins of the Sveta Sofia Church. Dating back to the 5th century, this vast, three-nave basilica was rebuilt in the 9th century as part of a huge complex that encompassed the bishop's palace. Today the ruins form the centrepiece of a busy plaza surrounded by cafes and artists' street stalls.

Christ Pantokrator Church   CHURCH
(ul Mesembria) Typical of the characteristic Nesebâr construction is the well-preserved Christ Pantokrator Church, built in the mid-14th century. An unusual feature at the eastern end is the frieze of swastikas, an ancient solar symbol. The church is now used as a commercial art gallery.

BLACK SEA COAST NESEBÂR

Archaeological Museum   MUSEUM
(www.ancient-nessebar.org; ul Mesembria 2; adult/child 5/3 lv; ⊙9am-8pm Mon-Fri, 9.30am-1.30pm & 2-7pm Sat & Sun Jul & Aug) Greek and Roman pottery, statues and tombstones, Thracian jewellery and ancient anchors are displayed here. There's also a collection of icons recovered from Nesebâr's numerous churches.

Sveti Stefan Church   CHURCH
(ul Ribarska; adult/student 5/2 lv; ⊙9am-7pm Mon-Fri, 9am-1pm & 1.30-6pm Sat & Sun) Built in the 11th century and reconstructed 500 years later, this is the best-preserved church in town, renowned for its beautiful 16th- to 18th-century murals, which cover virtually the entire interior. Try to come early, as it's popular with tour groups.

Sveti Spas Church   CHURCH
(Church of the Blessed Saviour; ul Aheloi; adult/child 3/2 lv; ⊙10am-1.30pm & 2-5pm Mon-Fri, 10am-3pm Sat & Sun) This modest, single-nave church was built in 1609, below ground level, as dictated by the Ottoman authorities of that time. It features some well-preserved murals depicting the life of Christ and the Virgin Mary.

Basilica of the Merciful Virgin   CHURCH
(ul Kraybrezhna) Overlooking the sea, the Basilica of the Merciful Virgin dates from the 6th century, and later became a monastery. The fortified tower alongside it was built as a response to pirate raids along the coast; eventually abandoned and partly swallowed by the sea, it was only rediscovered by archaeologists in the 1920s.

Sveta Paraskeva Church   CHURCH
(ul Hemus) A fine example of 13th-century architecture is the Sveta Paraskeva Church, which has only one nave and one apse. The building is now occupied by an art gallery.

Ethnographical Museum   MUSEUM
(ul Mesembria 28; adult/child 3/2 lv; ⊙10am-1pm & 2-6pm Mon-Sat) Inside a typical wooden National Revival building, built in 1840 for a wealthy merchant, this museum features exhibitions of folk costumes and traditional weaving.

🏃 Activities

Angel Divers   DIVING
(☎0888849341; www.angel-divers.com; ⊙9am-6pm May-Sep) Angel Divers, located in a small booth at the ferry port, is a PADI-certified diving company offering single dives for 90 lv and wreck diving (for certified divers) for

180 lv, as well as other specialist dives and longer courses.

🛏 Sleeping
In summer you'll need to book accommodation in advance. Private rooms are the best option for budget travellers – locals offering rooms meet tourists off the bus.

⭐ Hotel Tony   GUESTHOUSE $
(☎0889268004, 42 403; ul Kraybrezhna 20; r from 40 lv; ⊙Jun-Sep; ❄) In a great spot overlooking the sea, Hotel Tony is very reasonably priced, so it's regularly full in summer. Rooms are simple but clean, and the chatty host is very helpful.

Hotel Trinity Sea Residence   HOTEL $$
(☎46 600; www.trinity-nessebar.com; ul Venera 8; s/d/apt from 82/92/152 lv; 🅿❄🖥) This pretty National Revival–style wooden villa has spacious rooms and apartments, many with stunning sea views, and half- and full-board deals are available. Children under eight stay free, and video games and baby cribs are available.

Prince Cyril Hotel   HOTEL $
(☎42 220; hotelprincecyril@gmail.com; ul Slavyanska 9; d from 50 lv; ❄🖥) Located on a quiet, cobbled, souvenir-stall–free lane, this is a friendly place with a variety of rooms, all with TV and fridge, but not all with air-con; check a few out first and try to avoid the cramped, top-floor, fan-only rooms.

Royal Palace Hotel   HOTEL $$
(☎46 490; www.nessebarpalace.com; ul Mitropolitska 19; s/d 90/100 lv; 🅿⊙❄🖥) In the centre of the old town, the Royal Palace offers stylish and comfortable rooms with fridges and TVs (though there's only one single). There's a good restaurant and summer garden, and various package deals are often available.

Rony Hotel   HOTEL $$$
(☎44 000; www.hotelcaliforniasofia.com/rony; ul Chaika 1; s/d Jul & Aug 77/144 lv, Sep-Jun from 46/88 lv; ❄) Right behind the Archaeological Museum, the Rony is an old-style wooden villa with a dozen rooms – some of which have terraces and sea views – and a good restaurant. It books up quickly in summer.

🍴 Eating
All restaurants in Nesebâr are geared towards the passing tourist trade, and prices are roughly twice what you'll pay away from

the coastal resorts. Try to avoid those that employ touts.

Pri Shopite
BULGARIAN $$

(ul Neptun 12; mains 7-15 lv; ✍) Set in a traditional, tavern-style courtyard around a twisted, 300-year-old fig tree, this is a welcoming place with great food, including freshly caught fish, grills, steaks and vegetarian options.

Old Nesebâr
SEAFOOD $$

(✍42 070; ul Ivan Alexander 11; mains 8-15 lv) With two tiers of seating offering great sea views, this is a popular place for barbecues, grills and fish dishes, as well as salads and lighter meals.

Zlatnoto Runo
BULGARIAN $$$

(✍45 602; ul Rusalka 6; mains 8-20 lv; ⊘lunch & dinner) Overlooking the sea on the southeastern end of the peninsula, the 'Golden Fleece' serves a varied menu, including roast lamb and rabbit plus some inventive seafood dishes, such as octopus with blueberry sauce.

🛍 Shopping

In summer, almost every street of Nesebâr's old town is lined with hundreds of stalls selling all kinds of tourist tat, from cheeky t-shirts and knock-off watches to embroideries, pottery and paintings. The range is impressive, but price-wise it's far better to shop almost anywhere else. If you're after something a bit different, a few of the town's many churches now operate as more tasteful souvenir shops, open daylight hours in summer only.

ℹ Getting There & Away

Nesebâr is well connected to coastal destinations by public transport, and the town's bus station is on the small square just outside the city walls. The stop before this on the mainland is for the new town. From the bus station, there are buses to nearby Sunny Beach (1 lv, 10 minutes, every 15 minutes), Burgas (6 lv, 40 minutes, every 30 minutes), Varna (15 lv, two hours, seven daily) and Sofia (30 lv, seven hours, several daily).

Fast Ferry (www.fastferry.bg) operates a summer-only high-speed hydrofoil service to Sozopol (one way/return from 27/54 lv, 30 minutes, three to four daily) and Varna (one way/return 45/90 lv, 1½ hours, two daily).

Sunny Beach (Slânchev Bryag)
Слънчев Бряг

✍0554

Bulgaria's biggest purpose-built seaside resort, Sunny Beach is the Black Sea coast's hyperactive answer to the Spanish *costas*, and probably the most expensive place in the country. The appeal is clear, though, with several kilometres of sandy beach that attracts more international sun worshippers than any other resort in the country. The beach is one of Bulgaria's finest, with every imaginable activity from minigolf to parasailing, and restaurants and clubs abound. If you're just looking to top up your tan by day and go clubbing all night, this is the place to come. You won't even notice that you're in a country called Bulgaria.

As Sunny Beach is a package-holiday resort, pretty much everyone staying here will be on prebooked, often all-inclusive deals arranged in their home countries, and so no accommodation options are listed here; try nearby Nesebâr instead.

🏃 Activities

Numerous water sports are available on the beach, such as **parasailing** (solo/tandem 45/80 lv) and **jet skiing** (15 minutes about 50 lv). In summer, weekly **shows** (tickets 25 lv) of folk music, dancing and acrobatics take place in the Hotel Majestic at the far northern end of the beach.

Aqua Paradise
WATER SPORTS

(✍51 543; www.aquaparadise-bg.com; adult/child all day 28/16 lv, 3-7pm 20/10 lv; ⊘10am-7pm) Organised watery fun is on hand at Aqua Paradise, a huge water park on the southern outskirts of Sunny Beach with a variety of pools, slides and chutes. A free minibus, running every 15 minutes, makes pick ups at 10 signed stops around town.

Action Aquapark
WATER SPORTS

(✍26 235; www.aquapark.bg; adult/child all day 30/16 lv, from 3pm 22/11 lv; ⊘10am-7pm May-Sep) This big water park has 13 pools and numerous high-speed slides, chutes, fountains, waterfalls and tunnels. There's even a little zoo with ponies, goats and swans.

🍴 Eating

Restaurants in Sunny Beach are among the most expensive in Bulgaria, and, annoyingly, even normally uniform chains such as McDonald's and Happy Bar & Grill charge two to three times more than at their branches elsewhere. There are cheaper fast-food stalls dotted along the beach.

Fat Cat
PUB $$$

(mains around 10-20 lv; ⊘24hr) On the beachfront opposite the Glarus Hotel, this is a typically boisterous restaurant and pub aimed particularly at British tourists, with a menu of pizzas, steaks, curries and roast dinners.

Chilli Peppers STEAKHOUSE **$$$**
(mains around 15-30 lv; ☺9am-midnight) Popular 'Wild West Barbecue' joint serving up lots of steaks, sausages and grills in a mocked-up ranch-style setting. It's in the pedestrian thoroughfare known as 'Flower Street', near Hotel Kuban.

☆ Entertainment

Sunny Beach is famous for its clubs and there are plenty to choose from all over the resort.

Dance Club Mania CLUB
(www.danceclubmania.com; ☺11.30pm-6am) In the centre of Sunny Beach, this big, two-level club features international DJs and 3D laser shows.

Disco Orange CLUB
(www.orangedisco.net) Another typically brash Sunny Beach nightspot, near Hotel Strandja, playing dance, soul and '80s hits.

❶ Getting There & Away

The central bus station is just off the main road. City buses to Burgas (6 lv, 45 minutes, roughly every 30 minutes in summer) all go via Nesebâr; you can also get frequent buses to Varna (10 lv, two hours, every 30 minutes) and Pomorie (3 lv, 30 minutes).

❶ Getting Around

Trolleybuses (2 lv) shuttle along three numbered routes every 15 to 20 minutes between 9am and 11pm. There are a number of car-rental agencies on the main road, including **Sunny Trans** (☎71 082; www.rentacarsunny.com) opposite the Mariner Hotel; rates, including insurance and unlimited kilometres, start at 60 lv per day.

NORTHERN COAST

Varna   Варна

☑052 / POP 335,000
Bulgaria's third city and maritime capital, Varna is by far the most interesting and cosmopolitan town on the Black Sea coast. A combination of port city, naval base and seaside resort, it's an appealing place to while away a few days, packed with history yet thoroughly modern, with an enormous

park to amble round and a lengthy beach to lounge on. In the city centre you'll find Bulgaria's largest Roman baths complex and its finest archaeological museum, as well as a lively cultural and restaurant scene.

The city also makes an ideal base for day trips to nearby beach resorts such as Sveti Konstantin and Golden Sands (Zlatni Pyasâtsi), and the charming town of Balchik.

History

In 585 BC, Greeks from Miletus settled in the area of modern Varna, founding the city of Odessos, which thrived as a major commercial centre, taken over by the Romans in the 2nd century AD.

The city became a key port under the Byzantines, and gained its modern name of Varna (possibly derived from the word for 'water') during the period of the First Bulgarian Empire (681–1018). Varna was used by British troops as a port during the Crimean War (1853–56), after which Turkey allowed its allies Britain and France to sell their products throughout the Ottoman Empire, making Varna a great trading centre once more.

In 1866 a railway between Ruse and Varna was built, providing a direct route from the Danube to the Black Sea coast, and Varna became a major shipbuilding centre and port. In 1921 Varna was established as Bulgaria's first seaside holiday resort, and its status as the country's summertime playground was enhanced by the founding of the International Festival in 1926, which has been going strong ever since.

◉ Sights

Archaeological Museum MUSEUM
(ul Maria Luisa 41; adult/student 10/2 lv; ☺10am-5pm Tue-Sun Apr-Sep, 10am-5pm Tue-Sat Oct-Mar; ☐3, 9, 109) Exhibits at this vast museum, the best of its kind in Bulgaria, include 6500-year-old bangles, necklaces and earrings – said to be the oldest worked gold found anywhere in the world – Roman surgical implements, Hellenistic tombstones and touching oddments such as a marble plaque listing, in Greek, the names of the city's school graduates for AD 221.

Roman Thermae ANCIENT SITE
(cnr ul Han Krum & ul San Stefano; adult/student 4/2 lv; ☺10am-5pm Tue-Sun May-Oct, 10am-5pm Tue-Sat Nov-Apr) The well-preserved ruins of Varna's 2nd-century-AD Roman Thermae are the largest in Bulgaria, although only

DON'T MISS

PRIMORSKI PARK

Established in 1878, this large and attractive green space overlooking the sea stretches for about 8km, and is said to be the largest of its kind in Europe. It's full of promenading families and old ladies knitting lace in summer, and there are a number of attractions and lots of woodland paths to amble along.

The **Aquarium** (adult/child 4/2 lv; ☾9am-8pm), housed in a powder-blue art deco building, is an old-fashioned place with tanks filled with denizens of the Black Sea's depths. There's no English labelling.

Walking north, the **Terrarium Varna** (Natural Science Museum; adult/child 3/2 lv; ☾9.30am-11pm) has a collection of creepy crawlies, including snakes, spiders and scorpions.

Further north again, the small **Zoopark** (www.varna-zoo.com adult/child 1/0.70 lv; ☾8am-8pm; ☐409) features monkeys, camels, kangaroos and black swans, while another 500m to the north is the **Dolphinarium** (☑302 199; www.dolphinarium.festa.bg; adult/child 20/14 lv; ☾Tue-Sun; ☐409). It presents 40-minute shows (at 10.30am, noon, 3.30pm and 5pm) of dolphins performing various acrobatic tricks.

---

a small part of the original complex still stands. You can just about make out individual bathing areas and the furnaces, where slaves kept the whole thing going.

History Museum
MUSEUM
(ul 8 Noemvri 3; adult/child 4/2 lv; ☾10am-5pm Tue-Sun May-Oct, 10am-5pm Mon-Fri Nov-Apr; ☐20) Varna's ivy-covered History Museum is dedicated to city history between 1878 and 1939, with mock-ups of long-gone 1920s shops and offices, collections of photographs and postcards, and paraphenalia from local trades like brewing and printing.

National Naval Museum
MUSEUM
(bul Primorski 2; admission 5 lv; ☾10am-6pm Wed-Sun) The National Naval Museum hosts several galleries of model ships and uniforms. Anchors, artillery and helicopters can be seen rusting quietly in the grounds at the back, while the revered warship *Druzki,* which torpedoed a Turkish cruiser during the First Balkan War in 1912, is embedded in concrete outside.

Cathedral of the Assumption of the Virgin
CHURCH
(pl Kiril & Metodii; ☾6am-10pm; ☐3) Varna's cathedral (1886) is topped with golden onion domes. Note the murals (painted in 1950) and colourful stained-glass windows, though you'll have to pay 5 lv if you want to take photos inside.

FREE Roman Baths
ANCIENT SITE
(bul Primorski; ☐20) There's a walkway running around the ruins of this smaller Roman bath complex, built around the 4th century AD, but there's little to see other than some foundation walls.

Sveti Nikolai Church
CHURCH
(ul Knyaz Boris I) The pretty Sveti Nikolai Church, right in the city centre, is worth a visit for its saintly murals. It's always busy, and is a popular venue for weddings.

Ethnographic Museum
MUSEUM
(ul Panagyurishte 22; adult/student 4/2 lv; ☾9am-5pm Tue-Sun) This charming revival-era mansion built in 1860 houses an interesting collection of traditional folk costumes and furnishings, and displays on local customs, festivities and industries such as winemaking.

FREE Varna City Art Gallery
GALLERY
(Boris Georgiev Gallery; ul Lyuben Karavelov 1; ☾10am-6pm Tue-Sun; ☐14, 109) You can peruse two floors of 19th- and 20th-century Bulgarian art, including works by Vladimir Dimitrov and David Peretz, at this gallery. Various temporary exhibitions are held here too.

Beach
BEACH
Steps from Primorski Park lead down to the city's long, sandy beach, which is hugely popular with local sunbathers, paddlers and beach-volleyball players. There are also a couple of tiny, outdoor, steaming **mineral-water pools**.

Running alongside the beach is the long coastal lane, officially known as aleya Georgi Georgiev but more commonly referred to

Varna

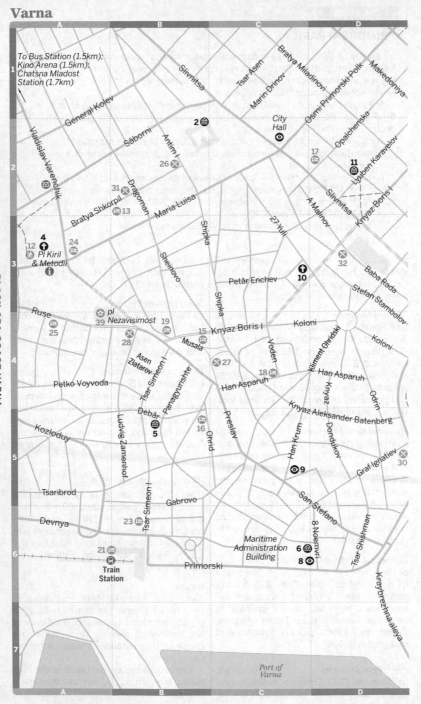

To Bus Station (1.5km);
Kino Arena (1.5km);
Chatsna Mladost
Station (1.7km)

Silvnitsa

Tsar Asen

Bratya Miladinovi

Marin Drinov

Osmi Primorski Polk

Makedoniya

General Kolev

City Hall

Opalchenska

Lyuben Karavelov

Vladislav Varenchik

Sâborni

Antim I

2

17

11

Lyuben Karavelov

26

Dragoman

31

13

Maria Luisa

Shipka

27 Yuli

A Malinov

Silvnitsa

Knyaz Boris I

Bratya Shkorpil

4

Pl Kiril
& Metodii

12

24

Sheinovo

Petâr Enchev

10

32

Baba Rada

Stefan Stambolov

Ruse

39

pl Nezavisimost

19

15

Knyaz Boris I

Koloni

Koloni

25

28

Musala

27

Voden

Kliment Ohridski

Han Asparuh

Asen Zlatarov

Tsar Simeon I

Panagyurishte

18

Han Asparuh

Petko Voyvoda

Han Asparuh

Knyaz

Knyaz Aleksander Batenberg

Odrin

Kozloduy

Ludvig Zamenhof

Debâr

5

16

Ohrid

Preslav

Han Krum

Dondukov

Graf Ignatiev

30

Tsaribrod

Tsar Simeon I

Gabrovo

9

Devnya

23

San Stefano

8 Noemvri

Tsar Shishman

21

Maritime Administration Building

6

8

Train Station

Primorski

Kraybrezhna aleya

Port of Varna

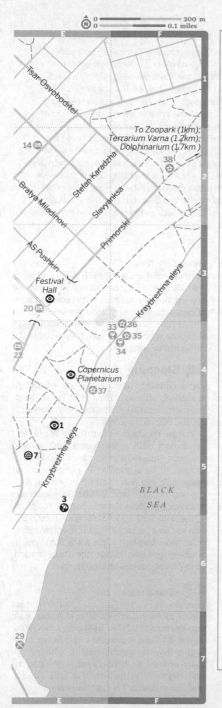

Varna

◎ Sights
1	Aquarium	E5
2	Archaeological Museum	B2
3	Beach	E5
4	Cathedral of the Assumption of the Virgin	A3
5	Ethnographic Museum	B5
6	History Museum	C6
7	National Naval Museum	E5
8	Roman Baths	C6
9	Roman Thermae	C5
10	Sveti Nikolai Church	C3
11	Varna City Art Gallery	D2

⊕ Activities, Courses & Tours
12	Free Varna Tour	A3

⊜ Sleeping
	Astra Tour	(see 21)
13	Flag Hostel	B2
14	Graffit Gallery Hotel	E2
15	Grand Hotel London	B4
16	Hotel Antik	B5
17	Hotel Astra	D2
18	Hotel Hi	C4
19	Hotel Oceanic	B4
20	Hotel Odessos	E3
21	Isak	A6
22	Modus Hotel	E4
23	Victorina	B6
24	Voennomorski Club	A3
25	Yo Ho Hostel	A4

⊗ Eating
26	Di Wine	B2
27	Dom na Arkitekta	C4
28	Morsko Konche	B4
29	Mr Baba	E7
30	Pri Monahinite	D5
31	Tanasi	B2
32	Trops Kâshta	D3

⊝ Drinking
33	Pench's Cocktails	F4
34	Punta Cana	F4

⊕ Entertainment
35	4aspik	F4
36	Copacabana	F4
37	Exit	E4
38	Open-Air Theatre	F2
39	Varna Opera House	A4

ROMAN BATHING

Like all self-respecting Roman cities, Odessos was graced with the very best public bathing facilities, and the vast *thermae* here were a visible, powerful symbol of the fruits – |and engineering skill – of Roman civilisation. Far from being simply a place to wash up, the baths were an integral part of civic life. They were a place to socialise, make business deals, eavesdrop on the latest gossip, snooze, read, eat and pick up male prostitutes. All classes were allowed, though men and women were admitted at different times. Larger baths, such as the one in Odessos, had a *palaestra,* or exercise hall, where wrestling and other athletic activities took place, often accompanied by music. Bathers would then rub themselves down with oil and sweat for a while in the *sudatorium* (a kind of sauna) before scraping it off with a strigil, examples of which are on show in the Archaeological Museum (p412). A plunge in the hot water of the *caldarium* would follow. They would then move on to the more bearable temperature of the *tepidarium*, finishing off with a dip in the icy *frigidarium*. The remains of these shallow pools can still be seen in Varna's Thermae (p412), as well as the furnace and hypocaust system that provided underfloor heating and hot water.

either as Plazhna aleya or **Kraybrezhna aleya**, which is the name we've used here. In summer, it's the centre of Varna's nightlife, lined with clubs, bars and restaurants.

🎭 Festivals & Events

Between May and October, Varna hosts the renowned **Varna Summer International Festival** (www.varnasummerfest.org). Established in 1926, the festival features outstanding events, including opera, the biennial International Ballet Competition (held in even-numbered years) and choral, jazz and folk music. Events are held at the Open-Air Theatre (p418) and in some of the nine halls in the massive **Festival Hall** (www.fccvarna.bg; bul Slivnitsa 2). Programs and information about buying tickets are well advertised beforehand in Varna and Sofia. The Festival Hall also hosts the **Annual International Film Festival** in late August and early September.

Other special events around the city include the **Songs about Varna Competition** and the **Days of Greek Culture Festival**, both held in March.

👣 Tours

FREE **Free Varna Tour** WALKING TOUR
(📞0887699875; www.freevarnatour.com; ⏰11am & 6pm Apr-Oct; 🚌3) Explore Varna on foot on these free, twice-daily walks, guided by friendly, English-speaking young volunteers. Leaving from in front of the Cathedral of the Assumption of the Virgin, the walks take about two hours.

Varna City Tour BUS TOUR
(www.varnacitytour.com; 2hr 13 lv; 24hr ticket adult/child 23/13 lv; ⏰Jun-Sep) This summertime hop-on, hop-off bus tour, with recorded multilingual commentary, runs between the resort of Albena and Varna, with several stops along the way. You can pick it up outside the cathedral in Varna.

🛏 Sleeping

Varna certainly has no shortage of accommodation, although the better (or at least, the more central) places get very busy during the summer months.

Private rooms are plentiful in Varna, and pensioners with spare rooms wait around the train station to greet new arrivals. Prices tend to be around 12 lv per person, but make sure you don't end up in some out-of-the-way suburb. **Isak** (📞602 318; info@accommodatebg.com; train station; r from 12 lv; ⏰9am-9.30pm May-Sep) and **Astra Tour** (📞605 861; train station; r per person from 12 lv, apt from 35 lv; ⏰7am-9pm Mon-Fri, to 7pm Sat & Sun), neighbouring agencies inside the train station, offer private rooms around town.

TOP CHOICE **Grand Hotel London** LUXURY HOTEL $$$
(📞664 100; www.londonhotel.bg; ul Musala 3; s/d Mon-Thu from 170/210 lv, Fri-Sun from 150/190 lv; P❄❀🐕🌐) Varna's grandest and oldest hotel is this five-star establishment, which originally opened in 1912. Rooms are spacious and elegantly furnished, if a little chintzy, and the restaurant is especially good.

Modus Hotel
LUXURY HOTEL $$$

(☎660 910; www.modushotel.com; ul Stefan Stambolov 46; s/d from 180/200 lv; P✈❄❅🌐; 🖥20) Just across the road from Primorski Park, Modus is a chic boutique hotel that has suitably stylish rooms with all the facilities you'd expect. Various discounts and package deals are offered, and there is also a gym, sauna and bistro.

Graffit Gallery Hotel
BOUTIQUE HOTEL $$$

(☎989 900; www.graffithotel.com; bul Knyaz Boris I 65; s/d/ste from 180/200/360 lv; P✈❄❅🌐; 🖥9) With its own art gallery, this modern designer hotel is certainly one of Varna's more colourful options. The large rooms on each of the four floors follow a different theme, and there's a spa and gym too. You can even choose from a pillow menu.

Hotel Astra
HOTEL $$

(☎630 524; www.hotelastravarna.com; ul Opalchenska 9; s/d 50/60 lv; ❄❅; 🖥9) A real bargain by Varna standards, this central, family-run hotel has 10 spacious and comfortable rooms, all with terraces, and basic but good-sized bathrooms.

Hotel Hi
HOTEL $$

(☎657 777; www.hotel-hi.com; ul Han Asparuh 11; s/d 80/112 lv; P❄❅) In a quiet neighbourhood south of the main thoroughfare, Hi is a friendly place featuring stylish, cosy rooms – some very small – with TVs and minibars.

Hotel Oceanic
CASINO HOTEL $$

(☎688 800; www.oceanichotelbg.com; pl Nezavisimost; s/d/apt 85/95/180 lv; ❄@❅) The centrally located Oceanic has cool, modern rooms with all the usual facilities, as well as some rather jazzy apartments. The big onsite casino and bookmakers' office may not be to everyone's taste, though.

Hotel Odessos
HOTEL $$

(☎640 300; www.odessos-bg.com; bul Slivnitsa 1; s/d/ste from 65/80/140 lv; P❄❅) Enjoying a great location opposite the entrance to Primorski Park, this is an older establishment with smallish and pretty average rooms, but it's convenient for the beach. Only the pricier 'sea view' rooms have balconies.

Flag Hostel
HOSTEL $

(☎0897408115; www.varnahostel.com; ul Bratya Shkorpil 13a; dm incl breakfast 22 lv; P✈❅; 🖥3, 9) The Flag is a long-established, sociable place with a young, international party atmosphere and three dorms, with single beds only (no bunks). Free pick ups from the bus and train stations are offered.

Yo Ho Hostel
HOSTEL $

(☎0886382905; www.yohohostel.com; ul Ruse 23; dm/s/d incl breakfast from 14/30/40 lv; @; 🖥109) Shiver your timbers at this pirate-themed place, with four- and 11-bed dorm rooms, two doubles and one single room. Free pick ups are offered, and staff also organise camping and rafting trips.

Voennomorski Club
HOTEL $

(☎617 965; ul Vladislav Varenchik 2; s 26-33 lv, d 35-60 lv; ❄; 🖥1, 409) Housed in a pale-blue building, the 'Naval Club' is something of a musty throwback to the days of the People's Republic, but the small rooms arc OK for the price and the central location is a plus.

Victorina
ACCOMMODATION SERVICES $

(☎0887721538, 603 541; http://victorina.borsabg.com; Tsar Simeon 36; s/d in private apt from 25/40 lv; ⊙9am-6pm Mon-Fri, to 5pm Sat, to 4pm Sun) Just north of the train station and highly recommended for renting good-quality rooms in private homes and apartments around the city centre.

Hotel Antik
HOTEL $

(☎632 167; www.antikvarna.com; ul Ohrid 10; s/d from 40/50 lv; ❄❅) A neat, family-run hotel just down the road from pl Nezavisimost, with basic but clean rooms; all come with TVs and refrigerators, and some have balconies.

✕ Eating

TOP CHOICE **Di Wine**
MODERN EUROPEAN $$$

(☎606 050; www.diwine.bg; ul Bratya Shkorpil 2; mains 12-30 lv; 🖥9) This formal but friendly restaurant is Varna's best fine-dining spot, with a big menu of tempting dishes, including rack of lamb, T-bone steaks, guinea fowl, salmon and trout as well as cheaper barbecue dishes. There are plenty of very good wines to try, too.

Tanasi
GREEK $$

(☎601 138; ul Bratya Shkorpil 16; mains 5-15 lv; 🖥9) This welcoming Greek restaurant has fresh white linen indoors, plus less formal outdoor seating. Featured dishes include stuffed aubergines, roast lamb, rabbit and various fish, and it also offers an excellent-value three-course set lunch for 5 lv.

Morsko Konche   PIZZERIA $$

(pl Nezavisimost; pizzas 5-10 lv; 🖥🍴) The 'Sea-horse' is a cheap and cheerful pizza place with a big menu featuring all the standard varieties, as well as some inventive creations of its own: the 'exotic' pizza comes with ba-nanas and blueberries.

Dom na Arkitekta   BULGARIAN $$

(ul Musala 10; mains 4-10 lv) 'The Architect's House' is a fine old wooden National Revival-style building with a leafy court-yard popular with local cats. Grills, steaks and salads are on the menu, plus more traditional 'delicacies' like chicken gizzards with onions.

Trops Kâshta   CAFETERIA $

(bul Knyaz Boris I 48; dishes 3-5 lv; 🍴) This branch of the dependable nationwide self-service canteen chain is the ideal place for cheap, simple food such as sausage and beans, chick-en chops and moussaka. There's no menu; just point at whatever takes your fancy.

Pri Monahinite   BULGARIAN $$$

(📞611 830; ul Primorski 47; mains 8-20 lv; 📞; 🚌20) Set in the courtyard of a little church, this is a classy place for roast lamb, grilled pork and other meaty offerings. It also has an ex-tensive wine list.

Mr Baba   SEAFOOD $$$

(📞614 629; mains 10-25 lv; ⊘8am-midnight; 📞; 🚌20) The coast-long trend for novelty ship restaurants has come to Varna, with this wooden-hulled venture stranded at the end of the beach off bul Primorski, near the port. It features a pricey but tasty menu of fish and steak dishes such as sea bass, trout and bluefish.

🍷 Drinking

Varna's trendiest bars are found along the beach on Kraybrezhna aleya, although many only have a brief existence in the summer sunshine. Popular hang-outs to sip seafront margaritas include **Pench's Cocktails** (Kray-brezhna aleya) and **Punta Cana** (Kraybrezhna aleya; ⊘6am-4am), while there are several cof-fee and cocktail bars along bul Slivnitsa.

☆ Entertainment

Exit (⊘10pm-6am), **4aspik** (📞0885800297; ⊘10pm-4am), specialising in Bulgarian folk-pop, and **Copacabana** (⊘10pm-5am), with a fondness for '70s and '80s music, are just a few of the many summertime clubs along Kraybrezhna aleya.

Varna Opera House   OPERA

(📞650 555; www.operavarna.bg; pl Nezavisimost 1; ⊘ticket office 11am-1pm & 2-7pm Mon-Fri, 11am-6pm Sat) Established in 1947, Varna's grand opera house hosts performances by the Varna Opera and Philharmonic Orchestra all year, except July and August, when some performances are staged at the Open-Air Theatre.

Open-Air Theatre   THEATRE

(Summer Theatre; 📞228 385; Primorski Park) Complete with mock ivy-covered Roman arches, this theatre hosts everything from ballet to rock concerts. Details are available at the adjoining ticket office.

Kino Arena   CINEMA

(www.kinoarena.com; bul Vladislav Verenchik 138; tickets 7-10 lv; 🚌148) On the top floor of the Grand Mall Varna shopping centre (right be-hind the main bus station).

ℹ Information

Internet Access

Internet Doom (ul 27 Yuli 13; per hr 1.60 lv; ⊘24hr) The most central of several branches around town, just behind the St Nikolai Church.

Media

The **Varna City Info Guide** is a free quarterly glossy booklet available at some hotel reception desks, with useful general information on the city and region, plus hotel, restaurant and club reviews. It also includes a handy tourist map.

Money

There are numerous banks with ATMs around the city centre, including **Unicredit Bulbank** (bul Slivnitsa) and **Biochim Commercial Bank** (bul Vladislav Varenchik).

Tourist Information

Tourist information centre (📞0887703242, 820 689; www.varnainfo.bg; pl Kiril & Metodii; ⊘9am-7pm; 🚌3) Plenty of free brochures and maps, and helpful multilingual staff.

ℹ Getting There & Away

Air

Varna's international **airport** (📞573 323; www.varna-airport.bg) has scheduled and charter flights from all over Europe, as well as regular flights to and from Sofia. From the centre, bus 409 goes to the airport.

Bus

Varna has two bus stations; the scruffy **central bus station** (bul Vladislav Varenchik 158; 🚌148) is about 2km northwest of the city centre. There are basic cafes and a **left luggage office** (central bus station; per hr 0.80 lv; ⊘7am-7pm).

Albena (5 lv, 45 minutes, several daily)
Balchik (5 lv, one hour, 16 daily)
Burgas (14 lv, two hours, four daily)
Kavarna (6 lv, 1½ hours, seven daily)
Plovdiv (27 lv, six hours, two daily)
Ruse (15 lv, four hours, five daily)
Shumen (8 lv, 1½ hours, three daily)
Silistra (9 lv, two hours, two daily)
Sofia (32 lv, seven hours, 20 daily)
Veliko Târnovo (18 lv, four hours, 20 daily)
Istanbul (60 lv, 10 hours, two daily)

The **Chatsna Mladost Station** (☑500 039) is about 200m along a road that starts almost opposite the central bus station. From here, frequent minibuses go to destinations such as Balchik, Kavarna and Burgas.Ticket prices are the same as from the central bus station.

Train

Facilities at Varna's **train station** (☑630 414; pl Slaveikov) include a left-luggage office and cafe.

Plovdiv (24.20 lv, seven hours, three daily)
Ruse (12.20 lv, four hours, two daily)
Shumen (6.50 lv, 1½ hours, 10 daily)
Sofia (23.60 lv, seven to eight hours, seven daily)

The **Rila Bureau** (☑632 348; ul Preslav 13; ⊘8.30am-5.30pm Mon-Fri, 8am-3.30pm Sat) sells tickets for international services and advance tickets for domestic trains.

ⓘ Getting Around

The bus and train stations are on opposite sides of the city, and linked by buses 1, 22 and 41. The most useful bus for visitors is 409, which connects the airport with Golden Sands (Zlatni Pyasâtsi) every 15 minutes between 6am and 11pm. This bus passes the central bus station in Varna and also stops outside Sveti Konstantin. It can be caught at designated spots on bul Vladislav Varenchik near the main post office, and along bul Knyaz Boris I. Bus 109 runs between the train station and Golden Sands.

If you need a rental car, **Hertz** (☑510 250; ⊘9am-6pm) and **Sixt** (☑599 490; ⊘9am-9pm) have offices at the airport.

Sveti Konstantin
Свети Константин

☑052

Sveti Konstantin is a small, sedate beach resort about 9km northeast of Varna, with hotels attractively spaced out amongst parkland. Established in 1946 under the name of Druzhba (Friendship), it was later renamed Sveti Konstantin i Elena, but is now more commonly known simply as Sveti Konstantin. It's less commercial than other resorts and has long been popular with older holidaymakers; it still has a number of 'rest homes' for retired civil servants and trade-union members, and the resort is famous for its therapeutic mineral waters and health treatments. There are several new resort hotels geared towards young families, but this isn't the place for water sports or raucous nightlife.

There are no street names in Sveti Konstantin and hotels are poorly signposted, although there is a map on a signboard by the bus stop. The centre of the resort is along the main road between the bus stop and the beach. Another road runs east from the bus stop to the Sunny Day Complex at the far end of the beach.

⊙ Sights & Activities

FREE **Sveti Sveti Konstantin & Elena Monastery**   MONASTERY
(www.varnamonastery.bg; ⊘dawn-dusk, closed morning Sun) This tiny church was built in the early 18th century on the site of a holy healing spring, though it has been rebuilt and remodelled since then. The spring remains, under the communion table. The church houses relics of St Valentine, as well as its patron saints.

Beach   BEACH
Much of the beach is carved up into private stretches of sand appropriated by the various hotels, but there are plenty of areas accessible to nonguests too. Parasols and sun beds cost 6 to 7 lv each. However, all the beaches tend to be small and bordered by jetties, breakwaters and rocky outcrops. There are no water sports available here.

🛏 Sleeping & Eating

Sirius Beach Hotel   HOTEL $$$
(☑361 224; www.siriusbeach.com; s/d 100/150 lv; P❊@≋) With its flashy glass tower and mock-up ship restaurant, the four-star Sirius is an unmistakable landmark. Set on a narrow curve of beach, it's a typical resort-style hotel, and there are indoor and outdoor pools, a kids' play area and a spa.

International House of Scientists Frederic Joliot-Curie   HOTEL $$
(☑361 161; www.ihsvarna.com; s/d 55/80 lv, renovated 85/95 lv; P☺❊@≋) Looking (and

ALADZHA MONASTERY

A major local attraction is **Aladzha Monastery** (adult/student 5/2 lv; ⊙9am-6pm Apr-Oct, to 4pm Tue-Sat Nov-Mar). Little is known about this bizarre rock monastery; the caves were first inhabited by 11th-century hermits, but what remains today was created during the 13th and 14th centuries, including some remarkable frescoes.

A signposted path (600m) leads to the three-level catacombs, accessed by stairways.

To walk to the monastery from Golden Sands, head up the road past the post office, cross the main Varna–Albena road, and follow the signs to 'Kloster Aladja' and the markings along the obvious trail. The walk takes an hour one way and wends its way through a wonderful, shady forest, part of the 1320-hectare Golden Sands Nature Park.

The road (3km) starts about 500m south along the Varna–Albena road from the start of the walking trail. The infrequent bus 33 from Varna to Kranevo drops passengers outside the front entrance of the monastery.

sounding) like a remnant of another era, this '60s tower block west of the bus stop nevertheless offers good value, and it's definitely worth the extra leva for the neater modernised rooms. It has a mineral-water pool, a pharmacy and a cactus garden. Various balneological treatments are available.

Hotel Panorama HOTEL **$$**
(☑361 025; www.panoramahotel.bg; s/d 60/74 lv; P🕸) Among the cheaper options, this older establishment faces the main road. Rooms are comfortable, if a little dated, but most have balconies and sea views. There are gardens at the back with steps leading down towards the beachfront area.

Mehana Marina BULGARIAN **$$**
(mains 6-12 lv;) Near the bus stop, this folksy restaurant features traditional Bulgarian and German fare, so there are lots of sausages. Fish dishes are also available.

ⓘ Getting There & Away

Buses 8, 9 and 109 leave regularly from the bus stop outside Varna's tourist information centre (p418) to Sveti Konstantin (1.60 lv, one hour). Bus 409 stops on the main road, near Hotel Panorama, on the way between Varna and Golden Sands.

Golden Sands (Zlatni Pyasâtsi) Златни Пясъци

Golden Sands (Zlatni Pyasâtsi), 18km up the coast from Varna, was Bulgaria's original purpose-built resort, with the first hotel opening here in 1957. Today it's Bulgaria's second-largest coastal resort, with a 4km

stretch of sandy beach, and some of the best nightlife on the coast. Virtually everyone staying in the resort will be on a prebooked package, and so no accommodation options are given here; try Varna or Sveti Konstantin instead.

🕴 Activities

The usual water sports, such as jet skiing (60 lv for 15 minutes) are available on the beach. Diving is also popular, and there are several outlets along the beach, including the PADI-certified **Harry's Diving Center** (☑356 701; www.divewithharry.com; ⊙May-Oct). Single dives, exploring the reefs just 30m offshore, cost 80 lv.

Aquapolis WATER SPORTS
(☑389 966; www.aquapolis.net; adult/child 33/16 lv, after 3pm 24/12 lv; ⊙10am-7pm) Near the main road, Aquapolis is a water park featuring lots of different pools, slides and other kid-friendly attractions, including a mini climbing wall. A minibus (1 lv, every 40 minutes) to Aquapolis picks up at various signed points around the resort.

✖ Eating

Eating out in Golden Sands costs about twice as much as in Varna, and there are plenty of unremarkable restaurants aimed at passing tourists along the seafront. Try **Taj Mahal** (mains around 5-10 lv) for Indian food, or **Chiflika** (mains 10-20 lv; ⊙24hr) for steaks and kebabs.

☆ Entertainment

Golden Sands has a lively clubbing scene, with numerous venues around the resort, many inside hotels. Restaurants and bars often provide live entertainment, with everything from Bulgarian folk ensembles to Elvis impersonators and Tom Jones tribute acts on the bill. **Arrogance Music Factory** (☑0885800275; www.arroganceclub.com; ⊙10.30pm-6am May-Oct) and **PR Club Admiral** (☑0899121501; ⊙10.30pm-6am) are just two of the more popular nightclubs.

ℹ Getting There & Away

Buses 109, 209, 309 and 409 leave Varna every 10 or 15 minutes between 6am and 11pm. The buses stop along the main Varna–Albena road at each main entrance to Golden Sands.

Balchik   Балчик
☑0579 / POP 12,100

After the vast, artificial resorts further down the coast, Balchik is a breath of fresh sea air. A small, pretty town and fishing port huddled below white-chalk cliffs, it's a low-key holiday spot that feels like a world away from the likes of Albena, whose lights can be seen winking across the bay at night. The main attraction here is the palace, with its lovely botanical gardens, a couple of kilometres down the coast. The biggest, fenced-off patch of sand (open 8.30am to 6.30pm) is in front of the Hotel Helios, just east of the centre. Otherwise, there are just a few scraps of artificial beach crammed with parasols – the rest of the very narrow shoreline consists of rubble and boulders – although there are several concrete jetties used by some tourists for sunbathing.

History

Greek traders who settled here in the 6th century BC initially called the place Krou-noi (meaning 'town of springs') but later changed the name to Dionysopolis in honour of the god of wine. The Romans came later and fortified the town, and viticulture remained an important local industry. In medieval times, Balchik (possibly meaning 'town of clay') thrived on the export of grain from the hinterlands. In 1913, the town (and the rest of the region) was annexed by Romania; it was literally sold back to Bulgaria in 1940 for 7000 'golden leva'.

◉ Sights

City Historical Museum   MUSEUM
(ul Vitosha 3; admission 2 lv; ⊙9am-noon & 1-5pm Mon-Fri) The diverse collection here includes Roman statuary, medieval pottery and vintage photographs of the town from the early 1900s.

Ethnographic Museum   MUSEUM
(ul Vitosha; admission 1 lv; ⊙9am-5pm Mon-Fri) This museum features folk costumes and displays relating to traditional trades and crafts such as fishing, barrel making and woodcarving.

🛏 Sleeping

Hotel Mistral   HOTEL $$
(☑71 130; www.hotelmistralbg.com; ul Primorska 8b; s/d 92/112 lv; ⊛❄🖥) One of the best waterfront hotels, the four-star Mistral is an upmarket place with large rooms, all with sea-facing balconies. Prices drop by up to half outside the summer season.

Hotel Regina Maria Spa   LUXURY HOTEL $$$
(☑460 065; www.reginamariaspa.com; r/ste 160/250 lv; P❄🖥❄) On the seafront, the four-star Regina Maria offers smart rooms in a variety of styles, all with sea views.

BLACK SEA COAST BALCHIK

WORTH A TRIP

ALBENA АЛБЕНА

With its lovely 4km-long beach and shallow water, the big purpose-built resort of Albena is a great place for water sports. On the downside, it's expensive and not particularly user-friendly for independent travellers, but that doesn't mean you can't drop by as a day visitor and take advantage of its facilities. Jet skiing, parasailing, waterskiing and surfing are all available, while Albena is also a base for diving; **Albena Diving Centre** (☑0888 980 409; www.bgdiving.com; ⊙9am-6pm May-Oct), based at Hotel Laguna Beach, offers diving packages (one/two dives 80/120 lv), plus a range of multiday courses, exploring wrecks and reefs. If that sounds a little *too* active, several hotels in the resort have excellent spa centres.

The bus station is around 800m from the beach and there are regular minibuses to/from Balchik (3 lv, 30 minutes) and Varna (5 lv, 45 minutes). Note that entry to the resort costs 3 lv if you arrive by private car.

Balchik

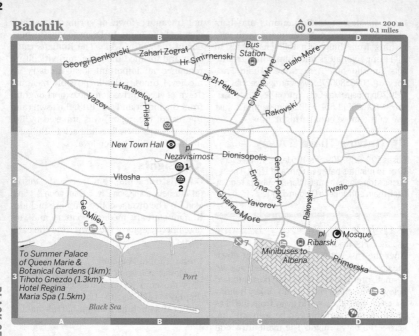

Balchik

⊙ Sights

1	City Historical Museum	B2
2	Ethnographic Museum	B2

🛏 Sleeping

3	Hotel Helios	D3
4	Hotel Mistral	B3
5	Irish Rover	C3
6	White House	A2

🍴 Eating

	Francis Drake	(see 4)
7	Old Boat	C3

Golfing packages and fishing trips can be arranged.

Hotel Helios   HOTEL **$$**
(☎76 970; www.heliosbg.com; d/apt 94/134 lv; P❄@☼) Occupying the only real patch of sandy beach in Balchik, Helios is a modern, resort-style hotel and all rooms have balconies, many with superb sea views. Prices drop by up to 50% out of high season.

White House   HOTEL **$$**
(☎73 822; www.whitehousebg.com; ul Geo Milev 18; s/d 50/80 lv; P❄) Situated on the seafront, this is a bright and breezy place with at-

tractive rooms, all with fridges and TVs and many with sea views. There's a busy restaurant at the front.

Irish Rover   INN **$**
(☎0888510530; www.balchikirish.com; ul Primorska 27; r Jul & Aug 30 lv, Sep-Jun 20 lv; ❄❅@) In the town centre, this is a lively Irish pub and popular party place, with several simple but serviceable rooms upstairs. Cheaper rates are available for longer stays.

🍴 Eating

The waterfront between the port and the palace is lined with restaurants, most offering fresh fish.

[TOP CHOICE] Tihoto Gnezdo   CAFE **$**
(mains from 3 lv; ⊙9am-11pm; ♪) On the shore near the palace, this simple little cafe serves light dishes like salads and omelettes (from 3.50 lv) as well as fish. Prices are much more reasonable than at most seafront restaurants.

Francis Drake   SEAFOOD **$$$**
(mains 10-30 lv; ⊙8am-midnight; ☎) The restaurant of the Hotel Mistral is the place for some classier cuisine. Fried turbot, smoked salmon and locally caught fish are among the offerings.

SUMMER PALACE OF QUEEN MARIE & BOTANICAL GARDENS

At the western end of the seafront, this little **palace** (Dvorets; admission 10lv; ⏰8am-8pm May–mid-Oct, 8.30am-6.30pm mid-Oct–Apr) was completed in 1926 by King Ferdinand of Romania for his English wife, Queen Marie (Balchik was then part of Romania). It was rumoured that Marie entertained her much younger Turkish lover here.

Size-wise, it's a relatively modest seaside villa, although the architecture – a blend of Bulgarian, Gothic and Islamic styles topped with a minaret – is unique. The half-dozen-or-so rooms on show contain original furnishings, including paintings by Marie, and several photographs of the queen striking dramatic poses in the grounds. Also here is a curious collection of local archaeological finds, including Roman pottery and mammoth bones.

Behind the palace are the extensive botanical gardens. Around 600 species of flora are featured throughout a series of themed gardens, including an impressive collection of cacti.

Also within the complex are a water mill, a classical-style nymphaeum, the tiny Chapel of Sveta Bogoroditsa and even a winery.

If you're travelling here by bus from the southern coast, get off at the bus stop opposite the palace – either look for the tour buses and souvenir stalls, or ask the driver to drop you off at the *dvorets* (palace). The entrance here leads into the top end of the botanical gardens. The other entrance is off the seafront promenade. Mugs, fridge magnets and postcards carrying Queen Marie's image can be had at shops at both entrances.

Old Boat
SEAFOOD $$

(mains 6-15 lv; ⏰8am-3am) With an attractive waterfront setting overlooking the harbour, this is a good place for fresh fish, such as grilled mackerel, shark fillet and bluefish.

❶ Information

The post office and telephone centre are on the main square, pl Nezavisimost. There's a branch of Unicredit Bulbank with an ATM opposite the bus station, and you can change money at **SG Expressbank** (ul Cherno More).

❶ Getting There & Away

Balchik's **bus station** (✆74 069) is at the top of ul Cherno More, a steep 1km walk from the port. Minibuses travel from Balchik to Albena (3 lv, 20 minutes, every 30 minutes), Varna (5 lv, one hour, hourly), Kavarna (4 lv, 30 minutes, four daily) and Sofia (36 lv, 10 hours, two daily). Rather more conveniently, minibuses to Albena also call at the bus stop on ul Primorska, outside the supermarket.

Kavarna   Каварна

✆0570 / POP 11,500

Kavarna, 17km east of Balchik, is a sleepy administrative town of little interest in itself, although it's famous (in Bulgaria) as the venue for the **Kaliakra Rock Fest** (www.kaliakrarockfest.com), which attracts international acts every June. It's also the most practical base for anyone wishing to explore the Kaliakra Cape.

The pedestrianised ul Dobrotitsa, running south from the bus station, is where you'll find the post office, banks and cafes. Halfway along, the **Church of Sveti Georgi** (ul Rakovski) is worth a quick look for its icons. Another low-key sight is the **History Museum** (ul Dobrotitsa 1B; admission 2 lv; ⏰9am-5pm Mon-Fri), displaying some Thracian and Roman oddments.

The seafront is around 3km or so downhill from town, and can be reached by hourly buses from the bus station if you don't fancy the walk. Impressive white cliffs watch over the harbour and sandy beach, which is patrolled by lifeguards.

There are four daily buses to Balchik (4 lv, 30 minutes), and hourly buses to Varna (6 lv, 1¼ hours). There are a few minibuses each day to Bâlgarevo and Shabla and one or two to Rusalka and Krapets. The border with Romania is closed along the coast here.

⛱ Sleeping

Thracian Cliffs Golf Resort & Spa
RESORT $$$

(✆058 510 510; www.thraciancliffs.com; apt from 394 lv; P❄✳🐾) Located in Bozhurets

THE LEGEND OF KALIAKRA

According to a local myth, as the Turks advanced on Kavarna in the 14th century, a group of 40 beautiful young women, fearing a life of slavery, dishonour or worse at the hands of the Ottoman soldiers, tied their long hair together and, holding hands, threw themselves off a cliff along the Kaliakra Cape. Some displays relating to this legend can be seen in Kavarna's History Museum (p423), and a monument at the Kaliakra Cape is dedicated to the women.

village, west of Kavarna, this sprawling all-suite resort is centered on a stunning 18-hole golf course, designed by Gary Player. The suites are large and luxurious and there are excellent restaurants on site. Windsurfing and waterskiing are available at the beach, if golf's not your thing.

Hotel Venera　　　　　　　GUESTHOUSE **$**
(☏87 003; www.venera-bg.eu; ul Chaika 6; r 20-30 lv; P❋@) Around 150m from the sea, Hotel Venera is among the better options in Kavarna.

Kaliakra Cape
Нос Калиакра

Kaliakra (Beautiful) Cape is a 2km-long headland (the longest along the Bulgarian coastline), about 13km southeast of Kavarna.

Most of the cape is part of the 687-hectare **Kaliakra Nature Reserve** (admission 3 lv; ☺24hr), the only reserve in Bulgaria that partly protects the Black Sea (up to 500m offshore). The reserve also protects fragile wetlands at Bolata and Taukliman (Bay of Birds), about 100 remote caves and over 300

species of bird. Between August and October you can spot migrating birds passing by, including storks and pelicans. Most of the year, the official lookouts along the cape and near Rusalka are ideal spots to watch numbers of increasingly rare dolphins.

Also in the reserve are the ruins of an 8th-century citadel, and some ruined churches. The history of the area is explained in some detail at the **Archaeological Museum** (admission free; ☺10am-6pm), wonderfully located inside a cave.

Anyone visiting the reserve must first go to the **Nature Information Centre** (☏057-44 424) in Bâlgarevo village, about halfway between Kavarna and Kaliakra Cape. The centre features a display (in English) about the flora, fauna and marine life of the Black Sea.

The tiny seaside town of Krapets, in between the protected areas of Lakes Shabla and Durankulak, and close to several archaeological sites, makes an excellent base for exploring the region. Try **Villa Kibela** (☏0888880281; www.villakibela.com; r 80-100 lv; P❋@☲), a welcoming place that also arranges walking tours and fishing trips.

The Danube & Northern Plains

Best Museums

» Ruse Regional Museum of History (p433)

» Sveti Sofronii Vrachanski Ethnographical & Revival Complex (p427)

» Archaeological Museum (p439)

» Historical Museum (p432)

» Transportation Museum (p433)

Best Places to Stay

» Hotel Drustar (p440)

» City Art Hotel (p434)

» Hotel Madona (p429)

» Pelican Lake Guesthouse (p439)

» Lopushanski Monastery(p428)

Why Go?

Much of northern Bulgaria is quiet, off-the-beaten-track territory and sees very few foreign visitors. It's a rewarding part of the country to explore, though you'll need plenty of time, patience or, most usefully, your own transport, to visit its more rural corners. Unspoilt mountain landscapes, wild nature reserves and peaceful monasteries are waiting for you to discover. The mighty Danube River shimmers along most of the country's border with Romania, and the urbane riverside city of Ruse, famed for its Viennese-style architecture and brimming with cafes and museums, is the gateway to Bucharest.

The enigmatic rock churches and rich wildlife of the vast Rusenski Lom Nature Reserve and, further east, serene Lake Srebârna, home to numerous rare bird species, are well worth visiting.

Away from the Danube, the bizarre rock formations at Belogradchik, the remote, charming monasteries at Lopushanski and Chiprovtsi and the dramatic hiking country around Vratsa are sure to delight outdoor enthusiasts.

When to Go

Vidin

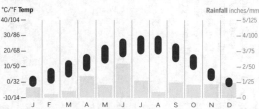

Mar–May Spring days are warm and pleasant, and festival season begins.

Jun–Aug Summers are hot and dry, and it's a great time for hiking and birdwatching.

Nov–Jan Winters can be harsh, but the countryside looks picturesque in the snow.

The Danube & Northern Plains Highlights

1 Marvelling at the wonders of **Belogradchik Rocks** (p429)

2 Going for a hike in the stunning countryside around **Vratsa** (p427)

3 Learning about the Russo-Turkish war in the museums of **Pleven** (p431), or enjoying the city's bars and cafes

4 Viewing the beautiful icons in the serene **Lopushanski Monastery** (p428)

5 Taking a look round the Russo-Turkish **Baba Vida Museum-Fortress** (p430) in Vidin

6 Discovering the elegant architecture, parkland and fine museums of **Ruse** (p432)

7 Visiting the unique rock churches at **Rusenski Lom Nature Park** (p437) and keeping an eye out for wildlife

8 Spotting rare waterfowl at **Srebârna Nature Reserve** (p438), a Unesco World Heritage site

9 Enjoying the views of the Danube and exploring the Roman and Byzantine ruins in **Silistra** (p439)

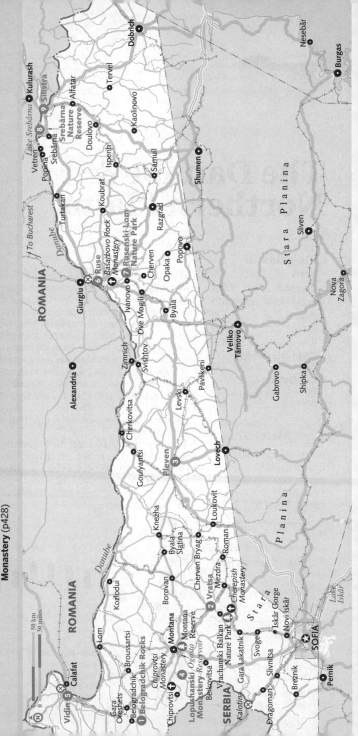

Vratsa
Враца

📞092 / POP 74,700

With its striking location just below a steep, narrow gorge in the Vrachanska Mountains, Vratsa makes a handy base for exploring the Vrachanski Balkan Nature Park, as well as Lopushanski and Cherepish Monasteries. It's a quiet, well-kept little town with plenty of laid-back pavement cafes, and there are a couple of worthwhile museums to visit too.

The centre of Vratsa is pl Hristo Botev, named in honour of the 19th-century revolutionary whose giant statue stands here. Cafes and civic buildings congregate around this square, though most of the action is further east along the pedestrian street of bul Nikola Voyvodov, which finishes at the market near the train station. Numerous banks here have ATMs.

South of the town centre on the way to the gorge, the **Natura Information Centre** (📞660 318; naturacenter@abv.bg; ul Pop Sava Katralfilov 26-29; ☺9am-noon & 1-5pm Apr-Oct, closed Sat & Sun Nov-Mar), located in a former mosque, provides information on walking routes and more general tourism information. For information, maps and advice, visit the Vrachanski Balkan Nature Park headquarters (p428).

⊙ Sights & Activities

Historical Museum
MUSEUM

(pl Hristo Botev; admission 3 lv; ☺9am-12.30pm & 1-6pm) The star of the show at Vratsa's museum is the **Rogozen Treasure**, a shining collection of Thracian silver jugs and plates, many featuring mythological scenes. Also here are neolithic clay idols, Roman pottery and displays relating to local hero Hristo Botev. The 17th-century tower outside doubles as the museum's souvenir shop.

Sveti Sofronii Vrachanski
Ethnographical & Revival Complex
MUSEUM

(ul Gen Leonov; adult/student 2/1 lv, free Fri; ☺9am-5.30pm Mon-Fri) This interesting museum complex consists of four National Revival era buildings displaying traditional costumes, instruments, toys, domestic interiors and silk-weaving apparatus. There's also a collection of vintage vehicles, including a sleigh and 19th-century carriages. The gardens are free to wander round; buy a ticket at the Vaznesenie School building and ask them to open the other houses for you.

Also accessible from the gardens is the **Sveti Vaznesenie Church**, which holds a particularly fine collection of 18th- and 19th-century icons, some by Zachary Zograf, all labelled in English.

Hiking
There's relaxed hiking trails in the forested hills southwest of the main square and tougher treks (several marked hiking trails exist) along the river road towards Ledenika Cave (p428) . Rock climbing – for the truly fearless only – is performed on the sheer mountain cliffs that straddle the road.

🛏 Sleeping & Eating

Hotel Hemus
HOTEL $$

(📞624 150; www.hotelhemus.com; pl Hristo Botev 1; s/d 50/60 lv; 🅿❄✳🖥🏊) This new three-star business hotel dominates the main square. Rooms are sparsely furnished but comfortable, and are reasonably priced for the central location. There's a small pool and a restaurant.

Hotel Chaika
HOTEL $

(📞621 369; www.chaika.net; at the gorge; d 42-62 lv, ste 68-154 lv; 🅿❄✳) The spectacular location at the mouth of the gorge is certainly appealing, the restaurant is excellent, and there's even a small boating-lake for guests. Sadly, the musty rooms with their hard, creaky beds let it down somewhat. It's about 2km out of town – a taxi from the bus/train station costs from 2 to 4 lv.

Trakiiska Printsesa
INTERNATIONAL $

(bul Nikola Voyvodov 12; mains 3-8 lv; 🍴) On Vratsa's main pedestrian street, this is a pleasant place for a variety of light meals. Salads, risottos, fish and pasta dishes are served. The chicken fettuccine is very good.

Pizza Corona
PIZZERIA $

(ul Targovska 2; pizzas 7-10 lv; 🍴) Facing the main square, Corona offers a big menu of pizzas, as well as pasta dishes and salads.

ⓘ Getting There & Away

The **bus station** (📞622 558) is 200m east of the train station. Buses travel hourly to/from Sofia (8 lv, two hours) and more frequently between 6am and 9am. One or two buses daily serve Gabrovo, Pleven and Lovech, plus four to Vidin.

Inside the **train station** (📞624 415), the **Rila Bureau** (📞620 562; ☺8am-4.30pm Mon-Fri) sells tickets for international trains and advance tickets for domestic services. Services include Sofia (five daily), Montana (six daily) and Vidin (four daily); the latter passes through Gara Oreshets, from where you can get to Belogradchik.

For more distant destinations, connecting to the nearby Mezra train station (20 minutes south) and changing there is recommended. From Mezra four daily trains serve northern Bulgarian destinations such as Pleven, Ruse (11.50 lv, seven hours) and Varna (15.70 lv), plus Silistra (18.20 lv, one daily). There are also frequent trains to Sofia (4.50 lv, two hours).

❶ Getting Around

Vratsa itself is easily walkable, though the gorge is 2km south of town; however, taxis are plentiful and cheap. Taxis are also useful to reach Ledenika Cave and Cherepish Monastery.

Vrachanski Balkan Nature Park

Numerous species of birds, 700 types of trees and about 500 caves distinguish this nature park of 288 sq km, southwest of Vratsa. While some of the rocky outcroppings are fragile, they're still open to rock climbers and hang-gliders. Unfortunately, the park's more accessible parts are marred by abandoned hotels and a disused chairlift.

Named after the Bulgarian word for ice (led), the **Ledenika Cave** (guided tours per person 5 lv; ⊙8am-6pm summer) is indeed sheathed in ice for much of the winter, but thaws out in summer when visitors on guided tours arrive to explore it. While most come on a sunny summer afternoon, a unique time to see Ledenika is for the periodic concerts held within its chilly confines.

The cave is about 15km (or three hours on foot) from the road that starts by the former Hotel Tourist in Vratsa, where it's signposted. The hourly bus from Vratsa to Zgorigrad will leave you near the cave if you alert the driver. The cafes also have directions to the new **Vrachanski Ecotrail**.

The **park headquarters** (☏666 5849; www.vr-balkan.net; ul Ivanka Boteva 1) provides information on hiking and caving expeditions.

Montana   Монтана

☏096 / POP 43,300

The main transport hub for Chiprovtsi or Lopushanski Monastery, this drab modern town was once known as Kutlovitsa then, from 1890, Ferdinand. While under the communists, it became Mihailovgrad, honouring a local socialist revolutionary. It was named

'Montana' following a 1993 referendum, after a nearby Roman settlement. There's little reason to stay, but 2km south of town, the modern lakeside **Ring Hotel** (☏588 861; www.ring-hotel.com; Augusta Lake; r from 100 lv; 🅿✴🖥) offers the best facilities. For cheaper rooms, try the central **Hotel Bulgari** (☏0885305600; ul Slavyanska 8; r from 45 lv; 🅿✴@), which also has a restaurant.

One pleasant local diversion along the road from Montana to Lopushanski Monastery is the **Ogosta Reservoir**. As Bulgaria's second-biggest artificial lake, it's popular for swimming and fishing.

From Montana's **bus station** (☏623 454) buses go almost hourly to Sofia, Vratsa and Vidin. Four or five daily buses serve Chiprovtsi, Kopilovtsi, Pleven and Belogradchik. The inconvenient **train station** (☏623 846) is on a spur track from the major line between Sofia and Vidin.

Lopushanski Monastery

Some 21km west of Montana, this small **monastery** (⊙8am-6pm), completed in 1853, enjoys a serene setting and holds icons painted by brothers Stanislav and Nikolai Dospevski. During the periodic rebellions against Ottoman rule, Lopushanski (also known as St John the Precursor) provided a safe haven for revolutionaries.

The monastery's **guesthouse** (Balova Shouma Inn; ☏0887397301 095-585 78; www.lopushanski-monastery.domino.bg; r per person 20-30 lv; ✴) is only metres from the monastery itself. It has 5 rooms and an apartment, with bathrooms and TVs. The attached cafe has indoor and outdoor seating, a peaceful location and decent food.

Chiprovtsi   Чипровци

POP 2000

Famous for its traditional carpets and quaint monastery, Chiprovtsi (Chip-rov-tsi) is little more than a rather quiet village tucked into the foothills of the Stara Planina (Balkan Range) mountains, but there are a few places to stay if you fancy resting up.

◉ Sights

FREE **Chiprovtsi Monastery**   MONASTERY
(admission free; ⊙dawn-dusk) Founded in the 10th century, this monastery, dedicated to Sveti Ivan Rilski (St John of Rila) was de-

stroyed and rebuilt several times over the years – what you see today dates largely from the early 19th century. It's roughly 6km northeast of Chiprovtsi village; take any bus between Montana and Chiprovtsi.

History Museum
MUSEUM

(ul Vitosha 2; admission 2 lv, free Thursday; ⊙8am-noon & 1-5pm Mon-Fri, 9am-5pm Sat-Sun) This small museum displays traditional costumes and colourful examples of the local Chiprovtsi carpets. Medieval ceramics, Roman coins and icons are also on show.

🛏 Sleeping & Eating

The guesthouse restaurants are the best places to eat. Chiprovtsi's few cafes are on the main square.

Torlacite Kâshta
GUESTHOUSE $

(☎0887892790; www.torlacite.com; ul Pavleto 31; d 30 lv; ℗) This attractive National Revival house has simple rooms set around a little courtyard garden, as well as a traditional *mehana* (tavern). If you have several days to spare, the owners offer carpet-weaving courses (65 lv per day, including accommodation and meals).

Pavlova Kâshta
GUESTHOUSE $

(☎095-542 242; videx_hotel@abv.bg; ul Pavleto 17; s/d 15/30 lv) The Pavlova Kâshta is a handsome white stone building offering basic, though airy and clean rooms. The adjacent *mehana* does good Bulgarian meals.

Tanchinata Kâshta
GUESTHOUSE $

(☎0888709044; roza.pavlova@abv.bg; ul Ropotomo 9; r 30 lv; ℗) There are just four homely rooms here, furnished in traditional style. There's a garden and barbecue for guest use, while meals can be arranged, as can a spot of carpet weaving.

ℹ Information

The **Chiprovtsi Tourist Information Centre** (☎095-52 910, 0885258405; tic.chiprovci@gmail.com), in the centre of town, provides information about local attractions, finds accommodation and may be able to help with buying the local handmade carpets.

ℹ Getting There & Away

Several daily buses connect Montana and Chiprovtsi. The road to Chiprovtsi from the Vratsa-Vidin Hwy (E79) starts 3km northwest of Montana. From the south, the turn-off is signposted 'Чипровски Манастир'; from the north, it's signposted 'Lopushanski' in English.

Belogradchik Белоградчик
☎093 / POP 5150

The crisp mountain air and the weird and wonderful rock formations rising from a lonely hill are what draw visitors to little Belogradchik, on the eastern edge of the Stara Planina mountain range. Although rather remote, Belogradchik's charms are starting to attract more visitors.

The **Tourist Information Centre** (☎64 294; milena-tourist_centre@abv.bg; ul Poruchik Dvoryanov 5; ⊙9am-5pm Mon-Fri) can help with information on local accommodation and supplies free maps and leaflets.

◉ Sights

Belogradchik Rocks
OUTDOORS

The massive Belogradchik sandstone and limestone rock formations cover an area of around 90 sq km and tower over the town. The rocks, standing up to 200m high, were sculpted over millions of years by natural compression and erosion, and their other-worldly appearance has inspired many local legends. The 'Monks', the 'Bear', the 'Shepherd Boy' and 'Adam and Eve' are just some of the named formations. The rocks are accessible by road, about 2km west of town.

Kaleto Fortress
FORTRESS

(admission 4 lv; ⊙9am-6pm Jun-Sep, 9am-5pm Oct-May) Almost blending in with the surrounding rocks is the Kaleto Fortress, originally built by the Romans and later expanded by the Byzantines, Bulgarians and Turks. Most of what you see today was completed in the 1830s. You can wander round three courtyards and explore the defensive bunkers; accessing the highest rocks involves a precarious climb up steep ladders.

History Museum
MUSEUM

(pl 1850 Leto; admission 1 lv; ⊙9am-noon & 2-5pm Mon-Fri) The history museum, housed in a National Revival building from 1810, displays folk costumes, jewellery and traditional local crafts such as woodcarving and pottery.

🛏 Sleeping & Eating

There are several guesthouses in and around town to choose from, most of which have decent restaurants. Nightlife is relegated to a few cafe-bars on the main street.

Hotel Madona
GUESTHOUSE $

(☎65 546; www.madonainn-bg.com; ul Hristo Botev 26; s 20-30 lv, d 40-60 lv; 🕏🍽) This cosy

LEGENDARY ROCKS

For centuries, the Belogradchik rock formations have fired the imaginations of local people. These twisting, contorted pillars of stone seem to take on the most curious shapes, both human and animal.

One legend tells the tragic tale of Valentina, a young nun renowned for her beauty. One day, during a holy festival, a young nobleman came along and was immediately smitten. The two began an illicit affair, which was discovered only when Valentina gave birth to a child in the convent. The Mother Superior and a council of monks decided to expel her. As she left, in tears, her lover came riding towards her on his white horse. At this moment, the sky turned black and terrifying thunder rent the air. The ground opened and consumed the convent, and everyone was turned to stone where they stood – including Valentina, who was transformed into the rock known today as the 'Madonna'.

guesthouse has six traditional-style rooms, 600m up from the main square (it's signposted). The restaurant is one of the best in town, and guests can hire mountain bikes for 7 lv per day.

Hotel Castle Cottage　GUESTHOUSE $$
(☎0898623727; www.castlecottage.eu; ul Tsolo Todorov 36; s/d 35/70 lv; P🐾) Standing not far from the fortress entrance, Castle Cottage is built in solid wood-and-stone traditional style. It offers one comfortable bedroom and two maisonettes, each individually designed, a log fire in winter and outdoor hot-tubs in summer.

Hotel Skalite　HOTEL $$
(☎094-691 210, 0884514154; www.skalite.bg; pl Vazrazhdane 2; s/d from 80/100 lv; P🐾@🐾) This modern four-star place in the town centre has the best rooms and facilities in Belogradchik, with a spa, gym, restaurant and appealing terrace bar. Prices rise slightly at weekends.

Drakite Guesthouse　GUESTHOUSE $
(☎63 930; www.drakite.com; ul Treti Mart 37; s/d from 25/35 lv) Run by a helpful English-speaking local who also organises fishing trips and transport, the guesthouse is 600m down from the Kaleto entrance and offers five basic rooms, two of which are en suite. The whole house can be rented for 175 lv per day.

Restaurant Elit　BULGARIAN $
(☎64 558; ul Yuri Gagarin 2; mains 4-6 lv; ⊙9am-midnight) Elit is the only dedicated restaurant in town and offers a variety of traditional Bulgarian dishes. It's a steep 600m walk up ul Vasil Levski and then off to the left.

ℹ Getting There & Away
From the **bus station** (☎63 427), three or four daily buses serve Vidin (5 lv, 1½ hours). A 6am bus serves Sofia via Montana (16 lv, four hours). The three daily buses that serve the train station, 9km away at Gara Oreshets (2 lv, 20 minutes), are timed to meet the Sofia-bound train. Several daily trains from Gara Oreshets serve Vidin (5 lv, 30 minutes), Vratsa (7 lv, 20 minutes) and Sofia (10 lv, 3½ hours).

A taxi from Belogradchik to Gara Oreshets train station costs 5 lv. For very early morning trains, taxis wait in front of the bus depot.

Vidin　Видин
☎094 / POP 48,000

Resting on a bend in the Danube in the far northwest of Bulgaria, Vidin feels a long way from anywhere, and unless you're crossing into Romania, there's little obvious reason for you to wend your way up here. The population has shrunk dramatically over the last decade or so, and it can appear forlorn and eerily deserted. Having said all that, Vidin does enjoy some fine riverside views and its one major attraction, the majestic Baba Vida fortress, is one of the best preserved in the country. The sprawling town square, pl Bdintsi, one block northeast of the train station, features an enormous communist-era monument, banks and shops.

◎ Sights

Baba Vida Museum-Fortress　FORTRESS
(adult/student 4/2 lv, combined ticket with Archaeological Museum 5 lv; ⊙8.30am-5pm Mon-Fri, 9.30am-5pm Sat & Sun) About 1km north of the centre, overlooking the river, the marvellously intact Baba Vida Museum-Fortress is largely a 17th-century Turkish upgrade of 10th-century Bulgarian fortifications, which in turn were built upon the ruins of the 3rd-century Roman fort of Bononia. There's little to see inside, but it's an atmospheric place. Watch out for uncovered holes and the sheer drops from the top.

Archaeological Museum　MUSEUM
(ul Tsar Simeon Veliki 12; adult/student 4/2 lv, combined ticket with Baba-Vida fortress 5 lv; ⊙9am-noon & 1.30-5.30pm Tue-Sat) Inside the former

Turkish prison, this little museum holds a scrappy collection of neolithic flints, Roman statue fragments, medieval swords and 19th-century rifles. There's no English labelling and it's worth a quick look only if you've bought the combined ticket with the Baba Vida fortress.

FREE **Contemporary Art Gallery** GALLERY
(Galeriya Nikola Petrov; admission free; ⊙9am-6pm Mon-Fri) A small contemporary art gallery, named after Bulgarian painter Nikola Petrov, with paintings by local artists. It's housed in a stately neoclassical building near the Hotel Bononia.

🛏 Sleeping & Eating

Anna-Kristina Hotel HOTEL **$$**
(☑606 038; www.annakristinahotel.com; ul Baba Vida 2; d from 84 lv; ℗❋@☎) Housed inside a century-old Turkish bathhouse set back from the river, the Anna-Kristina is a welcoming, if slightly formal, place with spacious rooms and smart modern bathrooms. There's a summer-only outdoor pool (10 lv extra) and a restaurant.

Old Town Hotel BOUTIQUE HOTEL **$$**
(Hotel Staryat Grad; ☑600 023; www.oldtownhotel.dir.bg; ul Knyaz Boris I 2; s/d/tr 60/80/100 lv; ❋☎) Centrally located near the Old Town Stambol Kapia gateway, this charming boutique hotel has just eight rooms inside a renovated townhouse, fitted with antique-style furnishings and original works by local artists.

Hotel Bononia HOTEL **$**
(☑606 031; www.hotelbononia.net; ul Bdin 2; s/d 36/39 lv; ❋) Just around the corner from the riverside park, the Bononia is an old-style hotel; even so it offers acceptable rooms that are good value. The hotel also has a decent restaurant.

Classic Pizzeria PIZZERIA **$**
(ul Aleksandar II 25; mains 5-15 lv) Opposite the Port Authority building on the riverbank, this is one of the better places in town, with a big menu of pizzas and pasta dishes, as well as locally caught fish.

❶ Getting There & Away

From Vidin's public **bus station** (ul Zhelezhnicharska) there are buses to Belogradchik (5 lv, 1½ hours, two to three daily). Nearby is the private Alexiev Bus Station, from where there are several daily buses to Sofia (20 lv, four hours)

via Vratsa (10 lv). Buses also run to Pleven (16 lv, four hours, one daily).

Fast trains travel to Sofia (13.80 lv, five hours, three daily) via Vratsa (8 lv, three hours).

To/From Romania
Finally completed in late 2012, the long-anticipated bridge between Vidin and Calafat, known as Danube Bridge 2, should be in full use from spring 2013. Meanwhile, the **ferry** (foot passenger/car 6/46 lv, 15 minutes, daily) provides the only daily service to Romania . The ferry terminal is 2km north of town; take a taxi (4 lv) from the train station's taxi rank. The boats theoretically depart every two hours, but won't leave unless they're full.

Cherepish Monastery

Founded in the 14th century, **Cherepish Monastery** (☑0897312770; admission free; guesthouse per person 20 lv) was, like Chiprovtsi Monastery, torched, toppled and rebuilt repeatedly during the Ottoman period. Like many other monasteries, it was used by rebels as a hiding place before and during the Russo-Turkish War (1877–78).

The monastery's little **museum** displays icons and has Bulgarian-language books about the monastery and local history. There's basic accommodation if you want to stay and meals are available.

The poorly signposted monastery is 600m from the eponymous roadside restaurant on the Mezdra–Zverino route. Buses from Sofia heading towards Mezdra, Vratsa, Montana or Vidin pass the monastery; disembark at the Zverino turn-off and wait for a connecting minibus, or walk west 6km. If driving from Sofia, the most aesthetically appealing approach is definitely the scenic if slower road through the stunning Iskâr Gorge, via Novi Iskâr.

Pleven Плевен

☑064 / POP 106,000
Roughly halfway between Sofia and Ruse, Pleven is mainly of interest as a transport hub, with good links to destinations across northern Bulgaria and beyond. It's a languid and fairly lacklustre place, though, and there's little incentive to stay, but if you do stop over, there are a few interesting sights and plenty of cafes in the extensive pedestrian centre. Bulgaria's highest temperatures are often recorded in Pleven, and summer in the city can be a little stifling.

The city is best known as the site of the decisive Siege of Pleven (or Plevna, as it was then known) between July and December 1877, when Russian and Romanian troops besieged and finally took the city from the Turks at the cost of more than 40,000 lives. After the city's fall, the rest of Bulgaria was soon liberated.

At the heart of Pleven is the expansive pl Vazrazhdane, which blends seamlessly into the pedestrian pl Svobodata. From here, ul Vasil Levski – also mostly pedestrianised – meanders northwards to the neighbouring bus and train stations on pl Republika.

Sights

Pleven's main pedestrian square, pl Vazrazhdane is dominated by the ornate neo-Byzantine **Mausoleum**, which holds the remains of the Russian and Romanian soldiers who died liberating the city in 1877. The square itself is one of the biggest in Bulgaria and features several impressive fountains and water cascades.

Historical Museum   MUSEUM
(www.plevenmuseum.dir.bg; ul Stoyan Zaimov 3; adult/student 2/1 lv; free Mon; ⊙9.30am-noon & 12.30-6pm Mon-Sat) A few blocks south of pl Vazrazhdane, this town museum houses 24 galleries of exhibits, including neolithic pottery, Roman mosaic floors, folk costumes, reconstructions of traditional rural homes and 19th-century furnishings and fashions.

Tsar Aleksander II House Museum MUSEUM
(ul Vasil Levski; 2 lv; ⊙9am-noon & 2.30-5pm Mon-Fri) Sitting in a city centre park, this modest cottage was where the Russian tsar, Alexander II, accepted the surrender of the Turkish general Osman Pasha after the 1877 Siege of Pleven. The four rooms have been restored to their 19th-century appearance and the tsar's uniform is on show in a glass case.

Sleeping & Eating

For its size, Pleven has a surprisingly poor choice of hotels and few decent restaurants. There are, however, plenty of bars spread along the main pedestrian thoroughfare.

Hotel Face   HOTEL $$
(☏801 613; pl Svobodata 12; r 60-80 lv; ✳@) On the main square, this oddly named family hotel has ten smallish but comfortable rooms above a busy restaurant and bar, some with balconies.

Hotel Rostov   HOTEL $$
(☏805 005; www.rostov.bg; ul Tsar Boris III 2; s/d/ste 60/80/120 lv; P✳☎) This socialist-era

concrete tower in the city centre has been partially renovated and offers small, serviceable rooms with TVs and fridges. Cheaper rooms, without air-con, are also available. There's a restaurant and nightclub on-site.

Pizza Tempo   PIZZERIA $
(ul Konstantinov 23; pizzas 5-10 lv; ✏) On the main road, east of the main square, this is an inviting place with a big menu of pizzas and pasta dishes.

Speedy Bar & Grill   BULGARIAN $
(ul Tsanko Tserkovski 17; mains 4-9 lv; ⊙10am-midnight) Grills, steaks, sausages, soups and salads are on the glossy illustrated menu at this city centre restaurant, which has plenty of outdoor seating. It gets busy in the evenings.

ⓘ Information

Tourist Information Centre (☏824 004; www.tourinfo.pleven.bg; pl Vazrazhdane 1; ⊙9am-5pm Mon-Fri) Helpful English-speaking staff hand out free maps and brochures here.

ⓘ Getting There & Away

Pleven's busy bus station is north of the town centre.
Burgas (30 lv, seven hours, one daily)
Lovech (5 lv, 40 minutes, hourly)
Ruse (11 lv, two hours, four daily)
Sofia (15 lv, three hours, five daily)
Veliko Târnovo (12.50 lv, two hours, three daily)
Vidin (16 lv, four hours, one or two daily)
Vratsa (10 lv, 2½ hours, three daily)

There are several trains daily to Sofia (13.50 lv, three hours) and Varna (16.80 lv, 4¾ hours, six daily). Travelling to Ruse involves changing at Gorna Oryakhovitsa (10.60 lv, five daily, 3½ hours).

Ruse   Pyce
☏082 / POP 182,500
One of Bulgaria's most elegant cities, Ruse (*roo-seh*), sometimes written 'Rousse', has more than a touch of *mitteleuropa* grandness not seen elsewhere in the country. It's a city of imposing *belle époque* architecture and neatly trimmed leafy squares, as if a little chunk of Vienna had broken off and floated down the Danube. Its past is abundantly displayed in several museums and in its ruined Roman fortress, standing guard high over the Danube.

The heart of Ruse is the grand pl Svoboda, dominated by the huge **Monument to Freedom**. Some 18 streets radiate out from the square, which is bisected by Ruse's main pedestrian street, ul Aleksandrovska. To the west lies the broad Danube. The train station and neighbouring Yug bus station are around 2.5km south of the city centre.

Ruse is also a base for visiting the nearby rock monasteries and other attractions at Rusenski Lom Nature Park.

History

Named Sexaginta Prista, or the Port of Sixty Ships, by the Romans, the fortress here stood guard over the Danube. The town declined under the Byzantines and Bulgarians, but its fortunes revived under the Turks, who called it Roustchouk. It developed great economic and cultural importance and, in 1866, became the first station on the first railway line in the entire Ottoman Empire, which linked the Danube with the Black Sea at Varna.

Ruse also became a centre for anti-Turkish agitation during the 19th-century uprisings when Bucharest, just a few hours to the north, was the headquarters of the Bulgarian Central Revolutionary Committee. By the end of the Russo-Turkish War (1877–78), Ruse was the largest, most prosperous city in Bulgaria; the legacy of those days lingers in the city's lovely turn-of-the-century architecture.

◎ Sights

Ruse Regional Museum of History   MUSEUM
(www.museumruse.com; pl Aleksandar Battenberg 3; adult/student 4/1 lv; ⊙9am-6pm) The 5th-century BC **Borovo Treasure**, consisting of sliver cups and jugs adorned with Greek gods, is one of the highlights of Ruse's interesting museum. Other artefacts on display include Thracian helmets, Roman statues and 19th-century costumes.

FREE **Sveta Troitsa Church**   CHURCH
(ul Zlatarov; ⊙7am-6pm) Built in 1632 below ground level – according to the Turkish stipulation that churches should be as unobtrusive as possible – Sveta Troitsa has a fine gilt wood iconostasis and wooden pillars painted to look like marble, as well as some well-preserved icons.

Roman Fortress of Sexaginta Prista   ARCHEOLOGICAL SITE
(ul Tsar Kaloyan 2; adult/student 2/1 lv; ⊙9am-noon & 12.30-5.30pm Tue-Sat) Closed for renovation at the time of research, little remains today of what was once a mighty Roman fort (AD 70), housing some 600 soldiers at its peak. You can still see some barrack walls and columns, and the enthusiastic custodian will show you around and bring it all to life.

Transportation Museum   MUSEUM
(ul Bratya Obretenovi 5; admission outside/indoor displays 4/2 lv; ⊙10am-noon & 2-5pm Mon-Fri) The unique Transportation Museum exhibits its vintage locomotives from the late 19th and early 20th centuries, as well as carriages that once belonged to Tsar Boris III, Tsar Ferdinand and Turkish sultan Abdul Aziz.

Museum of the Urban Lifestyle in Ruse   MUSEUM
(ul Tsar Ferdinand 36; adult/student 4/1 lv; ⊙9am-noon & 12.30-5.30pm) Built in 1866, this townhouse features some recreated period rooms, with 19th-century furniture, paintings and chandeliers upstairs. Downstairs there are changing exhibitions on social themes such as education, childhood and domestic life.

Pantheon of the National Revival   MONUMENT
(Park na Vazrozhdentsite; adult/student 2/1 lv; ⊙9am-noon & 12.30-5.30pm) The gold-domed Pantheon of the National Revival was built in 1978 to commemorate the 100th anniversary of the deaths of 453 local heroes who fought the Ottomans in the Russo-Turkish War. Inside you can see the marble tombs of revolutionary leaders and a small collection of swords and rifles, but nothing is explained in English.

Profit-Yielding Building   NOTABLE BUILDING
(pl Svoboda) This huge, gloriously titled neo-baroque building dominates the western end of pl Svoboda. Built between 1898 and 1902 by Viennese architects, it was intended as a home for the Dramatic Theatre (which is still here) and several shops. The rents from these were used to fund local schools, hence the name. These days it also houses a few restaurants.

✴ Festivals & Events

March Music Days Festival   CLASSICAL MUSIC
(www.marchmusicdays.eu; ⊙last two weeks of March) Two weeks of classical music at venues across the city.

Golden Rebeck Folklore Festival   MUSIC
(⊙early June) Traditional Bulgarian folk music gets a hearing at concerts in the city.

Ruse Jazz Bluezz Festival   JAZZ
(⊙September) International jazz and blues musicians show their skills at various venues.

Days of Ruse Festival   PERFORMING ARTS
(⊙early October) Music, dance and drama performances around Ruse.

Ruse

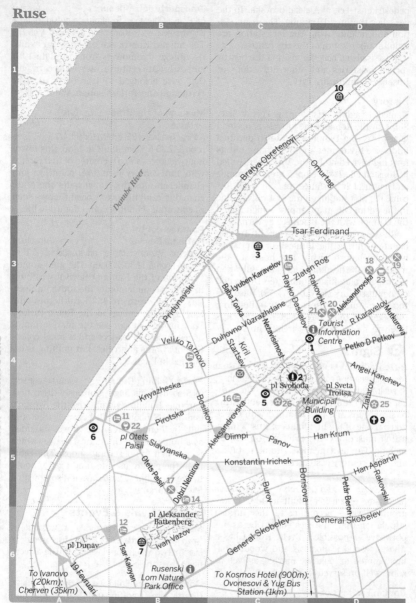

🛏 Sleeping

TOP CHOICE **City Art Hotel**   BOUTIQUE HOTEL $$
(☎51 9848; www.cityarthotel.com; ul Veliko Târnovo 5; s/d 68/90 lv; ❊☎) City Art offers 19 artfully styled rooms with trendy colour schemes,

giant headboards and upbeat philosophical quotations stencilled on the walls. The building is a renovated 19th-century hatmaker's shop on a quiet street near the centre. There's a Chinese restaurant, Bamboo, in the back courtyard.

THE DANUBE & NORTHERN PLAINS RUSE

Rooms are stylish, some with terraces, but it's a big place, and the labyrinthine layout can be confusing.

Anna Palace　　　　　　　　　HOTEL **$$**
(☏825 005; www.annapalace.com; ul Knyazheska 4; s/d from 80/100 lv; P❄@) In a bright yellow neoclassical mansion by the river terminal, the luxurious Anna Palace has large, slightly chintzy rooms. There are smaller, discounted attic singles.

Charlino Plaza　　　　　　　　HOTEL **$$**
(☏825 707; www.charlino-plaza.com; pl Dunav; s/d 50/70 lv; P❄☎) Rooms in this grand, Viennese-style mansion near the History

Cosmopolitan　　　　　BUSINESS HOTEL **$$$**
(☏805 050; www.cosmopolitanhotelbg.com; ul Dobri Nemirov 1-3; s/d from 90/160 lv; P❄☎☀) This modern business hotel has all the facilities and comforts you would expect, including a spa centre, pool and restaurants.

Museum are plainly furnished but cosy, and all come with TVs and fridges. There's also a restaurant, bar and garden.

English Guest House
B&B $

(875 577; vysachko@abv.bg; ul Rayko Daskalov 34; s/d/tr from 40/60/70 lv; P❄@) This British-run guesthouse has a selection of rooms in a renovated townhouse, including pricier en-suite rooms. It's a sociable place where guests can mingle over cups of tea in the garden.

Splendid Hotel
HOTEL $$

(825 970; www.splendid.rousse.bg; ul Aleksandrovska 51; s/d from 59/88 lv; P❄☎) On a side street near the main square, the Splendid is a slightly old-fashioned place offering comfortable if unspectacular rooms.

Kosmos Hotel
HOTEL $$

(871 871; www.hotelcosmos.bg; ul Borisova 122; s/d from 55/70 lv; P❄☎) Handy for the bus and train stations but a long walk from the centre. It has a restaurant downstairs.

✕ Eating & Drinking

TOP CHOICE Chiflika
BULGARIAN $$

(828 222; ul Otets Paisii 2; mains 6-25 lv; ☺11am-2am Mon-Sat, noon-1am Sun) Set in several rooms following an old-world *mehana* theme, with wooden benches, rugs, fleeces on the walls, and waiters in pantaloons, Chiflika is the best place in town for hearty traditional food. On the big menu are clay-pot meals, including an excellent chicken *gyuvetch*, soups, grills and more adventurous options like stewed lambs' intestines.

Ostankino
BULGARIAN $

(ul Aleksandrovska 76; mains 3-8 lv; ☺8.30am-midnight) Typical cheap and tasty Bulgarian food including sausages, grills, steaks, chicken and fish are served at this busy cafe with outdoor tables. It's a good place to enjoy a couple of cold beers, too.

Hlebozavod Ruse
FAST FOOD $

(ul Aleksandrovska; banitsa 0.70 lv; ☺6.30am-7pm Mon-Fri, 6.30am-2pm Sat) Ruse's best take-away snack shop draws locals all day, who come for the hot, freshly baked *banitsa* (cheese pasties).

Bamboo
CHINESE $

(Bambuk; 870 555; ul Veliko Târnovo 5; mains 6-10 lv; ☺11am-11pm; ☎✐) In the courtyard of the City Art Hotel, Bamboo offers the usual choice of Chinese rice and noodle dishes, which all come in big portions. The chicken with three kinds of mushrooms is good, and a takeaway/home delivery service is available. Watch out for mosquitoes if you sit outside in the evening, though.

Restaurant Veneziano
PIZZERIA $$

(ul Rakovski 13; pizzas 7-15 lv; ☎✐) Veneziano is the place to go for pizzas and pasta, with seating in an open internal courtyard, as well as a bar area.

Planet Food
FAST FOOD $

(ul Aleksandrovska 69; mains from 4 lv; ☺8am-11pm; ☎) The cheap and cheerful city centre restaurant has plenty of outdoor seating, and offers a menu of hamburgers, sandwiches, and chicken and chips type of dishes.

Coffee Time
CAFE

(ul Tsar Osvoboditel; ☺8am-3am; ☎) This trendy little coffee bar is always busy, with comfy sofas inside and seating outside. They also serve cocktails and light meals.

Club Admiral
PUB

(ul Slavyanska 5; ☺10am-midnight Mon-Sat; ☎) Describing itself as a 'Scottish pub', Admiral is a big, lively place with a traditional pub, smarter piano bar and a summer garden where food is also served.

☆ Entertainment

Ruse Opera House (825 037; pl Sveta Troitsa), open since about 1890 and one of the town's finest buildings, and the **Sava Ognyanov Drama Theatre** (pl Svoboda), are both well known for their quality productions. Buy tickets at the box offices, or through the Tourist Information Centre.

Art Club
LIVE MUSIC

(820 948; Youth Park; ☺9pm-3am) Just inside the park, this spacious bar is the place to go for live jazz music (Wednesday to Saturday).

➊ Information

There are numerous banks with ATMs and foreign exchange offices along ul Aleksandrovska and pl Svoboda, including **Unicredit Bulbank** (cnr ul Alexandrovska & pl Svoboda) and **Banka DSK** (pl Sveta Troitsa).

Polyclinic (834 200; ul Nezavisimost 2) Provides basic medical services.

Rusenski Lom Nature Park Office (872 397; www.lomea.org; ul General Skobelev 7; ☺9am-5pm Mon-Fri) Provides camping and hiking

DANUBE BRIDGE

Some 6km downstream from Ruse, this double-decker highway and railway bridge links the city with Giurgiu on the Romanian side of the Danube. Built in 1954, it was originally called the Friendship Bridge, and at 2.3km in length and towering 30m above the water, it's the longest steel bridge in Europe.

information and maps; can arrange trips to the Ivanovo Rock Monastery.

Tourist Information Centre (☑824 704; www.tic.rousse.bg; ul Aleksandrovska 61; ☺9am-6pm Mon-Fri, 9.30am-6pm Sat & Sun) The helpful tourist information office hands out free city maps and leaflets.

❶ Getting There & Away

Bus

The **Yug bus station** (☑828 151; ul Pristanishtna) has regular buses to Sofia (28 lv, five hours), Veliko Târnovo (10 lv, two hours), Pleven (11 lv, two hours) and Shumen (6 lv, two hours), Burgas (27 lv, 4½ hours, two daily) and Varna (15 lv, four hours, three daily). Buses and minibuses leave for Silistra (10 lv, about two hours) every hour or so. To get to the station, take trolleybus 25 or bus 11 or 12 from ul Borisova. A taxi will cost about 3 to 4 lv.

The **Iztok bus station** (☑844 064; ul Ivan Vedur 10), 4km east of the centre, has buses to nearby destinations such as Ivanovo and Cherven in the Rusenski Lom Nature Park. Take a taxi or city bus 2 or 13, which leave from ul General Skobelev, near the roundabout four blocks east of ul Borisova.

To/From Romania

The Ruse-based company **Ovonesovi** (☑872 000) runs two daily minibuses to Bucharest, leaving the Yug bus station and dropping off at Unitarii Plaza, outside Hotel Horoscope in Bucharest, rather than the bus station. Tickets are 20/30 lv one-way/return. Private taxis (90 lv one-way) from Yug bus station are more comfortable and convenient.

Train

From Ruse's grand **train station** (☑820 222; ul Pristanishtna) there are trains to Sofia (18.90 lv, six to seven hours, seven daily) and Varna (12.20 lv, four hours, two daily).

For Romania, three daily trains serve Bucharest (25 lv, 3½ hours). Show up at least 30 minutes before the train departure time for customs and passport checks.

In the station, the **Rila Bureau** (☑828 016; train station; ☺9am-5.30pm) sells international train tickets. It's best to buy a Bucharest ticket on the day of travel as there are sometimes delays. The train station's **left-luggage office** (☺6am-1.30pm & 2-8.30pm) is past the main buildings and in a smaller one up the hill. There's another branch of the **Rila Bureau** (☑834 860; ul Knyazheska 33; ☺9am-noon & 1-5.30pm Mon-Fri) in the city centre.

Rusenski Lom Nature Park
Природен Парк Русенски Лом

This 32.6 sq km nature park, sprawling south of Ruse around the Rusenski Lom, Beli Lom and Malki Lom Rivers, is a superb spot for birdwatching; 172 species are recorded here, including Egyptian vultures, lesser kestrels and eagle owls. It's also home to 67 species of mammals and 24 types of bats.

Most visitors, however, are drawn first to the park's cliff churches. While around 40 medieval rock churches exist in and around some 300 local caves, only a handful are accessible, the most famous being those of Basarbovo and Ivanovo. The park also contains the second-longest cave in Bulgaria, the Orlova Chuka Peshtera (Eagle Peak Cave), between Tabachka and Pepelina villages. Thracian and Roman ruins are also found here.

◉ Sights

Basarbovo Rock Monastery　MONASTERY
(☑082-800 765) The only working rock monastery in Bulgaria, Basarbovo is in the village of the same name 10km south of Ruse near the Rusenski Lom River on the road to Ivanovo Monastery.

Established some time before the 15th century, the complex has been much restored and extended over time. Visitors can see a rock-carved church with colourful icons and a little museum.

Ivanovo Rock Monastery　MONASTERY
(☑0889370006; Sveti Archangel Michael; adult/student 4/1 lv; ☺9am-noon & 1-6pm) Around 4km east of Ivanovo, this Unesco World Heritage–listed monastery is built inside a cave 38m above ground. It's about a 10-minute walk on a good trail through a forest to get there.

Built during the 13th century, it houses 14th-century murals regarded as some of the finest in Bulgaria, including a Last Supper scene.

Rusenski Lom Nature Park

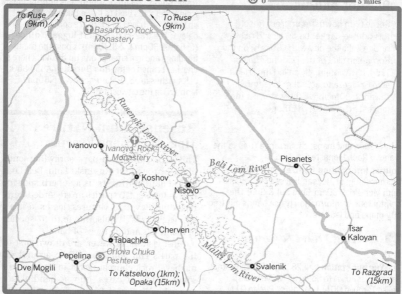

Cherven Fortress FORTRESS

(admission 4 lv; ⊙9am-noon & 1-6pm) Just outside the village of Cherven, 15km south of Ivanovo, are the remains of a remarkably intact 6th-century citadel. Several streets, towers and churches have also been discovered, and there are great views of the river valleys and hills from the top.

🛏 Sleeping

The nature park office in Ruse and Ivanovo's information centre provides information on accommodation, such as private rooms in Cherven, Pisanets, Nisovo and Koshov (20 lv per person) as well as small village guesthouses (from 40 lv per person) and the **hizha** (mountain hut; ☑0886 003 233; www.orlovachuka. eu; dm 8-10 lv) beside Orlova Chuka cave.

ℹ Information

Information Centre (☑081-162 203; Ivanovo town hall)

ℹ Getting There & Away

From the Iztok bus station in Ruse, two or three buses leave daily for Cherven, via Ivanovo and Koshov, between Monday and Friday (3 lv, 40 minutes). The best way to get to Ivanovo, however, is by train (every 30 minutes), as there are only three daily buses to Ivanovo in summer and fewer in winter. Frequent Razgrad-bound buses from Yug bus station pass through Pisanets, and for Nisovo, look for a bus leaving the Iztok station for Opaka.

Ask at the Ruse Tourist Information Centre for details on getting to Basarbovo via local bus directly from the city centre. In summer, hourly buses go to Basarbovo, though in winter they are less frequent.

Lake Srebârna & Around

Two of Bulgaria's most important waterways unite at Lake Srebârna, a shallow lake connected to the Danube by a narrow canal, and featuring unique types of vegetation and unusual floating islands made of reeds. The nearby village of **Vetren** is a good spot for fishing. There are plenty of hikes and other outdoor activities to be enjoyed. The large 80 sq km area around the lake, known simply as **Srebârna Nature Reserve**, is a Unesco World Heritage site.

Lake Srebârna hosts over 160 species of water birds, including colonies of endangered small cormorants, Ferruginous ducks and Dalmatian pelicans. There are elevated lookout posts set around the lake for birdwatching.

⊙ Sights & Activities

The **Museum of Natural History** (☎086-823 894; admission 2 lv; ☺9am-noon & 2-4pm Mon-Fri) in Srebârna village contains a few exhibits concerning local bird life and flora.

Guided birdwatching tours and nature walks (40 lv per group) are conducted by Englishman Mike Black of Pelican Lake Guesthouse. Mike can supply mountain bikes for local **cycling**, as well as **fishing** gear rentals and free temporary permits for fly-fishing.

For walkers, there's a relatively flat 4km-long **ecotrail** that starts from the beginning of the village and runs along the lake.

🛏 Sleeping & Eating

Srebârna village and nearby Vetren have several guesthouses and some decent places to eat.

Pelican Lake Guesthouse ᴛᴏᴘ ᴄʜᴏɪᴄᴇ B&B $$
(☎086772322, 0885671058; www.srebarnabirding.com; ul Petko Simov 16, Srebârna; s/d/ste 36/72/120 lv; ℗❄☏) The cosy English-owned Pelican Lake Guesthouse has two adjoining rooms with a shared bathroom. The hosts provide a wealth of local knowledge and activities, and birdwatching tours are free for guests. Breakfast is 8 lv extra and evening meals are available on request.

Kalimaritsa GUESTHOUSE $
(☎0888234985; www.housekalimaritsa.bg; d/apt 40/65 lv) A Vetren restaurant that doubles as a guesthouse, the Kalimaritsa's grapevine bedecked courtyard garden is lovely. Rooms are a bit musty and old-fashioned with their big floral carpets and garish fabrics, though they're passable for an overnight stay. Dining features grilled meats and fish (mains 5 to 8 lv).

Hotel Danube Pearl HOTEL $
(☎0888 652 867; www.danube-pearl.com; Popina village; d 40-50 lv; ℗❄☏) In the little village of Popina, just west of Vetren, this modern riverside hotel has ten comfortable rooms, as well as a small outdoor pool, gym and a restaurant. It's a scenic spot and good value.

Restaurant Stara Kâshta BULGARIAN $
(☎0886580001; ul Granichna 3; mains 4-6 lv, r 32 lv; ℗❄) This traditional *mehana* in Vetren offers a good selection of Bulgarian dishes. Basic, traditional-style rooms are

also available. It's signposted up a small driveway heading towards the river.

Restoran Diva BULGARIAN $
(ul Dunav 19; mains 3-7 lv; ☺7am-1am) This fairly basic place in the centre has no architectural appeal, but does have the best food in Srebârna, from salads to grilled meats.

ℹ Getting There & Away

There is no bus station in either Srebârna village or Vetren. Buses traversing the main Silistra–Ruse route drop off passengers on the roadside 1.5km from the centre of Srebârna village. Alternatively, local bus 22 from Silistra travels several times daily into Srebârna village.

To reach Vetren, enter Srebârna village and just keep following the main street, ul Dunavska. After 4km, you'll reach Vetren, which stops at the river.

Silistra Силистра

☎086 / POP 35,600

Sitting on the Danube, with picturesque views across the water to the forested Romanian shore, sedate Silistra feels a little out on a limb and foreign visitors are pretty thin on the ground. It's a pleasant, laid-back place, though, with some intriguing ruins and a couple of museums to explore, while the town's accommodation options are surprisingly good.

The grotty bus station and adjacent train station are 1.5km from the main square, pl Svoboda, where you'll find banks, the post office, cafes and shops.

⊙ Sights & Activities

Scattered **ruins**, including a hulking section of the 6th-century fortress wall and a number of early churches, can be seen between the main square and the riverfront.

Archaeological Museum MUSEUM
(ul Simeon Veliki 72; admission 2 lv; ☺9.30am-noon & 12.30-5pm Tue-Sat) Silistra's Archaeological Museum houses an impressive array of locally excavated Thracian and Roman artefacts, though you may need to knock to get staff to open up. Highlights include a curious Orphic sundial from the 3rd-century AD, bronze Thracian helmets and elaborate Roman chariot fittings.

Art Gallery GALLERY
(ul Simeon Veliki 49; admission 1 lv; ☺9-11.30am & 2-5.30pm Mon-Fri) The Art Gallery is in

THE DANUBE

The Danube is Europe's longest river at 2780km, and for 472km of its length it forms much of the border between Bulgaria and Romania. Called the Dunav by Bulgarians, it rises in the Black Forest of southwestern Germany and empties into the Black Sea. It travels through four capital cities (Vienna, Budapest, Bratislava and Belgrade) and ten countries (Germany, Austria, Slovakia, Hungary, Croatia, Serbia, Bulgaria, Romania, Moldova and Ukraine). No other river is shared by so many countries. The Danube's average depth is about 5m and the water rarely flows faster than 3km/h.

a grand yellow-and-white Viennese-style building on the central square. Inside you can view hundreds of 19th-century and contemporary Bulgarian artworks.

Sveti Sveti Petâr & Pavel Church CHURCH
(St Peter and St Paul Church; ul Hristo Smirnenski 16) This pretty pink church, a little further along from the Archaeological Museum, was built in the 1860s and is adorned with bright modern murals. It houses relics of a 4th-century local saint, Dasius, which were stolen by medieval crusaders and were returned to the church by the Pope only in 2001, after spending several centuries in Italy.

🛏 Sleeping & Eating

TOP CHOICE Hotel Drustar LUXURY HOTEL $$$
(☑812 200; www.hoteldrustar.com; ul Kapitan Mamarchev 10; s/d 130/160 lv; P🐕❄@🏊) This modern five-star hotel, set in parkland overlooking the Danube, offers attractive, spacious rooms with balconies; ask for a river view, and watch the aerial display put on by the numerous resident swallows. Facilities include a big outdoor pool and an excellent restaurant. Half-board packages are especially good value.

Hotel Danube LUXURY HOTEL $$$
(☑877 700; www.danube-hotel.com; pl Svoboda 1; s/d 80/140 lv; P🐕❄@🏊) Another five-star hotel, the Danube is a modern establishment, built in grand Viennese style. Rooms

have a plush, old-fashioned cosiness and are reasonably priced for what's on offer. There's a spa, pool, sauna, gym and restaurants, as well as a tempting pastry shop.

Hotel Silistra HOTEL $$
(☑833 033; hotel@bcsilistra.com; ul Dobruzhda 41; s/d/apt 45/64/90 lv; 🐕🏊) In the centre of town on the fifth floor of a shiny business centre, this place has nine big, fresh-looking rooms with laminated wood floors. There's a restaurant and nightclub on the ground floor.

Pizzeria Bellisima PIZZERIA $
(ul Dobruzhda; pizzas from 6 lv; ⏰7.30am-11pm; 🖋) Next door to the Hotel Danube, Bellisima has outdoor seating and a big menu of tasty pizzas, as well as a few pasta dishes and salads.

ℹ Getting There & Away

Hourly buses and slower minibuses leave Silistra **bus station** (☑820 280) for the Yug bus station in Ruse (10 lv, 1½ hours). Buses also head to Varna (9 lv, two hours, one or two daily), Sofia (33 lv, six hours, three or four daily) and Shumen (10 lv, two to three hours, two or three daily). From the **train station** (☑821 802), trains go to Ruse, via Samuil (9.90 lv, five hours, three daily).

From Silistra port to Călăraşi (in Romania), a ferry operates every few hours (15/2 lv per car/passenger). Fares are payable in euros or leva. Public transport on the Romanian side is not reliable, so the border crossing at Ruse is probably easier.

Understand Bulgaria

population per sq km

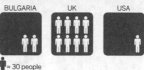

BULGARIA   UK   USA

≈ 30 people

Bulgaria Today

National Interests

» Population:
7.35 million

» Area: 42,823
sq km

» GDP per
capita: 15,981
lev (US
$10,700)

» Inflation:
7.3%

» Literacy rate:
98.2%

» Ethnicity
(2011): 84.8%
Bulgarian, 8.8%
Turkish, 4.9%
Roma, 1.5%
other

In joining the European Union in 2007, Bulgaria achieved the greatest goal of its post-communist incarnation. Bulgarians were rightly proud of this achievement, though any lingering europhoria has long since dissipated – no economic miracles have occurred, and the prevalence of decrepit and destroyed old communist-era factories by the roadsides hardly conjures up images of European affluence.

Yet there are signs of change too – the smoking ban in restaurants and bars, for example, is respected much more widely here than in neighbouring Romania, which also joined the EU in 2007. Sofia's expanding metro system now covers much of the city, making the capital easier to enjoy. And signs of 'progress' – which in 2013 included a projected 10 new shopping malls in Sofia alone – indicate that today's Bulgarians are happily drifting ever further from their former communist island.

Indeed, despite chronic complaints over the economy and corruption at high levels, Bulgarians have retained their wry sense of humour. One riotous example occurred in June 2011, when an unknown street artists gave an old Soviet fighters monument a makeover, repainting the figures as modern 'heroes' – Superman, Santa Claus, Ronald McDonald and more. Two years later, some of the paint can still be seen.

Bulgarians have always been considered a clever bunch in the scientific field. Early breakthroughs in robotics and computer sciences were made here and, most recently, the government announced a 10-year project to develop a national nanotechnology research and development centre in Sofia – making Bulgaria the first European country to do so. Oh, and to keep abreast of climate change developments Bulgaria keeps its own scientific research station – in Antarctica.

Habits

» Bulgarians say yes by nodding their head – from side to side.

» Wait staff in most restaurants don't usually serve bread unless you ask for it – and most don't expect tips either.

» As in other Orthodox Christian countries, the more devout may cross themselves three times when passing a church, and they also try to never exit a church with your their to the interior.

Top Music

Le Mystere des Voix Bulgares (1990) A now-legendary set of recordings from the national female choir.

Song of the Crooked Dance: Early Bulgarian Traditional Music 1927–42 A rare collection of vintage traditional tracks.

belief systems
(% of population)

80

Eastern Orthodox

9

No Religion

8

Muslim

3

Other

if Bulgaria were 100 people

85 would be Bulgarian
9 would be Turkish
5 would be Roma
1 would be Other

Tourism Optimism

Although the country has lost its novelty as a tourism destination, Bulgarians are still pondering its future potential. The Black Sea resort towns of Burgas and Varna are looking sharp and ever-posher eateries catering to well-heeled international travellers can be found in Sofia, Plovdiv and Veliko Tàrnovo.

The Bulgarian government has devoted funds and energy in recent years to TV and online marketing for Bulgarian tourism. The promising monastic tourism business got an exciting break in 2012, when the National Geographic Channel aired a fascinating special on the supposed relics of St John the Baptist, discovered in 2010 at a church site on the island of Sveti Ivan, off the Black Sea coast. (They were scientifically proven to date from the 1st-century AD from a man of Middle Eastern origin.)

The government is also ambitious about raising the country's profile as a golf destination. An international tournament will be held in the summer of 2013 at a swish resort whose clifftop course is said to be one of the most spectacular in the world.

Bulgarian tourism retains its old stalwarts as well – the Black Sea in summer, increasingly popular with Russians, and winter skiing in places like Bansko (popular with Russians, but also with plenty of Brits). Compared to other 'emerging destinations' in the region like Croatia and Montenegro, Bulgaria has not experienced a wild surge in prices and the country remains accessible for travellers of all budgets.

Interestingly, Bulgarians are showing increasing signs of enthusiasm about showing off their country: in Sofia and Varna, for example, friendly young university graduates volunteer to provide regular free tours of civic monuments and historic structures.

» Average life expectancy: 69 (m), 76 (f)

» Unemployment rate: 9.6%

» Highest point: Mt Musala (2925m)

» European country ranking in number of IT experts per capita: 1st

» Export: Bulgaria produces 10% of the world's rose oil

Top Books

A Street without a Name: Childhood and Other Misadventures in Bulgaria (Kapka Kassabova) An entertaining and thought-provoking memoir of one young woman's experiences growing up in Bulgaria in the last years of communism.

Circus Bulgaria (Deyan Enev) A surrealist collection of stories based on the legends and oddities of the Bulgarian reality and imagination.

Top Films

Sofia's Last Ambulance (2012) This documentary follows three Sofia paramedics challenged by an ever-dwindling budget.
The Peach Thief (1964) Vulo Radev's evocative romance set in World War I.

History

Bulgaria's strategic location and rich, forested landscape have made it an apple of envy for thousands of years, so it's no wonder that its military-political history is emphasised in the national narrative. However, there's much more to Bulgarian history than wars and (more recent) communist totalitarianism: the mysterious ancient Thracians were master goldsmiths and lovers of song and wine, while the Byzantine-inspired medieval Bulgarian tsars commissioned magnificent churches, fresco paintings and manuscripts in monastic literary schools. More recently, the National Revival period gave Bulgaria some of its most distinctive architecture and an artistic tradition that continues today.

Inhabited since neolithic times, Bulgaria has enjoyed brief but brilliant periods of greatness; during the medieval First and Second Bulgarian Empires, Bulgaria was among Europe's most powerful states. However, five centuries of subsequent Turkish occupation closed it to Western progress. The Orthodox Church largely preserved Bulgarian culture, prompting the 18th- and 19th-century National Revival period, reminding Bulgarians of their illustrious forebears.

Bulgaria's post-WWII experiment with communism deeply damaged the economy, society and national psyche, and the 1990s 'transition' period was difficult. However, it weathered the storm and two decades into its latest incarnation, Bulgaria is a NATO and EU member with significant foreign investment and a strong regional presence.

Beginnings

Cave excavations near Pleven and in the Stara Planina (Balkan Range) confirm human habitation since the Upper Palaeolithic Period (40,000 BC). However, archaeologists believe cave-dwelling neolithic peoples (6000 BC) were Bulgaria's earliest permanent settlers.

The best preserved examples are in Stara Zagora, where burnt grain finds indicate farming was undertaken. Bulgaria's Chalcolithic (copper-

TIMELINE	6000–5000 BC	4000–1000 BC	611 BC
	Bulgaria's earliest neolithic settlers occupy caves, abandoning them around 5000 BC for mud huts. Farming develops.	Thracian tribes dominate modern-day Bulgaria; around 3000 BC, settlements include coastal Mesembria; around 2000 BC they expand into Greece and Anatolia.	Greek settlers from the Anatolian city-state of Miletus establish Apollonia Pontica (Sozopol) òn the Black Sea coast – the first classical democracy on Bulgarian territory. All males over 18 can vote.

using) cultures developed during the fourth millennium BC; a superb collection of Chalcolithic artefacts – including possibly the earliest worked gold jewellery – is at Varna Archaeological Museum.

The Thracians

Several diverse tribes, the Thracians, settled in modern-day Bulgaria. Their earliest settlements were based around cave systems and 'sacred' springs. Later, they built more permanent villages with elevated, rudimentary fortresses. Herodotus records that Thrace's population was 'greater than that of any country in the world except India'; if unified, Thracian tribes could rule everywhere, he wrote.

Most powerful were the Sofia-area Serdi; the Getae, from the Danube region; and the Odrysai, from the Rodopi region. The tribes quarreled, but had a common culture, language and religious rites. They were feared warriors and horsemen. The 2nd-century BC Greek historian Polybius described the chronic wars of attrition between the Thracians and the Greek colonists at Byzantium (later, Constantinople, and then Istanbul).

Despite their warlike reputation, the Thracians had a softer, even more salacious side. Semi-mythical musician and underworld explorer, Orpheus, was born here: his talent for getting the party started worked seamlessly with that of wine god Dionysus, who was worshipped in orgiastic rituals. Polygamy and pre-marital promiscuity were encouraged for girls. Breathless ancient Greek historians also mentioned Thracians' lurid tatoos and recreational drug use (probably by inhaling burning hemp seeds).

The Thracians were accomplished artists and traded jewellery, copper and gold. Excavations around Shipka have unearthed an astonishing gold mask and the bronze head of a Thracian king. The Thracians also influenced Greek and Roman religion, while some Bulgarian names, like 'rila' (for Rila Monastery) and 'yantra' (the river through Veliko Tărnovo) probably originate from Thracian. However, lacking their own written record, the Thracians' history and culture remain opaque; since Thracian history is known largely from Greek sources, Greek scholars have long been tempted to 'Hellenicise' Thracian achievements.

Today's famous Thracian remains include tombs dating from about 4000 BC (in Varna's Archaeological Museum) and the 4th-century BC Kazanlâk one. The Shipka area is called the 'Valley of the Thracian Kings' for its Thracian burial mounds. Other Thracian artefacts lie in museums in Haskovo, Smolyan, Sofia and Sliven. Other settlement remains are at Burgas and Nesebâr on the Black Sea, and Plovdiv's Nebet Tepe fortress site.

Greeks, Macedonians and Romans

From the 7th century BC, Greek merchants seeking safe harbours and trade opportunities founded Black Sea ports like Apollonia Pontica

A Concise History of Bulgaria by R.J. Crampton is a scholarly and comprehensive overview of the country's history from prehistoric times to the present day.

HISTORY

335 BC	AD 46	293	443–47
Macedonian king Alexander the Great extends the Thracian holdings of his father Philip II by marching to the Danube, the northernmost border of his massive empire.	Rome annexes the eastern Balkans and modern-day Bulgaria is divided into provinces: Thrace (in the south), Moesia (in the north) and Ulpia Serdica (today's Sofia) as the capital of Inner Dacia.	Roman emperor Diocletian establishes the 'Tetrarchy' (rule of four), reorganising imperial administration. Regional 'capitals' are established, including Serdica (Sofia), which becomes important.	Forces of Attila the Hun cross the Danube, sweeping into Roman territory and sacking Serdica (Sofia) and Philipopolis (Plovdiv), forcing Rome to pay tribute in gold.

(modern-day Sozopol), Odessos (Varna), Mesembria (Nesebâr), Krounoi (Balchik) and Pirgos (Burgas). These ports exported wheat, fish and salt, while Greek pottery was traded for Thracian metalwork and jewellery.

The Greeks avoided Bulgaria's interior, however, being heavily outnumbered by Thracians there. Thus, few inland towns attest to Greek settlement. These include Pataulia (Kyustendil) and Danubian Silistra. Still, the Greeks did influence Balkan religion, arts and culture, and the Bulgarian language retains many Greek words and place names.

A more dangerous neighborhood adversary for the Thracians arose in the 4th century BC, when Macedonian King Philip II (and later his son, Alexander the Great) conquered Thrace. Philip's new capital, Philipopolis (Plovdiv) became an important military outpost. Odessos (Varna) and Serdica (Sofia) were also occupied.

Macedonian rule ended when Rome defeated them in 168 BC. In the mid-1st century AD, Romans occupied Mesembria (Nesebâr) and Odessos (Varna), site of Bulgaria's largest Roman ruins, the Thermae complex.

After AD 46, Bulgaria was divided into the provinces of Thrace, in the south, and Moesia, in the north. Roman fortifications arose at major Thracian and Greek towns along the Danube, such as Ruse and Bononia (Vidin), and at Debeltus (Burgas) along the Black Sea coast. The Romans burnt, but then rebuilt coastal Apollonia.

Ulpia Serdica (Sofia) subsequently became the Roman capital of Inner Dacia province (today's northwestern Bulgaria); the impressive Sveti Georgi Rotunda, or Church of St George, attests to this period. By the late 3rd century AD, Ulpia Serdica had become a major regional imperial capital, where Diocletian and subsequent emperors held court.

Bulgaria's other Roman towns include Sevtopolis (Kazanlâk), Ulpia Augusta Trayana (Stara Zagora), Nikopolis-ad-Istrum (north of Veliko Târnovo) and Trimontium (Plovdiv), site of a magnificent (and still working) amphitheatre. From the 3rd century AD onwards Goths, Visigoths, Vandals, Huns and other 'barbarians' wreaked havoc, though their raids were sporadic and short-lived.

Byzantium & the Bulgars: War & Peace

In AD 330 Roman emperor Constantine the Great founded Constantinople (modern Istanbul) at ancient Byzantium. Constantinople became the Eastern Roman Empire's capital, with a co-emperor ruling in Rome. Bulgaria (and most Balkan territory) fell under the eastern half. Up through the 6th-century rule of Emperor Justinian the Great, Bulgaria was relatively stable, and great structures like Sofia's original Church of Sveta Sofia were built. However, Slavs, Avars and Bulgars would increasingly threaten the Byzantine Balkans.

The Valley of the Thracian Kings by Georgi Kitov is an up-to-date account of the fascinating archaeological discoveries made in Central Bulgaria, with some beautiful colour photos

The Thracian 'Getae' tribe would send 'messengers' to their god, Salmoxis, by hurling them onto a row of upturned spears.

681	814	855	917
After Turkic Bulgar tribes sweep down from the Black Sea steppes, Khan Asparuh establishes the First Bulgarian Empire at Pliska. Centuries of chronic fighting with Byzantium ensue.	Khan Krum dies unexpectedly while preparing to besiege Constantinople; the Bulgars make peace two years later.	Byzantine monks Kiril and Metodii undertake a mission to the Moravian Slavs; their monk-disciples later create the Cyrillic alphabet in Ohrid, in Bulgarian-controlled Macedonia.	Boris' second son, Tsar Simeon (r 893–927) expands borders from Romania and Bosnia to the Peloponnese, becoming Europe's strongest power.

Around 632 Turkic Bulgars migrated southwest. These warlike Central Asian tribes were archetypical steppe nomads – skilled horsemen, archers and superstitious pagans. The Bulgars roamed from the Caspian Sea to the Black Sea steppes and, when united under Khan Kubrat, soon were roaming Bulgaria too. The Byzantines could not repel or assimilate this horde; the Turkic tribes gradually settled down, subjugating the Slavs, Greeks and Thracian remnants.

Khan (Tsar) Asparuh (r 681–700) created the First Bulgarian Empire (681–1018), based at Pliska near modern-day Shumen. The empire expanded south and west under Khan Tervel (r 701–718), who helped the Byzantine army repel an Arab advance on Constantinople.

Periods of bloody conflict and wary peace followed between Byzantium and the Bulgars, reaching a dramatic climax when Khan Krum 'The Dreadful' (r 803-814) besieged Constantinople after the Byzantines destroyed Pliska. However, while preparing a new offensive, Krum died unexpectedly; in Constantinople, the pagan ruler's untimely demise was interpreted as divine providence.

The early Turkic Bulgars practised pagan traditions, such as worshipping the spirits of their dead relatives.

A New Identity & New Heights

After Krum's death, several 9th century khans annexed further territory: Khan Omurtag (r 814–831) captured Hungary in 829, and Khan Presian's reign (r 837–852) ended with Bulgarian control over southeastern Europe, including modern-day Romania, Moldova, Macedonia and parts of Greece. Presian's territorial gains brought many Macedonian and other Slavs into his empire; along with Christianity's imminent arrival, this would dramatically change the Bulgars' ethnicity and culture.

Presian's son, Knyaz (Prince) Boris I (r 852–889) cleverly exploited the Constantinople–Rome rivalry; both sought spiritual control over Bulgaria, and Boris played both sides. In 863 he, his family and his court were baptised by Byzantine prelates, but only in 870 did Bulgaria officially go Orthodox, not Roman Catholic. Bulgaria's ruling class was soon immersed in Byzantine court practices, spirituality and culture. (Today, the Church considers Boris a saint).

Boris displayed further political acumen in sheltering the persecuted disciples of two Byzantine missionary monks, Kiril and Metodii (Cyril and Methodius), who in 885 were expelled from Moravia (in today's Slovakia) due to Papal machinations. Kiril and Metodii had in 855 gone to convert Moravia's Slavs to Orthodoxy, devising an understandable liturgical language (Old Church Slavonic). Under Boris' and later tsars' sponsorship, theological schools in Macedonia and Bulgaria would develop the Cyrillic alphabet. Bulgarian churchmen thus won freedom from both Rome and Constantinople, with the liturgy in their own emerging Slavic language, not Greek or Latin.

The 9th-century Bulgar ruler Khan Krum 'the Dreadful' earned his sobriquet from his ferocity in battle and his collection of enemy skulls – such as that of Byzantine Emperor Nicephorus – which he used as drinking vessels.

» Emperor Basil II

TIME & LIFE PICTURES / GETTY IMAGES ©

972

Byzantines capture and burn Bulgarian capital, Preslav; the leadership relocates to Ohrid, their capital until the Byzantine reconquest in 1018.

1014

Byzantine forces win decisively at the Battle of Kleidion/Belasitsa in southwestern Bulgaria, auguring the Bulgarian Empire's demise four years later.

1185-1396

Aristocrat brothers Asen and Petâr rebel against a weakening Byzantium, establishing the Second Bulgarian Empire, with Veliko Târnovo the capital. Tsar Ivan Asen II (1218–41) expands Bulgaria's borders.

Following Byzantine imperial practice, Boris retired to a monastery in 889 for his final years. However, when his son Vladimir tried to restore paganism, Boris deposed and blinded him. Younger brother Simeon (r 893–927) stretched Bulgaria's borders from the Adriatic to the Aegean, and the Dnieper River in the north. Ruling from a new capital, Preslav, Tsar Petâr (r 927–968) oversaw a cultural golden age of church building, fine arts and manuscript production. However, Preslav was badly damaged during 960s wars with the Kievan Rus and Byzantium and never recovered.

Dislocation & Decline

After Preslav's destruction, Tsar Samuel (r 978–1014) moved the capital to Ohrid (in modern-day Macedonia (his castle still towers above Ohrid's massive lake). However, he lost the 1014 Battle of Kleidion/Belasitsa to the Byzantines; according to a spurious legend, Emperor Basil II (r 976–1025) had 15,000 captured Bulgarian soldiers blinded and returned to

THE MYSTERIOUS BULGARS

The enigmatic Bulgars are a scholarly curiosity. In 2012 their lost culture and historical contributions were vividly recounted by Panos Sophoulis in his monograph, *Byzantium and Bulgaria, 775–831*. So who were these people?

According to Sophoulis, a University of Athens history professor, who spoke to Lonely Planet for this book, the Bulgars were 'steppe-warriors, culturally and linguistically related to the Eurasian nomads – and therefore, quite distinct from the Slavs'. They were distinguished by the 'political, social, military and religious traditions they brought from the steppes'. Elements of these traditions, 'like their fighting methods and titulature', survived even after the 864 conversion to Christianity. However, the professor notes, the Bulgar period lasted less than 200 years: 'And is insufficiently documented – a major obstacle for modern historians.' Nevertheless, he adds, 'Archaeology and epigraphy are constantly enriching our understanding of this period.'

The accepted view of the Bulgars having Turkic origins has irritated some Bulgarian scholars since the National Revival period; they could not accept being related, however distantly, to their former Ottoman oppressors. 'Some scholars refuse to accept that Asparukh and his warriors spoke a Turkic language,' says Souphoulis. Instead, the rival theory forwarded by these nay-sayers argues that the Bulgars were influenced by Iranian culture. However, despite being 'quite popular' in some circles, 'there is admittedly little solid evidence to support it,' notes Sophoulis.

What is certain, however, is that the mysterious Bulgars were transformed by their neighbours. 'From early on, Bulgars and their Slavic subjects interacted and intermarried. As a result, by the late 9th century, the Bulgars had been absorbed by the numerically superior Slavs,' says Sophoulis. Thus was born a new, Slavic-speaking culture – the descendents of today's Bulgarians.

1396	1598	1686	1762
Bulgaria's last native king, Tsar Ivan Shishman (1371–96), is defeated and Bulgaria is annexed by the Ottoman Empire, beginning 500 years of harsh Islamic rule.	The First Târnovo Uprising against Turkish rule briefly liberates Veliko Târnovo. A new tsar is crowned, but the revolt is brutally crushed. Thousands of Bulgarians flee to Wallachia.	Austrian victories against the Turks inspire revolts in northern Bulgaria, but the so-called Second Târnovo Uprising is squashed.	The National Revival era; monk Paisii Hilendarski's groundbreaking *Slav-Bulgarian History* captivates Bulgarians. By the 19th century, Bulgarian-language education (1840s) is allowed.

Samuel, who died of shock. While Samuel actually died months later, the defeat was impressive – Basil was nicknamed Voulgaroktonos ('Bulgar-Slayer' in Greek). In 1018, Ohrid fell, and Bulgaria was annexed.

Byzantium's later decline led Bulgarians aristocratic brothers Asen and Petâr to rebel; their Second Bulgarian Empire (1185–1396) had Veliko Târnovo as capital. Bulgaria now cast a wary eye westward. In the perfidious Fourth Crusade of 1204, Western knights invaded Constantinople, destroying the Byzantine state. In 1205, self-declared 'emperor' Baldwin of Flanders foolishly invaded Bulgaria: he was captured and terminally imprisoned in the tower at Tsarevets Fortress in Veliko Târnovo.

Asen's diplomatically savvy son, Tsar Ivan Asen II (r 1218–41), became southeastern Europe's most powerful ruler, and Veliko Târnovo became an important cultural centre. In 1230 he defeated Byzantine successor armies at the Battle of Klokotnitsa. After his death, however, Bulgaria disintegrated between Tatar and Arab invasions and internal fighting.

The Turkish Yoke

After 1362 Ottoman Turks swarmed into the northern Balkans; within 30 years, they possessed Bulgaria, holding it for five centuries.

Despite rosy modern revisionism depicting life under the Turks as actually quite a lot of fun, they regarded non-Muslims as second-class citizens, enjoying few rights and suffering harsh punishments for the most insignificant offences. Like most of the Balkans, Bulgaria was isolated from Christian Western Europe, and missed out on its cultural and intellectual advances. In all, up to half of Bulgaria's population was either killed or enslaved (young boys were kidnapped and converted into the sultan's Janissary guard, while the girls were taken into Turkish harems). Churches and monasteries were destroyed, closed, or turned into mosques. Sporadic uprisings were quashed ferociously, and many Bulgarians fled.

Ottoman aristocrats inhabited the cities, consigning Bulgarians to the mountains and villages. *Haidouks* (armed rebels) fought the occupiers from the hills. As elsewhere in Ottoman lands, the Turks courted mountain-dwelling populations in strategic regions like the Rodopi Mountains – here, Bulgarian converts to Islam (today's Pomaks) won exemption from taxes and enjoyed legal rights denied to their Christian neighbours.

Bulgaria's national, cultural and Christian identity survived largely because of monks in monasteries (like Rila) that the Turks tolerated or couldn't control. They carefully preserved rituals, traditions and important manuscripts, keeping Bulgarian culture alive until it could re-emerge safely.

Bogomilism was a medieval Bulgarian heresy based on dualism – the existence of two deities, one evil, the other good. In 1118, sect leader Basil the Bogomil was burned at the stake in Constantinople – an extremely rare punishment meant to intimidate his followers.

The Legend of Basil the Bulgar-Slayer (Paul Stephenson) offers a scholarly reinterpretation of the illustrious Byzantine emperor and his campaigns in Bulgaria.

1854–56	1876	1877–78	1878
The Crimean War brings British and French troops to Bulgaria, with Varna an important garrison; Turkey is compelled to open up Bulgaria to international trade.	Koprivshtitsa's April Uprising is suppressed; civilian massacres cause international outrage. The Ottomans reject Bulgarian autonomy at the November Constantinople Conference.	Russo-Turkish War; Tsar Alexander II's army invades Bulgaria and destroys Ottoman forces. The resulting Treaty of San Stefano envisages the Turks ceding 60% of the Balkan Peninsula to Bulgaria.	Only four months after San Stefano, Western European powers fearing Russian expansionism enforce the Berlin Treaty, drastically limiting Bulgarian land gains.

National Revival

The Bulgarian monasteries that had preserved Bulgarian culture and history sparked the 18th- and 19th-century National Revival. This re-awakening coincided with similar nation-state sentimentality in Western Europe, and was influenced by monk Paisii Hilendarski – his name was taken from his time at the Serbian-sponsored Hilandar Monastery in Greece.

Hilendarski collected information to compile the first history of the Slav-Bulgarian peoples in 1762. He roamed the land, reciting his history to illiterate people (the Turks forbade Bulgarian-language publications). It was an instant hit, stirring long-suppressed nationalist feelings. Hilandarski's emphasis on the great deeds of Bulgaria's medieval tsars fuelled populist pride.

By the early 19th century, the Bulgarian economy had grown, with merchants from Plovdiv and Koprivshtitsa supplying wool, wine, metals and woodcarvings to Turkey and Western Europe. An educated and prosperous urban middle class emerged, especially after the Crimean War, when the victorious allies persuaded Turkey to open up to foreign trade.

Bulgarian merchants built grand private homes and public buildings in the distinct National Revival style. Woodcarvers from Tryavna and painters from Samokov developed a unique Bulgarian style in designing them. Bulgarian art, music and literature also flourished, and Bulgarian-language schools were opened. Towns and villages built *chitalishti* (reading rooms), providing a communal forum for cultural and social activities and political chatter. Turkish recognition of an autonomous Bulgarian Orthodox Church followed in 1870.

Travels in European Turkey in 1850 by Edmund Spencer is a first-hand travelogue providing rare insight into the later years of Ottoman rule in the Balkans.

Revolution & Freedom

The 1876 April Uprising in Koprivshtitsa came after long planning by revolutionaries like Georgi Rakovski, Hristo Botev and Bulgaria's iconic

---

LADISLAS' CRUSADE & THE BATTLE OF VARNA

By the early 15th century, the Ottomans possessed Bulgaria, Serbia and Transylvania, with Hungary in their sights and Constantinople under siege.

Trying to save Europe, Pope Eugenius IV ordered a crusade. In 1443, King Ladislas of Hungary and Poland transported his 25,000-man army via Venetian ships. Victories in Serbia, and Sofia's capture forced Ottoman Sultan Murad II to concede Serbia and agree to a 10-year truce in 1444.

However, the Pope and other crusade sponsors wanted all Europe liberated, forcing Ladislas to break his agreement. With a smaller force, he marched to Varna; while the promised reinforcement fleet never arrived, one furious sultan accompanied by 80,000 soldiers did. Ladislas was killed, his army destroyed. Nine years later, Constantinople fell, and Ottoman expansion continued.

1885	1908	1912–13	1915–19
A bloodless coup sees Bulgaria reunited with the Ottoman-controlled southlands. Turkish armies mobilise, while a Serbian invasion is defeated. Bulgaria's new borders are internationally recognised.	Amidst internal Turkish political chaos, Prince Ferdinand declares full independence from Turkey and becomes tsar of the new Bulgarian kingdom.	Bulgaria and neighbouring states fight in the First Balkan War (1912), reclaiming territory. Dissatisfied with its share, Bulgaria attacks allies in the Second Balkan War (1913), losing hard-won territory.	Bulgaria joins the Germans in WWI; defeated, the Treaty of Neuilly punishes Bulgaria by awarding land to its neighbours, while the government faces crippling reparation payments.

hero Vasil Levski. The Turks indiscriminately massacred 30,000 Bulgarian civilians and destroying 58 villages.

Western Europe was outraged; Russia cited the massacre in declaring war on Turkey in 1877. Some 200,000 Russian soldiers died for Bulgarian freedom, as the Russian army (and its Bulgarian volunteers) crushed the Turks. With Russian forces only 50km from Istanbul, the Ottomans capitulated. In the Treaty of San Stefano signed on 3 March 1878, Turkey ceded Bulgaria 60% of the Balkans.

However, Russophobic Western European powers reversed this with the Treaty of Berlin signed on 13 July 1878. It awarded the area between the Stara Planina ranges and the Danube, plus Sofia, to an independent Bulgarian principality. The Thracian Plain and Rodopi Mountains became Ottoman 'Eastern Rumelia'. Macedonia, renamed 'Western Rumelia', also remained Ottoman, as did Aegean Thrace. This ill-conceived treaty infuriated every Balkan nation, sparking decades of war: between 1878 and WWII, Balkan countries (including Bulgaria) fought six wars over border issues.

The Shortest History of Bulgaria, by Nikolay Ovcharov, runs quickly through the high points of Bulgaria's past, cramming a lot of interesting facts into just 70 brightly illustrated pages.

HISTORY

The Nascent State

On 16 April 1879, Bulgaria's new national assembly adopted its first constitution. On 26 June, Germany's Prince Alexander Battenberg was elected head of state. On 6 September 1885 the Bulgarian Principality and Eastern Rumelia were reunified after a bloodless coup. Central European powers were angered by this contravention of the Berlin Treaty, and Turkish troops massed for war.

The Austro-Hungarian Empire incited Serbia to fight Bulgaria, but Serbian troops were quickly repelled; the Bulgarian army advanced deep into Serbia, prompting Austria to call for a ceasefire. The Great Powers finally recognised the reunified Bulgaria.

War and its Discontents

Alexander's forced abdication in 1886 brought Prince (later King) Ferdinand Saxe-Coburg-Gotha to power. Prime minister Stefan Stambolov helped accelerate economic development, while two important political parties were founded: the Social Democrats (the communist forerunners), and the pro-peasant Agrarian Union. On 22 September 1908, King Ferdinand I took advantage of the Young Turks revolt to declare complete independence from Turkey.

After a decade of guerrilla warfare against the Turks in Macedonia and Greece, Montenegro, Bulgaria, Greece and Serbia united in 1912. In this, the First Balkan War, Serbian troops easily swept down through Macedonia, and Greek naval power denied Turkey reinforcements. However, Bulgaria's invaluable infantry bore the brunt of the Turkish

Commmunist leader Georgi Dimitriov first became famous when he was accused, along with three others, of starting the infamous Reichstag fire in Berlin in 1933. Stalin later secured his release.

1923	1940	1941	1945–46
Prime Minister Aleksander Stambolyiski is assassinated by right-wing military supporters of Macedonian revolutionaries. A communist uprising is brutally repressed and the communist party banned.	Southern Dobrudzha, occupied by Romania since 1913, is returned to Bulgaria for a nominal fee; Bulgarian troops triumphantly enter Balchik and other towns.	After first declaring neutrality, Bulgaria joins the Axis powers after German troops are stationed along the Danube, and declares war on Britain and France, but not on the Soviet Union.	After winning 1945 elections, the communists under Georgi Dimitrov declare the People's Republic of Bulgaria, with Soviet backing.

counter-attack; this, and the Bulgarian obsession with Macedonia, caused a disgruntled Bulgaria to attack its allies (the Second Balkan War) in 1913. Quickly defeated, Bulgaria lost hard-won territory; Turkey grabbed back Hadrianople (today's Edirne) too.

Unsurprisingly, a bad-tempered Bulgaria joined the Central Powers (ironically, allying it with Turkey) in 1915. Bulgarian soldiers spent the next years staring down Allied troops at the frozen 'Salonika Front' (today's Macedonia–Greece border). However, by 1918 Ferdinand's pro-German policies forced his abdication. His son, Boris III, took over.

The 1919 Treaty of Neuilly awarded Aegean Thrace to Greece and southern Dobrudzha to Romania. Bulgaria was also humiliated by war reparations, inciting political and social unrest. The 'radical' ruling Agrarian Party renounced claims to Macedonia (now, divided between Greece and the newly established Kingdom of Serbs, Croats and Slovenes). A right-wing military coup followed in 1923. Two years later, at Sofia's Sveta Nedelya Cathedral, communist terrorists failed to assassinate Boris III, killing 123 innocent bystanders instead. In 1934 the right-wing Zveno group's military coup gave Tsar Boris dictatorial powers.

World War II

Bulgaria declared neutrality when WWII began. However, German troops advancing towards Greece menacingly massed along the Danube, and Hitler offered up Macedonia to entice Bulgaria, which, once again, joined the (losing) Germanic side.

Allowing the Nazis free passage, Bulgaria declared war on Britain and France, but not Russia. Bulgarian soldiers occupied Macedonia and northern Greece. In one of the more difficult episodes in modern Bulgarian history, these occupying troops deported 13,000 Greek and Macedonian Jews to the Nazi death camps, in order to delay doing the same with their own Jews, due to public opposition.

On 28 August 1943, one week after meeting Hitler, Tsar Boris III died. Boris' infant son, Tsar Simeon II, succeeded him. Allied air raids in winter 1943–44 damaged Sofia and other towns. A coalition government sought peace, but failed, leading Russia to declare war and invade. On 9 September 1944 the part-communist resistance coalition, the 'Fatherland Front', took power. Even before war's end, 'people's courts' saw thousands of 'monarch-fascist' supporters imprisoned or executed.

Red Bulgaria

The Fatherland Front won November 1945 elections, with communists controlling the new national assembly. Leader Georgi Dimitrov's Soviet-styled constitution declared the People's Republic of Bulgaria on 15 September 1946. The royal family were exiled. The Stalinist regime

Dictator Todor Zhivkov sought advice from an elderly Bulgarian mystic, Baba Vanga, who became famous for her predictions – allegedly including the date of Stalin's death, the break-up of the USSR and the 9/11 attacks. And she also revealed that earthly society is already infiltrated by space aliens.

Voices from the Gulag: Life and Death in Communist Bulgaria, edited by Tzvetan Todorov, is a collection of first-hand accounts of inmates, guards and bureaucrats of the communist system's horrors.

1958	**1978**	**1984**	**1989–90**
The government initiates a mass agricultural collectivisation programme – the 'Great Leap Forward' – promising a five-year modernisation plan in just three years.	In one of the most infamous Cold War espionage events, Bulgarian dissident Georgi Markov is assassinated in London with a poisoned umbrella tip by a Bulgarian secret agent.	A nationalistic campaign to assimilate the ethnic Turkish population causes a mass exodus of Turks, though many return after communism ends.	Democratic revolutions see Todor Zhivkov's communist regime collapse; nevertheless, the former communist Bulgarian Socialist Party's candidate, Zhelyu Zhelev, wins the first free elections.

held show trials for 'traitors', collectivised agriculture and undertook industrialisation and modernisation programs. Dimitrov's successor, Vâlko Chervenkov, was dubbed 'Little Stalin' for his unquestioning loyalty.

Dictator Todor Zhivkov's long rule (1954–89) saw prosperity under Soviet protection. Bulgaria received cheap oil and electricity, plus exporting and contracts with Eastern Bloc and Non-Aligned Movement states. However, the secret police became an instrument of Zhivkov's totalitarianism, dealing ruthlessly with dissidents and diaspora critics. The service was rumoured to have masterminded the 1981 assassination attempt on Pope John Paul II by a Turkish gunman. (However, Bulgaria has always denied this and conflicting theories exist). As the Soviet bloc weakened in the 1980s, and Bulgaria's economy too, nationalism surged, targeting Turks, Pomaks and Roma, who were pressured to adopt Bulgarian names. A Turkish exodus ensued, though many returned and prospered later.

See www.parlia
ment.bg and
www.govern
ment.bg for
English-language
information on
the workings of
government in
Bulgaria.

HISTORY

The Transition to the West

By 1989 *perestroika* had reached Bulgaria. On 10 November, an internal Communist Party coup dismissed Zhivkov, and the party allowed elections, renaming itself the Bulgarian Socialist Party (BSP). A broad opposition coalition, the Union of Democratic Forces (UDF) failed to unseat the BSP in the June 1990 parliamentary elections – making Bulgaria the first ex-Soviet state to resurrect communists.

While the incompetence of both blocs caused frequent changes in government, elections were generally irrelevant in transition-era Bulgaria, as power and wealth consolidated around overnight millionaires, bodyguards, former spies and other adventurers in the new 'capitalism.' Throughout the 1990s, an impoverished public held protests over government failures. In 1997, prime minister Ivan Kostov pledged to fight crime and corruption while attracting investment. However, doing this while making painful NATO- and EU-mandated reforms was difficult.

Boyko Borisov,
elected Bulgaria's
prime minister
in 2009, holds
a black belt
in karate and
has served as
president of the
Bulgarian Karate
Federation.

In 2001 Bulgarians elected their once-exiled king as prime minister. Simeon Saxe-Coburg had formed the National Movement Simeon II (NMSII) only two months earlier. His coalition included the Movement for Rights and Freedoms (MRF), the ethnic Turkish party of wealthy businessman Ahmed Dogan, and promised economic prosperity, plus NATO and EU membership. Although Simeon's popularity did not endure, those goals were reached – Bulgaria joined NATO in 2004 and the EU in 2007.

2001
Bulgaria's formerly exiled child-king, Simeon Saxe-Coburg, becomes prime minister.

2004
Bulgaria, along with other former Warsaw Pact nations, joins NATO.

2007
On 1 January, despite European misgivings over stalled reforms, Bulgaria joins the EU, becoming its first 'Cyrillic' country.

JEAN-CHRISTOPHE RIOU / GETTY IMAGES ©

» EU flag

Outdoor Activities & Wildlife

The Bulgarian Landscape

Bulgaria covers just under 111,000 sq km at the heart of the Balkan Peninsula, and in that relatively small area encompasses an amazing variety of landscapes and landforms. About a third of Bulgaria's terrain is mountainous and the country boasts seven distinct mountain ranges, each with a unique range of flora and fauna, and all covered with well-marked walking trails.

From the northern border with Romania, a windswept fertile plain gradually slopes south as far as the Stara Planina mountains, the longest mountain range in the Balkans, which virtually splits the country in two. To the south, the Sredna Gora mountains are separated from the main range by a fault in which the Valley of Roses lies.

Bulgaria's highest peak, Mt Musala (2925m), stands in the rugged and floriferous Rila Mountains south of Sofia, and is almost equalled in height by Mt Vihren (2915m) in the wild Pirin Mountains further south. The Rila Mountains' bare rocky peaks, steep forested valleys and glacial lakes are a paradise for hikers (and, in parts, skiers). The Rodopi Mountains stretch along the Greek border east of the Rila and Pirin Mountains and spill over into Greece. The fascinating Yagodina and Trigrad caves are geological highlights of the Rodopis, while Melnik's dramatic and unique sand pyramids are one of the more unusual sights in the Pirin region.

The Thracian plain opens onto the Black Sea coast. The 378km-long coast is lined with beaches and also features coastal lakes near Burgas, spectacular cliffs near Kaliakra and several sandy bays. Diving has become a popular activity here over recent years. In addition to the mighty Danube, which forms much of the border with Romania, the major rivers include the Yantra, which meanders its way through the town of Veliko Tărnovo; the Iskăr, which stretches from south of Samokov to the Danube, past Sofia; and the Maritsa, which crawls through Plovdiv.

The rare *silivriak* is also known as the Orpheus flower; legend says that its flowers were stained pink with the blood of the divine musician after he was hacked to pieces by the frenzied Bacchantes.

Activities

Bulgaria's mountainous, heavily forested terrain makes for great hiking, mountaineering and skiing, while on the Black Sea coast you can indulge in an array of water sports from paragliding to scuba diving. In addition, travel agencies organise a wide range of activity and special-interest holidays, taking in birdwatching, wildlife spotting, botanical and archaeological tours.

Hiking in Bulgaria

Hiking has long been a hugely popular activity in Bulgaria, with some 37,000km of marked trails to follow. The trans-European hiking trails E3, E4 and E8 all cross through the country, while the E3 trail, which begins in Spain, follows the crest of the Stara Planina range from Belogradchik eastwards to the coast at Cape Ermine, and is well signposted along the way. If you want to go the whole way, count on taking around 20 days or so. The E4 and E8 trails both pass through Rila National Park and offer varied scenery and difficulty.

Walkers are well supported, with numerous *hizhas* (mountain huts) along the more popular tracks, as well as in real wilderness areas. While some are very basic affairs, intended only as no-frills overnight shelter, others are more comfortable, sometimes with attached cafes. It's one of the more positive legacies of the old communist regime, which believed that hiking was a healthy and productive proletarian pastime.

> *Walkers are well supported, with numerous* hizhas *(mountain huts) along the more popular tracks*

The Rila Mountains are a rugged, rocky, heavily forested range with plunging glacial valleys and rich plant life. One of the most attractive and accessible walking routes heads into the Maliovitsa range, south of the small town of the same name and based around soaring Mt Maliovitsa (2729m).

Another relatively easy and very pleasant walk runs along the Rilska river towards Rila Monastery, passing through Kiril Meadow along the way.

The Pirins offer some of the very finest walking country in Bulgaria. It's an alpine landscape of glacial valleys and lakes, and the climate is blessed with a moderating Mediterranean influence.

The Sredna Gora is the highest, most visited section of the Stara Planina, with hundreds of marked tracks and the largest number of *hizhas*. The Stara Planina is noted for its sudden weather changes, and some of Bulgaria's highest rainfalls and strongest winds have been recorded here, so be prepared.

For organised hiking tours, contact Odysseia-In (p313) in Sofia.

Mountaineering

The Rila, Pirin and Stara Planina mountain ranges are the best places for mountaineering in Bulgaria. There are well over a hundred alpine peaks higher than 1000m in the Rila range, and breathtaking landscapes featuring streams and placid lakes. Note that snow and low temperatures persist at higher levels even into summer.

The Pirin Mountains feature almost a hundred peaks above 2500m. It's a typical alpine landscape of cirques and ridges. The northern face of Mt Vihren (2915m) is the most popular climb in this region and can be reached via Bansko.

The 550km-long Balkan Range (or Stara Planina; literally 'Old Mountains') cuts right across the country, and acts as a climatic barrier between the north and south of Bulgaria, with the northern side significantly colder. It's a huge, diverse area, covering 10% of Bulgaria's territory. Due to its relatively easy access (from Vratsa) and the variety of routes offered, the most frequented section of this mighty range is the Vratsa Rocks in the far west, the largest limestone climbing area in Bulgaria. Mt Botev (2376m), inside the Central Balkan National Park, is another popular climb, with easy access from Karlovo.

The Bulgarian Climbing & Mountaineering Federation (☑02-930 0532; www.bfka.org) in Sofia has information, advice and links to regional clubs.

Rock Climbing

There are numerous locations around the country where you can indulge in rock climbing, either independently or with a qualified guide – essential for some of the tougher areas. A good place to start is **www. climbingguidebg.com**, which has lots of information, advice and links.

See www.bul gariaski.com for comprehensive information about the country's skiing resorts and snow reports.

The main area for rock climbing is around Vratsa, where there are some 333 identified climbing routes and a variety of climbing conditions including alpine, sport and ice climbing. The area of Vratsata, on the road to the Ledenika Cave, has permanent bolts attached to the rock face.

Other areas include the Pirin Mountains, with 31 alpine and traditional climbing routes, although these are suitable only for experienced climbers. The north face of Mt Vihren, to the south of Bansko, is particularly challenging. Malîovitsa, in the Rila Mountains, is home to the Central Mountain School, which offers rock-climbing activities and guides in the Malîovitsa range. Again, these are quite serious climbs, and safety nets are provided. The Vitosha mountain range and the Stara Planina are the other main areas for rock climbing, with many different routes for climbers of varying abilities.

Skiing & Snowboarding

Bansko is the number one skiing and snowboarding resort in the country, with the most modern facilities, the longest snow season and the biggest international profile. There are now two ski centres: Chalin Valog (1100m to 1600m) and Shiligarnika (1700m to 2500m), roughly 10km from town and accessed from Bansko by gondola. All abilities are well catered for. Snow cover here lasts from December to May, helped in part by the use of artificial snow cannons. There's also a 5km cross-country ski track.

Pamporovo, sited at 1650m in the Rodopi Mountains, and with 25km of trails, is a family-friendly place and great for beginners. The more experienced will be drawn to the giant slalom run and, most difficult of all, the infamous 1100m-long Wall.

Nearby Chepelare is quieter, but it has 30km of cross-country tracks and some of the longest runs in Bulgaria. The Mechi Chal 1 (3150m) is a black-level run used for international competitions, while Mechi Chal 2 (5250m) is a combined red/green slope.

Borovets, in the Rila Mountains, is Bulgaria's oldest ski resort, and is a more basic affair. It has 45km of trails and a good ski school.

Just 10km from central Sofia, Vitosha is a convenient destination for weekending city folk and has slopes to suit all levels of skiers and snowboarders. Other, smaller (and cheaper) ski resorts include Govedartsi and Malîovitsa, which are mainly patronised by Bulgarian holidaymakers.

Water Sports on the Black Sea

During the summer, big Black Sea package resorts such as Sunny Beach (Slânchev Bryag) and Golden Sands (Zlatni Pyasâtsi), as well as some smaller seaside towns, offer organised water sports, including jet-skiing, waterskiing, parasailing and windsurfing. Often these are quite casual affairs set up at various points along the beaches.

Scuba diving has become popular in recent years, and there are several places along the coast where you can try it. As well as package resorts such as Albena (p421), popular tourist towns like Sozopol (p402) and Nesebâr (p410) are the places to go, and there's a new diving resort just north of Tsarevo (p406). As well as standard training courses and boat dives, there's also the opportunity to explore some wrecks at various points.

Birdwatching, Botany & Bears

Bulgaria is a haven for all kinds of wildlife, including such elusive creatures as brown bears and wolves, plus 400 species of birds (around 75% of the European total). Birdwatching is a popular hobby and several companies run birdwatching tours. The nesting period (May to June) and migration period (September to October) are the best times to come. The Via Pontica, which passes over Bulgaria, is one of Europe's major migratory routes for birds, while Atanasovsko Lake, north of Burgas, is the country's most important reserve, frequented by 314 species.

There are several companies running interesting wildlife tours, led by English-speaking professionals.

» Neophron (www.neophron.com) – Birdwatching, botany and bear-watching tours.

» Via Pontica Tours (www.viapontica.com) – Specialist birdwatching, butterfly, dragonfly, insect and botanical tours.

» Spatia (www.spatiawildlife.com) – Birdwatching and bat-, butterfly-, wolf- and bear-viewing tours.

» Wildlife Photography (www.cometobg.com) – Wildlife photography tours and workshops.

» Zig-Zag Holidays (www.zigzagbg.com) – Wildlife- and bear-viewing tours.

Wildlife

Though small, Bulgaria packs in a huge and diverse array of flora and fauna, helped by the varied climate and topography, relatively sparse human population, and the fact that almost a third of the country is forested.

Animals

Bulgaria is home to some 56,000 kinds of animal, including over 400 species of bird (about 75% of all species found in Europe), 36 types of reptile, over 200 species of freshwater and saltwater fish (of which about half are found along the Black Sea coast) and 27,000 types of insect.

Many larger animals are elusive and live in the hills and mountains, some way from urban centres, but if you are keen to see some natural fauna, join an organised tour. Alternatively, hike in the Strandzha Nature Park; the Rusenski Lom Nature Park, home to 67 species of mammal (about two-thirds of those found in Bulgaria); the Rila National Park; or the Pirin National Park, where 42 species of animal, such as European brown bears, deer and wild goats, thrive.

Bird lovers can admire plenty of our feathered friends at Burgas Lakes, the largest wetland complex in the country, and home to about 60% of all bird species in Bulgaria; the Ropotamo Nature Reserve, with more than 200 species of bird; Lake Srebârna, also with over 200 bird species; the Strandzha Nature Park, with almost 70% of all bird species found

The Bulgarian Society for the Protection of Birds (www.bspb. org) is a good source of bird news.

The Balkani Wildlife Society (www.balkani. org) is active in environmental conservation programs around the country and in raising public awareness of wildlife issues.

OUTDOOR ACTIVITIES & WILDLIFE

DANCING BEARS

The cruel practice of 'dancing' bears was officially banned in Bulgaria in 1993, and rescued bears now live in the **Dancing Bears Park** (www.vier-pfoten.bg) in Belitsa, in the Rila Mountains. Located around 33km northeast of Bansko (and 12km outside the village of Belitsa itself), the park is the largest of its kind in Europe, and visitors are welcome to join guided tours. You will need your own transport to visit. As well as helping these abused animals, the park also provides employment in a poor region of the country and it is hoped that this will become a significant ecotourism draw in the future. The park is partly funded by the Brigitte Bardot Foundation.

in Bulgaria; and the Rusenski Lom Nature Park, home to 170 species of water bird. White storks, black storks, Dalmatian pelicans, sandpipers, corncrakes and pygmy cormorants are some of the species that can be seen in these areas.

Common and bottlenose dolphins and harbour porpoises live in the Black Sea – though, sadly, in decreasing numbers.

ENDANGERED SPECIES

Bulgaria has one of the largest brown bear populations in Europe. Rough estimates put the figure at anything from 500 to 1000 individuals. There are thought to be around 300 bears in the southeastern Rodopis, and about 200 in the Central Balkan National Park. However, unless you're on a wildlife-spotting tour, you're extremely unlikely to see a bear.

There are thought to be up to 2000 wolves in the country, while numbers of the critically endangered Eurasian lynx are uncertain. Again, you'll be very lucky to see these animals in the wild.

Rare insects include the Bulgarian emerald dragonfly, discovered only in 1999. It is thought only to inhabit a small area of the Eastern Rodopi mountains and neighbouring areas of Greece and Turkey.

Various species of rare bird, including Egyptian vultures, lesser kestrels and great eagle owls, are protected in the Rusenski Lom Nature Park, while small cormorants, Ferruginous ducks and Dalmatian pelicans thrive in the Srebârna Nature Reserve. The imperial eagle is one of Bulgaria's most threatened birds – only around 30 pairs are believed to exist in the wild today. Saker falcons have been brought close to extinction in Bulgaria due to the illegal falconry trade and egg collectors; there are thought to be only 10 breeding pairs remaining.

Visit www.bulgariannationalparks.org for comprehensive information on Bulgaria's three national parks.

NATIONAL PARKS & NATURE RESERVES

NATIONAL PARK OR RESERVE	FEATURES	ACTIVITIES	BEST TIME TO VISIT
Central Balkan National Park	mountains, forests, waterfalls & canyons; wolves, otters, wildcats, rare birds & bats	hiking, caving & horse riding	May-Sep
Pirin National Park	mountains & lakes; bears & birds	hiking	Jun-Sep
Rila National Park	alpine forests & pastures; deer, wild goats & eagles	hiking	Jun-Sep
Ropotamo Nature Reserve	marshes & sand dunes; rare birds	boat trips & hiking	Apr-Jul
Rusenski Lom Nature Park	rivers, valleys & mountains; rare birds; rock churches	birdwatching & caving	Jun-Sep
Strandzha Nature Park	varied forest & beaches; birds & mammals; archaeological ruins	hiking & birdwatching	Jun-Aug
Vitosha Nature Park	mountain trails	hiking, skiing & snowboarding	Apr-Aug, Dec & Jan
Vrachanski Balkan Nature Park	forest, varied tree life & caves	hiking & caving	Jun-Sep

National Parks

The Bulgarian government has officially established three national parks – Rila, Pirin and Central Balkan – where the flora, fauna and environment are (in theory) protected. Besides the three officially protected national parks, which do not include any towns or villages, Bulgaria has 10 'nature parks', which do include permanent settlements, and nature reserves, which are unique managed ecosystems. The latter category receives the strictest protection, and access is often regulated or even prohibited.

Visual Arts, Crafts & Music

Bulgaria has an ancient tradition of icon painting and these religious images are still the most memorable examples of Bulgarian artistry. Five centuries of Turkish rule suppressed much of native Bulgarian culture, but the National Revival of the late 18th to 19th centuries saw a creative blossoming as writers and artists strove to reignite the national consciousness. During the communist era, however, most Bulgarians with artistic, literary, theatrical or musical talents were trained in the former Soviet Union and therefore heavily influenced by the Russians and socialist ideology. Today, artistic activity in Bulgaria is at an all-time high.

The remarkable late 9th-century ceramic icon of Sveti Teodor, found in Veliki Preslav, is regarded as one of the masterpieces of early Bulgarian art.

Icons & Religious Art

Most of Bulgaria's earliest artists painted on the walls of homes, churches and monasteries. The works of these anonymous masters are considered national treasures, and rare surviving examples can be seen in churches and museums across the country, including the lovely Boyana Church (p316), near Sofia.

Throughout the Ottoman occupation, the tradition of icon painting endured, as a symbol of national culture and identity. The highpoint for Bulgarian icon painting came during the National Revival period, and the most famous artist of the time was Zahari Zograf (1810–53), who painted magnificent murals in the monasteries at Rila, Troyan and Bachkovo. Many of Zograf's works were inspired by medieval Bulgarian art, though they display a more human (if often gory and sadistic) spirit, with naked sinners being inventively tortured by demons (a common and seemingly much-relished motif) alongside the calmer scenes of angels and saints. Zograf and others also produced smaller, devotional images both for churches and private homes.

The tradition of icon painting in Bulgaria continues to this day, and hand-painted icons by contemporary artists are sold at galleries, churches and street markets.

Find out about contemporary artists working in Bulgaria at www. modernbulgarian artists.com.

Painting & Sculpture

Bulgarian painting has had little exposure overseas, but well-regarded Bulgarian artists of the last 150 years include Vladimir Dimitrov (1882–1960), often referred to as 'The Master', Georgi Mashev, Michail Lutov and Zlatyu Boyadjiev. Dimitrov, who during his life was as famous for his asceticism as his art, is known for his colourful, sometimes psychedelic, images of 19th-century peasants, and you will see his work in galleries across Bulgaria.

Contemporary Bulgarian artists include the sculptor Todor Todorov and the abstract painter Kolyo Karamfilov. However, the most widely recognised modern Bulgarian artist is Christo.

Bulgarian sculpture developed in the 19th and 20th centuries, and one of the leading lights of the period was Andrei Nikolov (1878–1959), who was influenced by contemporary French styles. His home in Sofia is now a cultural centre and hotel. He designed the stone lion outside Sofia's Tomb of the Unknown Soldier and more examples of his naturalistic sculptures are on show in the city's National Art Gallery (p297).

Pottery

One of Bulgaria's oldest crafts is pottery, and the most distinctive style is known as *Troyanska kapka*, literally translated as 'Troyan droplet', after its town of origin and the runny patterns made by the paint on the glazed earthenware body. Developed in the 19th century, it's still produced both for everyday domestic consumption and as souvenirs. Everything from cooking pots, plates and jugs to vases, ashtrays and more decorative items can be bought at market stalls, and from souvenir shops and independent workshops. Easily identifiable, the pottery comes in a few basic colours, including a lovely cobalt blue, green, brown and yellow, and pieces are decorated with concentric circles, wavy lines and teardrops.

Carpets

Bulgarian carpets and rugs were first made as early as the 9th century, but were most popular and creative during the Bulgarian National Revival period. Sadly, weaving is a dying art, practised only by a dwindling band of elderly ladies who still work on handmade looms in a few remote villages such as Chiprovtsi, Kotel and Koprivshtitsa.

Carpets and rugs made in the southern Rodopi Mountains are thick, woollen and practical, while in western Bulgaria they're often delicate, colourful and more decorative. The carpet-making industry began in Chiprovtsi around the late 17th century, with patterns based mainly on geometric abstract shapes. The more popular designs featuring birds and flowers, commonly seen in tourist shops today, were developed in the 19th century.

For news about the Sofia Boys' Choir, see www. sofiaboyschoir. altpro.net.

Music

Choral Music

Bulgarian ecclesiastic music dates back to the 9th century and conveys the mysticism of chronicles, fables and legends. To hear Orthodox chants sung by a choir of up to 100 people is a moving experience. Dobri Hristov

---

CHRISTO & JEANNE-CLAUDE

The most internationally famous living Bulgarian artist is Christo Javacheff, known simply as Christo. Born in Gabrovo in 1935, he studied at Sofia's Fine Arts Academy in the 1950s and met his French-born wife, Jeanne-Claude, in Paris in 1958. They have worked in collaboration since 1961, when they created their first outdoor temporary installation, *Stacked Oil Barrels*, at Cologne Harbour. Since then, the couple, who moved to New York in 1964, have made a name for themselves with their (usually) temporary, large-scale architectural artworks, often involving wrapping famous buildings in fabric or polypropylene sheeting to highlight their basic forms. In 1985 they created *The Pont Neuf Wrapped*, covering the Parisian landmark in golden fabric for 14 days, while in 1995 the Reichstag in Berlin was covered entirely with silver fabric. In 2005, *The Gates*, an impressive installation consisting of 7503 vinyl gates spread over 32km of walkways, was unveiled in New York's Central Park. Christo and Jeanne-Claude are still working on major projects around the world, and current schemes still in the planning stage include *The Mastaba*, a gigantic stack of 410,000 multicoloured oil barrels – first conceived in 1977 – to be built in the desert in Abu Dhabi. For the latest news, see www.christojeanneclaude.net.

RECOMMENDED LISTENING

» **Bulgarian Folk Songs and Dances featuring Petko Radev and Petko Dachev** (2000) – a top-selling collection of traditional tunes

» **Orthodox Chants** (2004) by Orlin Anastassov and the Seven Saints Choir – sacred sounds from the young opera star and the highly respected church vocal group

» **Le Mystère des Voix Bulgares** (2001) – haunting melodies from the ladies' choir

» **Gadna Poroda** (2011) by Azis – pop-folk performed by Bulgaria's biggest *chalga* star

» **Folk Impressions** (2012) by the Sofia Boys' Choir – traditional folk songs from the renowned youth choir

» **Bulgarian Rhapsody Vardar** (2007) by Pancho Vladigerov – some of the composer's most popular works

(1875–1941) was one of Bulgaria's most celebrated composers of church and choral music, and wrote his major choral work, *Liturgy No 1*, for the Seven Saints ensemble, Bulgaria's best-known sacred-music vocal group, based in Sofia's Sveti Sedmochislenitsi Church.

The Sofia Boys' Choir, formed in 1968, brings together boys from various schools in the capital, aged 8 to 15, and has performed around the world to great acclaim. As well as their traditional Easter and Christmas concerts, they are known for their Orthodox choral music and folk songs.

Learn more about Seven Saints, Bulgaria's leading sacred-music vocal ensemble, at www.theseven saints.com

Folk Music

The vaguely oriental sounds of Bulgarian folk music offer an immediate and evocative aural impression of the country. Traditional instruments such as the *gaida* (bagpipes), *gadulka* (a bowed stringed instrument) and *kaval* (flute) normally feature. As in many peasant cultures, Bulgarian women were not given access to musical instruments, so they usually performed the vocal parts. Bulgarian female singing is polyphonic, featuring many voices and shifting melodies, and women from villages in the Pirin Mountains are renowned for their unique singing style. Regular folk-music and dance festivals are held around Bulgaria and are great opportunities to experience the culture.

Chalga

Music from *Le Mystère des Voix Bulgares* was included in the capsule aboard the *Voyager 2* space probe in the hope of reaching alien ears.

The most distinctive sound in Bulgarian contemporary music is the spirited, warbling, pop-folk idiom known as *chalga*. Influenced by Balkan, Turkish, Arabic and even flamenco rhythms, this is sexy, sweaty, repetitive dance music, and is looked down on by many Bulgarians, who consider it vulgar. Bands often feature a scantily clad female lead vocalist and play jazzed-up traditional Balkan tunes on instruments such as the electric guitar, clarinet and synthesizer. It's loud, brash and often self-consciously cheesy, and isn't to everyone's tastes, but there are plenty of clubs around Bulgaria that play little else, and it's pretty hard to avoid if you go anywhere near a TV or radio. One of the biggest names in contemporary *chalga* is Azis, a gay, white-bearded, transvestite Roma.

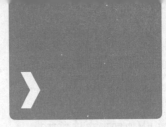

The Bulgarian People

The Bulgarian Character

Five centuries of brutal foreign occupation under the Ottoman Empire, and, more recently, four decades of totalitarian communist rule, might not be the happiest of back-stories, but the Bulgarians have maintained a strong pride in their history and traditions. Many express a worldly wise, cynical outlook on life and have a keen, dark sense of humour; high levels of corruption and uneven economic fortunes have taught them not to expect too much of politicians and bureaucrats.

Warm and open to strangers, Bulgarians are a welcoming and hospitable people, and most are genuinely concerned that you leave their country with only good impressions. They tend to be informal, easy-going and approachable, and parties and random get-togethers are common, usually involving plenty of alcohol. Bulgarians have rather freer attitudes towards personal space than most Western Europeans; don't be surprised if strangers ask to join you at tables in restaurants if no other seats are available.

Holidays of the Bulgarians in Myths and Legends by Nikolay Nikov is a fascinating account of the traditions and customs associated with all the major festivals.

Bulgarian Society

Like other Eastern European nations, Bulgaria remains a largely conservative and traditional society. Macho culture prevails, with often old-fashioned attitudes adopted towards women, and outright hostility towards gays and lesbians is not uncommon.

Rural life goes on much as it has done for the last century or so. You'll still see headscarfed old women toiling in the fields and donkeys pulling carts along the dirt tracks running through tumbledown villages. However, even the remotest areas are beginning to see the effects of foreign investment as ramshackle old houses are snapped up by developers for holiday homes and construction projects shoot up in and around the more popular areas.

Things are of course very different in the cities, where Western boutiques, casinos and strip clubs have proliferated. Pouting, scantily clad women are popular motifs used for advertising everything from alcohol to shopping centres, while a profusion of strip clubs and escort agencies has appeared in the big cities, colourfully touted in tourist magazines alongside reviews of restaurants and museums.

In A Street Without a Name, Bulgarian-born travel-writer Kapka Kassabova recalls her childhood under communism and offers a unique perspective on Bulgaria today.

Race in Bulgaria

Although it's been invaded and occupied by countless foreign powers throughout its long history, Bulgaria remains a fairly homogenous nation, with some 85% of the population declaring themselves Bulgarian.

In 1985 the communists mounted a program to assimilate the country's Turkish inhabitants by forcing them to accept Bulgarian names.

THE MACEDONIAN QUESTION

One topic that excites massive controversy in Bulgaria is the 'Macedonian question'. The historical region of Macedonia covered areas of modern-day northern Greece and south-western Bulgaria, as well as the Republic of Macedonia itself. For many Bulgarians there is no question – Macedonians are simply Bulgarians in denial, and their country really a part of the Bulgarian state, unfairly detached by bad luck and Great Power intrigue.

In 1945 the inhabitants of the Pirin region were named a Macedonian ethnic minority, and there were plans to merge Bulgaria and Macedonia into one country, though all this came to nothing in the end and by the 1960s the ethnic minority status was rescinded. The majority of people living in the Pirin region regard themselves first and foremost as Bulgarian, but movements for regional autonomy still exist. Ultra-nationalist parties such as the Internal Macedonian Revolutionary Organisation (IMRO) maintain that the state of Macedonia is part of Bulgaria.

Despite being the first country to recognise the independent Republic of Macedonia after it peacefully separated from Yugoslavia in 1991, Bulgaria does not recognise the Macedonian national identity or language.

Mosques were also closed down and even wearing Turkish dress and speaking Turkish in public were banned. Mass protests erupted, and in early 1989 about 300,000 Turkish Bulgarians and Pomaks left for Turkey (though many subsequently returned to Bulgaria when the repressive policies were overturned).

Relations between Bulgarians and the ethnic Turkish minority have improved since, but racial tensions remain, and far-right political parties have received increasing support over recent years. Their aggressively nationalistic rhetoric has been directed against both Turkish Muslims and Roma. There have also been violent attacks on Roma neigbourhoods.

Bulgaria's Roma, who form roughly 4% of the population, suffer disproportionate rates of unemployment, social deprivation, illiteracy, poverty and prejudice. They tend to live in ghettos and can be seen begging on the streets all over the country. Along with other East and Central European nations, Bulgaria signed up to the Decade of Roma Inclusion program (www.romadecade.org) in 2005, which attempts to improve conditions for Roma populations. Some success in providing employment has been claimed, but it remains to be seen if any lasting good comes out of it.

The Rodopi Mountains area is home to about 200,000 Pomaks, the descendants of Slavs who converted to Islam during the Ottoman occupation in the 15th century. In the past, they have been subjected to the same assimilatory pressures as the Turks. Some villages in the Rodopis are almost entirely Pomak.

The Orient Within by Mary Neuberger investigates the story of Bulgaria's Muslim minority population, their relationship with the modern state and ideas of national identity.

Religious Life in Bulgaria

Orthodox Christianity has been the official religion since 865, though modern Bulgaria is a secular state that allows freedom of religion. The vast majority of the population – around 76% – still professes adherence to the Bulgarian Orthodox Church, although only a fraction of this number regularly attend church services.

In the 2011 census, some 11% declared themselves atheist, while Protestant and Catholics together formed less than 2% of the Bulgarian population.

Roughly 10% of the population is Muslim – ethnic Turks, Pomaks and many Roma. Over the centuries the Islam practised in Bulgaria has incorporated various Bulgarian traditions and Christian beliefs and has become known as Balkan Islam.

There's also a tiny Jewish population, mainly living in Sofia.

Dunovism, founded in Bulgaria after WWI by Peter Dunov, is a religion combining Orthodox Christianity with yoga, meditation and belief in reincarnation.

Bulgarian Wine

Bulgaria's excellent wines are a product of its varied climate zones, rich soil and proud tradition. Foreign interest and investment in recent years have made Bulgarian wines increasingly known and appreciated abroad. Wine-loving travellers can sample them at rustic wineries, in gourmet urban restaurants and even at roadside stands.

History

Bulgaria's wine-making tradition goes back to the Thracians, who worshipped wine god Dionysus and planted grape varietals still cultivated today. Roman, Byzantine and medieval Bulgarian civilisations continued the tradition. While the Muslim Ottomans discouraged vintners, the 18th- and 19th-century National Revival period saw aristocratic mansions (some still in use) doubling as wine salons After a damaging late-19th-century phylloxera outbreak, French experts recommended which endemic varietals to continue (such as Mavrud, Pamid and Gamza). Today, modern techniques and know-how have helped make Bulgarian wines increasingly visible in foreign supermarkets.

The official website for Bulgarian wines is www.bulgarian wines.org.

Winemaking Regions

Bulgaria's five wine-producing regions have unique microclimate and grape varietals. Oenophiles can contact the wineries to arrange tastings, or find a specialised group.

Northern (Danube Plain)

Comprising the area between the Danube and the Stara Planina range, and hemmed in by the Serbian border and the eastern Dobrudzha Valley, this cool plains region boasts 35% of Bulgaria's vineyards. The signature Gamza is a light red dinner wine. Cabernet Sauvignon and Merlot are also crafted here, as are whites like Chardonnay, Riesling and Sauvignon Blanc. Other common northern wines include Muscat Ottonel, Aligoté and Pamid.

WINERIES

Vinprom Rousse Winery (☏082-884 250; www.vinpromrousse.com; ul Treti Mart 44, Ruse) Ruse's largest winery, Vinprom Rousse has modernised admirably since its 1998 privatisation. Among its best offerings are quality, Danubian Valley whites. It's especially known for the light local red, Gamza, but also produces Chardonnay, Sauvignon Blanc, Igni Blanc and Welschriesling, among others.

Lovico Suhindol (☏061-362 411; www.lovico.eu; ul Rositsa 156, Suhindol) In Suhindol village near Veliko Târnovo, this winery dating to 1909 produces over 6 million litres of wine and brandy annually. It specialises in the deep purple, slightly spicy Gamza (best after two or three years of ageing), Cabernet Sauvignon, Chardonnay and Muscat.

Eastern (Black Sea Coastal)

Running down the Black Sea coast from Romania to Turkey, this region features over half of Bulgaria's white grape varietals, with long summers and mild autumns creating ideal conditions for them. About 30% of Bulgaria's vineyards are here, in Targovishte, Preslav and Strandja. Dimyat, Traminer, Riesling, Muscat Ottonel, Sauvignon Blanc and Gewürztraminer are excellent local wines.

WINERIES

Chateau Euxinograde (☎052-393 165; Varna) Housed in the former royal palace north of Varna, this winery was established in 1891 by Prince Battenberg, then catered to the communist elite from 1944 to 1989. The 90-hectare Euxinograde complex includes a palace featuring elaborate period furnishings, botanical gardens with rare plants, and the wine collections of Prince Ferdinand and Tsar Boris III, which includes a Chateau Margaux from 1904. The winery's delicate Riesling and rich Traminer white are particularly good, as is its French-style brandy, Euxignac.

Degustatsija na vino is Bulgarian for 'wine tasting'.

LVK-Vinprom Targovishte (☎060-169 602; www.lvk-vinprom.com; bul 29 Yanuari 8, Targovishte) The Targovishte microregion, near Veliko Târnovo, has produced many prizewinning wines of late. LVK-Vinprom is the largest – visit the winery and its vineyards at nearby Kralevo. Targovishte wines, both red and white, make good dinner wines.

Domaine Boyar (☎02-969 7980; www.domaineboyar.com; Zlaten Rog 20-22, Sofia) This leading winery has won numerous awards at international fairs, and in 2005 became the official importer of champagnes for several European royal families. While Domaine Boyar operates vineyards in the eastern Black Sea region and on the Thracian plain, its tastings are held in Shumen-area vineyards. Professional guides detail the winery's history, and serve the winery's spectacular Chardonnay (among others).

The Valley of Roses (Sub-Balkan)

South of the Stara Planina mountain range and north of Plovdiv, this region's rich fields are perfect for producing dry whites, such as Misket – better here than anywhere else in Bulgaria.

Damianitza's 'No Man's Land' wine is made from grapes grown in the once off-limits border-zone fields between Bulgaria and Greece.

Thracian Lowland (South Bulgarian)

Beginning south of the Stara Planina range and extending to the Sakar Mountain and Maritsa River, this region enjoys hot, dry summers while the mountains protect it from cold northern winds. The Bessa Valley sub-region's winemaking tradition dates to the 5th-century-BC Thracian Bessi tribe. This region produces one of Bulgaria's most famous wines, the red Mavrud, plus Merlot, Cabernet Sauvignon, Muscatel and Pamid.

WINERIES

Bessa Valley Winery (☎088-949 9992; www.bessavalley.com; Ognyanovo village) Bessa Valley produces excellent Merlot, Syrah, Petit Verdot and Cabernet Sauvignon. Tasting tours involve seeing the impressive facilities, which include an enormous rotunda and arched pergola; the limestone cellar walls are flecked with the fossils of ancient sea creatures. The tour, involving sampling three wines accompanied by cheeses and meats, lasts two hours and costs 12 lv.

Todoroff Wine Cellars (☎02-850 4666; www.todoroff-wines.com) Just a tiny boutique winery when opened in 1999, Todoroff Wine Cellars is now among Bulgaria's best. Located in Brestovitsa, 15km southwest of Plovdiv, it's known for its juicy, red Mavrud. Vineyard tours may also include traditional cuisine, spa hotel accommodation and grape picking.

Struma River Valley (Pirin Mountains)

In Bulgaria's southwest, bounded by the River Struma and Pirin Mountains, this region is marked by an arid, Mediterranean climate and soil. The most famous wine here is Melnik's signature red, the Shiroka Melnishka Loza, while Cabernet Sauvignon and Merlot are also produced. The unique Keratzuda variety is indigenous to Kresna, a village between Blagoevgrad and Sandanski.

Winston Churchill used to order Melnik red wine by the barrel.

WINERIES

Damianitza (☑0746-300 90; www.damianitza.bg) The leading Melnik wine producer, Damianitza boasts innovations that include combining the local varietal with Cabernet Sauvignon, creating Ruen, and mixing Nebbiolo and Syrah varietals to create Rubin, among Bulgaria's best. At time of research, tours were limited due to renovations so check ahead.

BULGARIAN WINE

Bulgarian Cuisine

The Food & Cooking of Romania & Bulgaria by Silvena Johan Lauta features 65 easy-to-follow traditional regional recipes.

Fresh fruit, vegetables, dairy produce and grilled meat form the basis of Bulgarian cuisine, and, as well as home-grown Balkan traditions, it has been heavily influenced by Greek and Turkish cookery. Pork and chicken are the most popular meats, while tripe also features heavily on traditional menus. You will also find recipes including duck, rabbit and venison, and fish is plentiful along the Black Sea coast, but less common elsewhere.

Grilled Meats & Stews

Grilled meats (*skara*), especially pork, are among the most popular dishes served in Bulgarian restaurants, *mehana* (taverns) and snack bars. You can't escape the omnipresent *kebabche* (grilled spicy pork sausages) and *kyufte* (a round and flat pork burger), which are tasty, filling and cheap staples of Bulgarian menus, usually served with chips/fried potatoes (*pârzheni kartofi*) or salad. The *kyufte tatarsko*, a seasoned pork burger filled with melted cheese, is another variant. The Greek-influenced *musaka* (moussaka), made with minced pork or veal and topped with potatoes, is a quick lunchtime staple of cafeterias.

Shish kebabs (*shishcheta*), consisting of chunks of chicken or pork on wooden skewers with mushrooms and peppers, as well as various steaks, fillets and chops are widely available.

Meat stews and 'claypot meals' (hot, sizzling stews served in clay bowls) are traditional favourites. *Kavarma*, normally made with either chicken or pork, is one of the most popular dishes. Exact recipes vary from one region to the next, but the meat is cooked in a pot with vegetables, cheese and sometimes egg, and is brought sizzling and bubbling away to your table.

Pig, cow and lamb offal, in various forms, is a distressingly common feature of many a restaurant menu. If you're in the mood for something different, though, you could try such delights as stomach soup (*shkembe chorba*) or maybe some brain (*mozâk*) or tongue (*ezik*), which come in various forms, including in omelettes. Spleens and intestines also turn up in soups and grills.

Although it might seem one of the most 'traditional' Bulgarian dishes, the origins of *shopska* salad are unclear, and it may have been created as recently as the 1950s.

Salads & Starters

Salads are an essential part of most Bulgarian meals, and are often eaten as a starter, but some are so large that they could be a full meal in themselves. There's a bewildering array of salads available at most restaurants.

Shopska salad, which is made with chopped tomatoes, cucumbers, green peppers and onions and covered with feta cheese, is so popular it's regarded as a national dish. *Snezhanka* ('Snow White') salad is made with cucumbers and scoops of plain yoghurt, with garlic, dill and crushed walnuts; essentially a more solid version of *tarator* (chilled cucumber and yoghurt soup), a delicious and refreshing summertime dish.

Ruska (Russian) salad features boiled potatoes, pickles, eggs and chopped ham, while the hearty *ovcharska* salad includes ham, mushrooms, chopped tomatoes, cucumbers, peppers, cheese and olives. Rather lighter, and more common, green and Greek salads are served everywhere, and restaurants often have their own inventive concoctions worth trying.

Appetisers, or starters, are eaten before a meal, sometimes with a glass of *rakia* (fruit brandy). Plates of sliced, dried sausage (*lukanka*), stuffed vine leaves (*losovi sarmi*), roast peppers stuffed with cheese and egg (*chuska byurek*) and fried, breaded cheese (*sirene pane* or *kashkaval pane*) are all very popular.

Street Food

If you just fancy a quick bite, there's a wide choice of cheap and tasty street food available all over Bulgaria. By far the most popular takeaway snack is the *banitsa*, a flaky cheese pasty, freshly baked and served hot from simple counters and kiosks. They are often eaten for breakfast. Fancier bakeries will offer variations of the basic *banitsa*, adding spinach, egg, ham or other ingredients. Sweet versions (*mlechna banitsa*) are made with milk.

Sweet and savoury pancakes (*palachinki*), buns (*kiflichki*), filled with marmalade, chocolate or cheese and deep-fried doughnuts (*mekitsi*) are all worth sampling.

Bulgarians are great snackers and in big towns you will see old ladies in parks selling toasted sunflower seeds (*semki*) wrapped in paper cones. Steamed corn-on-the-cob is served on street corners and around parks, and bagel-like, ring-shaped bread rolls (*gevrek*) are commonly sold by street vendors.

Cheese & Yoghurt

Considering that there are only two traditional kinds of Bulgarian cheese, *sirene* ('white', brine cheese, similar to feta) and *kashkaval* ('yellow', hard cheese), it's amazing how much Bulgarians make out of these traditional ingredients, and how regularly it turns up on the menu. The lactose-intolerant and non cheese-lovers may need to read menus carefully.

Bulgarians claim to have invented yoghurt (*kiselo mlyako*; literally 'sour milk'), and, indeed, the bacteria used to make yoghurt is called *lactobacillus bulgaricus,* named in honour of its Bulgarian origins.

Traditional Bulgarian Cooking by Atanas Slavov gives more than 140 recipes you might like to try out, including all the favourites such as *kavarma*, *banitsa* and *shopska* salad.

VEGETARIANS

Vegetarianism remains an alien concept to most Bulgarians, but it's relatively easy to follow a meat-free diet here. On the down side, variety may be lacking, and those with an aversion to cheese may find their options very limited. Most restaurants offer a dozen or more salads, which are sometimes large enough for a main course. Omelettes, vegetarian pizzas and pasta dishes are common, but note that 'vegetarian' meals may simply mean that they include vegetables (as well as meat) or fish. Sometimes this designation doesn't seem to mean anything at all. Vegans will have to resort to self-catering.

Other tasty vegetarian meals and snacks include *sirene po shopski* (cheese, eggs and tomatoes baked in a clay pot), *gyuvech* (potatoes, tomatoes, aubergine, onions and carrots baked in a clay pot), *mish-mash* (scrambled eggs with peppers, tomatoes and cheese), *kashkaval pane* (fried breaded cheese), *chuska byurek* (fried, breaded peppers stuffed with egg, cheese and parsley), *bob chorba* (bean soup) and the ever-popular *banitsa. Tarator* (chilled yoghurt and cucumber soup) is a deliciously refreshing dish at any time of year.

Yoghurt is used in many sweet and savoury dishes, including salads and deserts, and drinking yoghurts are very popular; *ayran* is a refreshing, chilled, slightly salty, thin yoghurt drink that makes an ideal accompaniment to light meals.

Drinks

Coffee is the beverage of choice for most Bulgarians, though tea is also popular. Most common are the herbal (*bilkov*) and fruit (*plodov*) varieties; if you want real, black tea, ask for *cheren chai* and if you'd like milk, ask for *chai s'mlyako*.

Beer *(pivo* or *bira)* is sold everywhere, either in bottles or in draught *(nalivna)* form, which is generally cheaper. Leading nationwide brands are Zagorka, Kamenitsa, Ariana and Shumensko, while there are several regional brews, which are rarely available far beyond their home areas. Lower-alcohol fruit beers have become popular in recent years.

The national spirit is *rakia* (a clear and potent kind of brandy, usually made from grapes, although versions made from plums or apricots can also be found), and there are countless brands available. It's drunk as an aperitif, and served with ice in restaurants and bars, which often devote a whole page on their menus to a list of the regional *rakias* on offer.

Bulgaria produces huge quantities of both white and red *vino* (wine), which varies greatly in quality (see p465).

If you're looking for a quick and easy Bulgarian recipe, www.find bgfood.com gives instructions for several popular dishes.

Where to Eat & Drink

Restaurants

Most outlets providing seating describe themselves as restaurants, and this covers a pretty broad range of dining spots and every imaginable type of cuisine.

In the big cities and coastal resorts, most restaurants will offer menus in English and, occasionally, other languages. Reservations are rarely necessary, unless you are in a large group or the restaurant is especially popular. Bills will usually be 'rounded up', and a service charge of 10% is sometimes added. If it isn't, a small tip is expected.

Mehana

A *mehana* (tavern) is a more traditional restaurant, often decorated in a rustic style, adorned with rugs and farming implements, and offering only authentic Bulgarian cuisine. Some of these, of course, are tourist traps, luring foreign tourists with noisy 'folk shows' and waiters in fancy dress, though the genuine places provide a pleasant atmosphere in which to sample the very best local food. Look out for those frequented by locals.

Cafes & Markets

Cafes are cheaper affairs and include basic self-service cafeterias offering pre-cooked meals, soups and salads. In the cities, small basic cafes or snack bars offer drinks and snacks, sometimes with a few chairs outside, or just a table to lean on. Some bake their own produce, especially *banitsa*. Look out for signs reading закуска (*zakuska*; breakfast).

Self-caterers will find plenty of choice at Bulgaria's many street markets; this is where most locals do their shopping, and much of the produce will be fresh, locally grown and organic.

Survival Guide

Directory A-Z

Accommodation

Bulgaria offers pretty much every kind of accommodation option you can think of, from spartan mountain huts to the most opulent five-star hotels. Accommodation is most expensive in Sofia and other big cities, notably Plovdiv and Varna. Elsewhere, prices are still relatively cheap by Western European standards. If you're travelling independently around the country, one indispensable publication is the *Bulgaria B&B and Adventure Guidebook* (13.50 lv) published by the **Bulgarian Association for Alternative Tourism** (☑02-980 7685; www.baatbg. org; bul Stambolyiiski 20 B, Sofia), which lists sustain-able, family-run guesthouses all over Bulgaria. You can buy it at **Zig Zag Holidays** (☑02-980 5102; www.zigzagbg. com; bul Stamboliyski 20-V; ⊙9.30am-6.30pm Mon-Fri) in Sofia.

As you would expect, demand, and prices, are highest in the coastal resorts between July and August, and in the skiing resorts between December and February. Outside the holiday seasons, these hotels often close down, or may operate on a much reduced basis. So if you're thinking of staying in, for example, Pamporovo in September or Nesebâr in February, phone ahead to see what the current situation is.

There are several useful websites offering acccomo-dation information or online booking facilities.

» www.hotels.bg
» www.bgstay.com
» www.bgglobe.net
» www.bulgaria-hotels.com
» www.sofiahotels.net

Camping

Camping is not as popular as it once was in Bulgaria, and facilities at the campgrounds that do exist are often very basic. Most are open only between May and September. They are mainly popular with Bulgarian families, and are rarely convenient for anyone relying on public transport.

Camping in the wild (ie outside a camping ground) is technically prohibited but normally accepted if you're discreet and, most importantly, do not build wood fires (which attract attention and damage the environment).

Hostels

Backpacker hostels are increasingly popular in Bulgaria, and new establishments are appearing all the time.

Sofia has more hostels than anywhere else. You will also find hostels in Veliko Târnovo, Varna, Plovdiv and Burgas. Most are clean, modern and friendly places in central locations.

Hostelling International (HI; www.hihostels.com) can book you into hostels in Sofia and Plovdiv.

Hotels

Bulgaria has a wide variety of hotel accommodation at all prices. Usually, the most attractive, and often best value, places are the smaller, family-run hotels.

Many of the older, formerly state-run hotels – concrete monstrosities from the 1960s and 70s – have now been privatised and renovated. However, some are still shabby and run down, with antiquated plumbing and old-fashioned attitudes to customer service.

Some hotels do not offer single rooms or single rates

PRICE RANGES

The following price ranges refer to a double room with bathroom in high season. Unless otherwise stated, breakfast is included in the price.

Budget $ Under 60 lv

Midrange $$ 60 to 120 lv

Top End $$$ Over 120 lv

in a double room. If this is the case, only the rates for doubles are listed in this review. Suites normally have a separate lounge area and sometimes an extra bedroom.

Monasteries

About a dozen of the 160 monasteries around Bulgaria offer accommodation to anyone, of either sex, from pilgrims to foreign tourists. Some rooms are actually inside the monastery, such as at the Rila and Cherepish monasteries, or at guesthouses within metres of the monastery gates, for example at the Troyan, Dryanovo and Lopushanski monasteries. Some offer rooms only on a sporadic basis and availability may be unreliable; contact the monasteries directly to see if they have room. For information on Bulgaria's monasteries, including contact details and accommodation availability see www.bulgarianmonas teries.com.

Mountain Huts

Anyone, especially those enjoying long-distance treks or shorter hikes, can stay at any *hizha* (mountain hut). Normally a *hizha* only offers basic, but clean and comfortable, dormitory beds with a shared bathroom, which cost from 10 lv to 35 lv per person per night. Most are open only from May to October, but those situated at or near major ski slopes are often also open in winter.

Zig Zag Holidays (Map p298; ☑980 5102; www.zigzag bg.com; bul Stamboliyski 20-V, enter from ul Lavele; ☉9.30am-6.30pm Mon-Fri; Ⓜ Serdika) can arrange accommodation in the mountains and villages.

Private Rooms

Private rooms are mainly found in the cities and resorts along the Black Sea. Standards vary, but in the cities they will be in private flats in nondescript apartment blocks with shared bathroom facilities, and will tend to be away from the centre. In resorts such as Sozopol or Pomorie, private rooms are likely to be a more professional set-up and of a slightly higher standard, with private bathrooms. Rooms cost anywhere between 10 lv and 30 lv per person.

Stays in private rooms can often be arranged through an accommodation agency in a town centre, or at a bus or train station. Alternatively, you can keep an eye out for signs outside private homes advertising rooms available, either in Bulgarian (Свободни Стаи) or, quite often, in English or German. The pensioners who hang around outside bus and train stations offering rooms in their homes are invariably living on very low incomes, so by paying them directly, without the commissions taken by agencies, you will have the satisfaction of knowing that you're helping them get by and also making a positive contribution to this form of sustainable tourism.

These days, due partly to the increasing number of hostels, this kind of private room arrangement no longer appears to be on offer in Sofia and other inland cities.

Business Hours

Reviews list opening hours only if they differ from times given below.

Government offices 9am to 5pm Monday to Friday
Shops 9am to 6pm

Post offices 8am to 6pm Monday to Friday
Banks 9am to 4pm Monday to Friday
Restaurants 11am to 11pm
Bars 11am to midnight

Children

Bulgaria's Black Sea coast is the most family-friendly region of the country, with long, sandy beaches, water parks and other activities that will appeal to young children; bigger hotels here often have playgrounds and kids' clubs. More rural areas may also appeal to older children, as activities like horse riding, cycling and wildlife watching are available. All big towns have public parks with playgrounds, as well as attractions that children might enjoy, like zoos, which you can find in both Sofia and Varna.

» Most restaurants in Bulgaria welcome families with children, although few offer specific children's menus, and fewer still have such things as highchairs for babies. Again, you are more likely to find these kind of facilities in and around the Black Sea resorts and some places in Sofia. There are plenty of Western-style restaurants and international fast food chains if your little ones are fussy eaters.

» Most of the necessities for travelling with toddlers, such as disposable nappies (diapers), baby food and fresh or powdered milk are readily available in shops and supermarkets across the country.

BOOK YOUR STAY ONLINE

For more accommodation reviews by Lonely Planet authors, check out http://hotels.lonelyplanet.com. You'll find independent reviews, as well as recommendations on the best places to stay. Best of all, you can book online.

» Cots are often available in top-end, international chain hotels in the cities and are more common in hotels frequented by families in the coastal resorts.

» International car rental firms can provide children's safety seats for a nominal extra cost, but it's essential to book these in advance.

» Public nappy-changing facilities are rare and child-care (babysitting) agencies are common only among the expatriate community in Sofia. However, some top-end hotels may offer this service.

» Breast-feeding in public is not usual and may attract stares.

Customs Regulations

Whether you're inspected by customs officers depends on how you enter the country, but bona fide tourists are generally left alone. If you're travelling between Bulgaria and another EU country, then normal EU rules on what you can import or export apply.

If you enter or leave the country with more than 8000 lv on you (in any currency), you must declare it. Check with the customs service in your home country for advice on what you can import duty-free from Bulgaria.

For information about exporting unusual items (such as valuable archaeological artefacts) by air, contact the **National Customs Agency** (www.customs.bg).

Discount Cards

International Student (ISIC), Youth (IYTC) and Teacher (ITIC) discount cards can be used in Bulgaria, and offer a range of discounts on transport, accommodation, restaurants, shopping, entertainment venues and tourist attractions. Many places that accept these cards don't advertise the fact, so it's always worth asking. Cards may be bought in Bulgaria at branches of the **Usit Colours** (www.usitcolours.bg) travel agency. Check online at www.isic.org for current details and for participating companies.

» International Student Identity Card (ISIC) – available to full-time students of any age.

» International Youth Travel Card (IYTC) – available to anyone under 26 years of age.

» International Teacher Identity Card (ITIC) – available to schoolteachers and college lecturers.

Electricity

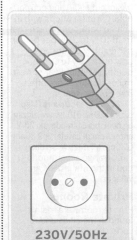

230V/50Hz

PRACTICALITIES

» The metric system is used for weights and measures.

» Videos work on the PAL system.

» *Vagabond* (www.vagabond.bg) is a glossy, English-language lifestyle magazine, published monthly and available at bookshops and newsstands in Sofia.

» More than 40% of Bulgarians smoke – one of the highest proportions in Europe. Since 2012, smoking has officially been banned in all public spaces, including restaurants, bars, hotels, cinemas and workplaces, but is still permitted at outside restaurant tables.

» Tune into the government-run TV channels (BNT1 and BNT2) or one of the private ones, including Nova Televisiya, BTV and TV7. Televisions in most – but certainly not all – hotel rooms can pick up a plethora of stations from around the region, so you can enjoy Romanian game shows, Greek movies and Turkish news programs, as well as BBC, Euronews, CNN, MTV and other international cables channels.

» The national radio station **Radio Bulgaria** (BNR; www.bnr.bg) has a daily one-hour English-language broadcast; listen online or check the website for details. In Sofia, tune into **BG Radio** (91.9FM; www.bgradio.bg), and for music, try **Jazz FM** (104FM; www.jazzfmbg.com), **Melody Radio** (93.4FM; www.melody bg.com) or **Classic FM** (89.1FM; www.classicfmsofia.com). **Darik Radio** (www.darikradio.bg), a nationwide network of stations that usually plays contemporary pop music, can be heard in Sofia (105FM), Varna (99.3FM), Burgas (104.5FM), Plovdiv (105.4FM), Ruse (107.9FM) and Veliko Tärnovo (106.6FM). International services that can be found on the FM band in Sofia include the **BBC World Service** (91FM).

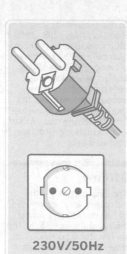

230V/50Hz

Embassies & Consulates

Australia (☎02-946 1334; austcon@mail.orbitel.bg; ul Trakia 37; ☐78)

Canada (☎02-969 9710; general@canada-bg.org; ul Moskovska 9; ☐20)

France (☎02-965 1100; www.ambafrance-bg.org; ul Oborishte 27-29; ⊞; 1)

Germany (☎02-918 380; www.sofia.diplo.de; ul Frederic Joliot-Curie 25; Ⓜ Joliot-Curie)

Greece (☎02-843 3085; www.mfa.gr/sofia; ul San Stefano 33; Ⓜ Kliment Ohridski)

Ireland (☎02-985 3425; www.embassyofireland.bg; ul Bacho Kiro 26-30; ☐20)

Macedonia (☎02-870 1560; todmak@bgnet.bg; ul Frederic Joliot-Curie 17; Ⓜ Joliot-Curie)

Netherlands (☎02-816 0300; www.bulgaria.nlembassy.org; ul Oborishte 15; ☐20)

Romania (☎02-971 2858; ambsofro@vip.bg; Bul Mihay Eminesku 4; ☐20)

Russia (☎02-963 0914; www.russia.bg; bul Dragan Tsankov 28; ☐18)

Serbia (☎02-946 1635; ambasada-scg-sofija@infotel.bg; ul Veliko Târnovo 3; ☐9)

Turkey (☎02-935 5500; www.sofia.emb.mfa.gov.tr; bul Vasil Levski 80; ☐94)

UK (☎02-933 9222; www.ukinbulgaria.fco.gov.uk; ul Moskovksa 9; ☐20)

US (☎02-937 5100; www.bulgaria.usembassy.gov; ul Kozyak 16; ☐88)

Food

Eating out in Bulgaria is remarkably cheap, at least for Western travellers, and even if you're on a tight budget you'll have no problem eating well. For more information see (p470).

Gay & Lesbian Travellers

Homosexuality is legal in Bulgaria; however, same-sex relationships have no legal recognition.

In common with other Eastern European countries, Bulgaria is a very conservative society, and opinion polls continue to suggest that a majority of Bulgarians have negative attitudes towards homosexuality; a recent poll found that 30% of employers would not hire gay workers, despite this discrimination being illegal.

Attitudes, among younger people at least, are slowly changing, and there are a few gay clubs and bars in Sofia and a couple of other major cities and an annual Gay Pride march in Sofia, although this has been the focus of protests and even violence in past years. One

of Bulgaria's biggest music stars, Azis, is an openly gay, transvestite Roma.

» www.gay.bg
» www.gayguidebg.eu
» www.gay-bulgaria.info
» www.sofiapride.info

Health

Vaccinations None required for travel to Bulgaria, but vaccination against typhoid may be recommended.

Health Insurance Citizens of other European Economic Area countries (EU plus Norway, Iceland and Liechtenstein) should pick up a European Health Insurance Card (EHIC) before they travel, which entitles you to the same immediate medical treatment that's available to Bulgarian nationals. However, you should also consider buying a policy that covers you for the worst possible scenario, such as an accident requiring an emergency flight home.

Health Care Availability Every major town and city has government hospitals of an acceptable, though not always high, standard. Private clinics are preferable.

Tap Water Generally safe and drinkable, but may have an odd taste. There have been reports of contamination in some rural areas. It's best to use bottled mineral water, which is widely available and cheap.

Pharmacies Common in towns across the country.

PRICE RANGES

The following price ranges refer to a standard main course. Unless otherwise stated, service charge is included in the price.

Budget $ Under 5 lv

Midrange $$ 5 to 10 lv

Top End $$$ Over 10 lv

Infectious Diseases

Rabies This is a potential concern considering the number of stray dogs running around Bulgaria. Do not approach feral dogs, but if you are bitten, seek medical attention immediately.

Tick-borne Encephalitis Spread by tick bites, this is a serious infection of the brain and is present in some rural areas of Bulgaria. Contraction risks are low, but if you are camping in rural areas, protect against bites by using sprays and wearing long-sleeved shirts and long trousers.

Insurance

A travel insurance policy to cover theft, loss and medical problems is a sensible idea. There are a wide variety of policies available, with some policies offering lower and higher medical-expense options, so check the small print.

Some policies specifically exclude 'dangerous activities', which can include scuba diving, motorcycling and even trekking. A locally acquired motorcycle licence is not valid under some policies.

You may prefer a policy that pays doctors or hospitals directly rather than you having to pay on the spot and claim later. If you have to claim later, make sure you keep all documentation. Some policies ask you to call back (via reverse charges) to a centre in your home country where an immediate assessment of your problem can be made.

Check that the policy covers ambulances as well as an emergency flight home.

Worldwide travel insurance is available at www. lonelyplanet.com/travel _services. You can buy, extend and claim online at any time – even if you're already on the road.

Internet Access

With the increasing availability of wi-fi, internet cafes have become something of a rarity in Bulgaria.

Most hotels and hostels offer free internet access to guests, and wi-fi hotspots may be found in many restaurants, cafes and other businesses. Some hotels offer laptops for guest use.

Where internet cafes do exist, access is usually cheap, between 2 and 3 lv per hour, although these are often cramped, smoky bunkers where teenage boys endlessly play violent and deafening computer games, and connections can be painfully slow.

Throughout this book, @ has been used to show premises which provide computers for internet access, or plug-in facilities for laptops, while 🛜 denotes places that offer wireless internet access.

Legal Matters

Bulgaria is a member state of the EU and more or less follows the same legal system as most of the rest of Europe. The days of blatant ripping off of foreign travellers are long gone; traffic police have to abide by a certain code of ethics, but residents do complain bitterly about corruption within some government departments, especially customs. If you do get into serious trouble with the police, it's best to contact your embassy.

Maps

Proper road maps are essential if you're driving around Bulgaria. One of the best is the *Bulgaria Road Atlas* (1:330,000), published in English by Domino.

If you are going to do some serious hiking, you will definitely need a detailed map. In Sofia, the best place to find these is **Zig Zag Holidays** (Map p298; 📞980 5102; www.zigzagbg.com; bul Stamboliyski 20-V, enter from ul Lavele; ⏱9.30am-6.30pm Mon-Fri; Ⓜ Serdika), which sells maps covering the various national parks and mountain ranges. Elsewhere, local travel agencies or tourist information centres are your best bet.

Money

The local currency is the lev (plural: leva), comprised of 100 stotinki. It is almost always abbreviated to lv. The lev is a stable currency. For major purchases such as organised tours, airfares, car rental and midrange and top-end hotels, prices are almost always quoted by staff in euros, although payment is possible in leva too. Bulgaria has no immediate plans to adopt the euro as its national currency. For current exchange rates, see p283.

ATMs

ATMs that accept major credit cards (ie Visa, MasterCard and American Express) are common, found in all sizeable towns and cities. The total amount you can withdraw depends on how much your bank will allow and on how much is in your account; the maximum allowed per day by most Bulgarian banks is usually 200 lv.

Black Market

With the currency stabilisation, no black market exists in Bulgaria. Foreigners may still be approached (especially in Sofia or Varna) and asked to change money, but this is illegal and there's a high chance you'll be given counterfeit leva, short-changed or robbed, so don't do it!

Cash

Bulgarian banknotes come in denominations of 2, 5, 10, 20, 50 and 100 leva. Coins come in 1, 2, 5, 10, 20 and 50 stotinki and 1 lev. Prices for smaller items are always quoted in leva or a fraction of a lev, eg on a bus ticket the fare will be listed as '0.50 lv' rather than '50 stotinki'.

When changing money, make sure that the foreign banknotes you have are not torn, marked or grubby, otherwise they may be refused or you may even be given a lower rate (without being told so in advance). Always make absolutely sure of the precise sum in leva you will receive before handing over any of your cash. Similarly, make sure that any leva given to you are not torn or marked. Foreigners may export and import up to 8000 lv (in any currency) without restrictions.

Credit Cards

Credit cards are commonly accepted in hotels, restaurants and shops in the big cities, towns and tourist resorts, but acceptance is less widespread in more rural areas. You cannot rely on using a credit card exclusively in Bulgaria; use it to get cash from banks and for major purchases only. Some places, particularly the more expensive hotels, will add a 5% surcharge to your bill if you use a credit card.

Moneychangers

Foreign exchange offices can be found in all larger towns, and current rates are always displayed prominently. They are no longer allowed to charge commission, but that doesn't always stop them trying; always check the final amount that you will be offered before handing over your cash. Avoid exchange offices at train stations, airports or in tourist resorts as rates tend to be very poor indeed.

The best currencies to take to Bulgaria are euros, pounds sterling and US dollars. You may have trouble changing less familiar currencies, such as Australian or Canadian dollars, but you should be able to find somewhere in a city such as Sofia, Plovdiv or Varna that will accept most major international currencies.

It's also easy to change cash at most of the larger banks found in cities and major towns; the exchange rates listed on the electronic boards in bank windows may offer slightly higher rates than foreign exchange offices, but they may charge a commission.

Tipping

Waiters normally round restaurant bills up to the nearest convenient figure and pocket the difference; the same applies to taxi drivers. In some restaurants a 10% service charge is already added, although this doesn't always stop the waiters from rounding up the bill again, or hovering expectantly for an extra tip. If it's not been added, and the service is good, add about 10%.

Travellers Cheques

Travellers cheques are a handy way to carry funds overseas, but are not as popular as they once were. They can only be changed at banks, not foreign exchange offices, and many only accept American Express and Thomas Cook, with commission rates of 3% to 5%.

Photography

Taking pictures of anything in Bulgaria that might be considered of strategic importance, such as military camps and border crossings, is not advisable. These days officials are much less paranoid about photography than they used to be, but use common sense when it comes to this issue. It's best to ask permission before taking close-up photos of people. For inspiration and advice about taking great photographs, take a look at Lonely Planet's *Travel Photography*.

Public Holidays

During official public holidays all government offices, banks, post offices and major businesses will be closed. All hotels, restaurants, bars, national parks/reserves and museums stay open (unless the holiday coincides with a normal day off), as do most shops and petrol stations; border crossings and public transport continue to operate normally.

New Year's Day (1 January)
Liberation Day (3 March)
Easter (March/April)
May Day (1 May)
St George's Day/Bulgarian Army Day (6 May)
Cyrillic Alphabet Day (24 May)
Unification Day (6 September)
Bulgarian Independence Day (22 September)
National Revival Day (1 November)
Christmas (25 and 26 December)

Telephone

To call Bulgaria from abroad, dial the international access code (which varies from country to country), add 359 (the country code for Bulgaria), the area code (minus the first zero) and then the number.

To make an international call from Bulgaria, dial '00' followed by the code of the country you are calling, then the local area code, minus the initial '0'.

To make domestic calls within Bulgaria, dial the area code, which will be between 2 and 5 digits long, followed by the number you wish to call. If you are making a domestic call from your mobile phone, you will also have to insert the country code (+359) first, unless you are using a Bulgarian SIM card.

To call a Bulgarian mobile phone from within Bulgaria,

dial the full number, including the initial '0'.

International directory inquiries (124)

International operator (123)

National directory inquiries – businesses (144)

National directory inquiries – residential (145)

National operator (121)

Mobile Phones

Mobile (cell) phones are as commonplace in Bulgaria as anywhere else, and many hotels, restaurants and other businesses give mobile numbers as their prime contact number.

Mobile telephone numbers have different codes (eg 087, 088 or 089) and are indicated by the abbreviations 'GSM' or 'mob'.

Bulgaria has three mobile service providers which cover most of the country.

Globul (www.globul.bg)

M-Tel (www.mtel.bg)

Vivacom (www.vivacom.bg)

Visitors from other European countries should be able to use their own mobile phones as usual, but do check your provider's roaming rates. Travellers from outside Europe may have to purchase a Bulgarian SIM card in order to use their handsets on the Bulgarian mobile network.

Phonecards

Prepaid phonecards, for use in public telephones, are available from newspaper kiosks and some shops in denominations ranging from 5 lv to 25 lv. Cards for domestic or international calls can be used in public phone booths and some also accept credit cards.

Time

Bulgaria is on Eastern European Time, ie GMT/UTC plus two hours, except during daylight saving time, when clocks are put forward by one hour between the last Sunday in March and the last Sunday in October. There are no time zones within the country.

Bulgaria is one hour behind Serbia and Macedonia, and at the same time as Romania, Greece and Turkey. Therefore, if it's noon in Sofia, it's 2am in Los Angeles, 5am in New York, 10am in London, 11am in Paris and 8pm in Sydney, not taking into account daylight saving (where applicable) in these countries. The 24-hour clock is commonly used throughout Bulgaria, and always used for bus and train timetables.

Toilets

With the exception of a few Middle Eastern-style squat toilets near the Turkish border, almost all toilets in Bulgaria are of the sit-down European variety. All hotels provide toilet paper and soap, but these are rarely offered anywhere else.

Public toilets are usually found at bus and train stations, underpasses and parks, and standards of cleanliness are generally poor. You will be charged between 0.30 lv and 0.50 lv per visit, sometimes more for toilet paper. Much better (and free) facilities are available within modern shopping malls. Western fast-food franchises such as McDonald's always have clean toilets with toilet paper.

Tourist Information

Bulgaria still doesn't have a dedicated Ministry of Tourism. Tourism is the responsibility of the Ministry of Economy and Energy.

The bigger cities, and some smaller towns popular with tourists, now have dedicated **tourist information centres**, which provide free maps, leaflets and brochures. National parks often have small information centres offering advice.

National tourism portal (www.bulgariatravel.org)

Burgas (www.tic.burgas.bg)

Varna (www.varnainfo.bg)

Plovdiv (www.plovdiv-tour. info)

Ruse (www.tic.rousse.bg)

Veliko Târnovo (www.veliko turnovo.info)

Travellers with Disabilities

Unfortunately, Bulgaria is not an easy destination for disabled travellers. Uneven and broken footpaths make wheelchair mobility problematic, and ramps and special toilets for those in a wheelchair are few and far between, other than in a handful of top-end hotels in Sofia and other big cities. Public transport is not geared towards the needs of travellers with disabilities.

One organisation worth contacting is the **Center for Independent Living** (www. cil.bg) in Sofia.

Visas

Citizens of other EU member states and Australia, Canada, Israel, Japan, New Zealand, the USA and several other countries can stay in Bulgaria visa-free for up to 90 days. Other nationals should check the current requirements with their nearest Bulgarian embassy or consulate before their departure. Visas cannot be obtained at border crossings. At the time of writing, Bulgaria was not a member of the Schengen zone, but its application to join was pending.

Visa Extensions

Visitors wishing to extend their visit to Bulgaria beyond the 90-day limit have to apply for a residence permit at the Immigration Office (☑02-982 3316; bul Maria Luisa 48; ☺9am-5pm Mon-Fri). This is likely to be a time-consuming, bureaucratic nightmare, and nobody here will speak anything but Bulgarian. It's probably far better to contact the Bulgarian Embassy in your own country for advice before you travel if you envisage being in the country for more than three months. The Bulgarian Ministry of Foreign Affairs (www.mfa.bg) has useful information, in English, on visas and other immigration matters.

Volunteering

If you're looking for a more satisfying holiday and you don't mind a bit of hard work, then there are a number of opportunities for volunteering in Bulgaria. Various international organisations have ongoing projects in the country, and there are also many local groups that welcome foreign volunteers.

World Wide Opportunities on Organic Farms (www.wwoofbulgaria.org) Can direct you to current projects and openings for volunteers on farms around the country.

Habitat for Humanity (www.habitatbulgaria.org) Organises house-building and community-based projects in poorer neighbourhoods.

Cadip (www.cadip.org) Canadian organisation running volunteer programs working in Bulgarian orphanages.

St James' Park (www.stjamespark.biz) A British-run venture in the village of Voditsa, in northern Bulgaria. It's an 'alternative' campsite and organic farm that welcomes volunteers, either (through WWOOF) working 30 hours a week for board and lodging, or doing smaller, casual jobs for free meals.

Peace Corps (www.peacecorps.gov) The US organisation offers projects working in education and community development.

British Society for the Protection of Birds (www.rspb.org.uk) Volunteers can work as field assistants in Bulgaria, mapping breeding birds.

Bulgarian Archaeological Association (www.archaeology.archbg.net) Find out about volunteering opportunities on archaeological digs in Bulgaria.

Women Travellers

In general, travelling around Bulgaria poses no particular difficulties for women. For the most part, sober men are polite and respectful. However, Bulgarian women won't normally go to a bar or nightclub unaccompanied and single foreign women may attract attention. If you do attract unwanted advances, saying *Omâzhena sâm* ('I am married') gives a pretty firm message.

Like most destinations in Eastern Europe, common sense is the best guide to dealing with possibly dangerous situations, such as hitchhiking, sharing hostel rooms and walking alone at night. For overnight train journeys, choose a sleeper compartment rather than a couchette. Young women in the big cities and coastal resorts are comfortable wearing miniskirts and low-cut blouses, but more modest apparel is advisable if you're travelling in more rural areas.

Feminine hygiene products, such as tampons, are widely available in supermarkets and pharmacies across the country.

Transport

GETTING THERE & AWAY

Most international visitors enter and leave Bulgaria via Sofia Airport, and there are frequent flights to the capital from other European cities. Bulgaria is also easily accessible by road and rail from neighbouring countries, and Bulgaria's railway is part of the InterRail system and so can be included in a longer European rail journey. Note, though, that at the time of research there were no trains operating between Bulgaria and Greece. There are regular ferry crossings across the Danube from Romania, which carry both vehicles and foot passengers.

If you prefer something more structured, an increasing number of companies offer organised tours and package holidays to Bulgaria.

Flights, cars and tours can be booked online at lonely planet.com/bookings.

Entering the Country

Bulgaria is a member of the EU, and so citizens of other EU nations, at least, will face minimal border formalities.

Delays are common at border crossings, and customs officials are generally an unfriendly and suspicious lot; expect to be questioned on what business you have in coming to Bulgaria and where you intend on staying.

Passport

There are no restrictions on any foreign-passport holders entering Bulgaria, other than the length of time they are allowed to stay. See p478 for information on which nationals require visas to visit Bulgaria. Passports should be valid for at least three months after the date of your arrival in the country.

Air

Bulgaria has good air links with numerous European cities, as well as some cities in the Middle East, with Sofia being the main entry point. There are currently no direct flights to Bulgaria from further afield, and so visitors from, for example, North America or Australia will need to pick up a connecting flight in Europe. Varna and Burgas have the only other international airports in Bulgaria, and these are particularly busy during the summer when they are used by charter flights.

Airports

Sofia Airport (www.sofia -airport.bg) The main point of entry to the country.

Varna Airport (www.varna -airport.bg) Domestic flights and seasonal flights to and from European destinations.

Burgas Airport (www. bourgas-airport.com) Mainly used for summer charter flights.

CLIMATE CHANGE & TRAVEL

Every form of transport that relies on carbon-based fuel generates CO_2, the main cause of human-induced climate change. Modern travel is dependent on aeroplanes, which might use less fuel per kilometre per person than most cars but travel much greater distances. The altitude at which aircraft emit gases (including CO_2) and particles also contributes to their climate change impact. Many websites offer 'carbon calculators' that allow people to estimate the carbon emissions generated by their journey and, for those who wish to do so, to offset the impact of the greenhouse gases emitted with contributions to portfolios of climate-friendly initiatives throughout the world. Lonely Planet offsets the carbon footprint of all staff and author travel.

Airlines

The Bulgarian national carrier is **Bulgaria Air** (www.air. bg). It has an unblemished safety record, and operates flights to destinations across Europe and the Middle East as well as domestic routes to the Black Sea coast. International airlines flying to Bulgaria include the following:

Aegean Airlines (www. aegeanair.com)

Aeroflot (www.aeroflot.ru)

Aerosvit (www.aerosvit. com)

Air Berlin (www.airberlin. com)

Air France (www.airfrance. com)

Alitalia (www.alitlia.it)

British Airways (www. britishairways.com)

Cyprus Airways (www. cyprusair.com)

easyJet (www.easyjet.com)

Lufthansa (www.lufthansa. com)

Tarom (www.tarom.ro)

Turkish Airlines (www. turkishairlines.com)

Wizz Air (www.wizzair.com)

Tickets

Air tickets to Bulgaria vary greatly in price, and it pays to shop around. You're likely to find the best deals online, and there are a few websites dedicated to Bulgarian flights.

» www.bulgariaflights.com
» www.flybulgaria.bg
» www.balkanholidays.co.uk

Land

Bus

Buses travel to Bulgarian cities from destinations all over Europe, with most arriving at Sofia. You will have to get off the bus at the border and walk through customs to present your passport. Long delays can be expected. When travelling out of Bulgaria by bus, the cost of entry visas for the countries con-

---

BORDER CROSSINGS

You can expect delays at each of Bulgaria's border crossings, especially if you are using public transport. Delays at the Turkish border tend to be longest. For information on visas, see p478.

Greece to Bulgaria
» Promahonas–Kulata
» Ormenio–Svilengrad
» Xanthi–Zlatograd

Macedonia to Bulgaria
» Deve Bair–Gyushevo
» Delčevo–Zlatarevo
» Novo Selo–Stanke Lisichkovo

Romania to Bulgaria
» Giurgiu–Ruse; toll-bridge
» Calafat–Vidin; ferry
» Calarasi–Silistra; ferry
» Kardam–Negru Vodă
» Durankulak–Vama Veche (accessible from Varna)

Serbia to Bulgaria
» Dimitrovgrad–Kalotina
» Zajc–Vrâshka Chuka (near Vidin)
» Klisura–Strezimirovtsi (near Pernik)

Turkey to Bulgaria
» Derekoy–Malko Târnovo
» Edirne–Kapitan Andreevo

---

cerned are not included in the prices of the bus tickets.

GREECE

The main departure/arrival points for buses to/from Greece are Sofia, Plovdiv, Burgas and Varna; several bus companies ply these routes. For information in English, see www.euro lines.bg.

» **Sofia–Athens** (108 lv, 12 to 14 hours)
» **Sofia–Thessaloniki** (50 to 60 lv, eight to nine hours)
» **Sofia–Patras** (125 lv, 14 to 15 hours)
» **Plovdiv–Athens** (120 lv, 15 hours)
» **Plovdiv–Thessaloniki** (60 to 70 lv, eight hours)
» **Burgas–Thessaloniki** (80 lv, 12 hours)
» **Varna–Athens** (127 lv, 20 hours)

MACEDONIA

Buses between Macedonia and Bulgaria arrive at and depart from Sofia and Blagoevgrad. Buses from Sofia go to Skopje (32 lv, six hours) and Ohrid (48 lv, nine hours). From Blagoevgrad, a daily service runs to Bitola (35 to 40 lv, seven to eight hours).

See www.matpu.com for more details (in Bulgarian) on buses to destinations in Macedonia.

ROMANIA

Regular buses to/from Romania depart from and arrive at Sofia, Ruse and Varna.

» **Sofia–Bucharest** (50 to 60 lv, nine hours)
» **Ruse–Bucharest** (20 lv, three hours)
» **Varna–Constanta** (20 lv, two to three hours)

SERBIA

Buses to/from Serbia depart from and arrive at Sofia (Serdika Bus Station, also known as the Trafik Market).

» **Sofia–Belgrade** (40 lv, eight hours)
» **Sofia–Niš** (25 lv, 2½ hours)

TURKEY

Several companies operate bus services to/from Turkey, and this is the quickest, most comfortable and safest way to travel between the two countries.

» www.nisikli.com.tr
» www.union-ivkoni.com
» **Sofia–Istanbul** (50 to 60 lv, 18 hours)
» **Burgas–Istanbul** (60 lv, seven to eight hours)
» **Varna–Istanbul** (60 lv, 10 hours)
» **Plovdiv–Istanbul** (40 to 50 lv, nine to ten hours)

Car & Motorcycle

In order to drive on Bulgarian roads, you will need to purchase a **vignette**, sold at all border crossings into Bulgaria, petrol stations and post offices. Petrol stations and car-repair shops are common around border crossing areas and along main roads. See p483 for information on road rules.

ROMANIA

Crossing the bridge from Giurgiu in Romania into Ruse will incur a toll of €6 (12 lv) per vehicle. Crossing in the opposite direction, from Ruse, costs €2 (4 lv). You are not permitted to cross at Giurgiu without transport.

Private **taxis** across the border from Ruse to Bucharest cost around 90 lv.

The new road and rail bridge (known as 'Danube Bridge 2') between Vidin and Calafat in Romania should be operational from mid-2013.

Train

Bulgarian International train services are operated by Bulgarian State Railways.

» **Bulgarian State Railway** (BDZ; www.bdz.bg)
» **Romanian State Railway** (CFR; www.cfr.ro)
» **Serbian Railways** (www.serbianrailways.com)

MACEDONIA

At present, no trains travel directly between Bulgaria and Macedonia. The only way to Skopje by train from Sofia is to get a connection in Niš (Serbia).

A rail line linking Sofia and Skopje was being planned at the time of research, but no completion date had been announced.

ROMANIA

Most visitors travel to/from Romania by train and either depart from or travel through Ruse.

» **Sofia–Bucharest** (60 lv, 10 hours)
» **Ruse–Bucharest** (25 lv, 3½ hours)

SERBIA

The Balkan Express (trains 490 and 491) travels between Belgrade and Istanbul, via Sofia. Trains 292 and 293 travel just between Belgrade and Sofia. The price for the journey between Belgrade and Sofia is about 60 lv on both trains.

TURKEY

At the time of writing, trains stop at Kapikule on the Turkish border, where a replacement bus service connects to Istanbul. The full train service should resume in late 2013.

The daily Bosfor (trains 498 and 499) travels through Bulgaria, between Bucharest and Istanbul, stopping at Ruse along the way.

From Ruse to Istanbul, the journey takes 16 hours and costs roughly 30 to 50 lv, more for a couchette.

The Balkan Express (trains 490 and 491) travels daily between Istanbul and Belgrade (Serbia), via Bulgaria, passing through Plovdiv and Sofia. The journey from Sofia to Istanbul takes 15 to 17

hours and costs roughly 60 to 70 lv.

Sea

Very few visitors enter or leave Bulgaria by sea. The only scheduled sea route into and out of Bulgaria is provided by a weekly cargo ferry between Ukraine and the port of Varna, which also accepts passengers and vehicles. Prices are in US dollars.

UKR Ferry (www.ukrferrry.com) cruises beyween Ilyichevsk, Ukraine, and Varna (about 30 hours, from US$70 to $200 per person).

Romania

There are two ferry services crossing the Danube between Romania and Bulgaria.

» **Silistra–Călăraşi** (2/15 lv per passenger/car, 10 minutes)
» **Vidin–Calafat** (6/46 lv per passenger/car, 15 minutes)

GETTING AROUND

Bulgaria is relatively easy and inexpensive to get around and vast network of trains, buses and minibuses cover pretty much the entire country, as long as you have plenty of time and patience to put up with poorer connections and slower services in rural areas. To explore the country more fully, you might want to hire a car within the country.

Airlines in Bulgaria

The only scheduled domestic flights within Bulgaria are between Sofia and Varna and Sofia and Burgas

Both routes are operated by **Bulgaria Air** (www.air.bg).

Boat

The only domestic sea transport in Bulgaria consists of a seasonal service between tourist towns on the Black Sea Coast. During the summer months, a private high-speed ferry service operates between the towns of Sozopol and Nesebâr, and between Nesebâr and Varna.

» **Fast Ferry** (www.fastferry. bg; 0877 908 004)

Bus

Buses link all cities and major towns and connect villages with the nearest transport hub. There are several private companies operating frequent modern, comfortable buses between the larger towns, while older, often cramped minibuses also run on routes between smaller towns. Buses provide the most comfortable and quickest mode of public transport in Bulgaria.

Union-Ivkoni (02-989 0000; www.union-ivkoni. com) Links most major towns and many smaller ones, including Sofia, Burgas, Varna, Plovdiv, Pleven, Ruse, Sliven and Shumen.

Biomet (02-868 8961; www. biomet.bg) Runs between Sofia and Veliko Târnovo, Varna, Burgas and Stara Zagora.

Etap-Grup (02-813 3100; www.etapgroup.com) Another extensive intercity network, with buses between Sofia, Burgas, Varna, Ruse and Veliko Târnovo as well as routes between Sofia and Sozopol, Primorsko, Tsarevo and Pomorie.

Car & Motorcycle

Probably the best way to travel around Bulgaria – especially when visiting remote villages, monasteries and national parks – is to hire a car or motorbike.

Union of Bulgarian Motorists (02-935 7935; www. uab.org) The main national organisation for motorists, though little information is available in English.

Bring Your Own Vehicle

If you do decide to drive your own car into Bulgaria, remember that car theft is very common and foreign cars especially are an immediate target. You will need all the original registration and ownership documents, or your vehicle may be impounded by the police. Before you can drive on motorways, you will need to purchase and display a **vignette** in your vehicle. For a car, this costs 10/25 lv for one week/one month. Vignettes can be bought at border crossings when first entering the country or at post offices once inside Bulgaria.

Note that under Bulgarian law, vehicles registered outside the EU are officially 'temporarily imported' when driven into Bulgaria, and if the vehicle is stolen while in the country, the owner will be liable for import duty.

Driving Licence

Drivers of private and rented cars (and motorcycles) must carry registration papers. Your driving licence from home is valid in Bulgaria, so an international driving licence isn't necessary (but it may be useful if you're driving elsewhere in Eastern Europe).

Car Hire

To rent a car in Bulgaria you must be at least 21 years of age and have had a licence for at least one year. Rental outlets can be found all over Bulgaria, but are most common in the bigger cities, at airports and Black Sea resorts. Prices start at around 50 to 60 lv per day. All major credit cards are normally accepted.

Insurance

Third-party 'liability insurance' is compulsory, and can be purchased at any Bulgarian border. Buying comprehensive insurance in your home country is a better

idea (but make sure it's valid in Bulgaria). The Green (or Blue) Card – a routine extension of domestic motor insurance for EU citizens, covering most European countries – is valid in Bulgaria.

The National Bureau of Bulgarian Motor Insurers (www.nbbaz.bg) has some useful advice (in English).

Road Conditions

Aside from the main highways, road conditions in Bulgaria can be very poor. Drivers must cope with potholes, roads under reconstruction, slow-moving vehicles, horses and carts and often erratic driving by other motorists.

You should never rely completely on road signs. They're often frustratingly ambiguous or nonexistent, and most are written in Cyrillic (except around major cities, along the Black Sea coast and at the borders). One useful map to take on your travels is the *Bulgaria Road Atlas* (1:330,000) published by Domino in Cyrillic and English, and widely available at bookshops in Bulgaria.

Road Hazards

Bulgaria's roads are among the most dangerous in Europe, and the number of road deaths each year is high. The worst time is the holiday season (July to September), with drink-driving, speeding and poor road conditions, inlcuding potholes, contributing to accidents. Sofia and roads along the Black Sea coast can be particularly nerve-wracking.

Road Rules

Road signs are rare, but official **speed limits** are enforced by traffic police and speed cameras have been installed on main routes.

» **Built-up areas** – 50km/h
» **Main roads** – 90km/h
» **Motorways** – 120km/h
There are a number of road rules you are required, by law, to follow.

BULGARIA ROAD DISTANCES (KM)

From \ To	Burgas	Dobrich	Gabrovo	Haskovo	Kulata	Kyustendil	Lovech	Pleven	Plovdiv	Ruse	Shumen	Silistra	Sliven	Smolyan	Sofia	Stara Zagora	Varna	Veliko Târnovo	Vidin	Vratsa
Vidin																				126
Veliko Târnovo																			328	193
Varna																		193	515	421
Stara Zagora																	316	126	388	251
Sofia																231	469	241	199	116
Smolyan															258	161	477	287	457	329
Silistra													248	474	443	279	248	110	429	300
Sliven														232	296	71	143	228	478	376
Shumen												113	135	356	381	218	90	140	429	329
Ruse											115	122	216	393	320	232	203	106	356	254
Plovdiv										298	283	396	159	102	156	88	398	192	355	237
Pleven									194	146	219	268	228	296	174	145	304	120	208	108
Lovech								35	150	150	225	272	193	261	167	180	313	85	243	119
Kyustendil							257	228	192	410	471	525	359	302	90	288	559	331	289	206
Kulata						154	350	313	272	503	564	619	419	207	183	348	652	424	382	299
Haskovo					346	289	206	180	90	293	302	374	132	141	234	61	371	187	433	316
Gabrovo				141	403	274	65	78	152	152	186	302	241	241	220	80	274	46	308	172
Dobrich			317	388	695	455	347	347	385	212	133	92	357	541	512	367	51	271	558	406
Burgas		185	234	213	520	462	334	357	270	263	148	262	114	357	385	182	134	224	464	451
Blagoevgrad	464	613	321	272	82	72	268	275	194	421	482	543	353	244	101	282	571	342	300	217

» Drivers and passengers in the front must wear seat belts, and motorcyclists must wear helmets.

» The blood-alcohol limit is 0.05%.

» Children under 12 years are not, by law, allowed to sit in the front seat.

» Between November and March, headlights must be on at all times.

» Mobile phones may only be used with a 'hands-free' system.

» If you have an accident, you must wait with your vehicle and have someone call the local traffic police. There have been many cases in recent years of corrupt traffic police targeting motorists, especially those in expensive foreign cars, and demanding on-the-spot 'fines' (or bribes) for alleged offences. This racketeering has resulted in dozens of arrests of serving traffic police officers, but is an ongoing problem. If you are approached in this way, and it looks like a scam, either ask to pay at a police station or insist on a receipt, with the officer's full details, at which point the 'charge' may well be dropped. There have also been reports of imposters masquerading as traffic police attempting to extort fines. Again, ask for ID before handing over any cash.

Hitching

Hitching is officially illegal in Bulgaria, but people still do it, and hitching in rural Bulgaria may be preferable to being restricted by infrequent public transport. As always, exercise caution and travel in pairs if possible. The upsurge in crime over the last few years has dissuaded some Bulgarians from offering lifts to hitchhikers. Bulgaria's borders are not particularly 'user friendly', and you may face extra questioning and delays if you are travelling in a stranger's vehicle, so

hitching across them in not recommended.

Local Transport

Buses & Trolleybuses

Private and public buses and minibuses ply routes between smaller villages, eg along the Black Sea coast and between urban centres and ski resorts in winter. Tickets for minibuses cost roughly the same as public buses but are usually bought from the driver. Destinations (in Cyrillic) and, often, departure times are indicated on the front window. Most minibuses leave from inside, or very close to, the major public bus station.

In Sofia, minibuses called *marshroutki* run between the city centre and the suburbs, acting like shared taxis. Most Bulgarian towns have cheap and efficient public bus services that tend to be quite crowded, as this is how most locals get around.

Trolleybuses, which operate in several city centres and draw their power from overhead cables, are little different from regular city buses in terms of comfort and reliability but they cost the same.

Taxi

Taxis, which must be painted yellow and equipped with working meters, can be flagged down on most streets in every city and town throughout Bulgaria. They

can be very cheap, but rates do vary. Taxis can be chartered for longer trips at negotiable rates, which you can approximate by working out the distance and taxi rate per kilometre, plus waiting time.

All drivers must clearly display their rates on the taxi's windows. These rates are divided into three or four lines:

» The first line lists the rate per kilometre from 6am to 10pm (about 0.50 lv to 0.70 lv per kilometre is average), and the night-time rate (sometimes the same, but often about 10% more).

» The second lists, if applicable, the call-out fee (of about 0.50 lv) if you preorder a taxi (almost never necessary).

» The third (or second-last) lists the starting fee (0.30 lv to 0.50 lv).

» The fourth (last) lists the cost for waiting per minute (0.15 lv to 0.30 lv). Some drivers try to overcharge unwary foreigners by claiming the meter 'doesn't work' (it must work by law) or offering a flat fare (which will always be at least double the proper metered fare). Dishonest drivers congregate outside airports, train and bus stations and big city centres and in the resorts along the Black Sea coast.

Train

Bâlgarski Dârzhavni Zheleznitsi (БДЖ) – the **Bulgarian State Railways**

TICKETS

All tickets are printed in Cyrillic. Other than the place of departure and destination, tickets also contain other important details:

» Клас – *klas* – '1' (1st class) or '2' (2nd class)

» Категория – *kategoriya* – type of train, ie T (express), 255 (fast) or G (slow passenger)

» Влак – *vlak* – train number

» Час – *chas* – departure time

» Дата – *data* – date of departure

» Вагон – *vagon* – carriage number

» Място – *myasto* – seat number

(BDZh; www.bdz.bg) boasts an impressive 4278km of tracks across the country, linking most sizeable towns and cities, although some are on a spur track and connected to a major railway line only by infrequent services.

Most trains tend to be antiquated, shabby and not especially comfortable, and journey times slower than buses. On the plus side, though, you'll have more room in a train compartment, and the scenery is likely to be more rewarding.

Trains are classified as *ekspresen* (express), *bârz* (fast) or *pâtnicheski* (slow passenger). Unless you absolutely thrive on train travel or you want to visit a more remote town, use a fast or express train.

Two of the most spectacular train trips are along Iskâr Gorge, from Sofia to Mezdra, and on the narrow-gauge track between Septemvri and Bansko. Railway buffs often go on these trips for no other reason than the journey itself.

Train travel in Bulgaria is a normally safe and enjoyable experience, but there have been reports of robberies, pickpocketing and minor annoyances (such as drunkenness) on some cross-border routes, such as to/from Turkey or Serbia. If you are travelling late at night, sit with other passengers rather than in an empty compartment, and if you are making a long overnight trip across the border, try booking a bed in a couchette.

Classes

First-class compartments seat six people, eight are crammed into 2nd class, and the intercity express has individual seats in an open carriage. Sleepers and couchettes are available between Sofia and Burgas and Varna but must be booked in advance. Fares for 1st class are around 25% higher than for 2nd class. The carriages won't be any cleaner, but it's always worth paying the extra just to have a bit more space.

Costs

Train travel within Bulgaria is cheap by Western European standards, with a 1st/2nd class express cross-country trip between Sofia and Varna costing approximately 30/37 lv. If you're travelling in a group (three or more people) you may get a small discount.

Reservations

For frequent train services between the main cities there is rarely a problem if you simply turn up at the station and purchase a ticket for the next train (but be careful to allow at least 30 minutes to queue up). Advance tickets are sometimes advisable on train services such as the intercity express to the Black Sea during a summer weekend. Advance tickets can be bought at specific counters within larger train stations and at Rila Bureaux in cities and major towns. Staff at Rila are normally far more helpful, knowledgeable and likely to speak English than anyone at a train station, so it's best to deal with Rila for advice, schedules and advance tickets.

Language

WANT MORE?

For in-depth language information and handy phrases, check out Lonely Planet's *Bulgarian Phrasebook*. You'll find it at **shop.lonelyplanet.com**, or you can buy Lonely Planet's iPhone phrasebooks at the Apple App Store.

Bulgarian is a member of the South Slavic language family, with Macedonian and Serbian as close relatives. It's the official language of Bulgaria, with 9 million speakers.

Bulgarian is written in the Cyrillic alphabet. The pronunciation is pretty straightforward for English speakers – just read our coloured pronunciation guides as if they were English, and you'll be understood. Note that ai is pronounced as in 'aisle', uh as the 'a' in 'ago' and zh as the 's' in 'measure'. Vowels in unstressed syllables are generally pronounced shorter and weaker than they are in stressed syllables. The stressed syllables are indicated with italics. Polite and informal options are provided where relevant, indicated by the abbreviations 'pol' and 'inf'.

BASICS

Hello.	Здравейте.	zdra·vey·te
Goodbye.	Довиждане.	do·veezh·da·ne
Yes.	Да.	da
No.	Не.	ne
Please.	Моля.	mol·ya
Thank you.	Благодаря	bla·go·dar·ya
You're welcome.	Няма защо.	nya·ma zash·to
Excuse me.	Извинете.	iz·vee·ne·te
Sorry.	Съжалявам.	suh·zhal·ya·vam

How are you?
Как сте/си? (pol/inf) kak ste/si

Fine, thanks. And you?
Добре, благодаря. do·bre bla·go·da·rya
А вие/ти? (pol/inf) a vee·e/te

What's your name?
Как се казвате/ kak se kaz·va·te/
казваш? (pol/inf) kaz·vash

My name is ...
Казвам се ... kaz·vam se ...

Do you speak English?
Говорите ли go·vo·ree·te lee
английски? ang·lees·kee

I don't understand.
Не разбирам. ne raz·bee·ram

ACCOMMODATION

Where's a ...?	Къде има ...?	kuh·de ee·ma ...
campsite	къмпинг	kuhm·peeng
guesthouse	пансион	pan·see·on
hotel	хотел	ho·tel
youth hostel	общежитие	ob·shte·zhee·tee·ye

Do you have a ... room?	Имате ли стая с ...?	ee·ma·te lee sta·ya s ...
single	едно легло	ed·no leg·lo
double	едно голямо легло	ed·no go·lya·mo leg·lo

How much is it per night/person?
Колко е на вечер/ kol·ko e na ve·cher/
човек? cho·vek

DIRECTIONS

Where's the (market)?
Къде се намира kuh·de se na·mee·ra
(пазарът)? (pa·za·ruht)

What's the address?
Какъв е адресът?   ka·*kuhv* e ad·*re*·suht

Can you show me (on the map)?
Можете ли да ми   *mo*·zhe·te lee da mee
покажете (на картата)?   po·*ka*·zhe·te (na *kar*·ta·ta)

How far is it?
На какво разстояние е?   na kak·*vo* ras·to·*ya*·nee·e e

EATING & DRINKING

I'd like (the)	Дайте ми	*dai*·te mee
..., please.	..., моля.	... *mol*·ya
bill	сметката	*smet*·ka·ta
drink list	листата с	*lees*·ta·ta s
	напитките	na·*peet*·kee·te
menu	менюто	men·*yoo*·to
that dish	онова блюдо	o·no·*va blyoo*·do

What would you recommend?
Какво ще   kak·*vo* shte
препоръчате?   pre·po·*ruh*·cha·te

Do you have vegetarian food?
Имате ли   ee·ma·te lee
вегетерианска храна?   ve·ge·te·ree·*an*·ska hra·*na*

| **I'll have ...** | Ще взема ... | shte *vze*·ma ... |
| **Cheers!** | Наздраве! | na·*zdra*·ve |

beer	бира	*bee*·ra
bottle	шише	shee·*she*
breakfast	закуска	za·*koos*·ka
cafe	кафене	ka·fe·*ne*
coffee	кафе	ka·*fe*
cup	чаша	*chas*·ha
dinner	вечеря	ve·*cher*·ya
eggs	яйца	yai·*tsa*
fish	риба	*ree*·ba
fork	вилица	*vee*·lee·tsa
fruit	плод	plod
glass	чаша	*chas*·ha
juice	сок	sok
knife	нож	nozh
lunch	обед	o·bed
meat	месо	me·*so*
milk	мляко	*mlya*·ko
restaurant	ресторант	res·to·*rant*
spoon	лъжица	luh·*zhee*·tsa
tea	чай	chai
vegetable	зеленчук	ze·len·*chook*
water	вода	vo·*da*
wine	вино	*vee*·no

Signs

Вход	Entrance
Изход	Exit
Отворено	Open
Затворено	Closed
Информация	Information
Забранено	Prohibited
Тоалетни	Toilets
Мъже (М)	Men
Жени (Ж)	Women

EMERGENCIES

| **Help!** | Помощ! | po·mosht |
| **Go away!** | Махайте се! | *ma*·hai·te se |

Call ...!	Повикайте ...!	po·*vee*·kai·te ...
a doctor	лекар	*le*·kar
the police	полицията	po·*lee*·tsee·ya·ta

I'm lost.
Загубих се.   za·*goo*·beeh se

Where are the toilets?
Къде има тоалетни?   kuh·de ee·ma to·a·*let*·nee

I'm sick.
Болен/Болна съм. (m/f)   bo·len/*bol*·na suhm

I'm allergic to ...
Алергичен/Алергична   a·ler·*gee*·chen/
съм на ... (m/f)   a·ler·*geech*·na suhm na ...

SHOPPING & SERVICES

Where's	Къде се	kuh·*de* se
the ...?	намира ...?	na·*mee*·ra ...
ATM	банкомат	ban·ko·*mat*
bank	банката	*ban*·ka·ta
department	универсален	oo·nee·ver·*sa*·len
store	магазин	ma·ga·zeen
grocery	гастроном	gas·tro·*nom*
store		
local	най-близкият	nai·*blees*·kee·yat
internet	интернет	een·ter·*net*
cafe		
newsagency	киоск	*kee*·osk
post office	пощата	po·*shta*·ta
tourist	бюрото за	*byoo*·ro·to za
office	туристическа	too·*ree*·stee·
	информация	ches·ka een·for·
		ma·tsee·ya

I'd like to buy (a phonecard).
Искам да си купя   *ees*·kam da see *koop*·ya
(една телефонна карта).   (ed·*na* te·le·*fon*·na *kar*·ta)

Can I look at it?
Мога ли да го
разгледам?
mo·ga lee da go
raz·gle·dam

Do you have any others?
Имате ли още?
ee·ma·te lee osh·te

How much is it?
Колко струва?
kol·ko stroo·va

That's too expensive.
Скъпо е.
skuh·po e

There's a mistake in the bill.
Има грешка в
сметката.
ee·ma gresh·ka v
smet·ka·ta

TIME & DATES

What time is it?
Колко е часът?
kol·ko e cha·suht

It's (two) o'clock.
Часът е (два).
cha·suhl e (dva)

Half past (one).
(Един) и половина.
(e·deen) ee po·lo·vee·na

At what time ...?
В колко часа ...?
v kol·ko cha·suh ...

At ...
В ...
v ...

yesterday ...	вчера ...	vche·ra ...
tomorrow ...	утре ...	oot·re ...
morning	сутринта	soot·reen·ta
afternoon	следобед	sle·do·bed
evening	вечерта	ve·cher·ta

Monday	понеделник	po·ne·del·neek
Tuesday	вторник	vtor·neek
Wednesday	сряда	srya·da
Thursday	четвъртък	chet·vuhr·tuhk
Friday	петък	pe·tuhk
Saturday	събота	suh·bo·ta
Sunday	неделя	ne·del·ya

January	януари	ya·noo·a·ree
February	февруари	fev·roo·a·ree
March	март	mart
April	април	ap·reel
May	май	mai
June	юни	yoo·nee
July	юли	yoo·lee
August	август	av·goost
September	септември	sep·tem·vree
October	октомври	ok·tom·vree
November	ноември	no·em·vree
December	декември	de·kem·vree

TRANSPORT

Public Transport

Is this the ...	Това ли е ...	to·va lee e ...
to (Burgas)?	за (Бургас)?	za (boor·gas)
boat	корабът	ko·ra·buht
bus	автобусът	av·to·boo·suht
plane	самолетът	sa·mo·le·tuht
train	влакът	vla·kuht

What time's	В колко часа	v kol·ko cha·suh
the ... bus?	е ... автобус?	e ... av·to·boos
first	първият	puhr·vee·yat
last	последният	po·sled·nee·yat
next	следващият	sled·vash·tee·yat

Where can I buy a ticket?
Къде мога да си
купя билет?
kuh·de mo·ga da see
koop·ya bee·let

One ... ticket	Един билет	e·deen bee·let
(to Varna),	... (за Варна),	... (za var·na)
please.	моля.	mol·ya
one-way	в едната
посока	v ed·na·ta
po·so·ka
return	за отиване
и връщане	za o·tee·va·ne
ee vruhsh·ta·ne

How long does the trip take?
Колко трае
пътуването?
kol·ko tra·ye
puh·too·va·ne·to

Is it a direct route?
Има ли прекачване?
ee·ma lee pre·kach·va·ne

At what time does it arrive/leave?
В колко часа
пристига/тръгва?
v kol·ko cha·suh
prees·tee·ga/truhg·va

How long will it be delayed?
Колко закъснение
има?
kol·ko za·kuhs·ne·nee·ye
ee·ma

Question Words		
How?	Как?	kak
What?	Какво?	kak·vo
When?	Кога?	ko·ga
Where?	Къде?	kuh·de
Who?	Кой? (m sg)	koy
	Коя? (f sg)	ko·ya
	Кое? (n sg)	ko·e
	Кои? (pl)	ko·ee
Why?	Защо?	zash·to

Numbers

1	един (m)	e·*deen*
	една (f)	ed·*na*
	едно (n)	ed·*no*
2	два (m)	dva
	две (f&n)	dve
3	три	tree
4	четири	*che*·tee·ree
5	пет	pet
6	шест	shest
7	седем	*se*·dem
8	осем	o·sem
9	девет	*de*·vet
10	десет	*de*·set
20	двайсет	*dvai*·set
30	трийсет	*tree*·set
40	четирийсет	che·*tee*·ree·set
50	петдесет	pet·de·*set*
60	шестдесет	shest·de·*set*
70	седемдесет	se·dem·de·*set*
80	осемдесет	o·sem·de·*set*
90	деветдесет	de·vet·de·*set*
100	сто	sto

Does it stop at (Plovdiv)?
Спира ли в (Пловдив)? *spee*·ra lee v (*plov*·deev)

How long do we stop here?
След колко време sled *kol*·ko *vre*·me
тръгваме оттук? *truhg*·va·me ot·*took*

What station/stop is this?
Коя е тази гара/ *ko*·ya e *ta*·zee *ga*·ra/
спирка? *speer*·ka

What's the next station/stop?
Коя е следващата *ko*·ya e sled·va·shta·ta
гара/спирка? *ga*·ra/*speer*·ka

Please tell me when we get to (Smoljan).
Кажете ми моля ka·*zhe*·te mee *mol*·ya
когато пристигнем *ko*·ga·to prees·*teeg*·nem
в (Смолян). v (*smol*·yan)

How much is it to ...?
Колко струва до ...? *kol*·ko *stroo*·va do ...

Please take me to (this address).
Моля да ме докарате *mol*·ya da me do·*ka*·ra·te
до (този адрес). do (*to*·zi ad·*res*)

I'd like a taxi ... Искам да *ees*·kam da
поръчам po·*ruh*·cham
такси ... tak·*see* ...

at (9am) в (девет часа v (*de*·vet cha·*sa*
сутринта) soo·treen·*ta*)

now сега se·*ga*

tomorrow за утре za *oot*·re

Please ... Моля ... *mol*·ya ...

slow down намалете na·ma·*le*·te

stop here спрете тук *spre*·te took

wait here чакайте тук *cha*·kai·te took

Driving & Cycling

I'd like to hire Искам да *ees*·kam da
a ... взема под *vze*·ma pod
наем ... *na*·em ...

bicycle един e·*deen*
велосипед ve·lo·see·*ped*

car една кола e·*dna* ko·*la*

motorbike един e·*deen*
мотопед mo·to·*ped*

How much for Колко струва *kol*·ko *stroo*·va
... hire? на ...да се na ...da se
наеме? na·e·me

hourly час chas

daily ден den

weekly седмица *sed*·mee·tsa

air въздух *vuhz*·dooh

oil масло *mas*·lo

petrol бензин ben·*zeen*

tyres гуми *goo*·mee

I need a mechanic.
Трябва ми монтьор. *tryab*·va mee mon·*tyor*

I've run out of petrol.
Нямам бензин. *nya*·mam ben·*zeen*

I have a flat tyre.
Пукнала ми се е *pook*·na·la mee se e
гумата. *goo*·ma·ta

Is this the road to (Rila)?
Това ли е пътят за *to*·va lee e *puh*·tyat za
(Рила)? (*ree*·la)

GLOSSARY

aleya – alley, lane

avtogara – bus station

banya – bath; often signifies mineral baths in general

BDZh – abbreviation for the Bulgarian State Railways

bul – abbreviation of boulevard; main street or boulevard

chalga – upbeat Bulgarian folk-pop music, based on traditional melodies but played on modern instruments

charshlya – a street or area of traditional craft workshops

dvorets – palace

dzhumaya – mosque

ezero (m), ezera (f) – lake

gara – train station

gradina – garden; often referring to a public park

haidouks – Bulgarian rebels who fought against the Turks in the 18th and 19th centuries

hali – indoor market

hizha – hut; often refers to a mountain hut

house-museum – a home built in a style typical of the Bulgarian National Revival period and turned into a museum

iconostasis (s), iconostases (pl) – a screen, partition or door in an Eastern Orthodox church that separates the sanctuary from the nave; often richly decorated

iztok – east

kâshta – house

khan – king within a Bulgar tribe, or the subsequent Bulgarian empires; also known as a *tsar*

kilim – hand-woven woollen carpet, normally with colourful geometric patterns

kino – cinema

knyaz – prince

krepost – fortress

mehana – tavern

obshtina – municipality; also another word for town hall

peshtera – cave

pl – abbreviation of ploshtad; town or city square

planina – mountain

Pomaks – literally 'helpers'; Slavs who converted to Islam during the era of Turkish rule

rakia – Bulgarian brandy, normally made from grapes, occasionally from plums or other fruit

reka – river

sveti (m), sveta (f) – saint

svobodni stai – 'free rooms'; advertised rooms for rent in private homes

Troyanska kapka – 'Troyan droplet'; traditional glazed pottery with a distinctive 'drip' design

tsar – see *khan*

ul – abbreviation of ulitsa; street

varosha – centre of an old town

veliko – great, large

vrâh – mountain peak

zakuska – breakfast

behind the scenes

SEND US YOUR FEEDBACK

We love to hear from travellers – your comments keep us on our toes and help make our books better. Our well-travelled team reads every word on what you loved or loathed about this book. Although we cannot reply individually to postal submissions, we always guarantee that your feedback goes straight to the appropriate authors, in time for the next edition. Each person who sends us information is thanked in the next edition – the most useful submissions are rewarded with a selection of digital PDF chapters.

Visit **lonelyplanet.com/contact** to submit your updates and suggestions or to ask for help. Our award-winning website also features inspirational travel stories, news and discussions.

Note: We may edit, reproduce and incorporate your comments in Lonely Planet products such as guidebooks, websites and digital products, so let us know if you don't want your comments reproduced or your name acknowledged. For a copy of our privacy policy visit lonelyplanet.com/privacy.

OUR READERS

Many thanks to the travellers who used the last edition and wrote to us with helpful hints, useful advice and interesting anecdotes

Roos Abelman, Richard Adams, Stefan Agneessens, Paul Alfrey, Albena Angelova, Reinier Bakels, Bob Barnes, Kirrily Beer, Kriss Bell, Adam Benbrook, Hannah Bennett, Arine Benschop, Martjan Bodegom, Akiko Brixey, Graeme Brock, Romelle Castle, Velislav Chorbadjiev, Huju Chuang, Mikkel Clausen, Ignacio Cobos, Robin Das, Assen Davidov, Anna Davies, A De Wolff, Folkert De Boer, Juun De Boer, Ioana Deac, Robbert Drieman, Gert Driessens, James Falk, Amie Ferris-Rotman, Linda Frederick Yaffe, Geer Furtjes, Marisa Galitz, Jose Gambe Tibayan, Videlina Gandeva, Emily Getty, Marciano Giancarlo, Lindsay Grant, Raoul Gunning, Cecilia Harlitz, Sacha Hather, Nir Hauser, Markus Haverkamp, Jennifer Hay, Hildegard Hornung, James Hughes, Mary Janssen, Diana Jeffery, Penny Johnson, Chris Jung, Joel Kleehammer, Wim Klumpenhouwer, Paul Korejcik, Michael Kuhnert, Shawn Lavoie, David Lewis, Jarvis Lim, Philipp Lohri, Steve Maher, Ashley Meyer, Pavel Mihalchev, Jack Mui, Thomas Münnich, Deborah Nedelcu, Kathleen Neumann, Peter Nuttall, Pär Nylander, Lloyd Orloff, Ben Owen, Cristian Pascu, Roxana Paun, Toma Peiu, John Percy, Mariana Petrova, Leif Pettersen, Emma Pettitt, Lynette & Les Price, Tessa Quartermaine, Tihomir Rangelov, Catalin Roman, Elizabeth Rudd, Klara Sceberras, Stephen Simblet, Vic Sofras, Thomas Stegenga, Sophie Stuerzer, Paweł Szczepański, Alenka Toinko, Arie Van Oosterwijk, Rianne Van Der Zanden, Ioan-luca Vlad, DC Wood, Hanneke Wilschut, Silke Wissing, Chris Young, Raya Yunakova, Martin Zeilinger, Mike Zerbe

AUTHOR THANKS

Mark Baker

I met many friendly and helpful people along the road. A complete list here would be impossible, but special thanks to Traian Orban at the Permanent Exhibition of the 1989 Revolution in Timişoara, as well as Paula Gusetu Nimigean and her husband Costy, Daniela Olariu, the staff at the Hotel Select in Tulcea, Iuliana Filote, Dorin Dumitrascuta, Mirela Petre, Bogdana Dobre, Elena Loghin and Irina Voicu.

Chris Deliso

Many people have provided invaluable advice, assistance and good cheer. Among many others in Bulgaria who deserve credit are Mitko, Andrew, Toshe and Rusalia Kirov. In Romania my thanks go out to Ioanna, Gigi,

Tania, Mihail and Vlad. This project could not have been finished without our ever-patient and helpful commissioning editor, Dora Whitaker, and coordinating author Mark Baker. My fellow authors Rick Watkins and Richard Waters also provided good comraderie. The hard-working cartography and production teams were also terrific.

Richard Waters

Special thanks to Cristina Ghivnici for her valuable insights, as well as my thanks to Lla and her charming family, Atti Alba, Rolling stone, Gabriel, Dan Marin, Sorana at Alburnus Maior, Duncan Ridgeley, Rada Pavel, Teofil Ivaciuc, Colin Shaw, Katharina and Ruxandra for staying up at night and translating creepy stories on my behalf.

Richard Watkins

Many thanks once more to Lubomir Popi-ordanov at the Odysseia-In travel agency in Sofia, for his hospitality, insight and advice. Thanks also go to Stela Stoianova, Ioanna Georgieva and Rositsa Lozanova at Zig-Zag Holidays for all their help before and during my trip around Bulgaria. I'd also like to thank Katerina and Yanica in Primorsko.

ACKNOWLEDGMENTS

Climate map data adapted from Peel MC, Finlayson BL & McMahon TA (2007) 'Updated World Map of the Köppen-Geiger Climate Classification', Hydrology and Earth System Sciences, 11, 163344.

Cover photograph: Corvin Castle, Hunedoara, Paul Biris/Getty Images©

BEHIND THE SCENES

This Book

This 6th edition of Lonely Planet's *Romania & Bulgaria* guidebook was researched and written by Mark Baker, Chris Deliso, Richard Waters and Richard Watkins. The previous editions were written by the same authors and Leif Pettersen. This guidebook was commissioned in Lonely Planet's London office, and produced by the following:

Commissioning Editor Dora Whitaker
Coordinating Editor Sophie Splatt
Coordinating Cartographer Julie Dodkins
Coordinating Layout Designer Carol Jackson
Managing Editors Barbara Delissen, Angela Tinson
Managing Cartographers Anita Bahn, Anthony Phelan, Adrian Persoglia, Amanda Sierp
Managing Layout Designer Chris Girdler
Assisting Editors Andrew Bain, Nigel Chin, Andrea Dobbin, Kate Daly, Cathryn Game, Helen Koehne, Sarah Koel
Assisting Cartographer Rachel Imeson
Cover Research Naomi Parker
Internal Image Researchers Nicholas Colicchia, Kylie McLaughlin
Language Content Branislava Vladisavljevic
Thanks to Laura Crawford, Lauren Egan, Ryan Evans, Larissa Frost, Jouve India, Annelies Mertens, Trent Paton, Martine Power, Kirsten Rawlings, Raphael Richards, Jessica Rose, Wibowo Rusli, Dianne Schallmeiner, John Taufa, Gerard Walker, Juan Winata, Wendy Wright

index

000 Map pages
000 Photo pages

N

NOTES

NOTES

how to use this book

These symbols will help you find the listings you want:

👁 Sights		☞ Tours		🍷 Drinking	
🐾 Beaches		🎊 Festivals & Events		☆ Entertainment	
🏃 Activities		🛏 Sleeping		🔒 Shopping	
🐢 Courses		✕ Eating		ℹ Information/Transport	

These symbols give you the vital information for each listing:

☎ Telephone Numbers	📶 Wi-Fi Access	🚌 Bus
🕐 Opening Hours	🏊 Swimming Pool	⛴ Ferry
P Parking	🥗 Vegetarian Selection	Ⓜ Metro
Nonsmoking	📖 English-Language Menu	Ⓢ Subway
❄ Air-Conditioning	👪 Family-Friendly	🚋 Tram
@ Internet Access	🐾 Pet-Friendly	🚆 Train

Look out for these icons:

TOP CHOICE Our author's recommendation

FREE No payment required

🌿 A green or sustainable option

Our authors have nominated these places as demonstrating a strong commitment to sustainability – for example by supporting local communities and producers, operating in an environmentally friendly way, or supporting conservation projects.

Reviews are organised by author preference.

Map Legend

Sights
- Beach
- Buddhist
- Castle
- Christian
- Hindu
- Islamic
- Jewish
- Monument
- Museum/Gallery
- Ruin
- Winery/Vineyard
- Zoo
- Other Sight

Activities, Courses & Tours
- Diving/Snorkelling
- Canoeing/Kayaking
- Skiing
- Surfing
- Swimming/Pool
- Walking
- Windsurfing
- Other Activity/Course/Tour

Sleeping
- Sleeping
- Camping

Eating
- Eating

Drinking
- Drinking
- Cafe

Entertainment
- Entertainment

Shopping
- Shopping

Information
- Post Office
- Tourist Information

Transport
- Airport
- Border Crossing
- Bus
- Cable Car/Funicular
- Cycling
- Ferry
- Monorail
- Parking
- S-Bahn
- Taxi
- Train/Railway
- Tram
- Tube Station
- U-Bahn
- Underground Train Station
- Other Transport

Routes
- Tollway
- Freeway
- Primary
- Secondary
- Tertiary
- Lane
- Unsealed Road
- Plaza/Mall
- Steps
- Tunnel
- Pedestrian Overpass
- Walking Tour
- Walking Tour Detour
- Path

Boundaries
- International
- State/Province
- Disputed
- Regional/Suburb
- Marine Park
- Cliff
- Wall

Population
- Capital (National)
- Capital (State/Province)
- City/Large Town
- Town/Village

Geographic
- Hut/Shelter
- Lighthouse
- Lookout
- Mountain/Volcano
- Oasis
- Park
- Pass
- Picnic Area
- Waterfall

Hydrography
- River/Creek
- Intermittent River
- Swamp/Mangrove
- Reef
- Canal
- Water
- Dry/Salt/Intermittent Lake
- Glacier

Areas
- Beach/Desert
- Cemetery (Christian)
- Cemetery (Other)
- Park/Forest
- Sportsground
- Sight (Building)
- Top Sight (Building)

Richard Watkins

Plan (Bulgaria); Sofia; Black Sea Coast; The Danube & Northern Plains; Understand (Bulgaria): Outdoor Activities & Wildlife, Visual Arts, Craft & Music, The Bulgarian People, Bulgarian Cuisine; Survival Guide (Bulgaria) Richard studied history at Oxford, and his first job after university was teaching English at a language school in Sofia. He has returned to Bulgaria several times since, and has now visited almost every corner of this welcoming country. On his most recent trip, he sweltered through a 40°C heatwave across northern Bulgaria and discovered a garden full of stone Lenins in Sofia. Richard has written for more than twenty guidebooks, including two previous editions of Lonely Planet's *Bulgaria*.

OUR STORY

A beat-up old car, a few dollars in the pocket and a sense of adventure. In 1972 that's all Tony and Maureen Wheeler needed for the trip of a lifetime – across Europe and Asia overland to Australia. It took several months, and at the end – broke but inspired – they sat at their kitchen table writing and stapling together their first travel guide, *Across Asia on the Cheap*. Within a week they'd sold 1500 copies. Lonely Planet was born.

Today, Lonely Planet has offices in Melbourne, London, Oakland and Delhi, with more than 600 staff and writers. We share Tony's belief that 'a great guidebook should do three things: inform, educate and amuse'.

OUR WRITERS

Mark Baker

Coordinating Author; Plan Your Trip (Romania); Bucharest; Wallachia; Crişana & Banat; The Danube Delta & Black Sea Coast; Understand (Romania): Visual Arts & Folk Culture, The Romanian Table, Survival Guide (Romania) Based permanently in Prague, Mark has lived and worked in Central Europe for more than 20 years, first as a journalist for *The Economist Group* and then for *Bloomberg News* and *Radio Free Europe/Radio Liberty*. He's a frequent visitor to Romania and a huge fan of the Danube Delta, Timişoara, Transylvania, and yes, even Bucharest, among other places. In addition to this book, Mark is coauthor of the Lonely Planet guides to Prague, Slovenia and Poland.

Chris Deliso

Moldavia & the Bucovina Monasteries; Plovdiv & the Southern Mountains; Veliko Târnovo & Central Mountains; Understand (Bulgaria): Bulgaria Today, History, Bulgarian Wine Chris is an American travel writer who writes widely about the Balkans and Mediterranean Europe. In addition to Bulgaria and Romania, he has contributed to Lonely Planet's guides to Greece, Crete, Western Balkans, Eastern Europe and Turkey. He has an MPhil with Distinction in Byzantine Studies from Oxford University.

Richard Waters

Transylvania; Maramureş; Understand (Romania): Romania Today, History, The Dracula Myth, Outdoor Activities & Wildlife, The Romanian People Richard is an award-winning travel journalist and works for the *Sunday Times*, *National Geographic Traveller*, the *Independent* and *Wanderlust*. You can see some of his work at www.richardwaters.co.uk. He first fell for the charms of Transylvania as an ardent horror buff. Curiosity took the cat to Bran Castle in the early '00s and he's been a sucker for the country's forests and folklore ever since, returning regularly. He lives with his fiancée and two children, Finn and Aggie, in the Cotswolds.

OVER PAGE MORE WRITERS

Published by Lonely Planet Publications Pty Ltd
ABN 36 005 607 983
6th edition – May 2013
ISBN 978 1 74179 944 6
© Lonely Planet 2013   Photographs © as indicated 2013
10 9 8 7 6 5 4 3 2 1
Printed in China

32953011930965